The Union Cavalry in the Civil War, Volumes I–III
Winner of the Jules F. Landry Award for 1985

Philip Henry Sheridan
Courtesy of the National Archives

STEPHEN Z. STARR

The
Union Cavalry
in the
Civil War

VOLUME II
The War in the East
From Gettysburg to Appomattox
1863–1865

Louisiana State University Press
Baton Rouge and London

Second printing (October, 1985)

Library of Congress Cataloging in Publication Data (Revised)

Starr, Stephen Z
  The Union cavalry in the Civil War.

  Bibliography: p.
  Includes index.
  CONTENTS: v. 1. From Fort Sumter to Gettysburg,
1861–1863.—v. 2. The War in the East, from Gettysburg
to Appomattox, 1863–1865.
   1. United States. Army. Cavalry—History—Civil
War, 1861–1865. 2. United States—History—Civil War,
1861–1865—Campaigns and battles. I. Title.
E492.5.S7   973.7′41   78-26751
ISBN 0-8071-0484-1 (v. 1)
ISBN 0-8071-0859-6 (v. 2)

This volume of
The Union Cavalry in the Civil War
is dedicated to the memory of
William H. Wright
April 29, 1902—July 23, 1980

Contents

Illustrations

Maps

Preface

THE FIRST VOLUME OF THIS STUDY, PUBLISHED IN 1979, describes the genesis of the Union cavalry in the summer and autumn of 1861, and the teething troubles, the early trials and tribulations, of a poorly organized, poorly equipped, poorly trained, and generally misused arm of the service. The volume then describes the operations of the Union cavalry in the area east of the Alleghenies from the early days of the Civil War to the close of the Gettysburg Campaign in July, 1863. The tale of these operations reveals the painfully slow emergence of technical competence at all levels except perhaps the highest, of increased and increasing self-confidence, of growing indications in the spring and summer of 1863, at Brandy Station, Aldie, Middleburg, Upperville, and lastly at Gettysburg, that through a pragmatic process of trial and error the Union cavalry had begun to find its way and was gradually establishing for itself a place in the sun.

The present volume takes up the story in late July, 1863, and describes the operations of the Union cavalry on both sides of the Blue Ridge to the April day in 1865 when, following the battles of Dinwiddie Court House, Five Forks, and Sayler's Creek, the formerly scorned, disprized cavalry, having become the cutting edge of the Union army, and led by Philip Sheridan, Wesley Merritt, George Custer, George Crook, Ranald Mackenzie, and a host of tough, battlewise regimental officers, brought to bay the proud Army of Northern Virginia and forced its surrender. As in the previous volume the story is told, whenever possible and appropriate, in the words of the men and officers whose hardihood, courage, and yes, devotion, brought about this result.

The next volume will tell the story of the Union cavalry as it fought the Civil War in what in the 1860s was "the West"—the vast area south of the Ohio River, bounded on the east by the Alleghenies and on the west by the Kansas-Missouri border. Comprised in that account will be the role of the Union cavalry, developing along basically similar but in some respects significantly different lines from its brethren in the East, in the closing campaigns of the war in Georgia and the Carolinas.

The present volume has had the benefit of a reading by, and the comments of, Dr. B. F. Cooling and (in part) Dr. R. J. Sommers, both of the U.S. Army Military History Institute, Carlisle Barracks, Pennsylvania. It is only fitting that a history of the Union cavalry in the Civil War be required to pass the scrutiny of distinguished scholars stationed at Carlisle Barracks, the site in the years before the Civil War of the U.S. Army's first cavalry school. The readiness of Drs. Cooling and Sommers to come to the aid of a beleaguered author who lacks any conceivable claim on their time and energies is deeply appreciated. Needless to say, it is not they but the author who is responsible for any and all errors of omission and commission in the present volume.

Mary Jane Di Piero of the Louisiana State University Press, who edited the first volume of this study, has (perhaps it would be more appropriate to say, "has nevertheless") agreed to edit the present volume as well, and to do her best to cope with the notions of a rather stubborn author. For what little compensation it may be to her, that same stubborn but repentant author begs to assure her of his affectionate gratitude.

I must end this Preface on a note of sadness. The dedication of the first volume of this study to Dr. T. Harry Williams was an expression of my admiration for an eminent historian and of my affection for a dear friend. It was intended to come to him as a surprise on the occasion of his retirement as Boyd Professor of History at Louisiana State University. There was, however, an unavoidable delay, and before a copy of the book could be presented to him, T. Harry Williams died. The present volume is dedicated to the memory of another dear friend, William H. Wright, who took time from a busy schedule to read with minute attention the manuscripts of each of my books and to point out in a wise, kindly, but never less than firm way passages which, as they stood, offended his unerring sense of clarity and good diction. I must go on with the concluding volume of this study without T. Harry's encouragement, usually expressed in two or three wry sentences in his barely legible handwriting, and without the comfortable knowledge that Bill Wright would save me from the embarrassment of committing grammatical and stylistic lapses. I cherish the memory of their friendship.

The Union Cavalry in the Civil War

I

Men of Valour

ON JULY 14, 1863, THE CONFEDERATE ARMY, BADLY DAM-
aged at Gettysburg in everything but spirit, was safely back in Virginia. The Army of the Potomac had had the Confederates at its
mercy for five days, but, paralyzed by the excessive caution of
Commanding General George Meade and five of his six corps
commanders, had allowed them to escape.[1] General Robert E.
Lee's invasion of the North had ended in a strategic defeat, but he
still commanded a powerful, veteran army, he was back on
friendly soil, and the war continued.

On July 17, three days after Lee had completed his crossing
of the Potomac, Meade began to follow. Completing the river
crossing on the nineteenth, the northern troops inched forward
as the Army of Northern Virginia, outnumbered more than two
to one, made a leisurely march up the Shenandoah Valley and
then crossed the Blue Ridge over Manassas Gap; by August 1 the
two armies were back where the long campaign had started, Lee
in and around Culpeper, Meade lining the east bank of the Rappahannock.[2]

1. The president, for one, saw clearly the reasons for Lee's escape. He
remarked to his secretary, John Hay, "We had them within our grasp. We
had only to stretch forth our hands and they were ours. And nothing I could
say or do could make the army move." Quoted in Kenneth P. Williams, *Lincoln Finds a General* (5 vols.; New York, 1949–59), II, 752.

2. Lee had 35,000 effectives exclusive of his cavalry, Meade about

The Confederate retreat had been effected with a minimum of interference. Colonel William Gamble, commanding the First Brigade of John Buford's First Cavalry Division, tried to block James Longstreet's corps at Chester Gap on the twenty-first, but was driven out of the way.[3] On the twenty-second, and on the two succeeding days, Meade received a stream of dispatches from his cavalry, giving in accurate detail the whereabouts of Lee's forces, corps by corps, and in one instance, regiment by regiment, and correctly identifying Culpeper as his destination.[4] Buford wrote that he was hampered by ignorance of the movements of his own army and a lack of instructions as to what was expected of him, while his chief, Alfred Pleasonton, was apparently confining his efforts as corps commander to reading his subordinates' reports and suggesting to General Andrew A. Humphreys, Meade's chief of staff, "Let us get off to Culpeper pretty soon, and I think we may yet gain Richmond before the month is out," a prognostication which, written five days before the end of the month, did not err on the side of pessimism.[5]

After two months of a hard campaign, with constant movement, long marches in midsummer heat, almost daily skirmishes and scouts interspersed with several full-scale battles, the Cavalry Corps was badly in need of a period of rest and recuperation. Men and animals were worn out; thousands of men were dismounted,

---

95,000. *Ibid.*, II, 753. A short time later, Lee retreated beyond the Rapidan.

3. *The War of the Rebellion: A Compilation of the Official Records of the Union and Confederate Armies* (128 vols.; Washington, D.C., 1880–1901), Ser. I, Vol. XXVII, Pt. 3, p. 741; hereinafter cited as *Official Records.* Unless otherwise indicated, all citations are to Series I. As commanding officer of the 8th Illinois, Colonel Gamble had issued an order prohibiting "card playing or gaming of any kind for money," which he described as "swindling or thieving of the most cowardly kind." Orders No. 42, July 22, 1862, in 8th Illinois Volunteer Cavalry, Regimental and Company Order and Letter Books, Record Group 94, National Archives. Hereinafter cited as 8th Illinois O&L Books. Hereinafter, as in volume I of this study, the word "Cavalry" will be omitted, in the text as well as in the notes, from the names of mounted regiments, unless it is needed to avoid confusion. Thus, we shall speak of the 1st New York, 2nd Ohio, etc., but of the 4th Kentucky Cavalry, to distinguish it from the 4th Kentucky Mounted Infantry.

4. *Official Records*, Vol. XXVII, Pt. 3, pp. 741, 742, 753, 763, 765, 775, 776.

5. *Ibid.*, 741, 769.

and thousands more were riding unserviceable horses. On July 31, 12,945 cavalrymen of all ranks were present for duty, divided among twenty-nine complete and nine partial regiments, constituting, as before, three divisions under Buford, David McM. Gregg, and Judson Kilpatrick, with three brigades in Gregg's division, two in Buford's and Kilpatrick's, but with the Reserve Brigade usually attached operationally to Buford's First Division, thus making it too in effect a three-brigade division.[6] Every regiment was badly under strength; typically, the 6th Pennsylvania had only 200 men present for duty.[7] Particularly ominous was the sharp decline in the number of experienced officers present with the colors. Six of the eight brigades were commanded by colonels; of the thirty-eight complete and partial regiments, six were commanded by lieutenant colonels, ten by majors, and seven (including the 6th Pennsylvania) by captains.[8] Charles Francis Adams wrote on August 2 that in the eight companies of the 1st Massachusetts, then in Colonel J. B. McIntosh's First Brigade of Gregg's division, there were only five line officers "left for duty . . . but then the companies are small, as mine, for instance, which puts fourteen troopers all told in the squadron ranks."[9]

As usual at the end of a campaign, there was a grave shortage of horses. Pleasonton estimated on August 4 that from three to four thousand animals would be needed by September 1 to make up the existing deficiency, plus the wastage to be expected by the end of the month with just "the ordinary duties of campaigning," and went on to point out, "One of the most serious drawbacks in the injury of horses has been the loss of shoes, and the difficulty of having the horses shod before they become lame. . . . A great assistance in this respect would be to furnish a sufficient number of fitted shoes. . . . The shoes sent to us have been

6. *Ibid.*, 804.
7. Samuel L. Gracey, *Annals of the 6th Pennsylvania Cavalry* (Philadelphia, 1868), 196.
8. *Official Records*, Vol. XXVII, Pt. 3, p. 804.
9. W. C. Ford (ed.), *A Cycle of Adams Letters, 1861–1865* (2 vols.; Boston, 1920), II, 67; "a year ago," Adams wrote, "this regiment landed in Virginia. Of all the officers we then had I am the only one who has always been with the regiment . . . and of all those officers, but . . . six are with us now."

such in many instances that they could not be used or fitted on the march."[10] This dispatch was addressed to a new official in the War Department, General George Stoneman, chief of the recently established Cavalry Bureau.

On July 28, 1863, the adjutant general issued the following General Orders No. 236:

1. A bureau will be attached to the War Department, to be designated the Cavalry Bureau.

2. This bureau will have charge of the organization and equipment of the cavalry forces of the Army, and the provision for the mounts and remounts of the same.

3. The purchase of all the horses for the cavalry service will be made by officers of the Quartermaster's Department under the direction of the chief of the Cavalry Bureau. Inspections of horses offered for the cavalry service will be made by cavalry officers.

4. Depots will be established for the reception, organization, and discipline of cavalry recruits and new regiments, and for the collection, care and training of cavalry horses. These depots will be under the general charge of the Cavalry Bureau.

5. Copies of inspection reports of cavalry troops, and such returns as may be at any time called for, will be sent to the [Cavalry] Bureau. . . .

6. The enormous expense attending the maintenance of the cavalry arm points to the necessity of greater care and more judicious management on the part of cavalry officers, that their horses may be constantly kept up to the standard of efficiency for service. Great neglects of duty in this connection are to be attributed to officers in command of cavalry troops. It is the design of the War Department to correct such neglects by dismissing from the service officers whose inefficiency and inattention result in the deterioration and loss of the public animals under their charge.[11]

General Montgomery C. Meigs may well have been the chief driving force behind the establishment of the new bureau. He had had to bear the brunt of the complaints, some justified and

10. *Official Records*, Vol. XXVII, Pt. 3, p. 840. Only ten days earlier, General Lee had written Jefferson Davis that half his cavalry was unserviceable for want of horseshoes. Thomas F. Thiele, "The Evolution of Cavalry in the American Civil War, 1861–1963" (Ph.D. dissertation, University of Michigan, 1951), 225.

11. *Official Records*, Ser. III, Vol. III, p. 580. General Orders No. 237, issued the same day, designated George Stoneman as chief of the Cavalry Bureau. *Ibid.*, 581.

some not, concerning the chronic shortage of remounts and what was claimed to be the poor quality of many of the horses furnished. Having horses inspected before purchase by qualified cavalry officers was a procedure General Meigs had been urging for a long time, but hitherto without success. No one knew better than he the great cost of the horses bought to replace wastage, much of which he knew to be preventable.

There were many reasons why the new bureau, set afoot, like many bureaucratic innovations, with the best motives and on the basis of flawless reasoning in the abstract, failed to bring about the reforms expected of it. To begin with, its authority lay athwart the routines and powers of too many vested interests: the Quartermaster's Department, the Ordnance Bureau, the commanders of armies, and, to a degree, even the state governors. Secondly, of the four chiefs the bureau had in the brief eight and a half months of its independent existence, two appear to have been poor choices, and a third accepted the post with the understanding that he would be released from it in not more than sixty days and given a field command.[12] Obviously, a new bureau, with organizational jealousies and conflicts to contend with, needed not only leadership of high quality but also a continuity of such leadership, a continuity the Cavalry Bureau did not receive.

As to the competence of the four chiefs of the bureau, Stoneman, the first, had been recuperating in Washington on sick leave since the conclusion of the Chancellorsville Campaign. His reports and dispatches as head of the bureau show a lack of the determination and drive needed to create an effective organization from scratch and to enforce its acceptance as the central organ of cavalry administration. Implicit also in these dispatches is the peculiarly bureaucratic failing of considering a well-worded statement of a case, or better still, a crushing rejoinder to a complaint, the equivalent of action. Secretary of War Edwin McM. Stanton, at any rate, did not have a high opinion of Stoneman's work, nor that of his successor, General Kenner Garrard, who held the post

12. Stoneman had the post from August 1, 1863, to January 2, 1864; Kenner Garrard from January 2 to January 29, 1864; James H. Wilson from January 29 to April 7, 1864; and August Kautz from the seventh to the seventeenth of April, 1864.

for less than a month. When the third incumbent, James H. Wilson, reported for duty, Stanton said to him:

I have sent for you because I understand you do not fear responsibility. My life is worried out of me by the constant calls of the generals in the field for more cavalry horses, and by the dishonesty of the contractors who supply us with inferior horses, or who transfer their contracts to subcontractors who do not fill them at all. . . . I want you to reorganize the business, drive the rascals out and put the cavalry service on an efficient footing. I don't want you to fail as Stoneman did, nor to say, as Garrard did: "I cannot hope to surpass the efforts of Stoneman." . . . I give you *carte blanche* and will support you with all the resources of the Department.[13]

It may be surmised that one of the bureau's failures Stanton had in mind was General Orders No. 237, a triumph of bureaucratic ambition over realism. The order, doubtless inspired, if not written, by Stoneman, directed:

Inspections will be made of all cavalry troops at the end of every month, reports of which . . . will be forwarded . . . to the head of the Cavalry Bureau. . . . These reports will exhibit the condition of the cavalry service in general, and especially the condition of the mounts. The reports shall state what service the troops inspected have done since last inspected; how many miles their horses have traveled within the month; what character of service has been required of them, and under what circumstances it has been rendered; what appears to have been the care taken of them . . . what has been the quantity and character of the . . . forage issued to them; if there have [sic] been any deficiency of forage, and who is responsible therefor, &c.; and shall convey any other information pertaining to the objects of the inspection which it may be advisable should come to the notice of the Bureau.[14]

With 174 cavalry regiments actually in the service on August 4, 1863, and 28 others, plus six separate battalions, then in process of formation, this was a manifestly impossible program. The reports were simply not forthcoming, nor could they have been, even in the winter months when cavalry activity was at a minimum. Moreover, even if the reports had been submitted as the order required, the monumental task of reading and analyzing

13. James H. Wilson, *Under the Old Flag* (2 vols.; New York, 1912), I, 327. It should be remembered, however, that Wilson wrote in his old age, and more than forty-five years after this conversation with Stanton.
14. *Official Records*, Ser. III, Vol. III, p. 581.

them, and initiating whatever action may have been indicated in each case, would have been utterly beyond the capability of a small bureau. Inevitably, the order remained a dead letter; "The information which has been obtained in regard to the condition of the cavalry," wrote Lieutenant A. J. Alexander, assistant chief of the bureau in November, 1863, "[is] very meager."[15]

The order directed further that a sufficient number of horses be purchased immediately "to meet the present and prospective wants of the service up to September 1," and that requisitions for remounts were to be channeled to the chief of the bureau, whose responsibility it would be to see that they were filled. Pursuant to paragraphs 2 and 3 of General Orders No. 236, officers from the Quartermaster's Department were assigned to the bureau to purchase horses in the principal markets (Washington, Pittsburgh, Buffalo, Detroit, Indianapolis, Augusta, Me., Chicago, St. Louis, and New York), and eleven cavalry officers—three lieutenants, six captains, a major, and a colonel—were detailed as inspectors.[16] Acting under paragraph 3 of the order, Stoneman chose a site for a cavalry depot at Giesboro Point, near enough to Washington "to be under the immediate supervision and control of the head of the Cavalry Bureau." He directed the construction there of stabling for sixteen thousand horses; a "dismounted camp where all new regiments . . . can be sent to be mounted, armed, accoutered and equipped, and to which men of the old regiments are sent to be refitted and again sent to the field," was constructed on a site adjacent to the depot. Existing facilities in St. Louis, large enough to accommodate ten to twelve thousand men and horses, were to be turned over to the bureau to serve as the main cavalry depot in the West, and Stoneman suggested the establishment of a third depot either in Louisville, Indianapolis, or Columbus, Ohio.

The provision of paragraph 4 of General Orders No. 236, that

15. *Ibid.*, 990.
16. *Ibid.*, 886. The colonel in question was William Gamble, who with considerable distinction had commanded the 8th Illinois and later the First Brigade of Buford's division. It was Gamble's brigade that opposed Heth's division on the Chambersburg Pike on July 1 at Gettysburg. Gamble's inspection assignment was temporary; he returned to a field command in the summer of 1864.

these depots be used for the "reception, organization, and discipline" of cavalry recruits and new regiments, and for the "collection, care, and training of cavalry horses," remained a dead letter. The depots fulfilled fairly well, even if not to everyone's satisfaction, their primary duty of supplying horses for the cavalry, including many thousands of rehabilitated animals, but they did not "train" horses in the sense that horses for European cavalry were trained by expert horsemen before being issued to the troops. Indeed, Stoneman's depots did not train the horses at all, and the bolting of untrained horses ridden by unskilled riders, the first time they were exposed to gunfire, remained a serious hazard in the Union cavalry to the very end of the war. Thus, Colonel Alfred Gibbs of the 19th New York reported after a skirmish near Manassas Junction, "The horses becoming unmanageable when the firing commenced, I lost five men with horses and equipments. My horses are too green to be serviceable as cavalry."[17]

With the war in its third year, making good the constant depletion of manpower was another major problem for the cavalry. Both of the usual methods of accomplishing this—the raising of new regiments and the recruitment of men for existing regiments —presented difficulties. The raising of new regiments, and a relatively infrequent variant, the raising of new battalions for existing regiments, was greatly favored by state governors. With upwards of forty officers needed for a new regiment, and thirteen for a new battalion, and that many commissions to be parceled out among the faithful, recruitment of a new unit was a political windfall whose advantages no governor was likely to overlook. Consequently, this was the favored procedure in the majority of states, and large numbers of new regiments were raised in 1863 and as late as the latter part of 1864. The War Department must share the blame with the governors for this situation, because of its habit of requisitioning from the states short-term (six-, nine-, and twelve-month) regiments to be raised in great haste to meet every real or fancied emergency. The training received by regi-

17. E. C. Barksdale, "Semi-Regular and Irregular Warfare in the Civil War" (Ph.D. dissertation, University of Texas, 1941), 110. Colonel (later major general) Gibbs, West Point Class of 1846, commanded the Reserve Brigade at various times and eventually rose to the command of a cavalry division.

ments raised in 1861 and 1862 was inadequate enough, but the absence of affirmative evidence to the contrary strongly suggests that the 1863 and 1864 regiments received even less and were sent into action with no training worthy of the name. The results were uniformly deplorable. James H. Wilson, whose Third Division included four of these newly raised regiments, wrote that when he got them, they were "entirely inexperienced . . . greener than grass," and that it took two of his veteran regiments, the 1st Vermont and the 5th New York, to "drive" them into action.[18]

The historian of the 1st Massachusetts was of the opinion that the raising of new units "not only brought into the field useless regiments, because wanting in drill and experience, but it usually furnished plenty of inexperienced field officers, of high rank."[19] Generals Henry W. Halleck and Grant were of the same opinion; when remounts were badly needed as the Wilderness Campaign was about to get under way, Halleck wrote Grant, "The Twenty-Second New York Cavalry, now at the depot, is entirely undisciplined and unfit for the field. I have ordered them armed as infantry, and their horses given to the Second Ohio . . . and to detachments of the Army of the Potomac."[20] The unfortunate New Yorkers were remounted a few months later and were assigned to Wilson's division; theirs was one of the newly raised regiments which, he claimed, had to be driven into action by his veterans. Grant expressed the opinion that "horses are worth more to . . . veteran cavalry, who have no horses, than men and horses [of a new regiment] together are. A new regiment will be worth something on foot, but less than their forage on horseback."[21]

The most scathing comment on "green" cavalry regiments in general, and on one of them in particular, was penned by Frederick Whittaker.

18. James H. Wilson, "The Cavalry of the Army of the Potomac," *Papers of the Military Historical Society of Massachusetts*, XIII (1913), 78. In addition to inexperience, these regiments were also handicapped by poor carbines. Wilson reports that their performance improved when he replaced their unreliable Smith carbines with Spencers.

19. Benjamin W. Crowninshield, "Cavalry in Virginia During the War of the Rebellion," *Papers of the Military Historical Society of Massachusetts*, XIII (1913), 23.

20. *Official Records*, XXXIII, 966.

21. *Ibid.*, Vol. XXVII, Pt. 2, p. 329.

In sending reinforcements to the field, heaven grant that they may not
be organized into fresh regiments, as they were . . . in 1864. . . . Formed
into new regiments to swell the vanity of more of those insolent in-
capables who so foully disgraced their uniform . . . such regiments
indulged in stampedes that members of the old corps would have
blushed to be involved in. At Five Forks . . . such a green regiment, six
hundred strong . . . [was] driven back in disgraceful panic . . . with
their colonel . . . at the head of the fugitives. An old regiment, depleted . . . to only forty-five carbines, was then advanced and held
the position . . . their officers had risen from the ranks, and the men
knew them; and the officers of the 20th Pennsylvania were appointed
from civil life, and were the first to quit the field.[22]

A four-company battalion, made up of recruits under officers
commissioned from civil life, was added to the 1st Massachusetts
in March, 1864. The regimental historian describes the result:

probably to induce men to enlist, Governor Andrew saw fit to recruit
new officers with the men. Consequently, when this battalion joined
the regiment, it was with entirely inexperienced company officers. . . .
Here were four hundred men and officers without any experience
whatever, utterly green, outnumbering the men in the eight other companies. It followed that when a detail was made for any purpose, one
of these inexperienced captains would outrank all the lieutenants in
the old command. . . . It turned out that in the first fifteen days of the
campaign of 1864 . . . this new battalion went all to pieces.[23]

The most common means of restoring the numbers of a regiment was to send home a recruiting detail of officers and enlisted
men to make the rounds of the towns and villages where the regiment had been recruited originally. The success of their efforts

---

22. [Frederick Whittaker], "A Volunteer Cavalryman," *Volunteer Cavalry: The Lessons of a Decade* (New York, 1871), 32. The "old regiment"
Whittaker speaks of may well have been the 6th Pennsylvania. Their own
historian's account of the fight at Five Forks has an epic quality befitting
his theme. "Our regiment was in the advance," he wrote, "and when, in
front of these formidable lines, the 6th Pennsylvania Cavalry for the last
time dismounted to fight on foot, there stood in the ranks but 48 men bearing carbines. These all went into the fight. There were no Nos. 4 left behind
to hold horses that day . . . the horses were given in charge to officers' servants and such other peaceful followers as could be borrowed for the occasion. Gracey, *Annals of the 6th*, 337.
23. Benjamin W. Crowninshield, *A History of the First Regiment of
Massachusetts Cavalry Volunteers* (Boston, 1891), 196–97. Two full companies, complete with new officers, were added to the 6th Ohio, also in
March, 1864. *Official Records*, XXXIII, 778.

varied with the amount of favorable publicity their regiment had received in the local papers, their own forensic skills, the state of the war at the moment, and the keenness of the competition. The same arts and wiles were used to attract recruits in 1863 and 1864 as had been used to raise the regiment originally.[24] A somewhat extreme case was that of William F. Cody, destined to become famous as "Buffalo Bill," whose "autobiography" records that "after haveing been under the influence of bad whiskey, I awoke to find myself a soldier in the Seventh Kansas. I did not remember how or when I had enlisted."[25]

A recruit fresh from the farm or workshop added to a company of veterans was far better off than one in a unit made up entirely of recruits like himself. The rough and ready schooling he received from the old hands helped him adapt to army life and gave him the campaigning wisdom they had had to acquire in a hard school. The 6th Michigan received more than two hundred recruits in early 1864; "being put in with the old men, they were worked into good soldiers before the [Wilderness] campaign opened, and proved to be as reliable and efficient as the veterans with whom they were associated."[26] An opposite judgment, and another demonstration of the lack of unanimity on practically any Civil War topic, was Charles Russell Lowell's contention that "for cavalry, raw recruits sent to a regiment in large numbers are worse than useless; they are of no account themselves and they spoil the old men."[27]

24. At times these recruiting missions were eminently successful. In March, 1864, the 1st New York got 250 recruits by this means. *Official Records*, XXXIII, 778. Vermont was one of the few states that assumed the responsibility of keeping filled the ranks of its regiments; as a result, the 1st Vermont was brought up to full strength, or nearly so, at fairly frequent intervals.

25. Stephen Z. Starr, *Jennison's Jayhawkers* (Baton Rouge, 1973), 294.

26. J. H. Kidd, *Personal Recollections of a Cavalryman* (Ionia, Mich., 1908), 233. The 7th Pennsylvania received so many recruits in April, 1864, that after the ranks of its twelve companies were filled enough recruits were left to make up four "supernumerary" companies. General Orders No. 21, April 11, 1864, in 7th Pennsylvania Volunteer Cavalry, Regimental and Company Order and Letter Books, Record Group 94, National Archives. Hereinafter cited as 7th Pennsylvania O&L Books.

27. Edward W. Emerson, *The Life and Letters of Charles Russell Low-*

The ideal solution would have been to give the recruits a few months, or even a few weeks, of training in a depot by veteran instructors before they were sent to join their units in the field. The language of paragraph 4 of General Orders No. 236 ("Depots will be established for the reception, organization, and discipline of . . . recruits") suggests that the War Department had some such plan in mind. Nothing came of it, however, for the scheme ran counter to the narrowly regimental pattern of army organization, the strong local roots and ties of every regiment, and their administrative isolation from each other. In the early weeks of the war, W. B. Franklin and Irvin McDowell had proposed that volunteer regiments be made up of three battalions, one of which was to remain in a base camp or depot to receive and train recruits, so that the two battalions in the field could be kept up to strength by a steady stream of adequately trained replacements.[28] This would have been an admirable scheme, especially for the cavalry, but it was too much in conflict with the political, organizational, and psychological realities of the United States of the Civil War years to have any chance of being adopted.

Manpower problems were troublesome enough, but the perennial shortage of "serviceable mounts" was even more so. The demands of the army, added to those of agriculture and trade, outgrew the limited supply of horses suitable for the cavalry. Prices rose from the 1861-1862 average of about $120, to $150 by the summer of 1863. Later in 1863, the president, by executive order, forbade the export of horses, and Secretary Stanton came up with the unhelpful notion of mounting the cavalry on mules.[29]

---

ell (Boston, 1907), 287. In the winter of 1863–1864, the 17th Pennsylvania received "many" new recruits. The regimental historian noted that "the very friendly and cordial feeling of comradeship that originally existed between the enlisted men and the officers was no longer a distinguishing feature. The lines drawn between the officers and new recruits became more marked. . . . Many of the recruits were of inferior intelligence, requiring the enforcement of more rigid discipline." Henry P. Moyer, *History of the 17th Regiment Pennsylvania Volunteer Cavalry* (Lebanon, Pa., 1911), 287.

28. See Vol. I, p. 76 of the present work. In 1872, the British army adopted this "linked battalion" system for its cavalry, as part of the so-called "Cardwell Reforms."

29. Allan Nevins, *The War for the Union: The War Becomes Revolution, 1862–1863* (New York, 1960), 476n, 477n.

Throughout the late summer and autumn of 1863, Pleasonton and his principal subordinates voiced the by now habitual complaint that entire brigades, already down to half strength because of the absence, legitimate or otherwise, of its men, were reduced further to half of that half, or even less, through the loss of horses. Thus, within ten days of the return of the Reserve Brigade to the army with every man mounted, General Wesley Merritt reported that he had "sent to the Quartermaster's Department, Washington . . . 471 disabled . . . horses. There are at least 100 more in the command. . . . The frightful loss among horses is owing to a disease which resembles 'hoof rot,' from the effects of which the finest appearing horses . . . become disabled in one day's march."[30] The day following this report, Buford informed Cavalry Corps headquarters that of the two thousand men in his division, all fully equipped and "available for duty," not more than half could be used for "arduous duty" by reason of the poor condition of their horses; that one of his brigades had been reduced from 1,488 mounted men to 850 in two weeks; and that he could not report the number of diseased horses in his division, because the "disease [hoof rot] is on the increase daily."[31] Kilpatrick's division, numbering 3,500 fully equipped and mounted troopers on June 29, was down to 2,100 men for duty on October 25. On the three previous days the division had sent 265 dismounted men to Giesboro Point; they "had their arms and equipments and were in every way ready for duty, but their horses, having been affected with the hoof disease and swelled tongue, were totally unserviceable."[32]

At the same time that Pleasonton's horses were being decimated by disease, the problem was being compounded by a grave shortage of forage. The horses of Gregg's division went without hay for twenty-one consecutive days. As Stoneman correctly pointed out, "no horses, however good and bought at whatever price, can stand this kind of treatment in a region where but lit-

---

30. *Official Records*, Vol. XXIX, Pt. 2, p. 353.
31. *Ibid.*, 400.
32. *Ibid.*, 400. The 1st Maine, then in the First Brigade of the Second Division, reported the number of its serviceable horses reduced from 556 to 275. *Ibid.*, XXXIII, 780.

tle, if any, grass can be procured."[33] No explanation was forth-coming, then or later, to account for the shortage.

These doleful reports were showering down on General Meade and were being passed on by him to the War Department at the same time that the Cavalry Bureau was sending large numbers of horses to his army. As in the days of the McClellan-Meigs contro-versy after the battle of Antietam, there were major discrepancies between the number of horses Stoneman claimed to have sent, and the number the Cavalry Corps claimed to have received. Stoneman wrote that in the six months from May 1 to October 31, 35,078 cavalry horses had been sent to the Army of the Potomac and pointed out that his figure did not include horses captured from the enemy or "taken from citizens" by the Cavalry Corps.[34] Within a day of Stoneman's report, and independently of it, Pleas-onton turned in a report of his receipts that was utterly irreconcil-able with Stoneman's figure. "Since April," Pleasonton wrote (that is, in seven months as against Stoneman's six), his corps had received "from all sources," presumably including horses taken from the enemy and from "citizens," a total of 18,676 horses, or just over half the number claimed by Stoneman.[35] A difference of a few hundred between the two figures might be ascribed to hasty record keeping by amateurs, but a difference of nearly 50 percent is beyond comprehension, and the Cavalry Bureau and the War Department might have been forgiven if, after seeing Pleasonton's report, they had thrown up their hands at what seemed a hopeless task.

General Halleck evidently did have that feeling. After seeing Stoneman's figures he pointed out that with the manpower of the Cavalry Corps ranging from ten to fourteen thousand in the same six-month period, every man in the corps had been remounted three times, or every two months. At that rate, he wrote, the 223 regiments of mounted troops in the service in November, 1863,

33. *Ibid.*, Vol. XXIX, Pt. 2, p. 419; see also 339, 418.

34. *Ibid.*, 398. The monthly figures claimed by Stoneman (May, 5073; June, 6,927; July, 4,716; August, 5,499; September, 5,827; October, 7,036) are significant. If accurate, they show that the Cavalry Corps received re-mounts with fair regularity and in substantial numbers.

35. *Ibid.*, 404. Pleasonton stated in the same report that his corps had lost 7,870 horses in action and had turned in 12,350 disabled animals.

would require 435,000 horses in 1864. He did not say, although
he might have, that at the then prevailing prices the 435,000
horses would cost the government more than $65,000,000, if so
many horses acceptable for cavalry service could be found at all,
which in itself was highly problematical. He did say, however,
and with ample justification, "The waste and destruction of cavalry horses . . . has proven an evil of such magnitude as to require
some immediate and efficient remedy"; the efficiency of the remedy he went on to propose, however, is open to question.[36] He
wrote:

The organization of the Cavalry Bureau, with frequent and thorough
inspection, it was hoped would in some measure remedy these evils.
To reach their source, however, further legislation may be necessary.
Probably the principal fault is in the treatment of their horses by the
cavalry soldiers. Authority should therefore be given to dismount and
transfer to the infantry . . . every man whose horse is, through his
fault or neglect, rendered unfit for service. The same rule might be
applied to cavalry officers who fail to maintain the efficiency of their
regiments and companies. The vacancies thus created could be filled
by corresponding transfers from the regular and volunteer infantry.[37]

One may sympathize with Halleck's desire to deal with a
seemingly insoluble problem, and unquestionably, mistreatment
and neglect were major causes of the appalling wastage of horses.
But the replacement of men guilty of this mistreatment and neglect, and of officers who tolerated it, would have been a cure worse
than the disease. Halleck left out of account the fact that it had
taken two years of war to bring many of these men and officers up
to a level of competence; transferring them to the infantry and
replacing them with footsoldiers might perhaps have given the
army better horsemasters, but surely not a better cavalry.

To deal with losses due to disease, Stoneman had caused an
order to be issued on his first day in office, for the appointment of
a "veterinary surgeon" to each regiment of cavalry, a step that

36. *Ibid.*, Ser. III, Vol. IV, p. 1041. Halleck took the 435,000 figure
from a report of Stoneman's in *ibid.*, Vol. XXIX, Pt. 2, p. 399. If the horse
population of the loyal states in 1864 was about the same as the 1860 cen-
sus figure of just under 4,700,000, the cavalry alone would have taken
nearly 10 percent of it in 1864, on the basis of the Stoneman-Halleck estimate.
37. *Ibid.*, Ser. III, Vol. IV, p. 1042.

might well have been taken in 1861.[38] The veterinarians were to be selected by the chief of the Cavalry Bureau on the recommendation of regimental commanders, a recommendation to be based on an examination of candidates by panels of three officers in every regiment. The system smacks of excessive centralization and red tape, but these flaws made no difference in the result, for, as Stoneman reported a short time later, there was a "deficiency of veterinary talent in the country, and . . . [an] impossibility of obtaining what little there . . . [was] for the compensation . . . allowed by the Government."[39]

The most important function of Stoneman's depots was to accept broken-down horses turned in by the cavalry and to reclaim as many of them as possible for reissue. Despite the problems inherent in such building projects—"the failure of contractors, the difficulty of procuring laborers, &c."—construction of the Giesboro Point depot proceeded with remarkable speed, and by mid-October it had "upward of 16,000" unserviceable horses in its stables.[40] As horses were delivered to the depot they were inspected, and those with a contagious disease were immediately shot. The others—many requiring nothing more than rest, decent care, and regular feeding—were reinspected when they were thought to be back in sound condition; some were sold out of the service, some were given to the Quartermaster's Corps or the artillery as draft animals, and only the best were set aside for reissue to the cavalry.

Not surprisingly, there were conflicting opinions on the quality of these "best" animals. On one occasion, George Custer complained that a detachment of eighty men had rejoined his brigade from dismounted camp on horses "the majority . . . [of which were] unserviceable, and . . . really a more indifferent lot than those sent to Washington as unserviceable." He went on to say that of the forty men of the 7th Michigan who were with this detachment when it left the depot, seventeen had to turn back, "on

38. *Ibid.*, 605; General Orders No. 259, August 1, 1863. The addition of veterinarians to cavalry regiments had been authorized by an Act of Congress of March 3, 1863.

39. *Ibid.*, III, 886.

40. *Ibid.*, 885–86.

account of the horses upon which they were mounted being unable to reach the army." Then for good measure he added, "numerous complaints reach me from regimental commanders against the inferior quality of horses sent to them . . . from the dismounted camp."[41]

Custer's report, forwarded by Pleasonton to General Meade and by him to Stoneman, elicited from the latter an endorsement that cannot be said to have met the problem. "I have understood," Stoneman wrote, "that Custer's brigades are great horse-killers, and it is very likely that the 17 horses were used up as stated, though they were considered serviceable when they left the depot."[42] Stoneman's reaction to another complaint of the same sort was even less helpful; he commented, "It was expected that [the reissue of horses] would cause complaint, but the Government has these horses on hand, and unless they are disposed of, they must either be kept and fed at great expense or must be reissued for further use."[43]

The most violent complaints, however, were reserved for the mechanics of the reissue system instituted by the Cavalry Bureau. Men who lost their horses, or whose unserviceable mounts were turned in to the Giesboro depot, were collected in the "dismounted camp" where they remained until they received horses to ride back to their units. In his usual firm but restrained fashion, Buford reported that "some of the dismounted men who went to Washington to be remounted have returned, and I learn that the officers and men are scattered all about the city."[44] Kilpatrick contended that a major reason for the decline of the numerical strength of his division was that his men had "learned to appreciate the easy life offered them at the Dismounted Camp, and take every opportunity to get there. They neglect their horses [and] lose their equipments, knowing in either case that they will be sent in to refit."[45] Custer's complaint was, characteristically, the least temperate. His brigade, he wrote, "suffers as much from the

41. *Ibid.*, Ser. I, Vol. XXIX, Pt. 2, p. 448.
42. *Ibid.*, 448–49.
43. *Ibid.*, 419.
44. *Ibid.*, 6.
45. *Ibid.*, 401.

influence and effect of the Dismounted Camp as it does frcm the weapons of the enemy . . . there are men in my command who have been captured by the enemy, carried to Richmond, and rejoined my command in less time than it frequently requires for men to proceed to Dismounted Camp and return mounted."[46]

Pleasonton's comment on the situation indicates his decision that in his capacity as commander of the corps he had to go beyond mere criticism and offer a remedy as well. It also reveals his readiness to disparage the work of his predecessor:

The poor quality of the horses sent from Dismounted Camp, and the want of care in the manner of forwarding them to the army, prove . . . the absolute failure of that enterprise and convince me that some other system must be adopted to keep the cavalry properly mounted and equipped. I . . . suggest that the entire business of fitting out the cavalry . . . be placed under the orders and control of the commanding general; that depots be established (within the actual limits of the army where practicable) where men who have lost horses and equipments can be readily re-equipped . . . instead of, as at present, lying sometimes for months together in a Dismounted Camp over which he has no control, and where it is reputed there is no discipline or order, and which officers and soldiers have learned to look to as a comfortable escape from the performance of duty in the field.[47]

There appears to be little doubt that the system of providing remounts for the dismounted men, and getting them back to their units, was faulty and lax, but Pleasonton's remedy was no solution, as Stoneman was obviously pleased to point out.

46. *Ibid.*, 448. The historian of the 6th Pennsylvania wrote of the dismounted camp: "Every cavalry soldier looking for a resting place goes to Remount Camp; there he knows that if he wants to go, he will be sent to his regiment, and if he wants to skulk, he has a better chance there than anywhere else. . . . There are always from 1000 to 1500 men in the camp, made up of squads and individuals from every cavalry regiment in the Eastern army. . . . To preserve . . . [the camp] in such discipline as our regiment was accustomed to was almost an impossibility with the means at hand." Gracey, *Annals of the 6th*, 297.

47. *Official Records*, Vol. XXIX, Pt. 2, p. 418. Gregg, who stayed out of the controversy, reported on October 24 that he had in his division 3,144 serviceable and 458 unserviceable horses, and that in the six weeks since September 18 he had lost in action 950 and had turned in as unserviceable 1,453 animals. He also stated that there was an "insufficiency of forage" for his division, which had received no hay whatever in the two weeks prior to the date of his report. *Ibid.*, 400–401.

Pleasonton's opinions in regard to the discipline of the dismounted camp, and also in regard to the quality of the horses issued . . . might possibly have more weight had they been founded . . . upon personal observation and inspection. The plan he proposes . . . necessarily indicates that he contemplates that in the future the Army of the Potomac shall remain stationary to protect . . . [his depots] from Stuart, or that his depots shall be of a portable character . . . and taken with the army in its various and uncertain movements.[48]

General Meade wrote the adjutant general that he concurred "with . . . [Pleasonton] in the opinion that the practice of sending the dismounted men to the camp at Washington has a most injurious and demoralizing effect upon the service, and I earnestly request that it be discontinued, and that the horses, arms, and equipments that may from time to time be required . . . be sent out as they are needed."[49]

The army commander having endorsed Pleasonton's proposal, Stoneman could not dismiss it out of hand; he wrote Meade that as the officer in command of the Army of the Potomac, he (Meade) would have to decide how the situation should be handled, and that his decision, whatever it might be, would "meet with the hearty cooperation of the Cavalry Bureau."[50] With that dispatch, the controversy, then in its third month, quietly faded away, leaving behind it frayed tempers and the situation precisely as it had been when the controversy began.

While the cavalry generals were conducting their war with the Cavalry Bureau, they also had to carry on the more important war with the Confederacy. A brief period of quiescence had followed the return of the armies from Pennsylvania to positions long familiar to them, the Union army on the east (or north) bank of the Rappahannock, Lee's infantry to the west (or south) of the Rapidan, and his cavalry between the two rivers. Everyone was in need of a rest; equipment and weapons had to be refurbished or replaced. Lengthy discussions on strategy between General Lee and President Jefferson Davis resulted in the detachment of Longstreet and two divisions of his corps to reinforce Braxton

48. *Ibid.*, 419.
49. *Ibid.*, 400.
50. *Ibid.*, 420.

Bragg's Army of Tennessee. Then, following the battle of Chicka-mauga in September, which Longstreet's men were instrumental in winning, two corps of Meade's army were also transported west, to Chattanooga.

The inactivity of the main bodies of the two armies did not mean a rest for the cavalry. There were constant minor clashes as the Union and the Confederate horse probed each other's posi-tions in an area well known to both. At the beginning of August, Buford, aggressive as always, crossed the Rappahannock and passed through the Brandy Station battlefield to within two and a half miles of Culpeper. His purpose, hampered by confused and misunderstood orders, was apparently to establish a bridgehead to permit the rebuilding of the Orange & Alexandria trestle at Rappahannock Station.[51] The operation was conducted in the midst of a heat wave "ruinous to horse-flesh" and not without an effect on Buford's temper. The uncalled-for interference of Gen-eral John S. Slocum with the movements of one of Buford's bri-gades caused him to let fly with a blast that, needless to say, was ignored; "I am disgusted and worn out with the system that seems to prevail. There is so much apathy and so little disposition to fight and cooperate that I wish to be relieved from the Army of the Potomac. . . . The ground I gain I wish to hold. . . . I am will-ing to serve my country, but I do not wish to sacrifice the brave men under my command."[52] Buford's equanimity was, however, restored by the Confederate cavalry; attacked at Brandy Station by a brigade of "Jeb" Stuart's corps on the afternoon of August 4, he reported, "The enemy's reconnaissance was an utter failure. My casualties are trifling. . . . The First and Reserve Brigades be-haved like heroes."[53]

Apart from scouts by both sides which led to almost daily col-lisions, each with its toll of a few men killed, wounded, or cap-tured, nothing of importance happened until mid-September. Gregg's division, with headquarters at Manassas Junction, pro-tected the line of the Orange & Alexandria; his people complained

51. The movement is covered in a long series of dispatches in *ibid.*, Vol. XXVII, Pt. 3, pp. 819–20, 821, 822, 827, 831, 834, 835, 839, 840.
52. *Ibid.*, 835, 834.
53. *Ibid.*, Vol. XXIX, Pt. 1, p. 22; see also 21.

of being worn out with an excess of picketing and long scouts in the heat.[54] The streams were at a late-summer low, fordable nearly everywhere, and no picket or reserve post was safe from a sudden attack by small squads of the enemy, guided by local inhabitants. There was a nightly toll of losses, caused on occasion by "improper dispositions, and . . . want of care and vigilance."[55] One such incident, in which a picket post of the 4th New York was surprised by a dash of the enemy across Kelly's Ford, with the loss of two of the New Yorkers killed, three wounded, and twenty-four captured with their horses, weapons, and all their equipment, led to the regiment being punished by having its regimental colors taken away.[56]

In mid-September, acting on a report that "the enemy has made a retrograde movement," Meade sent Pleasonton on a reconnaissance in force to Raccoon Ford on the Rapidan. The II Corps was ordered to follow the cavalry, to assist it in withdrawing safely if it met an enemy force larger than it was able to handle, but Pleasonton was cautioned not to "bring on a general engagement."[57]

Pleasonton was to begin his advance by attacking the Confederate cavalry at Culpeper. Stuart had received warning the night before that the Federals were about to move against him and was able to move his wagons and disabled horses out of danger. Pleasonton crossed the Rappahannock at daybreak, opposed by "Grumble" Jones's brigade, under Lunsford Lomax, and W. H. F. Lee's, under Colonel R. L. T. Beale. Attacking "with great spirit and rapidity," the Federals drove Lomax and Beale

54. *Ibid.*, Vol. XXVII, Pt. 3, p. 720; Frederick Denison, *Sabres and Spurs: The First Regiment Rhode Island Cavalry* (Central Falls, R.I., 1876), 281. Charles Francis Adams, on the other hand, wrote on August 8, "Summer picket is the pleasantest work we have to do, and is really charming. . . . The anxiety wears a little on one, for though one soon gets accustomed to the proximity of the enemy, the necessity of continued vigilance and perpetual preparation gets wearisome at last. Still, it is very pleasant, this getting away from camps, brigades and infantry, away from orders, details and fatigue duty, out to the front with no army near, the enemy before you and all quiet along your line." Ford (ed.), *A Cycle of Adams Letters*, II, 68–69.

55. *Official Records*, Vol. XXIX, Pt. 1, pp. 89, 103.

56. *Ibid.*, 114; see also Abner Hard, *History of the Eighth Cavalry Regiment, Illinois Volunteers* (Aurora, Ill., 1868), 273.

57. *Official Records*, Vol. XXIX, Pt. 2, p. 175.

back to and beyond Culpeper.[58] The 3rd Pennsylvania of McIntosh's brigade, Gregg's division, claimed to have captured three guns of a Confederate battery in this advance, but, their historians have written, Kilpatrick, "who had a newspaper reporter connected with his headquarters, sent North . . . a glowing dispatch claiming sole credit for the achievement."[59] Rival claims for such captures were commonplace and must be read with considerable skepticism, but given Kilpatrick's character and his usual mode of behavior, the Pennsylvanians' claim cannot be dismissed out of hand. The Federals at any rate reached the Rapidan early the following morning but were unable to force a crossing against the Confederate infantry and artillery posted on the far bank. They did learn from prisoners, however, that Richard Ewell's and A. P. Hill's corps were encamped near Orange Court House, and that Longstreet's corps had "gone south, destination said to be Tennessee."[60] Checked at the Rapidan, Pleasonton returned to the Rappahannock without incident.

On the twentieth, in anticipation of a forward move by his entire army, Meade ordered Pleasonton to return to the Rapidan with two divisions of cavalry and reconnoiter the area from Madison Court House down to Barnett's and Robertson's fords. He was to determine the position and numbers of the enemy, the state of the roads leading to the Rapidan, and "the character of the fords and of the ground on both sides where these fords cross the Rapidan, and the advantages such points afford for effecting a crossing in the face of the enemy."[61] Pursuant to this order, Buford moved south on the twenty-second on the road from Madison Court House to Gordonsville, expecting to join Kilpatrick's division at the crossing of the Rapidan at Liberty Mills. At Jack's

58. Henry B. McClellan, *I Rode with Jeb Stuart: The Life and Campaigns of Major-General J. E. B. Stuart* (Bloomington, Ind., 1958), 372; George M. Neese, *Three Years in the Confederate Horse Artillery* (New York, 1911), 210.

59. Regimental History Committee, *History of the 3d Pennsylvania Cavalry* (Philadelphia, 1905), 340; see also McClellan, *I Rode with Jeb Stuart*, 373. Kilpatrick claimed that one of the guns was captured by the 2nd New York and the other two by the 1st Vermont, both of his division. *Official Records*, Vol. XXIX, Pt. 1, p. 118.

60. *Official Records*, Vol. XXIX, Pt. 2, p. 177.

61. *Ibid.*, 215–16.

Shop, however, some distance north of the Rapidan, Buford encountered Confederate cavalry under Stuart. The Confederates attacked at once. While his men were charging Buford, but without being able to bring his advance to a halt, Stuart received word that another large body of Union cavalry had reached Liberty Mills and was directly behind him. The intruders were Henry E. Davies' brigade of Kilpatrick's division. Stuart had to halt his attack on Buford to deal with the threat in his rear. As soon as he did so, Buford went over to the attack, and Stuart was caught squarely between two fires. At one point in the ensuing action, Stuart's artillery, posted on a low hill, was simultaneously firing north at Buford and south at Davies, and his regiments of cavalry were charging in opposite directions, some north, some south, all within sight of each other.[62] Fortunately for Stuart, Lomax was able to drive Davies away from the road to Liberty Mills before Custer's brigade arrived, and the Confederates were able to escape across the Rapidan. .

A week after Stuart's narrow escape, General Lee learned from his spies that two corps of infantry had been detached from Meade's army; these were the XI and XII Corps, both small, sent to Chattanooga under Joseph Hooker. With the numerical odds less heavily weighted against him, Lee decided to take the offensive in order to prevent any further detachments from the Army of the Potomac to reinforce Grant in Tennessee and, at the same time, to free northern Virginia of the Union army.[63] The ensuing Bristoe Campaign began on October 9 with the crossing of the Rapidan by Lee's two corps of infantry.

It was General Lee's intention to repeat on a lesser scale the march around the right flank and to the rear of the Union army that had produced such spectacular results in the campaign against John Pope, and he had Stuart, with Wade Hampton's division under his immediate command, cover the right, or inside, flank of his advance.[64] Fitzhugh Lee's division, plus two brigades

62. McClellan, I Rode with Jeb Stuart, 374–75; see also William N. McDonald, A History of the Laurel Brigade (Baltimore, 1907), 174–76.
63. Douglas S. Freeman, R. E. Lee: A Biography (4 vols.; New York, 1941), III, 170.
64. Stuart exercised direct command of the division in the absence of

of infantry, were left behind at Raccoon Ford to keep Buford occupied.

Pleasonton's cavalrymen had come a long way in competence since the grim days of August, 1862; they discovered Lee's forward movement as soon as it began and at once reported it to Meade.[65] Stuart had scraps on the tenth with detachments of Kilpatrick's cavalry at Bethsaida Church and at James City and reached Culpeper on the morning of the eleventh. In the meantime, Meade's infantry had crossed to the east (north) bank of the Rappahannock, leaving Kilpatrick's division just east of Culpeper, facing Stuart, and Buford still facing Fitzhugh Lee across the Rapidan. On the tenth, Buford had crossed the Rapidan downstream of Lee's right on a reconnaissance in force, but had been driven back across the river and began to retreat north-eastward, toward Stevensburg and Brandy Station, with Lee in close pursuit.

Stuart, at Culpeper, finding Kilpatrick drawn up on open ground squarely across his path, rightly decided not to risk a frontal attack with two brigades of about fifteen hundred men against Kilpatrick's obviously much larger division.[66] He withdrew a short distance, turned west, then north, and then rode hard over a succession of country lanes toward the familiar position on Fleetwood Heights, on Kilpatrick's right flank and rear. It was not difficult for Kilpatrick to deduce Stuart's intention; he deployed into column to the rear and, at the best speed of his horses, made for Fleetwood Heights also.[67] The result was an extraordinary spectacle: the commands of Stuart and Kilpatrick, in plain sight of each other, riding hell for leather on converging roads toward the same destination.

Nor was this all. Buford was coming up from the southeast, followed closely by the twelve regiments of Fitzhugh Lee's com-

---

Hampton, who was recovering from the severe wounds he had received in the cavalry battle at Gettysburg on July 3.

65. By October 10 Meade knew that Lee had begun to march around his right flank. *Official Records*, Vol. XXIX, Pt. 2, p. 279.

66. Kilpatrick had just under 4,000 men. For Stuart's and Kilpatrick's numbers, see McClellan, *I Rode with Jeb Stuart*, 379.

67. *Official Records*, Vol. XXIX, Pt. 1, pp. 441, 443.

mand. Seeing the Stuart-Kilpatrick race up ahead, Lee decided that he could, by a change of direction, head off the Federal cavalry from the Rappahannock fords, and he too went racing toward Fleetwood Heights. The historian of the Laurel Brigade described the race:

Stuart . . . marched rapidly toward Brandy Station. . . . About a half mile to the right, on higher ground and on a line nearly parallel to Stuart's course appeared the serried masses of Kilpatrick's column. He was going at a rapid gait . . . and each step brought the forces a little nearer each other. As they moved along at a trot, gray and blue sent up shouts of mutual defiance, brandishing their sabres menacingly, and occasionally solitary horsemen rode out from either column and exchanged shots. . . . The sun shone brightly in a cloudless sky and its beams glancing from the myriad glittering sabres presented a scene of martial splendor.[68]

And this is how Lieutenant G. W. Beale, 9th Virginia, viewed the scene:

Probably no more interesting sight or exciting scene in cavalry warfare occurred in the long struggle than was here presented, than that of Stuart in pursuit of Kilpatrick, and Fitz Lee dashing forward to cut him off. The Federal column dashing down the road at full speed, Hampton's division in hot pursuit, and Lee's twelve regiments throwing themselves across the path of the Federal retreat—all in fastest motion, horsemen at the gallop, artillery at the gallop, battle flags borne swiftly above the dust, all made a sight to be remembered.[69]

As Stuart's and Kilpatrick's columns dashed forward, Stuart ordered the 12th Virginia to charge the Federals in flank. The charge slashed through the Federal column, "cutting off about 1,200 or 1,500 of the enemy," but the 4th and 5th North Carolina, sent by Stuart to help the Virginia regiment, were themselves charged with the saber and routed by a squadron of the 5th New York.[70] These charges and countercharges slowed down both

68. McDonald, *A History of the Laurel Brigade*, 180–81.
69. G. W. Beale, *A Lieutenant of Cavalry in Lee's Army* (Boston, 1918), 129.
70. *Official Records*, Vol. XXIX, Pt. 1, p. 443; see also McClellan, *I Rode with Jeb Stuart*, 380. Both Stuart and McClellan state that the 4th and 5th North Carolina were sent to support the 12th Virginia. Douglas S. Freeman's statement in *Lee's Lieutenants: A Study in Command* (3 vols.; New York, 1942–44), III, 251, that it was the 5th and 6th North Carolina, is a rare error in a superb work.

Stuart and Kilpatrick sufficiently so that Buford's column was the first to reach and occupy Fleetwood Heights. Thomas Rosser's brigade of Lee's division was right behind Buford; therefore, when Kilpatrick arrived near the hill, Rosser was squarely in his path, between him and the Rappahannock. The report of Colonel E. B. Sawyer of the 1st Vermont conveys the excitement as well as the confusion of the moment: "The scene began to grow interesting. . . . we were not only flanked on both right and left, and closely pressed in the rear, but right across the road we desired to travel we were confronted by a strong force. . . . we were surrounded."[71] But Colonel Sawyer was a veteran officer; his men too were veterans for the most part and were equal to the emergency. Sawyer halted his regiment and "addressed a few words to the officers and men," his calm courage producing the effect he wanted; the majors dressed their battalions, and the regiment "came into line in splendid order."[72]

The honors of this day on the Union side belonged to George Custer. Leading Kilpatrick's division, his brigade was approaching Brandy Station when a courier came galloping up from the head of the column "with the information that a brigade of the enemy's cavalry was in a position directly to . . . [his] front." This was a moment made to order for Custer and his own brand of personal leadership. He reported:

The heavy masses of rebel cavalry could be seen covering the heights in front of my advance . . . a heavy column was enveloping each flank, and my advance confronted by more than double my own number. . . . To . . . [Pleasonton] I proposed . . . to cut through the force in my front, and thus to open a way for the entire command. . . . My proposition was approved. . . . Leaving the 6th and 7th Michigan Cavalry to hold the force in rear in check, I formed the 5th Michigan Cavalry on my right . . . on my left I formed the 1st Michigan Cavalry. . . . After ordering them to draw their sabers, I informed them that we were surrounded, and all we had to do was to open a way with our sabers. They showed their determination and purpose by giving three hearty cheers. At this moment the band struck up the inspiring strains of Yankee Doodle, which excited the enthusiasm of the entire command to the highest pitch. . . . Simultaneously both regiments moved forward to

71. *Official Records*, Vol. XXIX, Pt. 1, p. 394.
72. *Ibid.*, 394.

the attack. . . . The enemy, without waiting to receive the onset, broke and fled.[73]

It was now late afternoon. Thanks to Custer, Kilpatrick and Buford had joined forces, and so had Stuart and Lee. The Federals were on Fleetwood Heights, but they still had to get to the river. The Confederates were all around them, and the Federal efforts to break out of the circle brought on a repetition on a smaller scale of the fighting of the June 9 battle of Brandy Station, with charges and countercharges in every direction by regiments, squadrons, and small groups separated from their units. The 5th, 6th, and 15th Virginia of Stuart's command each made five separate charges, all with the saber.[74] At nightfall, however, the Federals were still in firm possession of Fleetwood Heights, "protected by their artillery, which was handled with great skill."[75] Eventually Stuart and Lee withdrew, and the Federals vacated the hill and crossed the Rappahannock in good order.

Following this cavalry fight at Brandy Station, the Army of the Potomac continued its retreat, protected by a rear guard of G. K. Warren's II Corps and Gregg's cavalry division. Warren and Gregg had two hard fights with Confederate cavalry and infantry, at Sulphur Springs on October 12 and at Auburn two days later, in which Gregg sustained relatively heavy casualties of 17 killed, 117 wounded, and 447 captured or missing.[76] Neither of these actions is of any special interest from the standpoint of cavalry operations, but one was the scene of, and the other led to, incidents worthy of notice.

73. *Ibid.*, 390; see also Kidd, *Personal Recollections*, 207.

74. *Official Records*, Vol. XXIX, Pt. 1, p. 444.

75. McClellan, *I Rode with Jeb Stuart*, 383. Pleasonton lost 352 men taken prisoner at Brandy Station, in addition to his killed and wounded. *Official Records*, Vol. XXIX, Pt. 1, pp. 453–54. Buford returned to Brandy Station the next day. He reported his men "gratified" because "they were enabled to recover the bodies of some of their comrades who had fallen the day before, and to administer to and remove several wounded men, who had been neglected and who would undoubtedly have perished but for their timely assistance. It was truly gratifying to be able to recover these wounded men, and to bury the men that had been stripped and abandoned by the enemy." *Official Records*, Vol. XXIX, Pt. 1, p. 351.

76. Gregg reported that "of those reported as missing at Sulphur Springs, very many were killed and wounded." Obviously, therefore, he had

Ohio was to elect a governor in 1863. The candidates were War Democrat/Unionist John Brough, and Peace Democrat Clement L. Vallandigham, the latter running for office *in absentia*, from exile in Canada. The election attracted national attention as, in effect, a plebiscite on the war. Ohio was one of the northern states that allowed its soldiers to vote in the field. The 6th Ohio was posted as rear guard to protect the crossing of the Rappahannock by Gregg's division and was "closely beset by the enemy" when the men were called upon to cast their votes. Colonel Hampton Thomas of the 1st Pennsylvania, detailed to supervise the balloting, withdrew the Ohioans from the front a company at a time; as soon as a company had voted, back it went into the firing line, and another moved to the rear to cast its votes. When the votes were tallied, it was found that only three men of the regiment had voted for the peace candidate.[77]

The day after the rearguard action at Auburn on the fourteenth, Meade issued a general order praising "the skill and promptitude of Major-General Warren, and the gallantry and bearing of the officers of the Second Corps," but he failed to mention the important role of Gregg and his cavalrymen in the engagement. Gregg, ordinarily the least self-assertive of men—certainly in comparison with the glory-hunting Custers, Kilpatricks, and Pleasontons of the cavalry—decided that this was an intentional slight and should be challenged. He asked that a court of inquiry examine the manner in which he had performed his duties as commanding officer of his division, or that he be relieved of duty with the Army of the Potomac. Meade made the *amende honorable* the same day, by issuing another general order commending "the activity, zeal and gallantry, not only of the Second Division, but of the whole Cavalry Corps."[78]

---

been driven back and had been unable to collect his dead and wounded. *Official Records*, Vol. XXIX, Pt. 1, p. 359.

77. Hampton S. Thomas, *Some Personal Reminiscences of Service in the Cavalry of the Army of the Potomac* (Philadelphia, 1889), 15; see also Asa B. Isham, "The Cavalry of the Army of the Potomac," in Military Order of the Loyal Legion of the United States (MOLLUS), Commandery of Ohio, *Sketches of War History, 1861–1865* (7 vols.; Cincinnati, 1888–1910), V, 313.

78. *Official Records*, Vol. XXIX, Pt. 1, pp. 250, 360. James H. Wilson

On October 18, with the Federals hastily entrenching north of Bull Run and the Confederates concentrated near Manassas Junction, General Lee, mainly for logistical reasons, ordered a retreat to the Rappahannock. His cavalry was in its proper position, ready to protect the rear of the army. On the evening of the eighteenth, the day the retreat began, Stuart, still in direct command of Hampton's division, "received intelligence of an intended advance of Kilpatrick's division . . . with a column of infantry." The following morning Stuart began a leisurely rearward march toward Warrenton and sent word to Fitzhugh Lee, who was within supporting distance at Auburn, to join him. Lee countered with the suggestion that Stuart cross Broad Run on the bridge at Buckland Mills and retreat slowly toward Warrenton, drawing Kilpatrick after him; Lee would then attack Kilpatrick in flank and rear, and as soon as Stuart heard Lee's guns he too was to go over to the attack, trapping Kilpatrick between them.[79] Stuart accepted the suggestion but the plan did not work out exactly as Lee intended, because, after crossing the Buckland Mills bridge, Kilpatrick divided his division; Davies' brigade continued on Stuart's heels to within two and a half to three miles of Warrenton, but Custer and his brigade remained at the bridge to guard the crossing. Lee's attack fell on Custer, who put up a good fight against odds and succeeded in recrossing Broad Run without serious loss. Stuart on the other hand had much better success against Davies, whose men, strung out in a long column on a narrow road, stampeded and were chased on a dead run for about five miles, part of the brigade escaping by way of Buckland, and part toward Hay Market.[80]

Kilpatrick's report on what the Confederates promptly dubbed the "Buckland Races" was a masterpiece of obfuscation. To describe as a slow retirement Davies' five mile stampede, in which

wrote that Gregg was "somewhat lacking in enthusiasm and possibly in aggressive temper, but of far more than usual capacity." Wilson, *Under the Old Flag*, I, 364.

79. *Official Records*, Vol. XXIX, Pt. 1, pp. 451, 452, 464.

80. Freeman, *Lee's Lieutenants*, III, 260–63; McClellan, *I Rode with Jeb Stuart*, 393–95; William W. Blackford, *War Years with Jeb Stuart* (New York, 1945), 241–42; *Official Records*, Vol. XXIX, Pt. 1, pp. 451–52, 464, 473.

he lost 258 men taken prisoner, and to do so not once but twice in the same report, called for an attitude toward the truth out of the reach of any ordinary man.[81] Stuart's conclusion, though somewhat overdrawn, was not far from fact. "I am justified in declaring," he reported, "the rout of the enemy at Buckland the most signal and complete that any cavalry has suffered during the war."[82]

Among the eight wagons and ambulances captured by the Confederates in this encounter was Custer's headquarters wagon, containing his personal baggage and papers. "Some of the letters to [from?] a fair, but frail, friend of Custer's were published in the Richmond papers and afforded some spicy reading, though the most spicy parts did not appear."[83]

The Buckland fight on October 19 signaled the end of the Bristoe Campaign. On the same day, the Confederate infantry recrossed the Rappahannock, followed the next day by Stuart and the cavalry. The Army of the Potomac moved slowly forward on the heels of the Confederates, its commander satisfied with what had been a victory by default. He had shielded Washington and preserved his army in the face of another of General Lee's thrusts; with the latter eventually constrained to retreat—not by the Union army but by supply problems—the two armies once again faced each other across Rappahannock stream. Whether Meade might have accomplished more was another conundrum to be added to his cautious handling of the pursuit after Gettysburg. Meade, at any rate, was satisfied and became even more so three weeks later, when his infantry forced a crossing of the Rappahannock and caused Lee to pull back behind the Rapidan.

81. *Official Records*, Vol. XXIX, Pt. 1, pp. 382–83. Custer reports only the operations of his brigade and makes no mention of the rout of Davies, whose own report speaks only of "countermarching" his brigade when he heard the gunfire of Lee's attack on Custer and claims that with two of his regiments, the 2nd New York and the 1st West Virginia, he "attacked and drove back" Stuart's attack on what (after he turned to aid Custer) had become his rear. *Ibid.*, 387.

82. *Ibid.*, 452. Colonel Thomas H. Owen, commanding Williams C. Wickham's brigade, described Buckland as "the most signal cavalry victory of the war, as the enemy's cavalry, supported by infantry, was worse routed and demoralized than I have ever known them [to be] before." *Ibid.*, 387.

83. Blackford, *War Years with Jeb Stuart*, 242.

A period of inactivity now ensued and lasted until November 26, when the Union army was detected sideslipping to its left, through Stevensburg toward Germanna Ford and the area of the Chancellorsville battle. The Federals crossed the Rapidan at Germanna Ford, but then Meade did the unexpected; instead of turning left toward Fredericksburg, as General Lee thought he would do, he turned right, in what was obviously a move to flank Lee out of his position behind the Rapidan. Some time before, thinking such a move a possibility, Lee had directed Jubal Early "to study the defensive possibilities of Mine Run," a small stream winding its way through the western edge of the Wilderness to a junction with the Rapidan.[84] On the twenty-eighth, when Meade's advance reached Mine Run, it found the Army of Northern Virginia moving into position on the far bank. For the next two days the two armies busied themselves throwing up earthworks. Lee expected Meade to attack—what other purpose could the movement have had?—and, indeed, Meade actually ordered the attack but was persuaded out of it as a "useless slaughter" by G. K. Warren, whose corps was to be the spearhead. Since the Federals failed to attack him, General Lee decided to attack them, but at dawn the next day, as his men were getting ready to move forward, it was discovered that the Federals had decamped during the night. Thus ended the Mine Run Campaign, and thus too ended the fighting in the East in this most eventful year of 1863.

The role of the cavalry on both sides in the Mine Run Campaign had been of the slightest.[85] On the evening of the twenty-sixth, Custer, posted at Raccoon Ford, well to the south of Germanna, saw the Confederates massing infantry and artillery across the river, evidently in expectation of a Federal attempt to cross at that point; knowing that the crossing was to be made at Germanna Ford, Custer staged a charade for the benefit of the Confederates. Using one of the oldest tricks of the trade, he caused "fires to be built along the edge of the woods and . . . [his]

84. Freeman, R. E. Lee, III, 194.
85. The total casualties of the Federal cavalry in the campaign were 28 killed, 124 wounded, and 78 captured or missing. Official Records, Vol. XXIX, Pt. 1, p. 803. For reports on the operations of the Confederate cavalry in the campaign, see ibid., 898–901, 901–902, 903–904, 904–905.

band to play at different points . . . [after] dark, to give the impression that a strong force of infantry was . . . [there]."[86]

Far more significant, particularly for the future, than Custer's lively playacting was an action fought on November 27 by Colonel John P. Taylor's brigade of Gregg's division. The brigade was out beyond the left flank of the Union infantry, near Mountain Run, a small tributary of the Rapidan, flowing three or four miles to the west of, and nearly parallel to, Mine Run. The brigade found Stuart's cavalry near New Hope Church and was pressing it westward when, as Lieutenant Colonel John W. Kester of the 1st New Jersey reported, "the enemy withdrew his cavalry and advanced a division of infantry, which brought our advance to a check. I was then ordered forward with the regiment. . . . I dismounted the whole regiment and pressed forward . . . and I was just in time, as I met fragments of broken regiments falling back. . . . We then charged the enemy's infantry, driving him half a mile, and capturing 31 prisoners, and holding the ground until relieved by the Fifth Corps infantry."[87] General Gregg reported that three other regiments of the brigade, the 1st and 3rd Pennsylvania and the 1st Massachusetts, all on foot and "firing volleys from their carbines," participated in the attack for which Colonel Kester claimed the sole credit for his own regiment.[88]

The deployment of dismounted skirmishers to prepare the way for a mounted attack, or to operate on one or both flanks of a mounted attack, had become a commonly used tactical gambit. Also, dismounted cavalrymen in squadron or even regimental strength had been used to hold a position, as at Kelly's Ford and at Gettysburg, but Colonel Taylor's employment of a full brigade of four regiments to make a dismounted attack was a tactical novelty.

86. *Ibid.*, 811; see also 812.
87. *Ibid.*, 808.
88. *Ibid.*, 807. The historians of the 3rd Pennsylvania report that "It was amusing to behold the consternation of some of our prisoners who apparently had never before met dismounted cavalrymen at close quarters. They did not understand how we got in the shots from our breech-loading carbines so much more quickly and oftener than they with their muzzle-loading rifles." Regimental History Committee, *History of the 3d Pennsylvania*, 267.

The Confederate cavalry was on the verge of experiencing an identical tactical development. Stuart's every instinct favored the traditional mounted charge, sabers brandished and pistols drawn. But, as Douglas Southall Freeman has noted, the last few months of 1863 witnessed an important change:

Prior to the Bristoe campaign, the sharpshooters of the cavalry had been organized officially, and during the second battle of Brandy . . . they were dismounted by regiments and effectively used. . . . Again, in the "Buckland Races," Fitz Lee used some of his cavalrymen on foot. During the Mine Run operation . . . these tactics of dismounted action were developed. In the fighting of November 27, and again on the 29th and 30th, the troopers were led against the enemy by regular infantry approaches. From that time onward, as the necessities of the service demanded, the dismounted cavalrymen were frequently summoned to support the . . . infantry. It was hard on the troopers but it saved horses.[89]

Among northern cavalrymen there were two schools of thought on Colonel Taylor's innovation. After the New Hope Church fight, the historians of the 3rd Pennsylvania noted, "We had been fighting hard for more than five hours, and were thoroughly exhausted—tired as only dismounted cavalrymen, with their heavy boots and softened leg muscles could be."[90] More representative was the opinion of Frederick Whittaker, himself a traditionalist and a great devotee of the *arme blanche*:

The rapidity exhibited in going into action by dismounted cavalry is marvelous, and the simplicity and adaptability of the system admirable. The dash and impetuosity of the dismounted skirmish line is far beyond that of an infantry force of equal numbers. The men go into action perfectly fresh. . . . And when, after fighting for two or three hours and driving the enemy at a quick run, till the men are fagged out and a success gained, the open ground appears . . . and it becomes necessary to pursue . . . up come the horses. . . . The skirmish line is called in and mounted. The men, tired with running, can still ride as rapidly as ever. The horses have been resting and are able to press on. So that we combine the advantages of both infantry and cavalry.[91]

There is no indication that Colonel Taylor's decision, and similar

89. Freeman, *R. E. Lee*, III, 205.
90. Regimental History Committee, *History of the 3d Pennsylvania*, 369.
91. [Whittaker], *Volunteer Cavalry*, 16–17.

decisions on the other side, were based on theoretical considerations; these were, so far as one may judge, instinctive decisions, to deal with immediate tactical situations. A dismounted attack appeared to be the sensible thing to do. A crucially important aspect of Taylor's decision was that it enabled him to take maximum advantage of the firepower his men's carbines gave them. Thus was taken a major step in the evolution of a technique that was to become fully developed in the remaining months of the war, with a major impact on the role of cavalry in battle, and on the course of the Civil War itself.

II

"Winter and Rough Weather"

AT THE CONCLUSION OF THE MINE RUN CAMPAIGN, WITH major operations made impossible by the weather, the two armies settled down for the winter. The Union cavalry, its camps located in the neighborhood of Culpeper, Stevensburg, Brandy Station, and Warrenton, was to winter in a countryside that two years of war had turned into a barren, desolate wilderness, fouled with the refuse of long-abandoned camps, the fields uncultivated and overgrown with weeds, an occasional chimney to mark the site of what had been a farmhouse or mansion, all fences, livestock, and people gone, acres of stumps where forests had stood, and, as noted by a northern officer, "here and there . . . a little mound of earth, marked by a bit of board, on which is scrawled the name of the soldier who lies where he fell, in this desert region."[1]

Erecting shelter was naturally the first order of business in setting up a winter camp. As soon as a campsite had been assigned to a regiment and the officers had laid out the company streets, out came the axes, and the men, in groups of from three to six, set about constructing their log huts. Commanding generals differed greatly in their eye for a good campsite. Frederick Whittaker wrote that while his division was commanded by John

1. George R. Agassiz (ed.), *Meade's Headquarters 1863–1865: Letters of Colonel Theodore Lyman* (Boston, 1922), 48.

Buford, he could "never remember an uncomfortable camp," but when Buford was succeeded by an *infantryman*, General A. T. A. Torbert, there was a change; "It is safe to say that the whole time he commanded us, our division never had a comfortable camp."[2]

Whether the campsite assigned to them was good or bad, a well-drained slope or a swamp, sheltered from the winds or out in the open, near to or far from good water for the men and horses, the troopers built their huts to a pattern that, after two years of war, had become fairly well standardized.[3] Roughly twelve feet long by seven feet wide, the hut was built of logs, the side walls five or six feet high, the front and back walls rising to a peak eight or nine feet above the ground. The logs were chinked with clay or mud. The roof was sometimes thatched, but more commonly consisted of the men's shelter halves joined together, stretched over a ridgepole, and fastened as securely as possible to the side and end walls. The cabin was entered through a door of sorts, which was frequently nothing more than a blanket hung over the opening, and there were usually one or two windows. Built into the front wall, next to the doorway, was a stone or brick fireplace from which the smoke escaped, at least when the wind blew from the right direction, through a "stick" chimney daubed with clay or ordinary mud, or a brick chimney when bricks were available.[4]

The 1st New Jersey, building its huts near Warrenton, found that the supply of loose brick for fireplaces and chimneys fell far short of the demand, but "On the hill above the camp there stood that anomaly in a slaveholding society, a neatly built schoolhouse, disused at present. . . . Positive orders had been issued against wanton destruction of buildings, so it is certain that the First New Jersey Cavalry could not have assisted the hand of time in the destruction of this edifice; yet it is undoubtedly true that it

2. [Whittaker], *Volunteer Cavalry*, 60–61.

3. In a misguided attempt to enforce uniformity, the inspector general of the First Brigade, Second Division, issued a circular in November of the following year, laying down specifications for the huts the men were about to build for the third or fourth time. It is safe to assume that the specifications were ignored at least as often as they were followed. Circular, November 11, 1864, in 1st Massachusetts Volunteer Cavalry, Regimental and Company Order and Letter Books, Record Group 94, National Archives. Hereinafter cited as 1st Massachusetts O&L Books.

4. George A. Townsend, *Rustics in Rebellion* (Chapel Hill, 1950), 5.

crumbled fast away, as chimneys magically uprose throughout the camp."[5] Usually, but not always, the huts had flooring of some sort, boards when they could be found, split saplings, or pine boughs.

In addition to building their own huts, the enlisted men were also expected to build, or assist in building, housing for the officers. The 10th New York built "commodious quarters . . . for the commandant of the regiment, where the officers usually assembled in large numbers to pass the evenings—and other things."[6] The camp of the 1st New York Dragoons (19th New York) "presented a marvelous combination of architectural display, some of the officers' dwellings being quite pretentious. . . . There were some very tasty structures of the gothic order. . . . The buglers' squad erected a building 16 x 24 feet, and when completed . . . followed the fashion, gave a big house warming and had a big time."[7] Indeed, the only complaint the troopers of the 19th New York had was that they were joined with the "cowardly regulars" of the 1st, 2nd, and 5th United States in the Reserve Brigade; they were "disgusted" to have to associate with such a "foulmouthed set of blackguards," and their historian noted that "there existed no spirit of congeniality" between themselves and the Regulars.[8] What the Regulars thought of the 19th New York Volunteers is not on record.

The "Germans" of the 1st New York built a "music hall" where they met nightly for "social enjoyment" and gave concerts of "songs and stories" which were greatly enjoyed by the entire regiment.[9] The 5th New York built a chapel, and it is with evident gratification that their historian and erstwhile chaplain records

5. Henry R. Pyne, *The History of the First New Jersey Cavalry* (Trenton, 1871), 210–11.

6. Noble D. Preston, *History of the 10th Regiment of Cavalry, New York State Volunteers* (New York, 1892), 156.

7. James R. Bowen, *Regimental History of the First New York Dragoons*, (N.p., 1900), 113.

8. *Ibid.*, 102–103. The 6th Pennsylvania was the other regiment of volunteers in the brigade. They either got along better with the Regulars than did the 19th New York, or their historian (and chaplain) chose not to say anything derogatory about them in his regimental history.

9. William H. Beach, *The First New York (Lincoln) Cavalry* (New York, 1902), 282.

that at the conclusion of a temperance meeting held in it "a large number signed the pledge."[10] Kilpatrick had his division build a theatre; gaily decorated for the occasion, it was ceremoniously dedicated in February, 1864. In attendance were Vice-President Hannibal Hamlin and his daughter, the wife of the governor of Pennsylvania with a bevy of beauties in tow, numerous senators and congressmen with their wives and daughters, a large party from the British Legation, General Meade and his staff, and numerous guests of lesser note. The inevitable speeches were made, the host's being by common consent the most effective, and the festivities concluded with a minstrel show, a ball, and a lavish supper.[11]

Long before the winter was over the men had to go great distances for firewood to keep their huts warm. Yet their greatest trial was neither this nor the cold, but the eternal mud. It lay from four to as much as twenty inches deep in the company streets. The more enterprising regiments corduroyed the streets, but for the most part the men had to plow through the bottomless mud, and "wet feet were the rule rather than the exception."[12]

The chief victims of the winter were the horses. Some regiments went to the trouble of corduroying the horse lines, which at least saved the animals from having to stand in deep, cold mud for days on end.[13] There is an occasional mention in the records

10. Louis N. Boudrye, *Historic Records of the Fifth New York Cavalry, First Ira Harris Guard* (Albany, 1868), 93.

11. Samuel L. Gillespie ("Lovejoy"), *A History of Company A, First Ohio Cavalry, 1861–1865* (Washington Court House, 1898), 192; Virgil C. Jones, *Eight Hours Before Richmond* (New York, 1957), 5.

12. Edward P. Tobie, *History of the First Maine Cavalry* (Boston, 1887), 118. The everlasting snow, slush, and mud were hard on footwear. "The wide-bottomed, scow-like shoes" in which the 1st New York had "to navigate . . . [the] seas of Virginia mud would unexpectedly gape open in cracks." Beach, *First New York (Lincoln) Cavalry,* 72. The historians of the 3rd Pennsylvania complained that the "Government and the Quartermaster's Department were so derelict . . . that at one time, upon an inspection during the bitterest of cold weather, but fourteen pairs of serviceable boots could be produced in the regiment. Many were the times when the men turned out for duty with their feet tied up in pieces of cloth cut from other garments, or from grain sacks, to prevent them from freezing." Regimental History Committee, *History of the 3d Pennsylvania,* 389.

13. The 1st New Jersey was one such regiment. "Huge piles of pine logs were prepared as flooring . . . and as soon as there was a relaxation of

of the construction of a windbreak, and in a few cases, of an over-head shelter covered with pine boughs, to protect the horses from the worst of the weather. But providing some sort of shelter for the horses appears to have been left entirely to the enterprise or compassion of regimental commanders; the present writer has found not a single brigade, division, or corps order directing it to be done. And so the horses of the 1st Massachusetts, and of many another regiment, "were without shelter. They stood at the picket-rope in mud halfway up to their knees, and in the spring the sur-vivors were in bad condition." Indeed, one may wonder that there were any survivors at all.[14]

If cavalry commanders had been asked to justify their failure to provide shelter for their horses, they would doubtless have con-tended that winter camp was anything but a period of rest, that their men had more than enough to do to keep them fully occu-pied, and that they were shorthanded besides. This last was true enough. For although the strength of the corps as a whole re-mained fairly constant, many individual regiments were badly under strength.[15] Thus, the 1st Vermont had only 126 men pres-ent for duty on October 22, and in mid-February, after the arrival of 339 recruits had raised the total to above 500, only 206 vet-erans were present with the colors.[16] The 1st Pennsylvania was

---

the frost, on ground properly smoothed and sloped, a dry and strong layer of logs was placed along the picket ropes, affording a firm standing place for the horses. No covering could be provided for them, however, and through the wind, the rain and the snow they had to remain exposed to the weather. To save the cost of a few tarpaulins, the lives of many horses, worth thousands of dollars, were sacrificed." Pyne, *First New Jersey Cav-alry,* 211. The 1st New York also floored its horse lines, but not until the end of January. *Official Records,* XXXIII, 459.

14. Crowninshield, *A History of the First Regiment,* 102.

15. The Cavalry Corps reported 11,474 officers and men present for duty equipped on November 20; 11,520 at the end of the Mine Run Cam-paign; 13,383 at the year-end; and 11,229 on January 31, 1864. *Official Records,* Vol. XXIX, Pt. 1, p. 677; Pt. 2, p. 598; XXXIII, 462.

16. Report of October 22, 1863, in 1st Vermont Cavalry, Regimental and Company Order and Letter Books, Record Group 94, National Archives. Hereinafter cited as 1st Vermont O&L Books. The report explains that two officers and 108 men were absent (and had been absent for two months) "on duty with the Sixth Corps," one officer and 40 men were on duty with the post commissary, and 70 men had been sent to dismounted camp. The mid-February figure is from *ibid.,* Report of February 16, 1864. In January

down to "scarcely four hundred men present for duty."[17] In addition to all the usual reasons for a shortage of manpower, numbers were also reduced by a regular system of furloughs, in a revival of the plan instituted by Hooker the previous year. Also, with operations at a low ebb, the winter months were a good time to send recruiting parties back home.[18] Another major reason for absences, peculiar to the early months of 1864, was the veterans' furlough, to be described shortly.

At any moment throughout the winter, from a quarter to a half or more of every regiment was out on picket duty for periods of three days or longer and, when not absent from camp for that reason, was away on a scout, a reconnaissance, or an expedition to hunt guerrillas.[19] There were many other duties to be performed: guards had to be furnished for fatigue parties of infantry sent out for firewood; the camp had to be policed and dead horses buried; details had to be made for escort duty, to serve as orderlies, as "safeguards for the protection of forlorn females in their homes," or as " 'Bull Guards' to protect the large herd of beef cattle which the commissary department maintained to supply the army with beef."[20] Recruits had to be taught the rudiments of soldiering: the tactics, how to fold blanket and overcoat and strap them to the saddle, how to bridle and saddle the horses, and how and when to salute. Then too there was a steady diet of drill, weather

---

Colonel E. B. Sawyer wrote, "Owing to the number of officers absent on leave and on duty from the regiment, there are remaining only eight line officers on duty with their companies, and out of this number, two at least are constantly absent on picket duty; thus leaving a large proportion of the companies without a single officer." *Ibid.*, Letter of January 21, 1864. In October, 1863, the 6th Michigan had fewer than 100 men present for duty; "Many of the troops were commanded by lieutenants, some of them by sergeants, and one had neither officer nor non-commissioned officer." Kidd, *Personal Recollections*, 210.

17. William P. Lloyd, *History of the First Reg't. Pennsylvania Reserve Cavalry* (Philadelphia, 1864), 85.

18. Beach, *First New York (Lincoln) Cavalry*, 293; Pyne, *First New Jersey Cavalry*, 215.

19. Bowen, *Regimental History of the First New York*, 103; Crowninshield, *A History of the First Regiment*, 33; Lloyd, *History of the First Reg't.*, 85; Ford (ed.), *A Cycle of Adams Letters*, II, 104.

20. Circulars of January 29 and February 19, 1864, in 1st Vermont O&L Books, RG 94, NA.

permitting, as well as parades, reviews, inspections, schools for officers and noncommissioned officers, and "all manner of regulation fol-de-rol."[21] And lastly, time had to be found for personal grooming, officers being directed to see to it that their men's hair was cut "according to regulations."[22]

More than one regimental historian wrote of the winter of 1863–1864 as a season of unremitting hard work and exhausting duty, one even describing it as "without doubt the most severe and trying" in the entire history of his regiment.[23] Nonetheless, there is sufficient evidence of the pleasures of winter camp to justify the suspicion that the tales of the winter's labors and hardships are somewhat overdrawn. For the 1st New Jersey of Gregg's division,

winter quarters [were] . . . a time of rest. . . . having a comfortable cabin to retire to, where wet clothes could be removed and dry garments substituted; where cleanliness and decency could be preserved and the hours free from duty could be spent in reading or social relaxation, was a great advance upon the publicity and listlessness of the bivouac. . . . A depot for the sale of books, periodical magazines and daily papers was established . . . and sutlers made their appearance with the supplies most needed by the men. Regular food and regular hours took the place of the precarious rations and sudden vicissitudes of the campaign; and good order and proper discipline pervaded every department.[24]

As this regimental historian noted, the army being stationary and the work of the commissary officers being thereby simplified, the troopers were plentifully supplied with rations, and even the paymasters were able to make one or two of their infrequent appearances.[25] It is evident also that the men had time for recrea-

21. Bowen, *Regimental History of the First New York*, 123; Frederick Whittaker, *A Complete Life of General George A. Custer* (New York, 1876), 205; Kidd, *Personal Recollections*, 232; Preston, *History of the 10th Regiment*, 167; Orders No. 1, January 7, 1864, and Circular, January 20, 1864, in 1st Vermont O&L Books, RG 94, NA.

22. Circulars of January 29 and February 19, 1864, in 1st Vermont O&L Books, RG 94, NA.

23. Regimental History Committee, *History of the 3d Pennsylvania*, 382–83; see also Crowninshield, *A History of the First Regiment*, 32; Lloyd, *History of the First Reg't.*, 85.

24. Pyne, *First New Jersey Cavalry*, 212.

25. Tobie, *First Maine Cavalry*, 118; Crowninshield, *A History of the First Regiment*, 14; Boudrye, *Historic Records of the Fifth*, 92.

tion, to enjoy each in his own way. There were the ever-welcome boxes from home; there were books, magazines, and newspapers to read; and since this was distinctly a singing and musical age, there was always music. Glee clubs, minstrel groups, and string bands were organized and gave performances, as did the regimental and brigade bands.[26] There was opportunity too for religious services, and on the reverse of the moral coin, opportunity for cardplaying.[27] Horseracing flourished also, presumably on days when the footing was reasonably firm, accompanied by the inevitable betting.[28] Winter was also the time for wives of officers and enlisted men to visit their husbands.

The officers of Gregg's division established "club-rooms and reading rooms" in Warrenton, a town that did not lack other amenities.[29] Warrenton was the home of many of the members of Company H, 4th Virginia, but in the winter of 1863–1864 the Union was in possession.

There was a beautiful Episcopal church in the town, under the ministration of the Reverend Mr. Barton, at whose parsonage . . . a warm welcome was always ready for the officers, who gathered there to drink his excellent whiskey punch, while his charming wife chaperoned young members of the fair sex, who also gathered there to partake of her delicious egg-nog—and gain information for their friends. It was never supposed for an instant that the "secesh" girls were disloyal to the cause of their lovers, but this did not seem to interfere . . . with their appreciation of the attention of the gentlemen on the other side of the questions of the day. They were ever ready to discourse . . . of the gallantry and invincibility of their dear ones, and to predict the terrible disasters which were in store for the Northern intruders when they were to meet.[30]

In contrast to these pleasant evenings in the Reverend Mr. Barton's manse, Colonel J. P. Taylor had to report that "the guerrillas around Warrenton . . . [were] very troublesome, always attack-

    26. Bowen, *Regimental History of the First New York*, 113; Pyne, *First New Jersey Cavalry*, 212; Gracey, *Annals of the 6th*, 222.
    27. Gillespie, *A History of Company A*, 181; Tobie, *First Maine Cavalry*, 118.
    28. Gillespie, *A History of Company A*, 181.
    29. Pyne, *First New Jersey Cavalry*, 214.
    30. Regimental History Committee, *History of the 3d Pennsylvania*, 387.

ing . . . [his] pickets after nightfall. The citizens do all in their power to help and encourage these people."[31]

Warrenton also presented the Union cavalry with a moral and military dilemma. In January, Gregg wrote to Pleasonton that "the continued presence of Mosby's command in the vicinity" made it necessary for Colonel Taylor, whose brigade was established at Warrenton, to "confine the citizens of Warrenton within the lines of his pickets and to prevent citizens from without from entering the town."

There is in Warrenton a large population of women and children and old men. Cut off from all markets, very many . . . are suffering for the necessities of life. . . . I am constantly importuned by women to be allowed to purchase from the subsistence department. By existing orders this is not permitted. If the citizens of Warrenton are to secure their necessary supplies by commerce with the surrounding country, then will the security of the brigade be constantly threatened; if . . . the proper and ordinary precautions are observed for the security of the command, and the people of Warrenton kept within our lines, then it will be absolutely necessary to assist them in procuring the very necessaries of life . . . from the subsistence department.[32]

The records do not indicate what action, if any, was taken in response to Gregg's report, but there must have been at least an informal relaxation of the rules, for in mid-April, Captain R. F. Judson, commanding the cavalry outpost at Grove Church, complained bitterly, "It is through . . . people who are drawing commissary stores that the principal information of importance to the enemy is communicated to scouts and through them to the people across the . . . [Rapidan]. Quit issuing commissary stores to rebels . . . and the enemy's scouts . . . will become completely harmless."[33] It may be taken for granted that simply through the daily

31. *Official Records*, Vol. XXIX, Pt. 2, p. 467.
32. *Ibid.*, XXXIII, 364. A month earlier, Wesley Merritt reported that "almost all" the people in and around Culpeper were "suffering for the necessaries of life, and some will starve soon if their condition is not bettered by issues from the commissaries. Very few, if any, will take the oath of allegiance. . . . Nor would administering the oath . . . to such people do any good, for they would not probably consider themselves bound by it. . . . I do not allow these people to go out of the town limits, as they steal through the lines, and . . . give the enemy information." *Ibid.*, Vol. XXIX, Pt. 2, p. 551.
33. *Ibid.*, XXXIII, 857.

contact between Union cavalrymen and the people of Warrenton, Culpeper, and other towns, food found its way to the needy. The historian of the 1st New Jersey suggests as much when he writes, "There was scarcely a family . . . which was not under obligation to some officer of the brigade. . . . The natural instincts of humanity and . . . generosity were allowed by National officers and soldiers to flow forth in a thousand forms to soften the inevitable hardships of people really imprisoned within the town."[34] Was it a coincidence that toward the end of March, Merritt was ordered to move his brigade headquarters out of Culpeper and to require that his officers "now quartered in Culpeper . . . join their . . . commands"?[35]

Winter camp was of course the perfect setting for the lightning-fast propagation of rumors. One such rumor, more than ordinarily absurd—might it not have been a trial balloon?—had Pleasonton replacing General Meade as commander of the Army of the Potomac.[36] Winter camp also gave rise to such letters as the following, sent by the adjutant of the 1st Vermont to no less exalted a military potentate than Quartermaster General Montgomery Meigs.

I have the honor to transmit a special requisition for stationery for use of the adjutant's office of this regiment, to which I would respectfully ask your approval. The supply of stationery furnished . . . is inadequate to the demands of the official business transacted . . . in consequence of the numerous special and regular reports . . . [I am] required to prepare, and other increased official business. . . . The supply furnished . . . for the present quarter is entirely exhausted [this on February 5] and the adjutant is compelled to purchase stationery for public use. The stationery has been frugally used, and care taken that none is wasted.[37]

And, as the Army Regulations required, the adjutant had his eloquent letter duly copied into the order and letter book of his

34. Pyne, *First New Jersey Cavalry*, 213.
35. *Official Records*, XXXIII, 745.
36. Agassiz, *Meade's Headquarters*, 60. Another version of the same camp rumor listed Pleasonton, Winfield Scott Hancock, and John Sedgwick as Meade's possible successors. Allan Nevins (ed.), *A Diary of Battle: The Personal Journals of Colonel Charles S. Wainwright, 1861–1865* (New York, 1962), 308.
37. Letter of February 5, 1864, in 1st Vermont O&L Books, RG 94, NA.

regiment. One may hope that the greatly harassed General Meigs was able to manage a sympathetic smile when he read it.

The winter, too, was the time to deal with deserters. Of the 2,465 deserters of all arms returned to the Army of the Potomac between July 1 and December 31, 1863, 30 cavalrymen were tried by court martial, 22 of the 30 were found guilty, one of the 22 was sentenced to death (the sentence was not carried out), and the other 21 received lesser sentences.[38] Among the 21 were two troopers of the 3rd Pennsylvania, and the First Brigade of Gregg's division, to which the regiment belonged, was paraded to see the sentences carried out:

the sentence [was] . . . that half of their heads, including beards and moustaches, should be shaved off, that they be branded on the left hip with the letter "D" and then drummed out of the service. The brigade formed in a hollow square, in the centre of which were a blacksmith's forge to heat the irons, and two barbers with their implements; after the shaving and the branding the two men were marched along the several regimental fronts, the brigade band preceding them. . . . It was a sad, pitiable sight, but withal amusing.[39]

William E. Ormsby, a deserter from the 2nd Massachusetts, was dealt with more harshly; "captured in arms against the United States . . . [he] was convicted by drumhead court-martial" and immediately shot.[40]

The routine, pleasant or otherwise, of winter camp was rudely disturbed in December by a War Department announcement inviting veterans to reenlist. It was evident that despite Gettysburg, Vicksburg, and Missionary Ridge, the South was determined to go on fighting. The three-year terms of enlistment of the regiments mustered in in 1861—the regiments with the largest numbers of experienced officers and men—would begin to expire in the summer of 1864, and in a period of six or eight months the Union armies would lose a large percentage of their best and most re-

38. *Official Records*, Vol. XXIX, Pt. 2, p. 624. In contrast with the apparent leniency of the cavalry courts-martial, of the ninety-two infantrymen convicted of desertion, twenty-five were sentenced to death, and all twenty-five death sentences were carried out.

39. Regimental History Committee, *History of the 3d Pennsylvania,* 360.

40. *Official Records*, XXXIII, 336.

liable soldiers. To prevent this the army announced a policy whereby, if in any regiment, three fourths of the men having not more than fifteen months left to serve reenlisted for a new term of three years or the duration of the war, the regiment would retain its identity, organization, and officers and would be distinguished thereafter with the designation of "veteran" regiment— as, for example, Second Ohio Veteran Volunteer Cavalry. The men who reenlisted would be sent home in a body on a thirty-five-day furlough, would receive a United States bounty of $402 plus whatever additional bounties their states and localities might provide, and would be entitled to wear a special chevron identifying them as reenlisted veterans.

The announcement, as might be expected, set every mess and hut buzzing. On one side was the prospect of being free of the hazards and hardships of war in a few months; on the other was the continuation of those hazards and hardships in exchange for a long furlough and a sizable bounty. No doubt, as the historian of a western regiment of mounted infantry wrote, "there were . . . as many motives for reenlistment—in addition to patriotism pure and simple—as there were individuals. With a few it was a 'fad'. . . . Some hesitated till the example of others carried them over the ripple."[41] Charles Francis Adams may well have exaggerated when he wrote that "the reenlistment question has destroyed all discipline and nearly broken our hearts. It has reduced our regiment to a Caucus."[42] The result of the individual and group soul-searchings and debates was precisely what one could have predicted: the factor that seemed to weigh as much with the men as did patriotism, the furlough, and the bounty, was the personality, influence, and competence of their officers. Colonel Thomas C. Devin of the 6th New York, in which there was "great excitement" over the reenlistment question, had the regiment drawn up in line, "addressed" the men, and asked those willing to reenlist to step forward; nearly the entire regiment did so.[43] In the 3rd Pennsylvania, however, "the depressing circumstances attending the

41. William R. Hartpence, *History of the 51st Indiana Veteran Infantry* (Indianapolis, 1894), 199.

42. Ford (ed.), *A Cycle of Adams Letters*, II, 118.

43. Committee on Regimental History, *History of the Sixth New York Cavalry (Second Ira Harris Guard)* (Worcester, N.Y., 1908), 165.

kinds of work the men . . . were without interruption called upon to perform, militated against the success which had been hoped for," and only seventy-five chose to veteranize.[44] The 1st Massachusetts also failed to muster the necessary three quarters, but Charles Francis Adams was justifiably proud that his company "kept up to the mark."[45] A large majority of the 5th New York reenlisted, as did the 1st New York, but in the latter it was noted that the response varied from company to company; "in some . . . whose officers had proved efficient, almost every man determined to remain in the service . . . in others there was dissatisfaction. . . . There was dissatisfaction with one of the captains who had been unfortunate in every affair in which he had undertaken to lead. There was a general protest against re-enlisting under him."[46] But another company commander, Captain James H. Stevenson, was "very agreeably surprised," as he had every right to be, when the men of his company marched up to his tent in a body and offered to reenlist if he promised to remain with them, which he "very readily consented to do and nearly every man reenlisted at once."[47]

Alas for the patriotic troopers of the 1st New York (Lincoln) Cavalry! After they had veteranized, they learned that the 33rd New York Infantry had also reenlisted, but on condition that it be converted to a cavalry regiment. Not only was the condition agreed to, but the 33rd, being the first regiment from New York to veteranize, was assigned the honorable and totally undeserved title of "First New York Veteran Volunteer Cavalry." To have the right to bear a designation the *real* First New York Cavalry had earned by being the first mounted regiment raised in New York and had made illustrious in the tented field thus encroached upon, "provoked . . . [the] regiment beyond endurance." But even worse was to come. The *genuine* First New York Veteran Volunteer Cavalry found itself brigaded with the *bogus* First New York

44. Regimental History Committee, *History of the 3d Pennsylvania*, 390.
45. Ford (ed.), *A Cycle of Adams Letters*, II, 118.
46. Boudrye, *Historic Records of the Fifth*, 87; Beach, *First New York (Lincoln) Cavalry*, 303–304, 311.
47. James H. Stevenson,"*Boots and Saddles*": *A History of the First Volunteer Cavalry of the War, Known as the First New York (Lincoln) Cavalry* (Harrisburg, 1879), 243.

Veteran Volunteer Cavalry ("The idea of doughboys being called veteran cavalry!"), and utter confusion ensued. Each regiment received mail, baggage, supplies, and orders intended for the other, and "besides, the two regiments were always at swords points," and no wonder.[48]

Generally, however, the reenlistment program was successful enough. Many a trooper who resisted the temptation to sign up when the offer was first made jumped on the bandwagon when he saw his comrades preparing to depart on the thirty-five-day furlough. Consequently, in January and February most of the cavalry regiments were reduced to skeletons, with only the men who had decided not to reenlist and those not eligible to do so remaining in the field. On January 5, four cavalry regiments reported a total of 1,226 of their men absent on veterans' furlough.[49]

Winter or summer, cavalrymen lived in constant danger of attack by what they indiscriminately called "guerrillas," but were actually enemies of several different kinds. First were the scouting groups of regular Confederate cavalry. Next were the loosely organized bands of Partisan Rangers, the commands of John Mosby, James C. Kincheloe, John McNeill, Harry Gilmor, Charles T. O'Ferrall, Robert White, and others. Then there were furloughed Confederate soldiers visiting their families in occupied territory and not averse to picking up a Federal cavalryman's horse, weapons, and gear when the opportunity offered. Lastly, there were the guerrillas properly so-called, individuals and small, constantly changing *ad hoc* groups, who, innocent farmers and artisans by day, took advantage of terrain made to order for hit-and-run operations, by preference at night, to harry the enemy, partly for patriotism but perhaps mainly for profit. Quick in their movements, intimately familiar with every path, byway, and hid-

48. *Ibid.*, 254–55. The former 33rd New York Infantry should properly have been designated the 17th New York Cavalry. The writers of reports and dispatches reproduced in the *Official Records* tried to avoid confusion by referring to the "First New York (Veteran)" and the "First New York (Lincoln)," respectively. The same designations will be used hereafter in the present work.

49. *Official Records*, XXXIII, 338; Vol. XXIX, Pt. 2, p. 555. The four regiments were the 8th Illinois, 1st Maryland, and the 6th and 9th New York. The reenlisted veterans of several other regiments were already on leave, or were about to leave.

ing place, aided with information, food, and shelter by a friendly local population, all these types of "irregulars" were an ubiquitous, nerve-wracking menace.

In a class apart in the eyes of Federal soldiers were a subspecies of the breed of guerrillas, namely the bushwhackers—the "detestable" bushwhackers, the historian of a West Virginia cavalry regiment called them. "We did not object," he said, "to being shot at on general principles, but to have some unprincipled scoundrel, who was too cowardly to join the army and fight as a man, sneak around like a thief in the night and shoot from behind a tree or from some inaccessible position, was more than we could patiently stand."[50] Troopers away from camp on errands legitimate or otherwise were "constantly in danger of being captured and shot" by what they considered to be "thieving cutthroats," dressed by preference in Union army overcoats.[51] Kilpatrick had to warn Pleasonton's chief of staff in November, "The whole country . . . is full of bushwhackers, and several of my men have been killed or taken prisoner. Any messenger you send should have a strong escort."[52] Two days earlier, Pleasonton had issued a corps order in which he set forth that

The loss in officers and men sustained in this corps at the hands of guerrillas during the past few days demands the careful attention of all to prevent a recurrence. . . . Visiting in the families of the country . . . riding for pleasure, either alone or in small parties . . . will, therefore, be abstained from in future. Every house within or without the lines of the army is a nest of treason, and every grove a meeting place for guerrilla bands. . . . every effort will be made to confine all officers and men to such close attention to their duties as will remove all temptation to go beyond the lines of their respective commands.[53]

The men of the Union armies did not need manuals on guerrilla warfare to learn that the indispensable key to its success was

50. J. J. Sutton, *History of the Second Regiment West Virginia Cavalry Volunteers* (Portsmouth, W.Va., 1892), 56.
51. Bowen, *Regimental History of the First New York*, 105, 99; *Official Records*, Vol. XXIX, Pt. 1, pp. 656, 659; XXXIII, 248.
52. *Official Records*, Vol. XXIX, Pt. 2, p. 431.
53. *Ibid.*, 423. Buford reported on two occasions that "the whole country is infested with guerrillas, scouts, &c.," and that "guerrillas are very numerous hereabouts; to-day killed a sergeant who was out with a small party, foraging." *Ibid.*, Vol. XXVII, Pt. 3, pp. 734, 741.

a friendly civilian population. The historian of the 10th New York might have been speaking for the entire Cavalry Corps when he wrote, "The feeling against the citizens of the surrounding country was very bitter. It was generally believed that they were privy to the frequent murder of Union soldiers, if they were not the actual perpetrators of the crimes."[54] The 9th New York, stationed near Falmouth, notified the people of the neighborhood that "there must be no more bushwhacking at the peril of being driven out and their dwellings burned. After that there was no more of that kind of war while the 9th New York was there."[55]

General Herman Haupt, the engineering and transportation genius of the Civil War, trying to keep in operation the Orange & Alexandria, the lifeline of the Army of the Potomac, complained to Rufus Ingalls in July, 1863, that "attempts to throw off trains are made daily, and unless the practice can be broken up, there is no security in your communications. To operate the road with reasonable security, we must have the country patrolled by cavalry, and notice given to the inhabitants that in case of any further attempts to disturb the track or telegraph, all able-bodied residents within ten miles will be arrested and placed under guard."[56] Acting on Haupt's recommendation, Meade issued a proclamation notifying civilians living within ten miles of the railroad that they would be held responsible for any damage to the line and would be required to repair the damage; if, nevertheless, the "depredations" continued, they would be "put across the line" and their property confiscated.[57]

Fortunately for Virginians living in areas occupied by the Union army, such proclamations remained an empty threat. Those closest to the problem, the commanding officers of regiments and brigades of Union cavalry, felt that they were between the upper millstone of the guerrillas and the nether millstone of

54. Preston, *History of the 10th Regiment*, 168.
55. Newel Cheney, *History of the Ninth Regiment, New York Volunteer Cavalry* (Poland Center, N.Y., 1901), 135.
56. Herman Haupt, *Reminiscences of General Herman Haupt* (Milwaukee, 1901), 248; see also p. 251. Moving trains were so frequently fired into that they commonly carried infantry guards, ready to return the fire if they could see the attackers.
57. *Ibid.*, 254.

army commanders who wanted the guerrilla menace eradicated, but would not sanction the drastic methods that might have done the job. Colonel Horace Binney Sargent of the 1st Massachusetts wrote in the bitterness of his soul:

To-night I might, perhaps, report that there is not an armed rebel within the circuit of the country that the colonel commanding expects me to clear. To-morrow the woods may be full of them. Every man and horse must be sent within the lines, every house destroyed, every tree girdled and set on fire, before we can approach security. . . . Attila, king of the Huns, adopted the only method that can exterminate these citizen soldiers. . . . Regiments of the line can do nothing against this furtive population, soldiers to-day, farmers tomorrow, acquainted with every wood path, and finding friends in every house. . . . I can clear this country with fire and sword, and no mortal can do it in any other way.[58]

There were draconian messages and orders in plenty from on high. "Direct Colonel Bryan to catch all the bushwhackers he can and hang them"; "Use every exertion to suppress bushwhacking and guerrillas. Citizens found in arms with guerrillas will be shot on the spot," and many more, but regimental and brigade commanders knew better than to obey them literally.[59] No doubt there were occasions, never reported, when line officers and enlisted men administered vigilante justice to actual guerrillas and bushwhackers, or those suspected, rightly or wrongly, of being either, but the high command allowed itself to be inhibited by considerations of humanity and of the "laws of war" in dealing with the problem. Colonel Sargent was not given the authority to apply the methods of Attila. On the contrary, when Colonel C. H. Smith, Second Brigade, Gregg's division, was ordered to send a detachment to Auburn, where guerrillas had been reported, with instructions to search the houses in that vicinity, he was admonished to see to it that "The party . . . [is] . . . commanded by an officer who will perform this duty in a proper manner. You will instruct . . .

58. *Official Records*, Vol. XXIX, Pt. 1, p. 90.
59. *Ibid.*, XXXIII, 696; Vol. XXVII, Pt. 2, p. 790. General Orders No. 6, January 15, 1864, directed, "Every guerrilla or other rebel wearing the uniform of a United States soldier caught in the act of making war against any of the forces of this command will be hung upon the spot." The order was revoked on April 5 by Gregg, while he was temporarily in command of the Cavalry Corps. *Ibid.*, XXXIII, 806.

[him] to compel the search to be made without injury to persons or property."[60] General Meade asked Pleasonton to explain "by what authority the several cavalry commands arrest citizens . . . against whom there is no evidence of having been engaged in committing depredations or aiding those engaged in such practices, but who merely decline to take the oath of allegiance."[61] Poor Custer, who, it turned out, was the culprit, was obliged to explain, "Citizens whom I arrested several days ago and forwarded to . . . headquarters . . . have been paroled and returned to their homes. They regard their paroles no more than they do so much blank paper, and are as able to injure us by bushwhacking, &c., as they were before, if not more so. . . . I can suppress bushwhacking, and render every man within the limits of my command practically loyal, if allowed to deal with them as I choose."[62] The response from headquarters was a sharp rap across the knuckles for Custer; "the loose statements upon this subject contained in the letter of General Custer do not impress the major-general commanding with the suitableness of intrusting that officer with the discretion he suggests, of dealing with those within the limits of his command as he might choose."[63]

Doubtless General Meade's position was correct from a humanitarian standpoint, but it did not help the Federal trooper shot and killed from ambush, and the harassed Sargents and Custers may well have complained that they were expected to eradicate the guerrillas and bushwhackers with one hand tied behind their backs, and one eye on the Bill of Rights of the Constitution the South had spurned. The Union high command tried to abide by the rules of "civilized warfare" in fighting an enemy who had a minimum of respect for those rules, and it did not work.

And so, on the night of February 11, the westbound B & O express was derailed near Kearneysville by a band of twenty-five "guerrillas" led by Harry Gilmor, who held a major's commission in the Confederate army by virtue of his command of a Partisan Ranger unit. Gilmor's men did not burn the train, nor did they

60. *Ibid.*, 397.
61. *Ibid.*, Vol. XXIX, Pt. 2, p. 17.
62. *Ibid.*, 38.
63. *Ibid.*, 61.

bother to take away or to parole the soldiers on board, but they did relieve the conductor and the passengers of sizable sums of money, pistols, watches, and clothing, robbing everyone "except those in the ladies' car."[64] General Lee wrote of this exploit to Secretary of War Seddon that "no military object was accomplished after gaining possession of the cars, and the act appears to have been one of plunder. Such conduct is unauthorized and discreditable."[65]

By any standard, John Singleton Mosby stood head and shoulders above the generality of partisan or guerrilla leaders. A man of intelligence, he had a sense of the potential military value of guerrilla operations; he had written Jeb Stuart: "The military value of the species of warfare I have waged is not measured by the number of prisoners and material of war captured . . . but by the heavy detail it has already compelled . . . [the enemy] to make, and which I hope to make him increase, in order to guard his communications, and to that extent diminishing his aggressiveness."[66] This of course was true as far as it went. Mosby certainly spread apprehension and alarm among the Federals in his area of operations, and he frequently brought back valuable information from his forays behind their lines. His exploits earned him Stuart's extravagant praise, and General Lee, in recommending his promotion to lieutenant colonel, wrote that he was "zealous, bold and skillful, and with very small resources has accomplished a great deal," a commendation Mosby certainly deserved.[67] On another occasion, however, General Lee, who was nothing if not realistic in judging his subordinates' accomplishments, thought it proper to write, "I greatly commend . . . [Mosby's] boldness and good management . . . [but] his attention seems more directed to the capture of sutler's wagons, &c., than to the injury of the enemy's communications and outposts."[68] But perhaps capturing "sutler's wagons, &c." was Mosby's principal means of retaining the allegiance of a constantly changing group of a few dozen men

64. *Ibid.*, XXXIII, 151, 154.
65. *Ibid.*, 222.
66. *Ibid.*, Vol. XXIX, Pt. 1, p. 81.
67. *Ibid.*, Vol. XXXIII, 1113. Mosby was later promoted to colonel.
68. *Ibid.*, Vol. XXIX, Pt. 2, p. 652.

whom he led on his expeditions. Assuredly there was a glamour about his operations to which military historians, no less than Stuart, have proven susceptible, but it may be doubted if all his forays, to which may be added those of all other guerrillas, Partisan Rangers, and bushwhackers, accomplished anything more than to increase the cost and bitterness of the war.

Confederate General Tom Rosser, for one, had no illusions about the true military value of the guerrillas and their operations. Writing to General Lee in January, 1864, he observed:

During the time I have been in the valley I have had ample opportunity of judging the efficiency and usefulness of the many irregular bodies of troops . . . known as partisans, &c. . . . they are a nuisance and an evil to the service. Without discipline, order, or organization they roam broadcast over the country, a band of thieves, stealing, pillaging, plundering, and doing every manner of mischief and crime. They are a terror to the citizens and an injury to the cause. They never fight; can't be made to fight. Their leaders are generally brave, but few of the men are good soldiers, and have engaged in this business for the sake of gain. The effect upon the service is bad. . . . It keeps men out of the service whose bayonets or sabers should be counted on the field of battle.[69]

The endorsements of Generals Stuart and Lee on this scathing report indicated their agreement with Rosser, and at Lee's request the Confederate Congress repealed the Partisan Ranger Law on February 17, 1864.[70] Six weeks later, Lee recommended that all the Partisan Ranger groups except Mosby's (which was to be mustered into the regular service) be disbanded, on the ground that it was "almost impossible, under the best officers even, to

---

69. *Ibid.*, Vol. XXXIII, 1081. When Charles O'Ferrall set about raising his Partisan Ranger battalion, many of his recruits were "young fellows who . . . had become or were about to become liable to military service." Charles T. O'Ferrall, *Forty Years of Active Service* (New York, 1904), 86. In March, 1863, Mosby "gave notice of a meeting at Rector's Cross-Roads, in Loudon County." The sixty-nine men who responded "were representatives of nearly all the cavalry regiments in the army, with a sprinkling of men from the infantry, who had determined to try their luck on horseback." John S. Mosby, *Mosby's War Reminiscences: Stuart's Cavalry Campaigns* (New York, 1958), 98–99. It may be taken for granted that many of the sixty-nine were absent from their units without leave.

70. *Official Records*, XXXIII, 1082; Barksdale, "Semi-Regular and Irregular Warfare," 374.

have discipline in these bands . . . or to prevent them from becoming an injury instead of a benefit to the service, and the system gives license to many deserters and marauders, who assume to belong to these . . . companies and commit depredations on friend and foe alike."[71]

Whether as partisans or as members of the "regular service," Mosby and his men caused the Federals grief enough. On February 21, a 150-man detachment of the 16th New York and the 2nd Massachusetts met and defeated a group of 70 of Mosby's men, but on their return to camp they were ambushed by about 160 partisans, led by Mosby himself. He reported: "Distributing the different companies in positions where I could attack . . . [the enemy's] front, flank and rear simultaneously, we awaited the approach of the enemy. Soon the concerted signal . . . announced the time for attack. With a terrific yell . . . we dashed on the unsuspecting Yankees. Surprised and confounded, with no time to form, they made but a feeble resistance, and were perfectly overwhelmed by the shock of the charge. They fled in every direction."[72] Mosby claimed a "bag" of "at least 15 killed and a considerable number wounded, besides 70 prisoners . . . with all their horses, arms and equipments"; the Federals admitted the loss of 10 killed, 7 wounded, and "about 60" unaccounted for.[73] And this was only one of dozens of such onfalls. Scouting groups of Federal cavalry sent out to hunt for Mosby—one such group of 300 of the 1st New Jersey was guided by a prisoner who claimed to know where to find Mosby, and who was ordered shot if he led the Jerseymen into a trap—occasionally killed or captured some of his men, but Mosby himself led a charmed life.[74] In the long war

71. *Official Records*, XXXIII, 1252.
72. *Ibid.*, 160.
73. *Ibid.*, 159. A subsequent Federal report raised the number of men unaccounted for to seventy, matching Mosby's figure. A rapidly organized pursuit of the Partisan Rangers, who had a fifteen-hour start, was of course fruitless. *Ibid.*, 587.
74. *Ibid.*, 568–69; Vol. XXIX, Pt. 1, pp. 494, 658. In May, 1863, the 5th New York had an encounter with Mosby. Says the regimental historian, "the Fifth New York descended like an avalanche upon the guerrillas. Mosby was heard to exclaim, 'My God! It is the Fifth New York!' A hand-to-hand encounter took place, where Yankee sabers were used with fearful effect, and soon the Rebels broke and fled, entirely demoralized and panic-

of wits between him and the Federal cavalry the score remained heavily in his favor. Typical of his mode of warfare, except, in this case, for the lack of a clear-cut success, was a night attack on the camp of Cole's Battalion of Maryland cavalry, thus described by its historian:

It was two o'clock Sunday morning, January 10th, 1864 . . . when the tramp of horses' feet was heard on the icy road, but a few hundred yards distant. The night was dark and bitter cold. . . . The rebel yell resounded throughout the mountain fastness; Cole's camp was surprised . . . Mosby . . . had captured the pickets; he . . . fell upon the camp, and then fired a volley into the tents where Cole's men lay sleeping. . . . The rude awakening brought Cole's hardy veterans out into the snow. . . . Long experience in border warfare had taught . . . [them] to shoot at the horsemen, and not to attempt to mount their own . . . chargers. . . . the cry rang out on the frosty air, "shoot every soldier on horseback". . . . It was perfect hell! Every man cursing and yelling, and the horses were lunging and kicking in their mad efforts to get away. When one of the poor beasts would get wounded he would utter a piercing shriek that would echo throughout the mountains. Mosby's men had emptied their revolvers. The night was too dark for them to see to reload. . . . They were now completely at the mercy of Cole's Rangers, who were using their carbines with good effect. . . . The Rebels seeing that the bloody struggle was fruitless, the Confederate chief . . . gave the order to retire.[75]

It did not take cavalrymen long, after their first exposure to active service, to recognize the signs and portents of something out of the ordinary about to occur. Stanton P. Allen of the 1st Massachusetts explains:

Orders from brigade headquarters to have the horses well shod at once, meant a cavalry expedition into the enemy's country. Extra ammunition for the light batteries that belonged to the cavalry corps

---

stricken." Boudrye, Historic Records of the Fifth, 55. Boudrye's account is in the main factual, except for the exclamation he attributes to Mosby, which smacks of being the least likely exclamation to have been exclaimed in the Civil War.

75. C. Armour Newcomer, Cole's Cavalry, or, Three Years in the Saddle in the Shenandoah Valley (Baltimore, 1895), 93–96. The battalion received a congratulatory telegram from Halleck on their handling of Mosby's attack. General Jeremiah C. Sullivan's approval took a more tangible form; he sent Major Cole twenty gallons of whiskey to be distributed among his men. Ibid., 100, 102.

meant that the movement was to be a reconnaissance in force. The assembling of a division or two of infantry in battle trim near the cavalry outposts . . . showed that an attempt was to be made to gobble up another slice of the Confederacy or make a break in the communications of the rebels.[76]

From mid-February on, there were unmistakeable signs of a major move of some sort being in contemplation. Colonel Theodore Lyman, who, as a member of the commanding general's staff, saw the situation from a better, or at least higher, vantage point than did Trooper Allen, wrote home:

For some days General [Andrew A.] Humphreys has been a mass of mystery . . . doing much writing by himself, all to the great amusement of the bystanders, who had heard, even in Washington, that some expedition or raid was on the tapis, and even pointed out various details thereof. . . . A secret expedition with us is got up like a picnic, with everybody blabbing and yelling. . . . Kilpatrick is sent for by the President . . . everybody knows it at once; he is a cavalry officer; it must be a raid. All Willard's chatters of it. Everybody devotes his entire energies to pumping the President and Kill-cavalry! . . . So there was Humphreys writing mysteriously, and speaking to nobody, while the whole camp was sending expeditions to the four corners of the compass![77]

Colonel Lyman was definitely on the right track. He was in fact describing the gestation of what would be known as the "Kilpatrick Raid," or the "Dahlgren-Kilpatrick Raid." So far as the records show, the genesis of the raid was an order on February 11, 1864, for Kilpatrick to "proceed to Washington and report to the President, as requested by the latter."[78] Upon his return to the

76. Stanton P. Allen, *Down in Dixie: Life in a Cavalry Regiment in War Days* (Boston, 1888), 203.

77. Agassiz, *Meade's Headquarters*, 76–77. See also Kidd, *Personal Recollections*, 234: "Some time after the beginning of 1864, there began to be rumors of some daring expedition . . . to be led by . . . [Kilpatrick] . . . though nothing very definite leaked out as to what it was. . . . Hints were thrown out of an indefinite something that was going to happen." The destination of the raid appears to have been a well-kept secret. Captain John W. Phillips of the 18th Pennsylvania, who went on the raid, wrote on February 29, "Don't know yet where we are to go" and noted the next day, "I hear for the first time this morning that *Richmond* is our destination." John Wilson Phillips, "Civil War Diary," ed. Robert G. Athearn, *Virginia Magazine of History and Biography*, LXII (1954), 97.

78. *Official Records*, XXXIII, 552.

army five days later, Kilpatrick reported to General Gregg, in command of the Cavalry Corps in Pleasonton's absence on leave, that he had reported to the president on February 12 and was sent by him to Secretary Stanton, to whom, "at his request," he submitted a plan for a raid "to accomplish the double purpose of distributing the President's amnesty proclamation . . . [and] to destroy, as far as practicable, the enemy's communications, and attempt the release of our prisoners at Richmond."[79]

There is something strikingly unsatisfactory about this recital. The president was far from faultless in observing military protocol, but still, why should he bypass the general-in-chief, the commanding general of the Army of the Potomac, the officer commanding the Cavalry Corps, and a divisional commander in the corps senior to Kilpatrick and solicit from the latter a plan for an expedition of major importance? Unquestionably, the initiative must have come from Kilpatrick. Given his inordinate ambition, it would have been quite in character for him to think up the plan for a spectacular exploit with himself in the leading role, use his political friends to bring the plan to the president's attention, and arrange through them to have himself called to Washington to explain and sell it to the president and the secretary of war.[80]

However his visit to Washington had come about, upon his return to the army Kilpatrick submitted his plan to General Meade. He proposed crossing the Rapidan with a force of "not less than 4,000 cavalry and six guns"; he would then send a detachment to destroy the Virginia Central and the Richmond, Fredericksburg & Potomac at Frederick's Hall and Guiney's Station, respectively, while the main body moved "on Richmond" to release the prisoners. Meanwhile, the detachment that had been

79. *Ibid.*, 172. There were thought to be fifteen thousand Federal prisoners in Richmond. For the "amnesty proclamation" (correctly the Proclamation of Amnesty and Reconstitution) see Carl Sandburg, *Abraham Lincoln: The War Years* (4 vols.; New York, 1939), II, 482–84.

80. Colonel Kidd describes a visit to Kilpatrick's headquarters "about the middle of February" (unfortunately, he does not give a more precise date) of Senators Chandler of Michigan and Wilkinson of Minnesota. His further statement, "It is now known, as it was soon thereafter, that Kilpatrick had devised a daring scheme for the capture of Richmond, which had been received with much favor by the authorities in Washington," certainly suggests that the initiative came from Kilpatrick. Kidd, *Personal Recollections*, 234.

sent to Frederick's Hall would "proceed to Goochland Court-House, destroy the [James River] canal, cross the James, proceed down the south bank, destroy the arsenal at Bellona; also the Danville and Richmond and [the] Petersburg and Richmond Railroads." The two groups were then to meet, presumably in Richmond, and they and the released prisoners would either return to the army via Fredericksburg, or "seek temporary safety at West Point" on the Peninsula.[81]

A fascinating game of cat and mouse now began. Meade sent the plan to Pleasonton, who had evidently been hurriedly recalled from leave, for his comments, but Pleasonton confined himself to a laconic and noncommittal "Respectfully forwarded to Major-General Meade, as requested," a pretty clear indication of his desire to wash his hands of the whole affair. But Meade would have none of it. Back went the plan to Pleasonton with the notation, "The major-general commanding desires the views of the commander of the cavalry corps respecting the feasibility of the plan in writing."[82] Thus prodded, Pleasonton responded the next day that in his opinion the plan was not feasible, and that "in the present state of the roads and the facilities the rebels have," he could not recommend its acceptance. He pointed out that when Stoneman had made his raid nine months before, the Confederate army was pinned down, the country behind it was entirely clear, and "yet the damage done by the raid was repaired in a few days, while the loss to the Government was over 7,000 [?] horses besides the equipments and men left on the road." He added that although Kilpatrick intended to destroy the telegraph lines along his line of march, "the telegraph by way of Gordonsville and Lynchburg would soon notify the rebels in Richmond that . . . [the] cavalry was out, and before Kilpatrick could do much damage, their vulnerable points would be secured."[83]

Meade was now faced with an interesting dilemma. He had

81. *Official Records*, XXXIII, 172–73. Kilpatrick added that "from the information I have but lately received, and from my thorough knowledge of the country, I am satisfied that this plan can safely and successfully be carried out." Kilpatrick failed to state—and apparently no one bothered to ask him—how he expected to feed on their long journey to Fredericksburg or Fort Monroe the 15,000 prisoners he hoped to liberate.
82. *Ibid.*, 173.
83. *Ibid.*, 171–72.

before him a plan he knew was favored by the president and, by implication at least, by the powerful secretary of war.[84] Yet the plan had been reported on adversely by Kilpatrick's immediate superior—whether out of pique or on objective grounds, who could tell? What now was the army commander to do? Uncharacteristically, Meade decided to approve the plan; his formal orders to Kilpatrick directed that he "move with the utmost expedition possible on the shortest route past the enemy's right flank to Richmond, and . . . endeavor to effect an entrance into that city and liberate our prisoners." He then arranged for a diversion to help Kilpatrick, by advancing the VI Corps to Gordonsville and sending Custer with 1,500 men on a march to Charlottesville "to distract the enemy's attention and prevent the detachment of any force toward Richmond." Contrary to Pleasonton's opinion, Meade thought "it practicable by a rapid and secret movement that Richmond might be carried by a *coup de main*, and . . . [the] prisoners released before re-enforcements from either Petersburg or Lee's army could reach there," provided the raid was conducted with "secrecy, good management, and the utmost expedition."[85]

The army commander having given the plan his blessing, a great shower of orders descended upon the cavalry to assemble the 4,000-man force Kilpatrick was to lead. On February 26, the men in each regiment with the best horses were sent to Kilpatrick's camps at Stevensburg "by such routes and at such times . . . as . . . [to] insure their reaching him secretly."[86] The men were delighted when word of these orders got about; "Everybody was in excellent humor for nothing so delights the heart of a cavalryman as to go on a scout or a raid. It is easier to get a trooper or even a hundred for a raid than to get one to groom an extra horse."[87]

Ulric Dahlgren, who was to give his name as well as his life to the raid, was not quite twenty-two years old in February, 1864.

84. Curiously, the records contain not a single communication from General Halleck concerning this raid, or any indication that he was consulted about it.
85. *Official Records*, XXXIII, 170.
86. *Ibid.*, 598, 599, 600. Kilpatrick started with either 3,522 or 3,982 officers and men; the wording of his report is such that either interpretation is possible. *Ibid.*, 183.
87. Moyer, *History of the 17th Regiment*, 233.

He was the son of Admiral John Dahlgren and was studying for the bar when the Civil War broke out. Appointed aide-de-camp with the rank of captain to the staff of John Sigel, he saw action in 1862 in the Valley, at Second Bull Run, and in the defenses of Washington, In November, 1862, he was sent with a small group of cavalrymen to scout Confederate strength at Fredericksburg, and in Burnside's attack on December 13 he crossed the Rappahannock with the leading wave of Federal troops sent to silence the Confederate sharpshooters holed up in the town's riverside buildings. When Hooker replaced Burnside in command of the Army of the Potomac, Dahlgren transferred to Hooker's staff and, on June 7, 1863, carried to Pleasonton the orders that led to the battle of Brandy Station two days later. Dahlgren remained with Pleasonton for the battle and was mentioned in the most flattering terms in the latter's report. When Meade took over from Hooker he retained the latter's staff, including Dahlgren, who again distinguished himself just before the battle of Gettysburg by capturing a courier with important dispatches from President Davis and Adjutant General Samuel Cooper to General Lee. Attaching himself to Kilpatrick's division for the pursuit following the battle, he led the charge into Hagerstown on July 5 and was shot in the ankle, which necessitated the amputation of his right leg below the knee. While recovering in Washington, he was jumped two grades, becoming a colonel at age twenty-one. He also heard about the plans for Kilpatrick's raid. Still on crutches, he turned up at Kilpatrick's headquarters, asked to be taken along on the raid, and was enthusiastically accepted. Indeed, he was given command of the detachment that was to cross the James at Goochland and come upon Richmond from the south, an assignment that might perhaps have been given to a cavalryman with greater experience.

Kilpatrick's was not the only plan to liberate the Federal prisoners held in Richmond. Benjamin Butler, whose ability to think up such schemes was exceeded only by his inability to execute them, had his Army of the James at the tip of the Peninsula, well placed for such a move. In early February he organized an expedition made up of 4,000 infantry and 2,200 cavalry for that purpose, with the cavalry component, made up of parts of five regiments, being led by Colonel S. P. Spear, 17th Pennsylvania. In overall charge was General I. J. Wistar. The plan was elaborated in the most minute detail and took into account every contingency except the reaction of the enemy. Spear was ordered to start the movement on February 5; he was to "ride down," "surprise," or "capture" a series of picket posts and dash into Richmond. There he was to divide his command into detachments of 250–300 men. The task of each detachment was precisely spelled out and the streets and bridges they were to use on their respective errands were specified. One detachment was to destroy the navy yard and another was to release the prisoners in Libby Prison and on Belle Island; still others were to destroy the Tredegar Iron Works, public buildings and factories generally, and for good measure, one group was to "capture Jeff. Davis at his residence." The 4,000-man infantry was to follow Spear to Bottom's Bridge to await there the return of the cavalry with the liberated prisoners and Davis and escort them back to Fort Monroe.[88]

The one difficulty the plan failed to provide for involved Private William J. Boyle, 1st New York Mounted Rifles, who had killed a Lieutenant Disosway of his regiment. Boyle was tried, convicted, and sentenced to death, but the sentence had not been carried out because of a presidential order suspending executions in Butler's department. Then one of the guards allowed Boyle to escape. Boyle made his way to Richmond and, to assure himself of a friendly welcome, told the authorities that "large numbers of cavalry and infantry were concentrated . . . [at Fort Monroe] to take Richmond." As a result, when Colonel Spear and his troopers reached Bottom's Bridge on their way to Richmond, they found waiting for them a force of the enemy too large to be attacked. That was the end of the expedition, as Butler reported in indignant telegrams to the president and the secretary of war, blaming the failure of the plan on misplaced executive clemency and urging that the order suspending the carrying out of capital sentences in his command be revoked forthwith.[89]

Kilpatrick's luck was to be no better than Butler's. He started out from Stevensburg on the evening of February 28 and crossed

88. *Official Records*, XXXIII, 521–22.
89. *Ibid.*, 144.

the Rapidan without incident before midnight. Captain Joseph Gloskoski, Kilpatrick's acting signal officer and clearly a man of sensibility, thus described the march:

The first night of our march was very beautiful. Myriads of stars twinkled in heaven, looking at us as if in wonder why should we break the laws of God and wander at night instead of seeking repose and sleep. The moon threw its silvery light upon Rapidan waters when we forded it, and it seemed as if the Almighty Judge was looking silently upon our doings. . . . By the time we reached Beaver Dam Station, it grew dark and rain began to fall . . . [as] we moved on toward South Anna River . . . it stormed in earnest. Sharp wind and sleet forced men to close their eyes. The night was so dark that even the river in front could not be seen and trees on the roadside could not be distinguished. . . . Men depended entirely on the instincts of their horses.[90]

Despite the rain and sleet the roads remained in passable condition, and with the coming of daylight the main column made good progress. The march was "at a fast walk," but as Colonel J. H. Kidd of the 6th Michigan noted, that meant that only the head of the column moved at a fast walk; those behind frequently had to trot, or even gallop, to stay closed up; and Colonel Kidd added, "There was an air of undue haste—a precipitancy and rush not at all reassuring" about the march."[91] Nevertheless, telegraph lines were torn down and depots and track were destroyed, as planned. At ten A.M. on March 1, Kilpatrick reached the Brook Turnpike, five miles from Richmond. Three hours later, after a series of minor skirmishes, he was within a mile of the city. Here opposition stiffened, and so far as one can tell from the rather uncertain language of his report, Kilpatrick simply lost control; he was face to face with a tactical situation for which he was unable to find a solution. In General Meade's opinion, he "made no serious attempt to enter" the city; after losing "upward of 60" men killed and wounded, he retreated to Mechanicsville.[92] Late that evening, learning that there were no enemy troops between

90. *Ibid.*, 188.
91. Kidd, *Personal Recollections*, 240.
92. Kilpatrick's report is in *Official Records*, XXXIII, 183–87; Meade's comment is in *ibid.*, 171. Colonel Kidd was of the opinion that "Kilpatrick who, at the start, was bold and confident, at the last when quick resolution was indispensable, appeared to be overcome with a strange and fatal irresolution." Kidd, *Personal Recollections*, 249.

him and Richmond, he decided on a night attack on the city and was preparing to move when his rear was attacked by enemy cavalry coming from the direction of Hanover Court House. The attackers were Wade Hampton and a scanty force of something under 300 troopers; Hampton reported that his attack carried him into Kilpatrick's camp, where "horses, arms, rations and clothing were scattered about in confusion."[93] "Not knowing the strength of the enemy"—which was certainly excusable, since Hampton attacked at night in the midst of a snowstorm—Kilpatrick "abandoned all further ideas of releasing . . . [the] prisoners" and began a retreat down the Peninsula toward Butler's lines.[94]

Dahlgren, with 460 men in his detachment, had been given the assignment of riding ahead of the main column, crossing the James at Goochland, twenty miles above Richmond, and, after releasing the Belle Island prisoners, entering Richmond from the south. The wisdom of entrusting an extremely complex operation to the brave but inexperienced Dahlgren, unacquainted with the officers under him and they with him, and of making up his detachment of men from five different regiments not accustomed to working as a unit, may well be questioned.[95] In any event, Dahlgren was dogged by bad luck from the very beginning. On the second night out, 50 of his men lost the column in the dark but managed to rejoin in the morning. Then the Negro who was to guide the raiders to a ford across the James at Goochland either lost his way or intentionally misled them. Dahlgren, believing it to be the latter, had the man hanged by the roadside, but that did not produce a ford. Unable to cross and forced to stay north of the river, Dahlgren made his way inside the Richmond fortifications against steadily growing opposition, "losing heavily in killed and wounded," and was finally brought to a halt and forced to retreat. Trying to escape toward Gloucester Point, the column split up in the darkness. The larger group of about 260, ably led by Captain John F. B. Mitchell of the 2nd New York, made good its escape

93. *Official Records*, XXXIII, 201–202, 185; Kidd, *Personal Recollections*, 250. Colonel Kidd commented that Hampton's and Kilpatrick's statements on the former's night attack were "equally mythical."
94. *Official Records*, XXXIII, 185.
95. The 460 came from the 1st Maine, 1st Vermont, 5th Michigan, and the 2nd and 5th New York.

and joined Kilpatrick at Tunstall Station.[96] The smaller group of about 100, led by Dahlgren himself, made its way northward, harried by small squads of Confederate cavalrymen and home guards; on the night of the third it was ambushed near King and Queen Court House, Dahlgren was killed, and most of his men were rounded up and captured.[97]

Custer's diversionary raid was more successful than the main effort. Early on the afternoon of February 29, after crossing the Rivanna, he came to within three miles of Charlottesville where he found a "superior force of the enemy's cavalry, supported by four batteries . . . and a very heavy force of infantry."[98] By Confederate Major H. B. McClellan's account, these large forces of cavalry and infantry existed only in Custer's imagination, being in fact only the 1st Virginia and four batteries of field artillery, whose winter camp Custer had blundered upon. Whatever the actual strength of the enemy may have been, Custer at once ordered the 5th United States to charge them in flank. Led by Captain Joseph P. Ash, the charge captured the enemy's camp, six caissons, and two forges. The Confederates saved their guns, however. Deciding that enough had been done for glory, Custer recrossed the Rivanna, burned a number of mills and bridges, and after brushing aside at Madison a half-hearted effort, led by Stuart himself, to intercept him, "returned to camp without having suffered the loss of a man . . . [and with] over 50 prisoners and about 500 horses."[99]

96. *Official Records*, XXXIII, 194–97.
97. *Ibid.*, 205. The controversy concerning the papers found on Dahlgren's body, purportedly describing his intention to destroy and burn Richmond and kill Jefferson Davis and his cabinet, is outside the scope of the present work. Those interested in the subject may consult *ibid.*, 175, 176, 178, 217, 218, 223, and 224, and Jones, *Eight Hours Before Richmond*, passim.
98. *Official Records*, XXXIII, 161–63; McClellan, *I Rode With Jeb Stuart*, 399–402. On the second night of the march, "after spending two hours in marching one mile, General Custer determined to halt until daylight; rain mingled with snow fell during the entire night; we all had to lie upon the wet ground . . . unprotected from the pelting storm. The only wood accessible was green and wet, and it was impossible to have even a good fire; the rain froze on our clothes . . . so that by morning everything appeared to be cased in crystal." Gracey, *Annals of the 6th*, 226–27.
99. *Official Records*, XXXIII, 163.

Custer's column had an experience shared by every advance of northern cavalry into previously untapped southern territory; it attracted an ever-growing tail of "contrabands." Here is how the Reverend S. L. Gracey, chaplain of the 6th Pennsylvania saw them:

In the rear of our column, and only protected by the rear-guard, there followed hundreds of contrabands, of all shades, sexes, ages, &c. . . . It was impossible to keep them from joining the column, and our appearance in their neighborhood was the signal for their hasty preparation for flight from homes of bondage . . . to liberty. Old and young, male and female, in wagons and carts, on mules, horses, or oxen, trudging along on foot, any way and every way, hurrying on after the column, encouraging each other and enduring unimaginable hardships. As the advance of the enemy would press our rear-guard, the officers would urge them on, and their frantic efforts to keep up with the column were both pitiful and ludicrous in the extreme.[100]

With his command safe within General Butler's lines Kilpatrick's raid had come to an end, and not even he could claim that it had been a success. Its primary objective, the freeing of the thousands of prisoners held in Richmond, had not been accomplished. Against the destruction of a few bridges, depots, a few hundred yards of track and telegraph lines, and some supplies, had to be set the loss of 340 men, 583 horses, 594 rifles and carbines, 516 pistols, 505 sabers, and large quantities of miscellaneous gear.[101] Kilpatrick of course reported on March 3 that he had lost fewer than 150 men, and that his "entire command . . . [was] in good order, and need[ed] but a few days' rest."[102] But neither General Meade nor his staff were taken in by such whistling in the dark or mendacity; significantly, Meade had General Humphreys inquire of Pleasonton if "the instructions for General Kil-

100. Gracey, *Annals of the 6th*, 228.
101. *Official Records*, XXXIII, 187–88. The 5th New York sent forty on the raid and fourteen of them were taken prisoner; of the fourteen, one escaped, eight were exchanged, and five died in Andersonville. Boudrye, *Historic Records of the Fifth*, 115. The 1st Maine, which sent three hundred men—"the flower of the regiment . . . mounted on its best horses"—lost two killed, nine wounded, and thirty-eight missing, as well as two hundred horses. Samuel H. Merrill, *Campaigns of the First Maine and First District of Columbia Cavalry* (Portland, Me., 1866), 171, 186.
102. *Official Records*, XXXIII, 182.

patrick, as commander of the late expedition . . . sent to him through you, were duly received and acknowledged by him."[103] And, reflecting the opinions of Meade's staff, Colonel Lyman wrote on March 5, "Behold my prophecy in regard to Kill-cavalry's raid fulfilled. I have heard many persons very indignant with him. They said he went to the President with his plan; told Pleasonton he would not come back alive if he did not succeed; that he is a frothy braggart without brains and not overstocked with desire to fall on the field. . . . These charges are not new and I fancy Kill has rather dished himself."[104]

Colonel Lyman was mistaken in one respect. Kilpatrick had not quite dished himself. On March 14 he returned to the Army of the Potomac, still in command of the Third Division of the Cavalry Corps, and as ready as ever to gamble with the lives of his men. But it was not to be for long.

103. *Ibid.*, 176; Pleasonton's reply in the affirmative, *ibid.*, 177.
104. Agassiz, *Meade's Headquarters*, 79.

III

"The signs of war advance"

ON HIS VISITS TO GRANT'S HEADQUARTERS IN THE WEST, Assistant Secretary of War Charles A. Dana had become friendly with James Harrison Wilson, West Point 1860, a member of Grant's staff recently promoted to brigadier general. On January 17, 1864, Dana telegraphed Grant from Washington:

Will it be practicable for you to spare General Wilson for a time to come here and get the Cavalry Bureau into order and honesty? Of course the Department will make no order which will deprive you of the services of such an officer without your full consent, but the necessity for him is very great, and I know of no one else who can perform the duty as well as he. It is a question of saving millions of money and rendering the cavalry everywhere efficient. . . . He will be appointed chief of the bureau.[1]

Grant wired back the next day, "I will order General Wilson at once. No more efficient or better appointment could be made for the place."[2]

Wilson owed his new appointment to a combination of factors: his undoubted ability (of which no one was more conscious than he was himself), his knack of cultivating those in a position

1. *Official Records*, Vol. XXXII, Pt. 2, p. 115.
2. *Ibid.*, 131. The same day, General George Thomas wired Grant to ask if he could have Wilson to head the cavalry of the Army of the Cumberland. *Ibid.*, 131.

to further his career, the high opinion Dana had formed of his talents, and lastly, Secretary of War Edwin Stanton's dissatisfaction with the accomplishments of the Cavalry Bureau under its first two chiefs, Generals George Stoneman and Kenner Garrard. Wilson proceeded to Washington at once, and after an initial interview with the formidable secretary—an interview that might have shaken anyone with less than the young general's store of self-confidence—he went to work.

The first task Wilson undertook was to reorganize the system of inspecting horses offered for sale to the government; at each purchasing depot there was to be an inspection board made up of one regular and one volunteer cavalry officer, and a "citizen expert." Horses rejected by the board were to be branded, to prevent their being resubmitted for purchase. Next on Wilson's agenda came the horse contractors. The War Department regulations, habitually ignored or evaded, required successful bidders to deliver the number of horses they had undertaken to furnish and forbade subcontracting. After issuing a warning that these regulations would be enforced thereafter, Wilson had five defaulting contractors arrested and tried by court-martial; all five were found guilty and were sentenced to fines and imprisonment. "The incident," Wilson reported, "created a good deal of excitement among contractors and the politicians backing them" and thenceforth "the supply of cavalry horses became much more regular, and the quality greatly improved."[3]

One of the Cavalry Bureau's responsibilities was to supply weapons to the cavalry, but since the Ordnance Bureau supervised the manufacture and inspection of the arms, Wilson did not have the kinds of problems in this area that he had with the horse contractors. He rightly considered his major accomplishment as bureau head to be the adoption of the Spencer carbine as the standard cavalry firearm; this required surmounting the opposition of older and more conservative officers, who were convinced that the use of a repeater would lead to a great waste of ammunition. The supply of Spencer carbines never caught up with the demand, however, and some units were still having to make do

3. Wilson, *Under the Old Flag*, I, 330.

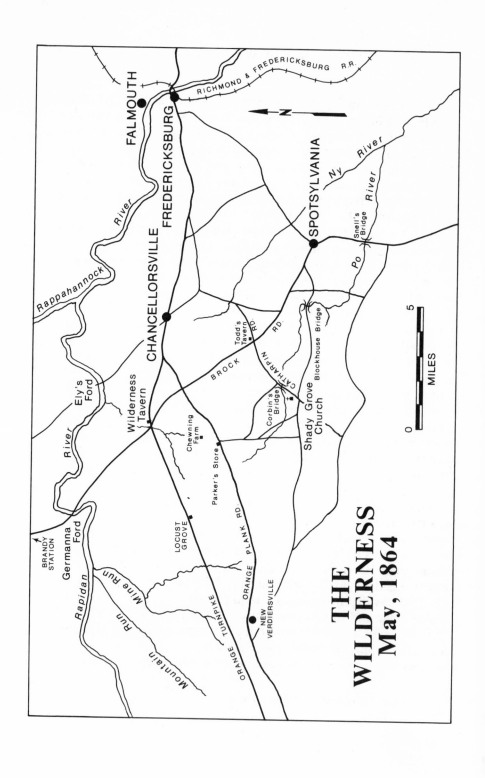

THE
WILDERNESS
May, 1864

FALMOUTH

FREDERICKSBURG

RICHMOND & FREDERICKSBURG R.R.

SPOTSYLVANIA

Ny River

River

Snell's Bridge

Po

CHANCELLORSVILLE

Rappahannock River

Ely's Ford

River

Wilderness Tavern

BROCK RD.

Todd's Tavern

CATHARPIN RD.

Blockhouse Bridge

Shady Grove Church

Corbin's Bridge

Chewning Farm

Parker's Store

LOCUST GROVE

ORANGE PLANK RD.

NEW VERDIERSVILLE

ORANGE TURNPIKE

Mountain Run

Mine Run

Rapidan

Germanna Ford

BRANDY STATION

N

MILES

0   5

with inferior weapons when the war ended.[4] Wilson's opinion of
the desirability of the change to the new carbine is amply supported by the testimony of other cavalrymen. In March, 1864,
after three years of war, Major Charles A. Wells of the 1st New
York (Lincoln) reported after a skirmish that "only a few of our
carbines (Staun's) can be relied upon . . . and [I] would respectfully recommend that a change of arm be made to one that can be
relied upon and give the men their old confidence."[5] The report
of an inspection of the 19th New York concluded with the recommendation that "Their unreliable Joslyn carbines should be turned
in, and the regiment supplied with others."[6]

Wilson's activities as chief of the bureau "touched every question that could arise in regard to the organization, equipment,
mounts, remounts, armament, instruction, efficiency, and stan-
dardization" of the cavalry, and the "care and recuperation" of
unserviceable horses. These activities kept him busy seven days a
week, but they somehow left time for a considerable amount of
politicking to promote Grant's elevation to lieutenant general,
and to have General William Farrar ("Baldy") Smith replace
Meade as commander of the Army of the Potomac.[7] The long term
impact of Wilson's work in improving the effectiveness of Federal
mounted troops, aside from the adoption of the Spencer carbine
and an improvement in the quality of the horses purchased, is
impossible to determine with any assurance; it was probably
minimal.

When Wilson took on the Cavalry Bureau assignment, it was
with the promise that after he had gotten "the machine in good
working order," which Dana estimated he could do in about sixty
days, he would be allowed to return to his post on Grant's staff.[8]

4. In early 1865, when Wilson was preparing for the Selma Campaign,
he applied "for a supply of Spencer carbines . . . to arm such regiments as
had a poor arm for an active fighting campaign; but these carbines did not
arrive in time," and Wilson had to take Spencers from regiments that were
to remain behind to arm John T. Croxton's brigade. Lyman B. Pierce, *History of the Second Iowa Cavalry* (Burlington, Iowa, 1865), 162–63.

5. *Official Records*, XXXIII, 233.
6. Bowen, *Regimental History of the First New York*, 136.
7. Wilson, *Under the Old Flag*, I, 332–35; Bruce Catton, *Grant Takes
Command* (Boston, 1968), 130.
8. *Official Records*, Vol. XXXII, Pt. 2, p. 115.

On March 10, however, well before the sixty days were up, Grant was promoted to lieutenant general and was called East to replace Halleck in command of the Union armies. Two weeks after his own arrival in Washington, Grant sent orders to Tennessee for Major General Philip Henry Sheridan to report immediately to the War Department.[9]

When Sheridan received Grant's summons, he had command of a division of infantry in the Army of the Cumberland. Born in 1831, the son of Irish immigrant parents, Sheridan grew up in Somerset, in southeastern Ohio, and entered West Point as a member of the Class of 1852. Suspended for a year after a fist-fight with his company sergeant, he graduated with the Class of 1853. He served in the infantry in the prewar years, was ordered East when the Civil War broke out, and held a series of humdrum staff appointments under Generals Samuel Curtis and Halleck until May, 1862, when fortune came his way; on the suggestion of General Gordon Granger, Governor Austin Blair appointed Sheridan colonel of the 2nd Michigan. Five weeks later, on July 1, in command of a cavalry brigade consisting of his own regiment and the 2nd Iowa, Sheridan fought and won the battle of Booneville against heavy odds. This fight made his reputation. The next day, General W. S. Rosecrans closed the report he sent General Halleck on the battle with the remark, "Sheridan ought to be made a brigadier. He would not be a stampeding general."[10] A short time later, Rosecrans joined Generals J. C. Sullivan, Gordon Granger, W. L. Elliott, and Alexander Asboth in the famous dispatch to Halleck, "Brigadiers scarce. Good ones scarcer. . . . [We] beg that you will obtain the promotion of Sheridan. He is worth his weight in gold."[11] Sheridan got his stars, his promotion being predated to July 1 to honor his victory at Booneville. His promotion, however, also removed him from the cavalry, and for the next eighteen months he commanded divisions of infantry, first in the Army of the Ohio and then in the Army of the Cumberland. His conduct in the battles of Perryville and Stone's River,

9. Richard O'Connor, *Sheridan the Inevitable* (Indianapolis, 1953), 144.

10. *Official Records*, Vol. XVII, Pt. 2, pp. 65–66.

11. *Ibid.*, 139.

and especially in the storming of Missionary Ridge, won him fame and promotion to major general.

Sheridan did not know he was being summoned to Washington to be given command of the Cavalry Corps of the Army of the Potomac. He was to write in his *Memoirs* that Alfred Pleasonton, his predecessor in that post, was one of the general officers "sent elsewhere" ("elsewhere" in Pleasonton's case being exile to the Department of the Missouri) because of the "many jealousies and much ill feeling, the outgrowth of former campaigns, [that] existed among officers of high grade in the Army of the Potomac."[12] General Henry E. Davies, Jr., wrote: "Even [Pleasonton's] success and the proofs he had given of the value of cavalry, when properly used and led, were not sufficient to overcome the force of traditions and customs, and among higher authorities the idea still prevailed that the mounted force was secondary to, and should be used for the protection, convenience and relief of the infantry. . . . Serious differences of opinion on these questions between Generals Meade and Pleasonton had from time to time occurred, and at last had gone so far that the latter . . . could no longer retain his command."[13] Grant's explanation of the way in which the change came about was quite different: "In one of my early interviews with the President I expressed my dissatisfaction with the little that had been accomplished by the cavalry so far in the war, and the belief that it was capable of accomplishing much more than it had done if under a thorough leader. I said I wanted the very best man in the army for that command. Halleck was present and spoke up, saying: 'How would Sheridan do?' I replied: 'The very man I want.' "[14]

These explanations clearly leave unsaid the real reasons for Pleasonton's removal. Not by any means a brilliant cavalryman, Pleasonton could nevertheless claim credit for the highly competent performance of his corps in the Gettysburg Campaign, and to that extent at least Grant's "dissatisfaction" was manifestly

12. Philip H. Sheridan, *Personal Memoirs of P. H. Sheridan* (2 vols.; New York, 1888), I, 339.

13. Henry E. Davies, *General Sheridan* (New York, 1895), 92–93.

14. Ulysses S. Grant, *Personal Memoirs of U. S. Grant* (2 vols.; New York, 1885), II, 133.

unfair. It is probably closer to the truth to assume that Pleasonton was removed because of the personal antagonisms he had aroused, both in the army and in the War Department. On no other basis can one account for Grant's request to Secretary Stanton the day after he had sent the wire summoning Sheridan to Washington, "that the order relieving General Pleasonton be made at once. I will then direct General Meade to place the senior officer of the cavalry corps in command of it until General Sheridan arrives."[15] The apparently pointless cruelty of this message is greatly at variance with the manner in which such situations were customarily handled.

Sheridan, five feet five inches tall, emaciated, and looking even younger than his thirty-three years, arrived in Washington on the morning of April 4 and immediately set out on his round of duty calls. His first visit was to General Halleck. Then he called on Secretary Stanton, who eyed "closely and searchingly" what must have struck him at first glance as a singularly unimpressive choice for the command of the Cavalry Corps. His third visit was to the president, who gave him a most cordial welcome, "offering both his hands." By the evening of the following day, Sheridan was at Cavalry Corps headquarters at Culpeper and at once issued formal orders assuming command.[16]

News that Pleasonton was gone and that they had a new commander named Sheridan spread with lightning speed among the regiments of the Cavalry Corps. Hardly any of the men had ever heard of him, and " 'Who's Sheridan?' was a very common inquiry."[17] Among the more knowledgeable upper ranks the arrival

15. *Official Records*, XXXIII, 721, 732, 733. Was there, perhaps, a connection between Pleasonton's abrupt removal and the rumors of a few weeks before that he was slated to succeed Meade in command of the Army of the Potomac?

16. Colonel Horace Porter of Grant's staff wrote that Sheridan "had been worn down almost to a shadow by hard work and exposure . . . he looked anything but formidable as a candidate for a cavalry leader." Horace Porter, *Campaigning with Grant* (New York, 1897), 23; Sheridan, *Personal Memoirs*, I, 347; *Official Records*, XXXIII, 806. The president evidently shared Grant's poor opinion of the cavalry of the Army of the Potomac. He said to Sheridan that "thus far the cavalry of the Army of the Potomac had not done all it might have done," and to Sheridan's distress, ended the interview "by quoting the stale interrogation . . . 'Who ever saw a dead cavalryman?' " Sheridan, *Personal Memoirs*, I, 347.

17. Bowen, *Regimental History of the First New York*, 135; see also

of the new commander was greeted with a combination of skepticism and hostility. General Davies recalled that the orders announcing Sheridan's assumption of command "were not received with much cordiality, or that the troops affected by them were pleased."

The corps had developed and improved by a system of evolution and survival of the fittest, and all the leaders it ever had under whom it had gained success . . . had been selected from its own ranks. . . . very little was known of . . . [Sheridan's] service. . . . It was not known that he had ever served with or in command of cavalry, and the prejudice . . . among mounted troops against being placed under the orders of an officer whose experience had been obtained in other arms of the service, affected to some extent his reception by his new command. Again, some experiences from which the Army of the Potomac had previously suffered had not induced the belief that the West was the point of the compass from which the advent of wise men bringing rich gifts of victory and success was to be confidently expected.[18]

The hostility to the new commander was not of long duration; Sheridan disarmed much of it by retaining most of Pleasonton's staff officers, and he won the good opinion of the men, especially of those who remembered John Pope, an earlier import from the West, by taking over without fuss or fanfare and without issuing grandiloquent, or in fact any, general orders. He reviewed each of the three divisions of the corps in a matter-of-fact way, and the men in the ranks approved of his "simple, unostentatious demeanor."[19]

The next change in the corps occurred on April 7. Wilson was relieved of duty as chief of the Cavalry Bureau, ordered to report to Grant "for assignment to duty," and was by him given command of the Third Division of the Cavalry Corps, replacing Kilpatrick. Despite the statement in Sheridan's *Memoirs* that Wilson

<hr />

Tobie, *First Maine Cavalry*, 248. Colonel Charles S. Wainwright, reflecting the general opinion in the upper ranks of the army, noted, "I know nothing . . . of . . . [Sheridan], but a change I think was needed; neither Pleasonton nor Stoneman proved themselves equal to the position." Nevins (ed.), *A Diary of Battle*, 341.

18. Davies, *General Sheridan*, 93–95.

19. Crowninshield, *A History of the First Regiment*, 202; Asa B. Isham, *An Historical Sketch of the Seventh Regiment Michigan Volunteer Cavalry* (New York, 1893), 211.

was assigned to him at his own request, a contemporary dispatch of his suggests that he did not learn of Wilson's appointment until it had already been decided upon by Grant.[20]

To be superseded as commander of the Third Division must have come as a bitter blow to Kilpatrick's pride, but after the failure of his Richmond raid, it should not have been unexpected. According to Wilson, he was "naturally chagrined," and the fact that Wilson was junior to him in rank made the humiliation even worse. Sheridan's statement that Kilpatrick was "anxious to be transferred to the West" and Wilson's that the transfer was made at Kilpatrick's own request must be taken with large grains of salt. The Army of the Potomac and its doings were prominently in the public eye and received the lion's share of the attention of those in power in Washington; given Kilpatrick's "simply boundless" ambition, separation from a position of high visibility must have been difficult for him to accept.[21]

Wilson's new appointment created other problems of military protocol. Three of the brigade commanders in the Cavalry Corps, namely, Wesley Merritt (his West Point classmate), Custer, and Davies, were all senior to him, their promotions to brigadier general antedating his by a few months. A basic rule of the army's command system was that an officer of lesser rank, or even a day's less seniority in the same rank, could not command an officer of higher rank or greater seniority. It was therefore necessary to transfer Henry Davies from the Third Division to the Second, and Custer and his entire brigade from the Third to the First. Colonel George H. Chapman and his brigade were moved bodily into the Third Division as the replacement for Custer and the Michigan Brigade, and Colonel Timothy M. Bryan, succeeded later by Colonel John McIntosh, replaced Davies in command of Wilson's First Brigade.

20. *Official Records*, XXXIII, 816, 753, 809, 815. On Wilson's departure, Colonel August Kautz, his second-in-command, took over as chief of the bureau. Within a week, however, following an urgent request from General Butler for a cavalry commander for his Army of the James, Kautz was promoted to brigadier general, relieved of duty in the Cavalry Bureau, and ordered to report to Butler. This was done despite General Halleck's objection that "There is no competent person to take . . . [Kautz's] place, and the difficulty of getting horses is daily increasing." *Ibid.*, 862, 865, 877, 879; see also Sheridan, *Personal Memoirs*, I, 352, and *Official Records*, XXXIII, 862.
21. Wilson, *Under the Old Flag*, I, 368, 361, 370.

In addition to these changes, on April 10, General A. T. A. Torbert, whose qualifications "as a commander of cavalry were not remarkable," was assigned to the command of the First Division, in succession to the greatly regretted John Buford, who had died in Washington on December 13, 1863.[22] Colonel Charles S. Wainwright had written in his diary on December 20, "The army and the country have met with a great loss by the death of . . . Buford. He was decidedly the best cavalry general we had, and was acknowledged as such in the army. . . . [He was] rough in his exterior, never looking after his own comfort, untiring on the march and in the supervision of all the militia of his command, quiet and unassuming in his manners."[23] Torbert's entire army career had been spent with the infantry; he was transferred—at whose behest the records fail to disclose—from the command of a brigade of New Jersey infantry regiments in the VI Corps to his new cavalry command. Wesley Merritt, who had commanded the division in Buford's absence, reverted to command of the Reserve Brigade.

It is important to note that Sheridan, whose wartime experience had been almost entirely that of a commander of infantry, entered upon his cavalry command with only one of his three divisions, the Second, commanded by an experienced cavalryman, David McM. Gregg. The First was commanded by an officer who lacked any cavalry experience whatever and was also new to the corps and his men. Commanding the Third was another newcomer, an engineer officer who had never commanded troops of any kind and whose appointment "gave particular offense . . . and led to hard feelings and complications which were not without influence in the cavalry operations and which did not entirely disappear till . . . [he] was relieved from duty with the Army of the Potomac."[24] Furthermore, the shuffling of brigade command-

22. Kidd, *Personal Recollections*, 261; *Official Records*, XXXIII, 830. Torbert, West Point Class of 1855, served in the infantry on the frontier. Appointed colonel of the 1st New Jersey Infantry on the outbreak of the Civil War, he was promoted to brigadier general in November, 1862. He saw action on the Peninsula, at Second Bull Run, South Mountain, Antietam, Rappahannock Station, and Mine Run. He had a respectable but by no means outstanding record in the Civil War as an infantryman.

23. Nevins (ed.), *A Diary of Battle*, 309.

24. Wilson, *Under the Old Flag*, I, 362. Wilson tells the story of a shocking expression of this hostility in *ibid.*, 365–67; another, and even

ers and of entire brigades from one division to another was bound
to have an unsettling effect on the cohesiveness, responsiveness,
and general efficiency of an arm of the service that had only recently begun to emerge from the shadows. These adverse factors
affected the performance of the corps for weeks to come; indeed,
it is greatly to the credit of the regimental officers and the enlisted
men under them that the corps performed as well as it did from
May 4 on.

So far as can be determined from his reports and writings,
Sheridan was not disturbed by these command changes, or by the
condition in which he found his new command. He wrote that the
"corps presented a fine appearance . . . and so far as the health
and equipment of the men were concerned the showing was good
and satisfactory, but the horses were thin and very much worn
down."[25] Sheridan's impression, or his memory of it after the lapse
of nearly a generation, may be contrasted with the report of Captain F. C. Newhall, who inspected the First and Third Divisions in
the same week in which they were reviewed by Sheridan. In the
First Brigade of the Third Division Newhall found "large deficiencies of carbines and pistols in all the regiments but one," the exception being the 1st Connecticut which had a full complement of
Smith carbines "reported by the officers as entirely unreliable"; in
Newhall's opinion these carbines were simply "worthless." The 1st
Connecticut had another and most unusual problem: how to deal
with eighty-five "recruits," all deserters from the Confederate
cavalry who, after enlisting in the Union army, had been assigned
to that regiment. The commanding officer, Major Erastus Blakes-
lee, did not trust them and was sure they would run away in any
action to avoid being captured by the enemy. In the Second Brigade, which "had become considerably disorganized . . . from the
effects of . . . Kilpatrick's raid and a too frequent change of commanders," there were "very large deficiencies of arms and horses,"
in addition to which the regimental camps were "very badly located" and in a "bad state of police."

---

worse, story, with Wilson's West Point classmate, Wesley Merritt, as the
villain, is to be found in Clarence E. Macartney, *Grant and His Generals*
(New York, 1953), 143.

25. Sheridan, *Personal Memoirs*, I, 353.

The First Brigade of the First Division, Newhall reported, was "very small," and its horses were "thin and . . . entirely unfit for any hard duty without rest and recuperation." In the Second Brigade there were "large deficiencies of horses and arms," but in Newhall's opinion, what horses this brigade did have were the best in either division. The horses of Merritt's Reserve Brigade were "used up and . . . in a deplorable condition for active duty," and the 19th New York of this brigade was armed with "unreliable and worthless" Joslyn carbines.

Newhall's general conclusion was that the two divisions and the Reserve Brigade were

not in condition to perform active duty with credit, on account of the condition of their horses and the deficiencies and in some cases inferior quality of fire-arms. . . . the regiments are so scattered and worn down that a proper supervision of officers is almost impossible, and the animals cannot be kept in condition. . . . Paper reports give no idea of the state of these commands. I am convinced that both divisions cannot put into line of battle 5,000 efficient cavalry at the present time.[26]

When Wilson took over command of the Third Division within a few days of Newhall's inspection, the conditions he found bore out fully the captain's findings. The division, Wilson wrote, was "badly run down. Its camps were badly placed and badly policed; its horses were overworked and exhausted; its equipment and clothing nearly used up, and its heterogeneous collection of carbines dirty and out of order. . . . the division itself was scattered"; of the 3,436 men present for duty, only 2,692 were mounted, 344 had disabled horses, and 744 were entirely dismounted.[27]

26. *Official Records*, XXXIII, 891–92. It is instructive to compare Captain Newhall's comments on the Third Division with a report Kilpatrick had turned in less than three weeks before, in which he claimed to have 4,293 fully armed and equipped men in the division and stated that he had 3,611 serviceable horses and 1,122 dismounted men, 680 of whom were fully armed and equipped and lacked only horses. Evidently Kilpatrick was not above turning in fudged figures (or allowing his subordinates to do so) to make the state of his division look substantially better than it actually was. *Ibid.*, 772.

27. Wilson, *Under the Old Flag*, I, 373; see also Wilson, "Cavalry of the Army of the Potomac," 37, and *Official Records*, XXXIII, 893. Wilson adds, "At the first morning inspection, I found but few officers attending stable call, while all routine duties were so poorly performed that I felt obliged to put one colonel in arrest and to admonish the rest that radical

Sheridan recognized that the horses were his principal problem. The cure, as he saw it, for the run-down condition and continuing wastage of the animals, was to persuade the army commander to relieve his corps of much of the picket duty it was being used for. In a stormy interview with General Meade, with whom any interview was likely to be stormy, he demanded that he be allowed to concentrate his regiments, so that he could use the entire corps to fight the enemy's cavalry. As he tells the story, Meade was "staggered" by the idea of the cavalry becoming an independent fighting arm of the service. The cavalry, he thought, was "fit for little more than guard and picket duty," and he wanted to know who would protect the trains, artillery reserve, and the front and flanks of the infantry if Sheridan's proposal were adopted. Sheridan replied that if permitted to use the cavalry as he wanted, he would "make it so lively for the enemy's cavalry" that they would cease to be a threat to the flanks and rear of the Army of the Potomac.[28]

Sheridan might have anticipated Meade's hostile reaction to what was in effect a declaration of independence on behalf of the cavalry. Meade held the traditionalist view that the cavalry, like the artillery, was an auxiliary of the Queen of Battles and had no independent role of its own. Sheridan, on the other hand, whom the peppery Meade probably looked upon as a brash young whippersnapper, was proposing for the cavalry the status of a self-contained army, allied to, but essentially independent of, the infantry. Moreover, these grandiose and heretical ideas were being presented by an officer whose experience with the cavalry consisted of a few short weeks in command first of a single regiment, and then of a two-regiment brigade of mounted troops. Hence, in addition to giving Sheridan's revolutionary proposal a chilly reception, Meade also made it evident that he expected the commander of his cavalry to be stationed at his own headquarters,

---

improvements must be made at once if they would save themselves from a similar fate." He also made requisition for five thousand Spencer carbines, but it was three months before he got them. Wilson, *Under the Old Flag*, I, 373–74.
    28. Sheridan, *Personal Memoirs*, I, 354–56; see also *Official Records*, Vol. XXXVI, Pt. 3, p. 787.

"practically as one of his staff, through whom he would give his detailed directions as, in his judgment, occasion required."[29] This was basically the way in which Pleasonton had been forced or was content to operate, but it was emphatically not Sheridan's idea of what his role should be.

Obviously, there was no middle ground on so fundamental an issue on which two equally strong-minded individuals held diametrically opposed views. The situation remained in *statu quo*, to be resolved later. But Sheridan's strong representations and Captain Newhall's devastating inspection report did bring about a change for the better. Sheridan referred to Newhall's findings in a formal request on April 19 that "the very long picket line of the First and Third Divisions . . . be at once diminished, so as to give rest to the horses and enable them to recuperate. . . . It is better to occasionally lose a cavalryman . . . than to render so many horses so unserviceable."[30] In a second dispatch the same day, Sheridan reported that his own inspection of the Second Division had disclosed the same state of affairs that Newhall had found in the First and Third: the horses of the division were in no condition to bear hard usage "and can be of but little service in the approaching campaign, unless they are promptly rested and fed."[31]

As a result of these representations, Meade authorized a substantial reduction of the picketing program.[32] The effects were highly beneficial. Even the brief two weeks of comparative rest, and the regular care and feeding the horses received before the start of the Wilderness Campaign, were sufficient to improve their condition significantly. The troopers too benefited from a few days of comparative rest and a refit, and mounts were received for many of the dismounted men.[33] Typically, in the 1st New Jersey, "the work of preparation for active service was carried on

29. Sheridan, *Personal Memoirs*, I, 356.
30. *Official Records*, XXXIII, 909.
31. *Ibid.*, 909.
32. *Ibid.*, 923.
33. For example, the "poor, tired, emaciated horses" of the 19th New York "were given eight or ten days of comparative rest; and even in so short a time, their improved condition was apparent." The regiment also exchanged their "unreliable and worthless" Joslyn carbines for Spencers. Bowen, *Regimental History of the First New York*, 136.

with energy. Constant drill revived the knowledge which had been fading from the memories of officers and men through the hard service of the campaign and the repose of winter quarters; frequent and rigid inspections disclosed . . . deficiencies . . . in the clothing, armament and equipment of the men which were at once carefully supplied."[34]

The one major difficulty Sheridan was unable to correct was his manpower situation. The thirty-one regiments in the corps nominally represented a large force of about 35,000 officers and men, but his actual strength was far less. Few of his regiments numbered more than 350, and many were smaller.[35] Thus, on April 30, four days before the start of the campaign, Sheridan had 12,424 cavalrymen present for duty equipped, plus 863 gunners manning eight batteries.[36] In the ensuing six weeks, from May 4 to June 14, the corps was to lose 482 killed, 2,269 wounded, and 1,219 captured or missing. Anyone with the desire to see a dead cavalryman could have satisfied his wish on any one of those forty-two days, in the Wilderness, at Spotsylvania Court House, Yellow Tavern, Hanover Court House, Ashland, Haw's Shop, Cold Harbor, and as far afield as Trevilian Station and Roanoke Station, and in the fields, forests, and roads between.

The Confederate cavalry Sheridan was eager to fight had had a difficult winter, and their complaints, loud and frequent, duplicated to an uncanny degree those of their blue-coated antagonists.

At the conclusion of the Gettysburg Campaign, in August, 1863, the cavalry of the Army of Northern Virginia became a corps in the technical sense by being divided into two divisions, one commanded by Wade Hampton and the other by Fitzhugh Lee, both promoted to major general. Hampton's division was given the brigades of James B. Gordon, Pierce M. B. Young, and

34. Pyne, *First New Jersey Cavalry*, 221–22; see also Lloyd, *History of the First Reg't.*, 86.

35. Crowninshield, "Cavalry in Virginia," 31. Wilson's division gained by the return of the 1st Vermont, which he justly called "one of the best cavalry regiments in the army," and it also had assigned to it the 22nd New York, because, Wilson wrote, it was "so green that no one else wanted it." Wilson, *Under the Old Flag*, I, 375; *Official Records*, XXXIII, 985.

36. *Official Records*, XXXIII, 1036.

Thomas Rosser; Lee's, the brigades of J. R. Chambliss, Lunsford L. Lomax, and Williams C. Wickham.[37] In the normal course of events, as commander of a corps Stuart could have expected promotion to lieutenant general, to place him on a level with James Longstreet, Ewell, and A. P. Hill, but for reasons that can only be conjectured, General Lee did not recommend Stuart for promotion, and he remained a major general.[38]

Like their counterparts in the Union army, Stuart and his chief subordinates had as their main concern the miserable condition of their horses. As early as the end of August, General Lee had written President Davis that "some days we get a pound of corn per horse and some days more; some none. Our limit is five [pounds] per day per horse."[39] Even the five pounds was only half the daily grain ration of the Federal cavalry mounts. In the late summer there was still grazing for the animals, but as winter closed in and put an end to the grazing, there was no appreciable improvement in the grain supply and there was little if any hay delivered to the army. Stuart wrote in February that in the preceding thirty days the horses of one of his brigades had received an average of eight pounds of corn and only one or two pounds of hay per horse per day.[40]

In January, Hampton complained officially to Stuart about the excessive amount of picket duty his division was required to perform. "The pickets from Gordon's brigade," he wrote, "have now to travel 40 miles to their posts. Forage has to be carried to their posts, as none can be obtained near them, and the mere travel is

37. Freeman, *Lee's Lieutenants*, III, 209–16. Gordon commanded what was actually Lawrence S. Baker's brigade; Young, M. C. Butler's; Chambliss, W. H. F. Lee's. Baker, Butler, and Lee were absent, recovering from wounds. Rosser had the brigade formerly commanded by "Grumble" Jones, who had been court-martialed and removed to western Virginia after a personal quarrel with Stuart.

38. D. S. Freeman considers as "the most probable explanation" of General Lee's failure to recommend Stuart for promotion his belief that command of the cavalry did not equal in importance, and hence should not equal in rank, command of a 20–30,000-man corps of infantry. *Ibid.*, 212. It is not unreasonable to suspect, however, that Stuart's ride around Hooker in June, 1863, was not without influence on General Lee's decision.

39. Charles W. Ramsdell, "General Robert E. Lee's Horse Supply, 1862–1865," *American Historical Review*, XXXV (1930), 764; see also Freeman, *R. E. Lee*, III, 251–52.

40. *Official Records*, XXXIII, 1164.

sufficient to prevent any improvement in the horses, if not to break them down."[41] Two weeks later Hampton called Stuart's attention to the "alarming decrease" in the strength of Young's brigade; within the previous twelve months, he wrote, "upward of 2,000 horses have been brought on to this brigade, besides those which were captured, and now not more than 500 men can be mounted on serviceable horses."[42] Young himself begged for permission to winter his brigade in South Carolina, writing that two thirds of his men were dismounted, and since it was impossible to procure mounts in Virginia the only way he could rebuild his brigade to a respectable strength was to take it where horses were still to be had. His plea was turned down both by Stuart and by General Lee, on the ground that the army was so short of cavalry that Young's brigade could not be spared. Stuart later relented, however, to the extent that in March he relieved the brigade of picket duty and sent it to Mathews and Middlesex counties to "recruit for thirty days."[43]

The Confederate system of requiring cavalrymen to furnish their own horses, combined with a galloping inflation that was already far out of control by the winter of 1863–1864, made it extremely difficult for a trooper who lost his horse in combat or by starvation to replace it, except by capture from the enemy. Henry Kyd Douglas tells the story of the Confederate cavalryman who, offered $5,000 "for a somewhat seedy looking steed, proudly reined up his bony Bucephalus, and exclaimed, 'Five thousand dollars for this horse! Why, I gave a thousand dollars this morning for currying him!'" No doubt the story is apocryphal, but as far as the going price of cavalry horses is concerned it does not exaggerate, for Douglas himself was offered $5,800 for a horse "worth, perhaps, $250."[44] One cavalryman, probably reflecting the

41. *Ibid.*, 1088. Hampton complained that "[Fitzhugh Lee's] Regts are very full & the duty will be light on them. I suppose, however, that some of Lee's Brigades will be kept at Richmond, as Stuart always manages to give them the lightest duty." Manly Wade Wellman, *Giant in Gray: A Biography of Wade Hampton of South Carolina* (New York, 1949), 137.
42. *Official Records*, XXXIII, 1140.
43. *Ibid.*, 1153, 1164.
44. Henry Kyd Douglas, *I Rode with Stonewall* (Chapel Hill, 1940), 272.

opinion of his fellows, wrote that "there were thousands of good horses in Virginia, in the hands of speculators, skulkers, and citizens generally, which should have been purchased or confiscated, and turned over to the cavalry; but this most important branch of the service was absolutely neglected, and went to pieces for want of horses, at the very time Sheridan was organizing a corps of the finest mounted infantry in the world."[45] The horses of the Confederate cavalry, gnawing the bark off trees to stay alive, were not alone in suffering from hunger in the winter of 1863–1864. Food for the men was desperately short also. In January, the 9th Virginia was furloughed in a body, so that the men could be fed by their families, and so that they could collect bacon, grain, cattle, and sheep to bring back to the army.[46] Clothing was as scarce as food; Colonel Elijah ("Lige") V. White of the Comanches tried every means he could think of to obtain uniforms for his battalion and at last managed to get a fourth of the amount needed, whereupon, in the cold December of 1863, "the spirit of discontent culminated in the Loudoun companies, and on the night of the 14th, about sixty of [Co's] A and C took regular French leave and went home."[47]

As the early Virginia spring came on and the fields turned green, the condition of the horses began to improve.[48] Nevertheless, as the Wilderness Campaign was about to open, Stuart's two divisions counted only something over 8,000 mounted men, against Sheridan's upwards of 12,000.

One great asset the cavalry of the Army of Northern Virginia possessed in the spring of 1864 was the skill of their commander, coupled with a remarkable symbiosis between him and themselves. Not all of Stuart's troopers approved of his personality; many disapproved of his taste for " 'spread-eagle' grand reviews,

45. John N. Opie, A Rebel Cavalryman with Lee, Stuart and Jackson (Dayton, 1972), 158–59.
46. R. L. T. Beale, History of the Ninth Virginia Cavalry in the War Between the States (Richmond, 1899), 108.
47. Frank M. Myers, The Comanches: A History of White's Battalion, Virginia Cavalry (Baltimore, 1871), 239.
48. The horses of Fitzhugh Lee's division, which was encamped "in a rich grazing district about five miles from Fredericksburg," had the benefit of several weeks of "wading in grass up to their knees." Luther W. Hopkins, From Bull Run to Appomattox: A Boy's View (Baltimore, 1908), 143.

which did no good except to give Yankee spies an opportunity to count the exact number of the cavalry . . . and to display the foppishness of Stuart," or they were repelled by his lack of dignity, his flamboyance, his "boastful vanity," and his taste for the company of "buffoons, a part he, himself, greatly affected."[49] Others were merely amused by his "clatter and gaiety." But all of them, whatever they thought of his personality or his behavior, had an implicit trust in his leadership in a fight. In their eyes, he was a "born cavalryman, dashing, fearless, clearheaded, enterprising, brilliant"; a shrewd, gallant commander with "capacity, skill, swiftness, *elan*" that no other cavalry commander possessed.[50] But now he and they were about to measure their talents and mettle against a new antagonist.

On April 22, Sheridan received preliminary orders to get ready for the forward movement of the army at an early date; he in turn ordered his division commanders to draw subsistence rations and 150 rounds of ammunition per man, to collect all surplus baggage for shipment to the rear, and to organize their dismounted men into foot battalions.[51] Ten days later Wilson was sent to scout all the major fords across the Rapidan; he reported everything quiet, with no sign of any unusual enemy activity along the river.[52] The same day the orders for the crossing of the Rapidan into the Wilderness were issued, with the role of each cavalry division carefully spelled out. Wilson was to have the responsibility of leading the way. At midnight, May 3/4, he was to cross the river at Germanna Ford, protect the crossing until the arrival of G. K. Warren's V Corps, then move forward into the Wilderness to Parker's Store on the Orange Plank Road and send out strong patrols on all the roads to the west and southwest, whence the Confederate army, coming from the direction of Mine Run and Orange Court House, was expected to approach. Gregg and the

49. Myers, *The Comanches*, 234; G. E. Govan and J. W. Livingood (eds.), *The Haskell Memoirs* (New York, 1960); see also Stephen Z. Starr, *Colonel Grenfell's Wars: The Life of a Soldier of Fortune* (Baton Rouge, 1971), 110–11.
50. Douglas, *I Rode with Stonewall*, 280, 194.
51. *Official Records*, XXXIII, 941.
52. *Ibid.*, Vol. XXXVI, Pt. 2, pp. 344–45.

Second Division were to cross at Ely's Ford, six miles downstream from Germanna, await the arrival of Hancock's II Corps, and then send out reconnaissances to the east and southeast in the direction of Fredericksburg and Spotsylvania. Torbert's First Division had the easiest assignment; until May 5 it was to remain north of the Rapidan, patrol the fords, and guard the enormous trains of the army.[53]

Since the use of cavalry to protect the trains was a major component of the chapter of frustrations that led to the famous Sheridan explosion of May 8, the size of these trains is worthy of mention. Quartermaster General Rufus Ingalls reported on May 3 that the army had 3,476 wagons and 591 ambulances; 4,076 horses and 20,184 mules were needed to draw these 4,067 vehicles. In addition to these animals, the army had 16,311 cavalry, 5,158 artillery, and 4,107 "private," that is, officers' horses.[54] To provide the regulation ration of grain and hay for these nearly 50,000 animals would have required the *daily* delivery of 477 tons of feed to the army. To do this many miles from railhead over execrable roads without impairing the flow of ammunition and food for the men was a manifest impossibility.

General Meade, preoccupied—perhaps to an excess—with the safety of his trains, had General Humphreys tell Sheridan on May 5 that he "had better draw in . . . [his] cavalry so as to secure the protection of the trains," and again the next day, "The cavalry . . . out on the plank road are now being driven in. . . . You must take immediate dispositions for the protection of the trains in this direction."[55] Sheridan, on the other hand, chafing under the restrictions on his freedom of movement that such orders implied, protested that he could not "do anything with the cavalry except to act on the defensive. . . . Why cannot infantry be sent to guard the trains and let me take the offensive?"[56] Meade's response merely rubbed salt into the wound; Sheridan was told that he was

53. *Ibid.*, 331; see also 334.
54. *Ibid.*, 355. It will be noted that Ingalls reported 16,311 cavalry horses with the army, whereas Sheridan reported that as of April 30, he had only 12,424 fully equipped and mounted officers and men. See preceding note 36. There is no explanation of this large discrepancy between the two figures.
55. *Ibid.*, 467, 515.
56. *Ibid.*, 428.

"authorized by existing instructions to make such offensive operations . . . as [are] consistent with the security of the trains. . . .
you are again authorized to detach any portion of your command
for offensive operations, cutting the enemy's communications,
&c."[57]

Meade and Sheridan were clearly at cross-purposes. It was
his entire command, not just portions of it, that Sheridan wanted
to use in "offensive operations." The mission to protect the trains
that Meade insisted upon not only made impossible the full-
blooded offensive Sheridan wanted and felt able to conduct, but
also caused a steady deterioration of his command. His subordinates were already complaining, and with good reason, that their
horses were starving. General Davies wrote after the war that "the
wagon trains . . . which were now . . . [the army's] sole dependence
for supplies, were utterly unable to provide and distribute the
forage required."[58] The 2nd Ohio, for example, a regiment new
to the Army of the Potomac, drew five pounds of forage per horse
—one fifth of a day's full ration—and even that not until May
11.[59]

Wilson, who was careful to draw attention to the contrast
between his own punctuality and what he described as "the rule
with the cavalry never to start at the time ordered," was at the
Rapidan just before midnight on the third of May; by 5:50 A.M.
on the fourth the last regiment of his division was crossing the
stream, and, as his orders required, he pushed southward to

57. *Ibid.*, 513.
58. Davies, *General Sheridan*, 69.
59. *Official Records*, Vol. XXXVI, Pt. 1, p. 893. The 2nd Ohio was a
veteran regiment; it had campaigned in Kansas, Indian Territory, Kentucky,
and Tennessee before it was shipped East in the spring of 1864 following its
veterans' furlough. There they "felt almost like strangers in a strange land.
Everything was so different from what we were used to. There were many
young staff officers that appeared to want to do something, but they did not
appear to know what to do but to make some fuss. They would gallop about
with an orderly behind them, giving orders about anything and everything,
and creating confusion. . . . When . . . [they] came about the 2nd Ohio . . .
cursing with their 'whoop-em-up' orders, they were received with remarks
and looks of contempt. They soon became scarce in that locality, and we
could now see why the cavalry of the Army of the Potomac had fallen into
bad repute." Isaac Gause, *Four Years with Five Armies* (New York, 1908),
221–23.

Parker's Store against negligible opposition.[60] He was now in the depths of the Wilderness. He discovered, as had Pleasonton a year earlier, that he was in an area "peculiarly unsuitable for the operations of cavalry, covered . . . in every direction with dense thickets that were impenetrable to horsemen and intersected by few and narrow paths which permitted of movement only in long-extended and thin columns, which could not be deployed."[61] Mounted fighting and saber charges were out of the question except for chance encounters of small patrols on the roads and paths or in an occasional small clearing. The cavalry did nearly all its fighting on foot against a similarly dismounted enemy, whom as often as not they could barely see in the dense undergrowth.

In dismounted action, much of which was at short range, possession of the Spencer carbines gave the Union regiments that had them a decided advantage over the enemy, psychological as well as material. In a fight on May 6 on the Brock Turnpike between Custer's Michigan regiments, reinforced by a portion of Thomas C. Devin's brigade, and Rosser's Confederates, the Spencers, used with "deadly effect," turned the scales; the action had begun with a generally successful attack by Rosser, but the attack was checked and his men were then driven back "in disorder."[62] On the previous day, the 5th New York, commanded by Lieutenant Colonel John Hammond and numbering scarcely 500 men, was guarding the approaches to Parker's Store from the direction of Mine Run and was able to stand off the advance of a full division of Confederate infantry. Realizing that the dense woods and the strength of the enemy would make mounted action impossible, Hammond dismounted all his men and spread them out in a loose skirmish line. "Their Spencer carbines made the dense woods ring, and told with fearful effect upon the enemy. Prisoners, afterwards captured from . . . [the] attacking division, swore that a whole brigade must have been in their front."[63] The regi-

60. Wilson, "Cavalry of the Army of the Potomac," 41; *Official Records*, Vol. XXXVI, Pt. 2, p. 377.
61. Davies, *General Sheridan*, 103.
62. Kidd, *Personal Recollections*, 264–71.
63. Boudrye, *Historic Records of the Fifth*, 122; *Official Records*, Vol. XXXVI, Pt. 1, pp. 875–77, 886. The three accounts of the action state vari-

ment was eventually forced back by sheer weight of numbers, but it had held the enemy in check for several hours.

With or without Spencers, it would not have been possible for Wilson's single division of cavalrymen to hold up for more than a short time the advance of the Confederate army, led by Stuart's cavalry and consisting initially of the corps of Ewell and Hill. On the morning of the fifth, after what appears to have been a successful encounter with Rosser's brigade, Chapman's brigade of Wilson's division came up against Confederate infantry near Craig's Meeting House and was driven back "in a very disordered state." In an uncommonly candid report, Chapman explained, "The confusion occasioned by getting a large number of led horses hastily back on one road was communicated to the men, and caused the men to break badly, of which the enemy was not slow to take advantage. We were driven back behind a line of battle formed by a part of the First Brigade, and subsequently retired to Todd's Tavern."[64] In protecting the rear of Wilson's division at Todd's Tavern, Davies' brigade of the Second Division lost 65 men, mostly from the 1st New Jersey, which charged the advancing enemy, and from the 1st Massachusetts, which between May 4 and May 11 lost 124 officers and men killed, wounded, and missing, of the 537 who began the campaign.[65]

The fortunes of Wilson's division were not helped by the newest of its regiments, the 22nd New York. The tragicomic adventures of that unfortunate regiment in the first few days of the campaign illustrate vividly the vice of exposing wholly untrained, untested units to combat in an extremely difficult terrain against veterans of three years of war. Some time after the regiment had its newly acquired horses taken away to provide mounts for veterans, it was remounted and assigned to the Third Division. On the third day of the campaign, exposed to artillery fire for the

---

ously that the regiment held up the Confederate infantry for three, five, and six hours. The regiment, however, paid a high price for its defensive prowess; it lost thirteen killed, twenty-two wounded, and 24 "known to have been captured, besides 15 or 20 from whom tidings have never since been heard. They were probably killed." Boudrye, *Historic Records of the Fifth*, 122.

64. *Official Records*, Vol. XXXVI, Pt. 1, pp. 877, 860, 897.
65. *Ibid.*, 857; Crowninshield, *A History of the First Regiment*, 211.

first time, the regiment stampeded, or, as its commanding officer reported, "retreated . . . with some precipitation and confusion."[66] Later the same day General Meade ordered Colonel Samuel Crooks of the 22nd under arrest "for having sent false information about the enemy."[67] It is not unlikely that the information Colonel Crooks sent was "false" simply because of his lack of experience. His next in rank, Major Peter McLennan, to whom Crooks was ordered to turn over command, fared even worse. He had to report that on the morning of the eighth the regiment "was fired upon by a concealed enemy from behind trees, stumps and logs. . . . I returned the fire, but the horses not having been trained to military noises, caused some confusion."[68] The result of two days of marching and skirmishing, without any serious engagement, was that the regiment not only lost 11 officers and men killed and wounded, but also had 97 missing. Nor was that all; it also lost 31 horses killed or "died of fatigue and want of forage," and, unbelievably, 241 horses *missing*.[69] As a crowning ignominy, General Winfield Scott Hancock reported on the afternoon of May 8 that the 22nd New York "certainly did not act well this morning, and . . . [Major McLennan] appeared stupid."[70]

The general shape of the fighting on May 4–7, "an affair of infantry musketry at close quarters," was one of alternating Union and Confederate attacks. When the firing died down on the evening of the sixth, with the "woods on fire in many places. . . . Choking smoke everywhere. And from the thickets . . . the cries of the wounded, frantic lest the flames reach them ere the litter-bearers did," the Union army, pinned down in the Wilderness, occupied an irregular line facing generally southwest along the Brock road, which ran from Germanna Ford to Spotsylvania Court House, a settlement located about eight miles southeast of the Union left flank.[71] The advantage after four days of battle lay with the Confederates. They had inflicted nearly 18,000 casualties on the enemy at a cost to themselves of 7,600. They had blunted the

66. *Official Records*, Vol. XXXVI, Pt. 1, pp. 893, 995.
67. *Ibid.*, Pt. 2, p. 509.
68. *Ibid.*, Pt. 1, p. 995.
69. *Ibid.*, 996.
70. *Ibid.*, Pt. 2, p. 532.
71. The quotation is from Freeman, *R. E. Lee*, III, 290n.

momentum of the Union army and had forced upon it a static battle under conditions that nullified its great numerical superiority. In a somewhat similar situation a year earlier, Hooker had surrendered the initiative to General Lee and retreated across the Rapidan in defeat and humiliation. But Grant was not Hooker.

During the fighting of the sixth and seventh, the entire Cavalry Corps was deployed near Todd's Tavern, located at the crossing of the Brock and Catharpin roads a little more than two miles below the southern end of the Union lines. Its assignment was to protect the left flank of the Union infantry and the trains in rear. For two days it held its own, and perhaps a little more, in a nearly continuous battle against Stuart's cavalrymen. All the fighting was dismounted, the men sheltering behind any cover they could find or improvise. One of Custer's officers described the cavalry action of these two days as "sulky, stubborn, bulldog fighting, entirely opposed to the brilliant methods by which Custer had gained his reputation, dismounted lines of skirmishers pressing grimly forward through tangled woods, firing at each other like lines of infantry, holding on to hasty breastworks of rails and fallen trees, and making but little progress."[72] On the forenoon of the sixth, Custer, aided by Devin, fought off an attack by Fitzhugh Lee's division near the intersection of the Brock and Furnace roads and, as Custer reported, "drove him in disorder from the field."[73] On the seventh, Gregg and Merritt, then Custer, then Torbert and Gregg, fought Fitzhugh Lee and Hampton at Todd's Tavern, and Sheridan sent a series of exuberant dispatches to headquarters, reporting their successes in glowing colors. One dispatch spoke of attacks "handsomely repulsed"; another, that "The cavalry is allright. So far they have handled the enemy very handsomely"; and a third, "I attacked the rebel cavalry . . . this afternoon, and after a sharp and hotly contested action, drove them in confusion toward Spotsylvania Court-House. Our cavalry behaved splendidly."[74] Such dispatches must ordinarily be taken with a grain of salt, but in this case Sheridan's enthusiastic re-

72. Whittaker, *George A. Custer*, 221. Whittaker adds (p. 222) that "[it] was noticeable in all . . . [these] battles . . . [that] the Confederate cavalry were not fighting with the obstinacy and vigor which characterized them in 1863."

73. *Official Records*, Vol. XXXVI, Pt. 2, p. 466.

74. *Ibid.*, 466, 515.

ports seem to have been fully justified; the effect of these fights on the morale of the Confederate cavalry was anything but favorable. Some of the officers captured at Yellow Tavern a few days later told their captors that their commands had been "entirely used up and demoralized, that they had the worst of every cavalry battle since the opening of the campaign."[75]

On the morning of the seventh Grant decided on the move that was to shape the contours of the campaign from that point on. He directed Meade to order the army to disengage after nightfall, a corps at a time, and by a night march around the right wing of the Confederate army occupy Todd's Tavern and Spotsylvania, both positions well to the south of General Lee's lines and hence between him and Richmond. The ensuing night march of Warren's and Hancock's infantry, in thick smoke and choking dust, over the narrow Wilderness roads, was hampered by the exhaustion of the men plus poor staff work and resulted in a tangle that brought on the Sheridan-Meade confrontation.

General Lee had already foreseen that Grant, checked in the Wilderness, would not retreat as Hooker had done, and that Spotsylvania would be his next objective. His orders on the seventh were thus the counterpart of Grant's. Longstreet had been severely wounded the previous day; his corps, now commanded by General R. H. Anderson, was ordered to leave its lines at nightfall, march to Spotsylvania, and occupy the town before the Federals could get there. To reach this settlement Anderson's infantry had to cross the unfordable Po River. They could do so on three bridges: Corbin's, two miles southwest of Todd's Tavern; Blockhouse, three miles due west of Spotsylvania; and Snell's, two miles due south of the settlement. In conformity with Grant's overall plan, Sheridan intended to seize all three bridges, establish strong bridgeheads beyond them, and thus deny their use to the enemy. Wilson was ordered to occupy Spotsylvania early on the morning of the eighth, then to move south and take possession of Snell's Bridge.[76] Gregg and Merritt, the latter commanding the First Division in Torbert's temporary absence, bivouacked at Todd's Tavern for the night, were to cross to the south bank of the Po on Corbin's Bridge in the morning; Gregg was to remain there

75. Crowninshield, A History of the First Regiment, 212.
76. Official Records, Vol. XXXVI, Pt. 1, p. 878.

to deny the use of the bridge to the enemy, and Merritt was to march downstream and seize and hold the Blockhouse Bridge.[77] There is no indication in the records that this excellent plan was communicated, as it should have been, to Meade or his staff.

Sheridan's plan in fact came to nothing. Wilson received his orders during the night, marched to Spotsylvania as directed, found Wickham's brigade of Fitzhugh Lee's division in possession, and drove it out of the village. That, however, was as much as he was able to do, for when he moved forward toward Snell's Bridge he found Anderson's infantry already across the river and blocking access to the bridge. Having been in possession of the village for a short time, Wilson was ordered by Sheridan to withdraw.[78]

What meanwhile of Gregg and Merritt? The flank march of the Union infantry having begun in accordance with Grant's orders, General Meade and his staff, riding ahead of the infantry, reached Todd's Tavern shortly before one A.M. on May 8. Gregg and Merritt were there, their regiments in bivouac in the woods over an area of several hundred acres, but they had received no orders from Sheridan. G. K. Warren's infantry was a short distance behind Meade, who then did what any army commander would and should have done. Two divisions of cavalry were encamped around the tavern, idle and without orders, and Sheridan was not there to be consulted. At one A.M., therefore, Meade issued orders directly to Gregg and Merritt, instructing them to move forward immediately, it being "of the utmost importance that not the slightest delay occur in opening the Brock Road beyond Spotsylvania Court-House, as an infantry corps . . . [was then] on its way to occupy that place." At the same time, however, he sent a courier to Sheridan to let him know that he had found the two cavalry divisions "without orders. They are in the way of the infantry, and there is no time to refer to you. I have given them the inclosed orders which you can modify to-day after the infantry corps are in position."[79]

Sheridan's orders to his two division commanders directing

77. Sheridan, *Personal Memoirs*, I, 365; *Official Records*, Vol. XXXVI, Pt. 2, p. 553.

78. *Official Records*, Vol. XXXVI, Pt. 2, p. 554; Pt. 1, p. 878; Wilson, *Under the Old Flag*, I, 393–94.

79. *Official Records*, Vol. XXXVI, Pt. 2, pp. 552, 551; for Sheridan's version, see *ibid.*, Pt. 1, p. 789.

the movement to Corbin's and Blockhouse bridges are marked "1 a. m.," as are Meade's. The records do not indicate when Gregg and Merritt received Sheridan's orders, but it must have been some time after they received Meade's. In a textbook sense Sheridan's orders were certainly superior to Meade's, which simply moved the cavalry forward, out of the way of the infantry, and produced a dreadful jam-up of horsemen and footsoldiers on the same pitch dark, narrow road. There can be no question, however, that as army commander Meade had a perfect right to issue whatever orders he chose to Gregg and Merritt when he found them without orders from their immediate superior. It must be remembered also that Meade informed Sheridan of his orders; indeed, he sent him copies of them.

There is a second point to be noted concerning Sheridan's one A.M. orders. They directed Gregg and Merritt to move out at five A.M. Assuming that they marched exactly on time, which was not by any means the invariable practice of the corps, it would have been nearly seven A.M. before they could have had secure possession of the two bridges. By that time they would have been too late. Sheridan did not know, and of course had no reason to know, that Anderson had chosen to make an all-night march, and would have been, as in fact he was, across the river before Sheridan's men could have reached the bridges.

Later in the morning Meade sent for Sheridan, and when the latter arrived at army headquarters at Piney Branch Church "a very acrimonious dispute took place between the two generals."

[Meade] had worked himself into a towering passion regarding the delays encountered in the forward movement, and when Sheridan appeared went at him hammer and tongs, accusing him of blunders, and charging him with not making a proper disposition of his troops, and letting the cavalry block the advance of the infantry. Sheridan was equally fiery. . . . His language throughout was highly spiced and conspicuously italicized with expletives.[80]

As Sheridan tells it in his *Memoirs*, with the spice and expletives naturally omitted, what he said to Meade was

80. Porter, *Campaigning with Grant*, 83–84. A less dramatic account is in R. V. Johnson and C. C. Buel (eds.), *Battles and Leaders of the Civil War* (4 vols.; New York, 1887–88), IV, 189, hereinafter cited as *Battles and Leaders*.

that he had broken up my combinations, exposed Wilson's division, and kept Gregg unnecessarily idle, and . . . such disjointed operations as he had been requiring of the cavalry . . . would render the corps inefficient and useless. . . . One word brought on another until, finally, I told him I could whip Stuart if he (Meade) would only let me, but since he insisted on giving the cavalry directions without consulting or even notifying me, he could thenceforth command the Cavalry Corps himself—that I would not give it another order.[81]

This unedifying set-to between the two generals may be ascribed at least in part to weariness; neither of them could have had much sleep the night before. In any case, Meade was notorious throughout the army for his vile temper. Still, Sheridan's tirade was not only insubordinate, it was also grossly unfair to Meade. Sheridan's statement in his *Memoirs* that Meade "modified the orders" he (Sheridan) had given Gregg and Merritt, and that he (Sheridan) was not "duly advised of these changes in Gregg's and Merritt's orders" is contradicted by the record, and is simply incorrect, or false, as one prefers.[82]

Grant's headquarters were also at Piney Branch Church, near Meade's, and after this bitter quarrel Meade walked over to Grant's tent and described the incident to him. When he quoted Sheridan's remark about going out to whip Stuart if Meade would turn him loose to do it, Grant remarked, "Did Sheridan say that? Well, he generally knows what he is talking about. Let him start right out and do it."[83] At ten o'clock the same evening, General Humphreys wrote out the orders that gave Sheridan the independence he wanted; he was directed "to immediately concentrate . . . [his] available mounted force, and . . . proceed against the enemy's cavalry."[84]

Early the following day, May 9, the Cavalry Corps was on its way south to have a fight with Stuart. Leaving behind his dismounted men and his more than 600 wounded, Sheridan set out on the independent expedition on which his heart was set.[85]

81. Sheridan, *Personal Memoirs*, I, 368–69.
82. *Ibid.*, 366.
83. Porter, *Campaigning with Grant*, 84. Grant makes no mention of the incident in his *Personal Memoirs*.
84. *Official Records*, Vol. XXXVI, Pt. 2, p. 552.
85. *Ibid.*, 551.

IV

The Face of Battle

ON THE NIGHT OF MAY 8, SHERIDAN ASSEMBLED HIS
three division commanders and declared, "We are going out to
fight Stuart's cavalry in consequence of a suggestion from me. . . .
We are strong, and I know we can beat him, and in view of my
recent representations to General Meade I shall expect nothing
but success."[1] This was self-confidence or brashness with a vengeance, but it was to find its justification in the result.

Sheridan started out on May 9 with approximately ten thousand mounted men and six batteries of horse artillery. Merritt
(Torbert was still absent) had the lead, followed by Wilson;
steady and reliable Gregg brought up the rear. Most of the men
were in high spirits; after five days of nearly unbroken fighting
dismounted in the Wilderness ("not a good place for a fair and
square fight," as one of them wrote) and moving from place to
place in a brushwood jungle where "on dark and rainy nights
horses would plunge into half-filled graves," they were happy to
be able to ride their horses in the bright sunlight, with blue sky
overhead.[2] Inevitably, after three years of war, there were exceptions to the general euphoria. One was Lieutenant J. M. Reynolds
of the 10th New York, who wrote years later:

1. Sheridan, *Personal Memoirs*, I, 370.
2. Allen, *Down in Dixie*, 271; Gause, *Four Years with Five Armies*, 229.

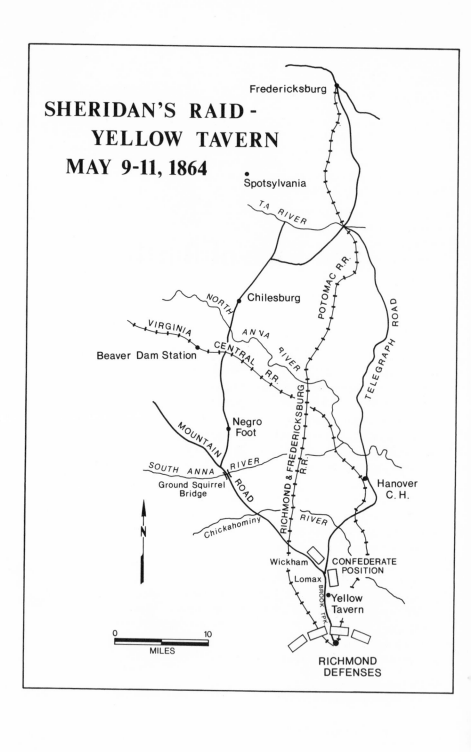

SHERIDAN'S RAID -
YELLOW TAVERN
MAY 9-11, 1864

Fredericksburg

Spotsylvania

T.A RIVER

POTOMAC R.R.

Chilesburg

NORTH

VIRGINIA

ANVA RIVER

CENTRAL R.R.

Beaver Dam Station

TELEGRAPH ROAD

RICHMOND & FREDERICKSBURG R.R.

Negro Foot

MOUNTAIN

SOUTH ANNA RIVER

ROAD

Ground Squirrel Bridge

Hanover C.H.

Chickahominy RIVER

N

Wickham

CONFEDERATE POSITION

Lomax

BROOK TPK.

Yellow Tavern

0   10
MILES

RICHMOND DEFENSES

How distinctly I recall our starting out on that hot Southern morning for . . . "the unknown" away from the main army. . . . All the novelty had departed, even patriotism was worn threadbare, our fighting appetites surfeited, and the end not yet. Two thoughts of that morning I shall always remember: First, the dread of being wounded . . . and falling into the hands of the enemy; second, that if Horace Greeley and Jeff Davis could be forced to represent sides and fight the thing to a finish I should feel happier.[3]

Orders were to keep to a walk, and the marching column stretched out over a distance of thirteen miles.[4] Colonel J. H. Kidd of the 6th Michigan noted, "To those of us who had been with Kilpatrick but a short two months before[,] the contrast . . . [between] Sheridan's manner of conducting a march with that of his predecessor was most marked. . . . This movement was at a slow walk, deliberate and by easy stages. So leisurely was it that it did not tax the endurance of men or horses. There was a steadiness about it that calmed the nerves, strengthened self-reliance, and inspired confidence."[5] The weather on May 9 was benign, the air mild and exhilarating, and the men "thought it was a holiday time we were having as we rode easily along, the most common topic of discourse being General Phil Sheridan. . . . It was the unanimous opinion that he had, at least, demonstrated one thing—that he knew how to march a cavalry force without exhausting [it]."[6] The one serious inconvenience was the stifling clouds of dust kicked up by the horses' hooves, "and the brief intervals of halt for water and rest were . . . seasons of delightful relief."[7]

Sheridan had decided that the surest way to bring the Confederate cavalry to battle was to ride southeast from Spotsylvania to the Fredericksburg-Richmond Telegraph Road, then south toward Richmond. This, he reasoned, would force Stuart to follow

3. Preston, History of the 10th Regiment, 200.
4. Allen, Down in Dixie, 279.
5. Kidd, Personal Recollections, 291.
6. Isham, "The Cavalry of the Army of the Potomac," 210. On the second night out, Wilson's and Gregg's divisions camped south of the South Anna River. Much to their amazement, the men were ordered to unsaddle. The historian of the 1st Maine comments, "This was something new on a raid, and the boys began to get acquainted with Sheridan." Tobie, First Maine Cavalry, 260.
7. Pyne, First New Jersey Cavalry, 236.

him. He hoped, however, to avoid battle until after he had reached the South Anna, or at least the North Anna, where he expected to find forage for his animals.[8]

At Jerrold's Mill, where the Telegraph Road crossed the Ta River, Sheridan took a side road leading southwest toward Chilesburg and the North Anna, which Merritt's division crossed before dark the first day. Beaver Dam Station, on the Virginia Central Railroad, was a short distance south of the river. Custer, in the lead, occupied the station, where he found and liberated 378 Union prisoners of war on their way to Richmond; he also found two trains and huge stocks of bacon and other foodstuffs— 1,500,000 rations, by Sheridan's estimate—as well as the reserve medical stores of Lee's army.[9] Custer's men took as much of the food as they could carry; everything else, trains, commissary, and medical stores, the station and its outbuildings, was put to the torch. The historian of the 6th New York noted:

> The scene here presented was one long to be remembered. . . . A portion of the regiment was in the saddle, drawn up in a line a few rods from the building[s] . . . others were dismounted and hastily tearing up the track on the right and left of the station, while others with carbine in hand were posted as pickets, ready to give the alarm in case of an attack by the enemy. . . . With the blazing buildings in front of us, the drenching rain falling, the thunder pealing overhead, and the blinding flashes of lightning, the situation can be better imagined than described.[10]

Before leaving the next morning, the entire division was set to work on the track and destroyed about ten miles of it.

The only opposition the First Division had encountered the first day out was small bodies of Confederate scouts and pickets, hovering ahead of and on the flanks of the marching column.

---

8. *Official Records*, Vol. XXXVI, Pt. 1, pp. 776–77.

9. *Ibid.*, 777; Sheridan, *Personal Memoirs*, I, 375. Custer also captured some forage for the "half-starved" horses. Wilson, *Under the Old Flag*, I, 419. The Confederate estimates of the rations lost at Beaver Dam Station were, as always in such cases, lower than the Yankees': 915,000 rations of meat and 504,000 of bread. Freeman, *Lee's Lieutenants*, III, 414. Some of the warehouses were set on fire by Confederate quartermaster troops when Custer arrived, to keep the supplies in them from falling into the hands of the Yankees. *Official Records*, Vol. XXXVI, Pt. 1, p. 812.

10. Alonzo Foster, *Reminiscences and Record of the 6th New York Veteran Volunteer Cavalry* (Brooklyn, 1892), 68–69.

These were brushed aside by the advance and flank guards.[11] The rear guard, Davies' brigade of Gregg's division, had a more difficult time of it. Stuart had been informed promptly by his pickets of the departure of the Federal cavalry, and within two or three hours Wickham's brigade was off in pursuit. Wickham caught up with the Federals at Jerrold's Mill, had a brisk fight with them there and later at Mitchell's Shop, but was unable to make an impression on the two rearmost Federal regiments, the 6th Ohio and the 1st New Jersey.[12] At the crossing of the North Anna, after Stuart had joined Wickham with the brigades of Lomax and Gordon, there was a more serious attack:

The commander of the rearmost battalion, who should have faced his men in the direction whence we had come, had grown careless . . . and had closed up to the main body around an angle of the road, without . . . taking any precautions against attack; when, with a yell, Lomax charged down upon them. Driven in upon the pack train of the brigade, they fell into complete disorder; and but for the trained presence of mind of the different regiments, there might have been a disastrous panic . . . [but] as General Davies galloped back, he found each regiment getting into position to resist the attack.[13]

These were veteran troops under experienced officers, able to respond quickly and effectively to an emergency. The attack was successfully beaten off and Wilson's and Gregg's divisions settled down to an undisturbed night's rest north of the river; the First Division, having crossed the river, bivouacked south of it.

To deal with the raiders, Stuart had with him half his corps— three brigades, a total of between four and five thousand men.[14] Why he chose to (or had to) leave behind the other half of his

11. On a march such as this in enemy territory, "The advance guard was formed in the usual order, one man alone in the advance, then two men a few yards behind him, then a sergeant and four men a few yards away, then a squad of eight men with a sergeant, then the company, then the regiment, and then the column, the different bodies being some twenty or thirty yards apart. Besides this arrangement, a corporal and four men in line of skirmishers marched in line with the advance of the column on either flank, always keeping in sight of the advance, and therefore at distances according to circumstances, being nearer the column in wooded country than where it was open." Tobie, First Maine Cavalry, 257.
12. McClellan, I Rode with Jeb Stuart, 409–10; see also Allen, Down in Dixie, 281–85.
13. Pyne, First New Jersey Cavalry, 237.
14. McClellan, I Rode with Jeb Stuart, 410.

corps does not appear in the records and is difficult to understand. On May 10, while Sheridan marched southeast through Negro Foot to the Mountain Road and the Ground Squirrel Bridge across the South Anna, Stuart sent James B. Gordon's brigade to follow on the heels of the Federals and impede their march as much as possible. He, with the brigades of Wickham and Lomax, took a longer route, marching east to Hanover Junction and then south on the Telegraph Road, with the evident intention of interposing his command between the Federals and Richmond.[15] By marching the legs off his horses and allowing his men the briefest possible rest at Hanover Junction (from "some hours after dark" until one A.M.) he managed to reach Yellow Tavern at about ten A.M. on the morning of the eleventh, with his men and horses dead tired.[16] The tavern was located about two miles north of the outer defense line protecting Richmond, near the point where the Mountain Road on which Sheridan was advancing joined the Telegraph Road and became the Brook Turnpike leading into Richmond.

Having reached the tavern ahead of the Federals, Stuart hesitated between two possible courses of action. He had with him two brigades of perhaps three thousand men.[17] He could form a line of battle either perpendicular to the Brook Turnpike with his back to Richmond, and endeavor to repel a head-on attack by Sheridan, or he could form to the east of, and more or less parallel to, the road and attack Sheridan in flank if he tried to march past him toward Richmond.[18] After learning that General Braxton Bragg, directing the defense of the city, believed that with the

15. *Ibid.*, 411.

16. Ten A.M. by Major McClellan's account; *ibid.*, 412. D. S. Freeman states that Stuart arrived at Yellow Tavern at eight A.M. Freeman, *Lee's Lieutenants*, III, 419.

17. According to Wilson, Stuart had "not more than two thousand five hundred men . . . under his personal command, while his other [that is, Gordon's] brigade was too far to the rear to give him any help." Wilson, *Under the Old Flag*, I, 408. Samuel H. Miller states, without citing a source, that Stuart had "some eleven hundred" men—an unbelievably low figure for seven regiments, even after every allowance is made for shrinkage due to straggling and the loss of men whose horses had given out. S. H. Miller, "Yellow Tavern," *Civil War History*, II (1956), 73.

18. There was a third course Stuart might have chosen: to retire into and help man the Richmond defenses, but it would have been wholly out of character for him to adopt so passive a role.

four thousand men of the city battalions, convalescents, and miscellaneous troops he already had, plus three brigades of infantry ordered up from Petersburg, he would be able to hold the fortifications, Stuart chose the latter alternative. Given Sheridan's great numerical superiority this was in any case the more promising deployment, but though the concept had much to recommend it Stuart's use of it was much below his usual high standard. A carefully timed, all-out attack from his flank position might well have been successful; if nothing more, it would have nullified to some degree the effect of Sheridan's three to one numerical superiority. But to occupy the flank position with his troops dismounted— with horseholders deducted, this reduced Stuart's already inadequate numbers by a further 25 percent—as he decided to do, and to remain on the defensive, allowing the Federals all the time they wanted to deploy and attack, was to sacrifice the advantage normally accruing from a position on the enemy's flank. It was not the Stuart of legend who placed the game so completely in Sheridan's hands and made a Federal victory virtually certain.[19] There is nothing in the records to indicate that Stuart entertained the idea of taking the offensive; if he did, he may well have decided that it was beyond the physical capabilities of his bone-weary command.[20] It is quite possible also that he himself was too tired to think through the problem with his usual clarity and decisiveness.

When the Reserve Brigade, commanded by Colonel Alfred Gibbs and leading the Federal column this day, arrived on the scene, perhaps an hour before noon, it found Stuart's two brigades deployed for battle.[21] There was no sign of the third of Stuart's brigades; Gordon was "assumed to be engaged with the enemy's rearguard," but if so, it was a good many miles from Yellow

19. "The whole command was dismounted except a portion of the 1st Virginia Cavalry, which was retained as a mounted reserve." McClellan, *I Rode with Jeb Stuart*, 413.
20. General John Schofield was told by Sheridan after the war that "Stuart had ridden hard all night . . . his men and horses [were] exhausted, while Sheridan had been resting and feeding his men and animals. In the morning Sheridan 'rode over' his exhausted antagonist." John M. Schofield, *Forty-Six Years in the Army* (New York, 1897), 154.
21. Freeman, *Lee's Lieutenants*, III, 420.

Tavern.[22] Of the two Confederate brigades present, Wickham's, posted to the west of the Telegraph Road, on rising ground behind a small stream named Turner's Run, faced south. Lomax was posted at an obtuse angle with, and to the south of, Wickham's left, on what Michigan Colonel Kidd described as a "very strong defensive position on a commanding ridge," protected by a patch of woods and a small tributary of Turner's Run.[23] Wickham had four regiments on the field, Lomax three. Lomax's right-hand regiment, connecting his position with Wickham's, was the 15th Virginia. It was astride the Telegraph Road and faced southwest; his other two regiments were east of the road and faced west, the direction from which Sheridan was advancing. The southern or left end of Lomax's line extended to within a short distance north of the Tavern. For artillery Stuart may have had as many as ten guns, most of which were posted on or near Lomax's position.[24]

The initial contact with the Confederates was made by the Reserve Brigade and a part of Colonel Thomas Devin's brigade of the First Division. Devin was ordered to move well out to the south of Lomax's position. One of his regiments, the 6th New York, reached and crossed the Brook Turnpike, then turned south, drove off a small group of Confederate cavalry, and pursued it as far as the Richmond defenses. The 17th Pennsylvania, another of Devin's regiments, turned northward and attacked the left flank of Lomax's southernmost regiment. At the same time the 5th and

22. *Ibid.*, 420. Gordon was anything but inactive, however, as Gregg's Second Brigade learned. "The boys were astir early," wrote a regimental historian; "Horses were groomed, breakfast was . . . eaten, and the march was about to be resumed, when rapid firing and the familiar yell from the rear was followed by a sudden breaking in upon our camp and regiment of a torrent of wild horsemen. In an instant the Tenth, too, was thrown into confusion and carried along with the bewildered mass. . . . None of the boys appear to have retained a very clear recollection of just how the thing occurred . . . but all agreed that the Regiment as a unit did not remain there long. . . . For a few moments it was every man for himself and the rebels take the hindmost. . . . The men of the different regiments were blended in the rush. It was one of those unaccountable panics which sometimes seize bodies of men. . . . a brilliant and determined little charge . . . caused a halt in the rebel advance that gave sufficient opportunity for the return of reason to the bewildered troops." Preston, *History of the 10th Regiment*, 177–78.
23. Kidd, *Personal Recollections*, 296.
24. Miller, "Yellow Tavern," 72–73.

6th Michigan of Custer's brigade attacked the 15th Virginia, at the opposite end of Lomax's line. The records are unclear and as usual contradictory, but they seem to indicate that the 15th Virginia was forced back some distance, with heavy casualties on both sides. It may be assumed that with the "hinge" unit of the Confederate line pressed back, the 5th and 6th Virginia on its left swung back to conform, and that thereafter Wickham and Lomax formed a continuous, more or less straight line facing south, Wickham to the west of the Telegraph Road and Lomax to the east of it.[25]

This preliminary action ended some time before two P.M., and for the next two hours there was a lull. More of Sheridan's regiments arrived, and as they deployed into position, Stuart's troopers had a brief and no doubt welcome rest. Meanwhile Custer, whose brigade had been moved to the right of the Union line, with Chapman's brigade of Wilson's division as its neighbor to the left, examined the Confederate position in his front. He saw before him Lomax's battle line "on a bluff in rear of a thin skirt of woods," with one gun on the bluff and two on the Telegraph Road. Custer decided that "a successful charge might be made upon the battery . . . by keeping well to the right."[26] He formed the 1st Michigan, mounted, in column of squadrons for a charge from the flank, and directed the 5th and 6th Michigan, which were dismounted and in a line facing Lomax, "to occupy the attention of the enemy . . . while the First charged the battery on the flank." Then, he reported:

The bugle sounded the advance and the three regiments moved forward. As soon as the First Michigan moved from the cover of the woods, the enemy divined our intention and opened a brisk fire from his artillery with shell and canister. Before the battery . . . could be reached there were five fences to be opened and a bridge to cross, over which it was impossible to pass more than 3 at one time. . . . notwith-

25. Kidd, *Personal Recollections*, 301–304, is to be contrasted with Mc-Clellan, *I Rode with Jeb Stuart*, 412. According to the latter, repeating what Stuart told him, "The enemy attempted to drive him from the Telegraph Road, but had been repulsed, after a most desperate hand to hand fight, by the sharpshooters of Fitz Lee's brigade [sic]."

26. This and the two quotations that follow are from Custer's report, *Official Records*, Vol. XXXVI, Pt. 1, pp. 817–18; see also McClellan, *I Rode with Jeb Stuart*, 413.

standing these obstacles, the First Michigan, Lieutenant-Colonel [Peter] Stagg commanding, advanced boldly . . . and when within 200 yards of the battery, charged it with a yell.

Colonel Stagg's "brilliantly executed" charge captured two of the enemy's guns; coupled with the simultaneous charge of the two dismounted regiments, it broke up Lomax's left and drove his entire brigade back a quarter of a mile across a ravine, on the far side of which his men rallied momentarily.[27] But now he was attacked all along the line; his left flank was charged by the 7th Michigan, while Chapman's brigade with the 1st Vermont, mounted, on the right, and the rest of the brigade dismounted, charged him in front.[28] At the same time Wickham was charged by the brigades of Gibbs and Devin. Stuart's entire line collapsed, and his two brigades were driven from the field.[29]

Stuart was spared the sight of the final defeat of his beloved command. When the charge of the 1st Michigan broke into Lomax's left flank, he rode there to rally his men. The charge of the other two Michigan regiments swirled past him and was met by a countercharge of the mounted portion of the 1st Virginia. As the men from Michigan, some mounted and some unhorsed, came running back past the handful of men Stuart had rallied for a

27. The comment that Colonel Stagg's charge was "brilliantly executed" is Sheridan's, *Personal Memoirs*, I, 378; see also *Official Records*, Vol. XXXVI, Pt. 1, p. 818.

28. Since Chapman's brigade was a part of Wilson's division, its work is emphasized in Wilson's description of the battle; "in an incredibly short time," he wrote, "we overbore his line, carried his position, and drove his men in confusion from the field. . . . Colonel Preston of the . . . [1st] Vermont led his splendid regiment in a mounted charge with flashing sabers against the enemy's center, while I directed the dismounted men against his right, with the result that we captured his guns, crumpled his dismounted line and broke it into hopeless fragments. Custer . . . charged abreast of Chapman farther to the right and was also fully successful, but while my men were pressing the enemy Custer halted to gather up the spoils and to sound paeans of victory." Wilson, *Under the Old Flag*, I, 407. Wilson was not one of Custer's admirers, a feeling Custer fully reciprocated.

29. Fitzhugh Lee was present at the fight (Lomax's and Wickham's brigades belonged to his division) but appears to have left direction of the battle in Stuart's hands. After the battle, he collected and organized the survivors and effected an orderly retreat northward across the Chickahominy. Nearly half of Lomax's and Wickham's brigades were casualties, killed, wounded, or taken prisoner. Miller, "Yellow Tavern," 80. Sheridan's losses too were large, totaling 704 killed, wounded, and missing.

stand, one of the dismounted troopers, Private John A. Huff of Company E, 5th Michigan, shot him with his pistol.[30] Fatally wounded, Stuart was carried to the rear, and after dark the following day he died.[31]

None of the major cavalry fights of the war, starting with Kelly's Ford in March, 1863, had resulted in a clear-cut victory for either side. After Brandy Station, Aldie, Middleburg, Upperville, Gettysburg, and the second fight at Brandy Station, both sides felt justified in claiming a victory. But the fight at Yellow Tavern had an unequivocal outcome. It was a battle of cavalry against cavalry, with no infantry present on either side, and the result was an indisputable defeat for the Confederates. They were badly outnumbered and outgunned, and they were physically exhausted before the fight even began, but the decisive factors were the self-confidence and drive—in short the morale—of the Federal rank and file. Like their commanding general, they expected nothing but success, and a gratifying success is what they achieved.

What skepticism about Sheridan's qualifications to command the corps had survived his management of the march south, disappeared in the warm glow of the Yellow Tavern victory; "the men were jubilant and enthusiastic over what had been accomplished. It was the first opportunity the cavalry of the Army of the Potomac had had to show what they could do under an efficient leader. The praises of general Sheridan were on every lip."[32]

The effect of Yellow Tavern on the Confederate cavalry is more difficult to assess. One writer has spoken of this battle as

30. Huff, who was mortally wounded in the battle of Haw's Shop on May 28, was forty-five when the war broke out; nevertheless, he enlisted in one of the four Michigan companies that became a part of Berdan's Rifles and won a prize as the best shot in the regiment. Mustered out after two years in Berdan's Rifles, Huff at age forty-eight enlisted in the 5th Michigan in the winter of 1863–1864. *Official Records*, Vol. XXXVI, Pt. 1, pp. 828–29.

31. McClellan, *I Rode with Jeb Stuart*, 413–17; see also the moving account in John W. Thomason, Jr., *Jeb Stuart* (New York, 1941), 498–501. For a dissenting opinion on Stuart's intervention in the battle, see T. T. Munford, "A Confederate Cavalry Officer's Views on 'American Practice and Foreign Theory,'" *Journal of the United States Cavalry Association*, IV (1891), 201.

32. Moyer, *History of the 17th Regiment*, 79.

more damaging to southern morale in general than the death of Jackson had been a year earlier, for "Jackson fell in the moment of victory; at Yellow Tavern, the Confederacy lost not only Stuart . . . but also the legend of its own invincibility in the arm that was the pride of every Southerner."[33] General Wilson wrote in his report that from the death of Stuart could "be dated the permanent superiority of the national cavalry over that of the rebels," and in 1913, with the perspective of nearly a half century, he cited Yellow Tavern as "the turning point in the history of the two cavalry forces operating in Virginia. The rebel cavalry was fairly beaten, and ever after was wary of meeting the Federal cavalry in an open field."[34] General Davies too was of the opinion that Yellow Tavern "had a lasting effect upon the conduct of the Confederate cavalry, as from that time until the close of the war it ceased to be distinguished for the enterprise and boldness in aggressive movement for which it was formerly remarkable, and in place of the frequent and successful raids upon our trains and communications to which it had been accustomed, it now found full occupation in defending itself from attack or attempting to check hostile demonstrations made by the Federal cavalry."[35] Sheridan himself considered that the defeat of Stuart made Yellow Tavern important, for under him, Sheridan wrote, "the cavalry of Lee's army had been nurtured, and had acquired such prestige that it thought itself well-nigh invincible; indeed, in the early years of the war it had proved to be so . . . and the discomfiture of Stuart at Yellow Tavern had inflicted a blow from which entire recovery was impossible."[36]

The performance of the Confederate cavalry at Haw's Shop less than three weeks after Yellow Tavern, at Trevilian Station in June, and on numerous occasions thereafter prove these claims of a major deterioration of its skill, dash, and morale to be vastly overdrawn. In any case, such comments ignore the fact that at Yellow Tavern only two of the six brigades of Stuart's corps were

33. Fletcher Pratt, *Eleven Generals* (New York, 1949), 136.
34. *Official Records*, Vol. XXXVI, Pt. 1, p. 879; Wilson, "Cavalry of the Army of the Potomac," 50.
35. Davies, *General Sheridan*, 115.
36. Sheridan, *Personal Memoirs*, I, 386–87.

defeated. Unquestionably, the southern cavalry no longer enjoyed in 1864 the great psychological edge—the "bulge," as they would have called it—over the Federal horse that had been theirs for three years. The odds in that respect were now to be more nearly even, but Yellow Tavern was a result of that leveling, not the cause. Since the advent of Grant to the East, the nature of the war had changed; it became a no-holds-barred, brutal slugging match, with no room in it for plumes, silk-lined capes, or deeds of derring-do. Moreover, the Confederate cavalry had already begun to show the effects of a steady attrition of numbers, a steady decline in relative strength in materiel, and, above all, of the tactical shift to more and more dismounted fighting, which not only nullified the advantage of superior southern horsemanship but actually shifted the advantage to the better-armed Federals, who not only seemed more at home in dismounted fighting, but were also enabled thereby to make maximum use of the increased firepower their breechloading and repeating carbines gave them.

The most serious injury sustained by the Confederacy at Yellow Tavern was the loss of Jeb Stuart. Many thought, and this account has indicated, that he had his shortcomings and faults. His strategic ability was modest, but his tactical sense, and above all his leadership qualities, were superb.[37] How well, or how poorly, he might have fared in the last year of the war, to what extent he might have been able to retain his buoyancy and his resourcefulness in the face of the ever more grim realities of the final months before the collapse, are unanswerable questions. His successors, Fitzhugh Lee, "Rooney" Lee, and particularly Wade Hampton, were cavalrymen of outstanding ability, but in any real sense Stuart had no successors. He was unique; there was only

---

37. Wilson's opinion of Stuart will be of interest: "He was a hardy, cheerful, and gallant leader, but by no means an invincible or even a model cavalryman. Like Kilpatrick, he generally overworked his men and horses in useless raids and seems never to have realized the advantage of operating in masses in close cooperation with the infantry. His failure to cover Lee's concentration at Gettysburg and his absence from that field have never been satisfactorily explained. . . . Although without previous military training, Hampton in the East and Forrest in the West were quite his equals in personal prowess and leadership, while Hampton was certainly his superior in administration and generalship. Wilson, *Under the Old Flag*, I, 409.

one Jeb Stuart, and assuredly he belongs in the southern pan-
theon at the side of Generals Lee and Jackson.

Sheridan now had the success he wanted. Fitzhugh Lee and the
survivors of the defeat at Yellow Tavern retreated across the
North Fork of the Chickahominy, four miles away. The Union
cavalry collected the wounded, buried the dead, cooked and ate
supper, and rested. Sheridan meanwhile thought out his next
move. He decided to march to Haxall's Landing on the James
River, a mile below the southern end of Malvern Hill, where he
expected to obtain much-needed rations and forage from Butler's
army on the other side of the James.[38] To reach Haxall he intended to march by country roads on the south side of the Chickahominy, between the inner and outer defenses of Richmond to
Fair Oaks Station. He had apparently toyed with the idea of trying to capture the city but decided against it; he remarked to Lieutenant Charles L. Fitzhugh, commanding one of his batteries, "I
could capture Richmond, if I wanted, but I can't hold it. . . . It
isn't worth the men it would cost."[39]

The march to Haxall's Landing began at eleven o'clock at
night, May 11, with Wilson's division in the lead. The route lay
southward along the Brook Turnpike to within five miles of Richmond and then along country lanes toward the Mechanicsville
Turnpike. Like all night marches, this one was trying, and indeed
more than usually so because of "extreme darkness," "pelting rain
and howling thunder."[40] As a result, there were "frequent and ex-
asperating" halts, and large gaps opened up between the regiments of cavalry and the batteries following them. A special hazard was the presence of "torpedoes" or primitive land mines—
buried artillery shells, set to explode by trip wires stretched across
the road—several of which actually exploded, killing and maim-
ing a number of horses and wounding a few men. Sheridan took
care of the problem by having "about twenty-five of the prisoners

38. Sheridan, *Personal Memoirs*, I, 379.
39. *Battles and Leaders*, IV, 191; see also *Official Records*, Vol. XXXVI,
Pt. 1, p. 778, and Porter, *Campaigning with Grant*, 120.
40. Sheridan, *Personal Memoirs*, I, 391; Phillips, "Civil War Diary,"
102.

. . . brought up and made to get down on their knees, feel for the wires in the darkness, follow them up and unearth the shells."[41] Then, just at daybreak, Wilson's advance was brought to an abrupt halt by a salvo of artillery from a battery of large-caliber guns in the Richmond defenses, less than two hundred yards in his front. Intentionally or in error, his guide had led the division into a trap.[42]

Realizing that it would be impossible to pass between the battery and the south bank of the Chickahominy, Sheridan ordered Custer to seize the Meadow Bridge, near Mechanicsville, to provide a crossing to the north bank of the stream. Custer found the bridge destroyed, and the Confederates in a "very strong position upon the opposite side, from which they commanded the bridge and its approaches with artillery, infantry and dismounted cavalry."[43] The dismounted cavalry were the troopers of Fitzhugh Lee's division who had fought at Yellow Tavern on the previous day.

Sheridan was now in an exceedingly tight corner. He was hemmed in on the south by the Richmond fortifications, manned by the three brigades of Confederate infantry brought up from Petersburg the previous day, plus four thousand or more city militia. Gordon's brigade resumed its attacks on Gregg's division, which was bringing up the rear of the Federal column, and barred any retreat westward.[44] Escape northward across the Chicka-

41. Sheridan, *Personal Memoirs*, I, 380. Chaplain Pyne of the 1st New Jersey recorded, "In our front the road had been thickly planted with torpedoes, which the rebel prisoners, very reluctantly, were employed in taking up; their timid groping and shrinking being a rather entertaining sight." Pyne, *First New Jersey Cavalry*, 242.

42. There are material discrepancies between Wilson's description of this incident in his *Under the Old Flag*, I, 411, and his wartime report in *Official Records*, Vol. XXXVI, Pt. 1, p. 879. Colonel McIntosh "had from the first suspected [the guide], kept him near him, and when their guns opened blew out his brains with a pistol." *Battles and Leaders*, IV, 191.

43. *Official Records*, Vol. XXXVI, Pt. 1, p. 819. In his own inimitable fashion, Custer thus described this incident in a letter to his wife: "Wilson proved himself an imbecile, and nearly ruined the corps with his blunders. Genl Sheridan sent me to rescue him." Jay Monaghan, "Custer's 'Last Stand': Trevilian Station, 1864," *Civil War History*, VII (1962), 246.

44. *Official Records*, Vol. XXXVI, Pt. 1, p. 854. The severity of Gordon's attack is attested by Gregg's loss of 157 officers and men killed and wounded.

hominy was seemingly blocked by the destruction of Meadow Bridge and by the troops in a commanding position on the far bank. One officer of the Reserve Brigade thought that this was "the tightest place in which the corps ever found itself"; for Captain John W. Phillips, commanding the 18th Pennsylvania in Colonel McIntosh's brigade, it was "a day of the greatest anxiety I ever experienced . . . all conspired to make things look gloomy."[45] But not so for Sheridan, who wrote that he "wished to demonstrate to the Cavalry Corps the impossibility of the enemy's destroying or capturing so large a body of mounted troops. . . . I felt perfectly confident that the seemingly perilous situation could be relieved. . . . Therefore, instead of endeavoring to get away without a fight . . . I concluded that there would be little difficulty in withdrawing, even should I be beaten, and none whatever if I defeated the enemy. In accordance with this view, I accepted battle."[46] Sheridan sent Merritt and his entire division to the bridge, with instructions to repair it, and told him that the crossing was to be made "at all hazards." Under a severe fire, which two of Custer's regiments endeavored without much success to keep down, the repairs were effected in "a few hours."[47] The bridge having been made passable, Merritt's three brigades crossed the river, and after a "hard contest," in which they sustained heavy losses, drove the Confederates from their position and pursued them for two miles, taking "many prisoners."[48]

While Merritt and Custer were opening an escape route northward, Wilson and Gregg had all they could handle in the south. Wilson's First Brigade, under Colonel McIntosh, was attacked by a brigade of infantry and some dismounted cavalry and driven back. The attack was eventually checked by the fire of Wilson's horse artillery and Gregg's troopers, fighting dismounted; Wilson too was able to rally his men, attack the Confederates in flank, and force them to break off the action and retreat to the protection of the fortifications.[49]

45. *Battles and Leaders*, IV, 191; Phillips, "Civil War Diary," 102.
46. Sheridan, *Personal Memoirs*, I, 384–85. Was this Sheridan's reasoning at the time, or is it ex post facto wisdom?
47. *Ibid.*, 382.
48. *Official Records*, Vol. XXXVI, Pt. 1, pp. 813–14, 777, 819, 835.
49. Sheridan, *Personal Memoirs*, I, 383; *Official Records*, Vol. XXXVI, Pt. 1, p. 880.

It was still well before noon when the firing ceased and the fight ended. The rains of the night had ended before sunrise, and after the smoke of battle cleared away the day "was all that Nature in her most generous mood could bestow. The rain had opened the curling leaves, the fields were resplendent with luxuriant grass, and beautiful gardens by the wayside gave forth a fragrance that was refreshing to the . . . exhausted men of Sheridan's cavalry."[50] Left in possession of the field of battle, Sheridan's troopers attended to the dismal after-battle chores of collecting the wounded and burying the dead. The horses were turned out to graze, and some of the officers and men had a special treat: they were able to read that day's Richmond *Inquirer*. Two enterprising newsboys, scenting a profitable trade, appeared on the scene and did a thriving business with the Yankees, who were amused to learn that "President Davis in person, and General Bragg . . . had taken the field against . . . [the Yankees, who] were surrounded, cornered; that not a man . . . should escape."[51]

Late in the afternoon, his men well rested after the exertions of the past twenty-four hours, Sheridan crossed Meadow Bridge with the divisions of Wilson and Gregg—the Reserve Brigade and Merritt's division were already across—and resumed his march to Haxall's Landing by way of Gaines's Mill and Bottom's Bridge. He reached the landing two days later, on May 14. The march was uneventful, for after Sheridan turned away from Richmond the Confederates paid no more attention to him. There were other difficulties, however. The small supply of oats Sheridan had brought along had given out long before. Some forage had been captured at Beaver Dam Station and along the road, but for the

50. Preston, *History of the 10th Regiment*, 181. In the course of Gregg's fight with the Confederate infantry and dismounted cavalry, the 10th New York "was ordered up to the guns as support. One battalion was on the dismounted line . . . the other two battalions sat their horses for moments that seemed like hours, the shot and shell from the rebel guns playing havoc in the ranks. Never did men exhibit more patience and nerve. . . . Although shot and shell from the enemy's battery went crashing through its ranks or plowed the ground beneath the horses' feet, shells burst over and around it in a terrorizing manner, not the least disposition to unsteadiness was manifested. Solid shot striking the ground in front of the regiment would ricochet over the heads of the men, causing the horses to fairly squat . . . and with extended nostrils tremblingly crowd together." *Ibid.*, 182.

51. Sheridan, *Personal Memoirs*, I, 385; Gracey, *Annals of the 6th*, 245.

most part the horses had had only grazing and, notwithstanding the carefully regulated slow pace of the march, were beginning to give out.[52] After reaching Haxall Sheridan turned in 341 animals as unfit to make the return trip to the army, but measured by the standards of previous raids by the Federal cavalry his losses in horses were amazingly small, not over four hundred out of a total of about ten thousand, "including killed in battle and abandoned on the road shot."[53] To the distress of many of the men, any horse unable to go on was destroyed, for most of these animals would have recovered with a few days' rest and adequate feeding, and therefore could not be left behind to become of use to the enemy.[54] Surgeon Elias W. H. Beck of the 3rd Indiana wrote his wife from Haxall's Landing, "So terrible to see every time a poor horse would give out by sheer exhaustion—out with a pistol & shoot him—break up the saddle & walk on."[55]

The men too suffered. They had left the army with three days' rations, but as was common with the cavalry and perhaps with the other arms of the service as well, many of the men managed to eat the three days' rations by the end of the first day or at best the second. The Confederate supplies at Beaver Dam Station that were not destroyed were carried off by Custer's brigade and apparently were not shared with the rest of the command. The corps arrived at Haxall's Landing on the sixth day after leaving Spotsylvania, and for the last three or four days the men by necessity tried to live off the country. For most of the way, however, the march took them through an "entirely destitute" area, where there was "nothing for man or animals"; the historian of the 17th Pennsylvania was "painfully impressed" with what he saw: "Deserted buildings, ruined churches . . . abandoned fields and workshops, neglected plantations, and the ragged, dejected, uncouth appearance of the few people who are to be seen at home, the almost entire absence of men and boys. . . . The people said it mattered but little to them which troops visited them, as the Rebels

52. *Official Records*, Vol. XXXVI, Pt. 2, p. 765.
53. *Ibid.*, Pt. 1, p. 781.
54. *Ibid.*, 792.
55. Elias W. H. Beck, "Letters of a Civil War Surgeon," *Indiana Magazine of History*, XXVII (1931), 134.

took all they could find and the Yankees treated them no better."[56] Even in country less devastated than the Peninsula foraging was not usually a reliable source of supply; on this march, as was often the case, some fortunate units and individuals "got plenty of fresh beef and corn by foraging," while others got little or nothing.[57]

Sheridan wasted no time at Haxall's Landing. He sent off jubilant dispatches to Generals Meade and Halleck, reporting his command "in fine spirits with its success" and giving an indication of his own fine spirits with the remark, "If I could be permitted to cross the James River and go southward I could almost ruin the Confederacy."[58] But another year of marches, battles, and losses was needed before he could make good on that bit of bragging, and at the moment other duties claimed his attention. The wounded and prisoners were sent downriver to Fort Monroe, rations and forage were received and distributed, and in the remarkably short time of three days, Sheridan was ready to start the return march to the army.

Sheridan's principal problem in planning the return journey was his uncertainty about the whereabouts of the Army of the Potomac. Eventually he learned from prisoners, citizens, and his own scouting parties that General Lee had retreated to the North Anna and that Grant was right behind him. Sheridan then knew where he had to go, and after an uneventful march he rejoined the army on the twenty-fourth, to receive a deservedly warm welcome from Grant and Meade.

Custer signaled his return by writing his wife, "When I think how successful I have been of late and how much has been said of my conduct and gallantry I think 'She will hear of it, and will be proud of her Boy!' That is all the reward I ask."[59]

The only noteworthy incident of the return journey was the crossing of the Pamunkey over the partially destroyed railroad bridge near White House, which two of Merritt's brigades repaired

56. *Official Records*, Vol. XXXVI, Pt. 2, p. 765; Moyer, *History of the 17th Regiment*, 247–48.
57. Tobie, *First Maine Cavalry*, 269; Phillips, "Civil War Diary," 103.
58. *Official Records*, Vol. XXXVI, Pt. 1, p. 777; Pt. 2, p. 765.
59. Monaghan, "Custer's Last Stand,'" 247.

and floored over in one day. To get the lumber for the job Merritt sent his troopers through the countryside with orders for every man to bring back one board or plank. Rations had again run short on the way north, and the resulting foraging in a country already ruined by three years of war was not a pretty thing to witness. Surgeon Beck wrote in a letter home, "We have been traveling 'round thro Kent & Hanover Countys destroying bridges & R Roads & robbing the poor people untill my heart is sick at the distruction of property & distress of the people"; and Captain Phillips noted in his diary, "The whole Cavalry Corps was sent out foraging. . . . Many instances of cruel treatment of citizens came to my knowledge. I did all I could to stop it."[60]

The Cavalry Corps returned to the army in time to take part in Grant's next forward move. After the costly fighting at Spotsylvania General Lee retreated below the North Anna, where his army formed up in a perfect defensive position, a V-shaped line six miles long, with its apex touching the river. Federal troops moving from one wing to the other to assault this line would have had to make a long march and cross the river twice, whereas Lee, with the benefit of interior lines, could reinforce a threatened wing in an hour or two. Lee showed no sign of an intention to launch an attack, and Grant concluded that for his own army to "make a direct attack from either wing would cause a slaughter of . . . men that even success would not justify."[61] Accordingly, he decided to sideslip to the southeast and to cross the Pamunkey downstream from the junction of the North and South Anna and the Little River. This move would once again place him between the Army of Northern Virginia and Richmond and would force Lee to vacate his unassailable position on the North Anna so as to interpose his army between the Federals and his own capital.

In preparation for the move of the infantry past Lee's right wing, Grant sent Wilson's division to the right of his own line with orders to manoeuver so as to create the impression that the

60. Beck, "Letters of a Civil War Surgeon," 158; Phillips, "Civil War Diary," 103. Sheridan reported that his "great difficulty" was "about forage and subsistence. I supposed there would be plenty between the Pamunkey and Mattapony Rivers, but . . . [was] mistaken. . . . I have one day's rations for my men; no forage for my horses." *Official Records*, Vol. XXXVI, Pt. 3, p. 121.
61. Grant, *Personal Memoirs*, II, 253.

left flank of the Confederate army was about to be attacked.[62] Gregg and Torbert (the latter had returned to the army and taken over command of the First Division) were given the task of seizing Hanovertown Ford, where the army was to cross the Pamunkey. This was successfully accomplished, and the army crossed the river without incident on May 28. On the same morning, uncertain of the location of the Confederate army, Grant ordered Sheridan to go forward on a reconnaissance toward Richmond and find it.[63]

Following Stuart's death, General Lee had to reorganize the command structure of his cavalry. On the basis of their performance first in brigade and then in divisional command, Hampton and Fitzhugh Lee had equal claims to succeed Stuart in command of the Cavalry Corps; to choose either would have been unjust to the other. Also, General Lee's son "Rooney" returned to duty, having recovered from his Brandy Station wound, and provision had to be made for him. General Lee solved both problems on May 14 by dividing the cavalry into three divisions of two brigades each, to be commanded by Hampton, Fitzhugh Lee, and "Rooney" Lee, respectively. Each division was to "constitute a separate command, and will report directly to and receive orders from the headquarters of the army," an awkward and obviously provisional arrangement.[64]

The armies were now approaching the northern edges of the area in which the Peninsular Campaign had been fought two years before. Haw's (also spelled Hawe's and Hawes') Shop was located a mile north of Totopotomoy Creek, on a crossroads three miles southwest of Hanovertown. Sheridan, looking for the Confederate army on May 28, marched past Haw's Shop. Gregg had the lead, and about three quarters of a mile beyond the shop, he came up against the divisions of Hampton and Fitzhugh Lee, both dismounted, "strongly posted in a dense woods, and in addition to defensive works [of logs and rails] were still further protected . . . by swamps," with their artillery in "advantageous positions." Manning a stretch of the Confederate line was Matthew C. But-

62. *Official Records*, Vol. XXXVI, Pt. 1, p. 880.
63. *Ibid.*, 793.
64. Wellman, *Giant in Gray*, 140; Freeman, *Lee's Lieutenants*, III, 436.

ler's brigade of mounted infantry of Hampton's division. The brigade was made up of the 4th, 5th, and 6th South Carolina, the men dressed in homespun and armed with the short Enfield rifle. The South Carolinians were in their first battle; their rifle fire, however, was so effective that they were mistaken for infantry, which, essentially, they were.[65] In an intense fire fight lasting between five and seven hours, in the course of which two hundred troopers of the 1st Pennsylvania fired off "upward of eighteen thousand rounds" of Spencer carbine ammunition, Gregg was unable to make headway against the desperate resistance of the Confederates.[66] At last, late in the evening, Sheridan ordered up Custer's brigade to reinforce Gregg. "Owing to the thick woods and dense underbrush," Custer reported, "it was impossible to maneuver the command mounted. The entire brigade was therefore dismounted and formed in line. . . . As soon as all the necessary dispositions had been completed," the men from Michigan, their brigade band playing, charged forward with a cheer and drove "the enemy from his position in great confusion."[67]

Haw's Shop, or Salem Church, as it is sometimes called, was the second victory of the Federal cavalry over the Confederate horse in just over two weeks, and on this occasion the numerical odds favored the men in gray. Federal casualties were high; Custer's brigade lost more men in this battle than in any other engagement of the campaign, and Gregg's division had 256 officers and men killed or wounded.[68] Indeed, by all accounts Haw's Shop saw "the severest cavalry fighting of the war."[69]

65. *Official Records,* Vol. XXXVI, Pt. 1, p. 854; U. R. Brooks (ed.), *Butler and His Cavalry in the War of Secession, 1861–1865* (Columbia, S.C., 1909), 350, 352.
66. Lloyd, *History of the First Reg't.,* 95. In his account of the fight, Sheridan paid tribute to the conduct of Butler's brigade; "these Carolinians," he wrote, "fought very gallantly in this their first fight." *Official Records,* Vol. XXXVI, Pt. 1, p. 793.
67. *Official Records,* Vol. XXXVI, Pt. 1, p. 821 (Custer's report); 854 (Gregg's Report).
68. *Ibid.,* 821, 854. According to D. S. Freeman, *R. E. Lee,* III, 365, the "gray troopers were greatly outnumbered." It is difficult to see how two *divisions* of Confederate cavalry could have been "greatly outnumbered" by Gregg's two brigades, plus Custer's brigade, the latter of which did not engage until the closing stage of the fight.
69. *Official Records,* Vol. XXXVI, Pt. 1, p. 861; *Battles and Leaders,* IV,

Hampton, who, as the senior major general present, commanded the Confederate cavalry in this fight, could by no stretch of the imagination claim a victory. Nevertheless, his capable direction of a hard-fought defensive battle made a favorable impression on the corps. Up to the time of Haw's Shop,

> the Cavalry Corps had not learned the style of their new commander, but now they discovered a vast difference between the old and the new, for while General Stuart would attempt his work with whatever force he had at hand, and often seemed to try to accomplish a given result with the smallest possible number of men, Gen. Hampton always endeavored to carry every available man to his point of operation, and the larger the force, the better he liked it. . . . under Stuart, stampedes were frequent, with Hampton they were unknown, and the men of his corps soon had the same unwavering confidence in him that the "Stonewall Brigade" entertained for their General.[70]

As soon as the fight at Haw's Shop ended, Sheridan started on a night march to Old Church, five miles to the southeast, and from there sent pickets forward another six miles toward Cold Harbor, which they found occupied by the enemy. It was clear to Sheridan that Union possession of Cold Harbor was "absolutely necessary" to secure the army's communications with the base at White House; roads from several different directions met at Old Cold Harbor, including roads leading toward "different crossings of the Chickahominy," which he thought it "indispensable" to secure.[71]

---

193. Colonel G. F. R. Henderson, biographer of Stonewall Jackson, has written that "there is no finer instance of . . . cavalry on the defensive than the resistance of . . . the Federals near Hawes' Shop." G. F. R. Henderson, *The Science of War* (London, 1913), 56. Colonel Henderson rightly cites Haw's Shop as a fine example of dismounted cavalry fighting on the defensive, though his praise should have gone to the Confederates, who were actually on the defensive. None of the reports in the *Official Records* mention any Confederate attacks (if Hampton or any other Confederate commander wrote a report on the action, it has not survived); nevertheless, D. S. Freeman states (*R. E. Lee*, III, 365), that "The Confederates threw the enemy back against his supports."

70. Myers, *The Comanches*, 291. Myers' identification of Hampton as commander of the Cavalry Corps is technically incorrect; Hampton did not receive that appointment until August 11, 1864.

71. Sheridan, *Personal Memoirs*, I, 403; see also *Official Records*, Vol. XXXVI, Pt. 1, p. 794. Sheridan's mention of White House refers to the fact that when Grant left the North Anna he changed his supply base from Fredericksburg to White House, at the head of navigation on the Pamun-

The Confederates had retreated behind Totopotomoy Creek and, recognizing the importance of Cold Harbor, just as Sheridan did, intended to hold it. On the afternoon of the·thirtieth there was a "sharp engagement" between Torbert's division plus the Reserve Brigade, and Confederate cavalry, in the wooded bottoms of Matadequin Creek, a tributary of the Pamunkey flowing eastward about four miles north of Cold Harbor. Butler's mounted infantry again bore the brunt of the fight and "held their ground with the same obstinacy they had previously shown," but the intervention of Custer's brigade again proved decisive; the 1st, 5th, and 7th Michigan "went forward with a yell," drove the Confederates from their position, and pursued them to within a mile and a half of Cold Harbor.[72]

The following morning Sheridan rode to Torbert's headquarters to make plans for the day's advance. Torbert and Custer told him that they had already worked out a plan for capturing Cold Harbor, and Sheridan at once approved it. The Confederate force holding the position consisted of Fitzhugh Lee's division of cavalry and Thomas L. Clingman's brigade of infantry, the latter being one of the units transferred from General P. G. T. Beauregard's command to reinforce the Army of Northern Virginia. Lee and Clingman had their men deployed on high ground, behind breastworks of "earth and rails," as was now the regular practice in both armies. The Torbert-Custer plan was to have Merritt's and Custer's brigades drive in the enemy's pickets and skirmishers and then make a frontal attack on the Confederate line while Devin, with two of his regiments, made a wide circuit to the left to "turn the enemy's right at all hazards, and get in among his led horses."[73] Merritt and Custer did what was expected of them, but the plan as a whole failed, Devin reporting that he found it impossible to carry out the turning movement. Torbert subsequently made quite evident his displeasure over Devin's failure to do his

key. White House had also been McClellan's supply base up to the beginning of the Seven Days battles in 1862.
    72. *Official Records*, Vol. XXXVI, Pt. 1, pp. 805, 822, 838; Sheridan, *Personal Memoirs*, I, 403–404.
    73. *Official Records*, Vol. XXXVI, Pt. 1, pp. 805, 784; see also Pt. 3, p. 412.

part, remarking in his report that it did "not appear that a very serious attempt was made to carry out . . . [his] designs."[74] Nevertheless, after Merritt and Custer came within range of the Confederate breastworks, Merritt thought he saw, and reported, an opportunity to turn the enemy's left. Told to go ahead, he sent the 1st and 2nd United States on a swing to his right. Advancing "under a galling fire from infantry and cavalry," the two regiments of Regulars, taking heavy punishment, turned Fitzhugh Lee's flank and caused him to pull back to avoid being surrounded.[75] As the Confederates began to leave the shelter of their breastworks Custer ordered a battalion of the 1st Michigan to charge with sabers drawn. "This charge," he reported, "had the desired effect. The enemy, without waiting to receive it, threw down their arms and fled, leaving their dead and wounded on the field."[76]

Sheridan's comment on this minor affair was deservedly laudatory: "The fight on the part of our officers and men was very gallant; they were now beginning to accept nothing less than victory."[77] The three commanding officers, Torbert, Custer, and Merritt, were also entitled to commendation; when they realized that their original plan would not work, they promptly improvised another and thereby got the result they wanted.

At nightfall that day, Sheridan had a fit of caution. He was at Cold Harbor with three brigades of cavalry which, with the losses since May 4, the dismounted men, and the stragglers deducted, could not have numbered more than about three thousand men. General Lee's entire army had reached Mechanicsville, less than six miles away, and was advancing toward him. After notifying General Humphreys that he did "not think it prudent to hold on"

74. *Ibid.*, Pt. 1, p. 805. Devin's explanation of his failure to carry out his part of the plan was that he was held up by a series of barricades across the roads he had to use; further, "There was no opportunity to use the saber. The nature of the country effectually prevented a mounted command from reaching the right flank of the enemy's position, and it was utterly impossible to force a passage up the road until the barricade had been carried and removed and the enemy driven from the woods." *Ibid.*, 839.
75. *Ibid.*, 849; see also Sheridan, *Personal Memoirs*, I, 405–406.
76. *Official Records*, Vol. XXXVI, Pt. 1, p. 822.
77. *Ibid.*, 794. In his report on the evening of the fight, Sheridan spoke of it as "a very handsome affair, and very creditable to General Torbert and his division." *Ibid.*, Pt. 3, p. 361.

where he was, he ordered Torbert to leave Cold Harbor and return to the position from which he had started that morning. The retreat began after dark, and the last of the command was just marching out of Cold Harbor when Sheridan received orders from Meade "to hold the place at all hazards." "So, at 10 p.m.," Captain (later General) Theo. F. Rodenbough of the Reserve Brigade noted, "weary and disgusted, having been on duty for eighteen hours, we moved back and reoccupied the old rifle-pits—at least part of the force did. The remainder were massed in rear, lying down in front of their jaded horses, bridle-rein on arm, and graciously permitted to doze. At 5 a. m., as things remained quiet in front, coffee was prepared and served to the men as they stood to horse." [78] Rodenbough did not mention that after returning to the position they had just vacated, and before being allowed to get some rest, the men were ordered to reconstruct in the dark the breastworks from which they had driven the Confederates earlier in the day. In some places, the breastworks were simply reversed; in others they were moved "to suit the circumstances of the ground" and rebuilt. [79]

At daylight, just as the officers' servants had "managed to broil a bone, butter a hoe-cake, and boil . . . coffee," the expected Confederate attack came in from the northwest, along the Bethesda Church Road. The center of Sheridan's line, on the lip of a ravine, was held by six hundred men of Merritt's brigade, dismounted. The 19th New York was armed with Spencers, the 1st and 2nd United States and the 6th Pennsylvania with Sharps carbines. In front of the brigade was timber, "large trees with but little undergrowth." The brigade, Rodenbough wrote, was "not aware of the character of the force about to attack . . . [them]. But the *morale* of the corps was so good and their confidence in Sheridan so great that when the order 'to hold at all hazards' was repeated, they never dreamed of leaving the spot." [80] The attackers

78. *Ibid.*, Pt. 3, pp. 411, 469; Sheridan, *Personal Memoirs*, I, 406–407; Grant, *Personal Memoirs*, II, 264; *Battles and Leaders*, IV, 193. Sheridan was nine miles from the nearest Federal infantry, and he learned from prisoners that Kershaw's division of Anderson's corps was between him and the left wing of the Union army.
79. Sheridan, *Personal Memoirs*, I, 408.
80. *Battles and Leaders*, IV, 193.

were three brigades, about 1,500 men, of Joseph B. Kershaw's division of infantry; "a sheet of flame came from the cavalry line. . . . The repeating carbines raked the flank of the hostile column while the Sharps single-loaders kept up a steady rattle. The whole thing was over in less than five minutes; the enemy . . . withdrew more quickly than they came, leaving their dead and wounded. We did not attempt to follow, but sent out parties to bring in the badly wounded, who were menaced with a new danger as the woods were now on fire."[81]

The Confederates paused to regroup and then mounted a second attack, but it was less determined than the first and was easily repulsed. By nine A.M. the footsoldiers of the VI Corps, sent to relieve the cavalry, began to arrive and took over the position. After reporting his success to General Meade, Sheridan was able to order his men to march to the rear.[82] The next evening he was at length forced to confess that his command had reached the limit of its endurance. He reported that his "men and horses are worn out. The men have been in the saddle since 4 o'clock yesterday morning, and the horses without water for the same period."[83]

While Torbert, Merritt, and Gregg were marching and fighting in advance of the left flank of their army, Wilson had the mission of shielding its right flank and rear and protecting its trains. On May 31 he was ordered to destroy the bridges of the Virginia Central and the Richmond, Fredericksburg & Potomac over the South Anna, and then to push on toward Richmond, destroying the railroads as he went until enemy opposition became too strong for him to handle. Once more poor staff work, or one of the accidents normal to operations in strange and poorly mapped country, caused problems. These orders did not reach Wilson, and when this was made evident by the arrival of a later dispatch from army headquarters, Wilson had to inform General Humphreys that he was unable to comply because he had "no appliances for the destruction of bridges."[84]

81. Ibid., 193; see also Sheridan, Personal Memoirs, I, 409–10.
82. Official Records, Vol. XXXVI, Pt. 1, p. 783.
83. Ibid., Pt. 3, p. 470.
84. Ibid., 414; Pt. 1, pp. 880–81. Wilson wrote in his reminiscences that the operation his orders called for was "of the first importance . . . [and] exposed me to the attack of the entire rebel cavalry, which, based on

After dark on May 31, Colonel McIntosh drove off "Rooney" Lee's division in a brisk action on Mechamp's (or Mechump's) Creek. McIntosh's attack was spearheaded by the 2nd Ohio, whose commander, Lieutenant Colonel George A. Purington, reported:

We moved forward under a heavy fire of shot and shell, until within 600 yards of the top of the hill, where the enemy were posted behind breastworks of rails, and at this period a general charge was ordered. . . . As we gained the crest of the hill our ammunition failed, and in some parts of the line the enemy were driven from their position with stones and clubs. . . . The battle, for the number engaged and . . . the nature of the ground over which it was fought, as it was composed of creeks and swamps, through which the men had to wade waist deep, and the superiority of the enemy's force (at least 3 to 1), was the severest I ever witnessed, and only evinces what Yankee cavalry . . . can accomplish when determined to win.[85]

Wilson concluded his own brief report of the action with the comment, "Colonel McIntosh deserves promotion as one of the most competent brigade commanders in the army."[86]

On June 1, having occupied Hanover Court House, Wilson sent Chapman's brigade to destroy the bridges over the South Anna, which was successfully accomplished (evidently the "appliances for the destruction of bridges" had at last been received, or others improvised), while with McIntosh's brigade he marched to Ashland, nine miles to the west, on the Richmond, Fredericksburg & Potomac. McIntosh's troopers had hardly begun to tear up the track when they were attacked by "Rooney" Lee's division, reinforced by Rosser's brigade and backed by a force of infantry. After a hard fight lasting nearly the whole day Wilson was worsted. By using Chapman's brigade, returned from the South Anna,

---

Richmond, had the short line against me from start to finish. The proper tactical use of cavalry under the circumstances was to send the entire corps to assist in the work committed to me. This would have enabled it to destroy the bridges and railroad effectively in a few hours and would have given us, besides, an opportunity to crush or drive Hampton into the fortifications of Richmond or to compel him to take refuge behind Lee's army." *Under the Old Flag*, I, 429–30. The criticism is unjust, for, as has been seen, Gregg and Torbert kept Hampton and Fitzhugh Lee fully occupied from May 28 to June 1, and Wilson had only "Rooney" Lee's division to deal with.

85. *Official Records*, Vol. XXXVI, Pt. 1, pp. 894–95.
86. *Ibid.*, Pt. 3, p. 414.

to distract the Confederates' attention by an attack on their rear, he managed to extricate McIntosh, but by the end of the day he had been driven some distance east of Hanover Court House.[87]

The initial enemy attack at Ashland had struck the 2nd Ohio. Having shown its prowess in the offensive the previous day, the regiment now had a chance to show what it could do on the defensive. Forced back to the village, it held out grimly until driven out by an overwhelming volume of fire. The Ohioans lost forty-five men in this day's fight, to add to the twenty-five they had lost the evening before. Not until midnight, "tired and worn out, having had nothing to eat in twenty-four hours," did they reach camp.[88]

Two days later, on June 3, the battle of Cold Harbor was fought, a senseless frontal assault on a well-entrenched, thoroughly prepared enemy, in which the Army of the Potomac lost five thousand men in fifteen minutes. Cold Harbor was an infantry battle (or slaughter) in which the cavalry played no part. The 3rd Pennsylvania, however, was posted behind a section of the Federal line, on provost duty. "It was probably one of the most horrible days of our whole experience," their historians have written; "The piles of dead, the immense number of wounded, the ghastly spectacle of blood and suffering, can never be effaced from our minds. In many respects our duty was harder to bear than if we had been in the charging line. We were witnesses of the terrible carnage without the excitement of the fighting . . . the rear of a line of battle in an assault is one of the most horrible places imaginable."[89]

The bloody check at Cold Harbor made Grant conclude that he could not hope to defeat decisively Lee's army in the Chicka-

87. *Ibid.*, Pt. 1, pp. 881, 900–901.
88. *Ibid.*, 895. Purington called attention in his report to the "necessity of having some organized system of ordnance sergeants or men detailed, whose duty it shall be to keep cavalry commands well supplied with ammunition during engagements. Men armed with the breech-loading weapon will necessarily fire a greater number of rounds than those armed with muzzle-loading pieces, and it is utterly impossible for a cavalry man to carry more than from 60 to 80 rounds upon his person, and when dismounted and away from his horse this supply can be easily exhausted in a few hours' firing." *Ibid.*, 895.
89. Regimental History Committee, *History of the 3d Pennsylvania*, 433.

hominy swamps north of Richmond, and he decided to sideslip to the left once again, march past the southern flank of the Confederate army, cross the James, and lay siege to Richmond from the south and east. To cover this manoeuver, Wilson, reinforced by a mixed bag of 1,400 infantry, between 1,200 and 1,500 unarmed stragglers, "an indifferent force of dismounted cavalry regiments, and about 1,500 good cavalry," the whole commanded by Colonel Louis Palma di Cesnola, was sent to make a demonstration on the northern flank of the Confederate army.[90] This movement led to a series of fights with Confederate infantry on June 3 at Haw's Shop, Salem Church, and Via's House. On June 4, Wilson went into camp on the Salem Church Road and reported, "My horses have been out of forage [some] thirty hours; my men out of rations [over] a day, and being hard at work with the enemy ever since crossing the Pamunkey. Most of my horses have been kept saddled over forty-eight hours, and my command needs rest."[91] Wilson's men and horses were not to get the rest they badly needed, for on June 4 and 5 Grant decided to take his army across the James River, which led to new plans and more hard work for the Cavalry Corps.

90. *Official Records*, Vol. XXXVI, Pt. 3, pp. 558–59, 559–60, 561, 562; Sheridan, *Personal Memoirs*, I, 411–12; Wilson, *Under the Old Flag*, I, 429–34. Colonel di Cesnola, wounded and taken prisoner at Aldie on June 17, 1863, had been exchanged, and as he was returning to take command of his regiment, the 4th New York, he was given command of this group of "casuals" to take back to the army.

91. *Official Records*, Vol. XXXVI, Pt. 3, pp. 541, 558–59.

V

"Grim-Visaged War"

BY MOVING HIS ARMY SOUTH OF THE JAMES, GRANT IN-
tended to pin Lee to the defenses of Richmond, whose safety, he
knew, "would be a matter of the first consideration with the executive, legislative and judicial branches of the so-called Confederate
government."[1] To simplify the movement, he deemed it advisable
to draw as much of the Confederate cavalry as possible away from
the Chickahominy and Lee's army. Grant reasoned that the best
way to bring this about was to send his own cavalry on a raid to
the Virginia Central Railroad, as far west as Charlottesville.[2] The
raid's subsidiary purpose would be to break up both the railroad
and the James River Canal and thus interdict the flow of supplies
from the West and from the Shenandoah Valley to Lee's army
and to the civilian population of Richmond, swollen by a large in-
flux of refugees. On June 5, therefore, Sheridan received the following orders: "With two divisions of your corps you will move
on the morning of the 7th . . . to Charlottesville and destroy the
railroad bridge over the Rivanna . . . you will then thoroughly
destroy the railroad from that point to Gordonsville toward Hanover Junction, and to the latter point, if practicable."[3] Grant him-

1. Grant, *Personal Memoirs*, II, 281–82.
2. Sheridan, *Personal Memoirs*, I, 416.
3. *Official Records*, Vol. XXXVI, Pt. 3, p. 628.

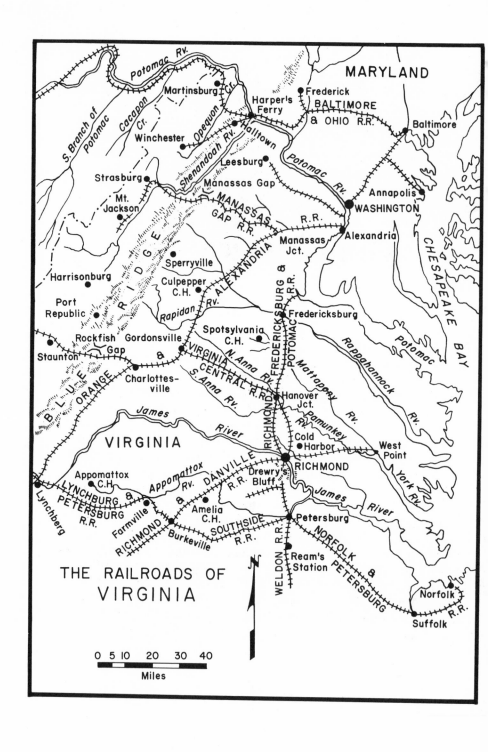

THE RAILROADS OF
VIRGINIA

0 5 10 20 30 40
Miles

self explained to Meade, who passed these directions on to Sheridan, "The object of the . . . expedition . . . is to effectually break
up the railroad connection between Richmond and the Shenandoah Valley and Lynchburg. To secure this end . . . [Sheridan]
should go as far as Charlottesville and work upon the Lynchburg
branch and main line to Staunton. . . . It is desirable that every
rail . . . should be so bent and twisted as to make it impossible to
repair the road without supplying new rails."[4]

The following day, in an interview with Sheridan, Grant added to these orders that he was to unite at Charlottesville with
General David Hunter's army, which had had a successful engagement with Confederate troops at Staunton and had then been
ordered by Grant to "turn east . . . [to] the Lynchburg branch of
the Va. Central road . . . [and] move eastward along the line of the
road, destroying it completely" and, after effecting a junction with
Sheridan at Charlottesville, join the Army of the Potomac.[5]

Sheridan decided to take with him the divisions of Torbert
and Gregg, leaving Wilson behind to handle whatever duties
Grant required of the cavalry as his army marched to and across
the James.[6] Left with Wilson was the large contingent of dismounted men of the other two divisions, reducing the mounted
strength of the raiders to "about six thousand officers and men,"
two thousand fewer than the number with which Torbert and
Gregg had started the campaign just a month before.[7] Casualties

4. *Ibid.*, 599. These directions were keyed to the railroad network of
west-central Virginia. The Virginia Central ran northwest from Richmond
to Orange, where it joined the Orange & Alexandria. From Orange southwest to Charlottesville, the two roads shared a common track. At Charlottesville they separated, the Virginia Central running west through Rockfish
Gap into the Shenandoah Valley to Staunton and beyond, whereas the
Orange & Alexandria ran south to Lynchburg where it intersected the Virginia & Tennessee. The latter ran east from Lynchburg to Burke's Station,
where it met the Richmond & Danville, and was continued east by the
Southside Railroad as far as Petersburg, where it connected with the Richmond & Petersburg.
5. Grant, *Personal Memoirs*, II, 282–83.
6. *Official Records*, Vol. XXXVI, Pt. 3, p. 630.
7. Sheridan, *Personal Memoirs*, I, 417; *Official Records*, Vol. XXXVI,
Pt. 3, p. 661. For reinforcements sent to the Cavalry Corps from May 1 to
June 7, see *Official Records*, Vol. XXXVI, Pt. 3, pp. 665–66. T. F. Rodenbough states that the divisions of Torbert and Gregg numbered "about eight
thousand men." *Battles and Leaders*, IV, 233. This appears to be a serious

SHERIDAN'S TREVILIAN STATION RAID
WILSON'S SOUTHSIDE RAILROAD
RICHMOND & DANVILLE RAILROAD RAID

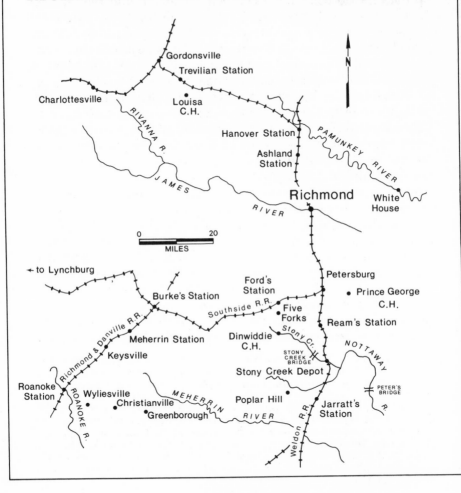

had been heavy, especially at Yellow Tavern, Meadow Bridge, Haw's Shop, and Cold Harbor, but the loss of horses had been even greater, and the efforts of the Cavalry Bureau to make good the losses had fallen short of the demand.

It had become evident also that the War Department, which meant in essence Secretary Stanton himself, had become disenchanted with the bureau, or at least had lost faith in its ability to perform the miracles expected of it when it was established the previous summer. As has been mentioned, within a week of taking over from Wilson as chief of the bureau, Colonel Kautz, an able administrator, was sent to command the cavalry of the Army of the James, despite General Halleck's protests. Responsibility for the procurement of horses for the cavalry then reverted to the Quartermaster's Department, and Lieutenant Colonel James A. Ekin, who had had an excellent record while in charge of the quartermaster's depot at Indianapolis, was given supervision of the purchase and inspection of cavalry horses.[8] The functions of the bureau "relating to the organization, equipment and inspection of cavalry" were to be undertaken "by a cavalry officer especially assigned to that duty" and reporting directly to General Halleck, who was directed to perform "the duties of chief of the Cavalry Bureau" in addition to his other functions and responsibilities.[9]

These changes meant the end of the bureau as it was originally intended to function, but not the end of the problem of supplying horses to the cavalry as fast as all the hazards of an active campaign destroyed the horses they had. On May 1 Halleck informed Grant that 425 animals had been shipped to the army the previous day and that 200 more would be sent daily thereafter.[10] Colonel Elkin was ordered "to proceed . . . to the various points where horses are purchased . . . and . . . [devote] his personal energies to the sending forward of the necessary animals . . . [and to] cause arrangements to be made for buying in open market at

---

overestimate, but less so than the nine thousand men with which Sheridan is credited in Wellman, *Giant in Gray*, 189.

8. *Official Records*, Series III, Vol. III, p. 899.

9. *Ibid.*, 299.

10. *Ibid.*, Series I, Vol. XXXVI, Pt. 2, p. 319.

any point not yet visited by agents of the Cavalry Bureau, where . . . [he] may find it practicable to procure horses."[11] Colonel Ekin's expedition produced the desired results, for on June 4 Halleck was able to report to Grant that in May, 6,683 cavalry horses had been sent to the Army of the Potomac, in addition to the horses supplied to cavalrymen remounted in Washington, and that 1,000 more were about to be shipped to White House.[12] Some of these, no doubt, were horses nursed back to reasonable health at the Giesboro depot, and others were horses taken from new regiments to mount veterans, greatly to the distress of the losers. The 13th Ohio Mounted Infantry, the 13th Pennsylvania, a Massachusetts regiment of black cavalry, the 1st Delaware, and the 21st Pennsylvania all lost their horses and were made to serve as infantry.[13] Colonel W. H. Boyd of the 21st Pennsylvania, who had risen to that post from a captaincy in the 1st New York (Lincoln), for which he had recruited two companies in the summer of 1861, wrote in the anguish of his soul to General William F. ("Baldy") Smith:

I arrived . . . [in Washington] with a full regiment, over 1,200 men, fully armed and equipped, and well mounted and well drilled and disciplined, expecting to be sent to the front as cavalry. To-day we were ordered to turn in our horses and arms and to-morrow to draw muskets and act as infantry. I have been in the cavalry service now nearly three years, and have done as much as many other officers more favored. I feel the humiliation very sorely. Can you do anything for me? . . . If you can do anything for me with General Grant I will ever feel grateful.[14]

11. *Ibid.*, Series III, Vol. IV, p. 228.
12. *Ibid.*, Series I, Vol. XXXVI, Pt. 3, p. 569. In his report for the fiscal year ending June 30, 1864, General Meigs wrote, "During the first eight months of 1864, the Cavalry of the Army of the Potomac was supplied with two remounts, nearly 40,000 horses. The inspection now enforced provides good, serviceable horses. The waste in active service is still too great; but as the cavalry has improved in discipline and knowledge, it is believed that the horses last longer. The broken-down horses . . . able to bear transportation are sent to the rear . . . about 50 per cent. of the horses which reach the depots disabled and broken down are returned ultimately to the military service. *Ibid.*, Series III, Vol. IV, p. 889. (If Meigs's figure of forty thousand was correct, as presumably it was, it would represent much closer to three remounts than two.)
13. *Ibid.*, Series I, Vol. XXXVI, Pt. 3, pp. 590, 602; Pt. 2, pp. 328, 907.
14. *Ibid.*, Pt. 3, pp. 110–11.

Leaving no stone unturned, Boyd had W. Howard King, surgeon of his regiment, wire Colonel Herman Biggs, General Smith's chief quartermaster and doubtless a friend of the surgeon's, "For God's sake get my regiment mounted. It is dismounted for no offense."[15]

If the historians of the 3rd Pennsylvania are to be believed— their blithe tale strains one's capacity for belief—their regiment of veterans arranged for its own remount by playing what these historians call the game of "Old soldier":

The unnamed regiment . . . had just arrived from Washington, where it had had the pick of everything in the way of fresh equipment. Its horses were new, fresh, and in splendid condition, and in all respects of better quality than ours. . . . The wood road which the column had . . . taken was narrow and the night dark. . . . As soon as the unnamed regiment was overlapped . . . our men—those who were after remounts at least—jumped off their own horses, threw the unsuspecting new-comers out of their saddles, mounted their horses, and rode off at top speed. A tremendous row ensued.[16]

Sheridan and his six thousand troopers departed on their expedition at daybreak on June 7. The men were "provided with three days' rations, intended to last five days, and with two days' grain for their horses."[17] It should be said now that they received army rations when they reached White House on their return march on June 21, fifteen days after their departure; hence for the greatest part of fourteen days they had to live off the country and find forage for their animals.

Over the years and in a hard school the men had learned the advantages of traveling light. On this march, too, "every man put as little burden upon himself and horse as possible, carrying nothing that he could do without. If he had a preference for a

15. *Ibid.*, 145. The records do not indicate the result of Colonel Boyd's and Surgeon King's efforts. As of May 31, 1864, the 21st Pennsylvania was not listed either as part of the Army of the Potomac or the Army of the James.

16. Regimental History Committee, *History of the 3d Pennsylvania*, 421.

17. Sheridan, *Personal Memoirs*, I, 417. Each man also carried forty rounds of ammunition. The reserve ammunition, amounting to sixty rounds per man, was carried in wagons. *Ibid.*, 417; *Official Records*, Vol. XXXVI, Pt. 1, p. 794.

blanket, he left behind his overcoat; or if the overcoat was thought indispensable, the blanket was thrown out. Cooking utensils were . . . reduced to a pint tin cup and half of a canteen, which latter, with a split stick, served for a frying and stewing pan."[18] The raid began at the start of a long period of hot, dry weather. For forty-seven days, "from June 3 to July 19, no rain . . . [fell] . . . and the weather was intensely hot. The dust was many inches deep on all the roads and rose in suffocating clouds when disturbed by marching columns. . . . The heat, dust, want of water and scanty food . . . caused a greater loss in horses than that sustained in action."[19]

The march was made at a walk, as the march to Yellow Tavern had been. Nevertheless, "even on the first day there was much suffering from the extreme heat and dryness of the weather; and the horses had to be watched carefully to save them as much as possible from the effect of over-exhaustion and of reckless riding. . . . On the next day's march some horses began to give out and drop by the wayside, forcing their riders to accompany the command for the rest of the journey on foot."[20]

Sheridan chose to march northwest along the north bank of the North Anna. He planned to cross the river at Carpenter's Ford and to strike the Virginia Central at Trevilian Station, four miles west of Louisa Court House and eighteen miles southeast of Gordonsville. He intended to tear up the Virginia Central track from Trevilian Station back to Louisa Court House and then march cross-country, bypassing Gordonsville, to Cobham's Station and tear up the approximately sixteen miles of track between that point and Charlottesville.

On June 9 Sheridan learned from prisoners that the Confederate cavalry had "left its position on the south side of the Chickahominy, and was marching . . . toward Gordonsville."[21] The information was correct. Hampton had learned of Sheridan's

18. Isham, "The Cavalry of the Army of the Potomac," 198.
19. Davies, General Sheridan, 129.
20. Pyne, First New Jersey Cavalry, 260. "We had marched daily at 5 o'clock A.M., not reaching camp often until after dark, after such days of heat and dust as choke one to look back upon." Gracey, Annals of the 6th, 265.
21. Sheridan, Personal Memoirs, I, 418.

departure during the night of the seventh or on the morning of
the eighth. He at once notified General Lee, who ordered him to
follow the raiders with his own and another division. Hampton
took it for granted that Sheridan had Gordonsville and Charlottesville as his destination and marched at a fast pace with his own
division to head him off, directing Fitzhugh Lee to follow with his
division as speedily as possible.[22] By the evening of the tenth, by
hard marching and with the benefit of a shorter, more direct
route, Hampton had accomplished his objective; he reached the
Virginia Central three miles west of Trevilian Station and hence
was between Sheridan and both Gordonsville and Charlottesville.
The same evening Fitzhugh Lee arrived near Louisa Court House
and went into camp at a point about six miles from Trevilian
Station.[23]

On the first two days of their march the Federals were in an
area that had been stripped bare of forage, and the horses were
fed only the grain the men had brought with them. On the morning of the ninth, however, after the command crossed the Rich-
mond-Fredericksburg Telegraph Road and marched toward
Childsburg, it came into an "undevastated region." Foraging parties were sent out on both sides of the line of march, "occasionally making discoveries of horses and mules, regularly bringing
in supplies of provisions and corn. . . . Though the extra distance
traveled and the speed sometimes required were a severe strain
on the horses, these supplies had to be secured; and at the expense of a few animals the rest were kept alive."[24] In addition to
the "official" foraging, there was also foraging for private account:

the orders against taking horses from the column, except by permission or by order, were so stringent and so rigidly enforced, that private
foraging had to be done on foot, which, however, did not prevent it
from being quite extensively done. Adventurous and hungry boys
would start off in advance of the column in the morning, and scour
along the line of march as well as they could, leaving their horses to be
led along the column by comrades, recompensing the comrades for the
trouble by dividing the spoils with them on their return, which oftentimes was not till the command had halted for the night. . . . On the

22. *Official Records*, Vol. XXXVI, Pt. 1, p. 1095.
23. *Ibid.*, 1095.
24. Pyne, *First New Jersey Cavalry*, 261.

whole the men did not suffer a great deal from hunger, while many of them lived on the fat of the land.[25]

On the evening of the tenth the Federals bivouacked on the road running along the South Anna toward Trevilian Station. Sheridan had deduced from "the boldness of the enemy's scouting parties" that the main force of the Confederates was nearby.[26] It was evident that there would be a collision the next day.

The confused and confusing battle of Trevilian Station, fought on June 11, is uncommonly difficult to describe. Unlike other cavalry battles, Upperville or Gettysburg, for example, it had no definable shape. At one time or another, regiments and whole brigades were attacking the enemy from the rear, or were themselves attacked from the rear, or were attacking and being attacked at the same time, or they had some portion of the enemy surrounded or were themselves surrounded. The reports and accounts of the battle by the two sides are more than usually irreconcilable, to the point where the puzzled historian is tempted to conclude that they describe two entirely different battles.

At daylight on the eleventh, Sheridan's command was in motion southward, on the Carpenter's Ford-Trevilian Station road, with the Reserve Brigade and Devin's brigade of the First Division in the lead. Custer's brigade marched roughly parallel to the main body, on a narrow "woods road" about a mile to the left (east) and leading also to Trevilian Station.[27] Characteristically, Sheridan meant to find and attack the enemy.[28]

But Hampton did not wait to be found. Counting Lee's division, he had with him 4,700 officers and men and three batteries with a total of twelve guns.[29] Knowing as he must have, by the evening of the tenth if not sooner, that Sheridan had two divisions plus the Reserve Brigade with him, he probably suspected that his command and Sheridan's were roughly equal in size, and he therefore decided to seek out and attack Sheridan. He planned

25. Tobie, First Maine Cavalry, 282–83.
26. Sheridan, Personal Memoirs, I, 419.
27. General Torbert claimed credit for sending Custer forward on the "woods road" that brought him to Hampton's rear. Official Records, Vol. XXXVI, Pt. 1, p. 807.
28. Sheridan, Personal Memoirs, I, 420.
29. Wellman, Giant in Gray, 198. General Rosser's figure of "about 5,000" is essentially the same as Wellman's. Battles and Leaders, IV, 239.

to move out before dawn with Butler's and P. M. B. Young's brigades on the Carpenter's Ford Road, with Rosser's brigade moving on a parallel road on his left, and attack Sheridan at Clayton's Store, located at a crossroads three miles northeast of the station. He chose Clayton's Store as his goal because a road that Lee could take from Louisa Court House met the Carpenter's Ford Road at that point. Hampton sent Lee word of his plan and directed him to march his division up to Clayton's Store, where he would be well placed to attack Sheridan in flank as Butler and Young attacked him frontally. Rosser's function on Hampton's left was to block any attempt by Sheridan to try to bypass Hampton and march toward Gordonsville or Charlottesville.[30]

There were two flaws in Hampton's theoretically excellent plan. It failed to allow for the fact that Lee had twice the distance to cover to reach Clayton's Store as did Butler and Young; as a result, Lee was still two or three miles from the rendezvous when the battle began.[31] The second and more important flaw was Hampton's tacit assumption that Sheridan would wait quietly at Clayton's Store to be attacked; the plan did not allow for the possibility, or indeed probability, based on his conduct in the previous month, that Sheridan would himself be the aggressor.

The focal point of the ensuing events was Custer's brigade. Unknown to Hampton, Butler, and Young, as they marched confidently forward to Clayton's Store, Custer, screened from view behind the dense woods to their right, was marching in the opposite direction. In short order, in sight of Trevilian Station, he found himself in a position cavalrymen dream about: squarely in the enemy's rear. There in front of him was the station and, just beyond the tracks a short distance to the south, were the trains, the artillery caissons, and the led horses of Hampton's division.[32] This was a situation made to order for Custer; without a moment's hesitation he ordered Colonel Russell A. Alger to charge the trains with his regiment, the 5th Michigan. "The regiment was immediately closed up," Colonel Alger reported, "and charging down the Gordonsville road, the enemy was found in force.

30. *Official Records*, Vol. XXXVI, Pt. 1, p. 823.
31. "It appears . . . that Fitz Lee, who should have closed up on Hampton, was late in getting out that morning." *Battles and Leaders*, IV, 234.
32. *Official Records*, Vol. XXXVI, Pt. 1, p. 823.

After a desperate resistance for a moment, he was routed, and the fight became a running one, kept up for a distance of 4 miles. In this charge about 800 prisoners, 1,500 horses, 1 stand of colors, 6 caissons, 40 ambulances, and 50 army wagons, were captured, and men left guarding them. Many prisoners broke their arms upon surrendering."[33] In the excitement of the charge, Colonel Alger, "acting under the impulses of a pardonable zeal," failed to halt at the station, as he had been ordered to do, and galloped on so as to increase his captures.[34] As a result, one of Fitzhugh Lee's regiments, coming up from Louisa Court House, got between Alger and the rest of Custer's brigade, recaptured all the prisoners, led horses, and trains Alger had captured, and, for good measure, captured the men Alger had left behind to guard his trophies. Alger himself, with a dozen of his officers and men, managed to escape and, after making a circuit of more than twenty miles, rejoined the command late in the day. A group of twenty-eight of his men, cut off near Louisa Court House, "abandoned their horses, and after remaining in the woods two days, started on foot . . . for Alexandria, where they arrived after a week's hard marching. The whole distance was made in the night, they secreting themselves in the woods during the day, subsisting upon a very small amount of corn meal, obtained from negroes."[35]

Before Custer's and Alger's adventures began, the two forces advancing upon each other on the Carpenter's Ford Road collided. According to Sheridan, Torbert, and Merritt, they attacked the Confederates and drove them back about a mile, where, Torbert reported, the enemy "took up a position in a dense woods . . . where it was with the greatest difficulty that a man could get through even if there had been no enemy in front."[36] According to Hampton, on the other hand, his own men were the aggressors; Butler, he wrote, "met the enemy, whom he drove handsomely until he was heavily re-enforced and took position behind works. Young's brigade was sent to re-enforce Butler, and these two brigades pushed the enemy steadily back, and I hoped to effect a

33. *Ibid.*, 831.
34. *Ibid.*, 823.
35. *Ibid.*, 831.
36. *Ibid.*, 897; Sheridan, *Personal Memoirs*, I, 420.

junction with Lee's division at Clayton's Store in a short time; but while we were driving the enemy in front it was reported to me that a force had appeared in my rear."[37] It must be assumed that General Hampton's report, intended to be accurate, was based on incorrect information; it may or may not be significant in that connection that the records do not contain any reports on the battle by Fitzhugh Lee, Butler, Rosser (who was severely wounded in the battle), or Young.[38] At any rate, the subsequent course of the fighting becomes incomprehensible if General Hampton's report is taken as correct. What probably happened was that Butler's South Carolina Mounted Infantry met and drove back Merritt's skirmishers and were then driven back themselves when they came up against the main body of the Reserve Brigade. What appears to be fully established is that at the end of these preliminaries, the 1,300 men of Butler's brigade, and perhaps portions of Young's, were drawn up in line in the woods, not more than a half mile north of the station, and were under heavy attack by Merritt's brigade. If Hampton's account were correct, they would have been a mile or more farther north and would not have been on the defensive.

Hampton now learned of Custer's presence in his rear and of the attack on his trains. He sent word to Rosser to leave his position on the flank, march back to and across the railroad, and keeping to the south of the station, attack the intruders from that direction; he also withdrew some of the troops facing Merritt, to attack Custer from the north.[39] At the same time Fitzhugh Lee, apparently on his own initiative, rode for the sound of the guns; instead of going north to Clayton's Store, he turned west and made for the station via the Gordonsville road. This brought him on to Custer's position from the east.

Custer was now in desperate straits. He had with him only the 1st and 7th Michigan and part of the 6th. The 5th had become scattered, and part of the 6th, which he had sent to aid Alger, had been cut off from the rest of the brigade. With but two regiments and part of a third, he was surrounded by Rosser's brigade on the

37. *Official Records*, Vol. XXXVI, Pt. 1, p. 1095.
38. See, however, *Battles and Leaders*, IV, 237–39.
39. *Official Records*, Vol. XXXVI, Pt. 1, p. 1095.

south and west, Lee's division on the east, and the troops Hampton had withdrawn from the line facing Merritt on the north. "The enemy having shown himself in heavy force on all sides," he reported, "I was compelled to take up a position near the station from which I could resist the attacks of the enemy, which were now being made on my front, right, left, and rear. . . . The smallness of my force compelled me to adopt very contracted lines . . . [which] resembled very nearly a circle. The space over which we fought was so limited that . . . the entire ground was in range of the enemy's guns."[40]

While Custer was fighting for his life and managing somehow to keep from being overrun, Merritt and two regiments of Devin's brigade on his right were being held off by the South Carolinians in their front.[41] Sheridan sent Colonel J. Irvin Gregg's brigade of the Second Division to add weight to the attack and a short time later sent Davies' brigade of the Second Division to attack Fitzhugh Lee's right and thereby relieve some of the pressure on Custer.[42] These dispositions broke the deadlock. J. Irvin Gregg's brigade came in on Merritt's left; he, Merritt, and Devin launched a simultaneous attack, broke through the Confederate line in their front, and established contact with Custer. Their charge drove part of the enemy into Custer's lines, and the men from Michigan had the hard-earned satisfaction of taking about five hundred of them prisoner. The rest of Hampton's division was driven westward, through and beyond the station. Then Davies struck Lee's right and drove his division back toward Louisa Court House and hence away from Hampton.[43]

Writing many years after the event, General Wilson exercised

40. *Ibid.*, 823–24. Fitzhugh Lee's troopers not only recaptured the horses, wagons, etc., and freed the prisoners the 5th Michigan had captured, but they also captured Custer's trains and headquarters wagon, which contained his spare uniforms and his personal correspondence.

41. A trooper of the 1st Massachusetts wrote, "Hampton's men had improved the time and a strong line of breast-works had been thrown up. Butler's rebel troopers were armed with 'long toms' which they used with deadly effect, being able to drop our boys before the latter could get within carbine range. . . . One brigade armed with Enfield rifles and posted behind earthworks ought to be a match at any time for more than an entire division of dismounted cavalry." Allen, *Down in Dixie*, 366.

42. Sheridan, *Personal Memoirs*, I, 421–22.

43. *Official Records*, Vol. XXXVI, Pt. 1, p. 855. David Gregg's two brigades lost 109 officers and men killed and wounded in these attacks. Tor-

his wit in a friendly way at Custer's expense: "According to unofficial reports the rest of Sheridan's corps had a very lively time
in endeavoring to get Custer out of trouble, while Custer, with his
usual energy, was endeavoring to assist those out of trouble who
had been sent to assist him."[44] More representative of the general
opinion in the corps, however, was General Torbert's comment,
"Much credit is due to General Custer for saving his command
under such trying circumstances."[45]

If possession of Trevilian Station and of the track for some
distance on either side of it, after driving off the divisions of Lee
and Hampton in opposite directions, can be considered a Federal
victory, then a victory was what Sheridan's tactical skill and the
hard and costly fighting of his men had achieved.[46] General Butler himself concluded that the day's fighting "ended disastrously"
for Hampton. The historian of Butler's brigade, however, decided
that Sheridan had "met a crushing defeat" and quoted with obvious relish General Rosser's postwar pronouncement to the effect
that "Sheridan displayed no skill in manoeuvering; it was simply
a square stand-up fight, man to man, and Hampton whipped him.
. . . Sheridan was not only whipped . . . but routed. . . . If Sheridan
had been even a tolerably fair general he would have taken advantage of the scattered condition of Hampton's command and
destroyed him."[47] General Thomas T. Munford, a more objective
commentator, wrote that the Trevilian Station battle "has been
regarded by the Confederates as the proudest achievement of
their cavalry during the war," and Hampton himself claimed that
"Sheridan was defeated at Trevilian."[48]

---

bert's and Merritt's losses were high also, but were not reported separately
for the fight of the eleventh.

44. Wilson, "Cavalry of the Army of the Potomac," 57.

45. *Official Records*, Vol. XXXVI, Pt. 1, p. 808.

46. Other indications of a Federal victory were that the Confederates
left their dead and "nearly all" their wounded on the battlefield; the Federals also captured "20 officers, 500 men, and 300 horses." *Ibid.*, 784. Further in the same report, however, (p. 785), Sheridan speaks of a total of
370 prisoners, but does not explain the discrepancy between the two figures.

47. *Battles and Leaders*, IV, 238; Brooks, *Butler and His Cavalry*, 239,
256–57. The losses of Hampton's division were 59 killed, 238 wounded, and
295 missing. *Official Records*, Vol. XXXVI, Pt. 1, p. 1096. There is no statement in the records of Lee's casualties.

48. Munford, "A Confederate Cavalry Officer's View," 202; *Official
Records*, Vol. XXXVI, Pt. 3, p. 903.

As often happened after a prolonged battle, a shower of rain fell during the night "and the stifling dust was nicely laid."[49] Fitzhugh Lee took advantage of the hours of darkness to take his division on a wide swing around the Federals, who were in bivouac at and around the station, and join Hampton. During the forenoon of the twelfth, Sheridan's troopers tore up the track to the east as far as Louisa Court House, and to the west for a mile or so.[50] Meanwhile Hampton and Lee deployed their troops at Mallory's Cross Roads, about two miles west of Trevilian Station, in anticipation of a possible move by Sheridan toward Gordonsville or Charlottesville.[51] This alone effectively disposes of the Confederate claims of victory in the previous day's fighting.

While his men were destroying the railroad Sheridan had to decide what to do next. From prisoners captured the previous day he learned that Hunter, instead of marching toward Charlottesville and hence toward him, was going away from him, toward Lynchburg; he also learned that John C. Breckinridge's division of infantry, on its way to the Valley, was either at Gordonsville or at Charlottesville and thus in a position to block his further progress west. Sheridan concluded that the intended junction of his command and Hunter's was beyond "all reasonable probability" and therefore decided "to abandon that part of the scheme, and to return by leisurely marches, which would keep Hampton's cavalry away from Lee while Grant was crossing the James River." His judgment was swayed further in the same direction "by the burden which was thrown on me in the large number of wounded —there being about five hundred cases of my own—and the five hundred prisoners that I would probably be forced to abandon, should I proceed farther. Besides, the recent battle had reduced

49. Myers, *The Comanches*, 303.
50. Sheridan was careful to state in his report that the destruction of the track "was thoroughly done—ties burned and rails rendered unserviceable." *Official Records*, Vol. XXXVI, Pt. 1, p. 784. On the other hand, with the benefit of postwar but secondhand knowledge, General Wilson wrote, "it is claimed that . . . [Sheridan] broke . . . [the railroad at Trevilian's] up thoroughly, but I think it is a question of doubt whether he succeeded in breaking the track at all . . . if he did, it was broken in such an inadequate manner that it was repaired in a few hours." Wilson, "Cavalry of the Army of the Potomac," 58.
51. *Battles and Leaders*, IV, 238.

my supply of ammunition to a very small amount—not more than enough for one more respectable engagement."[52]

Having decided to return to the army, Sheridan's next problem was to choose his route. His first thought was to march northwest to Mallory's Ford on the North Anna, cross the river there, follow the Catharpen Road to Spotsylvania, and go from there to White House. He therefore sent Torbert and Merritt west to secure the country road leading to Mallory's Ford.

Moving forward in midafternoon, Torbert and Merritt found the Confederate cavalry in position at Mallory's Cross Roads, a short distance west of the point where the road to Charlottesville branched off the main Gordonsville road. Generals Lee and Butler (the latter being in immediate command of Hampton's division) had laid out an L-shaped defense line, Butler's own brigade sheltered behind the railroad embankment and facing north, Young's and Rosser's brigades and Lee's division lined up south of the railroad track, facing east, and protected by "breast-works of fence-rails and such materials as were available."[53] Merritt attacked from the north toward the railroad embankment, while Devin and Custer attacked Young, Rosser, and Lee. The Confederate skirmishers were driven in on both sides of the L, but neither the repeated attacks of Merritt's, Custer's, and Devin's men —seven attacks were made before the fighting stopped—directed mainly against the angle in the enemy line, nor the help of Davies' brigade, sent by Sheridan to reinforce Torbert, were able to drive the enemy from their position.[54]

52. Sheridan, *Personal Memoirs*, I, 423. Wilson's comment on this was, "After the results of the day [June 11] were known, it was found that the Federal cavalry had lost quite a large number of men killed, wounded and missing. For this and other causes not fully explained, Sheridan resolved to give up the object of his expedition." Wilson, "Cavalry of the Army of the Potomac," 57.

53. *Battles and Leaders*, IV, 238. Lee's division blocked both the Gordonsville and the Charlottesville roads.

54. *Ibid.*, 238–39; *Official Records*, Vol. XXXVI, Pt. 1, pp. 824–25, 842, 851; Sheridan, *Personal Memoirs*, I, 424. Torbert stated in his report that the Confederate cavalry "had been re-enforced by one or two regiments of infantry from Gordonsville." *Official Records*, Vol. XXXVI, Pt. 1, p. 809. General Torbert was misinformed; there were no infantry with Hampton. Colonel Kidd wrote, correctly, that although there was some reason to think that a part of Breckinridge's infantry had reinforced Hampton, he himself

The historian of the Charleston Light Dragoons—the famous
"Drags"—a mere dozen survivors of whom, commanded by a non-
commissioned officer, made up a "company" of the 4th South
Carolina Mounted Infantry, described the sixth Federal attack:

The enemy advanced in force to finish the job. . . . They concentrated
on Butler's Brigade. . . . One body marched . . . with beautiful precision, in close order, shoulder to shoulder, the [carbines] . . . held hori-
zontally at the hip and shooting continuously. . . . a few steps in advance strode the leader . . . and he counted time to keep his troopers in
regular step. . . . somehow, no bullets . . . could hit him and when any
of his men dropped, the rest closed up beautifully and marched
straight on . . . this brave fellow had almost reached the breast-work,
when suddenly he stopped . . . and then all at once the legs gave way
and he collapsed upon the ground, an inert, lifeless thing. Immediately his men broke and ran.[55]

After their seventh and final attack was beaten off, the Federals
began to withdraw, free of any interference by the Confederates,
but, according to Hampton, leaving their "dead scattered over the
whole field, with about 125 wounded on the ground and in temporary hospitals."[56] The Confederates made no attempt to pursue.

The stout fight put up by the enemy at Mallory's Cross Roads
made it clear to Sheridan that he could not hope to get to Mallory's Ford without another fight the next day. Another battle
would use up his remaining stock of ammunition, a risk he was
not prepared to run. He therefore decided to make for Carpenter's
Ford, the way he had come, and go from there to the Catharpen
Road. The retreat began in the night; the North Anna was crossed
in the morning, after which Sheridan ordered a badly needed
halt. The horses, which had gone without feed or water for the

---

was "of the opinion that the 'infantry' was Butler's dismounted cavalry
which, when in a good position, as they were that day, could do as good
fighting as any infantry in the confederate service." Kidd, *Personal Recollections*, 361; see also Pyne, *First New Jersey Cavalry*, 265.

55. Edward L. Wells, *A Sketch of the Charleston Light Dragoons from
the Earliest Formation of the Corps* (Charleston, 1888), 69–70.

56. *Official Records*, Vol. XXXVI, Pt. 1, p. 1096. "Pursuit by my command was out of the question," Butler wrote; "We had been engaged in this
bloody encounter . . . without food or rest . . . in the broiling sun of a hot
June day, and recuperation was absolutely necessary." *Battles and Leaders*,
IV, 239.

preceding forty-eight hours, were watered, unsaddled, and turned out to graze.

Sheridan brought away from Trevilian Station 370 prisoners and 377 of his wounded, "all that could be transported," and left behind "three hospitals containing many rebel wounded, and 90 of . . . [his own] that were non-transportable, with medicines, liquor, some hard bread, coffee and sugar."[57] There being only eight ambulances available, most of the wounded rode "in old buggies, carts, and such other vehicles as could be made available. . . . the suffering was intense, the heat of the season and dusty roads adding much to the discomfort. Each day we halted many times to dress the wounds of the wounded and to refresh them as much as possible, but our means for mitigating their distress were limited."[58]

Thus, in addition to the nearly six thousand troopers who were expected to shift for themselves for food, there were more than seven hundred wounded and prisoners to be fed. The command had to depend entirely on foraging to stay alive, and as usual the results varied greatly from unit to unit. The march was through "the most exhausted and desolate region through which we had ever passed, even in Virginia," wrote the historian of the 1st New Jersey; "There was scarcely any grazing, and no corn for the horses, and nothing by which the men could eke out their scanty rations of pork and hard bread."[59] The 19th New York, on the other hand, fared very well indeed; their historian noted, "We took but three days' rations, but . . . lived like kings for fifteen days. In fact, the boys prefer being their own commissaries on such expeditions."[60] But as had been the case before and would be again, foraging could be a grim business, as a trooper of the 4th Pennsylvania recalled:

foraging parties . . . on the flanks of the column . . . literally "cleaned out" the section of anything edible for man or beast. . . . There were

57. *Official Records*, Vol. XXXVI, Pt. 1, pp. 785, 797. As to the Federal wounded left behind, Sheridan reported, "I regret to say that the surgeons left in charge were not well treated by the enemy, and that the hospitals were robbed of liquors and stores." *Ibid.*, 797.
58. Sheridan, *Personal Memoirs*, I, 428.
59. Pyne, *First New Jersey Cavalry*, 266.
60. Bowen, *Regimental History of the First New York*, 189–90.

rather rough deeds perpetrated by us . . . at this time, out of sheer necessity. The people being very poor, at best, were now entirely destitute
of provisions, and we thus gave them fair prospects of a famine. We
were obliged to appropriate for our own uses, all they had. . . . mad-
dened by the intrusion, what few men were left in the country, hov-
ered around in the shape of guerrillas, picking up any stray foragers
they found, and making summary examples of them. . . . it was no
uncommon sight to see our dead comrades suspended conspicuously
from the limbs of trees along our line of march, and labelled, "Such
will be the fate of every forager caught."[61]

At a later stage of the march, in King and Queen County, "many
of our foragers who straggled out a little from the main body were
found with their throats cut hanging on trees, or otherwise man-
gled and mutilated."

The heat and dust on the return march were even harder to
bear than they had been on the way west. Everyone, the troopers,
the wounded, the prisoners (who took turns riding the troopers'
horses so that they could keep up with the column), and the Negroes of both sexes and all ages—"like the locusts of Egypt for
number; where on earth they all came from no one could tell"—
who followed the "Yankee sogers" to freedom, all suffered equally.[62] The dust was so thick at times, one historian commented,
that "we could not see ten feet ahead, or even distinguish our file
leader."[63]

As always, however, the chief sufferers were the horses. They
gave out by the hundreds, day after day, and were shot without
mercy, the losses being "immense." The Confederates estimated,
probably conservatively, that in the eight days of the retreat Sheridan left "on the average, twelve dead horses to the mile; that besides his losses . . . at the battle, twelve hundred were shot . . . on
his retreat; but he took quite that number from the citizens along
his route, and in a manner that no other man than a Sheridan or
a Sherman would have done."[64]

61. This and the following quotation are from William Hyndman, History of a Cavalry Company (Philadelphia, 1870), 203, 207; "The foraging
had to be done by squadrons, the bushwhackers were so thick." Crowninshield, A History of the First Regiment, 222.
62. Battles and Leaders, IV, 235; Bowen, Regimental History of the
First New York, 190; see also Pyne, First New Jersey Cavalry, 266.
63. Bowen, Regimental History of the First New York, 190.
64. Tobie, First Maine Cavalry, 289; Myers, The Comanches, 306

The march continued, day after weary day, on the north side of the North Anna, through Spotsylvania and Bowling Green, and on the north side of the Mattapony to King and Queen Court House, where Sheridan learned on the eighteenth that supplies were waiting for him at White House.[65] He arrived there, at last, on the twenty-first.

During the eight days that Sheridan took to cover the hundred miles from Trevilian Station to White House, Hampton kept pace with him, but remained south of the rivers so as to keep his command between Sheridan and the Union army. "During several days," Hampton reported, "while we marched on parallel lines I constantly offered battle, which . . . [Sheridan] studiously declined."[66] Just what form the offers of battle took is not described, nor does General Hampton explain why he did not choose the most effective way of offering battle by crossing the river and attacking the Federal column. There is no indication in the records that Sheridan knew he was being offered battle; indeed, General Rodenbough has written that "the enemy came in sight but once during the entire march."[67] Nevertheless, Hampton might have been more aggressive had he not had the same problem with his mounts as did Sheridan; his horses too were starved and suffering from the heat, hundreds were broken down and unfit, and he did not have quite the same freedom as Sheridan had to seize horses from the villages and farms along his route.[68]

When Sheridan arrived at White House, Grant had already crossed the James and was establishing a new base for his army at City Point. There were still left at White House, however, more than nine hundred army wagons and some miscellaneous troops, and when Sheridan reported his arrival there he was sent orders to break up the base and escort the wagons and troops across the

---

(Myers might well have added to his list of those responsible for a merciless seizure of horses from the civilian population Forrest, Morgan, Wheeler, and even Stuart in Pennsylvania); Crowninshield, A History of the First Regiment, 229; see also Wellman, Giant in Gray, 149.

65. Sheridan, Personal Memoirs, I, 426–27; Official Records, Vol. XXXVI, Pt. 1, p. 797.

66. Official Records, Vol. XXXVI, Pt. 1, p. 1096.

67. Battles and Leaders, IV, 235.

68. Wellman, Giant in Gray, 150; McDonald, A History of the Laurel Brigade, 259.

Peninsula and the James to City Point.[69] It was known that Hampton had reached General Lee's army, and both General Meade and Sheridan realized that if his command "had any spirit left" he would probably attack the long train of wagons and its escort as they moved slowly across the Peninsula.[70] To guard against such an attack, Sheridan had David McM. Gregg's division march along roads to the right of the one to Charles City Court House that the wagons, convoyed by Torbert's division, were to take. On the twenty-fourth, a clear, hot, dusty day, Torbert was attacked by a brigade of Hampton's cavalry as the train was passing through Charles City Court House, and at the same time Gregg, at St. Mary's Church, was attacked by Hampton with the rest of his cavalry, and Confederate infantry in support. Concerned about the safety of the wagons and evidently under the impression that the attack on Torbert by a single brigade was the precursor of a much heavier attack, Sheridan told Gregg that he was not to expect any reinforcements.[71]

Fortunately for Gregg, Hampton did not have his command properly organized for the attack until midafternoon, which gave the Federal troopers time to throw up the inevitable breastworks. Gregg had his entire division deployed in line of battle—"there were no disengaged men"—when the attack struck him. Fighting in extreme heat which "prostrated many . . . and produced some deaths," the Federals successfully held off the Confederate cavalrymen and their supporting footsoldiers for about two hours. It then "became evident," in Gregg's words, "that the contest was too unequal to maintain it longer"; in fact, he was driven out of his lines. The led horses, caissons, and as many of the wounded as there was transportation for (all the dead and many of the wounded had to be left behind) were started back to Charles City Court House, eight miles away. Those troops still able to put up a fight retreated by sections, "in confusion . . . completely routed" in Hampton's version, "in the best possible order, without confu-

69. *Official Records*, Vol. XXVI, Pt. 3, p. 784.
70. *Ibid.*, 787; Pt. 1, p. 798.
71. *Ibid.*, Pt. 1, p. 855. Sheridan wrote that "Gregg . . . on discovery of the enemy's superior numbers sent message after message to me concerning the situation, but the messengers never arrived, being either killed or captured, and I remained in total ignorance till dark of the straits his division was in." Sheridan, *Personal Memoirs*, I, 434.

sion or disorder" in Gregg's.[72] The historian of the 10th New York, who was not under any necessity to maintain a reputation as a general, described the retreat in the following terms:

[When the retreat began] we came to a line the staff officers had formed. We passed through this . . . then formed another line. Soon the line we had passed came running through us; and so the retreat was kept up, running and fighting, a distance of about six miles, when the Johnnies stopped chasing us. Our men were completely exhausted. . . . Some died of heat and over-exertion during the night. . . . We realized for the first time how it felt to get a good sound thrashing and then be chased for our lives, somewhat as we had served the Rebs at Trevilian Station two weeks before.[73]

The fight the Second Division put up, coupled with the exhaustion of Hampton's men, saved the wagons, an achievement for which Sheridan gave Gregg full credit.[74] During the night of the twenty-fourth and on the following morning the wagons—which, Sheridan wrote, "ought never to have been left for the cavalry to escort after a fatiguing expedition of three weeks"—were ferried across the James.[75] Sheridan's two divisions followed, and the campaign, which had begun nineteen days before, was at last concluded.

The Trevilian Station expedition fell considerably short of the overly ambitious goals Grant's wishes and General Meade's orders of June 5 had set for it. The battle of June 11, despite Confederate claims to the contrary, was without question a Federal success; not so, however, the fighting on June 12. The campaign as a whole was undoubtedly a failure, and it was absurd of Sheridan to term it a "constant success."

Sheridan used his report of the campaign to set forth his thoughts on the subject of foraging. They are worthy of quota-

72. *Official Records*, Vol. XXXVI, Pt. 1, pp. 855–56, 1097; see also *ibid.*, Vol. XL, Pt. 2, p. 688.
73. Preston, *History of the 10th Regiment*, 213–15.
74. "[Gregg's] steady, unflinching determination to gain time for the wagons to get beyond the point of danger was characteristic of the man, and this was the third occasion on which he had exhibited a high order of capacity and sound judgment since coming under my command." Sheridan, *Personal Memoirs*, I, 435. Gregg's division sustained heavy casualties at St. Mary's Church: 225 dead, wounded, or missing. *Official Records*, Vol. XXXVI, Pt. 3, p. 794.
75. Sheridan, *Personal Memoirs*, I, 436.

tion, to demonstrate the extent to which a tough realism had replaced the romantic notions of 1861:

In these marches we were obliged to live to a great extent on the country . . . consequently many hardships were necessarily brought on the people. . . . I do not believe war to be simply that lines should engage each other in battle, as that is but the duello part—a part which would be kept up so long as those who live at home in peace and plenty could find the best youth of the country to enlist in their cause . . . and therefore do not regret the system of living on the enemy's country. These men or women did not care how many were killed, or maimed, so long as war did not come to their doors, but as soon as it did come in the shape of loss of property, they earnestly prayed for its termination. As war is a punishment, if we can, by reducing its advocates to poverty, end it quicker, we are on the side of humanity.[76]

But this philosophising came later. While Sheridan was still in the process of crossing the James, he was faced with the more immediate problem of how to rescue his Third Division.

76. *Official Records*, Vol. XXXVI, Pt. 1, p. 801.

VI

"The Sound of the Trumpet"

THE STORY OF THE UNION CAVALRY PRESENTED SO FAR has dealt mainly with operations and conditions east of the Blue Ridge, a screen and a barrier that was as much psychological as material. Nevertheless, there was a constant interaction between operations to the east and to the west of the barrier, and a constant movement of troops backward and forward across it.

The 25-mile wide Shenandoah Valley, lying between the Blue Ridge on the east and the Alleghenies on the west, was a well settled, well cleared, hilly belt of fertile land, running from the Potomac southward for about 125 miles, a land of family farms large and small, rich in grain and livestock. The Valley was also a broad highway, over which marched the contending armies of the North and South, Joseph E. Johnston and Robert Patterson in 1861, Stonewall Jackson, John Fremont, and Nathaniel Banks in 1862, Richard Ewell, A. P. Hill, and Longstreet in 1863, and at all times and seasons the Partisan Rangers, guerrillas, and bushwhackers of the Confederacy. For the Army of Northern Virginia, the Valley was not only a vitally important granary, but also the ready means of access to the Potomac, the Chesapeake & Ohio Canal, and the Baltimore & Ohio Railroad, the lifelines to the West of Washington, and hence of the Army of the Potomac. It was through the Valley that Confederate armies could most read-

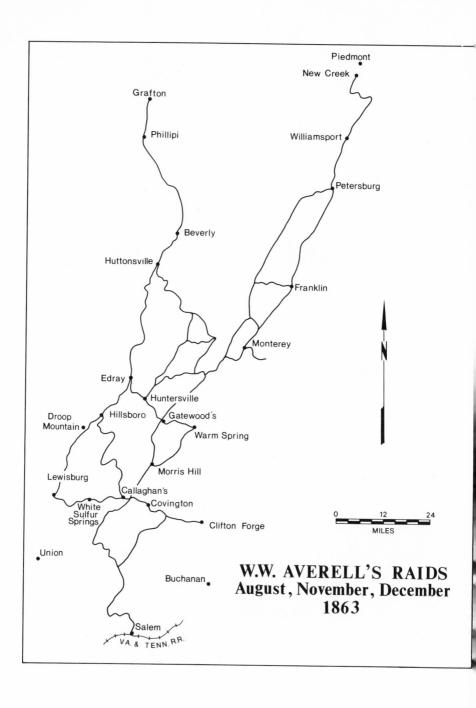

Piedmont

New Creek

Grafton

Phillipi

Williamsport

Petersburg

Beverly

Huttonsville

Franklin

Monterey

Edray

Huntersville

Droop
Mountain

Hillsboro

Gatewood's

Warm Spring

Lewisburg

Morris Hill

Callaghan's

White
Sulfur
Springs

Covington

Clifton Forge

Union

0   12   24

MILES

Buchanan

W.W. AVERELL'S RAIDS
August, November, December
1863

Salem

VA. & TENN. R.R.

ily invade Maryland and Pennsylvania, as they had done in 1862 and 1863 and were to do again in 1864, threatening not only Washington, but also Baltimore, Harrisburg, and even Philadelphia.

Beyond the Allegheny Mountains, extending west into Kentucky and north to the Ohio River, lay the Appalachians, a jumble of steep-sided, heavily forested ridges, more or less parallel, trending generally from northeast to southwest and separated by valleys that were frequently mere narrow troughs between high ridges. This was a sparsely settled, backwoods region, primitive by the standards of the Virginia Tidewater and Piedmont. After the attack on Fort Sumter and passage of the Virginia Ordinance of Secession, the representatives of that state's western counties initiated a movement to remain in the Union by separating from the rest of the state. In June, 1861, in a convention held in Wheeling, they established the "restored [Unionist] Virginia," for which they chose the name "Kanawha," changed later to West Virginia. At the time of its formation the new state's forty-eight counties (not formally admitted into the Union until June, 1863) had a white population—many of southern, pro-Confederate sympathies—of 355,000. Their 19,000 slaves represented less than 5.5 percent of the total population, whereas in Confederate Virginia slaves accounted for upwards of 38 percent of the total. The separation of West Virginia from the Old Dominion, though outwardly an expression of pro-Union feeling, was brought about by a complex of factors: differences in "historical backgrounds, intrastate sectionalism, geography, climate, topography, economic relations, and social diversities."[1]

West Virginia became a battleground in the first summer of the war. In July, 1861, George B. McClellan won a brilliant but small success at Rich Mountain and Carrick's Ford in the north-central part of the new state, which led to his promotion later in the same month to the command of what was to become the Army of the Potomac. Thereafter West Virginia became a military backwater. General Jacob D. Cox gained control of the Kanawha River valley for the Union; the West Virginia Panhandle, sandwiched

1. J. G. Randall, *Lincoln the President* (2 vols.; New York, 1945), II, 12.

between the loyal states of Pennsylvania and Ohio, had been safely in Union hands from the beginning and remained so to the end. The more vulnerable points on the crucially important line of the Baltimore & Ohio, running westward through Grafton and Clarksburg to Parkersburg on the Ohio River, were protected by Union infantry, some in fixed posts and others shuttling forward and back in an effort, futile more often than not, to cope with the frequent Confederate raids against the line. Guerrillas and bushwhackers, Union as well as Confederate, were everywhere.

West Virginia had little to recommend it as a theatre of war. Its scenery of high, wooded ridges and fertile, well watered valleys was magnificent, but its roads were few and poor, its settlements, few and far between, mere hamlets in the wilderness, and its people poor and ignorant. Nonetheless, the state had a strategic value, particularly for the North. It lay on the flank of a long stretch of Confederate territory; from bases in West Virginia, Union armies were in a position to move southeast toward Staunton and the upper Shenandoah Valley and the Virginia Central Railroad, or south toward the Virginia & Tennessee Railroad, which ran in a northeast-southwest direction across the southeastern corner of the state.[2] But conditions were never right for the North to take full advantage of these strategic opportunities. Rugged terrain and poor communications were handicaps that could have been overcome, as they were overcome farther west, but not so the opinion of the Union high command that operations in West Virginia were a military sideshow compared to the campaigns east of the Blue Ridge, along the Mississippi, and in central and eastern Tennessee. There was a momentary gleam of greater possibilities in the spring of 1862, when West Virginia and some contiguous territory were raised to the status of the "Mountain Department" and assigned as a command to John C. Fremont. With thirty-five thousand troops at his disposal, Fremont planned a two-pronged drive against the Virginia & Tennessee Railroad and thence southwest to Knoxville, but this logistically visionary scheme was wrecked, and Fremont's military career along with it, by Stonewall Jackson's Valley Campaign. Thereafter, the department relapsed into inactivity.

2. T. Harry Williams, *Hayes of the Twenty-third: The Civil War Volunteer Officer* (New York, 1965), 69.

The lack of importance the Union army leadership attached to West Virginia was demonstrated by the assignment to commands in the area of officers whose performance in more important posts had been judged less than satisfactory. Thus, William W. Averell, whom Joseph Hooker relieved as commander of the Second Division of the Cavalry Corps because of what Hooker considered to have been his failures at Kelly's Ford and in the Stoneman raid, was exiled to the command of a cavalry brigade in what had by then been reconstituted as the Department of West Virginia. Shortly thereafter, Alfred Duffié, who was deemed to have mishandled his role in the fighting at Aldie-Middleburg, was also relegated to a West Virginia cavalry command.[3]

When Averell and Duffié reported to take up their new assignments, the Department of West Virginia was commanded by Brigadier General Benjamin F. Kelley. Conditions in the department were well illustrated by the makeup of General Kelley's forces. Brigadier General E. Parker Scammon's division, divided into five detachments posted at five widely separated locations, had in its First Brigade, commanded by future president Colonel Rutherford B. Hayes, three regiments of infantry, a battery of artillery, two companies of the 1st West Virginia, and one of the 3rd West Virginia. The Second Brigade consisted of three regiments of infantry and a battery of artillery. The Third Brigade was made up of the 2nd West Virginia and the 34th Ohio Mounted Infantry. The division was thus a "legion," consisting of all three arms under a single command. Brigadier General Henry H. Lockwood's "Maryland Heights Division" had in its First Brigade two companies each of the 1st Connecticut and the 6th Michigan, one company of the 2nd Maryland, three regiments of infantry, and two batteries of artillery; similarly, the Second Brigade contained two mounted units, the "Maryland Battalion (Potomac Home Brigade)" and the Loudoun (Virginia) Ranger Battalion, plus three infantry regiments and two batteries. Colonel Andrew T. McReynolds' command at Martinsburg, not designated as a division, had an infantry brigade of five regiments, and a separate force of cavalry and artillery made up of the 1st New York (Lincoln) and the 12th Pennsylvania, plus detachments of the 1st

3. Duffié's orders to report for duty in West Virginia were dated August 14, 1863. *Official Records*, Vol. XXIX, Pt. 1, p. 49.

and 3rd West Virginia and one company of the "Maryland Battalion" cavalry. Colonel Jacob M. Campbell's brigade, portions of which were to be found at Moorefield, Petersburg, and Romney, had in it three independent companies of cavalry; Colonel Nathan Wilkinson's brigade, at Clarksburg, Grafton, and Parkersburg, had the 4th West Virginia, joined to two regiments of infantry; and Colonel John E. Wynkoop's 20th Pennsylvania was stationed in lonely independence at Sir John's Run.[4] Averell himself was given command of a unit designated the "Fourth Separate Brigade," consisting of two regiments of infantry, two batteries, the 2nd, 3rd, and 8th Regiments of West Virginia Mounted Infantry, the 16th Illinois, an independent company of Ohio cavalry, and one company of the 1st and three of the 3rd West Virginia, the whole numbering 3,855 officers and men present for duty on August 31, 1863.[5]

This roster of the forces at General Kelley's disposal shows clearly that the army high command considered the troops in West Virginia an essentially defensive force, to deal with Confederate raids into the area, to keep the large prosecession portion of the population under control, and to try to cope with the ubiquitous guerrillas and bushwhackers. The scattering of units around the western and northern perimeter of the state could no doubt be justified in part by the rugged terrain and poor communications, but the mixing of cavalry and infantry in the same brigades or divisions, the wide dispersion of individual regiments and battalions of cavalry, and the breaking up of cavalry regiments by the assignment of one or two companies to one brigade or division, and one or two more to another, can only be explained on the theory that the Union forces in West Virginia were considered to be merely a garrison and were not intended to operate in an offensive role. By late summer, 1863, the demonstration by Hooker and Meade of the greatly increased effectiveness of cavalry, particularly in the offensive, when grouped into brigades and divisions, was sufficiently well known and understood. Hence the fragmentation of cavalry in West Virginia must be assumed to be

4. *Ibid.*, 139–41. All the data cited are as of August 31, 1863. General Kelley's command, designated officially as the VIII Army Corps, had on that date 24,096 officers and men present for duty. *Ibid.*, 138.
5. *Ibid.*, 140, 138.

the result of deliberate design, not of ignorance of a potentially better arrangement.

William Averell had a special incentive to show the world what he could do in his new command, for he had to demonstrate that he had been the victim of a glaring injustice at Hooker's hands. He assumed command of his "brigade" at Weston, West Virginia, on May 23. On the same date, three of the infantry regiments in the brigade, the 2nd, 3rd, and 8th West Virginia, were ordered to be converted to mounted infantry, and Averell's troubles began.[6] The three regiments were sent to a "camp of instruction" near Clarksburg and received their horses in the astonishingly short time of two weeks. Saddles, bridles, and other cavalry gear did not arrive, however, until a week after that. By that time the Gettysburg Campaign was in full swing, and General Ewell's corps, leading the Confederate march toward Pennsylvania, was approaching Winchester. A sequence of poorly worded orders from General Robert C. Schenk's headquarters in Baltimore directed Averell to "push eastward, with all the means of re-enforcing . . . [he could] command, to New Creek."[7] Some of the handicaps under which Averell made the ensuing march are worthy of mention, being quite typical of conditions under which the Union forces in West Virginia had to operate, then and later; except in a major emergency, regiments and batteries there were the poor relations of the eastern armies. Averell reported that the 3rd and 8th West Virginia had been transformed from infantry to "cavalry in . . . forty-eight hours, by mounting the men upon green horses"; moreover, "The horses . . . were not shod," and, he pointed out, "Horses cannot travel over the rugged roads of this country without shoes, without breaking down very soon." Even the "ordnance stores" of the two regiments "had been unnecessarily delayed."[8]

Duffié, who had been sent to Charleston, West Virginia, to

6. In the reports of Union officers, these and other West Virginia regiments are frequently referred to with the qualifying word "West" omitted. See, for example, the reference to the "Third and Eighth Virginia" in one of Averell's reports, *ibid.*, Vol. XXVII, Pt. 2, p. 206. In Confederate reports, on the other hand, West Virginia regiments in the Union army are sometimes referred to as, for example, "9th Virginia (bogus)." *Ibid.*, XXXIII, 1288.

7. *Ibid.*, Vol. XXVII, Pt. 2, p. 208.

8. *Ibid.*, 206.

command a four-regiment cavalry brigade, found only two regiments, the 34th Ohio Mounted Infantry and the 2nd West Virginia, plus four companies of the 3rd and two of the 1st West Virginia, actually in camp. Six other cavalry companies—three of the 3rd, two of the 1st, and one of the 2nd West Virginia— were posted in a number of widely separated locations, with the result, Duffié wrote, that "those companies are never drilled, and discipline is unknown to them." The caissons and gun carriages of his artillery, "having been in the service for nearly three years, are completely worn out"; his requisitions for supplies went unfilled, with the result that the 2nd West Virginia, for example, was "unfit for duty, having not a single cartridge." Lastly, the wagons issued to his regiments at the beginning of the war were worn and patched beyond repair, and his transportation was therefore "worthless."[9]

For most of the month of July, Averell's brigade marched and countermarched in the Williamsport-Martinsburg-Winchester area, keeping an eye on the Confederate army as it retreated south after Gettysburg. Then, on August 12 and 14, Averell was sent orders to take his command south to Huntersville, in Pocahontas County, West Virginia, to "attack and capture, or drive . . . out of the county" the troops of Colonel William L. Jackson and, in his march through Pendleton County, to destroy the saltpeter and gunpowder works located there. Then, after disposing of Jackson, and unless he decided that the movement was "impracticable," he was to go on to Lewisburg, in Greenbrier County, "and dispose of any force of the enemy that may be there stationed." Averell was directed to take with him only hardtack, coffee, and sugar, and to rely for fresh meat and forage on requisitioning and captures from the enemy. The mission completed, he was to return to Beverly for a resupply and rest and was then to operate "against Staunton or [John D.] Imboden, as may be deemed best."[10]

Averell's departure on this expedition was delayed by supply

9. *Ibid.*, XXXIII, 403–405. And yet, within a week of this discouraging report Duffié reported that his command was "generally in good condition," that it was "fully supplied with horses, arms, and equipments," and that its horses were well fed, groomed, and shod. He did add, however, that "in some cases much delay occurs in getting . . . requisitions filled." *Ibid.*, 456.
    10. *Ibid.*, Vol. XXIX, Pt. 1, pp. 38, 39.

problems. He needed horseshoes, horseshoe nails, clothing, small-arms ammunition (eventually, he had to leave with no more than thirty-five rounds per man), ammunition for his artillery, and even salt. Most of his wants having been supplied, he set off on the eighteenth. After an uneventful five-day march, "although constantly annoyed by shots from guerrillas who infested the bushes along the way," Averell reached and occupied Huntersville on the twenty-second.[11] Colonel Jackson did not wait to be attacked and captured, but retreated in some haste in the direction of Warm Springs and Millborough, leaving his "Camp Northwest" to be destroyed by Averell's troopers. Deciding that there was little chance of overtaking Jackson, Averell marched south toward Covington and White Sulphur Springs, from where he expected to reach Lewisburg. On the morning of the twenty-sixth, however, as his leading unit—the column behind it was strung out for a distance of four miles on the narrow Callaghan's and White Sulphur Springs Turnpike—had just crossed Allegheny Mountain to the east of White Sulphur Springs, it was met at Rocky Gap by Colonel George S. Patton's nineteen hundred-man brigade of Virginia infantry.[12] An all-day fire fight ensued, neither side being able to budge the other, and toward evening both sides ran low on ammunition. Tactically, the engagement was a Confederate victory, inasmuch as Averell's progress toward Lewisburg was effectively blocked; indeed, after the firing died down late in the evening, he concluded that a retreat would be the better part of wisdom. He decided, however, not to leave until morning, because it would be "impossible to retire during the night without disorder."[13]

11. *Ibid.*, 34. The historian of the 2nd West Virginia Mounted Infantry wrote of this march, "[The regiment] made the march direct to Huntersville . . . meeting with the hidden enemy in the bushes and on the hillsides, not knowing what moment the last call should come to a brave comrade." Frank S. Reader, *History of the Fifth West Virginia Cavalry, Formerly the Second Virginia Infantry, and Battery G, First West Virginia Light Artillery* (New Brighton, W.Va., 1890), 203. (The 2nd [West] Virginia Infantry became first the 2nd West Virginia Mounted Infantry and was then renamed the 5th West Virginia Cavalry.)

12. *Official Records*, Vol. XXIX, Pt. 1, p. 55. For a sketch of the battlefield, see *ibid.*, 1016. Averell believed that Patton had a force of 2,500; he gave his own, actually engaged, as 1,300. *Ibid.*, 37.

13. Averell's report, *ibid.*, 35–36; for the Confederate reports, see *ibid.*, 53–66. Averell's casualties at Rocky Gap were 26 killed, 115 wounded,

Probing attacks in the morning showed the enemy still in position, whereupon "every arrangement was made in rear for a prompt withdrawal."

The ambulances loaded with wounded, the caissons, wagons, and long columns of horses were placed in proper order upon the road, details made for the attendance of the wounded, trees prepared to fall across the gorge when our artillery should have passed, and commanding officers received their instructions. . . . At 10:30 o'clock the order to retire was given, and in forty-five minutes from that time my column was moving off in good order, my rear guard at the barricades repulsing the enemy's advance twice before it left the ground. Successive barricades were formed, and my column reached Callaghan's about 5 p. m., where it was halted, fires built, and the men and horses given the first opportunity to eat in thirty-six hours.[14]

Averell reached Beverly on August 31, after a retreat that may not have been quite so deliberate and orderly as his narrative suggests. In his description of the arrangements for starting the retreat, he neglected to mention that he left behind at Rocky Gap fifty-seven of his wounded. He did write, however, that following the halt at Callaghan's "after dark the fires were left burning and the column took the road to Warm Springs."[15] Abandoning one's wounded, a night march, and fires left burning to deceive the enemy may be taken as indications of a more severe enemy pressure and a greater anxiety about the safety of his command than Averell was willing to admit.

Through September and October Averell and Duffié remained quietly at Beverly and Charleston, respectively. On October 26, however, acting on wishes "intimated" by General Halleck, General Kelley ordered Averell to proceed "as soon as . . . [he could] possibly get ready" to Lewisburg, "attack and capture, or drive away, the rebel force stationed at that place," and, after forming a junction with Duffié who was ordered to meet him at Lewisburg with two regiments of cavalry, two of infantry, and a battery, to go on to Union, in Monroe County, and thence to the Virginia &

---

and 67 captured or missing; Patton's, 20 killed, 129 wounded, and 13 missing. *Ibid.*, 41, 56.
    14. *Ibid.*, 36–37.
    15. *Ibid.*

Tennessee Railroad bridge over New River, the destruction of which was the principal goal of the expedition. A special incentive for the destruction of the bridge was Longstreet's presence in east Tennessee with two divisions of the Army of Northern Virginia; a serious break in the Virginia & Tennessee would cut off his communications with the East, except by the roundabout route through Atlanta.[16]

Averell left Beverly on November 1 with four regiments and a separate battalion of mounted troops, two regiments of infantry, and two batteries. He marched south to Huntersville, but from there, instead of turning eastward as he had done in August, he took the direct road to Lewisburg through Mill Point and Hillsboro. There was some opposition from William Jackson's troops, but it did not become a serious hindrance until the morning of November 6, when the column reached Droop Mountain and found the road over the mountain to Lewisburg blockaded by Jackson's command, General John Echols' brigade of infantry, and a portion of the 14th Virginia from Albert G. Jenkins' brigade.[17] An examination of the ground caused Averell to conclude that a frontal attack uphill, across two and a half miles of cultivated fields, on Echols' position on top of the mountain was impractical. He therefore sent his two infantry regiments—the 28th Ohio and the 10th West Virginia—1,175 strong, and commanded by Colonel Augustus Moor of the Ohio regiment—on a wide circuit to the west, to attack Echols' left flank and rear.[18]

Making a nine-mile march "in a zigzag line along ditches and behind fences," Moor managed to get within twenty-five or thirty yards of the Confederate flank before his approach through the trees and dense underbrush was detected. Without taking time to

16. *Ibid.*, 499, 501–502. Duffié, who had a shorter distance to travel, was given his orders on October 30. The two columns were intended to arrive at Lewisburg simultaneously on the afternoon of November 7.

17. Echols' brigade was the unit commanded by George S. Patton as senior colonel in the fight at Rocky Gap on August 26.

18. *Official Records*, Vol. XXIX, Pt. 1, pp. 505–506. General Echols stated that he had seventeen hundred men at Droop Mountain and claimed that he was opposed by seven thousand under Averell, the latter figure being a gross exaggeration, not uncommon in the reports of officers on both sides. Averell actually had between three and four thousand men, and he in turn believed that Echols had "about 4,000." *Ibid.*, 500, 501.

deploy, Moor ordered a charge, and "with cheers completely drowning the hideous yells of the enemy," his men surged forward.[19] At the sound of Moor's attack, Averell sent forward the 2nd, 3rd, and 8th West Virginia Mounted Infantry in a dismounted charge up the mountain. The twin charges were decisive. Echols was driven out of his position in "total rout . . . [his] forces, throwing away their arms . . . scattered in every direction," according to Averell; or, if one prefers Echols' version, he "gave orders to the troops to fall back slowly." His carefully modulated language makes it evident, however, that the retreat, whether ordered by him or spontaneous, was both rapid and chaotic, and in the course of it many of his men simply disappeared into the woods. In any event, the portion of Echols' command that remained together made an all-night march back to Lewisburg and kept right on going to the hamlet of Union, fifteen miles farther south.[20]

Duffié had left Charleston with his four regiments on the morning of November 3. He was delayed somewhat by "blockades in the road," but by the evening of the sixth was within fifteen miles of Lewisburg. Having learned that Averell was fighting the enemy on Droop Mountain, he did the correct thing: starting his march at three A.M. on the seventh, he pushed forward as fast as his men could march, "with the purpose of placing . . . [his] command in the enemy's rear, that we might capture their whole force between . . . [his own] forces and those of General Averell."[21] Unfortunately for Duffié's excellent intentions, Echols was too fast for him; when Duffié entered Lewisburg at about nine A.M., Echols had already marched through the town and was well on his way to Union. Duffié pursued, but the Confederates had a two hours' start and all he was able to accomplish was the capture of a few men of their rear guard, two caissons, and 110 head of cattle.

Averell and his command reached Lewisburg on the afternoon

19. Ibid., 511.
20. Averell itemized his casualties at Droop Mountain as 30 killed, 88 wounded, and 1 missing. Echols merely stated that his casualties totaled 275 killed, wounded, and missing and added the stereotyped phrase, greatly favored by defeated commanders, "the loss of the enemy was much greater." Ibid., 503, 511.
21. Ibid., 523.

of the same day and found "as much destruction going on as if the town had been given over to plunder." The culprits were evidently Duffié's men. Colonel James M. Schoonmaker of the 14th Pennsylvania and his provost marshal succeeded, however, in stopping the destruction and "in partially restoring order."[22]

The destruction and looting by Duffié's men were not the only unpleasant aspects of the expedition. It also gave Averell the opportunity to display the pettiness and propensity for backbiting that were a part of his complex character, and may at least partially explain his failure to rise as high as his opportunities in the cavalry would have allowed. He had won a well planned, well executed engagement at Droop Mountain and could certainly afford to be generous. There was no reason, and no excuse, for him to write, as he did, that Duffié reached Lewisburg at ten P.M., "capturing a few stragglers and such material as the enemy was unable to remove in his flight" and to imply that Echols' escape was Duffié's fault.[23]

Nor was this all. It was still midafternoon when Averell arrived at Lewisburg. It may be taken for granted that Duffié reported to him the results of his pursuit of Echols toward Union earlier in the day, but not until the next morning did Averell decide to move forward to Union, as his orders required. This produced another unaccountable discrepancy in the reports. According to Duffié, *he* was ordered to pursue; he marched out and, leaving his infantry behind on the road, got to within eight miles of Union with his cavalry when he was ordered by Averell to return to Lewisburg, being ordered subsequently to march his entire command back to Meadow Bluff, where he had bivouacked on the night of the sixth.[24] According to Averell, however, he himself moved out on the morning of the eighth with his "whole com-

22. *Ibid.*, 519.
23. In fairness to Averell, it should be said that the "10 P.M." may be an error for ten A.M., either in his report or in the printed version in the *Official Records*. In any case, he implies that Duffié was to blame for Echols' escape. Duffié was of course equally unfair and petty, stating in his report, "Had General Averell, instead of attacking the enemy in force and making a general engagement [at Droop Mountain] engaged him lightly, detaining him until my command reached Lewisburg, it is my opinion that we might have captured almost the entire rebel force." *Ibid.*, 524. Obviously, there was no love lost between the two men.
24. *Ibid.*

mand" to march to Union, but, he wrote, "General Duffié reported his command as unfit for further operations, as his infantry had but one day's rations, and was so exhausted as to be able to march only 10 miles per day. My own infantry was encumbered with the prisoners, captured property, and *matériel*. I therefore ordered General Duffié to retire to Meadow Bluff, and Colonel Moor to return to Beverly." For this or some other reason Averell decided to go no farther and to return to his base. He made the return march via White Sulphur Springs, Callaghan's, Franklin, and Petersburg to New Creek on the Baltimore & Ohio, where he arrived safely on November 17.[25]

Averell's account strongly suggests that the state of Duffié's command was his main reason for giving up the pursuit of Echols and the attempt to destroy the Virginia & Tennessee bridge over New River. Duffié had indeed reported that his infantry was "footsore and without rations (by reason of their wagons having broken down)"[26] But Averell was pursuing an enemy he had driven from a strong defensive position "in total rout" less than forty-eight hours before; he had at his disposal the four regiments he had taken with him on this raid, plus a battalion of cavalry, Duffié's two cavalry regiments, and the two infantry regiments— presumably not footsore or without rations—of his own command, a respectable force of upwards of four thousand men. If Averell had had the drive and the instinct for the jugular of a Sheridan, or a Forrest, or a Custer, he could have left his prisoners and captures at Lewisburg, to be guarded by Duffié's footsore infantry, and gone after Echols and on to the bridge with the rest of the combined command.

Why did he fail to do this? He was told at Lewisburg on the evening of the seventh that Echols was "promised heavy reinforcements" at Dublin, Virginia, roughly forty-five miles south of Union on the Virginia & Tennessee—the location of the New River bridge. Such information, or rumor, was notoriously unreliable, but added to his other difficulties, real or imagined, it was enough to cause Averell to decide that he had done enough and that it would not be prudent for him to go farther.[27] The main

25. *Ibid.*, 507.
26. *Ibid.*, 523.
27. *Ibid.*, 504.

objective of the expedition had not been accomplished, but on his return to New Creek Averell was apparently able to persuade General Kelley to accept without demur the propriety of his decision not to go on to Dublin. It is significant, however, that in his report to General Halleck, Kelley spoke of the "most commendable spirit and gallantry" the *troops* had displayed on the expedition, but, despite Averell's creditable performance at Droop Mountain, made no mention of his leadership, not even in the stereotyped language commonly resorted to in such cases.[28]

Whatever may be thought of General Halleck's gifts as general-in-chief, he must be given high marks for persistence. On December 5, within two weeks of Averell's return to New Creek, "in pursuance of . . . [General Halleck's] intimated wishes" General Kelley once again ordered Averell to take his command south through Petersburg, Franklin, and Monterey, "to the line of the Virginia and Tennessee Railroad, at Bonsack's Station, in Botetourt County, or Salem, in Roanoke County, and there destroy the railroad as thoroughly as practicable." As part of an elaborate program of deception worked out by Averell, Kelley ordered General Scammon to move his division from Charleston to Lewisburg and Union, as a threat to the railroad at Dublin, and General Jeremiah C. Sullivan to send his cavalry and two regiments of infantry up the Shenandoah Valley to Harrisonburg, as a threat to Staunton. Colonel Moor, still at Beverly with the 28th Ohio and 10th West Virginia Regiments of infantry, was ordered south to Droop Mountain to assist Scammon at Lewisburg. Colonel Joseph Thoburn, with two regiments of West Virginia infantry, was to join Averell for the first part of the march south and was then to remain behind at "some selected point" with the major portion of Averell's trains, to await his return. Indeed, the Kelley-Averell plans provided for every contingency but one: they failed to take into account the near certainty of bad weather in December in the West Virginia mountains.[29]

Averell had had a few days' advance notice of the intended movement, "but owing to the meager supplies of horse-shoes, nails, coal, and forges . . . and the shortness of the time allowed, the mounted forces of the brigade were but poorly prepared to

28. *Ibid.*, 501.
29. *Ibid.*, 920–21, 923, 916.

make a long march." Nonetheless, the brigade departed from New Creek on the morning of the eighth, with the 2nd, 3rd, and 8th West Virginia Mounted Infantry, the 14th Pennsylvania, Major Thomas Gibson's independent battalion of cavalry, and Captain Chatham T. Ewing's battery making up the column. The weather was "bright and beautiful," but Averell had "many misgivings on account of our poor condition to overcome the weary distances and confront the perils incident to such an expedition."[30] Justified or not, such misgivings were hardly a promising state of mind for the commander of a more than usually hazardous enterprise; quite different in spirit from Sheridan's "I shall expect nothing but success." Despite Averell's forebodings, however, all went well at first except for the weather, which did not remain "bright and beautiful"; it turned cold on the eleventh and the next day brought a severe rain storm, which continued for the three following days.

Colonel Thoburn and his infantry and most of Averell's trains were left behind at Monterey, the half-way point to Salem, on the twelfth, after the troopers had been issued sufficient rations for themselves and forage for their horses to last, supposedly, until their return to Monterey. At the same time there was a combing-out of the command; "all men and officers unfit for severe duty were sent back to New Creek, only the able bodied, well equipped and well mounted going forward."[31]

For most of the way south Averell avoided the main roads and followed what he called "secluded" roads—rough paths running beside mountain streams or atop ridges. Sensible from the standpoint of security, the use of these backwoods trails nevertheless had its disadvantages. On the way down Back Creek, for example, in the twenty-three miles from just below Monterey to Gatewood's, the men had to ford the creek, "which was swollen very high and was very swift," no less than thirteen times. By then a thorough wetting had become a serious affair, for it had turned "intensely cold, the wind blew hard from the north," and the rain, continuing to fall, was mixed with sleet and snow.[32]

The head of the column was preceded by "vigilant scouts,

30. Ibid., 926; Reader, History of the Fifth West Virginia, 222.
31. Reader, History of the Fifth West Virginia, 222.
32. Ibid., 223.

armed with repeating rifles, mounted upon fleet horses, who permitted no one to go ahead of them."[33] As a result of their efforts
and with the aid of the bad weather, the approach of the column
was not detected by the enemy until it was within four miles of
Salem. Indeed, so free was the march from enemy interference
that Averell had the leisure to notice and admire the magnificent
mountain scenery around him. Marching along the top of Sweet
Spring Mountain, a long ridge south of the springs of that name,
he was enraptured by what he saw: "From the top of this mountain a sublime spectacle was presented to us. Seventy miles to the
eastward the Peaks of Otter reared their summits above the Blue
Ridge, and all the space was filled with a billowing ocean of hills
and mountains, while behind us the great Alleghanies, coming
from the north with the grandeur of innumerable tints, swept
past and faded in the southern horizon."[34]

On the morning of the sixteenth, riding with an advance party
of 350 cavalry and a section of artillery, Averell entered Salem.[35]
There were no Confederate troops in the village, and the Federals
were able to set about the work of destruction without hindrance;
Averell sent parties along the railroad four miles to the east and
twelve miles to the west to burn bridges, break up culverts, and
tear up the track "as much as possible in six hours" and, he might
have added, with limited manpower.[36] Five bridges were burned,
but it was found that the device that had been issued to twist track
so that it could not be straightened by rerolling was too weak to
do the job properly, and the men had to fall back on the more

33. *Official Records*, Vol. XXIX, Pt. 1, p. 928. Some of these scouts
wore Confederate uniforms. Reader, *History of the Fifth West Virginia*, 223.
34. *Official Records*, Vol. XXIX, Pt. 1, p. 927.
35. Averell did not mention in his report that to get to Salem by the
morning of the sixteenth his men rode all through the night of the fifteenth.
As a result, "the condition of the troops was bad. Many horses were broken
down, more lame, [and] some of the men were obliged to walk." Reader,
History of the Fifth West Virginia, 224–25.
36. According to Reader, Averell's main body did not reach Salem
until noon and started on the return march at "about 3 P.M." Even if
Averell had put his entire force of about twenty-five hundred men (*Official
Records*, Vol. XXIX, Pt. 1, p. 931; Reader's figure of fifteen hundred, in *History of the Fifth West Virginia*, 225, is either erroneous or a misprint) to
work tearing up the track, they could not have caused much damage in so
short a time.

common but less destructive method of heating the rails in the middle so that they could then be wound around the nearest tree or telegraph pole; this, however, "was but [a] partial success" in the limited time available.[37] On the other hand, the depot at Salem, two large warehouses adjacent to it, three cars, "the water-station, turn-table, and a large pile of bridge timber and repairing material" were set on fire, and Averell carefully itemized the quantities of supplies that went up in flames, the flour, wheat, corn, oats, meat, salt, clothing, cotton, and wagons, plus large quantities of leather, harness, shoes, saddles, tools, oil, tar, "and various other stores." Needless to say, the quantities of destroyed supplies reported later by Commissary Captain James Wade of the Confederate army bear little resemblance to Averell's figures.[38]

Having accomplished the object of the expedition, Averell now had the problem of deciding on the route to follow to get back to his base. His men and horses were worn out, having covered the last eighty miles to Salem in thirty hours with little sleep or rest since leaving Monterey five days before. Hence, leaving Salem late on the afternoon of the sixteenth, Averell stopped after a seven-mile march to give his people and animals a night's rest. To add to his difficulties, a heavy rain began to fall during the night and continued for the next twenty-four hours.

As far north as New Castle, about twenty-five miles by road from Salem, Averell followed the route he had taken on the march south. The road ran along the Craig's Creek bottoms; the column, Averell wrote, "was caught in the many windings of Craig's Creek, which was now swollen to a dangerous torrent, which uprooted trees and carried them away. Heavy caissons were swept down the stream, and great exertion and skill were required to save them . . . [the] command, drenched, muddy and hungry, arrived at New Castle about sundown on the 18th, in miserable condition

37. *Official Records*, Vol. XXIX, Pt. 1, p. 928.
38. Averell claimed to have destroyed 2,000 barrels of flour, 10,000 bushels of wheat, 100,000 bushels of shelled corn, 50,000 bushels of oats, 2,000 barrels of meat, 1,000 sacks of salt, etc. Captain Wade's figures were 143 barrels of flour, 150 bushels of wheat, 130 bushels of corn, and no oats. *Ibid.*, 928, 929. Wade did, however, qualify his figures with the statement that they were "not exact, but they are as near the true amount as I can get until my records are made up."

to make the march before us."[39] The historian of the 2nd West Virginia Mounted Infantry provides a graphic account of the troopers' struggle with Craig's Creek:

[The stream] was full of slush, ice and driftwood. . . . The road crossed the creek seven times within a distance of ten or twelve miles . . . and there was no alternative but to ford the wild stream. The water was mid-rib deep on the large horses, and the current so strong that the animals had to be kept with their breasts up the stream and worked across sideways. If the current . . . [was] permitted to strike the horses sideways . . . horse and rider were carried downstream, and a number of men were drowned in this way. . . . The weather was so cold, part of the time below zero, that the clothing of the men was frozen stiff soon after leaving the water. The horses were covered with icicles and trembling from the cold. . . . After a few crossings . . . it was with difficulty the horses were forced into the stream, and they were whipped and spurred to compel obedience.[40]

This was a cavalry operation in the winter of 1863—a far cry from the gaudy expectations of romance and glamor of the summer of 1861.

Much of the ammunition carried by the command, in the men's pouches and in the wagons, was ruined by the rain and by the crossings of Craig's Creek. Hence Averell had to plan his onward course so as to avoid, if possible, any serious fight with the enemy.[41]

General Samuel Jones, in command of the Confederate Department of Western Virginia, took charge of the effort to catch the raiders. He had learned on December 12 of Scammon's advance from Charleston and Moor's from Beverly, and on the fifteenth of Averell's approach to Salem.[42] He concluded, quite correctly, that Scammon's and Moor's movements were mere feints, and since he had neither the time nor the troops to intercept Averell before he reached Salem, Jones devoted his efforts to preventing the raiders' escape. In response to his pleas to Richmond for help, Fitzhugh Lee and his two brigades of cavalry, Imboden's brigade, the Rockville Home Guards, and Jubal Early with two

39. Ibid., 928–29.
40. Reader, History of the Fifth West Virginia, 225–26.
41. Official Records, Vol. XXIX, Pt. 1, p. 929.
42. Ibid., 941–42, 949.

brigades of infantry were hurried west. Jones had under his own control the regiments of Colonels Jackson and John McCausland, and Echols' brigade. With these units of his own, which Averell outnumbered by a considerable margin, Jones blocked the raiders' way north by the route they had followed on their way south. To escape they would either have to make a wide circuit through rugged country to the west, or else, by taking a more direct route past Echols' eastern flank, take their chances on crossing Jackson's River (considered unfordable at that time of the year) by capturing the bridges across it either at Covington or at Clifton Forge. Jones, who knew that Early was on his way to help him, but did not know that Fitzhugh Lee and Imboden had also been ordered to his support, sent a dispatch to Early on the morning of the nineteenth, describing in detail the position of his troops and suggesting that Early deploy his infantry to block the Jackson's River crossings that Averell was likely to try to use. Averell had the good fortune to capture this dispatch the same day and thus learned where Jones's troops were located. Jones's suggestion that Early send a "force to Morris Hill and a strong picket to Callaghan's," and the information that Jones had ordered a portion of his "small mounted force" to send word to Early if the raiders tried to escape by way of Clifton Forge or Covington, allowed Averell to infer that the last two of these points were guarded lightly or not at all. He therefore decided to march to Covington, gambling, with the odds clearly in his favor, that he could get there, capture a bridge, and get across the river before Early could intervene.[43]

Early of course did not receive Jones's dispatch. Furthermore, he encountered delays in moving his two brigades westward by rail from Staunton and by late in the evening of the nineteenth had gotten only as far as Millborough Depot, twenty-five miles northeast of Covington. Also, as it turned out, Lee and Imboden were completely out of the hunt. On the strength of erroneous reports they received from Echols on the evening of the eighteenth to the effect that Averell had turned back to Salem, they decided that he would try to escape eastward from there and rode south to Buchanan to intercept him. By the time the error was rectified and

43. *Ibid.*, 929–30. Averell implies that he made his decision to cross Jackson's River at Covington before he saw Jones's intercepted dispatch.

they turned back, Averell was two days' march ahead of them.[44]

In the meantime, at about midnight on the eighteenth Averell had reached a point about twelve miles north of New Castle. There he had to stop to allow his men to build fires and thaw out, but he resumed the march after a short halt "in the darkest and coldest night . . . [the] command had yet experienced."[45] At nine in the evening of the nineteenth, after a thirty-mile march, he reached Covington. For the last two or three miles, the road he was on ran through "a deep, narrow defile . . . and [was] so narrow that it was with the greatest difficulty for any one to pass from the rear to the front. The road bed was covered with ice, and it was impossible to prevent the horses from falling."[46]

The events at Covington on the evening of the nineteenth are extraordinarily difficult to reconstruct from Averell's report, and there are no reports by his subordinates to resolve the questions and doubts his report raises. What apparently happened is that some distance south of Covington the Federal column encountered "300 mounted rebels" (presumably a home guard unit), drove them north, and seized the two bridges across Jackson's River. Colonel Jackson had tried to protect both bridges by dividing his regiment between them, stationing himself midway between the two crossings. The bridges had been prepared for burning, and when the Federals appeared Jackson ordered them fired, but the messenger carrying the order was captured and in the absence of orders the bridge guards failed to act. It would seem, however, that some of Averell's men were already across the river when Jackson ordered the bridges burned, so that his orders would have been too late in any event.[47]

Then came one of the puzzling aspects of the affair. Three of Averell's regiments, Gibson's battalion, and the artillery crossed the river, but the 14th Pennsylvania, stragglers from the other regiments, and all that was left of the trains remained south of the river. Why they did not cross, or were not ordered to do so, is

44. *Ibid.*, 970, 971.
45. *Ibid.*, 929.
46. Reader, *History of the Fifth West Virginia*, 226–27.
47. Colonel Jackson's handling of the defense of Covington appears to have been singularly inept and aroused "great indignation" among the townspeople. *Official Records*, Vol. XXIX, Pt. 1, p. 946; see also pp. 950–54.

nowhere explained in Averell's narrative; he merely reports that they were "detained" "by the darkness and difficulties," which, however, had not prevented the rest of the command from crossing.[48] Jackson took advantage of the situation by making a night attack on the laggards, taking 119 of them prisoner. Later in the night, apparently, the rest of the contingent tried to fight its way through to one of the bridges, but all three of the attacks it made were repulsed.[49]

Another mystery surrounds the events of the morning of the twentieth. "Finding it impossible to dislodge the enemy as long as the bridges remained," Averell ordered them destroyed, notwithstanding that a sizable number of his men, as well as his ambulances and trains, were still on the other side. He did send orders to them "to swim the river, or come . . . over the mountain around the bend" but his failure to explain where the enemy was located that morning or why they had to be "dislodged" makes incomprehensible his order to destroy the bridges and thereby sacrifice a portion of his command.[50]

Having received Averell's orders, Lieutenant Colonel William Blakely, commanding the 14th Pennsylvania, chose to try to "swim the river." Before starting he destroyed all the wagons and ambulances; then, when he reached the stream, he found it "swollen and full of floating ice and drift."

Several of the Fourteenth Pennsylvania Cavalry plunged into the river to cross, but some of them were drowned in the attempt. A citizen had been asked if the river was fordable at this place, when he stated that it was perfectly safe, which led to the drowning of our men. The citizen was at once thrown in and was drowned. A woman who lived near the burned bridge was then asked to inform us where we could find a fording place, which she at first refused to do; but upon threatening to burn her house, she told us there was a ford some distance up the river.[51]

48. *Ibid.*, 924.
49. *Ibid.*, 930–31, 953–54.
50. *Ibid.*, 931.
51. Reader, *History of the Fifth West Virginia*, 227. Six of the seven men the command lost by drowning belonged to the 14th Pennsylvania; four of the six were drowned at Covington. The casualties of the entire command were 7 wounded, 7 drowned, 122 taken prisoner (119 at Covington), and 1 missing. *Official Records*, Vol. XXIX, Pt. 1, p. 932.

The crossing whose existence the woman revealed under duress was Holloway's Ford, two miles upstream from the supposed ford the Federals had first tried. Colonel Blakely and his men reached Holloway's without molestation and got across the river. Confederate Quartermaster Major Edward McMahon, who visited Covington several days later, was told by the local people that Blakely was able to escape because Jackson's men, "instead of gathering up stragglers . . . were running about plundering and gathering up property abandoned by the enemy, and . . . almost every crime has been perpetrated by . . . [Jackson's] command from burglary down to rape."[52]

His command reunited at Callaghan's, Averell marched away northwestward. He had learned of the presence of an enemy force east of Huntersville, thirty miles north of where he then was. He was marching along the east bank of the Greenbrier River and decided that if he could get across it to the west bank and reach Marling's Bottom (now Marlinton) he would be safe. The problem was finding a place to cross the unbridged stream. The historian of the 5th West Virginia tells how this was accomplished:

A [Negro] boy perhaps twelve years old, said he knew a way across Greenbrier River by a ford far above Lewisburg. . . . The boy led us up Oggle Creek and down Anthony's Creek, over the Alleghany Mountains—high, rough, wild and icy. The horses were taken from the artillery and long ropes attached; men were dismounted, and drew the pieces up and down that fearful mountain path. Our advance reached the Greenbrier River at dark the evening of December 20. We found the stream swollen and full of floating ice. . . . Cakes of ice ten to fifteen feet square, and heavy enough to submerge a horse, were constantly passing. The order came to plunge in and cross. This was accomplished without loss.[53]

The Greenbrier was crossed on the morning of the twenty-first, opposite Hillsboro. The command bivouacked at the northern foot of Droop Mountain that night and went on toward Edray the following day. From that point north to Beverly, another forty miles away as the crow flies and farther by the winding, twisting, hilly paths the command had to use, the hardihood of the men was

52. See map, *Official Records*, Vol. XXIX, Pt. 1, p. 947, and also p. 496.
53. Reader, *History of the Fifth West Virginia*, 228.

tested to the limit. The road had become a "glacier . . . traversed with great difficulty and peril. The artillery was drawn almost entirely by dismounted men during the 23d and 24th."[54] Averell had sent couriers on ahead to Beverly to ask that rations and forage be sent forward to meet him. This was successfully accomplished "after extreme hardships," and from the twenty-fourth until the twenty-sixth, when the raiders at last reached Beverly, the men and animals had something to eat after being "without rations eight days in a wild, desolate region which furnished barely enough to prevent starvation."[55]

In terms of the hardships suffered by the men, the Salem Raid, now concluded, was probably the most severe and testing enterprise of its kind in the entire war. Half jokingly, Averell said in the dispatch he sent from Edray that up to the twenty-second his men had "marched, climbed, slid and swum 355 miles"; in his formal report he wrote, "The officers and men . . . endured all the sufferings from fatigue, hunger, and cold with extraordinary fortitude, even with cheerfulness. The march of 400 miles . . . was the most difficult I have ever seen performed. The endurance of the men and horses was taxed to the utmost."[56]

The descriptions in the history of the 5th West Virginia of the crossings of Craig's Creek, Jackson's River, and the Greenbrier make it evident that the hardships the men had undergone were if anything more severe than Averell's rather stilted account indicates. But what did they have to show for their sixteen days of unrelieved misery, for the seven men drowned, and the other casualties? They took two hundred prisoners, but kept only eighty-four; the others had to be turned loose "on account of their inability to walk."[57] They captured about 150 horses, far short of the number they themselves lost. They destroyed some quantity of supplies, substantially less, apparently, than they estimated.

54. *Official Records*, Vol. XXIX, Pt. 1, p. 931. In an earlier dispatch, Averell had written, "For three days my guns were dragged, almost entirely by the men, over roads so slippery that horses could gain no foothold, and some limbs were broken and men otherwise injured by their falling." *Ibid.*, 925.
55. *Ibid.*, 931, 925.
56. *Ibid.*, 925, 931–32.
57. *Ibid.*, 925.

These, however, were incidentals. The objective of the expedition, and the justification for all the hardships and casualties, was to break up a stretch of the Virginia & Tennessee Railroad and interrupt communications between Virginia and Knoxville. This was not accomplished, nor could it have been in the few hours Averell spent in Salem. If General Jones's account is to be believed, and there is no reason why it should not be, the "damage done the railroad was repaired in three or four days. The railroad was rather improved than injured by the raid, as the few small bridges [destroyed] were in such condition that they were scarcely safe, and would have required rebuilding very soon."[58]

The raid, at any rate, had a most heartening aftermath. On arriving at Beverly Averell reported to General Halleck, "The clothing of my men has been ruined in this expedition by being torn, burned, wet and frozen, and I request that the Quartermaster's Department be directed to make them a New Year's gift of a new suit throughout."[59] Halleck rose to the occasion; the command had complete new outfits for the New Year and not a cent was charged against the men's clothing allowances.

58. *Ibid.*, 945.
59. *Ibid.*, 925.

VII

"War . . . is toil and trouble"

FROM THE BEGINNING OF THE WILDERNESS CAMPAIGN to the end of the war a year later, Grant's constant desire was to have broken up the railroads from the north, west, and south that kept the people of Richmond and Petersburg alive and brought General Lee the food and supplies he needed to keep on fighting. One manoeuver after another, as far afield as the Shenandoah Valley and West Virginia, and order after order expressed Grant's determination to have these railroads destroyed and kept out of operation as long as possible. By the summer of 1864 the railroads of the South—roadbed, locomotives, and rolling stock—were in deplorable condition; they were nevertheless vital to the survival of the Confederacy, as both Grant and General Lee well understood.

When Sheridan with two of his divisions and the Reserve Brigade departed on the railroad-breaking expedition that ended at Trevilian Station, he left behind with the Army of the Potomac all his dismounted men, Wilson's Third Division, and on call in case of need General August V. Kautz's small cavalry division of the Army of the James.[1]

As the only major body of mounted troops left with the army, the Third Division was kept fully occupied protecting its advance

1. Kautz had been made chief of cavalry of the Army of the James on April 30, 1864. *Official Records*, XXXIII, 930.

to the James. As Grant's infantry crossed the river, Wilson's over-worked horsemen, after crossing the river themselves, were even ordered to recross to perform the humiliating duty of guarding the army's "great herd of cattle."[2] After a week of almost continuous marching, scouting, picketing, and skirmishing in the midsummer heat, the division was exhausted. Wilson had to report on June 17 that for several days he had been without forage and on short rations, that his men had been on duty without a break for three days and nights, and that he needed desperately a short rest, so that he could unsaddle his horses, draw supplies, and allow his men and animals a chance to recover.[3] He received permission to do so, but by the twentieth Grant was writing Meade that as soon as Wilson was able to move, he was to make a raid to the Weldon, Southside, and Richmond & Danville railroads.[4] After reading Grant's order, which Meade had forwarded to him, Wilson reported that his division was ready for "light work," but would need until the twenty-second to prepare for the kind of expedition Grant had requested. In the same dispatch he asked that at least one brigade of Kautz's division be added to his command for the raid, and he asked for the "necessary implements" for breaking up track.[5]

A month earlier Kautz had led his division on a raid against the Weldon and the Norfolk & Petersburg railroads and had burned the 210-foot bridge of the latter over the Nottoway River. Two days after returning from this raid he was off on another, against the Richmond & Danville. On this raid, only moderately successful, Kautz and his men marched from thirty to forty miles a day for six days and brought back with them several hundred mules and a "large number" of Negroes. In his report on the two raids Kautz said he was pleased with the fighting qualities of his men, but deplored their "disposition to pillage and plunder . . . and a want of proper officering on the part of the officers to check this tendency."[6] Immediately after his return from the second raid, Kautz reported that "from 500 to 1,000 [of his] horses . . .

2. *Ibid.*, Vol. XL, Pt. 1, pp. 13, 18, 19, 24.
3. *Ibid.*, Pt. 2, pp. 71, 139, 140.
4. *Ibid.*, 232, 255.
5. *Ibid.*, 256.
6. *Ibid.*, Vol. XXXVI, Pt. 2, pp. 697, 171–75.

[were] disabled so as to be unfit for use for several weeks, and quite a number . . . never will be fit for service."[7] Such losses were the usual price paid for any cavalry raid, successful or not.

On June 20 Grant directed General Butler to send as much of Kautz's division as he could spare to Wilson for the forthcoming raid. Butler, who was not always so accommodating, outdid himself on this occasion; he sent Kautz's entire division of 2,414 officers and men.[8] Colonel Robert M. West commanded the First Brigade, made up of the 3rd New York and the 5th Pennsylvania; Colonel Samuel P. Spear commanded the Second Brigade, containing the 11th Pennsylvania and the 1st District of Columbia.[9] Wilson was unkind enough to describe the command as a "so-called division," "small and poorly organized," and, on a later occasion, as the "wildest rag-tag and bob-tail cavalry I ever saw."[10] There was apparently some justification for these strictures, for Kautz himself reported three weeks later that "in addition to the great variety of arms and caliber" in his command, there was also a "great deficiency of proper arms. . . . Repeated requisitions for carbines have been made but have not been filled." He went on to point out that "Without a serviceable carbine cavalry is almost useless in the wooded country in which it is required to operate."[11] Whether Wilson's own division was in a better state of appearance or discipline than Kautz's is debatable, but from the standpoint of its armament it was not much better off than Kautz's "rag-tag

7. *Ibid.*, 939.

8. *Ibid.*, Vol. XL, Pt. 2, pp. 257, 267.

9. *Ibid.*, Pt. 1, p. 730. The 1st District of Columbia had the distinction of being the only cavalry regiment armed with the sixteen-shot Henry rifle. Because of its armament, half the regiment had been used as infantry; they were given horses and assigned to take part in the Wilson raid "before they had been drilled in the saddle at all. . . . At four o'clock P. M. of the twentieth [of June], an order was received to be ready to march at an hour's notice. At nine o'clock our horse equipments arrived from Washington. The different parts of the saddle were in different boxes, and so unacquainted were the men with horse gear, that many of them were unable to adjust the various parts without assistance . . . yet three hours later they started on the celebrated "Wilson Raid." Merrill, *Campaigns of the First Maine*, 233–34; see also Tobie, *First Maine Cavalry*, 332.

10. Wilson, *Under the Old Flag*, I, 456; Wilson, "Cavalry of the Army of the Potomac," 59.

11. *Official Records*, Vol. XL, Pt. 3, p. 245.

and bobtail." At this very time, a mere detachment of the 1st Massachusetts had to request cartridges for its three different types of carbines.[12]

On June 21 Wilson was handed detailed orders for his expedition. He was to move out at two A.M. on the twenty-second, take the shortest route to Burkeville, where the Southside intersected the Richmond & Danville, and from there destroy both roads in both directions, to the greatest possible extent. He was reminded, "The destruction of these roads to such an extent that they cannot be used by the enemy . . . during the remainder of the campaign is an important part of the plan." Later the same day he was told that Kautz would join him, but he was ordered to detach from his own division and leave behind "an effective command of about 800 men for the execution of reconnaissance and such other duties as may be required of it."[13]

In light of the eventual fate of the operation it is important to note factors that cast a shadow over it even before it started. General Meade appeared to have misgivings about the wisdom of the raid from the very start. In his response to Grant's initial suggestion (not yet an order) for the expedition, he wrote, "Where do you suppose the enemy's cavalry to be? And do you not think that with the knowledge of Sheridan's withdrawal [from Trevilian Station] Hampton will be drawn in to Richmond, ready to be thrown on any raiding party?"[14] The next day, after Grant had decided that the raid should be made, Meade again voiced his concern. It was known by then that Hampton was near White House on the Pamunkey, only forty miles from Petersburg; "I

12. *Ibid.*, Pt. 2, p. 310; the dispatch is dated June 22, 1864.
13. *Ibid.*, 285. Wilson left behind the 3rd New Jersey and the 18th Pennsylvania, a total of 1,146 officers and men. Wilson, *Under the Old Flag,* I, 458. The 3rd New Jersey, known originally as the "First United States Hussars," was mustered in, 1,200 strong, on February 10, 1864, and joined the Army of the Potomac at the end of April. "The seams and edges of their jackets were trimmed with yellow lace, while the breast was ornamented with parallel stripes of the same material, running cross-wise about one inch apart, with loops at the sides and center, surrounding brass buttons. Hence they received the name of 'Butterflies.' " Asa B. Isham, "Through the Wilderness to Richmond," MOLLUS, Commandery of Ohio, *Sketches of War History, 1861–1865* (7 vols.; Cincinnati, 1888–1910), I, 206–207; see also John Y. Foster, *New Jersey and the Rebellion* (Newark, 1868), 661 ff.
14. *Official Records*, Vol. XL, Pt. 2, p. 232.

trust," Meade wrote, "Sheridan will keep Hampton occupied," and he added, in an oblique but unmistakeable expression of his concern, that if "Sheridan were here"—if, that is, the entire Cavalry Corps could be sent on the operation—it could get as far west as Lynchburg.[15] Meade had evidently drawn the correct conclusion from the success of Sheridan's Richmond raid—the value of concentration—a lesson Grant had not yet learned.

Wilson too was worried about Hampton. Just before starting out he wrote General Humphreys, "If Sheridan will look after Hampton I apprehend no difficulty." Wilson was also concerned about the possibility that on his return he would find Confederate infantry blocking the most direct roads back to the Union army, and he stipulated that Union infantry be sent to hold these roads open for him. He was assured that this would be done.[16]

The historian is fortunate to have as sources for the Wilson raid not only the full reports of the major participants and the somewhat *ex parte* account in Wilson's autobiography, but also a view of the raid from the ranks, in the exceptionally detailed, vivid and intelligent narrative of Roger Hannaford, quartermaster sergeant of Company M, 2nd Ohio, of Colonel John B. McIntosh's First Brigade. On June 21, Hannaford reports, "Every body seemed in a hurry. The surgeon was examining the men & all not fit for duty were being sent back to City Point; there were . . . rations to be drawn, also requisitions to be made out for clothing, then drawn and issued. The butchers were killing beeves, the Q[uarter] M[asters] were running around wildly . . . broken down horses [were] being condemned & turned over to the Q[uarter] M[asters] and it was plain to be seen some move was to take place." It was midnight when these preparations were at last completed and the men could settle down to sleep. Within an hour, however, at one A.M., the bugles blew reveille. Two hours later, an hour behind schedule, the march began, with the men, not surprisingly, riding along "more asleep than awake."[17]

The first few hours of the march westward were uneventful

---

15. *Ibid.*, 267; see also Pt. 1, p. 620.

16. *Ibid.*, Pt. 2, p. 286. Wilson wrote, in the same dispatch, "The ammunition issued to my command is very defective."

17. Stephen Z. Starr (ed.) "The Wilson Raid, June, 1864: A Trooper's Reminiscences," *Civil War History*, XXI (1975), 219, 220.

and free from interference by the enemy. Reams' Station, on the Weldon Railroad, reached in midmorning, "was a pretty little place . . . the houses were inhabited, with nice yards & fruit trees around, blooming with flowers."[18] Nearly a year later the 2nd Ohio passed through the village again, and Hannaford noted the change:

Oh! how different was its appearance . . . not a single inhabitant was there, the houses were most of them destroyed or in ruins, fences all gone, an open common . . . in place of the lawns & neat gardens, the neat little Church completely "gutted," the seats scattered all over the woods . . . the woods in the vicinity of the station was [sic] torn & rent from the effects of shot & shell . . . the underbrush scarred & cut up with "Minnie balls," while old knapsacks, haversacks, canteens, gun stocks & twisted & broken barrels, intermingled with the skeletons or putrid remains of horses told of war, horrid stern war.[19]

On June 22, 1864, only the station buildings were put to the torch, and the track on either side was torn up for a short distance; the destruction Hannaford describes came about later in the year. Another trooper of the 2nd Ohio, commenting on the tearing up of the track, recalled that the men "received positive orders from the staff as to how the work should be done, but it was evident that they had no experience in that line . . . in which we had taken our first lesson in Kentucky and Tennessee. We car- ried out orders for a short time, but it was too tedious, and was soon abandoned for a more expeditious method. We made such fine headway that our method was adopted by the other troops."[20]

Marching through "very pretty" country, "farms in good order, fences all up, and the wheat just ready to cut," the raiders neared Dinwiddie Court House early in the afternoon, when the rear guard was attacked by Rooney Lee's cavalry. The attack was not pressed and was beaten off with ease. A few miles farther on the raiders reached Ford's Station, on the Southside Railroad, where they found two freight trains loaded with supplies for the army.

18. *Ibid.*, 220.
19. *Ibid.*, 220–21. Most of the destruction Hannaford describes was the effect of the fighting in and around Reams' Station August 17–24, 1864.
20. Gause, *Four Years with Five Armies*, 277. Gause does not explain what the 2nd Ohio's "method" was, or wherein it differed from the method the staff wanted them to use. His comment is a good illustration of the sense of superiority western soldiers had toward the "effete" Army of the Potomac and all its works.

After burning the trains, station buildings, a woodpile, and a saw-mill, they followed the track westward until nearly midnight, tearing it up and heating and bending the rails on burning piles of crossties. It was well past eleven o'clock at night, after a march of over fifty miles on an "exceedingly hot" day, "the roads dusty and the sun beating down with a blistering intensity," that a halt was called at last. The regiments were drawn up in line, the horses remained saddled and bridled (Wilson had evidently for-gotten the lesson of Sheridan's march to Yellow Tavern), and the men slept as best they could, lying on the ground in front of their horses, with the reins over their arms.[21]

Well before daylight on the twenty-third Kautz's division was sent on ahead to the crossing of the two railroads at Burkeville. While Colonel George H. Chapman's Second Brigade fought off another attack by Rooney Lee's pursuing cavalry, McIntosh's men tore up the track of the Southside Railroad as they too moved westward. McIntosh's troopers were dismounted in turn, a bat-talion at a time, and given a certain length of track "to do." As Hannaford reports, "We had no time to do a right good job; so we would turn the road, iron & ties all together; this is easy enough after you get it started."[22] Shortly before noon of what was an-other "very, very warm" day, at Black & White's Station, the men were given time to cook and eat dinner. Storage sheds at the sta-tion, loaded with tobacco and cotton "belonging to the Confeder-ate Gov't." were burned. Progress that afternoon was slow, for Lee's cavalry, which had interposed itself between Kautz and Wilson, had to be driven out of the way; this was not accom-plished until dark.[23]

The next day, the twenty-fourth, after a "really good night's rest," Wilson's division overtook Kautz's. The latter had reached Burkeville the previous afternoon, burned the depot, and de-stroyed the Richmond & Danville track for "several miles" north and south of the junction.[24]

The twenty-fourth was only the third day of the raid, but al-

21. Wilson, *Under the Old Flag,* I, 460; Starr, "The Wilson Raid," 221.
22. Starr, "The Wilson Raid," 222.
23. Wilson, *Under the Old Flag,* I, 461; *Official Records,* Vol. XL, Pt. 1, pp. 621, 626, 645.
24. Colonel West of Kautz's division reported that the men of his bri-gade were kept at work in two shifts all through the night of the twenty-

ready the horses were giving out. Hannaford recorded that "it was the duty of the rear-guard to shoot all these . . . we shot on the average one horse every quarter of a mile." After noting that "at least one half" of the horses destroyed could have been saved by "a few days, yes, in many cases only a few hours" of rest, Hannaford described an aspect of cavalry service that potential recruits were probably not warned about:

It seemed too that some [of the] poor brutes understood the fate in store for them, for they would stagger along in advance of us for sometimes two or three miles . . . sooner or later, however, they would again give up, and staggering in some fence corner wait for us to pass. Now came the opportunity some of the [men] seem to delight in, as riding up close they would present their carbines or pistols and fire. At times the shot would be effectual, and the poor faithful . . . servant would fall prone. . . . Oftener the first shot would not drop the poor brute, and he would start forward . . . as though new life instead of his death wound had been given him, and I have seen them rush in the midst of the column, the blood streaming from the mouth and nostrils . . . where they would stagger along . . . dropping at last from sheer weakness.[25]

Wilson's division joined Kautz's at Meherrin Station, on the Richmond & Danville ten miles southwest of Burkeville, and the united command marched southwestward to Keysville where they bivouacked for the night. The march was resumed at first light on the twenty-fifth and followed the line of the railroad toward Roanoke Station. The roadbed of the Richmond & Danville was constructed in a manner not uncommon in its day. Crossties were first laid, as they are at present; the track proper consisted of strap iron fastened to the tops of long wooden stringers, 5″ by 7″ in cross-section, which were mortised into the crossties. Hannaford explains that since the "stringers were mostly pine, it was a very

third to destroy two and a half miles of track. "The work was very hard," he wrote, "owing to the scarcity in some places of fence rails or other dry wood, and also the great weight of the track." *Official Records*, Vol. XL, Pt. 1, p. 733. On the other hand, Wilson wrote that "one or two of . . . [Kautz's] impatient or careless colonels, under the burning sun, did not do their work as well as they should have done. The Third Division, however, completed the destruction." Wilson, *Under the Old Flag*, I, 461.

25. Starr, "The Wilson Raid," 223–24. As early as the twenty-third Wilson had detachments out on both sides of the line of march, impressing horses.

easy matter to destroy the road, by simply laying down fence rails alongside the stringers & putting fire to it. The fire destroyed the stringers, burnt the ends of the ties off, and the iron was warped & badly twisted." [26]

Beyond Keysville, Kautz's command, in the van, burned depots, bridges, sawmills, turntables, wood piles, water tanks, and trestles, while Wilson's men attended to destroying the track. Hannaford describes how this was managed:

each Regiment was given a certain distance to burn, and when it was finished they would pass on until they again came to the front, where another distance would be allotted to them. . . . It was a most terrible hot day, and carrying fence rails & wood a distance was no desirable work. . . . After our portion would be finished, we would put fire to the piles . . . and march forward through fire & smoke and under a broiling sun a mile to a mile and a half where another [stretch] would be allotted to us. . . . A great part of the way we could find no water, and many of the boys began to give out. At last, what with the intense heat and our fatigue, R. R. burning, except under the most favorable circumstances, was abandoned, and we marched along just as we saw proper, every man for himself. . . . all our wish was our horses, as almost fainting from the combined effects of hunger & the intense overpowering heat we dragged ourselves along. [27]

The latter part of Hannaford's narrative illustrates the difference between the breaking up of a railroad as it appears in commanding officers' reports and memoirs, and the actual facts as they are recorded by the enlisted men who did, and sometimes did not, do

---

26. *Ibid.*, 225; see also Boudrye, *Historic Records of the Fifth*, 146: "The work was comparatively easy, owing to the peculiar construction of the road. . . . The labor of tearing up and burning could be done in half the time it would take on the ordinary roads. Decidedly encouraged by such advantages, the boys applied themselves faithfully to the accomplishment of their task. Every foot of the road was destroyed from Meherrin to Keysville."

27. Starr, "The Wilson Raid," 225–26. In contrast, Wilson was to write, "The wood was thoroughly dry, and the soil having no moisture in it at all, every foot of that road from the point we struck it till we abandoned it was absolutely destroyed." Wilson, "Cavalry of the Army of the Potomac," 61. Lieutenant Colonel George A. Purington's (2nd Ohio) report substantiates Hannaford's grim account. Purington wrote that the labor performed by his men "under a burning sun and over hot fires was extremely exhausting, and many of the men have not and never will recover from its effects." *Official Records*, Vol. XL, Pt. 1, p. 642.

George A. Custer
Courtesy of the Library of Congress

John B. McIntosh
Courtesy of the Library of Congress

Charles E. Capehart
Courtesy of the Library of Congress

Henry E. Davies, Jr.
Courtesy of the Library of Congress

William W. Averell
Courtesy of the Library of Congress

A. T. A. Torbert
Courtesy of the National Archives

the work. Nevertheless, in this instance, the destruction was sufficiently thorough.

While Hannaford and his comrades were wrecking the railroad, and Chapman's brigade, in the rear, fought off another attack by Rooney Lee, Kautz reached the Roanoke River in the afternoon.[28] Here, at Roanoke Station, the railroad crossed the river on a long wooden trestle, the destruction of which would have been a far more damaging blow to the South than the destruction the raiders had already wrought. On Wilson's side the river was bordered by a half-mile wide belt of flat bottom land planted in wheat, over which the roadbed was carried to the bridge on a high embankment. On the opposite side the river flowed at the foot of a high, steep bank. Two forts, one on each side of the track and armed with six guns, were situated on top of the bank and were protected by a triple line of rifle pits. The arrival of the raiders had been anticipated, and the forts and rifle pits were manned by nearly a thousand home guards and Confederate infantry, commanded by Captain Benjamin L. Farinholt.[29]

Wilson gave Kautz's division the job of burning the trestle. Kautz in turn ordered Colonel West's brigade to reach the trestle by crossing the bottom land to the right of the railroad embankment. Colonel Spears's brigade was to advance to the left of it. The two brigades, dismounted, worked their way forward to within two hundred yards of the trestle under a heavy fire from Farinholt's riflemen and artillery. There, Colonel West formed an assaulting column, "and directed it up the embankment in the hope that by a quick move . . . it might obtain possession of the . . . bridge sufficiently long to fire it. The men tried repeatedly to gain a foothold on the railroad, and to advance along the sides of the embankment, but could not. The height of the railroad embankment enabled the enemy from their position down by the river's edge . . . to sweep the sides and track with a terrible fire."[30]

This attempt to reach the bridge, in which Kautz sustained a

28. The Roanoke is sometimes referred to in the records as the Staunton River.
29. *Official Records*, Vol. XL, Pt. 1, pp. 621, 627, 731, 734, 764–65; Wilson, *Under the Old Flag*, I, 463.
30. *Official Records*, Vol. XL, Pt. 1, p. 734; Wilson, *Under the Old Flag*, I, 463.

large loss of men killed and wounded, as well as many prostrated by the heat, was condemned by the men as useless, and they held Wilson to blame. It must be remembered that most of them were veterans, as capable as any general of recognizing a hopeless venture. Hannaford, for one, decided that a "[g]eneral of good judgment would have never after developing the enemy's strength and position . . . ordered the second attack; many a brave mans life was uselessly lost here, and our ambulances and wagons crowded with wounded, all of whom were afterward abandoned to the enemy."[31]

With Kautz's men pinned down to the embankment and unable to reach the bridge, Wilson sent scouts up and down the river to look for a crossing place whence Farinholt's position could be turned. The river was too wide and deep to cross except over a ford or a bridge, and the scouts could find neither. Meanwhile, Rooney Lee's attacks on Chapman's brigade, still protecting the rear, continued. In view of these circumstances, Wilson decided that he had done as much as could reasonably be expected of him and that it was time to retreat.

Now came the crunch. Wilson had advanced nearly a hundred miles from his base, his men and animals were worn out, and his retreat would be impeded by "something like two hundred" wounded in ambulances and all sorts of vehicles picked up along the way, and by a large and constantly growing tail of contrabands. Rooney Lee's cavalry, which had dogged his footsteps for four days, remained in contact and would doubtless keep its own army fully informed of the raiders' route and progress, thereby making it inevitable, barring extraordinary good fortune, that they would be intercepted before they could reach the Army of the Potomac.

Wilson's route on the outward march had been west to Burkeville, then southwest to Roanoke Station. For the return journey he decided on a more southerly route: southeast to Wyliesville (or Wyliesburg), Christianville, and Greensborough, north across the Meherrin River at Saffold's Bridge, then east by way of Smoky Ordinary and Poplar Hill toward Jarratt's Station on the Weldon Railroad, well to the south of the left flank of the Union forces

31. Starr, "The Wilson Raid," 227.

investing Petersburg. About five miles short of the Weldon Railroad, Wilson would have to make a choice; he could march east to Jarratt's Station, Peter's Bridge across the Nottoway, Blunt's Bridge over the Blackwater, and thence to the left rear of the Union army; or he could take a shorter, more direct route by turning north five miles from Jarratt's Station, crossing the Nottoway on the "Double Bridges," and taking a road that crossed the Weldon Railroad just north of Stony Creek Depot and led to Prince George Court House, Wilson's original point of departure.[32]

The return march began at about eleven P.M. on the night of the twenty-fifth and until past noon of the twenty-eighth was quite uneventful. The roads the raiders used led through countryside as yet untouched by war; hence foraging was productive, and men and animals had plenty to eat.[33] Lee was taking a more northerly route back to the Weldon Railroad, and the only enemy the Federals saw on the twenty-sixth and twenty-seventh were small scouting groups Lee sent out to keep an eye on their progress. The main problem was the heat, "so terrible," Hannaford wrote, "that we had to move very slowly, yet fast enough to keep out of the way of the enemy. . . . Horses were continually staggering & falling with the heat. . . . If it had not been that we were continually capturing horses fully half of the command would have been dismounted; as it was a number were now footing it."[34] The Negroes marching along behind the column were also a

32. For Wilson's route, see U.S. War Dept, *Atlas to Accompany the Official Records of the Union and Confederate Armies* (3 vols.; Washington, D.C., 1891–1895), II, Plate LXXIV, No. 1. See also *Official Records*, Vol. XL, Pt. 1, p. 632.

33. In that day of generally unmarked roads and lanes, stragglers, foragers, and rear guards were helped to find their way back to their units by means of the following technique: "when we would come to a forked road, or when we turned off into some other road, a thing we were constantly doing, a couple of rails would be laid across the road we did not go on, which would [be a] sufficient guide to all foraging parties, stragglers, the rearguard, &c." Starr, "The Wilson Raid," 229.

34. *Ibid.*, 228. The historian of the 5th New York wrote, "The day has been very warm, many horses 'played out' by the way. They were invariably shot, and replaced by horses and mules captured in the country. Scouting parties and flankers are constantly replenishing the column with instalments of fresh, fat animals, which the people have not the time or adroitness to hide." Boudrye, *Historical Records of the Fifth*, 147.

cause for concern. Once again it is Roger Hannaford who relates, "About the third day . . . the slaves began gathering in . . . droves, men, women & children; many of them had appropriated . . . horses & wagons; some few had carriages, some carts, &c., in which they had their families. . . . [By June 27] The Negro Brigade [was] swollen to about 1200 and hourly increasing. . . . Such an army had they almost become that Wilson had appointed Officers to take charge of them, and now they were marching by fours in column."[35] At some time on the twenty-seventh, Wilson was told by Negroes met along the way that there was only a small force of Confederate infantry at Stony Creek Depot, supported by two small detachments of cavalry.[36] This information caused him to make the fateful choice of the route via the Double Bridges, instead of the longer route via Jarratt's Station which Sheridan thought he should have taken. Given the ensuing events, and the fact that Wilson was eventually forced to take the Jarratt's Station route, it is difficult not to agree with General Sheridan, notwithstanding that his opinion smacks of wisdom after the event.[37] In view of Wilson's concern before he left over the difficulties he might have to face on his return, his choice of the potentially more dangerous Stony Creek route is not easy to understand.

Having made his decision, Wilson sent forward "a small detachment" to Stony Creek Depot to clear the way across the railroad for the main body. The detachment ran into unexpectedly powerful opposition; it was able to secure the crossing over Stony Creek, but in the woods at Sappony Church, two miles west of the railroad, it was brought to a halt by John R. Chambliss' brigade of cavalry, reinforced by about two hundred infantry. From prisoners Wilson learned that Chambliss had behind him the full strength of Hampton's and Fitzhugh Lee's divisions of cavalry. In an effort to break through Wilson eventually deployed his entire command, but in frequently heavy fighting that went on intermittently until midnight, he was unable to budge Chambliss.[38]

35. Starr, "The Wilson Raid," 227–29. Most of the wagons, carriages, and carts were confiscated after the fight at Roanoke Station to provide transportation for the wounded for whom there was no room in the ambulances.
36. Wilson, *Under the Old Flag*, I, 465.
37. Sheridan, *Personal Memoirs*, I, 465.
38. Hannaford repeats the rumor that General Kautz expressed his

Now Wilson was faced with another critical decision. His way east to the Army of the Potomac via Stony Creek Depot was effectively blocked, forcing him to seek another route across the railroad. Should it be to the north or to the south of where he was? Once again he made what turned out to be, and should probably have been anticipated to be, the wrong choice. At midnight he pulled Kautz's division out of the line facing Chambliss and ordered it to march north ten miles—that much closer to the Confederate lines defending Petersburg—and break through to the east at Reams' Station. Wilson's own division was to remain behind at Sappony Church until daylight to hold Chambliss, Hampton, and Fitzhugh Lee in check and was then to follow Kautz.[39]

In the course of the afternoon of the twenty-seventh, Hannaford and another trooper were assigned the job of keeping the trains, officers' servants, and camp followers of McIntosh's brigade ("a very large and motley throng . . . nearly as long a column as the whole Brigade") in order and moving. The subsequent adventures of Hannaford and his partner illustrate vividly the desperate confusion behind the line of battle on a night of peril and chaos. Hannaford wrote:

In a short time we came to a forked road. . . . Going a short distance, we were halted, drawn off on the side . . . and told to be in instant readiness to go on at a moments warning. . . . It must have been about 1 oclock A. M. when a Staff Officer came along giving orders to get into the road, mount & be ready to start . . . so arousing myself I went up along the road, booting the darkies . . . into a condition of wakefulness,

disapproval of Wilson's handling of the fight at Sappony Church, "that is, of first throwing in a single Regiment, & then another, allowing them to be beaten in detail." Starr, "The Wilson Raid," 241.

39. Wilson, *Under the Old Flag*, I, 465–66. Hannaford also records the rumor that at this point in the action, Kautz urged Wilson "to destroy our wagon trains, spike the guns, take only ambulances enough to convey . . . [the] wounded and then he offered to safely lead the column in the hours of darkness to the east of the R. R., but . . . General Wilson would not [listen]." Hannaford adds, "Whether these rumors were true or not I cannot say, but they were extensively circulated among the men and generally recd as gospel truths, heightening the mens admiration of Kautz and their dislike of . . . Wilson." Starr, "The Wilson Raid," 241. Allowance must be made for Hannaford's pro-Kautz, anti-Wilson bias; nonetheless, to the present writer, this rumor, as well as the one quoted in the preceding note 41, appear entirely believable.

seeing them out in the road and mounted. . . . Very soon after mounting the train started, but the latter part soon got lost from the advance.
. . . We went not far before we turned off to the left. . . . The road we
were on was a narrow woods road & the heavy pines completely over-
arched it, so that it was black & dark as Egypt; soon one of the wagons
lost the road, drove in among the trees & . . . was smashed all to pieces.
. . . A few hundred yards farther we were brought up standing, and
our utmost exertions could not make the train move on. The firing still
kept [up] with more vigor if possible than ever, & mingling with it was
the occasional roar of artillery. Every one was trying to get ahead,
cries of "we are on the wrong road"; "no we aint, we are right"; "I tell
you were wrong" were constantly heard; at last a Staff Officer volunteered to go back and find out. While waiting his return, the advance
of the 2nd Brigade pack train mingled with stragglers came up in our
rear. Soon they began crowding on us . . . they edged around our flank,
[and] crowded up until we were wedged up in a perfect jam. The musketry was seemingly getting closer, and a regular panic . . . was the
result. . . . such swearing & cursing, it was really awful . . . many of
the teamsters had lighted candles, showing a scene perfectly indescribable. Every one that could, now pushed ahead . . . and although
we were not certain where we were going, yet it was everybody for
himself & the devil take the hindmost.[40]

Scenes such as these, although not often described so graphi-
cally, were nevertheless an inescapable part of cavalry operations. In this instance the chaos was the product not of a lost battle, but of a sudden change of plans that had to be executed under
the worst possible conditions; only a heavy downpour and deep
mud were lacking to make an utterly grim situation.

The fact that in his memoirs Wilson saw fit to minimize the
force he expected to face at Stony Creek Depot suggests that he
came to realize in time, but not to admit, that he had made the
wrong choice in trying to break through at that point. Assistant
Secretary of War Charles A. Dana, always a strong supporter of
Wilson's, repeated in a letter to Secretary Stanton a remark of
General Grant's to the effect that "Wilson . . . [was] as likely as
any other man to get safely out of a tight place."[41] On this June

40. Starr, "The Wilson Raid," 230, 231, 232. It will be recalled that the
substitution of pack mules for wagons was one of Hooker's cavalry innovations, intended to make the cavalry more mobile. The idea was not a success
and was officially abandoned June 4, 1863; *Official Records*, Vol. XVII,
Pt. 1, p. 7. Wilson, however, had both wagons and pack mules on this raid.
41. *Official Records*, Vol. XL, Pt. 1, p. 28.

night, however, Wilson showed greater ingenuity in getting *into* a "tight place" than in getting out of it.

Before daylight on the twenty-ninth word came back from Kautz that the road to Reams' Station was clear, and Wilson ordered his own division to disengage and march north to join Kautz.[42] McIntosh's brigade was in actual contact with Chambliss' line of battle. Chapman's brigade lay behind improvised breastworks six hundred yards behind McIntosh.[43] Ordered to withdraw, McIntosh asked Chapman to remain in position until the First Brigade had marched to the rear and then to fall in behind it for the march to join Kautz. McIntosh's withdrawal in the thick woods and the darkness would have been difficult enough under the best of circumstances; it was doubly so on this occasion because his men, who had been marching and fighting for twenty-four hours, were exhausted and close to demoralization.[44] Nevertheless, they effected their withdrawal in fair order but made enough noise to alert the Confederates to what was happening, and Chambliss took advantage of the situation by delivering a powerful attack on Chapman's front, left flank, and rear. The flank attack drove a wedge between the two Federal brigades and also separated most of Chapman's men from their led horses; as a result, many of the men were captured. Chapman himself had a narrow escape; with only three hundred of his men he rejoined the main body at about noon, after a long march by a "circuitous route."[45]

In the meantime Kautz, after sending Wilson the dispatch to let him know that the road to Reams' Station was unobstructed, arrived within a short distance of the station and found not the Union infantry Wilson hoped would be there, but two brigades of Confederate infantry of William Mahone's division, backed by

42. Wilson, *Under the Old Flag*, I, 466. There is a conflict of evidence as to when McIntosh was ordered to pull out. He reported it as "about 2.30 o'clock," whereas Wilson had it as "about daylight." In view of what ensued, McIntosh's version is more likely to be correct. *Official Records*, Vol. XL, Pt. 1, p. 636; Wilson, *Under the Old Flag*, I, 466.
43. *Official Records*, Vol. XL, Pt. 1, p. 636.
44. Starr, "The Wilson Raid," 231.
45. *Official Records*, Vol. XL, Pt. 1, pp. 646, 628. One of Chapman's officers told Sheridan that "the brigade was completely broken up and dispersed." *Ibid.*, Pt. 2, p. 574.

artillery and sent to that point at Wade Hampton's suggestion.[46] There was a flurry of firing followed by a Confederate attack on Kautz's lead regiment, which was beaten off by a well-executed countercharge; nevertheless, Kautz concluded that it would not be possible for him to break through and that "there seemed no other course left except to intrench and hold on . . . until relieved by the Army of the Potomac."[47] To carry word of the raiders' predicament to General Meade, whose headquarters were only eight miles from the station, Captain Edward W. Whitaker of the 1st Connecticut, a member of Wilson's staff, volunteered for the perilous duty of making his way through the Confederate lines in broad daylight.[48]

For an account of the march of Wilson's exhausted and disheartened division to Reams' Station we must turn once again to Roger Hannaford:

Crossing the bridge [over Stony Creek], evidences of a regular panic began to be noticeable . . . the road was filled with stragglers, darkies, &c. . . . Nearing Reams' the appearance became worse & worse. . . . The panic visibly increased among the disorganized mass, and the fright of many of the negroes was nearly painful to witness. . . . I plainly saw that the whole Division was disorganized, one great & principal cause being the want of confidence felt in our Commanding General. . . . The feeling against him was bitter in the extreme.[49]

At about noon the entire command, troops, stragglers, trains, and contrabands, was reunited in the fields and swampy woods to the west of Reams' Station. Hampton and Fitzhugh Lee had also moved northward, and now Wilson was hemmed in on three sides: Rooney Lee and Fitzhugh Lee to the north and northeast, Mahone's infantry to the northeast and east, and Hampton to the south.[50] With disaster staring him in the face, Wilson had an agonizing decision to make. Should he ask his severely shaken,

46. *Ibid.*, Pt. 1, p. 808.

47. *Ibid.*, 732.

48. Captain Whitaker's gallant attempt was successful. He was given an escort of forty men of the 3rd New York for his ride and half of them got through with him. He reached General Meade's headquarters at 11:30 A.M.

49. Starr, "The Wilson Raid," 233–34; see also Luman H. Tenney, *War Diary* (Cleveland, 1914), 123.

50. For the position at Reams' Station, see sketch map in *Official Records*, Vol. XL, Pt. 1, p. 633.

disorganized, physically exhausted command for a major effort and, with the menace of enemy cavalry on both flanks, try to break through the ranks of the well rested, fresh Confederate infantry to the east? Or should he attempt a possibly even more risky retreat, and if so, where? The decision he first made is more creditable to his heart than to his head. He ordered McIntosh "to take the First Brigade and force the enemy's lines." A careful examination of the terrain and of the Confederate position convinced McIntosh that there was no hope of a successful attack; not until then did Wilson face up to the inevitable and order a retreat.[51]

In preparation for the attempt to escape—for it was that, more than a retreat—Wilson ordered the troopers' ammunition pouches filled and then had the trains burned. The ambulances and other vehicles, with their loads of wounded, were parked along a nearby stream to be left behind under the charge of the surgeons.

While the trains were being set on fire, McIntosh's brigade lay in a double skirmish line facing in three directions, north, east, and south. Seeing behind them the thick clouds of smoke from the burning trains and hearing the "terrible uproar" of the cartridges and shells exploding as the fire reached them, the men realized that "things were getting into an acknowledged desperate straight [sic]," and the effect on their morale was "plainly visible."[52]

The critical situation in which the raiders now found themselves provides the ultimate test of discipline, and they were equal to it. To the extent that their own exhausted state and the actions of the enemy permitted, they maintained cohesion and followed orders. To make his escape, Wilson decided to march straight west about five miles to the Stage Road, then south to the Double Bridges across the Nottoway, and, finally, east by way of Jarratt's

51. *Ibid.*, 636. It is instructive to compare McIntosh's report, in which Wilson's order to break through is repeated, with Wilson's, in which the order is not mentioned. What Wilson wrote instead was, "In company with Colonel McIntosh I carefully reconnoitered the enemy's line, but after examining it closely could see no reasonable hope of breaking through it." *Ibid.*, 623. When Wilson came to write his autobiography, however, he told substantially the same story as McIntosh. Wilson, *Under the Old Flag*, I, 470.

52. Starr, "The Wilson Raid," 235.

Station, the route he would have been wise to follow two days earlier. But getting away from Reams' Station proved to be more difficult than Wilson may have anticipated. Chapman, who was to lead the way with what was left of his brigade, had already marched away, and McIntosh was about to follow when he was attacked by Confederate infantry, which had been sent on a wide swing to the west in an effort to complete the encirclement of the raiders.[53] Leaving the 2nd Ohio, the 5th New York, and Lieutenant Charles L. Fitzhugh's Battery E, 4th United States Artillery to hold what had been his front, McIntosh deployed the 1st Connecticut and the 2nd New York to check the attack of the Confederate infantry.[54] These moves were successful and McIntosh was able to extricate himself, but in the process the two pairs of regiments became separated; the 1st Connecticut and the 2nd New York followed and eventually joined Chapman, whereas the other two regiments joined Kautz.

Kautz's division, with the two regiments of McIntosh's brigade plus a scattering of men belonging to other units of the Third Division under their wing, was the first major group of raiders to reach safety. In his report, General Kautz said merely, "Finding that I could not get to the stage road, I immediately determined to turn the enemy's left [i.e., southern] flank and thus seek to enter our lines. This was done without opposition. We crossed the railroad between Reams' Station and Rowanty Bridge and reached our lines soon after dark."[55] But there was more to General Kautz's

53. Hannaford describes the scene: "we were ordered to our horses, and after standing by them ten minutes or so, were ordered to mount. We had just done so when crash, bang came a volley from the pine woods in our left rear . . . while with an infernal yell, here came a long line of graybacks . . . running so as to cut us off from the road we had advanced on. It was a most complete surprise. . . . In less time that it takes me to write it, they were among the wagon train, capturing the ambulances & all our wounded & many who were not wounded who had not time to escape. General Wilson & Staff & a large number of stragglers . . . just managed to mount & get away." Ibid., 235.

54. Lieutenant Fitzhugh was eventually forced to spike and abandon his guns. His report of the raid was forwarded by Wilson with the endorsement, "No blame whatever can be attached to the officers or men of this battery for its loss, but, on the contrary, they are worthy of the highest praise for their good conduct and gallantry." Official Records, Vol. XL, Pt. 1, p. 654.

55. Ibid., 732. Rowanty Bridge was approximately half way between Reams' Station and Stony Creek Depot.

escape than his overly modest, laconic report would suggest. Hannaford supplies the telling details. The enveloping movement of the Confederate infantry having been momentarily checked,

In the open field in the rear . . . a rapid consultation was held among the Officers, and . . . General Kautz took command. . . . In the meantime the enemy . . . were making their way . . . toward us. . . . the side [on which they] had not attacked us was very swampy, and any person looking at it would judge it impossible for the cavalry to push themselves through such a tangled, swampy jungle. But it was our only chance. . . . So in we plunged. . . . As first we entered it, the[re] sat our old Colonel, [i.e., Kautz] and not one of our Regiment but felt infinitely better when they understood he was in command; he was sitting [with a] leg thrown over his horse's neck, and seemingly as cool as though the situation was perfectly agreeable. He had a pocket map of Virginia spread over his knee, while in his left hand he was holding a mariners compass, and was looking at the sun . . . then . . . he pointed out the course.[56]

This imperturbable, confident and hence confidence-inspiring leadership had its reward. After a hard cross-country ride of seven hours, Kautz and the men with him—many of them asleep in their saddles—reached the Federal lines at 9:30 P.M. and were safe. Hannaford was one of those who rode along more asleep than awake; "before I dropped again to sleep," he wrote, "I saw drawn off the road-side and hidden by the shadow of the bushes . . . a man on horse-back, his horses head turned outward. . . . I knew it was a vidette . . . and now indeed the feeling of perfect security thrilled through my bosom. I could scarcely for a few moments contain myself . . . and soon my joy was succeeded by deep thankfulness to God for his great mercy and goodness in bringing me safely though such innumerable dangers."[57] These were the words of a deeply religious soldier who had seen comrades killed, who knew himself what it meant to be wounded, and who knew also, as most troopers did by the summer of 1864, what

56. Starr, "The Wilson Raid," 236–37. Kautz had been colonel of Hannaford's regiment, the 2nd Ohio; Wilson criticized him as "a typical infantryman and never a success as a cavalry commander." Wilson, *Under the Old Flag*, I, 510–11.

57. Starr, "The Wilson Raid," 239–40; see also *Official Records*, Vol. XL, Pt. 2, p. 512. In addition to those who escaped with Kautz and Wilson, officers and men, singly and in small groups, made their way into the Federal lines; they were turning up for days after July 1.

it meant to be taken prisoner and sent to Andersonville or Salisbury.

Those who escaped from Reams' Station under Wilson had a more difficult time of it. Led by the 1st New Hampshire and the 1st Vermont, the only two regiments that retained their organization, the division, with hundreds of its men on foot and accompanied by the provost guard, stragglers, and details of Kautz's division, plus about twelve hundred Negroes, marched south "in a cloud of suffocating dust." The fugitives reached the bridge over Stony Creek without molestation by the enemy, but while they were in the process of crossing, Fitzhugh Lee's cavalry appeared and attacked the large crowd still on the north bank of the stream waiting to cross. A panic ensued; the narrow bridge "at once became filled with a mass of footmen, black and white, mingled among the horsemen. Many were pushed over its sides, and fell upon the rocks or into the stream below."[58] Many more, unable to fight their way to the bridge, became victims of the vicious brutality of Lee's troopers. Wilson wrote merely that "It is reported that . . . [the Negroes] who were unable to get across the bridge were sabered or shot by the rebels"; but the tales Hannaford heard from members of his regiment who escaped with Wilson's column were more explicit and hence more shocking:

it would appear that the rebel cavalry would leave [off] pursuing a "Yankee" at any time for the pleasure of shooting down a negro, and our boys saw them shot down like so many mad dogs . . . the men were shot down without mercy. . . . The women and children were made prisoners, after being beaten & abused most shamefully; many were knocked senseless by a stroke from the back of a sabre, or a stroke from the butt of a gun. The reports that were given by eye-witnesses were horrible, sickening & heartrending.[59]

Wilson's retreat had gotten under way on the afternoon of the

---

58. G. G. Benedict, *Vermont in the Civil War* (2 vols.; Burlington, Vt., 1886–88), II, 654.

59. *Official Records*, Vol. XL, Pt. 1, p. 629. Wilson later told Dana that "the rebels slaughtered without mercy the negroes they retook." *Ibid.*, 31. Troopers of the 1st Vermont reported, "The enemy shot and sabred the negroes without mercy." Benedict, *Vermont in the Civil War*, II, 654. Hannaford's version is in Starr, "The Wilson Raid," 241. About four hundred of the Negroes escaped and reached safety.

twenty-ninth. Eleven hours later, having crossed the Nottoway and then the railroad, the column halted some distance east of Jarratt's Station. After a brief, two-hour rest, the march was resumed at first light on the thirtieth toward the Blackwater River, through an unbroken forest, over roads "obscure and difficult to follow."[60] Blunt's Bridge over the Blackwater, which the raiders reached in the dead of night in the early hours of July 1, had been burned, but rough-and-ready repairs made it passable. Beyond the Blackwater there was no more danger from the enemy, and when Wilson ordered a halt near Fort Powhatan early in the afternoon, after a 125-mile march in sixty hours, the entire command "for the first time in ten days . . . unsaddled, picketed, fed, and went regularly to sleep."[61] Wilson himself fell asleep in the midst of writing a dispatch to General Humphreys announcing his return from the raid.

Captain Whitaker's arrival at General Meade's headquarters on the morning of June 29 with news of Wilson's desperate situation set off a flurry of orders—to General Horatio G. Wright to send one of the divisions of his VI Corps to Reams' Station post haste and to follow with his other two divisions as soon as possible, and to Sheridan, who was still north of the James, to hurry to Wilson's rescue. Wilson's fate, however, was decided before any of these moves could bring him the help he needed.[62] The next word Meade and Grant had of Wilson's predicament came from Kautz, late the same evening. In his dispatch announcing his own safe return, Kautz used the expression, "this afternoon . . . we were surrounded and overpowered," and until Wilson himself reported two days later his arrival behind the Federal lines with what was left of his command, the Union high command remained highly apprehensive about his fate.[63] Sheridan was urged

60. Wilson, *Under the Old Flag*, I, 473.
61. *Ibid.*, 479.
62. *Official Records*, Vol. XL, Pt. 2, pp. 499, 500, 504, 506, 510, 511, 512; see also Wilson, *Under the Old Flag*, I, 468, and *Official Records*, Vol. XL, Pt. 1, p. 169.
63. *Official Records*, Vol. XL, Pt. 2, p. 512; Pt. 1, p. 28. Grant refused to believe these reports; Dana thought them improbable, but at the same time he reported to the War Department that Wilson had been "surrounded and destroyed." Wilson himself called Kautz's report "an overdrawn account." *Ibid.*, Pt. 1, p. 28.

on the evening of June 30 to "move . . . in the direction in which the enemy is reported to have followed General Wilson, and endeavor to ascertain definitely where his command is and make every effort in your power to extricate his force and secure its return."[64] Sheridan responded that he would "move in the morning but it will be at the risk of dismounting. . . . My horses are worn out. Some of them have been without forage for forty-eight hours. I am satisfied that . . . Wilson cannot keep any considerable body of his command together. I thought it best to keep open the roads leading to the south, so that small parties can come in as they are now doing."[65] What Sheridan reported about the state of his horses was doubtless true, but his dispatch certainly did not evince any great concern for Wilson's fate; indeed, it can be described as amazingly dispassionate and even callous. Wilson himself had that opinion of it, which he expressed at great length in his memoirs; General Meade too implied it in a dispatch to Grant.[66]

Unbelievable as it may seem, even Kautz was asked to help. Less than twenty-four hours after his own escape, he was ordered to "assist General Sheridan in extricating General Wilson." With ample justification for doing so, Kautz asked Grant to have the order revoked; "My command is in no condition to do anything," he wrote; "Men and horses have had nothing to eat for forty-eight hours and they are exhausted from loss of sleep . . . we can do nothing more."[67] Grant evidently had the order canceled, but Wilson described Kautz's plea as "weak and contemptible in the last degree," and, he added, Kautz "simply lay down and quit."[68] Wilson's bitterness is understandable enough, but it does not excuse his gross unfairness to a fine soldier.

64. *Ibid.*, Pt. 2, p. 517.
65. *Ibid.*, 573.
66. Wilson, *Under the Old Flag*, I, 486–521; *Official Records*, Vol. XL, Pt. 2, p. 517. In Sheridan's opinion, "Wilson's retreat from the perilous situation at Ream's station was a most creditable performance—in the face of two brigades of infantry and three divisions of cavalry—and in the conduct of the whole expedition the only criticism that can hold against him is that he placed too much reliance on meeting our infantry at Ream's station, seeing that uncontrollable circumstances might, and did, prevent it being there." Sheridan, *Personal Memoirs*, I, 444.
67. *Official Records*, Vol. XL, Pt. 2, p. 540.
68. Wilson, *Under the Old Flag*, I, 511, 510.

With no help from any part of the Union army, both Kautz and Wilson escaped from dire peril. They did so, however, with the loss of all their artillery, trains, and supplies, and all their wounded left behind to be captured by the enemy. They sustained a total of 1,445 casualties, nearly 25 percent of the force with which they started out. Wilson had 33 killed, 108 wounded, and 674 captured or missing; Kautz, 48 killed, 153 wounded, and 429 taken prisoner or missing.[69] What did the operation accomplish? It has always been called a cavalry raid, presumably because the units that made it were officially designated regiments of cavalry, but it was a "cavalry raid" in name only. It was actually a mounted infantry operation. The horses provided transportation, and uncertain transportation at that; when there was fighting to be done, at Roanoke Station, Stony Creek Depot, and Reams' Station, it was done on foot. Wilson learned after the war from General J. M. St. John, in charge of Confederate military railroads, that his raid "was the heaviest blow of the kind that ever befell the Confederacy . . . with all the resources at [St. John's] command it was nine weeks, or sixty-three days, before a train from the south ran into Petersburg on either road."[70] Sheridan wrote that "the wrecking of the railroads . . . was most complete, occasioning at this time serious embarrassment for the Confederate Government"; he thought, however, that the losses Wilson sustained were too high a price to pay for the damage he had been able to cause.[71] General Meade described the raid as a "brilliant success"; he regretted "the disaster at the termination of the expedition" but, unlike Sheridan, felt that the "heavy injuries inflicted on the enemy were . . . ample compensation for the losses sustained."[72] Grant's reaction was identical to Meade's, and his approval took the tangible form of recommending Chapman's and McIntosh's promotion to brigadier general, which was granted in short order.[73]

Perhaps the most durable effect of the raid was beneath the

69. *Official Records*, Vol. XL, Pt. 1, pp. 232, 238.
70. Wilson, *Under the Old Flag*, I, 462–63.
71. Sheridan, *Personal Memoirs*, I, 444.
72. *Official Records*, Vol. XL, Pt. 1, p. 169.
73. Grant wrote that he regretted "the disaster, but the work done by Wilson and his cavalry is of great importance . . . it will take the enemy several weeks to repair the damage done the South Side and Danville roads." *Ibid.*, Pt. 2, p. 560; Pt. 3, p. 421.

ken of general officers, but it was recognized by a lesser mortal, Trooper Hannaford. Summing up the accomplishments of the raid as he saw them, he wrote:

We . . . did an immense deal of damage and destroyed large [quantities of] supplies of all sorts . . . many saw & grist mills & contents . . . beside large quantities of corn, oats &c., & quantities of tobacco & cotton. . . . We passed over that portion of Virginia just as the wheat harvest was or should have been in progress, and by disarranging the labor, most of which followed us, an immense . . . loss must have been the result. . . . it may be said [that] on each side of our line of march for at least twenty miles we stripped the country of its able-bodied labor in its time of utmost need.[74]

But the raid also had an unpleasant aftermath. It was common knowledge among the men that the foraging and the hunt for replacement mounts had led to the customary excesses, and also, that at Marysville on June 25 a detachment of the 2nd New York "broke open stores, released two civil prisoners, and did many things out of the way."[75] On July 4, General Seth Williams sent Wilson on Meade's instructions a copy of an "editorial article" in the July 2 Richmond *Inquirer*, describing "several instances cited with particularity" of depredations committed by Wilson's men and asked for an explanation.[76] General Williams' dispatch was unexceptionable in tone; nevertheless, Wilson took great umbrage and produced an indignant reply, which led off with the rhetorical flourish that he could "scarcely realize" that his own conduct and that of his command could be "seriously arraigned upon charges made in a journal notoriously venal and unscrupulous in its efforts to sustain the cause of the public enemy." He then proceeded to cite the orders he had issued to prohibit and prevent "straggling, marauding and pilfering." Candor nevertheless compelled him to state his belief that "there exists in our cavalry service an organized band of thieves, who are under no restraint whatever, and who have been skillful enough so far to elude every attempt to arrest. . . . I have heard vague rumors—in one instance of plate having been taken, and of several where

74. Starr, "The Wilson Raid," 240.
75. Tenney, *War Diary*, 121.
76. *Official Records*, Vol. XL, Pt. 2, p. 632.

money was stolen."[77] The good repute of the troops that had gone on the raid was not helped by this admission, nor by the report of Wilson's acting assistant inspector general, who had to confess that "Much straggling was constantly observed" and implied strongly that the brigade and regimental commanders made little effort to enforce the commanding general's antistraggling, antimarauding, antipilfering orders.[78]

General Kautz, who was also asked for a report, responded with facts instead of rhetoric, writing that on the outward march, when his division had the advance, "General Wilson called my attention to the fact that there was much pillaging found to have taken place after my command had passed." On the return march, however, when the Third Division had the lead, Kautz's attention was repeatedly "called to houses that had been robbed before . . . [his own] command came up." Kautz added that in his opinion, the "outrages" committed by his and Wilson's men did not in any instance "exceed those committed by [John Hunt] Morgan's command in his raid through Indiana and Ohio" a year before.[79]

After receiving Wilson's report, and without waiting for Kautz's, General Meade beat a hasty retreat. He had General Williams inform Wilson that his report was "entirely satisfactory," and that it had not been his (Meade's) intention "to reflect in the slightest degree" upon Wilson's conduct or that of his troopers. With that somewhat lame evasion the incident came to a close.[80]

---

77. *Ibid.*, Pt. 3, pp. 15–16.
78. *Ibid.*, 80; see also Wilson, *Under the Old Flag*, I, 528–30.
79. *Official Records*, Vol. XL, Pt. 1, p. 113. Kautz, then colonel of the 2nd Ohio, had been involved in the pursuit of Morgan on the latter's Indiana-Ohio raid.
80. *Ibid.*, 68. On the day Meade's apology was sent to Wilson, Dana wrote Secretary Stanton that Grant was coming to the conclusion that Meade would have to be removed from the command of the Army of the Potomac because he aroused such hostility and resentment among his subordinates by his insulting behavior toward them. The conversation in which Grant made this remark concerned the Meade-Wilson correspondence cited earlier. *Ibid.*, 35–36.

VIII

"A soldier, and afeared?"

WHEN GRANT, AS NEWLY APPOINTED GENERAL-IN-CHIEF, began to issue orders for the campaign of the spring of 1864, which he planned as a simultaneous advance of all the Union armies "toward one common center," one of his directives went to Major General Franz Sigel, darling of German-Americans and also of Confederate commanders who had the good fortune to be pitted against him. After a number of defeats and failures unmarked on his part by any display of military competence, Sigel commanded the Federal forces in that graveyard of Union military reputations, the Shenandoah Valley. His Department of West Virginia was one of four military departments within fifty miles of Washington that divided and confused the responsibility of protecting the capital, the Baltimore & Ohio Railroad, and generally, the area to the north of the Army of the Potomac as it moved south against the Army of Northern Virginia and Richmond. Sigel had twenty-six thousand troops of all arms under his command, "generally recruits, recently organized regiments, or such as were thought to be of least value to the armies engaged in active service."[1]

Grant's orders to Sigel were to march south in the Shenandoah Valley to Staunton, on the Virginia Central Railroad. There he was

1. Davies, *General Sheridan*, 137.

to be joined by General George Crook, who, starting from Charleston, was to march south to the Virginia & Tennessee Railroad which he was to destroy and then turn east to unite with Sigel. Assembling a field force of seventeen thousand for his march up the Valley, Sigel set forth on May 2. He got as far as New Market, where on May 15 he was soundly beaten by a smaller force under John C. Breckinridge and retreated in considerable disorder to Strasburg, at the northern end of Massanutten Mountain.[2] There he was relieved of his command and replaced by General David Hunter.

William Averell, in command of the cavalry of the Department of West Virginia, had returned to his base at Beverly on the day after Christmas from his Salem raid. Within a few days thereafter, Fitzhugh Lee, still in the Valley after his unsuccessful chase of Averell earlier in the month, went on a raid of his own. Starting on the last day of 1863, he rode north to Moorefield and Petersburg. The roads were sheets of ice; nevertheless, he captured an ordnance train and returned with a herd of cattle, horses, and mules, and with welcome supplies of bacon, hardtack, horseshoes, and nails. Averell, who had just moved from Beverly to Martinsburg, was asked to try to intercept the raiders but had to report that he had only a few usable horses; he thought, in any case, that on the ice-covered roads infantry could march faster and farther than cavalry and suggested that he be allowed to send after the raiders those of his men who had shoes and were able to walk.[3]

Averell was prevented or inhibited from pursuing Lee by more than the state of the roads, the inclement weather, and the condition of his horses, worn out by the raid to Salem. Rightly or wrongly, and probably rightly, he was convinced that he had a poor lot

2. For an excellent account of Sigel's brief campaign and defeat, see William C. Davis, *The Battle of New Market* (New York, 1975), *passim*; see also *Official Records*, Vol. XXXVII, Pt. 1, p. 475, and Sigel's own account, "Sigel in the Shenandoah Valley in 1864," *Battles and Leaders*, IV, 487–91.

3. *Official Records*, XXXIII, 329. On January 3, 1864, Imboden's brigade and McNeill's partisans captured a Union wagon train near Williamsport. At the end of the month, Rosser's brigade, aided by McNeill's and Gilmor's partisans, made another raid on Williamsport and captured ninety-three supply wagons, forty-two of which, however, were smashed and burned. *Ibid.*, 335, 33; see also Samuel C. Farrar, *The Twenty-Second Pennsylvania Cavalry and the Ringgold Battalion* (Pittsburg, 1911), 159.

of troops to work with. He had little confidence in the pickets of the 12th Pennsylvania, and he reported the Ringgold Battalion as "without any organizing talent at its head," suggesting that it be "assigned to one of the large cavalry commands for organization and discipline."[4] Five companies of the 22nd Pennsylvania, ordered to report to him, arrived "unarmed, dismounted and unequipped."[5] On March 1, he notified the Cavalry Bureau that he needed two thousand horses, and more importantly, after being assigned on March 15 to the command of the First and Fourth Divisions of the department, he asked Adjutant General Lorenzo Thomas for several good brigade commanders. Those he had, he wrote,

have neither the rank nor the experience to fit them for the important duties that are devolved upon them; duties that are the more onerous because of the inefficiency of their subordinates. The results are a want of discipline, neglect of duty, and waste of precious time and valuable material . . . as an assemblage of men from all classes and conditions of civil life are as soon as mounted upon horses called cavalry, and expected to perform the duties that legitimately belong to that arm. More especially in cavalry than in any other arm does everything depend on the officers, who should be energetic, industrious, intelligent and persevering.[6]

Averell did not get the brigade commanders he asked for, but his comments on the "inefficiency" of officers could have been echoed with equal justice by every other cavalry commander in the Union army, as indeed they were. It would appear, however, that Averell had more cause than most for his complaint. Two days before he wrote General Thomas, he had received a most gloomy report on the state of his command from Captain W. H. Brown, his assistant inspector general.

[The] horses . . . are in a very bad condition, and this is caused purely

4. *Official Records*, XXXIII, 321, 537. The Ringgold Battalion was eventually added to the 22nd Pennsylvania, losing its independent status. *Ibid.*, 751. The Ringgold men, who had been in the service since the beginning of the war, bitterly resented the consolidation of their battalion with what they called "militia" and resented even more the replacement of their free and easy ways by "the restrictions and discipline of large military camps." Farrar, *The Twenty-Second Pennsylvania*, 183, 185.
5. *Official Records*, XXXIII, 751.
6. *Ibid.*, 629, 679, 703.

by the negligence of the officers. . . . The grooming is generally wretched, and from the looks of the horses, the feeding and watering is [sic] worse. . . . The horses of the 14th Pennsylvania were tolerable, but I noticed a most lamentable ignorance in many officers as regarded the condition of their companies; indeed, throughout the day I found sergeants and even corporals called upon for reports with which captains of companies should at all times have been perfectly conversant. . . . throughout the command the morning reports . . . are incorrect. . . . I am confident there are more men in the division fit for duty than appears on the paper.[7]

Although the order giving Averell command "of all the cavalry forces of the First and Fourth Divisions" was not specific on the point, it was apparently intended—or so at least Averell interpreted it—as doing away with the "legion" type of organization in the department and establishing the cavalry as a separate command. Averell promptly requested authority to call his new command a "cavalry division"; he explained that "the cavalry of this department, like the same arm in the Army of the Potomac, have been scattered and broken up until they have lost all confidence in themselves. What they need now as much as anything is a revival of their esprit de corps; they should get the idea that their arm is independent in itself, able to do anything, and as worthy of a special name as any other."[8]

After a mild debate, Averell was allowed to have his way, and his command was officially designated a cavalry division. His organizational problems, however, were only beginning. Only three days later he was ordered to change the composition of his new division; of the regiments assigned to him less than two weeks before, he was to select six for what would then be his division; what was to become of the regiments he did not select was not indicated.[9] Averell thereupon chose the 1st New York (Lincoln), 1st New York (Veteran), 21st New York, 12th and 14th Pennsylvania, and 1st and 6th West Virginia. The fact that he chose seven regiments instead of six was only an additional complication in a

7. Ibid., 674–75. For difficulties with line officers of the cavalry in general, see Stephen Z. Starr, "Hawkeyes on Horseback: The Second Iowa Cavalry," Civil War History, XXIII (1977), 222–25.
8. Official Records, XXXIII, 715; approval was granted on March 23 (ibid., 720).
9. Ibid., 746.

situation already sufficiently confused, but it was accepted without comment, and the division was formally constituted on April 12.[10] Two weeks went by, and then another reorganization was ordered. General Julius Stahel had been appointed chief of cavalry of the department on March 25. He was allowed to enjoy the powers and privileges of the post for a month and a day, but was then released from that assignment and given command of what had been until then Averell's division. This now became the *First* Cavalry Division, but two of its regiments were taken away from it and replaced not by two, but by four others. At the same time, Averell was given command of what was constituted as the *Second* Cavalry Division, made up of the 1st, 5th, and 7th West Virginia, the 14th Pennsylvania, the 8th Ohio as one of its brigades and General Alfred Duffié's brigade as the other.[11] The cavalry, rank and file, to say nothing of the unfortunate clerks in the War Department, must have found it a sore trial to keep up with this dizzying succession of changes.

On March 29 there were twelve regiments of cavalry—5,441 officers and men "present for duty equipped"—in the Department of West Virginia. Of these, two regiments and the Ringgold Battalion were trying with moderate success to guard an 18-mile stretch of country between the Upper Potomac and Parkersburg. Three regiments were stationed in the Kanawha Valley, and the rest of the cavalry was stationed at a number of points between the Shenandoah and Cacapon rivers.[12] Not surprisingly, Sigel, preparing for the campaign that was to come to an inglorious end at New Market, intimated that he needed more cavalry than he had and, to make certain that he was clearly understood, asked in a subsequent dispatch that the 20th and 21st Pennsylvania be transferred from the Department of the Susquehanna to him, to enable him to cope with guerrillas and bushwhackers. General Grant sent him word the same day that the two regiments he asked for were being ordered to report to him.[13]

10. *Ibid.*, 847.
11. *Ibid.*, 986.
12. *Ibid.*, 762.
13. *Ibid.*, 766. The two regiments had been raised as six-month units at the time of Lee's invasion of Pennsylvania in the summer of 1863; they were remustered in February, 1864, as three-year regiments. C. E. Dorn-

Whatever pleasure the general-in-chief's prompt and favorable action on his request for cavalry reinforcements may have caused Sigel could not have been of long duration. When the 20th Pennsylvania left Chambersburg for Charleston two days after Grant's dispatch, it was reported as "neither mounted except one squadron, nor armed, except with sabers," and it may be assumed that the 21st Pennsylvania was in no better condition.[14] Duffié, to whom the two Pennsylvania regiments were ordered to report, had informed the Cavalry Bureau at the end of January that his "cavalry and mounted infantry . . . [were] fully supplied with horses, arms and equipments. . . . The horses have been well fed and groomed, and well shod," but now, only two months later, he had a different story to tell; he not only had nothing to spare to supply the newcomers' wants, but on March 27 he had wired Sigel a plea for horses for the troopers he already had and followed it up with a second wire the same day, begging to have forwarded to him without delay "the arms and horses required to place . . . [his] command efficient for field duties."[15]

Averell's supply situation was no better than Duffié's. He reported on April 11, when he had command of the previously mentioned seven-regiment division, that he needed 3,500 horses to mount the men actually present, plus another 1,000 horses for the men he expected "to return," perhaps from veterans' furlough; he also needed 2,142 carbines, 1,562 revolvers, and 250 sets of horse equipments.[16]

When it is remembered that the war was about to enter its

busch, *Military Bibliography of the Civil War* (3 vols.; New York, 1971), Vol. I, Pt. 4, p. 30.

14. *Official Records*, XXXIII, 793.

15. *Ibid.*, 452, 751, 756.

16. *Ibid.*, 840. The figures Averell gave as the number of horses he needed are incomprehensible. Assuming the impossible, that he had no horses at all, to need either 3,500 or 4,500 horses for seven regiments would mean that the regiments averaged 500 or 643 men each, impossibly high figures for the spring of 1864. Even the 2,142 carbines he said he needed seems an exorbitant figure. Perhaps Averell operated on the theory that to get his actual wants met, he had to ask for twice as many horses and carbines as he needed. The details of his request show that two of his regiments, the 1st New York (Lincoln) and the 1st West Virginia, were armed with Spencers and the others with Burnside carbines.

fourth year, that the massive industrial resources of the North had been mobilized long since to supply the wants of the armies, that the quartermaster's and ordnance organizations in Washington and in the field had outgrown the fumbling amateurishness of 1861 and 1862, and that the Cavalry Bureau had been in existence for nearly a year, it is difficult to understand why the 12th Pennsylvania should have been sent in the spring of 1864 for service in the field with "about 10 men in each company mounted," or why the 8th Ohio (the 44th Ohio Infantry converted to a cavalry regiment) should have arrived in Charleston as "a fine and full organization, but not yet equipped with horses and arms."[17]

The Department of West Virginia was the happy hunting ground of the best and most active of the Confederate Partisan Ranger groups—White's, McNeill's, Gilmor's, and of course Mosby's—and their nearly unbroken record of successes, due frequently to the carelessness or ineptness or both of their antagonists, makes a dismal tale. It is the merest truism that these groups enjoyed every advantage—the aid of the local population, thorough familiarity with the countryside, superior horsemanship, freedom to operate independently of larger units, no concern with road-bound logistics, a terrain made to order for their type of warfare—but an additional advantage they should not have had, certainly not so late as the spring of 1864, was the seeming lack of ability of Union cavalry officers to anticipate and to deal with their attacks. Incident after incident illustrates the point. Thus, Major Hanson W. Hunter of the 6th West Virginia was sent out with a detachment of 151 of his troopers to "capture or destroy" a band of about 100 guerrillas. He surprised them in Winchester as they were feeding their horses.

The rebels, however, escaped and were followed for a mile beyond the town, when the attack was abandoned, and . . . [the] men brought back to . . . town, when . . . [Hunter] left them to enter a house, where he remained for some time, without having taken any precaution

17. *Ibid.*, Vol. XXXVII, Pt. 1, pp. 370, 520. Brigadier General Max Weber, who wrote the dispatch concerning the 12th Pennsylvania, remarked in the same dispatch that the regiment was "known as one of the worst in the service, that it would run at the first alarm," and that its 400 recruits were "good for nothing—worse than useless."

against surprise except leaving a detachment as a rear guard. The enemy, availing himself of the carelessness and utter lack of common sense . . . charged upon the rear guard, threw it upon the main body, which . . . was quickly thrown into confusion, and 27 men were lost in the disgraceful and dastardly flight of 151 men before less than 100.[18]

Hunter was placed in arrest and recommended for dismissal from the service, but that did not help matters; the damage, material and moral, had already been done. Three months later, a 100-man picket reserve of the same ill-omened 6th West Virginia was surprised by McNeill, who carried off 60 of the men and all 100 horses, complete with their equipment.[19]

On May 22, Captain Michael Auer of the 15th New York allowed his picket reserve of about 50 men "to be disgracefully surprised and captured by a party of the enemy . . . the reserve picket guard not firing a shot, and the result being the loss . . . of 11 men, 45 horses and some small arms."[20] A week later, a 120-man detachment of the same regiment, escorting a train of 16 wagons loaded with "medical and subsistence stores," was waylaid near Newtown by Gilmor's guerrillas. The escort was driven off with the loss of 1 man killed, 9 wounded, and 10 missing; the 16 wagons and their contents, and 96 army mules, became the partisans' trophies.[21]

Mosby himself commanded in still another humiliation of the Federal cavalry. He arrived at Centreville on the morning of June 24, a half hour after Lieutenant Matthew Tuck with 40 troopers of the 6th New York rode through the village. A mile or so beyond, Tuck and his men stopped in a newly cut field of hay to let their horses feed. The animals were unbridled, some of the men lay down for a nap, and others climbed trees across the road for a

18. *Ibid.*, XXXIII, 263. In his report of the incident, Averell speaks of Major Hunter's "criminal carelessness."
19. *Ibid.*, Vol. XXXVII, Pt. 1, p. 162.
20. *Ibid.*, 527. Auer received a dishonorable discharge, but it was voided by the president. Major Henry Roessle of the same regiment was dishonorably discharged because of the same incident, for having "grossly neglected his duty while in command of pickets," but his discharge too was voided by the president. *Ibid.*, 532.
21. *Ibid.*, 161, 565. The Pennsylvanians claimed that they were outnumbered by the enemy. That claim, nearly always made in similar situations, must be viewed with considerable skepticism.

feast of ripe cherries. One man, posted as the single sentry, sat on a fence "in a very poorly chosen position." Having learned all this from the friendly townspeople, Mosby "sent a part of his men rapidly on, who dashed into the field, shooting the man on post, and making such a panic that no resistance was attempted." Three of Tuck's men were wounded and left behind by the partisans, five others escaped on foot, and "all the horses and the rest of the men and arms" were captured.[22]

Another exploit of McNeill's and the ineffectual Federal response to it are described by the historian of the veteran Ringgold Battalion, which a short time before had been consolidated with the 22nd Pennsylvania, commanded by Colonel Jacob Higgins. On May 5, McNeill with 60 of his men captured a Baltimore & Ohio train in Bloomington, Maryland, placed guards on the train, and ordered the engineer to move slowly toward Piedmont, West Virginia, a short distance to the east. The rest of the partisans "followed immediately in the wake of the train, thus hidden from observation," and surprised the Federal garrison at Piedmont, which surrendered without putting up any resistance. The mail train, arriving a short time later, was captured and burned, as were the railroad shops and buildings and two freight trains loaded with army stores. Word of the raid reached General Sigel on the evening of the sixth, thirty-six hours later. He ordered a "scout" of 450 cavalry to Moorefield and Petersburg "to cut off the raiders." The 22nd Pennsylvania was ordered to saddle up and be ready to march at a moment's notice.

We were kept in this position until 3:30 a. m. of the 7th, when we marched out in the direction of Moorefield . . . with a train of 20 wagons. . . . Had this scout been ordered out in charge of . . . Major Work [of the veteran Ringgold Battalion] . . . it would have moved promptly a few minutes after the order had been issued and there would have been no . . . wagon train. . . . We reached Moor[e]field late in the afternoon of the 8th when we found McNeill's force on a point southwest of town. . . . We formed immediately . . . and with the precision of a dress parade advanced toward the enemy. . . . When we were within a short distance of . . . [them] they skedaddled . . . and in less time than it takes to tell it, they were lost in the woods.[23]

22. *Ibid.*, 168–69.
23. Farrar, *The Twenty-Second Pennsylvania*, 198–201.

Before these melancholy incidents occurred, or while they were occurring, the larger course of the war swept on. The advance of the West Virginia armies ordered by Grant got under way on schedule. General Crook, in overall command of the movement from the Kanawha Valley, had been protesting all through the month of April that a shortage of horses would prevent Averell, who was to command the cavalry phase of the operation, from doing his part. At one point Crook asked for permission to buy horses in Ohio, writing to Sigel that if additional horses were not procured, the cavalry operation would "have to be abandoned for want of sufficient mounted force." Crook's dispatches were echoed by Sigel, who wrote Grant on April 12 that "at least one-third of our cavalry is dismounted, and we cannot buy as many horses and as fast as we want them."[24]

Despite all these difficulties, enough horses had been collected by one means or another by the end of April to give Averell a mounted force of 2,479 "picked men" in two brigades, one under Duffié and the other under Colonel James M. Schoonmaker, plus a separate 400-man composite unit made up of men from the 5th and 7th West Virginia.[25] Before starting out on May 5, Averell issued a general order for the guidance of his men. "First, on the march," he told them, "guard carefully against sudden and violent changes of gait, which soon tire and break your horses. Second, in camp or bivouac, first look after the wants of your horses, and be silent that all may rest. Third, in action listen to the commands of your officers, and be always ready, with your arms in good order." This helpful and practical advice should not have been needed in the fourth year of the war, but it must be assumed that Averell had reason to think it necessary. He weakened the thrust of the order with pompous rhetoric, however, adding, "As your commanding officer, I feel the load of heavy responsibility; but relying upon your strength, I am confident that I shall bear it easily."[26]

The goal of Averell's share of the overall plan was to break up the Virginia & Tennessee Railroad at Saltville, in the southwest-

24. *Ibid.*, 820, 900, 938, 844.
25. *Ibid.*, Vol. XXXVII, Pt. 1, p. 41.
26. *Ibid.*, 364–65.

ern corner of Virginia. His expedition, however, was plagued by supply problems from the start. On the fourth day of his march "over pathless mountains and . . . tortuous streams," in a "region almost . . . destitute of supplies," Averell learned from deserters and prisoners that John Hunt Morgan and W. E. ("Grumble") Jones, well informed of his strength and plans, were waiting for him at Saltville with 4,500 men. He concluded that he could not take the town by surprise, nor, with cavalry alone, could he expect to carry the earthworks the Confederates had had time to construct around the town. He therefore decided to change his objective; he would try to strike the railroad at Wyethville, where he would also be in a position to prevent Morgan and Jones from moving east to intercept Crook and his infantry.

Averell reached Wyethville on the afternoon of May 10 and discovered that Jones and Morgan had gotten there ahead of him; they occupied an "admirable position" which blocked his access to the railroad. He thought, apparently with reason, that they outnumbered him two to one. Just what happened thereafter is far from clear. Averell reported that notwithstanding the odds against him he attacked, and that after "the field was maintained four hours" the enemy "retired."[27] It is significant, however, that it was not at Wyethville, but at Christiansville, thirty-five miles to the northeast, that Averell reached the railroad and destroyed it "as much as practicable" (which it may not be too uncharitable to translate as "very little indeed") for a distance of four miles. Moreover, Morgan, who implied that he was in command at Wyethville, wrote his wife on the evening of the fight, "If we had 2 more hours of fighting, would have captured the entire force. My men fought magnificently, driving them from hill to hill. It was certainly the greatest sight I ever witnessed to see a handful of men driving such masses before them. Averell fought his men elegantly, tried time & time again to charge but our boys gave them no time to form."[28] None of this—and Morgan was hardly a model of accurate reporting—is reflected in Averell's report.

27. In addition to "about 114" killed and wounded at Wyethville, Averell also lost "a few men" by drowning, in crossing "frequently unfordable" mountain streams. *Ibid.*, 42.
28. Cecil F. Holland, *Morgan and His Raiders* (New York, 1942), 317.

On May 15, Averell joined Crook at the town of Union.[29] In a congratulatory order nearly as long as his report, Averell paid the conventional tribute to the good conduct of his men on the march and in the fight at Wyethville, but he ended on a note most unusual in such orders. He thanked "those officers and men . . . who . . . treated the inhabitants of the country with that courtesy, dignity, and magnanimity which is [sic] inseparable from true courage and greatness." But, he went on, "Those few unworthy persons who have disgraced themselves and us by acts of lawless pillage should receive the scorn and contempt of every honorable soldier in the command."[30]

Alfred Duffié, who reinforced Averell's divisonal congratulatory order with a special congratulatory order to his own brigade even more grandiloquent and fulsome than Averell's, felt it necessary also to inform General Crook that his men were "without clothing or shoes, the horses are worn down, their equipment destroyed, and everything in bad condition." A strange litany of shortages to come at the start of the grand coordinated campaign intended to end the war, but nothing more than a representation of the normal state of the cavalry in West Virginia. Then, however, came a more personal note. "I have been," Duffié wrote, "under the command of General Averell since the expedition started, but have been without a written order. . . . When I joined him, I understood it to be only for the present expedition, and that when it should end my command would again be my own. . . . This is now my great desire. I wish to be relieved from duty

29. The account in the text of Averell's abortive Saltville Raid is based on his report, *ibid.*, 41–42. One of his troopers wrote, "Our ammunition being exhausted or rendered useless by the incessant rains . . . [Averell] decided to start on the return march. . . . Our rations and forage had been exhausted, and the country was so poor that only an inadequate supply could be had. Our clothing was soaked with rain and our feet so badly swollen that our boots had to be cut open to get them off. One hundred and eighty-eight men were . . . barefooted . . . such raids, owing to the long distance we were compelled to cover, certainly cost us more than the harm done the enemy." Sutton, *History of the Second Regiment*, 117–18.

30. *Official Records*, Vol. XXXVII, Pt. 1, p. 43. "Owing to the miserable condition" of the teams and wagons supplied to him, Averell was able to take along only four days' rations for his men and one and a half days' forage for the animals. To start out on a ten-day campaign with food enough for four made "acts of lawless pillage" inevitable.

under General Averell, and to be ordered to report to you with my command."[31] This was most unusual language to use in an official dispatch, even in a service in which backbiting and feuding among members of the higher command were fairly common. Duffié's desire to be relieved of duty under Averell was in fact satisfied, but not in the way he might have expected. General Julius Stahel was wounded on June 5 in the battle of Piedmont and incapacitated for service in the field, and on June 9 Duffié replaced him in command of the Second Cavalry Division.[32] It may be added that Duffié's dislike of Averell was cordially reciprocated, and when, at an early date, Averell had the opportunity to even the score, he did not fail to take advantage of it.

While Averell was on his way to Wyethville, George Crook, with 6,000 infantry, defeated the Confederate forces opposing him on May 9 on Cloyd Mountain. A future president of the United States, Colonel Rutherford B. Hayes, commanding a brigade of Ohio and West Virginia troops, particularly distinguished himself in this action.[33] On the following day, Crook accomplished the primary objective of his part of the operation by demolishing the New River Bridge, eight miles east of Dublin. From there he marched east, intending to join Sigel at Staunton. However, as has been mentioned, Sigel was defeated on May 15 at New Market, which caused Secretary Stanton to urge that he be replaced forthwith by General David Hunter. Grant's orders to that effect were duly issued on May 19.

On taking over command in the Valley, Hunter's primary task was to resume the advance that his predecessor had been unable to effect. Hunter was a veteran of the guerrilla war on the Kansas-Missouri border, which was conducted by both sides with a ferocity unknown in Virginia. To protect his rear and his line of communications from guerrilla attacks, Hunter decided that he had to put the fear of God into the guerrillas' base of support, the pro-Confederate people of the Shenandoah Valley. On the night of

31. *Ibid.*, 43–44, 500–501.

32. At some point not disclosed by the records, the divisions of Averell and Duffié exchanged numbers. Averell's became the First Division, and Duffié's (formerly Stahel's), the Second.

33. For Crook's report, see *Official Records*, Vol. XXXVII, Pt. 1, pp. 9–13; see also Williams, *Hayes of the Twenty-third*, 174–80.

May 23 one of his trains was fired on from a house in the village of Newtown. The next morning, Major Timothy Quinn, 1st New York (Lincoln), was ordered to proceed to Newtown, ascertain from which house the shot had been fired, "burn the same with all . . . [its] outbuildings," and notify the populace that if the incident was repeated, "the commanding general will cause to be burned every rebel house within five miles of the place at which the firing occurs."[34]

Less than a week later, Gilmor, as has been mentioned, captured near Newtown a sixteen-wagon convoy from its escort of the 15th Pennsylvania. This led Hunter to order Major Quinn to detail two hundred of his men to return to Newtown and burn "every house, store and out-building in that place, except the churches and the houses and out-buildings of those who are known to be loyal citizens of the United States"; the houses and outbuildings of all rebels between Newtown and Middletown were also to be burned down.[35] The reaction of the men detailed for this expedition might have surprised General Hunter:

It began to be suspected that the purpose of this expedition was to burn . . . [Newtown]. There were murmurings of disapproval. Burning houses of citizens was not the business of soldiers. . . . The apprehensions of the object of the move were confirmed when silently, and more like a funeral procession than a marching army, the column moved into . . . the town. . . . The old people and children were standing in the doorways with an expression of mute helplessness on their faces. . . . The officers consulted together and decided to disobey the order of General Hunter. . . . It was found that the Union men wounded in the attack on the train had been carefully nursed in these homes. It seemed best to have the people take the oath of allegiance to the Union, and spare the town. . . . It was a relief to all when the column headed toward the south and the houses in the town still standing.[36]

34. *Official Records*, Vol. XXXVII, Pt. 1, p. 528.
35. *Ibid.*, 557.
36. Beach, *First New York (Lincoln) Cavalry*, 355–56; see also Stevenson, *"Boots and Saddles,"* 278. Both Beach and Stevenson state that Major Joseph K. Stearns commanded the detachment. Later in the campaign, when Captain Franklin G. Martindale, on what the regimental historian says was the "direct and positive orders of General Hunter," burned down the residences of Andrew Hunter, Colonel Edmund Lee, and A. G. Boteler, "Hunter's burning of residences was condemned in the strongest terms by the men of his command." Beach, *First New York (Lincoln) Cavalry*, 393. In October, Sheridan ordered the burning of every house within a radius of three miles

The troopers of the New York regiment may have considered the retaliatory burning of houses as not "the business of soldiers," but neither they nor the members of other cavalry regiments were averse to victimizing "enemy" civilians, the disloyal and the loyal alike, in other ways. General Hunter had to call Stahel's attention to the "numerous and grave" complaints against his cavalry "for unauthorized pillaging. It is represented that the men sent out in regular foraging parties break away from their officers and straggle into houses, carrying off dresses, ornaments, books, money, and doing wanton injury to furniture; and that some not sent out, do also straggle beyond the camps in squads, and commit similar depredations."[37]

General Hunter had taken over command of Sigel's beaten army on the evening of May 21 at Cedar Creek and announced to the War Department that he had ordered Crook and Averell to move on Staunton, where he intended to meet them and then march east via Charlottesville and Gordonsville to join the Army of the Potomac.[38] His own advance to Staunton began on June 4. The following day he met and defeated "Grumble" Jones at the village of Piedmont, an action in which Jones's small army lost more than 1,000 men taken prisoner, and, by Hunter's estimate, 600 killed and wounded, General Jones being among those killed.[39] The day after the battle Hunter occupied Staunton and destroyed "the railroad bridges and depots, and public workshops and factories in the town and vicinity."[40] Crook and Averell arrived on June 8, increasing Hunter's command to a total of about 17,500 of all arms.

There had been no improvement in the condition of Averell's

---

of the place near Dayton where his topographical engineer, Lieutenant John R. Meigs, was killed. The historian of the 5th New York, which was designated to carry out the order, wrote, "This was the most heart-sickening duty we had ever performed. Splendid mansions in great number . . . were laid in ashes. . . . The execution of such orders, however just and right, has a very demoralizing effect upon the men." Boudrye, *Historic Records of the Fifth*, 176–77.

37. *Official Records*, Vol. XXXVII, Pt. 1, p. 555.
38. *Ibid.*, 508, 507.
39. *Ibid.*, 95, 96; see also *Battles and Leaders*, IV, 485–86.
40. *Official Records*, Vol. XXXVII, Pt. 1, p. 95.

cavalry since the end of the Saltville-Wyethville expedition. With 3,200 mounted and 1,200 dismounted men he had waited for two weeks at Lewisburg on half rations, for supplies that "owing to the miserable, inadequate and insufficient transportation furnished from the Kanawha" failed to arrive. Not only was he short of rations, but he also needed shoes for 600 of his men, 378 of whom, Duffié reported, were already barefoot, and he needed "many other articles of clothing," as well as horseshoes and horseshoe nails. Then, to add indignity to his very real supply problems, when he arrived at Staunton he was ordered to "see that all private property and dwellings in the vicinity of . . . [his] camp has a guard, to prevent soldiers from marauding. No soldier will be allowed to enter the town without a pass from division headquarters. When horses are sent into town to be shod they must be sent under the charge of a commissioned officer." This order of Hunter's makes it evident that it did not take him long to learn what to expect of his cavalry when they came within reach of the property of the local population.[41]

Averell himself, however, received an expression of Hunter's confidence. He was asked on June 9 to prepare a plan for the capture of Lynchburg at the end of a five-day campaign. The request came about as a result of Hunter's decision, pursuant to the discretion Grant had given him, to march to Richmond via Lynchburg instead of taking the more direct route via Charlottesville and Gordonsville, as he had originally intended to do. As soon as General Lee learned that Hunter was moving in the direction of Lynchburg, he sent first Breckinridge's division, and then Jubal Early and his 8,000-man corps—troops he sorely needed at Richmond—to protect the threatened city.[42] This was an indication of the strategic soundness of Hunter's choice of the Lynchburg route. It will be recalled, however, that the ultimate goal of Sheri-

41. Ibid., 145, 578, 607.
42. "On June 12, when . . . [General Lee] learned that Hunter had picked up Crook and had gone on to occupy Lexington . . . [he] ordered Jubal Early to take his army corps . . . to Lynchburg with all speed . . . the prospect of losing Lynchburg and the railroad network that centered there was unendurable, and on June 13, while Grant's army was marching for the James, Early and his 8,000 infantry were going far away to the west." Catton, Grant Takes Command, 298; see also Freeman, R. E. Lee, III, 396, 401.

dan's raid to Trevilian Station was to effect a junction with Hunter; this might have been accomplished had Hunter taken the Charlottesville-Gordonsville route, but by going to Lynchburg he moved away from Sheridan instead of toward him.

The plan for capturing Lynchburg Averell proposed was that all but Duffié's division of Hunter's army should move south on a number of parallel roads running generally through the middle of the Valley, while Duffié marched south along the western foot of the Blue Ridge, "making demonstrations at the various gaps"; he was then to move to the east side of the Blue Ridge by way of White's Gap, cross the James River below Lynchburg and come up to the town from the southeast, destroying the track of the Southside Railroad as he went. Meanwhile the main body would cross the Blue Ridge near the Peaks of Otter, cross the James above Lynchburg, circle around to meet Duffié, and attack the town from the south.[43]

When on the seventeenth Hunter reached Lynchburg, Breckinridge and Early were already there. Attacking side by side, Averell and Crook got to within three miles of the city by nightfall, but there they were held and then had to fight off a powerful counterattack mounted by the Confederates. Duffié also reached Lynchburg on the seventeenth and launched his attack to the left of Averell and Crook, along the Forestville Road, but his attack, in which his men used up all their ammunition, was no more successful than Crook's and Averell's had been.[44] The Federals did not renew their attacks on the eighteenth; indeed, they had to fight off another Confederate counterattack. Also, Hunter learned from prisoners of Early's presence in Lynchburg, and, so he reported, it became evident to him "that the enemy had concentrated a force at least double the numerical strength of mine, and what added to the gravity of the situation was the fact that my troops had scarcely enough ammunition left to sustain another well-contested battle."[45] Hunter was greatly in error in believing

43. *Official Records*, Vol. XXXVII, Pt. 1, p. 146.
44. *Ibid.*, 141–43, 99.
45. *Ibid.*, 100. Actually, with all his troops deployed, Hunter would have outnumbered the defenders by nearly two to one. For two conflicting assessments of Hunter's decision not to press the attack, see Grant, *Personal Memoirs*, II, 304, and John B. Gordon, *Reminiscences of the Civil War* (New York, 1905), 300.

that the Confederates outnumbered him; nonetheless, acting on his belief he gave up the effort to capture the town and decided to retreat. He chose not to return to Staunton, the way he had come, but to march west over the mountains to Charleston. From there, and with a great deal of difficulty owing to low water in the Kanawha and the Ohio, he eventually moved his army by boat to Parkersburg and then east by rail to Cumberland, Maryland. The effect of this eccentric retreat was that from the day it began, on June 18, until past July 14, Hunter's army was out of the war.[46]

Averell's report on this campaign is a curious document. After explaining the plan he had drawn up at General Hunter's request, he writes that he gave Duffié "complete and comprehensive verbal instructions with regard to the route he was to take and the services his division was to render. He was also furnished with memoranda to assist his memory." Given the nature of the operation, or, for that matter, of any fairly complex military operation, this was no more than what should have been done as a matter of course. But, says Averell, Duffié was out of touch with the main body from June 11 on; in fact, having "lost himself on the extreme left," he was not "found" until the morning of the eighteenth. Without actually saying so, Averell implies, no doubt intentionally, that Duffié mishandled in some fashion the role assigned to him and was therefore responsible for the failure of the operation.[47]

Naturally, no hint of any failure on his part is to be found in Duffié's report. He speaks of sending off messages to General Hunter on June 10, 11, and 17; moreover, his report is peppered with such phrases as "Failing to receive any communication from

46. General Hunter's report of the campaign is in *Official Records*, Vol. XXXVII, Pt. 1, pp. 98–103. His total casualties were 940, of which the cavalry's share was 25 killed, 198 wounded, and 133 missing. *Ibid.*, 106. His retreat took the army through sparsely inhabited mountain country. The march was made in severe heat and on starvation rations. Captain James H. Stevenson, 1st New York (Lincoln), who commanded the rear guard, "counted five hundred horses and mules, abandoned by our army, which I was obliged to have shot. They were only worn out with fatigue and hunger, and could have been recruited . . . by a little care." Stevenson, *"Boots and Saddles,"* 287.

47. *Official Records*, Vol. XXXVII, Pt. 1, pp. 147–48. At one point on the march to Lynchburg, Duffié's division had been "led in the wrong direction, it was thought intentionally, by the citizen guide, whose life paid the penalty of the act." Sutton, *History of the Second Regiment*, 130.

department headquarters," and "had failed to receive any orders as to what I should do."[48]

Here was an impressive bill of particulars, presented by Averell, to prove Duffié guilty of gross incompetence and disobedience of orders. Assuredly, Duffié had serious shortcomings as a cavalry commander, but it is nevertheless evident that Averell was out to paint his performance in the blackest possible colors. Lacking information from an unbiased third party, one can only suspect that although there was doubtless some basis for Averell's criticisms, express or implied, they are probably exaggerated and inspired by the bad blood between the two men. Whatever Averell's reason or excuse may have been, he quite clearly conducted a personal vendetta against Duffié. There is a strong hint in the records that General Hunter was of that opinion; in a June 19 order to Averell he stated that thereafter Duffié would receive his orders "direct from the major-general commanding" (i.e., Hunter himself), and not through Averell.[49] On July 2, shortly after the arrival of the command at Charleston, a general order placed Duffié "under the exclusive orders" of Hunter and assigned Averell and his division to the command of General Crook.[50] Clearly, a history of cavalry operations must at times be a record of something more than campaigns and battles; the personal dislikes and feuds that made it impossible for some officers to work in harmony with certain others are an essential if unpleasant part of the story.

On June 27, while Hunter's troops were still on their retreat to Charleston, Averell found time to compose a dispatch for the benefit of the commanding general, which, despite its self-serving conclusion, deserves to be quoted at length. "I beg leave to say a few words to you about the cavalry of this department," Averell wrote,

Hastily organized and but partially equipped, and with inexperienced officers, it has never been properly fitted for the field. During last winter the supplies of horses, equipments and arms were meager and irregular. . . . Since May 1, this cavalry has marched 800 miles, over a region filled with every obstacle to cavalry operations. . . . It is difficult

48. General Hunter acknowledged on June 13 receipt of a dispatch of Duffié's "of 5 o'clock this morning." *Official Records*, Vol. XXXVII, Pt. 1, pp. 633, 140, 141.
49. *Ibid.*, 651–52.
50. *Ibid.*, Pt. 2, p. 9.

to procure horses. The demands of other armies will cause ours to be neglected. The assemblage of so many fragments of regiments is in many respects objectionable . . . I, therefore, think it will be well to mount the best regiments entirely, dismounting the least effective for the purpose, and organizing the cavalry of the department into one division instead of two. The dismounted regiments can replace infantry . . . and can be mounted as soon as practicable under the charge of some officer who is qualified for organization.[51]

Averell's assessment of the problems of the cavalry of the department, and the remedy he proposed, were sound enough. It is of course unnecessary to ask whom he had in mind for the command of the single active division of cavalry, or the name of the officer to be relegated to the role of "organization."

The return of the Third Cavalry Division from the Wilson Raid, in what other cavalrymen of the Army of the Potomac judged to be "a demoralized and almost disorganized condition," marked the beginning of a month's lull in cavalry operations along the James.[52] Sheridan was directed to attend to the reorganization of Wilson's division and to get the entire Cavalry Corps in condition for active service.[53] The Third Division was certainly in need of reorganization; many of its troopers were wandering about in the rear areas of the army, causing Provost Marshal Marsena R. Patrick to order the arrest of troopers of the division who came to City Point, or who were already "in that neighborhood."[54] The condition of Torbert's and Gregg's divisions, just returned from Trevilian Station, was in many respects as bad as Wilson's. Sheridan reported on July 3 that the corps was "unfit for service."

The larger portion of the command has marched continually for nearly sixty days. The horses are . . . jaded and must have rest. Most of the horses have lost their shoes, and, in fact, the whole command should be reshod. The men have also suffered and require rest, and above all things, clothing. I have a large number of men who have been barefooted for the last two weeks. The men can soon get into condition, but it will require from twelve to fifteen days to get the horses in good working condition.[55]

51. *Ibid.*, Pt. 1, pp. 679–80.
52. Crowninshield, *A History of the First Regiment*, 229.
53. *Official Records*, Vol. XL, Pt. 2, pp. 675, 612.
54. *Ibid.*, 577.
55. *Ibid.*, 613.

A mere five—not twelve or fifteen—days later, Meade inquired of Sheridan, "what will be the earliest day on which your command will be in condition for service, and the number of officers and men you will then have available? It is important that . . . [I] should know this, and also that your corps should be made available at the earliest practicable moment."[56] Sheridan replied that in an emergency he could turn out nine thousand men, but that his command was not yet fit for hard work.[57] Regardless of Sheridan's difficulties, the war had to go on, and on July 11 he was ordered to send one of his divisions—he chose Gregg's—on a reconnaissance beyond the left flank of the army, to try to locate A. P. Hill's corps.[58] Three days later he was directed to "get ready at the earliest possible moment" for a raid as far south as Weldon, North Carolina, against General Lee's communications. Kautz's division was to join the Cavalry Corps for this operation, and as evidence that the lesson of Wilson's misfortunes had been taken to heart, Sheridan was asked to inform Meade "what force in infantry you consider necessary to co-operate with you in starting, and at what point it should be directed, and how long it should continue its operations to render its assistance effectual."[59] Sheridan replied the same day that he could move with between eight and nine thousand men on the morning of the sixteenth, but before that day came, the expedition was called off.

A major problem for the cavalry of the Army of the Potomac in that month of July, 1864, was a lack of water. Due to a long dry spell and excessive heat, the smaller streams on both sides of the James were drying up. Sheridan himself reported that in the vicinity of Prince George Court House, where his corps had been ordered to camp, there was no water for the men or the animals; the Blackwater, normally a sizable stream, had "dried up so much that after watering one regiment the water became so thick and bad that the horses would not drink it."[60] Manpower was another problem. Large numbers of men were absent from their regiments for one reason or another; many were dismounted, many were

56. *Ibid.*, Pt. 3, p. 80.
57. *Ibid.*, 112.
58. *Ibid.*, 166, 167, 196, 197, 216.
59. *Ibid.*, 241.
60. *Ibid.*, Pt. 2, p. 613.

sick, many were without weapons, many were away on detached service, and throughout the summer those members of regiments raised in 1861 who had not "veteranized" were being discharged upon the expiration of their three-year terms of enlistment.[61] On July 6, Sheridan reported that he had shipped to Washington 2,927 of his sick, "mostly without arms," and two weeks later he wrote Meade:

[I] urgently request the return of the mounted and dismounted cavalry of . . . [the] corps now at Washington City and vicinity. . . . Those mounted can be of little service to the Government, as they are without organization or officers. The dismounted men . . . if sent here . . . can be mounted as the horses arrive, the best first, and the balance, kept under good discipline, available at all times. . . . We have about Washington 6,000 or 7,000 men without horses, in consequence of which they are a burden instead of a benefit to the Government.[62]

Shortly before the end of July, Grant complied with Sheridan's request; he directed Halleck to have sent to the army all cavalrymen, mounted or not, belonging to Sheridan's corps.[63] Still, the manpower figures were not all on the debit side of the ledger, as "many hundred convalescent wounded and sick men returned from hospital to duty."[64] Horses were being received also, not nearly as many as were needed, but enough to mount sizable numbers of troopers; at the same time, a period of rest and plentiful forage greatly improved the condition of all the animals.[65]

61. *Ibid.*, Pt. 3, pp. 50, 68. Among the units mustered out in the summer were the 1st, 3rd, 6th, and 8th Pennsylvania, 1st New Jersey, and 3rd Indiana. Some of these regiments left behind with the army their recruits and men not yet eligible for muster-out, organized into battalions bearing the designation of the parent regiment. It will thus be proper to speak, for example, of the 6th Pennsylvania as still with the army, but it should be borne in mind that it was now a mere battalion, not a regiment.

62. *Ibid.*, 338. Having large numbers of cavalrymen dismounted was not confined to the Federals. In the summer of 1864, more than a quarter of General Lee's cavalry was also dismounted. Ramsdell, "General Lee's Horse Supply," 772; see also Wellman, *Giant in Gray*, 152.

63. *Official Records*, Vol. XI, Pt. 3, p. 409.

64. Kidd, *Personal Recollections*, 370.

65. According to Sheridan, he received a total of only 1,900 horses. Sheridan, *Personal Memoirs*, I, 446. It was at this time that the War Department decided to buy the horses of the cavalrymen who owned their animals. The horses of the 3rd Indiana and the 9th New York were appraised and bought at prices ranging from $100 to $185. William N. Pickerill, *History of the Third Indiana Cavalry* (Indianapolis, 1865), 157; Cheney, *History of the Ninth Regiment*, 195. Forage for the horses was sometimes ob-

Clothing and supplies of all kinds arrived, but not always in the right sequence; the first item of "clothing" to reach Wilson's division was a supply of chevrons for the noncommissioned officers, and it was ordered, not by any means for the first time or the last, that they wear them. The "dirty, ragged and barefooted men . . . remarked that it would be better to buy shoes and underclothes for barefooted and naked men than to decorate them with those stripes."[66] Then supplies from the Christian and Sanitary commissions arrived by the boatload, and the cavalry got its share of such unaccustomed delicacies as pickles, canned, dried, and fresh fruit, canned meats, condensed milk, cocoa, butter, new potatoes and other vegetables, as a relief from the monotony of salt pork, hardtack, and coffee.[67]

Only two major cavalry operations, both abortive, were mounted by the Army of the Potomac in July. Both operations had their origin in Grant's wish to exploit the explosion of the Petersburg Mine, the most shamefully mishandled operation in American military history.[68] To get as many as possible of Lee's infantry away from the area in which the mine was to be exploded, and at the same time to further his constant objective of breaking up the railroads leading into Richmond and Petersburg, Grant ordered Winfield Scott Hancock, his most dependable corps commander, to cross to the north side of the James with the II Corps and with Gregg's and Torbert's divisions of cavalry. Hancock's footsoldiers were to open a path northward for the cavalry, who were then to destroy once again the Virginia Central bridges over the North and South Anna and the Little River. The infantry in the meantime were to be positioned to protect the rear of the cavalry and to cover its retreat after the bridges had been destroyed.[69] The opera-

---

tained in ways the authorities might not have sanctioned. The 1st Maine, on picket with a field of oats in front of their picket line and a Confederate cavalry unit on picket on the other side of the same field, declared an informal truce, "rode out into the field, dismounted, shook hands, and went to cutting grain." Tobie, *First Maine Cavalry*, 304.
66. Gause, *Four Years with Five Armies*, 298.
67. Cheney, *History of the Ninth Regiment*, 193, 196.
68. For the Petersburg Mine, see *Battles and Leaders*, IV, 545–67; Bruce Catton, *A Stillness at Appomattox* (Garden City, N.Y., 1953), 219–25, 235–53.
69. *Official Records*, Vol. XL, Pt. 3, pp. 437, 448; Grant, *Personal Memoirs*, II, 310; Sheridan, *Personal Memoirs*, I, 446–47. Kautz was ordered

tion prospered at first, but General Lee reacted swiftly to the threat and moved well over half his infantry, also Rooney Lee's and Fitzhugh Lee's cavalry, across the James to deal with the raid. Sheridan scored a minor victory in an engagement with the divisions of C. M. Wilcox, Henry Heth, and Kershaw on the Darbytown Road, but the presence in strength of Confederate infantry and cavalry north of the James made impossible an advance of the Union cavalry to the bridges. Hancock and Sheridan therefore agreed to call off the operation and recrossed the James with their troops.[70] An interesting aspect of the Darbytown Road fight, sometimes called the first battle of Deep Bottom, was Sheridan's use of the Duke of Wellington's favorite stratagem. Torbert and Gregg, supported by Kautz, made a mounted attack on Kershaw's division, posted on the west bank of Bailey's Creek, but were driven back to a north-south ridge below the east bank of the stream. When the cavalrymen crossed the crest of the ridge, they were "quickly dismounted, and the men directed to lie down in line of battle about 15 yards from the crest. . . . When Kershaw's men reached the crest such a severe fire was opened on them . . . that they . . . gave way in disorder."[71]

The second cavalry operation was timed to coincide with the actual explosion of the mine, scheduled for the dawn of July 30. Sheridan was ordered to join Wilson with the divisions of Torbert and Gregg during the night of the twenty-ninth on the left wing of the Union army; at daylight the Cavalry Corps was to attack the right flank of the Confederate forces defending Petersburg. The rationale of the cavalry attack was sound, since it would have pinned down the Confederate troops stationed to the south of the mine and thus kept them from coming to the aid of the troops at or near the site of the explosion. Since, however, the frontal attack of Ambrose Burnside's troops following the explosion was an abject, costly failure, the cavalry operation was called off.[72]

---

to join Gregg and Torbert after they crossed the James. Sheridan was in overall command of the cavalry phase of the operation.

70. *Official Records*, Vol. XL, Pt. 3, pp. 531, 532, 569; Sheridan, *Personal Memoirs*, I, 447; Freeman, *R. E. Lee*, III, 465–66.

71. Sheridan, *Personal Memoirs*, I, 447.

72. *Official Records*, Vol. XL, Pt. 3, pp. 616, 668, 671, 672; Sheridan, *Personal Memoirs*, I, 451.

Sorely disappointed as Grant was by the gross mismanagement of the fight at the Crater—he wrote Halleck that "Such an opportunity for carrying fortifications I have never seen and do not expect again to have"—he wasted no time bemoaning the failure of the plan.[73] The bulk of Lee's forces were still north of the James, which suggested to Grant an opportunity to put the Weldon Railroad out of commission. He wrote to Meade, "This will . . . be a favorable opportunity to send a corps of infantry and the cavalry to cut fifteen or twenty miles of the Weldon railroad. Instruct the cavalry to remain for this purpose. . . . They should get off by daylight tomorrow morning, and strike the road as near Petersburg as they can to commence work. I cannot yet help feeling that if our cavalry should get well round the enemy's right . . . we may yet take Petersburg."[74] But Meade had to respond with a report of "difficulty and objections all around, with both infantry and cavalry."[75] Gregg, in command of the Cavalry Corps in the absence of Sheridan due to a brief illness, reported on the thirtieth that his horses had had no water since the previous day and that it was absolutely necessary to move the corps that evening to some point where the horses could be watered.[76] Hancock, whose infantry was to accompany the cavalry on the expedition, reported that one division of his corps was in the lines; "It took till midnight to put it in last night, and probably take as long to relieve it. My troops are very tired, owing to the two long night marches and loss of sleep. These are the facts and I leave it to you to decide the case."[77] These reports caused Meade to place the burden of the ultimate decision on Grant; he sent him copies of the two reports and commented that he had "but little hope of effecting anything in the way of a raid. . . . Besides, I think the enemy's infantry will be back before night, if not already here. I have, however, given the necessary orders for the movement tomorrow."[78]

On this same thirtieth of July Grant wrote Meade, on the strength of information sent him by Halleck, that Jubal Early's

73. Quoted in Catton, *Grant Takes Command*, 325.
74. *Official Records*, Vol. XL, Pt. 3, p. 637.
75. *Ibid.*, 639.
76. *Ibid.*, 670.
77. *Ibid.*, 648.
78. *Ibid.*, 648.

forces had begun "crossing the Potomac at the different fords above Harper's Ferry"—an operation to be described in the next chapter—and that enough infantry and artillery were available in and near Washington to deal with the threatened invasion, "but no cavalry to depend on." Consequently Grant ordered Meade to have one of Sheridan's divisions proceed at once to City Point to embark for Washington. With the cavalry thus weakened, and in face of Gregg's and Hancock's discouraging reports and Meade's misgivings, Grant also authorized the cancellation of the Weldon Railroad raid.[79]

Pursuant to Grant's instructions to Meade, Torbert and the First Division were ordered to leave at once for Washington. Their departure, followed within a day by the departure of Sheridan himself, and within a week by the removal to Washington of Wilson's division, opened a new and important chapter in the history of cavalry operations in the East.

79. Ibid., 639, 640, 649, 669, 672; Vol. XXXVII, Pt. 2, p. 509. At the end of July the Cavalry Corps reported 11,111 of all ranks "present for duty," 4,287 in the First Division, 4,215 in the Second, and 2,609 in the still badly under-strength Third. The corps also had 569 artillerymen, manning twenty-seven guns. Ibid., Vol. XL, Pt. 3, p. 728.

IX

"The battle to the strong"

WHEN GENERAL DAVID HUNTER DECIDED TO RETREAT from Lynchburg westward to Charleston instead of going north down the Shenandoah Valley, he left that much-traveled military thoroughfare leading to the Baltimore & Ohio Railroad, the Chesapeake & Ohio Canal, and Maryland, Pennsylvania, and the city of Washington beyond the Potomac wide open for General Early. This was an opportunity Jubal Early was not likely to neglect, nor did he. For three days he followed Hunter's retreating army as far as Lewisburg and beyond and then made the wise decision that there was no military advantage in pursuing an army that was taking itself out of the war as fast as it could go. He gave his men a day's rest and then started down the Valley with the divisions of John C. Breckinridge, John Echols, Robert E. Rodes, S. Dodson Ramseur, and John Gordon; indicative of the ominous shrinkage of Confederate manpower was that the five divisions mustered but ten thousand muskets among them, the strength of two Confederate divisions of a more prosperous past. For cavalry, Early had a total of four thousand troopers, many of questionable reliability.

Early's march down the Valley met practically no opposition until July 6, when he crossed the Potomac into Maryland and turned east through Frederick toward Washington. Three days later at the crossing of the Baltimore & Ohio over the Monocacy

River, some two miles southeast of Frederick, he defeated General Lew Wallace's scratch force, which, however, also included the Third Division of General Horatio Wright's VI Corps, rushed north from the Petersburg trenches.[1] The road to Washington was now open, and on the eleventh Early reached the fortifications on the northwestern edge of the city. Notwithstanding the formidable appearance of the forts facing him, Early decided to attack at "earliest dawn" the next day, but learning that the rest of the VI Corps had arrived in Washington and was manning the forts, he thought better of it, called off the attack, and began his retreat to Virginia. This summary of the events of the first month of what developed into the Valley Campaign of 1864 provides the framework for the Federal moves to counter a totally unlooked-for invasion.

General Christopher C. Augur, in command of the Washington defenses, had little to work with. Except for the VI Corps, he had practically no mobile troops, and the heavy artillery regiments of the Washington garrison had been depleted to provide reinforcements for the Army of the Potomac.[2] He had a small cavalry brigade commanded by a most capable officer, Colonel Charles Russell Lowell, Jr., of the 2nd Massachusetts, made up of Lowell's own regiment plus the 13th and 16th New York. The scanty troops of the Middle Department (Baltimore), a second-rate force at best, had been defeated at Monocacy Junction and could not be relied upon for help. For effective aid there were only two sources available to Augur: General Hunter's troops in the Department of West Virginia and the Army of the Potomac.

The reader will recall that it was not until July 14, two days after Early began his retreat from Washington, that Hunter's army began to arrive in the East after its roundabout journey from Lynchburg; moreover, its point of assembly was Cumberland, one hundred miles as the crow flies from Washington and much

1. Lieutenant Colonel David R. Clendenin, who led a detachment of the 8th Illinois in the battle, reported, "The force pursuing me was McCausland's brigade. Stahel's cavalry I could not bring into action, and ordered them to the rear. . . . The Loudoun Rangers are worthless." *Official Records*, Vol. XXXVII, Pt. 1, p. 221.

2. Halleck wrote Grant that the "garrisons of Washington and Baltimore are made up of troops entirely unfit for the field." *Ibid.*, Pt. 2, p. 384.

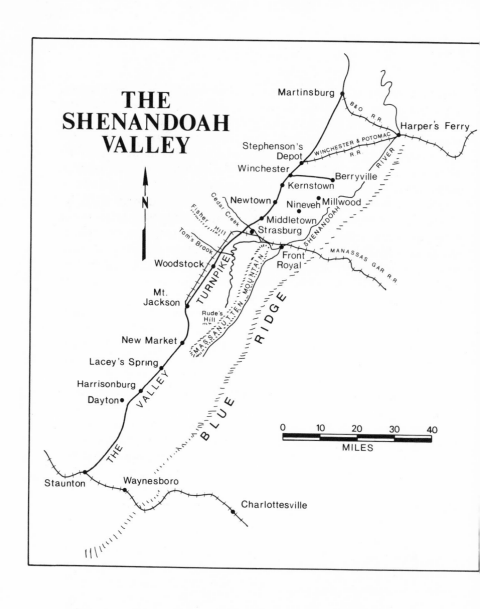

THE
SHENANDOAH
VALLEY

N

Martinsburg

B & O R.R.

Harper's Ferry

Stephenson's
Depot

WINCHESTER & POTOMAC R.R.

Winchester

Berryville

Kernstown

Newtown

Nineveh

Millwood

SHENANDOAH RIVER

Cedar Creek

Middletown

Strasburg

Fisher Hill

Tom's Brook

Woodstock

Front
Royal

MANASSAS GAR. R.R.

TURNPIKE

MASSANUTTEN MOUNTAIN

Mt.
Jackson

Rude's
Hill

New Market

RIDGE

Lacey's Spring

Harrisonburg

Dayton

VALLEY

BLUE

| 0 | 10 | 20 | 30 | 40 |

MILES

THE

Staunton

Waynesboro

Charlottesville

farther by road or rail. In addition to being too late and too far from the scene of action, Hunter's troops, certainly his cavalry, were in poor condition for a campaign against Early's tough veterans. There is no official statement in the records of the condition of Averell's cavalry as it reached Cumberland, but the historian of one of his regiments, the 2nd West Virginia, writes that the division, "much disorganized, worn out by long marches, poorly equipped, wretchedly mounted, and armed with inferior weapons, was almost worthless."[3] Duffié's report of his operations from July 14 to July 27 is a long litany of the failures and stupidities of his officers and, more to the point, of the endless shortages and other difficulties he had to contend against. "I have been unable," he wrote, "to secure . . . grain for my horses, and during part of the time, not even hay. The horses . . . were unshod. . . . My command had just returned from Lynchburg . . . and were completely worn down. . . . The horses are thin . . . and without shoes. The men are without the necessary clothing. . . . An entire remount is required. All the regiments are badly scattered, dismounted detachments . . . being stationed at various points within and without the department."[4]

There was a third source of reinforcements General Augur could draw on in an emergency, namely the dismounted cavalrymen from every regiment of Sheridan's corps, waiting for remounts and equipment at Camp Stoneman. As soon as Early's approach was reported, Colonel William Gamble, in command of the camp, became the recipient of daily and hourly dispatches, of which the following may serve as samples. "[July 4] You will at

3. Sutton, *History of the Second Regiment,* 144.
4. *Official Records,* Vol. XXXVII, Pt. 1, pp. 322–25. The following are examples of the failures of Duffié's subordinates: 1. "through the shameful mismanagement and neglect of Capt. [Samuel] Montgomery, 20th Pennsylvania . . . one squadron, which was picketing the rear of Ashby's Gap . . . was captured by Mosby's guerrillas, with all their horses, arms, and equipments." 2. The plan to capture a detachment of Confederate cavalry at Kernstown "was . . . frustrated by Lieutenant-Colonel Alonzo W. Adams of the 1st New York (Lincoln). . . . I must here remark that the stupidity of this officer has been repeatedly manifested whilst under my command." 3. "Colonel [Jacob] Higgins, commanding the Second Brigade . . . by his shameful mismanagement . . . caused a disgraceful stampede . . . resulting in the abandonment and burning of some twenty wagons."

once organize the dismounted cavalry of your command into one or two battalions, and arm and equip them as infantry, for temporary service at Harper's Ferry. This must be done at once, so that they can leave by to-morrow morning." Another, on July 9: "Draw all the horses the Cavalry Bureau has for issue, and mount and equip as many men as you can with them, and do it as quickly as possible. Send for clothing, if necessary, at the same time, but do not delay for it. Report a battalion ready for the field by 1 o'clock to-day." And another, the next day: "arm, with as little delay as practicable, all dismounted men in your camp, and send them to report to Major-General [Alexander McD.] McCook. . . . The men are to go with their cavalry arms." And yet another, the same day: "The major-general commanding directs that 1,000 dismounted men in your camp, armed as cavalry, be sent at once to the Reserve Camp. . . . It is absolutely necessary that this detachment move without delay."[5] These orders, and numerous others in the same series, seem to rest on the assumption that Colonel Gamble had an inexhaustible supply of dismounted cavalrymen at his disposal. The men he was able to send had to be thrown together, catch-as-catch-can, into improvised squadrons and battalions, under strange corporals, sergeants, and officers. Nevertheless, the men were veterans for the most part, and they did good service. For example, on July 11 six hundred dismounted men, all of whom happened to be from General Gregg's Second Division and were commanded by Major George C. Briggs, 7th Michigan, drove Early's skirmishers away from the northern fortifications of Washington.[6]

Early's retreat removed the immediate threat to the capital and gave the Cavalry Bureau breathing space to announce a new inspection policy. A special inspector, representing the bureau, was to be assigned to every department that had a sizable body of cavalry; he would have the duty of collecting and consolidating

5. *Ibid.*, Pt. 2, pp. 34, 143, 168. In addition to the troops Colonel Gamble furnished, the Army of the Potomac sent on July 6, three thousand dismounted cavalrymen to Harper's Ferry. *Ibid.*, 80–81. General Halleck directed the Cavalry Bureau to have these men mounted on horses to be impressed in Maryland. *Ibid.*, 99.
6. *Ibid.*, Pt. 1, p. 231. General Alexander McD. McCook characterized Major Briggs's action as "handsomely done."

the monthly inspection reports of brigade inspectors general and submit the consolidated reports to the department commander "in person." The commander in turn was to forward the reports to the Cavalry Bureau with whatever "remarks . . . he may see fit to place thereon." In addition, the special inspectors were to visit,

if possible, each regiment in their departments, at least once a month, and make an informal inspection, rendering themselves thoroughly conversant with the military bearing, discipline, and efficiency of officers and regiments. . . . In case of a scarcity of horses . . . [they] will recommend the dismounting of the most inefficient regiments, entire, and the turning over their good horses to the best regiments, with a view to their being placed on duty as infantry, thereby avoiding the necessity of dismounted camps. All inefficient officers will be reported that they may be recommended for rebuke or dismissal.

The special inspectors were also to establish depots for the reception of unserviceable horses, to receive and forward requisitions for horses and ordnance stores, and in general to "correct all abuses to which cavalry is subject."[7] This was a formidable set of responsibilities indeed, but was it reasonable for the bureau to expect that department commanders, to say nothing of cavalry officers, would allow these "outsiders" to operate effectively? The scheme—as such schemes always are—was initiated with the best of intentions, but so far as the records show it failed to accomplish its laudable purposes.

The new inspection policy did, however, give General Butler the occasion to address one of his inimitable letters to Captain E. V. Sumner, who had the unenviable distinction of being appointed special inspector of cavalry for the Army of the James. After making clear his poor opinion of the entire plan, Butler went on to tell Sumner that "if the Cavalry Bureau . . . had chosen to examine my inspector-general's reports . . . they would have found every item of intelligence there which . . . you are required to give, saving always your opinions upon the efficiency and propriety of action of my cavalry officers, and I know that the opinion which you will give as your own, being those [sic] of a young

7. *Ibid.*, Pt. 2, pp. 393–94. In the distribution of horses and "ordnance stores," "preference . . . [was to] be shown to those regiments which take the best care of their horses and arms."

cavalry officer . . . will be modestly and properly expressed." One can readily picture General Butler's grim smile, or leer, as he fired off his closing salvo: "I desire . . . to call your special attention to the insufficiency of arms with which my cavalry is furnished, and if the bureau can have any effect in promoting the efficiency of cavalry it can do more in this direction than in any other, and in answering my requisitions for horses, which have been before them for three months without any notice."[8]

After leaving Washington Early crossed the Potomac back into Virginia, moved west into the Valley, and settled down at Berryville. On his march to Washington he had collected $220,000 ransom from the towns of Hagerstown and Frederick, filled his supply wagons, and destroyed all the highway and railroad bridges his cavalry could reach. His chief concern at this time was the state of his mounted troops. He had not quite 4,100 cavalry divided into five brigades, varying in strength from 562 to 1,132, under John C. Vaughn, John D. Imboden, John McCausland, Bradley T. Johnson, and William L. Jackson. At a later stage of the campaign, Early was to attribute all his misfortunes to the inefficiency of the greater part of his cavalry.[9] How much of this inefficiency was due to lack of discipline, how much to poor leadership, and how much to other causes is impossible to determine, but all these factors were present in some measure. Writing after the war about his ill-fated campaign, Early said, "All my operations had been impeded for the want of an efficient and energetic cavalry commander."[10] Major General Robert Ransom had the command for a short time but had to relinquish it due to ill health. When he reached Richmond he urged a major reorganization of Early's cavalry, which he hoped would have the double effect of teaching it to fight and getting rid of "indifferent officers."[11] General Bragg forwarded Ransom's proposals to Early with the discouraging comment that "too radical a change may produce dissatisfaction in those commands raised mostly in the country now held by the enemy and cause many desertions. At the same time

8. *Ibid.*, Vol. XL, Pt. 3, p. 269.
9. *Ibid.*, Vol. XLIII, Pt. 1, pp. 1003–1004, 558.
10. Quoted in Freeman, *Lee's Lieutenants*, III, 568.
11. *Official Records*, Vol. XLIII, Pt. 1, p. 1004.

it is felt that some stringent measures are necessary to secure discipline and prevent disaster."[12] Four months passed without a response from Early, or any action by him on Ransom's recommendations, and in those four months discipline was not established and disaster was not prevented.[13]

At this point, General Lee decided to strengthen the cavalry in the Valley by adding to it the divisions of Fitzhugh Lee and Wade Hampton and by giving Hampton the overall cavalry command under Early. Hampton and his division thereupon left for the Valley, but they had to be recalled; Rooney Lee's division and the independent brigades of John W. Geary and James Dearing, left behind at Petersburg, were not strong enough to cope with David McM. Gregg's Federal horse.[14] Given Hampton's abilities as a leader and a cavalryman, the outcome of the entire Valley Campaign might well have been different had it not been necessary for General Lee to recall him to the James.

With Early's retreat to Berryville there came a brief lull in operations in the Valley, interrupted by a brilliant little victory gained by Averell on July 20. Advancing from Martinsburg with 1,350 infantry and 1,000 (later increased to 1,300) cavalry, he attacked Ramseur's division of infantry and the cavalry brigades of Vaughn, Imboden, and Jackson at Stephenson's Depot, north of Winchester, and routed them, capturing four guns, 267 unwounded and 130 wounded prisoners, with a loss to his own command of 214 killed, wounded, and missing.[15] Four days later it was the Confederates' turn: Early defeated Crook in an action at Kernstown and forced him to retreat to the Potomac. Averell's and Duffié's divisions were involved in Crook's defeat and gained no glory in the fight; General Hunter wrote to Halleck, "The cavalry and the dismounted men . . . behaved in the most disgraceful manner, their officers in many instances leading them off."[16]

12. *Ibid.*, 1008.
13. *Ibid.*, 1004.
14. *Ibid.*, 996–97, 999. Fitzhugh Lee was already in the Valley. It was intended that Matthew C. Butler should succeed to the command of what had been Hampton's division.
15. Averell's report is in *ibid.*, Vol. XXXVII, Pt. 1, pp. 326–27. Ramseur also lost 73 men killed.
16. In his report of the fight Averell made a special point of stating that by his personal exertions he was able to save three guns which had been abandoned by a battery serving with Duffié's cavalry. *Ibid.*, 328.

Following his victory at Kernstown Early advanced to Martinsburg, and Grant, faced with the possibility that the Confederates might again cross the Potomac, decided to leave the VI Corps in the Valley. Colonel Gamble was bombarded once again with orders to organize all the dismounted cavalrymen in his camp to reinforce the VI Corps infantry and was able to collect and send forward three improvised battalions, totaling 1,363 effectives.[17] Inspired by his Kernstown victory to resume the offensive, Early sent McCausland's and Johnson's brigades across the Potomac on a raid to Chambersburg, Pennsylvania. In retaliation for Hunter's burning of residences and of the buildings of the Virginia Military Institute, they were to demand a ransom of $100,000 in gold or $500,000 in greenbacks; if the money was not forthcoming, they were to burn down the town. The raiders reached Chambersburg on July 30, and when the inhabitants were unable or unwilling to pay, the town was put to the torch.[18] Whatever one may think of the morality—even the military morality—of Early's orders, the behavior of McCausland's and Johnson's troopers at Chambersburg and on the march there and back would not have given the many admirers of the Horsemen in Gray cause to rejoice. General McCausland apparently turned a blind eye to the many outrages going on around him, but Bradley Johnson did not. He wrote, "Every crime in the catalogue of infamy has been committed, except murder and rape. Highway robbery of watches and pocket books was of ordinary occurrence. . . . Pillage and sack of private dwellings took place hourly."[19] And he added that the men behaved just as badly on friendly Virginia soil as they did in Maryland and Pennsylvania.

Charles D. Rhodes, *History of the Cavalry of the Army of the Potomac* (Kansas City, 1900), 127. In the fight itself and the subsequent retreat, the two divisions lost 18 killed, 95 wounded, and 56 missing. *Official Records*, Vol. XXXVII, Pt. 1, p. 289.

17. *Official Records*, Vol. XXXVII, Pt. 2, pp. 435, 448, 449.

18. *Ibid.*, Pt. 1, pp. 331–35. It must be placed on record that Colonel William E. Peters, 21st Virginia, flatly refused to obey his commanding officer's orders to have his men start fires in the town. Freeman, *Lee's Lieutenants*, III, 572.

19. Quoted in Freeman, *Lee's Lieutenants*, III, 573, but see Farrar, *The Twenty-Second Pennsylvania*, 307.

The only sizable body of Federal cavalry that had any chance of overtaking the raiders was Averell's division, which, however, was as usual beset by problems. Averell had to ask on July 27 to have the 8th Ohio, portions of which were stationed at Beverly, Baltimore, and Hagerstown, brought together at one place; he also pointed out that the arms of the Beverly detachment were "almost useless."[20] To increase his numbers he asked General Darius N. Couch, commanding the Department of the Susquehanna, to lend him all the mounted companies he could spare for a few days to perform picket duty, so that he could concentrate his division "for offensive or defensive operations." Couch obliged by sending two independent cavalry companies, but the loan was hardly what Averell had hoped for; one of the companies, Edward B. Sanno's, was "stampeded" at Williamsport the following day and Couch sent George D. Stroud's company with the caveat that Stroud "is said to be of unsound mind."[21]

Notwithstanding that his command was as usual "broken down" even before he started, Averell overtook the raiders on the morning of the thirty-first as they were about to burn down Mc-Connellsburg; he attacked immediately, killed and captured "several" of the raiders, and saved the town.[22] Contact was apparently lost later in the day, but reestablished in the evening at Hancock; by then Averell's horses were "used up" and his men had been without rations for two days.[23] After a slight brush with their pursuers, Johnson and McCausland marched through the night toward Cumberland. For six more days the pursuit continued, in heat so severe that on August 1 General Hunter wrote that six men in one of his brigades of infantry had died of sunstroke on a

20. *Official Records*, Vol. XXXVII, Pt. 1, pp. 472, 475. Late in August, 477 men of the regiment were reported as armed with the Union carbine, "a worthless arm," for which they had only fifteen cartridges per man; they had neither pistols nor sabers. *Ibid.*, Vol. XLIII, Pt. 1, p. 908. At the end of October, the portion of the regiment still at Beverly tried to defend the settlement against an attack by a sizable Confederate force. The report of the action states that some of the Ohioans had "no arms, and the greater number who were armed had only the Union carbine, which is . . . an entirely unreliable weapon." *Ibid.*, 647.
21. *Ibid.*, Vol. XXXVII, Pt. 2, pp. 477, 484, 507.
22. *Ibid.*, 534.
23. *Ibid.*, 568, 569.

march to Frederick.[24] Averell himself reported to Hunter on August 6 that he was following the enemy toward Moorefield, that he had lost 100 horses the previous day and had only 1,600 mounted men left, but he closed the dispatch with the soldierlike remark that he would "follow and fight . . . [the enemy] if it kills every horse and man in the command."[25]

Averell's perseverance paid off when he caught up with the raiders the following morning at Moorefield. Attacking at daybreak, he scattered the two Confederate brigades to the four winds and captured three battle flags, 420 prisoners including 38 officers, 400 horses and their equipment, large quantities of small arms, and the battery of four guns the raiders had with them.[26]

On this occasion at least, the conventional claim in Averell's report that the enemy "broke," "fled in the wildest confusion," was "driven to the mountains" and "scattered through the woods" seems to have had a firm basis in fact. A reporter for the Richmond *Whig*, who was present at Moorefield, wired his editor that McCausland and Johnson were "stampeded and routed . . . [the] men scattering in wild disorder and confusion and running in different directions."[27] And the effects, immediate and long-term, of Averell's victory were also significant. With the defeat and dispersion of his two strongest brigades, the strength of Early's cavalry was at once reduced from about four thousand to under two thousand. Early judged the moral results to be even more serious; Moorefield, he wrote, "had a very damaging effect upon my cavalry for the rest of the campaign."[28] Whether his cavalry's poor performance was due to the "damaging effect" of Moorefield or the Federals' great numerical superiority or a creeping feeling of hope-

24. *Ibid.*, 564.
25. *Ibid.*, Vol. XLIII, Pt. 1, p. 713.
26. Averell's report of the action is in *ibid.*, 493–95. On August 1, Duffié was ordered to join Averell in the pursuit. *Ibid.*, Vol. XXXVII, Pt. 2, pp. 565, 585. In Averell's congratulatory order following Moorefield, he makes prominent mention of the 1st New York (Lincoln) for its "brilliant charge." *Ibid.*, Vol. XLIII, Pt. 1, p. 503.
27. *Ibid.*, Vol. XLIII, Pt. 1, p. 991.
28. Quoted in Freeman, *Lee's Lieutenants*, II, 574. Early was left with "only about 1,700 mounted men" until Fitzhugh Lee joined him with another 1,200. Jubal A. Early, *Autobiographical Sketch and Narrative of the War Between the States* (Philadelphia, 1912), 416.

lessness, it is true that every major engagement from Moorefield to the end of the campaign produced a large bag of unwounded Confederate cavalrymen taken prisoner.

The events of August and September, insofar as they were to involve Averell and his relations with Sheridan, should be viewed in the light of the fact that the only two victories won by the Union in the Shenandoah Valley from the time of Hunter's retreat from Lynchburg until Sheridan's great victory in the battle of the Opequon on September 19, were won by Averell; moreover, both at Stephenson's Depot on July 20 and at Moorefield on August 7 he was in sole command.[29]

Early's advance to the Potomac for the second time in a month caused Grant to propose putting an end to the confused command structure around Washington by combining the four separate departments of Washington, West Virginia, the Susquehanna, and the Middle Department into a "Military Division" under a single head.[30] His first choice to head the division, General William B. Franklin, was vetoed by the president and the secretary of war. Grant then gave General Meade to understand that the post would be his. But Grant changed his mind. Under circumstances that showed one of the less attractive sides of his character, he gave the command to Sheridan. Judged by its results, he made an inspired choice; it is impossible to think that Meade could have accomplished what Sheridan did in the Valley. Nevertheless, the unpleasant deviousness with which Sheridan's appointment came about should not be ignored, as it has generally been.

In a dispatch that has become famous in the literature of the Civil War, Grant informed Halleck that he had selected Sheridan for the Valley command; "I want Sheridan put in command of all the troops in the field," Grant wrote, "with instructions to put himself south of the enemy and follow him to the death. Wherever the enemy goes, let our troops go also."[31] The promotion of Sheri-

29. It is not without interest that in his memoirs Grant wrote that General Benjamin F. Kelley, in command of what was called the "Reserve Division" at Cumberland, who was not anywhere near Moorefield, "met and defeated" McCausland and Johnson; nowhere does Grant mention Averell in connection with this affair. Grant, *Personal Memoirs*, II, 316.

30. *Official Records*, Vol. XXXVII, Pt. 2, pp. 433–34.

31. *Ibid.*, p. 558.

dan to what was initially intended to be only the command of the forces in the field and not of the Military Division, but was changed to "temporary" command of the division when General Hunter asked to be relieved, was accepted with considerable misgivings by Secretary Stanton and the president, both of whom thought the thirty-four-year-old Sheridan too young for so responsible a position.[32]

Sheridan assumed his new command at Monocacy Junction on August 7.[33] Two divisions of General William H. Emory's XIX Corps had been brought from Louisiana to reinforce the Army of the Potomac but were diverted to Washington when Early's threat to the capital developed. August 4 found them encamped at Monocacy Junction. Captain John W. DeForest of the 12th Connecticut Infantry of the XIX Corps wrote,

Near us are Hunter's and Crook's troops, both in a fagged-out and demoralized condition, ragged, famished, discouraged, sulky, and half of them in ambulances. They have been marched to tatters, they say, besides being overwhelmed and beaten. . . . The Sixth Corps, one of the best in the Army of the Potomac, is lying near us. They seem to be badly demoralized by the severe service and the disastrous battles of the campaigns in Virginia. Their guns are dirty; their camps are disorderly clutters of shelter tents; worst of all, the men are disrespectful to their officers. I heard a private say to a lieutenant, "I'll slap your face if you say that again." These fellows lurk around our clean, orderly camps and steal our clean, bright rifles. I went over to the nearest brigade to complain about this and to recover lost ordnance stores. "Looking for guns, Cap?" drawled a sergeant. "Well, if you find a clean gun in this camp, you claim it. We hain't had one in our brigade since Cold Harbor."[34]

Such was the state of much of Sheridan's infantry when he took over the Valley command. If Grant, who met Sheridan at Monocacy Junction to give him his instructions, or if Sheridan himself, noticed the condition of the instrument with which the enemy was to be driven south, no mention of it appears in their respective memoirs.

32. Sheridan, *Personal Memoirs*, I, 463.
33. On August 7 the Middle Military Division was established, with Sheridan as its "temporary" commander; he assumed command the same day. *Ibid.*, Vol. XLIII, Pt. 1, p. 719.
34. John W. DeForest, *A Volunteer's Adventures* (New Haven, 1946), 163–65.

Sheridan had met with Halleck in Washington on August 3, while on his way to take up his command. He remarked to Halleck that "for operations in the open country of Pennsylvania, Maryland, and Northern Virginia, cavalry is much better than infantry."[35] Torbert and the First Division of the Cavalry Corps had been ordered to hasten to Washington on July 30, but the movement of these nearly forty-three hundred cavalrymen, their horses, and all their impedimenta did not go as fast or as smoothly as might have been desirable. Grant asked Meade on August 1 why, despite his explicit orders that the cavalry be embarked first, the artillery of the division was the first to be shipped. He included in the same message his decision to give Sheridan the Valley command, which Meade had had every reason to think would be his; this did nothing to sweeten Meade's temper, and he replied with a tart message that a copy of Grant's orders had been given Sheridan, who "will undoubtedly be able to give some satisfactory explanation of the variation from the orders given."[36] Nevertheless, Torbert's cavalrymen began arriving at Washington on August 2, and that gave rise to another problem: Torbert, with good reason, "apprehend[ed] difficulty" getting his command out of Washington if he attempted to march them through the city in small detachments as each shipload arrived. To avoid the manifold temptations of the capital, he asked that a camp be set up below the city where his men could be collected and then marched around the city to Tennallytown.[37]

Grant's and Sheridan's attention was, however, claimed by a far more serious problem than Torbert's. With Sheridan slated to be in overall command of all the troops of the Military Division, who was to command his cavalry? Averell's and Duffié's divisions and Colonel Lowell's brigade were already in the field and Torbert's division was arriving. Acting on a request from Sheridan, Grant was about to order Wilson's division to the Valley also. This would make a cavalry force of four divisions plus an extra brigade, perhaps as many as twelve thousand troopers. Providing the cavalry with a unified organization and a single head in command had been the making of the mounted troops of the Army of the

35. *Official Records*, Vol. XXXVII, Pt. 2, p. 582.
36. *Ibid.*, 559.
37. *Ibid.*, 573.

Potomac. The idea had at long last become accepted and was to be carried out in the Valley. But who was to be the "single head in command"? The question had evidently been in Grant's mind, and he and Sheridan must have had some discussion of the problem, for on August 7 he wired the latter, "Do not hesitate to give commands to officers in whom you repose confidence, without regard to claims of others on account of rank. If you deem Torbert the best man to command the cavalry, place him in command and give Averell some other command, or relieve him. . . . What we want is prompt and active movements after the enemy."[38] Clearly, the respective claims of Averell and Torbert had been considered. Both men had the substantive rank of brigadier general of volunteers, but Averell was senior in that rank, and he also had the brevet rank of major general. Hence in keeping with the hierarchical system of the army, the top cavalry command in the Valley should have been his. Grant's August 7 dispatch, however, makes it evident that the decision had gone against him. How and why such decisions are made is seldom recorded, nor is there anything in the records in this case to indicate why Torbert—an uninspired choice—was preferred. Neither Grant nor Sheridan had ever served with Averell, nor, so far as is known, were they personally acquainted with him, but there were few secrets in the tightly knit fraternity of West Pointers, and no doubt they were told enough about Averell by those who had served with or under him to create doubts about his competence, reliability, personality, or willingness to work in harness—doubts that his generally good record in his West Virginia command could not overcome. It will be seen presently that as the Valley Campaign progressed, instead of doing his utmost to disarm what he must have recognized as Sheridan's deliberate intention to "get" him, Averell seemed to go out of his way to provide Sheridan with ammunition.

A mysterious aspect of the choice of Torbert to command Sheridan's cavalry is the status of David McM. Gregg, whose

38. *Ibid.*, Vol. XLIII, Pt. 1, p. 719. According to Sheridan, Grant feared "discord on account of Averell's ranking Torbert" and authorized him to relieve the former. Sheridan says that he decided not to do so, hoping "that if any trouble of this sort arose, it could be allayed, or at least repressed . . . since the different commands would often have to act separately." Sheridan, *Personal Memoirs*, II, 44–45.

claims, on the basis of his rank, experience, and record, to receive
the Valley post were greater than either Torbert's or Averell's. Was
he or was he not considered for the post? Was it offered to him,
and if so, did he turn it down? If he was not offered the post, why
was the offer not made? We do not know.

Torbert's appointment as chief of cavalry of the Middle Military Division was announced on August 8.[39] When, if at all,
Averell, who was then on his way from Moorefield back to Cumberland and thence by rail to Hancock, was told officially of the
appointment is not known. On the nineteenth, however, after receiving a number of orders from Torbert—his junior in rank—he
wrote Colonel J. W. Forsyth, Sheridan's chief of staff:

As I have received no order placing me under General Torbert's command, and as my commission is senior to his, I do not think it proper
to obey his orders until I am shown by some law or order that it is
proper that my rank should be ignored. . . . I trust that you will understand that my only motive in declining to obey the orders of a junior is
dictated by a sense of duty to myself and from no disrespect to General
Torbert or others. Will you be good enough to instruct me, if I am
wrong, at your earliest convenience?

Four days later, Forsyth told Averell in a curtly worded dispatch
that he was to report to Torbert and that all orders he received
from Torbert were to be "obeyed and respected."[40]

For the first five weeks after Sheridan's arrival in the Valley,
his and Early's marches and countermarches resembled the elaborate choreographic evolutions of eighteenth-century warfare. On
August 10, Sheridan, having concentrated his troops at Harper's

39. *Official Records*, Vol. XLIII, Pt. 1, pp. 501, 744. It is to be noted
that Sheridan's cavalry was not officially designated a corps. This no doubt
was because Torbert's (later Merritt's) and Wilson's divisions, notwithstanding their transfer to the Valley, remained technically part of the cavalry of the Army of the Potomac, and Averell's and Duffié's divisions belonged to the Department of West Virginia.

40. *Ibid.*, 502, 503. The day after receipt of the dispatch from Averell,
Sheridan wired Secretary Stanton that "Averell is senior to General Torbert,
my chief of cavalry. This causes a difficulty which can but be overcome by
conferring the rank of [major general by brevet] on Torbert. Will you have
the kindness to do so?" *Ibid.* Torbert was not brevetted a major general
until the following spring. Sheridan's idea would not have solved the problem in any case, because Averell's brevet would have antedated Torbert's,
and he would therefore have still been the senior.

Ferry, marched south toward Berryville. Early, whose army lay at Martinsburg, astride the Baltimore & Ohio and within an easy march of the Potomac, immediately reacted to this threat to his right and rear and fell back, first to Bunker Hill and then to Winchester. When Sheridan turned west from Berryville and threatened Winchester from the southeast, Early retired to Fisher's Hill below Strasburg, the best east-west defensive position in the Valley. Sheridan followed, but on August 14 a dispatch from Grant to Halleck, forwarded to him by special courier, brought the information that two divisions of Confederate infantry under General Richard Anderson, plus Fitzhugh Lee's cavalry division were on their way to the Valley via Culpeper to reinforce Early. Now it was Sheridan's rear that was threatened, and he reacted by retreating to Halltown, four miles west of Harper's Ferry. Early, joined by Anderson and Lee, marched north on Sheridan's heels and, after skirmishing with him at Halltown for three days, marched north to Kearneysville, past Sheridan's position, and sent Lee forward to Williamsport on the Potomac. For the next several days Sheridan thought that Early would again cross the Potomac into Maryland and he made his dispositions accordingly. Early, however, withdrew to Bunker Hill and Stephenson's Depot north of Winchester. There were isolated encounters between parts of the two armies, but with both sides in need of a period of rest, things remained quiet until mid-September.[41]

At the start of these operations Sheridan had for cavalry only Torbert's division, commanded by Wesley Merritt after Torbert's elevation to chief of cavalry, and two regiments of Lowell's brigade.[42] One of Sheridan's first dispatches in his new command went to Halleck to tell him that he had found things 'in confusion" with the cavalry "all scattered," but that he had collected "a large number," among them Duffié's and Averell's divisions, the former of which had "been doing nothing up about Hancock." He closed

41. For Sheridan's reports, see *ibid.*, 17–24; see also Sheridan, *Personal Memoirs*, I, 477–84, 488–99.
42. Merritt assumed command of the First Division on August 9. *Official Records*, Vol. XLIII, Pt. 1, p. 438. The third regiment of Lowell's brigade, Colonel Henry M. Lazelle's 16th New York, was stationed near Falls Church with the responsibility of keeping in check the guerrillas in that area.

a dispatch to General Augur, asking that the 8th Illinois be sent to him, with the remark, "I find that the cavalry has been so scattered up here that it is no wonder it has not done well." Augur had to tell him that the 8th Illinois had been scattered worse than any; six of its companies were with Lew Wallace near Baltimore, four were guarding the Potomac between Great Falls and the Monocacy, another was at Port Tobacco trying to stop smuggling across the Potomac below Washington, and the twelfth was with the Army of the Potomac.[43]

Averell, who asked to be allowed a few days to "reorganize, remount and equip" his command, which, he said, would double its strength, received permission to remain at Martinsburg while the rest of the army followed Early up the Valley; he was of course asked to get the job done as quickly as possible.[44]

Wilson was ordered on August 4 to disengage from the left of the Union lines at Petersburg and to join Sheridan in the Valley.[45] The division reached City Point the next day and shortly after midnight began to embark for the trip to Washington. The horses were loaded on the steamers

by means of tackle and pulleys; they were . . . let down on the lower deck on a level with the boiler & machinery. It was an ugly, tedious job & dangerous. . . . no accomodations were on board for cooking so we had to eat our pork raw with our hard-tack, and Oh! . . . do without our coffee. After finishing my apology for a dinner, I was ordered below to feed and water the horses. Notwithstanding the open hatchways the place was like an oven, especially back toward the boilers . . . the thermometer would have reached at least 150° and . . . [the horses] were crowded together as close as they could stand; it is a wonder all did not die, instead of one.[46]

Not until the evening of August 12 did the last of Wilson's division reach Giesboro; it is to be noted that seven days were needed to transport a division of about three thousand men and their horses from City Point to Washington. Wilson took advantage of his presence in the capital and of his friendships in the

43. *Ibid.*, 737–38, 728; Pt. 2, p. 43.
44. *Ibid.*, Pt. 1, pp. 725, 734–35, 788, 423.
45. *Ibid.*, 516.
46. Roger Hannaford, "Reminiscences," The Cincinnati Historical Society, Cincinnati, 115(c)–116(a).

Cavalry Bureau and the War Department to have the First (Mc-
Intosh's) Brigade of his division rearmed with the Spencer carbine. The change was "highly pleasing to most of the boys, but
some grumbled at their great weight . . . they were nearly twice
as heavy as our Burnsides."[47] Indeed, a short while later, by which
time sixteen regiments and an independent battalion of Sheridan's
cavalry were armed fully, and three more regiments partially,
with the Spencer, Torbert ordered the men to carry their guns instead of strapping them to their saddles, which rendered many
horses "unserviceable by sore backs."[48]

The change from the dreary Tidewater about Richmond and
Petersburg, with its "scorching sun, its choking dust and ugly pine
swamps," to the "bracing air," the "crystal waters, the rolling
wheatfields and the beautiful blue mountains" of the Valley delighted the men.[49] They left an area that the war had turned into
a noisome desert, seamed and scarred with trenches, earthworks,
and the detritus of abandoned camps for one that despite three
years of war retained a look of fertility—a land of good farms, a
rolling landscape of great variety and beauty, whose lived-in, well
cultivated appearance the marches and countermarches of the
armies had not succeeded in destroying. But such a land also had
its temptations. Wilson sent word to General McIntosh, "Complaints reach here that your men are roaming around the country,
robbing the orchards, corn fields, &c. You will please have it
stopped, and place safeguards on whatever grounds you may
judge necessary, so as to prevent all unlicensed proceedings of

47. *Ibid.*, 117(d).
48. J. O. Buckeridge, *Lincoln's Choice* (Harrisburg, 1956), 116; *Official Records*, Vol. XLIII, Pt. 2, p. 51. The excellence of the Spencer has been
mentioned previously, but it is appropriate to quote here a letter Wilson
wrote General Alexander S. Dyer on January 2, 1865: "There is no doubt
that the Spencer carbine is the best fire-arm yet put into the hands of the
soldier, both for economy and maximum effect physical and moral. Our best
officers estimate one man armed with it the equivalent to three with any
other arm. I have never seen anything else like the confidence inspired by it
in the regiments and brigades which have it. A common belief among them
is if their flanks are covered they can go anywhere."
49. Gracey, *Annals of the 6th*, 275–76. The change was even more
pleasing to the 3rd Massachusetts, which, as part of the XIX Corps, had
been brought to the Valley from the Louisiana swamps. James K. Ewer, *The
Third Massachusetts Cavalry in the War for the Union* (Maplewood, Mass.,
1903), 195.

any kind."[50] In all likelihood the order remained a dead letter, for McIntosh had his own way of dealing with such problems, as one of his men has recorded:

At a farm house close by, there was abundance of hay, the owner soon grew frightened at the manner it took unto itself legs & walked away, so hurried off to the Commander of the Brigade, desiring a safeguard; Genl McIntosh heard him but was very busy, desired him to wait and he would in a few minutes attend to his case; after some 25 or 30 minutes gave orders that one of the Prov[ost] Guards should be sent with him; remarking to his Officers after the man was gone that he guessed all the boys had hay by this time & those who had not, ought to go without.[51]

One of Wilson's regiments, the 5th New York, had an exceptionally favorable introduction to the Valley. While still in Washington it was ordered to escort Colonel Norton P. Chipman, who had been chosen to deliver to Sheridan Grant's message to let him know that two divisions of infantry and one of cavalry had left Richmond to reinforce Early.[52] To make certain that this important dispatch got to Sheridan through country overrun with Confederate guerrillas, it was deemed necessary to provide Chipman with an escort of a full regiment of cavalry, and the 5th New York was assigned to the job. Starting before daylight on August 13, riding at "great speed" in keeping with the urgency of the dispatch carried by Chipman, the regiment reached the eastern foot of Snicker's Gap through the Blue Ridge well after dark the same day. "It was night," the regimental historian has written, "and not a breath of air stirred in the heavy foliage of the trees. No sound was heard save the song of the katydid and the heavy tramp of our horses. . . . The moon shone brightly, flooding the mountain tops with her silvery beams. . . . From the summit of the gap, the Shenandoah Valley, filled with the hazy light of the moon, presented a scene that was perfectly enchanting."[53] Near Berryville the regiment rode past the "burning remains of a supply train which Mosby had captured and destroyed that day," a demonstration of the need for a strong escort.

Averell, whose difficulties, some of his own making and some

50. *Official Records*, Vol. XLIII, Pt. 1, p. 787.
51. Hannaford, "Reminiscences," 121(b).
52. *Official Records*, Vol. XLIII, Pt. 1, p. 787.
53. Boudrye, *Historic Records of the Fifth*, 162–64.

not, grew progressively worse as the campaign developed, stepped off on the wrong foot at the very beginning. After reaching Martinsburg on August 14 he notified Sheridan's chief of staff that a third of his horses were "totally unfit for further service" and would have to be "abandoned" if, as ordered, he continued his march to Harper's Ferry. He expected to receive a thousand horses at Martinsburg within the next five or six days, and supplies of forage and facilities for shoeing the horses were much better at Martinsburg than at Harper's Ferry, he said. So he had decided to remain there.[54] For a subordinate officer who had been ordered to one point to declare that he intended to remain at another, instead of asking permission to do so, was undiplomatic at the very least. Averell was showing a lack of tact, if not an insubordinate disposition, in dealing with a hot-tempered superior who, in his first independent command, was in the process of retreating to the Potomac and had become the target of "mutterings of dissatisfaction" and "adverse criticisms pouring down from the North," which, however blithely he may have shrugged them off when he wrote his memoirs many years later, would not have sweetened his disposition or made him more patient with a fractious subordinate.[55]

Then, with Sheridan's army in the Halltown lines and Early believed to be meditating another invasion of the North, came something worse. Sheridan wanted a careful watch kept over the approaches to the Potomac and the fords Early might use to cross the river. Consequently he sent Averell, who in the meantime had moved from Martinsburg to Shepherdstown, a series of three orders. The first, on the night of August 17/18 from Torbert, told him to retire to Charlestown. The second, the next morning, signed by Colonel Forsyth, ordered him to "move . . . [his] command to the north side of the Potomac, if necessary, and cover the country from Williamsport to Sharpsburg." The third, a day later and also signed by Forsyth, said, "the general rather desires that the enemy should cross; all that he wants is early information of

54. *Official Records*, Vol. XLIII, Pt. 1, p. 804. Averell's dispatch was referred to Torbert (Averell was informed accordingly), who approved his remaining at Martinsburg. *Ibid.*, 827.

55. Sheridan, *Personal Memoirs*, I, 492.

the character and number of troops that pass over."[56] Averell would have been well advised to question the last two of these orders. Did they supersede his orders from Torbert? What precisely did Sheridan want him to do? Was he to remain south of the river or cross over? What did "if necessary" mean? Unfortunately, Averell asked no questions; he decided that Sheridan wanted to lure Early across the Potomac, and since the fords could be watched better from north of the river, he proceeded to cross over. And now came a blunt dispatch written by Sheridan himself. "I do not know," it said, "why you moved your cavalry from Shepherdstown. If there was a necessity it was not known to me, and you have not informed me. . . . Report to me at once where you are and why you moved from Shepherdstown."[57] Averell later wrote that he was "amazed and pained" by the message, "as it evinced an undue readiness on the part of . . . [Sheridan] to find faults in my official conduct."[58] At the moment, however, in a politely worded reply, he explained that he had moved in accordance with his understanding of Sheridan's wishes, that he regretted the misunderstanding, and that his only desire was to "render the most assistance to" the commanding general.[59] Nevertheless, the damage was done, and it should not be forgotten that these exchanges occurred at the same time that Averell was questioning Torbert's right to issue orders to him.

Fortunately for the good name of everyone concerned, more was happening in the Valley than these bickerings. The marches of Sheridan's army to Fisher's Hill and back again to the Potomac led through good cavalry country; this gave Sheridan the opportunity to use his cavalry either alone or in combination with

56. The three orders are in *Official Records*, Vol. XLIII, Pt. 1, pp. 502, 501, 502.
57. *Ibid.*, 503. Without waiting for Averell's reply, Sheridan wired Halleck, who may well have passed the message on to Grant, "To-day, for some unknown reason and without necessity . . . [Averell] moved from Shepherdstown somewhere without informing me—perhaps to Hagerstown —giving unnecessary alarm by his movement." *Ibid.*, 857.
58. *Ibid.*, 497.
59. *Ibid.*, 503–504. On August 25, Sheridan ordered Wilson to do precisely what Averell had done, namely to watch the Potomac fords from Sharpsburg to Williamsport by crossing over to the north bank of the river. *Ibid.*, 517.

the infantry, to a greater extent and far more aggressively than any army commander in the East had done previously. Moreover, all the tasks he assigned the cavalry were closely allied to the operations of the army as a whole; unlike Grant and others before him, he did not waste the strength of his mounted troops on eccentric operations.

Throughout the Valley Campaign Sheridan's cavalry enjoyed an overwhelming numerical superiority over Early's mounted troops. The returns for the month of August showed Merritt and Wilson with 8,262 officers and men "present for duty"; Crook's Department of West Virginia reported 6,472 mounted troops, about half of whom, in the divisions of Averell and Duffié, were attached to Sheridan's army; and the Department of Washington had 4,622, perhaps as many as a third of whom were actually with Sheridan.[60] As students of the Civil War well know, expressions like "Present for duty," "Present for duty equipped," etc., in strength reports are a statistical quicksand for the unwary; they bear little relation to the numbers actually present and available for combat at any given moment. And indeed, in mid-August, by which time Wilson's division had reached the Valley, Sheridan claimed that he had only 7,500 cavalry.[61] Nevertheless, the "official" figures make it evident not only that Sheridan's cavalry outnumbered Early's by as much as three or four to one, but also that Sheridan's field army had the highest ratio of cavalry to infantry and artillery that any army enjoyed, or was to enjoy, in the Civil War.

Great as was the numerical superiority of Sheridan's cavalry over Early's, its superiority in firepower was nothing short of awesome. And, more important than either, it had an entirely new spirit and morale, for through the strange alchemy of leadership, Sheridan, who had yet to win his first victory, had managed to win the confidence and raise the spirits of his army. Colonel Lowell, whose brigade in the course of one twenty-four-day period in this campaign was "in a fight of more or less importance" every day, and who in the same twenty-four days had fifteen horses killed under him, wrote as early as August 9, "Everything is in

60. *Ibid.*, 974.
61. *Ibid.*, 812.

chaos here, but under Sheridan is rapidly assuming shape. It was a lucky inspiration of Grant's or Lincoln's to make a Middle Military Division and put him in command of it. . . . It is exhilarating to see so many cavalry about and to see things going right again." A month later, Lowell wrote again, "I like Sheridan immensely. Whether he succeeds or fails, he is the first General I have seen who puts as much heart and time and thought into his work as if he were doing it for his own exclusive profit. He works like a mill-owner or an iron master."[62]

Colonel Chipman, Secretary Stanton's aide-de-camp who remained with the army as an observer and sent daily reports to the secretary, wrote on August 25, "Sheridan's army is in splendid condition, well in hand and manifesting the greatest anxiety for a fight. There is a feeling of entire confidence in their leader, and regiments talk about being able to whip brigades. Sheridan really has a very fine army here, and the universal good spirits that prevail and anxiety to fight manifested would make it a hard army to compete with."[63] Be it noted that this report was written three weeks to a day after Captain DeForest's dismal portrayal of the same army.

Sheridan's cavalry had its full share of stragglers and "skulkers," men who had urgent business elsewhere when shells and bullets were flying about; men who, like the eleven troopers of the 22nd Pennsylvania, "had to march about the camp for hours, carrying a rail, while a guard rode after them, being punishment for running from the skirmish line," or like the "command" of two hundred dismounted cavalrymen Lieutenant Joseph Lane of the same regiment had collected, submitting after the battle of Monocacy the report, "Killed 0; wounded 1; missing 163."[64] But there were also cavalrymen of an incredible toughness, men like Trooper Franklin Dickson, Co. A, Cole's Maryland Cavalry. Severely wounded in the fight at Kernstown on July 24, Dickson was sent to the hospital at Winchester:

The doctor in charge . . . decided his arm should be amputated. Dick-

---

62. Crowninshield, "Cavalry in Virginia," 21; Emerson, *Charles Russell Lowell*, 322, 336 (the second letter is dated September 5).
63. *Official Records*, Vol. XLIII, Pt. 1, p. 907.
64. Farrar, *The Twenty-Second Pennsylvania*, 355, 269.

son refused . . . and overheard the surgeon tell one of his attendants that the enemy would be in town in a short time and those in the hospitals would be prisoners. Dickson, although suffering with his shattered arm, got out of the window and took possession of an ambulance that was standing at the door . . . and placing the reins in one hand, drove out of Winchester . . . as the Confederates came in at the other end of the town. On arriving at Martinsburg he reported to the surgeon in charge of the hospital. . . . After examining the arm, which had become greatly inflamed, he said that his life depended upon the amputation of it. Dickson again refused . . . and walked from Martinsburg to Williamsport, Md., a distance of twelve miles, taking a stagecoach at that place to Hagerstown and from thence to Frederick in an army wagon. At the hospital in Frederick, the surgeon operated upon the arm; an old Army surgeon stating the arm might be saved.[65]

And Dickson, whose third wound this was—one of his previous wounds was a severe saber cut over the head—saved his arm.

It was in the Shenandoah Valley under Sheridan that the Union cavalry in the East truly came into its own. From August 10, when the advance up the Valley began, until the end of December, when winter snow and cold closed down operations for the year, the cavalry was constantly in action. It fought in mounted actions, it made massed charges with the saber—in the manner in which the recruits of 1861 thought all cavalry fighting was done—and it fought dismounted. It beat the Confederate cavalry in the open field, and it learned to fight and beat the much tougher Confederate infantry.

To strengthen Merritt's division, which included the brigades of Custer and Thomas C. Devin and the greatly depleted Reserve Brigade of Regulars, Torbert added to it Colonel Lowell's brigade, made up of the 2nd Massachusetts, 22nd Pennsylvania, Cole's Maryland Cavalry, and a detachment of the 14th Pennsylvania.[66] Thus reinforced, Merritt had the first serious engagement of the campaign on August 16. He was attacked at Cedarville, near Front Royal, by two brigades of Joseph B. Kershaw's infantry and Williams C. Wickham's brigade of cavalry. Merritt drove the attackers across the Shenandoah River, "killing and wounding about 300 men, capturing nearly 300 prisoners and 2 infantry battle

65. Newcomer, *Cole's Cavalry*, 140–41.
66. *Official Records*, Vol. XLIII, Pt. 1, p. 422. On August 15, Duffié reported to Torbert with his division, which was down to nine hundred men. *Ibid.*, 423.

flags," at a loss of only sixty of his own men.[67] In a jubilant dispatch to Grant, Sheridan wrote, "The cavalry engagement in front of Front Royal was splendid; it was on open ground; the saber was freely used. Great credit is due to Generals Merritt and Custer and Colonel Devin."[68]

On August 25, Wilson's and Merritt's divisions met Breckinridge's division near Kearneysville. McIntosh's brigade attacked dismounted, Chapman's brigade and Merritt's division partly mounted and partly dismounted. The Confederates were driven back nearly a mile, with a loss of sixty men taken prisoner. The next day, Colonel Lowell, working with Crook's infantry, charged Kershaw's division and took seventy prisoners, including seven officers.[69] Two days later it was again Merritt's turn; he met Fitzhugh Lee's cavalry at Leetown and drove it "with the saber" through Smithfield and across Opequon Creek.[70] For two weeks, from September 3 to September 19, the main armies were inactive, but not so the cavalry; as Sheridan wrote in his report, his horsemen were "employed every day in harassing the enemy . . . [their] opponents being principally infantry. In these skirmishes the cavalry was becoming educated to attack infantry lines."[71]

The most striking feat of arms of the Federal cavalry at this stage of the campaign occurred on September 13. Its hero was John McIntosh, who deserves a special place of honor in any account of cavalry operations in the East.[72] He had commanded

67. *Ibid.*, 19, 438, 472–73, 423. Merritt states in his report that Lomax's brigade, as well as Wickham's, was in the fight.

68. *Ibid.*, 822.

69. *Ibid.*, 517, 440, 425. According to Torbert, Kershaw also lost 250 killed and wounded in the second fight.

70. *Ibid.*, 426, 440–41. On August 24, the 1st New York (Lincoln) was taken from Duffié's division and added to Averell's; the 12th Pennsylvania, also taken from Duffié, was assigned to General Stevenson at Harper's Ferry. Since only two weeks earlier Duffié's division had numbered only nine hundred, the removal of these two regiments left him with only a handful of men. This remnant was ordered dismounted, and Duffié was directed to take them to Cumberland to establish a "camp of instruction." *Ibid.*, 896.

71. It was in the Valley Campaign that the Federal cavalry, in the opinion of Colonel G. F. R. Henderson, "struck the true balance between shock and dismounted tactics." Henderson, *The Science of War*, 55.

72. John Baillie McIntosh was a native of Florida, born in 1829. He served as a midshipman in the Mexican War. At the outbreak of the Civil War he was commissioned second lieutenant in the 2nd United States, from

Wilson's First Brigade as its senior colonel and continued to do so after his well-deserved promotion to brigadier general. There were those in the Third Division who thought that Wilson owed to him whatever successes he achieved.[73] Six days after his exploit of September 13, about to be described, while rallying his men in the battle of the Opequon he was seriously wounded. The wound required amputation of a leg, and he was lost to the cavalry service. One of his men, John W. Phillips of the 18th Pennsylvania, paid him a tribute any officer would have been proud to receive; "His loss," Phillips wrote, "cast a gloom over all who knew him. . . . In every place he was the same kind, brave man & gallant officer. He had won, and fairly too, on many a field the stars he wore. His Brigade *loved* him, and would follow him wherever he led."[74]

In the process of retreating after his second advance to the Potomac, Early reached Winchester. On September 13 Sheridan sent a strong force on a reconnaissance from Summit Point toward the town and ordered John McIntosh and his brigade forward on a similar mission on the Berryville-Winchester road. Leading the advance of his brigade with detachments of the 2nd Ohio and the 3rd New Jersey, McIntosh charged across the Opequon and up the steep rise leading to Winchester, beyond the stream. He found Confederate cavalry posted on the high ground to the west of the creek and flushed them out, taking thirty-seven prisoners. Continuing his advance, he broke through an infantry screen stationed behind the cavalry and surrounded and captured the entire 8th South Carolina Infantry of Kershaw's division, complete with its colonel, thirteen line officers, ninety-two enlisted men, and the regimental battle flag.[75]

---

which he transferred to the 5th United States. In November, 1862, he succeeded Averell as colonel of the 3rd Pennsylvania and from May, 1864, on commanded the First Brigade of the Third Division.

73. "Our Div[ision] when under . . . [Wilson's] command had no reputation, or but little, & that little being due to Col. McIntosh." Hannaford, "Reminiscences," 178(d). Isaac Gause, also of the 2nd Ohio, who was sent with a message to Wilson on September 13, wrote, "I arrived at headquarters at the same time General Wilson did. . . . The same old air of excitement and timorousness that always prevailed at his headquarters came with him." Gause, *Four Years with Five Armies*, 312–13.

74. Phillips, "Civil War Diary," 112.

75. For the official reports of the action, see *Official Records*, Vol. XLIII, Pt. 1, pp. 529–30, 427, 517; Pt. 3, p. 77.

General McIntosh's fine feat is recorded in the formal language of official reports and also in the more personal accounts of two participants, both of whom were troopers of the 2nd Ohio. The first of these accounts is that of Corporal Isaac Gause, who allows, indeed encourages, the inference that it was he himself who, practically single-handed, surrounded and captured the 106 South Carolinians. Having ordered them to surrender, Gause "dismounted, ran into the woods, took the flag, and marched the prisoners out."[76] Gause's reward for the capture of the flag was favorable mention in General McIntosh's report, a journey to Washington to deliver the flag to the War Department, a new uniform, a thirty-day furlough, and the Congressional Medal of Honor.

A more factual, more vivid, and certainly more dispassionate account of the capture is to be found in Trooper Hannaford's reminiscences, which also contain a friendly but unflattering comment on the hygienic state of the captives. Hannaford records for posterity that "a flock of ten year old 'billy goats' . . . could not have 'stunk' worse than these Johnnies. It is a fact that many of the men appeared as though water & they were strangers." As to the capture of the flag, Hannaford reports, "When lying in the thicket . . . [the South Carolinians] hid their flag[,] covering it with leaves, but some Corp[oral] of Co. G [actually Co. E] of our Reg-[imen]t happened to be passing through the woods after the 'rebs' had left, and kicked his foot against it, thereby uncovering enough to show its character[;] of course he picked it up & that was all he did do." The historian is free to make his choice between the two accounts.

The most striking point in Hannaford's recital of this day's events—the report of a sober, matter-of-fact, deeply religious individual, ten years older than the majority of his fellow troopers—is in its close. "We returned to camp," he writes, "More than well satisfied with ourselves; it was really a good day's work; no one but those who have been engaged in it can have the least idea how exhilarating is man hunting."[77]

However successful the Federal cavalry may have been in

76. Gause's version of the capture of the 8th South Carolina Infantry and their battle flag is in his *Four Years with Five Armies*, 309–16.
77. Hannaford, "Reminiscences," 153(d), 155(a). In fairness to

their encounters with Early's cavalry and infantry, neither the arrival of Sheridan nor the great increase in Federal strength in the Valley did anything to improve their sorry record in dealing with the Confederate partisans, guerrillas, and bushwhackers. On the contrary; they merely provided more and better targets. Brigadier General John D. Stevenson, in command at Harper's Ferry, wrote on August 17, "no small party or train with a small guard is safe."[78] General Merritt had to direct Colonel di Cesnola, temporarily in command of his Second Brigade, to "give strict orders that no men go more than a half a mile from camp, save in organized parties. . . . The guerrillas have murdered ten or twelve of our men . . . already."[79] No supply train was safe; for example, the train of the First Division's Reserve Brigade, guarded by a "battalion of 100 days men," was attacked in broad daylight and totally destroyed on August 13 by Mosby near Berryville. Mosby was able to "run off" about 350 mules.[80] Divisional commanders had to send dispatches to Sheridan's headquarters with a strong escort of at least fifteen men and an officer.[81]

Ideas for dealing with the ubiquitous menace were not lacking. Wilson suggested to McIntosh that he "leave some wagons with picked men concealed in them somewhat in rear as a decoy for bushwhackers."[82] Colonel Henry M. Lazelle, convinced of the hopelessness of keeping the guerrillas under control by conventional methods, urged that detachments of cavalry be moved to "desirable forest covers, always at night," to ambush the partisans and guerrillas.[83] General Grant, who could afford to take a Olympian view of the problem, wired Sheridan, "The families of most

Gause, it should be said that McIntosh credited him with the "capture," not the mere finding, of the flag. *Official Records*, Vol. XLIII, Pt. 1, p. 530.

78. *Official Records*, Vol. XLIII, Pt. 1, p. 826.

79. *Ibid.*, 865. The order is dated August 20.

80. *Ibid.*, 489, 836.

81. *Ibid.*, 848.

82. *Ibid.*, 818. At this time also Wilson set up a divisional group of scouts under the command of Captain T. A. Boice, 5th New York. Each regiment of the division was asked to recommend five men ("only such . . . as are sure to be a credit to their regiment and the division in every particular") for this "special duty." *Ibid.*, Pt. 2, p. 33.

83. *Ibid.*, 389.

of Mosby's men are known . . . they should be taken and kept at Fort McHenry . . . as hostages for the good conduct of Mosby and his men. Where any of Mosby's men are caught hang them without trial." Later the same day Grant had another idea; "If you can possibly spare a division of cavalry," he wrote Sheridan, "send them through Loudoun County, to destroy and carry off the crops, animals, negroes, and all men under fifty years of age capable of bearing arms. In this way you will get many of Mosby's men. . . . If not already soldiers, they will be so the moment the rebel army gets hold of them."[84] For the moment, Loudoun County remained unscathed, but Sheridan did not appear to need Grant's encouragement to carry out the hangings. The very day of Grant's dispatch he wired him that he had "hung one and shot six" of Mosby's men, and two days later, he added, "Guerrillas give me great annoyance, but I am quietly disposing of numbers of them."[85] The general-in-chief's thoughts on the subject appeared to filter down the chain of command, if, indeed, there was any need for high-level coaching, for a short time later Captain Richard Blazer, commanding a body of "Independent Scouts," reported a successful engagement with Mosby at Myers' Ford; "I have 6 prisoners; the circumstances are such that I am compelled to send them in."[86] Clearly, the prisoners would not have been "sent in" if "circumstances" had been different.

Sheridan's Valley Campaign is memorable not only for his truly spectacular victories, but also for the deliberate course of devastation he carried out. Grant's original instructions for the campaign stipulated, "In pushing up the Shenandoah Valley . . . it is desirable that nothing should be left to invite the enemy to return. Take all provisions, forage, and stock wanted for the use of your command. Such as cannot be consumed, destroy."[87] In

84. *Ibid.*, Pt. 1, p. 811. In compliance with this second suggestion, Sheridan issued a circular on August 19 to the effect that "All ablebodied male citizens under the age of fifty who may be suspected of aiding, assisting, or belonging to guerrilla bands . . . will be immediately arrested . . . and forwarded to these headquarters as prisoners of war, to be confined in Fort McHenry." *Ibid.*, 843, 843–44.
85. *Ibid.*, 822, 841.
86. *Ibid.*, 615.
87. *Ibid.*, 628. On July 14, Grant had written Halleck that "[Early]

compliance with this directive, which, he said, he "endorsed . . . in all its parts," Sheridan ordered Torbert, whose cavalry was to bring up the rear in the mid-August retrograde movement to Halltown, to "give the necessary order for the destruction of all the wheat and hay south of a line from Millwood to Winchester and Petticoat Gap. You will seize all horses, mules, and cattle. . . . No houses will be burned, and officers in charge of this delicate, but necessary, duty must inform the people that the object is to make the Valley untenable for the raiding parties of the rebel army."[88] Merritt, whose division actually had to do the work, noted in his report, "This duty, not among the most agreeable assigned to soldiers, was thoroughly though delicately done; no private property, save that mentioned, being injured; nor family molested by any soldier . . . to my knowledge."[89] It was just as well, perhaps, that General Merritt added the "to my knowledge" escape clause. Nevertheless, the destruction wrought by the Federal cavalry in the course of the two weeks of this retreat was only a foretaste of the far more extensive destruction of the succeeding months.

---

should have upon his heels . . . everything that can be got to follow, to eat out Virginia clear and clean . . . so that crows flying over it for the balance of this season will have to carry their provender with them." *Ibid.*, Vol. XXXVII, Pt. 2, pp. 300–301. Six weeks later, in a dispatch to Sheridan, Grant was more specific: "Do all the damage to railroads and crops you can. Carry off stock of all descriptions, and negroes, so as to prevent further planting. If the war is to last another year, we want the Shenandoah Valley to remain a barren waste." *Ibid.*, Vol. XLIII, Pt. 2, p. 202.

88. Sheridan, *Personal Memoirs*, I, 487; *Official Records*, Vol. XLIII, Pt. 1, p. 816.

89. *Official Records*, Vol. XLIII, Pt. 1, p. 440; see also Sheridan, *Personal Memoirs*, I, 485–88. On August 28, the 8th Illinois and the 16th New York were sent to the Middleburg-Upperville area on a hunt for guerrillas. Major John M. Waite, who was to command the expedition, was instructed, "The special object of your scout is to destroy . . . the sources from which Mosby draws men, horses and support. . . . You will arrest and bring in all males capable of bearing arms and conveying information, between the ages of eighteen and fifty. . . . impress all wagons, and bring them in loaded with forage; destroy all crops of hay, oats, corn and wheat which you cannot bring in, and seize all horses." *Official Records*, Vol. XLIII, Pt. 1, p. 942.

X

"Swifter than eagles, stronger than lions"

UNION GENERAL JOHN BEATTY REMARKS IN HIS REMINIS-
cences of the Civil War that he knew "absolutely that many of the
reports . . . [of Civil War actions were] base exaggerations—romances, founded upon the smallest conceivable amount of fact.
They are simply elaborate essays, which seek to show that the
author was a little braver, a little more skillful in the management
of his men, and a little worthier, than anybody else."[1] With equal
justice General Beatty could have included postwar memories and
memoirs as a continuation of these exaggerations and romances.
Union and Confederate officers, high and low, all tended to recall
the events of the war, and particularly their roles in it, through a
mythopoeic haze, with, more often than not, a generous dose of
self-justification thrown in. Nor were enlisted men wholly free of
this failing. One regimental historian has written what every other
practitioner of that esoteric branch of literature might well have
echoed: "As the work has progressed," wrote the author of the 9th
Illinois regimental history, "I have found it very difficult to har-
monize the facts as given in letters and diaries, with the recollec-

---

1. John Beatty, *Memoirs of a Volunteer, 1861–1863* (New York, 1946),
222; for a particularly blatant example, see *Official Records*, Vol. XLIII, Pt.
I, pp. 300–307.

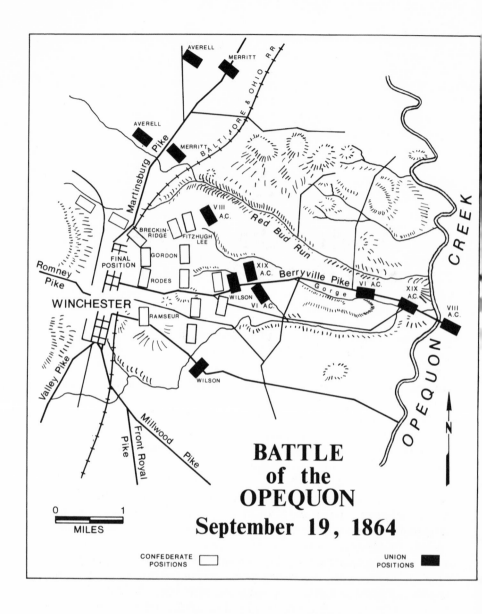

AVERELL

MERRITT

BALTIMORE & OHIO R.R.

AVERELL

MERRITT

Martinsburg Pike

VIII A.C.

BRECKIN-
RIDGE

FITZHUGH
LEE

Red Bud Run

GORDON

FINAL
POSITION

XIX
A.C.

RODES

Berryville Pike

VI A.C.

Romney
Pike

Gorge

XIX
A.C.

WILSON

WINCHESTER

VI A.C.

VIII
A.C.

RAMSEUR

CREEK

Valley Pike

WILSON

OPEQUON

Millwood Pike

N

Front Royal Pike

**BATTLE
of the
OPEQUON**
September 19, 1864

0   1

MILES

CONFEDERATE
POSITIONS

UNION
POSITIONS

tions of comrades."[2] As one moves upward on the ladder of military rank, the need to glamorize appears to grow less, but the need to justify (excused as an obligation "to set the record straight") grows correspondingly greater.

A conspicuous example of the Civil War as myth occurs in General-in-Chief Grant's *Personal Memoirs*. On September 15, 1864, with Sheridan backed up to the Potomac and Early's foot-soldiers and cavalry roaming at will north of Winchester, Grant decided to visit the Valley. His reason for doing so, he writes, was the impossibility of getting orders to Sheridan "to make a move" transmitted through Washington without having them "stopped there and such orders as Halleck's caution (and that of the Secretary of War) would suggest" substituted.[3] Perhaps General Grant had actually persuaded himself that this was the reason for his journey, notwithstanding that a steady stream of his messages and orders to Sheridan, and Sheridan's messages to him, had passed through the War Department telegraph office without any apparent sign of having been tampered with or watered down.[4] The suspicion may be permitted that Grant's real reason for the journey was quite different from what he claimed it to be. Sheridan, his own choice for the Valley command, had been given the post reluctantly, in deference to his wishes, by the president and the secretary of war. Sheridan had now had the command for five weeks and was seemingly no nearer the accomplishment of the mission assigned to him—the destruction of Early's army—than he had been on his first day in his new post. He had followed Early up the Valley and then meekly marched back down, followed closely by Early, to hole up in the Halltown defenses. Early himself thought, quite mistakenly as he was to learn to his cost, that Sheridan "lacked enterprise." The northern press, as has been mentioned, was loud in its criticism of the untried appointee who had not only failed to come to blows with the Confederate army but allowed it to return unhindered to the Potomac.

2. Edward A. Davenport, *History of the Ninth Regiment Illinois Cavalry Volunteers* (Chicago, 1888), vii.
3. Grant, *Personal Memoirs*, II, 327.
4. Messages between Grant at City Point and Sheridan in the Valley were transmitted via the War Department Telegraph Office in Washington.

And so Grant went to the Valley in mid-September—and did so with "a plan of campaign for Sheridan" in his pocket—not for the reason he gave, but in an effort to salvage his own status and to justify an appointment whose seeming failure was a reflection on his own judgment and a blow to his own prestige, already shaken by the apparently fruitless slaughter of the Wilderness Campaign. If it be objected that the "Victor of Appomattox" was incapable of harboring such mean motives, the reader is urged to suspend judgment until Grant's inexcusably brutal treatment of General George H. Thomas, from equally mean motives, is examined later in this narrative.

As it turned out, Grant made a needless journey. When he and Sheridan met at Charlestown, the latter already had a plan of his own and announced with the utmost confidence that he was ready to "whip" Early. Grant's plan remained in his pocket. Reassured (or bowled over) by Sheridan's exuberant self-confidence, he returned to City Point.[5]

When Sheridan rode to meet Grant, he already knew that the infantry reinforcements General Anderson had brought to the Valley were on their way back to Richmond. He then learned from Averell that Early was marching north to Martinsburg with two of his divisions of infantry and had left only Ramseur's division of infantry at Winchester to protect his base.[6] Sheridan now saw an opportunity to defeat Early in detail, and at two A.M. on the nineteenth set his army in motion.[7] Against the single division of Confederate infantry posted across the Berryville Pike on a plateau one and a half miles east of Winchester, with Lomax's cavalry on its right and Fitzhugh Lee's on its left, Sheridan sent Wilson's cavalry division, followed in order by the VI and XIX Corps, and the infantry, designated the VIII Corps, of George Crook's Army of West Virginia. This made a total of seven divi-

5. Grant, *Personal Memoirs*, II, 428.
6. *Official Records*, Vol. XLIII, Pt. 2, pp. 105, 106. Early marched to Martinsburg with Rodes's and Gordon's divisions to drive off the repair gangs working to restore service on the Baltimore & Ohio. *Battles and Leaders*, IV, 522. The fourth of Early's infantry divisions, Breckinridge's, was stationed at Stephenson's Depot.
7. *Official Records*, Vol. XLIII, Pt. 2, pp. 102–103.

sions (twenty brigades) of Union infantry and a two-brigade division of cavalry, the latter accompanied by six batteries of horse artillery. Led by Wilson, the army was to advance on the Berryville Pike, which west of the crossing of Opequon Creek climbed for about three miles through a narrow and steep ravine or "cañon," heavily wooded on both sides, to the plateau on which lay the Confederate infantry and the town of Winchester. Wilson was to clear the crossing of the Opequon and the upper end of the ravine; having done so, he was to give way to his own left and thus provide a corridor through which the VI and XIX Corps could debouch to the right and attack Ramseur, while Crook's infantry swung to the left and then around to the Valley Turnpike south of Winchester, thereby blocking Ramseur's best available escape route.

The two essentials for complete success were, first, for Wilson to drive off the outlying Confederate forces blocking the Opequon crossing and the exit from the long ravine, to allow the infantry following him to get through the ravine without hindrance and to deploy on the plateau beyond; and second, for Wright's, Emory's, and Crook's infantry and artillery to make the climb up the ravine with reasonable speed, get into battle formation, and launch their attack promptly.

To make success even more certain Sheridan planned a double envelopment. He sent Torbert with Merritt's division and the Reserve Brigade downstream (north) to cross the Opequon over Stevens' and Lock's fords. From there they were to march west to Stephenson's Depot, where they were to be met by Averell's division marching south from the direction of Martinsburg; the two divisions of mounted troops were then to move toward Winchester on a path that would bring them down on Ramseur's left flank and rear.[8]

The most important of a number of difficulties that caused Sheridan's plan to be executed differently from the way he had intended occurred at Martinsburg on the morning of the eigh-

8. Stevens' and Lock's fords are so named in Sheridan, *Personal Memoirs*, II, 11. Torbert calls them Seiver's and Locke's fords; *Official Records*, Vol. XLIII, Pt. 1, p. 427. They are also called Ridgeway's and Locke's fords, in G. E. Pond, *The Shenandoah Valley in 1864* (New York, 1883), 164.

teenth, when Early learned that Grant and Sheridan had met two days before at Charlestown.[9] He concluded at once that the meeting portended an early move by Sheridan against him and he therefore ordered the divisions of John B. Gordon and Robert E. Rodes to return by forced marches to Winchester, twenty miles away. Hence Sheridan's attack the next day was met by Early's entire force, instead of only a fraction of it. Even so, when fully deployed, Sheridan was to have an overwhelming, roughly three to one superiority in numbers, 43,000 rifles and sabers against 16,000. The second hitch was the result of bad management. A member of General Wright's staff, or perhaps the general himself, saw fit to order the entire wagon train of the VI Corps to follow the infantry, and the "miles" of wagons, inching along the steep rise on the narrow road through the ravine, blocked the advance of the XIX and VIII Corps.[10] As a result, the VI Corps infantry, attacking as soon as it reached level ground on top of the ravine, was left without support. Sheridan, who in this as in all his battles, seemed to be everywhere at once, rode back himself to see why Emory's and Crook's men were delayed. What he saw called for all his ample stock of expletives. The road was hopelessly jammed with a tangle of wagons, mules, swearing teamsters and staff officers. Sheridan ordered all the wagons off the road into the ditches, bushes, and trees alongside, and General Cuvier Grover's division, leading the XIX Corps, was at last able to snake its way up the ravine, followed by General William Dwight's division and then by the five brigades of Crook's command. The holdup in the ravine had caused a six-hour delay, which cost Sheridan the opportunity to overwhelm Ramseur's division before Gordon's and Rodes's divisions could reach him.

When the head of the XIX Corps emerged at last from the ravine, and Emory deployed his men to the right of the VI Corps, they had to fight for their lives to meet an attack launched by Early against the loosely held joint between the two Federal corps. The Confederate attack drove a deep salient into the Union line and created a serious crisis. Sheridan managed to restore the situ-

9. *Battles and Leaders*, IV, 523.
10. DeForest, *A Volunteer's Adventures*, 173; see also *Battles and Leaders*, IV, 507.

ation by ordering Emory Upton's brigade of the First Division, VI Corps, to pivot on its right and attack the southern face of the salient. He was also forced to deploy the VIII Corps to the right of the XIX Corps, instead of using it, as he had intended, to make a wide turning movement around the opposite flank. David A. Russell, Upton's division commander, was killed, and Upton, a twenty-five-year-old brigadier general three years out of West Point, took his place. In the course of directing the attack of the division's three brigades, Upton was gravely wounded by a shell fragment that laid open his thigh and narrowly missed the femoral artery. Paying no attention to Sheridan's order to go to the rear and have his wound attended to, Upton had his staff surgeon apply a tourniquet to his leg and had himself placed on a stretcher and carried about the field, so that he could continue to direct the division until the close of the action.[11] Casualties in these successive attacks and counterattacks were heavy on both sides.

With the Confederate salient eventually wiped out and the hostile lines back in their original positions, there was a lull in the action, in the course of which Crook finally reached the position on Emory's right that had been assigned to him. As soon as he had done so, Sheridan ordered the three corps commanders to attack in succession, starting with Crook, and to direct their attacks in a half-wheel to the left, so as to envelop the left flank of the Confederate infantry and force them into the bottleneck of the streets of Winchester, and into the waiting arms of Wilson's troopers who, Sheridan hoped, would have blocked the Valley Turnpike south of the town.[12]

Nine days before the battle Torbert had reported 6,465 officers and men present for duty equipped in the two divisions of cavalry—Wilson's and Merritt's—under his immediate command; with the 2,500 officers and men of Averell's Second Division of the Army of West Virginia added, Sheridan had approximately nine thousand mounted men at his disposal.[13] They were

11. Stephen E. Ambrose, *Upton and the Army* (Baton Rouge, 1964), 41. Upton was promoted to major general by brevet the day after the battle. Never was promotion more richly deserved.
12. Sheridan, *Personal Memoirs*, II, 19–25; *Official Records*, Vol. XLIII, Pt. 1, p. 47.
13. For Torbert's numbers, see *Official Records*, Vol. XLIII, Pt. 1, p. 61.

now to demonstrate what well led, intelligently used, largely veteran cavalry could do *as* cavalry in the traditional sense, in a full-scale battle.

Wilson discharged faultlessly the duty he had been assigned in Sheridan's battle plan. Moving out on time, with McIntosh's brigade in the lead, he crossed Opequon Creek against negligible opposition and made his way up the ravine. The Confederates occupied a strong position behind earthworks on a ridge just to the west of the point at which the road emerged from the ravine, "commanding the road and the open fields on both sides of it." In the predawn darkness, guided only by the flashes of the defenders' guns, McIntosh attacked with his entire brigade, partly mounted and partly dismounted, and drove the Confederates from their position.[14] With the ridge now securely in Wilson's possession, the VI Corps was able to debouch from the ravine and deploy for its attack on Ramseur.

Meanwhile Torbert, who had also moved out at two A.M., ran into stiff opposition in his effort to cross the Opequon. A Federal reconnaissance of the fords a few days earlier had caused the Confederates to anticipate an attempt to cross the stream at those points. Strong detachments of infantry of General Gabriel C. Wharton's brigade of Breckinridge's division were therefore sent to the fords to dig and man rifle pits on their side of the stream. Merritt decided to force a crossing at Seiver's (or Stevens') Ford with Devin's brigade and Colonel Lowell's Reserve Brigade. Lowell led the attack, dismounted men in front, followed by the 5th United States and a portion of the 2nd Massachusetts, mounted. The Confederate infantry were driven out of their rifle pits and a railroad cut they used as a trench, and the crossing was made good.

Custer and his brigade, attempting to cross three quarters of a mile downstream at Lock's Ford, had a more difficult time of it.

Averell's strength is given as "about 2,500" by Sheridan in a September 13 report (*ibid.*, 62). On September 23, according to Colonel Wm. H. Powell, who succeeded Averell in command of the division, its strength was 2,287, all ranks (*ibid.*, 506).

14. *Ibid.*, 518; Wilson, *Under the Old Flag*, I, 551–53. "McIntosh," Wilson reported, "displayed the highest qualities of a cavalry officer in this morning's work." *Official Records*, Vol. XLIII, Pt. 1, p. 518.

Wharton's infantrymen were on the alert, and there was no chance of rushing the ford by surprise. Custer dismounted the 6th Michigan and moved it to the crest of a hill overlookng the ford, to try to keep the Confederates down with their carbine fire while the 25th New York and the 7th Michigan rushed the ford, mounted. The New Yorkers got to the near bank of the stream, where they were brought to a halt by the "heavy fire" of the defense. They and the Michigan regiment behind them gave way "in considerable confusion." Custer now called upon Colonel Peter Stagg and the 1st Michigan "to accomplish what two regiments had unsuccessfully attempted." Helped by the covering fire of the 6th Michigan, Stagg and his men galloped into the stream, reached the opposite bank, and captured the rifle pits and a considerable number of prisoners.[15] Dislodged from the fords, Wharton's infantrymen retreated about a mile in the direction of Winchester; joining the other two brigades of their division, they "took position behind a heavy line of earthworks," where they succeeded in bringing Merritt's advance to a halt.

Averell, with his two brigades, made an unopposed crossing of Opequon Creek near Smithfield, five miles below Lock's Ford. From there he rode west to Bunker Hill, where he turned south toward Winchester. His advance along the Winchester-Martinsburg Pike was contested by Fitzhugh Lee with two weak brigades; nevertheless, Averell made steady progress and reached a point from which he could easily have enveloped the left flank and rear of Breckinridge's infantry, facing Merritt.[16] Greatly outnumbered and in imminent danger of being flanked by Averell, whose divi-

15. *Official Records*, Vol. XLIII, Pt. 1, p. 454; see also Kidd, *Personal Recollections*, 385–88. Other accounts of the crossing, however, differ in important respects from that given in the text. Colonel Kidd writes that while the 1st Michigan was preparing for its charge, "it was discovered that the Confederates were leaving their cover and falling back. Lowell had effected a crossing at another ford and was threatening the flank of the force in our front." Kidd, *Personal Recollections*, 388–89. Averell stated in his report that after he had crossed the stream and reached Stephenson's Depot, his "attention was attracted by heavy firing to . . . [his] left and rear, which was soon ascertained to be General Torbert endeavoring to cross the Opequon. . . . Attacking the enemy opposed to Custer promptly in rear he was enabled to cross and join my left." *Official Records*, Vol. XLIII, Pt. 1, p. 498. More than a cavalryman's courage is needed to decide which of so many conflicting accounts of the same event is most likely to be correct.

16. It is significant that nowhere in Merritt's report, written after Aver-

sion alone was as large as his own, Breckinridge had no choice but to order a retreat.

Averell's division was now abreast of Custer's; in the meantime also, Devin's brigade had followed Lowell's across the Opequon. And now, at about two P.M., five brigades of Federal cavalry, Devin on the left, next to him Lowell, Custer in the center, and on the right the brigades of Colonels William H. Powell and James M. Schoonmaker of Averell's division, an unbroken front more than a half mile long of mounted men in three lines, moved like a tidal wave toward the left and rear of Early's infantry, who were fighting for their lives in the face of the frontal attacks of Crook's, Emory's, and Wright's infantry and repeated "demonstrations" by Wilson's cavalry on their right flank.[17] Here and there the advance of the Federal cavalry was held up momentarily by small groups of Confederate infantry or cavalry, or a section or a battery of artillery, taking advantage of fences, ditches, patches of timber, or whatever other cover offered, but they faced hopeless odds and were either surrounded and captured or driven back step by step toward the main body of their own infantry, fighting before Winchester.

Much of the area through which Merritt and Averell had fought their way was wooded, but south of Stephenson's Depot most of the land had been cleared and was under cultivation. As the Federal cavalry emerged from the woods into the afternoon sunlight, some two miles north of Winchester and squarely on the flank of Early's sorely beset infantry, they presented a spectacle unique in the Civil War. Every man of the five brigades was mounted and in his place; there were no horseholders to thin the ranks. It was a scene and an occasion made to order for George Custer's lush eloquence, which could on occasion be as scarlet as the neckerchief he affected. He wrote:

At this time most . . . of the brigades moved in brigade front, the regiments being in parallel columns or squadrons. One continuous and heavy fire of skirmishers covered the advance . . . while the line of brigades as they advanced across the open country, the bands playing the

_____

ell had been relieved of his command, is there any mention of Averell or of his division.

17. Lowell's command, made up of his own 2nd Massachusetts, the 6th Pennsylvania, and the 1st, 2nd, and 5th United States, was technically a

national airs, presented in the sunlight one moving mass of glittering sabers. This, combined with the various and bright-colored banners and battleflags . . . furnished one of the most inspiring as well as imposing scenes of martial grandeur ever witnessed upon a battle-field. . . . Upon our left and in plain view could be seen the struggle now raging between the infantry lines of each army, while at various points columns of light-colored smoke showed that the artillery on neither side was idle.[18]

Taking advantage of a patch of woods, the Confederate cavalry, now united, made a stand across the Martinsburg Pike in an effort to stem the advance of the horsemen in blue. Fitzhugh Lee, in overall command (he was to be severely wounded in the ensuing melée) had a choice of two nearly equally hopeless alternatives: to remain on the defensive or to attack. He chose the latter and ordered a charge. His troopers, relying on carbine and pistol, drove through the line of Federal skirmishers and a "portion" of Custer's brigade. Indeed, Averell was to claim that members of his staff and several of his orderlies were "engaged for some time in rallying . . . [Custer's] cavalry."[19] Lee's attack broke up the parade-ground regularity of the Federal advance; it could not, however, do more than delay the inevitable.[20] As his troopers were

---

brigade, but with a total strength of about six hundred, it was no larger than one fair-sized regiment. *Official Records*, Vol. XLIII, Pt. 1, p. 455.

18. *Ibid.*, 456; see also Kidd, *Personal Recollections*, 390–91; Beach, *First New York (Lincoln) Cavalry*, 427–28; Farrar, *The Twenty-Second Pennsylvania*, 374 ; Bowen, *Regimental History of the First New York*, 230–32, this last being a verbatim copy, without the courtesy of quotation marks, of Custer's report.

19. *Official Records*, Vol. XLIII, Pt. 1, p. 498.

20. Merritt, in a report glowing with self-satisfaction over the work of his division that day, wrote, "When approaching the field near Winchester, the enemy's cavalry (reinforced) again met our advance, when the Second Brigade charged it, which charge, being closely followed up by the First Brigade . . . drove the rebel horsemen pell-mell over their infantry and out of sight into the town. . . . At this time . . . the field was open for our cavalry operations such as the war has not seen, such as all good cavalry officers long to engage in. . . . A six-gun battery of the enemy was playing away rapidly toward our left front. This was ordered to be charged, but before the order could be executed it withdrew, and the charge was directed on the enemy's infantry, which was attempting to change front to meet us. . . . Devin . . . burst like a storm of case shot in their midst showering saber blows on their heads and shoulders . . . and routing them in droves in every direction." *Ibid.*, 444–45.

beaten back by the masses of Federal cavalry, "the country for a mile was full of charging columns—regiments, troops, squads— the pursuit taking them in every direction where a mounted enemy could be seen."[21] At one point the Federal horsemen saw a strange spectacle, probably unmatched in the Civil War: General Breckinridge's infantry had formed a hollow square to resist the blue horsemen coming at them from all sides.[22]

The Confederate infantry, notwithstanding their relative numerical weakness, had managed to more than hold their own against the frontal assault of the Federal footsoldiers, but the descent of masses of Federal cavalry on their flank and rear was too much for their fortitude. General Early reported that "as soon as firing was heard in rear of our left flank the infantry commenced falling back along the whole line, and it was very difficult to stop them"; summing up the course of the battle, he added, "In this fight I had already defeated the enemy's infantry, and could have continued to do so, but the enemy's very great superiority in cavalry and the comparative inefficiency of ours turned the scale against us."[23] In his postwar reminiscences Early described his discomfiture in terms which suggest that both as a military man and as one reconverted to American patriotism he harbored a personal grievance against Sheridan. "Little Phil" had failed to measure up to Early's standard of the generalship to be expected of an American army commander. Sheridan's victory should have been more decisive than it was. Given Sheridan's "immense superiority in cavalry," a "skillful and energetic commander" would have crushed Ramseur and destroyed or captured, bag and baggage, Early's entire force.[24]

It was evident to all the participants in this battle, both at the time and in retrospect, that the intervention of the Federal cavalry was the decisive factor in producing Sheridan's victory. The cavalrymen themselves, high and low, were certain that they had

21. Kidd, *Personal Recollections*, 391.
22. Douglas, *I Rode with Stonewall*, 310; *Official Records*, Vol. XLIII, Pt. 1, p. 554.
23. *Official Records*, Vol. XLIII, Pt. 1, p. 554; see also Early, *Autobiographical Sketch*, 426–27: "We deserved the victory and would have had it, but for the enemy's immense superiority in cavalry, which alone gave it to him."
24. Early, *Autobiographical Sketch*, 427.

won the battle and exulted accordingly.[25] Their losses had been heavy: 65 killed, 267 wounded, and 109 missing in Merritt's division alone, but that division also laid claim to the capture of 775 prisoners, seven battle flags, and two pieces of artillery.[26] There was glory for everyone; the president wired Sheridan, "Have just heard of your great victory. God bless you all, officers and men"; the secretary of war sent his congratulations on the "brilliant victory" and notified Sheridan of his appointment to the rank of brigadier general in the Regular Army and the change of his command of the Middle Military Division from temporary to permanent. Grant too wired congratulations on the "most opportune" victory, which, he said, "wipe[d] out much of the stain upon our arms by previous disasters in that locality."[27] The only serious disappointment of the battle was Wilson's inability—excusable, given the numerical weakness of his division, the desperate resistance he faced, the "ravines, stone fences and rough country" over which he had to fight his way, and the darkness—to get his men across the Valley Turnpike south of Winchester; had he been able to do so, most of Early's army might well have been captured.[28] As it was, Early reported 1,818 of his infantry and gunners missing, many and probably most of whom were taken prisoner in the battle and subsequent pursuit, and he had no data on the losses in captured and missing of his cavalry.[29]

General Wilson, whose comments on his contemporaries in

25. "The battle . . . was . . . finally decided by the cavalry, the first instance in which such was the case." Whittaker, *George A. Custer*, 234.

26. Losses: *Official Records*, Vol. XLIII, Pt. 1, p. 60. There is a lack of agreement on Averell's casualties. He himself, doubtless anxious to magnify his role in the battle, claimed 250 of his men killed, wounded, and missing. Torbert, hostile to him throughout, went out of his way to correct the figure to a total of 32. Strangely enough, however, Torbert also reduced Merritt's total loss from 441 to 311. *Ibid.*, 498, 435.

27. Lincoln and Stanton, *ibid.*, 61; Grant, *ibid.*, 61–62. Sheridan was promoted to brigadier general in the Regular Army (Regular Army ranks, unlike ranks "of Volunteers" were to be retained after the war ended) within twenty-four hours after Grant "urge[d]" that it be done. *Ibid.*, Pt. 2, pp. 118, 131. Sheridan's command of the Middle Military Division was changed to "permanent" by General Orders No. 259 of September 21. *Ibid.*, 131.

28. Wilson, *Under the Old Flag*, I, 556.

29. *Official Records*, Vol. XLIII, Pt. 1, p. 555. In addition to the missing, the infantry and artillery also lost 226 killed and 1,567 wounded. Given the confusion following a major defeat, and an even more severe defeat only three days later, the accuracy of Early's figures is open to question.

high command rarely erred on the side of an excess of charity, was critical of the role of the Federal infantry in the battle— "slow and timid . . . [and] badly handled"—and less than enthusiastic about Sheridan's generalship—"with all his energy and dash Sheridan was not yet the whirlwind of battle he afterward became." Nonetheless he gave Sheridan full credit for the tactics that produced the victory. "Winchester was the first battle of the war," he wrote, "in which the cavalry was properly handled in cooperation with the infantry."[30] After the hesitancy of Sheridan's predecessors and contemporaries in high command, McClellan, Hooker, Meade, and even Grant—all, in fact, except the unfortunate John Pope—to exploit or even to recognize the full potential of their mounted forces, this was a notable step forward and a harbinger of the glories to come.[31] In General Davies' words, the Opequon was "a rainbow of promise"; Colonel G. F. R. Henderson, the British biographer of Stonewall Jackson and a military theorist whose pronouncements on the Civil War are entitled to the highest respect, cited Sheridan's handling of his cavalry in combination with the infantry a model of tactical skill.[32]

Early's army, greatly reduced in numbers and with many of its infantry unarmed, made its escape in the night to Fisher's Hill, twenty miles south of Winchester and two miles below Strasburg. The "hill," actually an uneven ridge running east and west, rising in a steep bluff from the bed of Tumbling Run at its northern foot, blocked the Valley for its full width of about three and a half miles from Massanutten Mountain on the east to Little North

30. Wilson, *Under the Old Flag*, I, 557–58. In a paper read in 1913, Wilson said, "Taking it all in all, Winchester was a beautiful battle . . . the only other fight in which the cavalry performed its proper part was at Nashville." Wilson, "Cavalry of the Army of the Potomac," 84. It should be noted, however, that at Nashville the Union cavalry fought dismounted; only at Winchester (and later at Cedar Creek, and in some of the engagements of the Appomattox Campaign) did the Federal cavalry fight mounted, in the traditional way.

31. "It was the first time that proper use of . . . [the cavalry] had been made in a great battle during the war." Kidd, *Personal Recollections*, 393–94.

32. Davies, *General Sheridan*, 164; Henderson, *The Science of War*, 275.

Mountain on the west. A naturally strong defensive position, Fisher's Hill was further strengthened with breastworks along its crest that the Confederates had constructed while they held the position in August. Early had been able to carry away from the battle of the Opequon nearly all his artillery; despite his numerical weakness—he had about twelve thousand men left after the fight on the nineteenth—he was confident that he could hold the position which gave the defense every advantage, protected as it was by steep-sided mountains on both flanks and the steep rise from Tumbling Run in front.

On the day following its victory at the Opequon, the Union army reached Fisher's Hill. Wright's and Emory's corps took up positions north of Tumbling Run, facing the center and right of Early's line; Crook bivouacked in heavy timber a short distance to the rear. After a careful survey of Early's position, Sheridan decided to move Wright and Emory forward to create the impression that he was planning a frontal assault, while he moved "Crook, unperceived if possible, over to the eastern face of Little North Mountain, whence he could strike the left and rear of the Confederate line."[33] Averell, who had been posted with his division on the right and somewhat to the rear of the Federal line, claims credit in his report for suggesting the idea, but there are good grounds for believing that it was actually proposed by Crook.[34] To make the flank attack succeed, Crook's march had to be hidden from the signal station overlooking the entire area that Early had established on top of Massanutten Mountain. This Sheridan was able to accomplish by having Crook march during the night of the twentieth into another large stand of "heavy timber north of Cedar Creek, where he lay concealed all day the 21st"; at break of day on the twenty-second, Crook moved with his two divisions under cover of the dense woods and ravines along the eastern foot of Little North Mountain until, late in the afternoon, he reached a point well to the rear of the roughly one thousand dismounted cavalry of Lunsford Lomax's division whom

33. Sheridan, *Personal Memoirs*, II, 35.
34. *Official Records*, Vol. XLIII, Pt. 1, p. 499; but see Williams, *Hayes of the Twenty-third*, 268; according to the latter, the flank attack was proposed by Crook, with Rutherford B. Hayes as his spokesman.

Early had deployed to hold what he thought was the relatively safe western end of his line.[35] Lomax discovered the approach of Crook's infantry when they were still a half-mile away. He acted quickly to meet the threat by moving his men from their northward-facing line along the crest of the ridge to a new line facing west, the direction from which Crook's command was advancing; he sent word at the same time to Ramseur, commanding the division of infantry immediately to his right, that he had done so and asked him to send some of his men to occupy the position he had vacated. However, before Ramseur's infantry could get there, Averell's men scrambled over the undefended crest. Lomax was thus caught between two fires, Crook in his front and left, and Averell on his right and rear.[36] His scanty force would have had little chance of holding its own against either attack; to fight off the simultaneous assault of three Federal divisions, coming from three directions, was impossible. The Federal divisions were small; still, they counted nine thousand carbines and rifles against Lomax's one thousand. As Lomax's men broke to the rear, they exposed successively the left flank and rear of Ramseur's, John Pegram's, and Gordon's divisions, all of whom, as Early reported, "got into a panic and gave way in confusion."[37] The "confusion" soon turned into an all-out rout, far worse than it had been at Winchester three days before. Early's casualties in killed and wounded were modest—a total of 240—but he lost twelve pieces of artillery and about a thousand of his infantry and gunners taken prisoner or missing. Once again he had no data on the losses of his cavalry, but he thought them to be "slight."[38]

The fight at Fisher's Hill cannot properly be called a battle, but for Averell it had a sorry aftermath. As Early's routed army fled through the night toward Woodstock, ten miles to the south,

35. Sheridan, *Personal Memoirs*, II, 36–37; *Official Records*, Vol. XLIII, Pt. 1, pp. 611, 363. Lomax had on Fisher's Hill only one (Imboden's) brigade of his division.
36. *Official Records*, Vol. XLIII, Pt. 1, p. 611. Sheridan's first report to Grant, sent off at 11:30 P.M. on September 22, mentions the roles of Crook and of the VI and XIX Corps, but not Averell's contribution to the victory. *Ibid.*, Pt. 2, p. 142.
37. *Ibid.*, Pt. 1, p. 556; see also 558.
38. *Ibid.*, 556.

Averell, by his own account, pursued for seven miles, capturing prisoners, guns, wagons, and ambulances; then, in the absence of orders from Sheridan "or anyone else," he halted for the night.[39] Why a major general of cavalry, West Point-trained, a cavalry-man before the war and with three years of combat experience in the Civil War under his belt, should have needed orders from any-one to do anything but press on after the fleeing enemy as long as his own men and horses were capable of movement, is a point Averell has not bothered to explain. There was "hot pursuit" of the enemy by Wright's and Emory's infantry, as Sheridan record-ed, and, not surprisingly in light of the sequel, he wrote that "without good reason . . . [Averell] had refrained from taking any part whatever in pursuing the enemy . . . and in fact had gone into camp and left to the infantry the work of pursuit."[40] Clearly, Averell's claim of a seven-mile pursuit and Sheridan's of no pur-suit at all are in direct conflict; which of the two is incorrect, and whether it is so by intent or otherwise, are questions which in the absence of independent evidence cannot be answered. It would seem, however, on Averell's own showing that he did not press the pursuit with the determination the circumstances called for and Sheridan had the right to expect.

On the morning of the twenty-third, having organized his troops—many of whom had thrown away their arms in their flight to Woodstock—into some sort of order, Early resumed his retreat toward Mount Jackson. Sheridan sent Devin's brigade of Merritt's division in pursuit. Two miles short of Mount Jackson Devin was brought to a halt by the Confederate rear guard. Sheri-dan told Devin that Averell, whom he thought to be "close at hand," would be hurried forward to help him. But, says Sheridan, Averell was not close at hand at all; indeed, he did not reach Devin until three P.M., and even this did not occur until there had been "some hot words" between the two generals and Averell had been told to "proceed to the front at once, and in conjunction with Devin, close with the enemy."[41] Averell's report gives a somewhat detailed, and so far as one may judge from internal evidence

39. *Ibid.*, 499.
40. Sheridan, *Personal Memoirs*, II, 43.
41. *Ibid.*

alone, factual account of these "hot words." Sheridan, in a rage, wanted to hear neither explanations nor excuses for Averell's delayed arrival. Averell on his part was anything but conciliatory. Typical of the exchanges between the two men was the following, as reported by Averell:

I replied that I had received no information or instructions from him. He stated that he could not find me. I asked him if he had tried, to which he made no reply, but stated that the rebel army was a perfect mob, which would run away upon the firing of a single gun, and that he desired me to go and put in my cavalry. I assured him that I never hesitated to put it in when there was any chance of success . . . [but that] I did not entertain the opinion that the rebel army was a mob.[42]

James R. Bowen of the 19th New York claimed to have overheard "the entire conversation" and wrote in his regimental history that "it can be stated from positive knowledge that while Averell maintained a calm and civil demeanor, Sheridan manifested unreasonable anger, refusing to listen to any explanations."[43]

Averell eventually joined Devin, took command as the senior officer, and "putting . . . [his] division in action, the enemy was driven beyond the town."[44] So Averell has it, but according to Sheridan, Devin "was pushing the Confederates so energetically that they were abandoning Mount Jackson, yet Averell utterly failed to accomplish anything. Indeed, his indifferent attack was not at all worthy the excellent soldiers he commanded."[45] It may be asked why, if Devin was already "pushing the Confederates so energetically," it was so urgently necessary to have Averell support him. Whether or not Averell attacked with the requisite energy must remain a matter of judgment and doubt. Devin was an eyewitness, but his report sheds no light on the subject.[46] In Sheri-

42. *Official Records*, Vol. XLIII, Pt. 1, p. 500.
43. Bowen, *Regimental History of the First New York*, 240; Bowen prefaces his account of what he overheard with: "Right at this time, General Torbert . . . had also failed to meet Sheridan's expectations and thus incurred his displeasure. Irritated and angered by these failures, it would seem he sought some object upon which to vent his spleen; and instead of removing the really incompetent Torbert, that splendid fighter, the gallant Averell, became the victim of his pent-up wrath." It should be noted that Bowen's regiment belonged to Merritt's, not Averell's division.
44. *Official Records*, Vol. XLIII, Pt. 1, p. 500.
45. Sheridan, *Personal Memoirs*, II, 43.
46. For Devin's report, see *Official Records*, Vol. XLIII, Pt. 1, p. 476.

dan's judgment, Averell did not, and unfortunately for the latter, Sheridan was the superior officer and his opinion was decisive. By Sheridan's own admission, however, Averell *did* attack, and the Confederate rear guard, which had been able to hold Devin in check for some time, was compelled to retreat beyond Mount Jackson.

Then came the final act of "Averell Agonistes." Sheridan learned (actually from a report Averell sent him) that Early's entire army was in bivouac in a strong position on high ground south of Mount Jackson, that a "division" of his army, supported by five pieces of artillery, was moving forward to counterattack Devin and Averell, and that a message from a "signal officer" had informed Averell that a Confederate brigade or division was moving around to envelop his right. Averell informed Sheridan that in view of these developments he was about to break off the action, move to the rear, and go into camp "where water and forage could be obtained, and where the command could rest securely until morning, as they had had but little forage for two days."[47] This was a red rag to the bull with a vengeance; it was not fighting the enemy as Sheridan understood the term, and he responded with a dispatch calculated to raise blisters. "Your report and report of signal officer received," Sheridan wrote; "I do not want you to let the enemy bluff you or your command, and I want you to distinctly understand this note. I do not advise rashness, but I do desire resolution and actual fighting, with necessary casualties, before you retire. There must now be no backing and filling by you, without a superior force of the enemy actually engaging you."[48] "Some little time" after sending off this note, Sheridan learned that without waiting for a reply to his own report, Averell had indeed retreated and gone into camp. He there and then sent orders relieving Averell of his command, directing him to depart at once to Wheeling, there to await further orders, and assigning Colonel William H. Powell, 2nd West Virginia, to the command of the division.[49]

47. *Ibid.*, 500, 43–44. Devin's report corroborates Averell's statement that (in Devin's words) "a large force of infantry was plainly visible bivouacked around the town." *Ibid.*, 476.

48. *Ibid.*, 500.

49. Colonel Powell assumed command of the division and Averell left (taking with him all the division's records and its entire staff excepting the

In his report on the campaign Averell charged that the order relieving him of his command—an order, he wrote, which "trampl[ed] upon . . . [his] record and upon all military courtesy and justice"—was merely the final step in a vendetta whose object was to advance Torbert at his expense, and which had begun even before Sheridan took command of the Middle Military Division.[50] The charge, especially the latter part of it, may well have been true, but Averell obviously failed to recognize the extent to which his inconceivably senseless behavior on September 22–23 contributed to his own downfall.

Sheridan informed Grant two days after the event that he had relieved Averell because "instead of following the enemy when he was broken at Fisher's Hill, so that there was not a cavalry organization left, he went into camp, and let me pursue the enemy for a distance of fifteen miles with infantry during the night."[51] When he came to write his memoirs, he thought it incumbent upon him to claim a broader justification for his action, explaining,

The removal of Averell was but the culmination of a series of events extending back to the time I assumed command of the Middle Military Division. . . . Averell's dissatisfaction began to show itself immediately after his arrival at Martinsburg, on the 14th of August, and, except when he was conducting some independent expedition, had been manifested on all occasions since. I therefore thought that the interest of the service would be subserved by removing one whose growing indifference might render the best-laid plans inoperative.[52]

There is no question but that Averell had proven himself a difficult subordinate, willful, intractable, and unpredictable. More-

chief surgeon) on September 24. Before leaving, Averell issued a most creditable farewell order to the division. *Ibid.*, 506; Pt. 2, p. 158.
    50. *Ibid.*, Pt. 1, pp. 500–501.
    51. *Ibid.*, 29. This passage occurs in a lengthy report to Grant written by Sheridan himself, not by one of his staff officers. In his formal report on the campaign, he wrote that "Averell's division . . . for some unaccountable reason went into camp immediately after the battle [of Fisher's Hill]. General Averell reached Devin's command at about 3 P.M., and in the evening returned with all the advance cavalry . . . to a creek half a mile north of Hawkinsburg, and there he remained until the arrival of the head of the infantry column." *Ibid.*, 49.
    52. Sheridan, *Personal Memoirs*, II, 44–45.

over, at critical times, as he had shown before at Kelly's Ford and in the Stoneman Raid preceding Hooker's crossing of the Rapidan, his actions, or more correctly, his inertia, indicated either a failure of nerve, an overactive imagination, or at least a lack of determination to carry through to the end an operation that had been assigned to him. Averell was simply not Sheridan's kind of fighting man. And yet Sheridan's explanation stops a long way short of clarifying what he himself recognized as the real source of his problems with his balky subordinate. Why had the inexperienced Torbert been preferred by Grant and himself over Averell, his superior in rank and experience, for the top cavalry command in the Valley? And was Averell's lack of aggressiveness on the twenty-third the real cause of his downfall? Unquestionably, it was a major factor, but James R. Bowen's surmise may well be right, namely, that Averell was relieved not because of his inertia, or what Sheridan considered to be such, but because he was the handiest target for the latter's rage on learning that Torbert had failed to carry out an assignment that might have made possible the capture of Early's entire army.[53]

Early had deployed his army atop Fisher's Hill on the twentieth in the reasonable expectation that it could hold its own there against any direct assault, but he knew that he would be in a critical situation if the Federals, moving up the narrow Luray Valley on the far side of Massanutten Mountain, should cross one of the numerous passes through the mountain south of Fisher's Hill and come down on his rear. To prevent this he sent Fitzhugh Lee's cavalry, commanded by Williams Wickham after Lee was wounded on the nineteenth, to Milford in the Luray Valley to block any Federal advance by that route.[54] The strategic possibilities opened up by the Luray Valley—first demonstrated by Stonewall

53. It will be of interest to note in connection with Averell's dismissal, that his erstwhile enemy, Alfred Duffié, after being shelved by assignment to the command of a camp of dismounted cavalry at Hagerstown in October, 1864, was captured by Mosby on the twenty-fourth of the same month. Sheridan reported to Halleck that Duffié was "captured by his own stupidity" and requested his dismissal from the service as "a trifling man and a poor soldier." *Official Records*, Vol. XLIII, Pt. 2, pp. 399, 466, 475. Duffié must have had friends in high places, for he was not mustered out until August, 1865.

54. *Ibid.*, Pt. 1, p. 555.

Jackson two years before—were as clear to Sheridan as they were to Early. On the twenty-first, while his infantry moved into position facing Fisher's Hill, Sheridan sent Torbert with two brigades of Merritt's division to join Wilson, who had previously been posted to Front Royal at the northern end of the Luray Valley. Torbert's orders were to drive Wickham out of his way, move up the Luray Valley, and cross Massanutten Mountain into the main Valley at New Market, nearly thirty miles south of Fisher's Hill, which would place him squarely athwart Early's only available line of retreat toward Harrisonburg and Staunton.

Before Torbert joined him in the early evening of the twenty-first, Wilson had already driven Wickham out of Front Royal and for a distance of about six miles south in the Luray Valley, in one of the strangest cavalry operations of the Civil War. To get at the enemy at daybreak on the twenty-first, his troopers had to cross both branches of the Shenandoah in fog so dense that they "could not see thirty yards."[55] Wilson made the fog serve his cause with a stratagem which it is safe to say he did not get out of any manual of cavalry tactics. He had the inspiration to order all his buglers— there were about 250 of them in the division—to blow the charge. The effect was similar to that of Joshua's trumpets at Jericho; no walls came tumbling down, but, as Wilson believed, "As the hills reechoed the bugle notes and the shouting of the captains, the air was filled with a swelling volume of sound, which might well have frightened a larger force than the one before us. Ten thousand men could not have made a greater noise and as it came from all sides the enemy broke and ran in all directions."[56]

One of those fascinated by this novel method of attack was Roger Hannaford. Reveille that day, he recorded, was

at 2 A.M. Got breakfast & moved out. . . . A damp heavy fog arising from the river enveloped [us]. . . . As soon as it was fairly light we . . . crossed the N[orth] fork of the Shenandoah. . . . Where the road enters the [South Fork] was Gen[era]l Wilson, in a state of great excitement, by him was the H[ead] Q[uarte]rs . . . bugler, blowing . . . "the charge," Wilson calling to him to "blow charge, blow charge I say, damn you, blow charge," then turning he would give a rapid order to one of his

55. Wilson, *Under the Old Flag*, I, 558–59.
56. *Ibid.*, 559.

staff, then flying around would ride up to the poor bugler with damn you why dont you blow charge? while *he* was as red in the face as a turkey cock & had no wind left, being scarcely able to make a feeble sound on his instrument, but not a moments rest would little Wilson give him . . . the scene was so ridiculous as to call forth universal laughter.[57]

Whether the propelling force came from Wilson's bugles or his troopers' carbines, Wickham did not halt in his retreat until he reached Gooney Run, flowing in a "rocky chasm many feet deep and impassable for any creature except mountain goats" to its junction with the South Fork of the Shenandoah, which flows along the eastern foot of Massanutten Mountain. Wickham had had time to burn the bridges across Gooney Run and to dig in above it. The Luray Valley, never more than a narrow trough, becomes at Gooney Run "a mere gorge, impracticable for any kind of troops, except on the pike."[58] With the bridges gone and Confederate guns lining the far bank of the stream, Wilson's advance was brought to a halt. He was joined in the evening by Torbert, with the Reserve and Custer's brigades. A frontal assault being manifestly out of the question, Torbert sent Custer back north with instructions to cross the Shenandoah, then march south along the west bank of the stream about two miles to McCoy's Ford, well to the south of Gooney Run, recross the stream there, and attack Wickham from the rear. But Wickham's lookouts spotted Custer's move and he retreated, this time to the south bank of Overall's Run, above the village of Milford. Torbert crossed Gooney Run the next morning and followed. What he saw when he examined Wickham's new position made him hesitate. He reported that the Confederates were now even more strongly posted than they had been at Gooney Run,

their left resting on the Shenandoah, which runs so close under . . . [Massanutten] mountain it was impossible to turn it, and their right rested against a high mountain . . . their line was very short, and the banks of the creek so precipitous it was impossible for the men to get across in order to make a direct attack. In addition to their naturally strong position they were posted behind loophole breastworks, which

57. Hannaford, "Reminiscences," 163(d)–164(b).
58. Wilson, *Under the Old Flag*, I, 554; *Official Records*, Vol. XLIII, Pt. I, p. 519.

extended clear across the valley. Not knowing that the army had made an attack at Fisher's Hill, and thinking that the sacrifice would be too great to attack without that knowledge, I concluded to withdraw.[59]

Torbert's failure to carry out his assignment threw Sheridan into a rage when he learned of it the morning after the fight at Fisher's Hill, but in contrast to his treatment of Averell later in the day for what he saw as a similar offense, he was satisfied merely to have his chief of staff tell Torbert, "If you had gone down the Luray Valley, as the general thought you would, we would have captured nearly all of Early's army. . . . [He] directs that you push down the Luray Valley without regard to horseflesh. You can connect with us at some place below . . . [Woodstock] and obtain your rations and forage."[60] In his dispatch to Grant announcing his Fisher's Hill victory, sent on the night of the twenty-second, Sheridan wrote, "If General Torbert has pushed down the Luray Valley according to my directions, he will achieve great results." In a second dispatch to Grant the next day—a dispatch in which he failed to mention that he had relieved Averell of his command—he wrote, "I have been disappointed in the cavalry operations which were to have formed a part of this battle."[61] Another day passed, and Sheridan wrote to Grant from Harrisonburg, "Torbert's cavalry overtook me this evening. Its operations in the Luray Valley, on which I calculated so much, were an entire failure."[62] There was no return dispatch from Grant suggesting that Sheridan replace Torbert with someone in whom he had confidence.

59. *Official Records*, Vol. XLIII, Pt. 1, p. 428. Torbert calls Overall's Run "Milford Creek" in his report.
60. *Ibid.*, Pt. 2, p. 156. In this and the next dispatch cited, "pushed down" the Luray Valley is used for "pushed up." In Valley terminology, south is "up," north is "down." Sheridan's own words for his reaction to the news of Torbert's failure at Milford were that he was "astonished and chagrined." Sheridan, *Personal Memoirs*, II, 41.
61. *Official Records*, Vol. XLIII, Pt. 1, p. 27. In his report on the campaign, Sheridan wrote, "Unfortunately, the cavalry . . . was unsuccessful, and only reached so far as Milford, a point at which the Luray Valley contracts to a gorge, and which was taken possession of by the enemy's cavalry in some force. Had General Torbert driven this cavalry or turned the defile and reached New Market, I have no doubt but that we would have captured the entire rebel army." *Ibid.*, 48.
62. *Ibid.*, Pt. 2, p. 170.

Not until many years later, when Sheridan wrote his memoirs, did he express a forthright opinion on Torbert's "failure."

The only drawback [of the fight at Fisher's Hill] was with the cavalry, and to this day I have been unable to account satisfactorily for Torbert's failure. No doubt, Wickham's position near Milford was a strong one, but Torbert ought to have made a fight . . . but it does not appear that he made any serious effort at all to dislodge the Confederate cavalry; his impotent attempt not only chagrined me very much, but occasioned much unfavorable comment throughout the army.[63]

Nonetheless Torbert, unlike Averell, retained his command. No doubt there were reasons—personal likes and dislikes, friendships and enmities, army or Washington politics—to account for the difference, but what those reasons were is lost beyond recovery.

63. Sheridan, *Personal Memoirs*, II, 41–42. A sample of the army comment Sheridan referred to was that of Colonel Kidd of the Michigan Brigade: "Torbert made a fiasco of it. He allowed Wickham . . . with at most two small brigades, to hold him at bay and withdrew without making any fight to speak of. . . . If Custer or Merritt had been in command it would have been different." Kidd, *Personal Recollections*, 396.

XI

"The action of the tiger"

AFTER THE DEBACLE AT FISHER'S HILL, LARGE NUMBERS of Early's men took to the woods to avoid capture and were lost to the army, at least temporarily, and this was in addition to those killed, wounded, or taken prisoner. What was left of the Confederate army retreated up the Valley, pursued by Sheridan. Any serious resistance to the Federals' progress, other than rearguard actions, was out of the question. Early realized this, and on the morning of September 25 he sideslipped to the Blue Ridge and took up a position at the eastern foot of Brown's Gap. He expected to be joined there by Kershaw's division and Wilfred E. Cutshaw's battalion of artillery, hurrying to the Valley to provide a desperately needed reinforcement for his "shattered" and "exhausted" army. Other reinforcements came in the shape of Lomax's cavalry from Harrisonburg, and Wickham's and William E. Payne's horsemen from the Luray Valley. Notwithstanding the accession of these mounted units, however, Early commented again, in a justifiably gloomy dispatch to General Lee, on Sheridan's "superiority in cavalry," which, he said, gave the Union commander "immense advantage." In his reply Lee promised shipments of shoes, arms, and ammunition, plus cavalry reinforcements (Thomas L. Rosser's small brigade), but he also urged Early to improve the effectiveness of the cavalry he already had by "instructions and discipline" —a vain hope.[1]

Notwithstanding the mild shock of Averell's sudden departure and the disappointment of Torbert's failure at Milford, the Federal cavalry and indeed the entire army were in good heart. Torbert himself, after the mild rebuke administered to him by Sheridan's chief of staff, resumed his advance up the Luray Valley, found a way to flank Wickham out of the Overall's Run position, and on the afternoon of September 25—"many hours later than . . . [he] had been expected"—joined the main army.[2]

After a second spectacular victory in three days, the men, including some who had remained skeptical after the battle of the nineteenth, were "converted to the belief that . . . Sheridan . . . [was] not only a brilliant cavalry rider, an impetuous fighter, and the impersonation of warlike energy, but that he . . . [was] also a careful, deliberate, pains-taking soldier, thoroughly versed in tactics and strategy, whose fiery zeal . . . [was] controlled by most unusual discretion."[3] Among the cavalry, belief in themselves went with belief in Sheridan; the men felt that they were not only capable of meeting and resisting Confederate troops, but that they now had the power "to inflict crushing defeats . . . and inflict blows and cause losses that were irreparable, and which, if continued, promised a speedy close of the war."[4]

With Early hugging the base of the Blue Ridge, Sheridan was free to march up the Valley as far as he wished. Posting Crook's corps and Merritt's and Powell's cavalry to protect his left and rear, he sent Torbert with Wilson's division and the Reserve Brigade forward to occupy Staunton and destroy the iron bridge of the Virginia Central over the South Fork of the Shenandoah at Waynesboro.[5] Staunton was duly occupied on the twenty-sixth; the next day, in "fine, bracing weather," Torbert reached Waynesboro, burned down the railroad depot and some government build-

1. *Official Records*, Vol. XLIII, Pt. 1, p. 558, 559.
2. Sheridan, *Personal Memoirs*, II, 49.
3. Aldace F. Walker, *The Vermont Brigade in the Shenandoah Valley, 1864* (Burlington, Vt., 1869), 122–23.
4. Davies, *General Sheridan*, 173.
5. Sheridan, *Personal Memoirs*, II, 49; *Official Records*, Vol. XLIII, Pt. 1, p. 49.

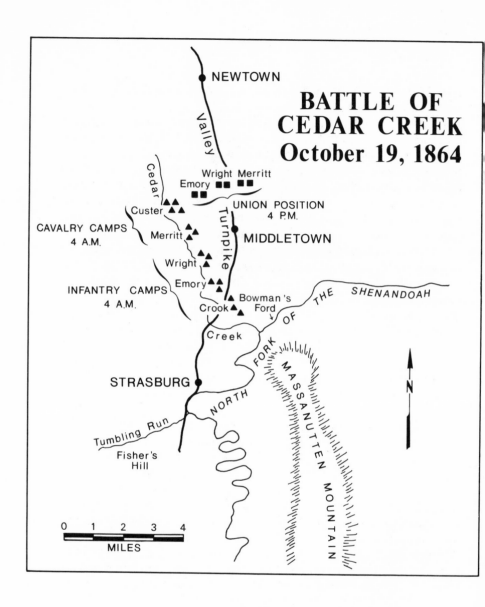

NEWTOWN

BATTLE OF
CEDAR CREEK
October 19, 1864

Valley

Cedar

Wright Merritt
Emory ■■ ■■
■■

Custer ▲▲
▲▲

UNION POSITION
4 P.M.

CAVALRY CAMPS
4 A.M.

Merritt ▲
▲

Turnpike

MIDDLETOWN

Wright ▲
▲

INFANTRY CAMPS
4 A.M.

Emory ▲▲
▲▲

Crook ▲▲

▲ Bowman's
Ford

OF   THE   SHENANDOAH

Creek

FORK

MASSANUTTEN MOUNTAIN

N

STRASBURG

NORTH

Tumbling Run

Fisher's
Hill

0   1   2   3   4

MILES

ings, partially destroyed the bridge, and tore up some track. Late in the afternoon, however, he was fiercely attacked by "a strong force of cavalry, infantry and artillery" that Early, who had doubtless learned that the Federals had sent only cavalry to Waynesboro, had brought down from Brown's Gap.[6] Torbert's pickets were driven in and at dark, instead of staying to fight as Wilson thought he should have, he decided to retreat.[7] The march north in the night was full of peril, especially for the rear guard, but the entire command managed to reach Spring Hill at daylight after a march of more than twenty miles in pitch darkness.[8]

The last few days of September brought major command changes to Sheridan's cavalry. On the twenty-sixth, Custer was assigned to the command of what had been Averell's division, replacing Colonel Powell. Without question, Custer had earned promotion from command of a brigade to command of a division. It could not have been pleasant for Colonel Powell to be superseded after three days by an "outsider," but Custer was his senior in rank and a Regular besides, and he had to make the best of it. On the previous day, Grant had wired Sheridan instructions to send either Torbert or Wilson (the telegram named them in that order) to command W. T. Sherman's cavalry in the West; Sheridan replied on October 1 that he had chosen Wilson as "the best man for the position" and had already ordered Wilson to report to Sherman, Custer to take command of the Third Division, and Colonel Powell to resume command of the Second Division.[9]

The change of commanders from Wilson to Custer pleased the men of the Third Division; the troopers of the 1st Vermont, for example, welcomed the advent of the "fiery Custer," although, or perhaps because, "they knew it meant mounted charges, instead of dismounted skirmishing, and a foremost place in every fight."[10] Roger Hannaford wrote shortly after the war,

6. *Official Records*, Vol. XLIII, Pt. 1, pp. 519, 429. The attackers were John Pegram's division of infantry and Wickham's cavalry.
7. "Torbert, instead of fighting, gave orders to retire, as he alleged, in compliance of orders from Sheridan." Wilson, *Under the Old Flag*, I, 561.
8. *Ibid.*, 562–63; *Official Records*, Vol. XLIII, Pt. 1, p. 519.
9. *Official Records*, Vol. XLIII, Pt. 1, pp. 170, 249, 218. Custer had not actually assumed command of the Second Division when he was given command of the Third.
10. Benedict, *Vermont in the Civil War*, II, 660–61. The 8th New York was another regiment that welcomed the change; "The boys liked General

Our Div[ision] when under . . . [Wilson's] command had no reputation, or but little. . . . The "Mich[igan] Brig[ade], 1st Div[ision]" bore the palm, every soldier in it glorying in its proud reputation while under the command of Gen[era]l Custer. . . . our Div[ision began] in 3 or 4 days after Custer took command that series of glorious heroic deeds that ended with Lee's surrender, making a record that was blazoned over the country, its soldiers even now wishing no greater honor than to be known as belonging to "Custer's Div[ision]."[11]

One day in the spring of 1865, Hannaford happened to be riding stirrup to stirrup with a trooper of the Michigan Brigade, which was still, as it had been, part of the First Division. "Why," said the man from Michigan, "since Custer left the 1st Division, it has done nothing. . . . now . . . all you hear about is the 3d Division, the 3d Division captured so many cannon, Custer's Division captured so many battle flags, nothing but the 3d Division, while the 1st Division is scarcely heard of. The fact is you have Custer now." And, Hannaford added on his own behalf,

I well knew he spoke the truth, for while Wilson had command of the 3d Division . . . scarcely a member of it would willingly acknowledge his connection with it, but now it was very different. Every member felt proud to be known as one of Custer's division. . . . Why, we ask, should these things be so? The material of the Division was the same then as now; in truth, we had lost many veterans since then, & rec'd some recruits, so really the material may be said to have been better then. The fact is, the whole difference [was] in the commanders. Wilson was universally considered to be an unlucky man. We never went into a fight but that we expected to be beat. We neither had confidence in him or ourselves, but with Custer . . . we never began but we felt sure of victory.[12]

Custer had left West Point in July, 1861, as the "goat" of his class. Now, scarcely more than three years later, he received com-

---

Custer, there was some get up and get to him. He used the saber a great deal, which the boys . . . liked." Henry Norton, Deeds of Daring, or, History of the 8th New York Volunteer Cavalry (Norwich, N.Y., 1889), 93–94.

11. Hannaford, "Reminiscences," 178(b). Hannaford invariably spelled Custer's name "Custar." Here, and throughout the text, Hannaford's spelling has been corrected. The brigade of the 1st, 5th, 6th, and 7th Michigan, plus the 25th New York, commonly called the Michigan Brigade, had been Custer's command before he was promoted to division commander.

12. Stephen Z. Starr (ed.), "The Last Days of the Rebellion," The Cincinnati Historical Society Bulletin, XXXV (1977), 9–11.

mand of a division of cavalry from one of the most exacting of army commanders. Custer's habit of calling attention to himself with flamboyance in dress and behavior may have helped his upward progress in 1861 and 1862, but his promotion in 1864 was due to his solid qualities as a commander of cavalry. One of the earliest of his biographers, himself a former officer in the Cavalry Corps, wrote, "Custer was to take up the division which had so far, under Wilson's lead, only held its own with respectability and was to transform it into the most brilliant single division in the whole Army of the Potomac . . . and [they were] so much impressed with the stamp of his individuality that every officer in the command was seen to be aping his eccentricities of dress."[13]

Having sent off a telegram congratulating Sheridan on his victory at Fisher's Hill, and having celebrated it by ordering the firing of hundred-gun salutes with live ammunition by the armies before Richmond and Petersburg, Grant initiated a lengthy exchange of messages with him on the question of what the Army of the Shenandoah, having seemingly cleared the Valley of the organized forces of the enemy, was to do next.[14] A telegram of Grant's on the twenty-sixth directed Sheridan to "make a great effort" to have his cavalry destroy first the railroads around Charlottesville and then the James River Canal wherever they could reach it.[15] Sheridan saw in this message the thin edge of the wedge to have his army move east of the Blue Ridge, draw its supplies over the Orange & Alexandria Railroad, and operate against Richmond by way of Charlottesville and Gordonsville. He protested, partly because after leaving sufficient troops to ensure the security of the Valley, and immobilizing additional troops to protect the line of the Orange & Alexandria, he would have been left with too small a force to mount a successful campaign against Richmond from the west. He also believed that he lacked sufficient transportation to be able to maintain an army beyond Harrisonburg.[16] Eventual-

13. Whittaker, George A. Custer, 250.
14. The statement in the text is slightly anachronistic, in that Sheridan's forces were not officially designated the Army of the Shenandoah until November 17, 1864. Official Records, Vol. XLIII, Pt. 2, p. 638.
15. Ibid., Pt. 1, p. 202.
16. Sheridan, Personal Memoirs, II, 53–54; Official Records, Vol. XLIII,

ly, but with considerable trouble, Sheridan persuaded Grant to accept the strategy he himself favored, namely that the Valley Campaign be considered as at an end, that he retreat down the Valley "desolating the Shenandoah country so as to make it untenable for permanent occupation by the Confederates," and, when that task was completed, to send off the bulk of his forces to reinforce Grant before Petersburg.[17]

The debate on strategy settled in his favor, Sheridan began his retreat on October 6. The infantry led the way, marching along the Valley Turnpike; behind them came the cavalry, "stretched across the country from the Blue Ridge to the eastern slope of the Alleghanies."[18] Merritt had been ordered previously to "destroy all mills, all grain and forage . . . drive off or kill all stock, and otherwise carry out the instructions of Lieutenant-General Grant . . . which means 'leave the Valley a barren waste.' " To add weight to the order, he was now given a copy of Grant's August 26 directive to Sheridan ("Do all the damage to railroads and crops you can. Carry off stock of all descriptions, and negroes, so as to prevent further planting. If the war is to last another year, we want the Shenandoah Valley to remain a barren waste"). Wilson was sent a shorter version of the same orders.[19]

The day before Sheridan's retreat began, General Rosser and his "Laurel Brigade" joined Early, his troopers, according to Sheridan, "all bedecked with laurel leaves."[20] Never was that classic symbol of victory bestowed more prematurely. Upon reaching Early, Rosser improved on the laurel leaves; he proclaimed him-

---

Pt. 2, p. 249; Pt. 1, pp. 34, 50. An inadequate account of these exchanges is in Grant, *Personal Memoirs*, II, 335–36.

17. Sheridan, *Personal Memoirs*, II, 54–55; *Official Records*, Vol. XLIII, Pt. 1, p. 30; Pt. 2, p. 266. Wilson thought the strategy urged by Sheridan mistaken. "There is now little doubt," he wrote, "that he might have continued the pursuit till he had driven Early back on Lee instead of putting that off until six months later." Wilson, *Under the Old Flag*, I, 560. Confederate General Gordon was of the same mind: "[Sheridan's] twenty-six days of apparent indecision, of feeble pursuit, of discursive and disjointed fighting after his two crushing victories, are to me a military mystery." Gordon, *Reminiscences of the Civil War*, 328.

18. Sheridan, *Personal Memoirs*, II, 55–56.

19. *Official Records*, Vol. XLIII, Pt. 2, pp. 202, 203.

20. Sheridan, *Personal Memoirs*, II, 59n.

self, or allowed himself to be proclaimed, "the Savior of the Valley."

Having reported to the army commander, Rosser was ordered to "pursue the enemy, to harass him and ascertain his purposes."[21] With his own brigade, the two brigades of Fitzhugh Lee's division and the two of Lomax's under his command, a respectable total of between four and five thousand men, Rosser attacked Merritt's and Custer's rear guards with some success. On the seventh he reported that he had driven the enemy "handsomely, capturing several wagons, ambulances, and nine forges with their teams, a number of horses, about fifty prisoners, besides killing and wounding a considerable number."[22]

This success of Rosser's and his continued harassment of the Federal rear guards the next day were too much for Sheridan. On the evening of the eighth he called Torbert to his headquarters and told him to go out at daylight the next day and either "whip the rebel cavalry or get whipped." Moreover, said Sheridan, he intended to ascend Round Top Mountain, from which a good view of the surrounding area could be had, and, like the Persian King Xerxes at Salamis, watch the battle.[23]

When Sheridan decided that Rosser should be "chastised," Merritt's division was encamped on both sides of the Valley Turnpike just north of a tributary of the Shenandoah named Tom's Brook. Custer's division lay six miles farther north and to the west, along the foot of Little North Mountain. Torbert ordered Custer to make a night march to reach Merritt's position by daylight and then to attack the three brigades, under Rosser himself, that held the Confederate left. At the same time Merritt was to attack the two brigades of Lomax and the brigade of Bradley Johnson in his front.[24]

Custer reached his assigned position in time to allow the Fed-

21. *Official Records*, Vol. XLIII, Pt. 1, p. 559.
22. *Ibid.*, 553. Rosser's successes on October 7 and 8 are not reflected in Torbert's, Merritt's, or Custer's reports.
23. *Official Records*, Vol. XLIII, Pt. 1, p. 431; Sheridan, *Personal Memoirs*, II, 56. The reader is invited to supply the adjectives and adverbs clearly missing from the official version of Sheridan's remarks to Torbert.
24. Powell's division, then in the Luray Valley, was not present at Tom's Brook.

eral attacks to be launched at seven A.M. His was the more difficult task, since he faced Rosser's between 3,000 and 3,500
troopers, compared to the 1,000 to 1,500 whom Merritt faced.
Moreover, the Confederates facing Custer were posted on "a high
and abrupt ridge of hills running along the south bank" of Tom's
Brook, with strong detachments of dismounted men lining stone
walls and breastworks of rails and logs at the foot of the ridge
and a second line of barricades along the crest, the latter being
strengthened with six pieces of artillery "strongly supported by
columns of cavalry."[25]

Custer's phase of the action opened with an artillery duel in
which the Confederates gained the advantage, mainly, as he reported, because of the "extreme defectiveness" of the ammunition
of his own guns, Batteries B and L, 2nd United States Artillery.[26]
Nonetheless, Custer ordered forward the 5th New York, 2nd Ohio,
and 3rd New Jersey of Colonel Alexander C. M. Pennington's
(formerly McIntosh's) brigade, to make a frontal assault on
Rosser's lines. The three regiments were unable to make any headway, so Custer sent the 18th Pennsylvania and the 8th and 22nd
New York to turn the enemy's left flank, at the same time moving
up Colonel William Wells's Second Brigade to add weight to the
frontal attack of Pennington's three regiments. With everyone in
position, the charge was blown and the entire division moved forward. Rosser's center held, but his left-hand regiments, seeing
themselves about to be flanked and their line of retreat cut, "broke
in the utmost confusion" and, followed shortly by the rest of the
command, "sought safety in headlong flight."[27]

While Custer fought his battle on the right wing, Merritt, on
the left, sent his Reserve Brigade forward in an enveloping movement against the enemy's right, attacking frontally at the same
time with his First and Second Brigades. Here too the Confederate regiments in the center held their ground, but those on the
right, attacked in flank by the Reserve Brigade, gave way in some
disorder, which soon involved their neighbors to the left.

These initial successes enabled both Custer and Merritt to

25. *Official Records*, Vol. XLIII, Pt. 1, pp. 431, 520.
26. *Ibid.*, 520.
27. *Ibid.*, 521.

cross Tom's Brook into the open country beyond, "a magnificent place for a cavalry fight . . . [with] room to deploy, smooth ground to ride on, all the rail fences . . . [gone].[28] Both Federal divisions now attacked mounted and were met with mounted counter-charges by the Confederates. Merritt and Custer, however, had the upper hand. They outnumbered the enemy nearly three to two, they had the initiative, and they relied mainly on the saber, whereas many of their antagonists—Lomax's men in particular—had no sabers, and their rifles were useless in a melée.[29] The fighting swayed back and forth for nearly two hours, but again the Confederate regiments on the two flanks were beaten back, their center gave way to avoid being surrounded, and the engagement became a grand rout and chase. Small groups of gray troopers tried to rally and made a stand here and there, but these were quickly overwhelmed. The ensuing pursuit, known to the Federals forever after as the "Woodstock Races," did not end until it had carried twenty miles to the south on Custer's side and twenty-six on Merritt's, and the survivors, those who had not been captured or taken refuge in the woods along the way, found safety with Early's infantry. At the cost to themselves of only 9 killed, 48 wounded, and none missing, the Federals took 350 prisoners, captured all but one of Rosser's twelve guns and everything else he had on wheels—supply wagons, ambulances, headquarters wagons, and caissons.[30]

Tom's Brook gave the Federal cavalry a chance to exult over a victory that belonged to all of them. Custer, Merritt, and Torbert were all able to boast of what Sheridan described as a "brilliant engagement . . . in which the enemy was routed beyond my power to describe."[31] Nor did the cavalry generals have to warm themselves in the glow of their own lavish hosannahs alone; Secretary Stanton sent Sheridan, his officers and men, the thanks of the

28. Whittaker, *George A. Custer*, 257.
29. The returns for the end of September showed the First and Third Divisions with a total of 6,343 cavalrymen, rank and file, "present for duty," plus 543 in the horse artillery. *Official Records*, Vol. XLIII, Pt. 2, p. 248. Rosser had between four and five thousand under his command.
30. *Ibid.*, Pt. 1, pp. 60, 431. Sheridan claimed 330 prisoners in his report; in his *Personal Memoirs*, II, 58, he gives the number as 300.
31. *Official Records*, Vol. XLIII, Pt. 1, pp. 32, 431, 448, 521.

War Department for their "brilliant victory," adding that they had become "the efficient arm in this war that . . . [cavalry] has proved in other countries," an encomium that, with Cedar Creek, Nashville, and the Appomattox and Selma campaigns still in the future was somewhat premature.[32]

On the Confederate side, poor General Early must by this time have bethought him of Judges 5:20: "The stars in their courses fought against Sisera." On the basis of preliminary and obviously incomplete information he reported to General Lee that Rosser had been defeated ("he is, I understand, falling back in good order," Early wrote, which was anything but correct), and added the disconsolate comment,

the enemy's cavalry is so much superior to ours, both in numbers and equipment, and the country is so favorable to the operations of cavalry, that it is impossible for ours to compete with his. Lomax's cavalry are armed entirely with rifles and have no sabers, and the consequence is that they cannot fight on horseback, and in this open country they cannot successfully fight on foot against large bodies of cavalry; besides, the command is and has been demoralized all the time. It would be better if they could all be put into the infantry; but if that were tried I am afraid they would all run off.[33]

The historian of the Laurel Brigade credits Rosser's calm and competent direction of his rear guard with preventing a "panic" at Tom's Brook, which makes one wonder about the point of vantage from which he saw the battle.[34] Trooper George Baylor of the same

32. *Ibid.*, 62. A mildly dissenting voice was that of John DeForest: "I was amused at the wrath of a young West Pointer when (after Tom's Brook) we congratulated him on the fact that Sheridan could make even the cavalry fight. 'Sheridan had nothing to do with it,' he asserted. 'Torbert was just about to pitch into the Rebs when Sheridan happened to come along.' " DeForest, *A Volunteer's Adventures*, 198.

33. *Official Records*, Vol. XLIII, Pt. 1, p. 559. On the matter of sabers, Frederick Whittaker of the Federal cavalry agreed with General Early. "Ill fared it with Rosser and his men," Whittaker wrote, "that they received . . . [Custer's charge] at a halt, and trusted to fire for their defence. . . . The completeness of the victory was owing to . . . [the fact that] Rosser, in common with most Confederate officers, distrusted the sabre, which was rarely used by the Confederate cavalry after Stuart's death, and not enough during his life." Whittaker, *George A. Custer*, 260–61.

34. McDonald, *A History of the Laurel Brigade*, 308. It does appear, however, that the three brigades under Rosser's immediate command did not panic as badly as those facing Merritt.

brigade, on the other hand, was of the opinion that "with a good leader," the Laurels might at least have saved their artillery.[35] Gunner George M. Neese, while still on the way to the Valley with his battery, had written that "if . . . [Sheridan] has the men he had at Trevilian Station, there will be some tough work on the boards yet this fall, for his cavalry is made out of firstclass fighting stuff"; his fears were well founded, and he wrote after Tom's Brook, "The shameful way that our cavalry . . . fought, bled and died a-running rearward was enough to make its old commander, General J. E. B. Stuart, weep in his grave. Ring down the curtain on that scene, for the cavalry played a regular exeunt act."[36]

Tom's Brook was fought after the Union cavalry, pursuant to Grant's and Sheridan's orders, had begun to lay waste the Valley from Harrisonburg northward. Sheridan has borne the odium for this devastation, but in his dispatches to Grant concerning it, he was usually careful to ascribe it to "your instructions."[37] As early as October 7, he informed Grant from Woodstock that his cavalry had "destroyed 2,000 barns filled with wheat, hay, and farming implements; over seventy mills filled with flour and wheat," and, in addition to slaughtering 3,000 sheep for the immediate needs of his men, had driven off 4,000 head of stock plus "a large number of horses." Not only the main Valley, but the smaller valleys paralleling it—Luray, Little Fort, and Page—had been made "untenable for a rebel army."[38] This destruction, in an age when the margin between sufficiency and destitution was narrow, was a tragedy for many. A single regiment, the 19th New York, marching from Port Republic to Mount Crawford, burned 82 barns containing grain and hay, 72 stacks of grain and hay standing in the fields, 5 flour mills, 2 sawmills, and an iron furnace, and drove off 321 head of cattle and 200 sheep. A few days later, the New

35. George Baylor, *Bull Run to Bull Run, or, Four Years in the Army of Northern Virginia* (Richmond, 1900), 42.
36. Neese, *Three Years in the Confederate Horse Artillery*, 317, 322. Neese's high opinion of the Union cavalry was shared by Henry Kyd Douglas, who wrote, "We soon found out that . . . [Sheridan's cavalry] was more to be feared than his infantry—better soldiers all through." Douglas, *I Rode with Stonewall*, 313.
37. For example, *Official Records*, Vol. XLIII, Pt. 1, p. 29.
38. *Ibid.*, 30. The Page Valley was attended to by Colonel Powell's division; *ibid.*, 508.

Yorkers, working as a team with another regiment, burned 115 barns, 206 stacks of grain and hay in the fields, 18 flour and grist mills containing an estimated 18,000 bushels of grain, plus some woolen mills and sawmills. The smoke of burning buildings filled the Valley from one side to the other, as far as the eye could see.[39]

Orders were orders, and the orders to burn and destroy were generally obeyed, but the men, and in some cases even their officers, made their own exceptions. Here, for example, is a detachment of the 2nd Ohio, sent to burn barns in the neighborhood of Dayton:

many barns . . . were not burned; I know also for I saw it, that Co[mpany] D often helped the folks that afternoon remove their furniture when the barn stood so near the house as to endanger the latter, & at one place . . . I saw the boys tugging & working . . . helping an old lady to move her furniture, as they had rec'd orders to burn the barn & this stood near the house, but as it was near evening, when the Officer left them, the boys all left, not one of them would fire the barn.[40]

Indeed, not only in their postwar writings, but even at the time, neither the men nor their officers made any secret of their great distaste for organized incendiarism. The historian of the 1st New York (Lincoln) wrote, "Men who never flinched in the hottest fight declared they would have no hand in this burning."[41] Colonel James H. Kidd spoke of the burning as "a disagreeable business," and he ended his description of the burning of a mill in Port Republic and the narrowly averted destruction of the houses clustered around it with a passage that does him credit.

What I saw there is burned in my memory. Women with children in their arms, stood in the street and gazed frantically upon the threatened ruin of their homes, while the tears rained down their cheeks. The anguish pictured in their faces would have melted any heart not seared by the horrors and "necessities" of war. It was too much for me

39. Bowen, *Regimental History of the First New York*, 242–43. "This 6th Day of Oct[.] we marched slowly, often making short halts, for the burning details were scattered for miles on either flank, & as we came to the top [of] each gentle swell . . . & look[ed] around, it was no uncommon sight to see at least 50 barns on fire. . . . By noon a heavy cloud of smoke hung over the whole valley like a pall." Hannaford, "Reminiscences," 180(c)–181(a).

40. Hannaford, "Reminiscences," 179(d)–180(a).

41. Beach, *First New York (Lincoln) Cavalry*, 438; see also Williams, *Hayes of the Twenty-third*, 283–84.

and at the first moment that duty would permit, I hurried away from the scene. General Merritt did not see these things, nor did General Sheridan, much less General Grant.[42]

Occasionally a farmer, driven to frenzy, tried to protect his property. One man "stood on a hay stack and fired into the marching column, and it is needless to say he fell riddled with bullets. Another man stood in his barn door and shot the soldier that was ordered to set the barn on fire. He was tried by court martial"; the man's fate is not difficult to guess.[43]

The deliberate, planned devastation of the Shenandoah Valley has deservedly ranked as one of the grimmest episodes of a sufficiently grim war. Unlike the haphazard destruction caused by Sherman's "bummers" in Georgia, it was committed systematically, and by order. Perhaps the superb natural beauty of the Valley—even the beauty of its name—and the fact that it was mainly small farmers who were affected, made the devastation even more repellent than it actually was. It was said in contemporary newspaper accounts—not, however, by the cavalrymen who had to do the work—that the devastation was so thorough that a crow flying over the Valley would have to carry his rations with him.[44] But, later in the year, after Early had retreated to Waynesboro and the Army of the Potomac had gone into winter quarters, a "citizen of Woodstock" remarked to Roger Hannaford, "You folks don't work the thing right, you only seem to see the main pike, there are hundreds of folks living over in the bottoms, that you never see, the very richest part of the valley, where there are hundreds of acres of splendid corn untouched, while we that live on the pike are literally stripped of everything."[45]

On October 10, Sheridan's infantry, in its march north, reached and crossed Cedar Creek, a tributary of the North Fork of the

42. Kidd, *Personal Recollections*, 399.
43. Gause, *Four Years with Five Armies*, 327.
44. See page 263, note 87.
45. Hannaford, "Reminiscences," 235(d); Hannaford adds: "One thing should be remembered & that is that at the time (the first week of Oct[.]) the valley was burned out, the immense crop of corn was standing in the fields & that this with the exception of the very small quantity used by us as we fell back was intact." *Ibid.*, 236(a).

Shenandoah, roughly halfway between Strasburg and Middletown and just over three miles north of Fisher's Hill. On the twelfth, based on his understanding with Grant, Sheridan ordered General Wright to start the VI Corps on its journey to reinforce the Army of the Potomac.[46] On the fifteenth, at Stanton's request, Sheridan himself left for Washington, accompanied as far as Front Royal by all his cavalry, who were to proceed from there across the Blue Ridge to raid the Virginia Central in the Gordonsville-Charlottesville area. The next day, however, General Wright, left in command at Cedar Creek, forwarded to Sheridan a message "planted" by the Confederates, which was intended to make him believe that Longstreet was about to join Early for an attack on his army. Sheridan suspected that the message was spurious, but to be on the safe side he called off the cavalry raid on the Virginia Central and sent Torbert back to Cedar Creek. He himself went on to Washington to meet with Stanton and Halleck.[47]

With the objective of thwarting Sheridan's "purposes if he should contemplate moving across the [Blue] Ridge and sending troops to Grant," Early, whose losses at the Opequon and Fisher's Hill had been made good by the return of convalescents and stragglers, plus the arrival of Kershaw's infantry and Cutshaw's artillery, decided to attack the Union army in its camps north of Cedar Creek.[48] His own army was in its old Fisher's Hill position. On October 17, General John B. Gordon and Captain Jed. Hotchkiss, Early's topographical engineer, climbed the northernmost tip of Massanutten Mountain. "With strong field glasses, Gordon and

46. These orders were countermanded the next day by Grant's order instructing the Army of the Shenandoah to take a position "far enough south to serve as a base for future operations upon Gordonsville and Charlottesville"; the VI Corps remained at Cedar Creek. Sheridan, *Personal Memoirs*, II, 59–60; *Official Records*, Vol. XLIII, Pt. 2, p. 345.
47. Sheridan, *Personal Memoirs*, II, 59–66; *Official Records*, Vol. XLIII, Pt. 1, pp. 51–52.
48. *Official Records*, Vol. XLIII, Pt. 1, p. 561. Early's decision to attack the enemy and "surprise him in camp" was made partly because lack of forage made it impossible for him to remain at Fisher's Hill, and partly because he was too pugnacious to retreat without giving the Federals another battle. *Battles and Leaders*, IV, 526. General Davies wrote that "the nearest point from which subsistence could be procured . . . [by Early] was Staunton—ninety miles in his rear, and too distant to admit of providing for the army by wagon transportation." Davies, *General Sheridan*, 188–90.

Hotchkiss could see the entire Union army, its breastworks, gun emplacements, and lines of tents; General Gordon counted the enemy's guns, and he "could see distinctly the three colors of trimmings on the jackets . . . of infantry, artillery and cavalry, and locate each, while the number of flags gave a basis for estimating approximately the forces with which . . . [Early's army would have to] contend in the proposed attack."[49]

The peculiar topography of the area surveyed by Gordon and Hotchkiss, which had governed the layout of Sheridan's camps, also suggested the highly imaginative mode of attack proposed by Gordon and adopted by Early. Flowing generally north in a series of great loops past the eastern edge of Fisher's Hill, the North Fork of the Shenandoah makes a sharp turn eastward past the northern foot of Massanutten Mountain. Cedar Creek flows southeast and joins the Shenandoah almost directly in line with the foot of Massanutten. A strip of ground, barely wide enough for a footpath, lies between the steep foot of the mountain and the right bank of the Shenandoah. A belt of fairly level ground, sloping upward, reaches from the left bank of the river to the high ground overlooking the creek on which Crook's corps was encamped. Because of the generally northwest to southeast line of the creek, the camps of the XIX and VI Corps, in that order, were echeloned to the northwest of Crook's, the XIX Corps camps overlapping Crook's for some distance. The level ground between the southeastern end of Crook's camps and the Shenandoah was unoccupied because General Wright failed to follow Sheridan's suggestion that he move Powell's cavalry division from Front Royal into that space. The existence of this gap was an important element in General Gordon's plan for the attack.

On the day Gordon climbed Massanutten, Early tried a novel stratagem. Rosser's scouts had reported the presence along the "Back Road"—a road that ran close to the foot of Little North Mountain, roughly parallel to and about three miles west of the Valley Turnpike—of a division (actually Custer's) of Union cavalry. Early decided to try to gobble up this seemingly isolated unit and on the night of October 16 sent Rosser with two brigades of

49. Gordon, *Reminiscences of the Civil War*, 333–34.

cavalry to do it; but, either because of the numerical weakness of the two mounted brigades, or his disenchantment with his cavalry, Early had Rosser carry along a brigade of infantry, the foot-soldiers mounted behind the saddles of the cavalrymen.[50] After an all-night ride, just before dawn Rosser was where he wanted to be, squarely in rear of where Custer's camp was reportedly located, but he found only the debris of an abandoned camp. Custer had moved the previous day, and the only trophies of Rosser's expedition were a picket reserve of a major and twenty-five troopers taken prisoner.[51]

The known presence of nearly all its cavalry on the Union right and the information brought back by Gordon and Hotchkiss from their viewing of the Union camps determined the shape of the battle of Cedar Creek. The topography of the ground above the left bank of Cedar Creek ruled out a frontal attack. An attack on the Union right was ruled out also, because, Early said, "the greatest part of the enemy's cavalry was on his right, and Rosser's attempt had caused that flank to be closely picketed." The Federal left was therefore the logical point of attack, notwithstanding the difficulties of terrain that an attack on that flank would have to overcome. As General Early reported, "To get around the enemy's left was a very difficult undertaking . . . as the [Shenandoah] river has to be crossed twice, and between . . . [Massanutten] Mountain and the river, where the troops had to pass . . . there was only a rugged pathway. I thought, however, that the chance of success would be greater from the fact that the enemy would not expect a move from that direction."[52]

The decision to aim the attack at the Federal left was of course Early's to make, but—a point not mentioned in his report—he made it at the powerful urging of General Gordon, who insisted that if Early adopted this plan of attack "and would press it to its legitimate results, the destruction of Sheridan's army was inevi-

50. *Official Records*, Vol. XLIII, Pt. 1, p. 56. Torbert says that Rosser made the expedition with three brigades of cavalry; he evidently mistook the brigade of infantry riding pillion for a third brigade of cavalry. *Ibid.*, 432.

51. *Ibid.*, 432.

52. *Ibid.*, 561. The First Division had been ordered to join Custer on the right of the army and apparently did so on the seventeenth or eighteenth.

table."[53] The tactical recommendation of an officer with General Gordon's superb record was entitled to the utmost respect, especially when, as in this instance, he not only offered to assume full responsibility if the plan failed, but also to lead the attack himself. He proposed that, leading his own division (to be commanded by General Clement A. Evans) and the divisions of Ramseur and John Pegram, the three divisions to be preceded by General William E. Payne's cavalry brigade of three (small) regiments, he would cross the Shenandoah at the foot of Fisher's Hill, follow the right bank of the river around the foot of Massanutten, and cross back to the left bank of the river at Bowman's Ford. After this second crossing, and when deployed on the rising ground beyond the ford, he would be well to the rear of the eastern end of Crook's camps and in an ideal position to attack them.

The attack, it was agreed, was to be made in semidarkness, just before dawn. It was hoped that the surprise would be aided by fog, usual in river valleys at that time of the year. To reach attacking position before dawn, Gordon was to set out at nightfall. The men were to be ordered to leave behind all belongings likely to make a clatter and warned to speak only when necessary, and then in whispers. While Gordon made his flank march, Kershaw's division, to which Early attached himself, was to move forward through Strasburg and cross Cedar Creek a half mile above its mouth to attack Crook's left at the same time that Gordon attacked his rear. All of Early's artillery, Gabriel C. Wharton's division in support, was to be brought forward to the right bank of Cedar Creek upstream of Kershaw and open on the Union camps as soon as the Federal artillery was turned to fire on Gordon and Kershaw. Rosser was to move up Cedar Creek and demonstrate against the Federal cavalry in order to keep it pinned down and unable to interfere with Gordon's and Kershaw's attacks. Lunsford Lomax was sent with his division—numbering nearly half of Early's 3,900-man mounted force—to march via Front Royal to Newtown

53. Gordon, *Reminiscences of the Civil War*, 335. Neither in his official report nor in his article "Winchester, Fisher's Hill, and Cedar Creek" in *Battles and Leaders*, IV, 522–30, did General Early credit Gordon with the suggestion of the flank march to attack the Federal left. The overall plan for the attack, he claimed, was his own. *Battles and Leaders*, IV, 526.

or Winchester, clearly the same kind of assignment Sheridan had given Torbert at Fisher's Hill. Commanding officers' watches were synchronized to make certain that all attacks went in at the right moment.[54]

Every facet of this exceptionally bold and complex plan—without question one of the most intricate battle plans of the Civil War—worked to perfection. Even the weather cooperated; the night march of Gordon's flanking force was greatly eased by a bright moon, just past the full, floating in a clear sky, and the hoped for dense fog settled in just before the attacks were to be launched.[55] With Payne's cavalry leading the way, Gordon's infantry splashed across Bowman's Ford, deployed, and fell upon Crook's "unprepared and unsuspecting Federals, great numbers of whom were still asleep in their tents."[56] Attacked at the same moment by Kershaw, those of Crook's men who were not shot down or captured took to their heels. With Gordon blocking the Valley Turnpike behind them, their only escape route was to the northwest, straight into the XIX Corps camps. A standing order of that corps required its men to stand to arms at daybreak when in the presence of the enemy; hence, unlike the VIII Corps, the XIX was not caught unprepared. General Emory, blinded by the dense fog and guided only by the sound of musketry, lined up his two divisions to face in the direction from which the attackers seemed to be advancing. However, the total collapse of Crook's corps and Gordon's rapid advance exposed Emory's left and rear, and his men were greatly unsettled by the stampede of Crook's men through their lines; some of his units broke, and with his ranks in considerable disorder he was forced to fall back. In doing so he uncovered the turnpike bridge over Cedar Creek, which then made it possible for Wharton to cross and join in the attack.

54. Freeman, *Lee's Lieutenants*, III, 609, 598; *Official Records*, Vol. XLIII, Pt. 1, p. 613, 561; *Battles and Leaders*, IV, 526.

55. "It was a perfect night, bright and clear, the air was crisp and transparent. A more serene and peaceful scene could not be imagined. The spirit of tranquillity seemed to have settled down, at last, upon the troubled Shenandoah." Kidd, *Personal Recollections*, 409. It was to be the last night on earth for 644 Yankees and no one knows how many "Johnnies."

56. Gordon, *Reminiscences of the Civil War*, 339. In the opinion of a Union cavalry officer, the surprise was complete because the pickets on the left were too few in number and not posted far enough out. [Whittaker], *Volunteer Cavalry*, 98.

Since General Wright commanded the army in Sheridan's absence, his VI Corps was commanded by General George W. Getty.[57] Being farthest from the initial Confederate attack, Getty had time to organize a coherent front, but with his left flank compromised by the direction of Gordon's advance, the best his three divisions could do was to make a reasonably orderly, fighting retreat northwestward, with occasional pauses to fight off the enemy; eventually, they came to a halt some distance beyond Middletown.

By midmorning, five hours from the start of the attack, Early —or more accurately, Gordon—had achieved a spectacular victory. Of the three corps of Federal infantry, Crook's was scattered to the four winds; part of Emory's had fled and the rest was badly disorganized; only the VI Corps, severely damaged, remained as an organized force. Early's men had possession of the Federal camps and supplies, they had captured thirteen hundred prisoners and eighteen pieces of artillery.[58] A bright autumn sun had burned off the early morning fog; surrounded on all sides by the signs of a great triumph—and that too a month to a day of the bitter defeat on the Opequon—Early, who knew his history of the Napoleonic wars, was heard to exclaim, his face radiant with joy, "The sun of Middletown! The sun of Middletown!"[59]

Behind the reasonably firm front put up by the VI Corps, all was chaos. Thousands of men, many of them unarmed, were streaming to the rear, singly and in small groups, an "appalling spectacle of a panic-stricken army—hundreds of slightly wounded men, throngs of others unhurt but utterly demoralized, and baggage wagons by the score . . . in hopeless confusion."[60] The 2nd Ohio, reduced to scarcely more than a hundred mounted men, was sent to try to halt and turn back the stream of fugitives, but their efforts were futile; "many were stopped but not long for so many were thronging back that it was impossible."[61] In John DeForest's

57. General Wright's place was actually taken by General James R. Ricketts, who was badly wounded early in the battle and was then succeeded as corps commander by General Getty. Getty led the corps until, upon General Sheridan's return, Wright resumed its command.
58. *Official Records*, Vol. XLIII, Pt. 1, p. 561.
59. Freeman, *Lee's Lieutenants*, III, 603. The reference was of course to the "sun of Austerlitz."
60. Sheridan, *Personal Memoirs*, II, 75–76.
61. Hannaford, "Reminiscences," 198(a).

considered opinion, shared by many others, including General Early himself, "If Early could now have launched upon us a powerful cavalry, he would have made a great sweep of prisoners and might have converted our retreat into a rout"—or, more accurately, converted what was already a rout into an irretrievable disaster.[62] But, fortunately for the Army of the Shenandoah, Early did not have a powerful cavalry at his command; moreover, the Confederate infantry were nearly as badly disorganized by victory as their antagonists by defeat. An unknown but large number, including many officers, gave way to an irresistible impulse and left the ranks to plunder the captured camps.[63]

At about ten o'clock there came a lull in the fighting. Gordon begged Early to order an attack on the VI Corps to complete the victory, but Early chose not to do it; as General Gordon recalled many years later, Early responded to his arguments for an attack with "No use in that; they will all go directly."[64] Whatever Early may have said, and whatever his reasons may have been for not pressing his advantage—unquestionably he should have done so, as he himself recognized when it was too late—the firing became sporadic and the stage was set for Sheridan's heroics, which, thanks to the inherently dramatic impact of a victory snatched from the very jaws of disaster, and thanks too to Thomas Buchanan Read's poem, "Sheridan's Ride," became the stuff of legend and made Cedar Creek second only to Gettysburg as the most glamorous Union victory of the Civil War.[65]

Now, however, it is necessary to turn to the crucial role of the Federal cavalry in the battle and in the eventual Union victory. It will be recalled that the First and Third Cavalry Divisions were,

62. DeForest, A Volunteer's Adventures, 214. See also Early, Autobiographical Sketch, 451; J. G. Harbord, "The History of the Cavalry of the Army of Northern Virginia," Journal of the United States Cavalry Association, XIV (1904), 489.

63. Official Records, Vol. XLIII, Pt. 1, p. 562. In Battles and Leaders, IV, 528, Early wrote that "a great number" left the ranks to plunder. His statement is reinforced by the testimony of Henry Kyd Douglas, I Rode with Stonewall, 316–17, but is denied with some heat by General Gordon, Reminiscences of the Civil War, 363–72. Freeman, Lee's Lieutenants, III, 64, 69n, considers Gordon's thesis "late but convincing."

64. Gordon, Reminiscences of the Civil War, 341.

65. See, for example, the first paragraph of Colonel Kidd's chapter on the battle of Cedar Creek, written in 1886, in Personal Recollections, 403.

on the morning of October 19, stationed on the Federal right. After Rosser's predawn attack on the seventeenth, both Custer and Merritt were alive to the possibility of further trouble in their sector. At four A.M. on the nineteenth, the 7th Michigan, picketing Cupp's Ford across Cedar Creek, was attacked.[66] The gunfire at the ford, followed a short time later by the sound of much heavier gunfire to the southeast, alarmed the cavalry camps. The call "To horse" brought the two divisions to readiness for immediate action. While waiting for orders from Torbert, both Custer and Merritt sent their escort companies and members of their staffs to turn back the "immense number of infantry stragglers" streaming to the rear behind them; for a short time, Devin's entire brigade was sent on that errand. Apart from that unrewarding employment the cavalry remained inactive until between nine and ten o'clock when General Wright ordered Torbert to move the two divisions from the right to the left flank. On his own responsibility, Torbert left behind Colonel Wells with three regiments of the Second Brigade of Custer's division to deal with Rosser; the rest of the cavalry, the regiments in column of battalions, took post to the left of the Valley Turnpike, three quarters of a mile north of Middletown. There they were exposed to "a very destructive fire from the enemy's artillery, the loss in horses being particularly heavy," but their presence at that point protected the left flank of the VI Corps; Custer was to report that he was "confident" that "but for the cavalry the enemy would have penetrated to the rear of . . . [the] army, which at that time was in no condition to receive an attack from any direction."[67]

Sheridan had spent the morning of the seventeenth in Washington in consultation with Stanton and Halleck, whom he was able to persuade to take his side in opposing the campaign east of

66. Cupp's Ford is called "Cupp's Mill" in some reports.
67. Kidd, *Personal Recollections*, 449, 523, 415–16. An incident of the cavalry deployment on the left deserves mention. As Colonel Devin's brigade was being forced back along the turnpike, the Second Brigade of Colonel Powell's division, coming from the direction of Front Royal, arrived on the scene. Devin, fearful that the Confederates would turn the Union left, asked Colonel Alpheus S. Moore, commanding the brigade, "to dismount his command and seize and hold the stone walls crossing the road. . . . [Moore] protested that his men had great objections to fighting dismounted and declined to accede to . . . [Devin's] request." *Official Records*, Vol. XLIII, Pt. 1, pp. 478, 434; see, however, Merritt's report, *ibid.*, 450.

the Blue Ridge that had been urged upon him by Grant. But, un-easy about the situation of his army at Cedar Creek, he left at noon by special train for Martinsburg, where he spent the night. The next morning, with a three-hundred-man escort as protection against guerrillas, he rode the twenty-eight miles to Winchester. A courier from Cedar Creek arrived there in the evening with word that all was peaceful at the front, and "greatly relieved," Sheridan went to bed.[68] He was awakened early in the morning by an officer with the report that artillery firing had been heard in the direction of Cedar Creek. Sheridan thought the gunfire indicated the recon-naissance in force that he knew Wright had ordered for that morn-ing, but as the firing continued he became more and more uneasy and, after a hasty breakfast, started for Cedar Creek. Only a mile or two south of Winchester he encountered the first wave of the men and wagons escaping from Cedar Creek, and he decided to ride to the front at a gallop with his aides-de-camp and twenty of the best-mounted men of his escort. The road, he saw, was "thickly lined with unhurt men, who having got far enough to the rear to be out of danger, had halted, without any organization, and begun cooking coffee." When they saw him galloping toward the front, "they abandoned their coffee, threw up their hats, shouldered their muskets, and . . . turned to follow with enthusiasm and cheers."[69]

There are two versions of the language Sheridan used as he rode past the coffee-boilers. The first is his own: "I said nothing except to remark. . . . 'If I had been with you this morning this dis-aster would not have happened. We must face the other way; we will go back and recover our camp.' " The second version is that of an eyewitness, reported in a letter written the same day: "God *damn* you, don't cheer me! If you love your country, come up to the front! God *damn* you, don't cheer me! There's lots of fight in you men yet! Come up, God damn you! Come up!"[70] The second version is not only more in character but is also more in keeping with the time-honored cavalry standard of rhetoric.

68. Sheridan, *Personal Memoirs*, II, 67.
69. *Ibid.*, 80. Sheridan rode his black horse "Rienzi" on this famous ride.
70. *Ibid.*, 81; a letter of Union army surgeon C. H. Parry, quoted in Bruce Catton, *Never Call Retreat* (Garden City, N.Y., 1965), 393.

There was to be a lengthy debate after war over the apportion-
ment of credit for the dramatic about-face in the fortunes of the
day at Cedar Creek. One school, headed by Sheridan himself, held
that it was *his* intervention from about 10:30 on, *his* rallying of a
beaten army, *his* realignment of his forces, *his* orders, that produced the eventual Federal victory.[71] The other school gives General Wright the lion's share of the credit, contending that the early-
morning panic had run its course, the stragglers were returning to
their units, the VI Corps had organized a solid front against the
enemy, and that even before Sheridan's arrival, Wright, with a
firm grip on the situation, had begun to make arrangements for a
counterattack.[72] It may be well to point out that neither school
gave sufficient credit to General Early, whose incomprehensible
inactivity after ten A.M. was as much as anything else responsible
for the ultimate Federal victory.

What is beyond dispute is the electrifying effect that Sheridan's
arrival at Cedar Creek—and he made certain that as many as possible of the men saw him—had on his troops. Testimony on this
point is unanimous. From the commanding officer of the Michigan Brigade: "Sheridan dashed along in front of the infantry for
the purpose of letting the army know that he was there. . . . I was
not near enough to hear . . . but whatever may have been his exact
words, the enthusiasm which they aroused was unmistakeable.
The answer was a shout that sent a thrill across the valley."[73]
From a trooper of the 2nd Ohio: "It was . . . as near as I could
judge about 11 oclock . . . when great cheering was heard along
the front of the . . . infantry line & we could hear cheer after cheer
come down the line toward us. . . . Of course eager questioners
wanted to know what the cheering meant? why Sheridan is come
. . . 'thank God, thank God!' is the cry of . . . many tongues."[74]

71. For example, "Sheridan's arrival, and his immense enthusiasm,
effected a wonderful change in the beaten army. Much of the work of reorganization was already effected, but there was little hope that an advance
could be made. A stand, and a stubborn defense of what was left, was the
utmost that could apparently be hoped for. It required the magic of Sheridan's name and genius to transform defeat into such complete victory."
Whittaker, *George A. Custer*, 267.
72. For example, Gordon, *Reminiscences of the Civil War*, 345.
73. Kidd, *Personal Recollections*, 420.
74. Hannaford, "Reminiscences," 200(a)–(b).

From Major (later General) G. A. Forsyth, 8th Illinois, an aide-de-camp of Sheridan's and one of his companions on the ride from Winchester: "[Sheridan's] appearance was greeted by tremendous cheers from one end of the line to the other, many of the officers pressing forward to shake his hand. He spoke to them all, cheerily and confidently, saying, 'We are going back to our camps, men, never fear. I'll get a twist on those people yet. We'll raise them out of their boots before the day is over.' "[75] The effect was magical. Without question Sheridan, like no other commanding officer in the Union army—not excepting McClellan—had the gift of making his men somehow feel that they were "greater than they knew."

Sheridan's one thought after he reached the front was to mount a full-scale counterattack at the earliest possible moment, using as his startline the position about two miles northwest of Middletown that Getty's division of the VI Corps was then holding. To that end he sent Custer's division back to the right flank and ordered the First and Third Divisions of the VI Corps and, as fast as they could be collected and marched to the front, the brigades of the XIX Corps, to prolong Getty's line to the right.[76] When these evolutions were completed, the Federal infantry was deployed west of the Valley Turnpike in a two-mile arc facing southeast. Merritt's cavalry, east of the pike, was in line with Getty's left; Custer, on the right, was nearest to Cedar Creek.

Prior to Sheridan's arrival, Merritt had placed the Reserve Brigade, under Colonel Lowell, in the center of his line, with Colonel Kidd's Michigan Brigade on its left and Devin's brigade on its right. While in this position, the entire division was pounded by artillery fire that Merritt described as "truly terrific; it has seldom been equaled for accuracy of aim and excellence of ammunition"; his own horse artillery was "overpowered at times by weight of metal and superior ammunition."[77] Facing Lowell's small brigade were some of Wharton's infantry, "strongly posted behind fences . . . [and] piles of logs" and the houses of Middletown.[78] In front of

75. George A. Forsyth, *Thrilling Days in Army Life* (New York, 1900), 151.

76. Sheridan, *Personal Memoirs*, II, 84.

77. *Official Records*, Vol. XLIII, Pt. 1, p. 450.

78. Kidd, *Personal Recollections*, 418.

the division, south of Middletown, the ground dropped away to a broad depression through which ran a small creek. Beyond it was a wide area of level ground, bounded on the south by a steep-sided ravine. A short distance south of the ravine, and beyond a second ravine, the ground rose toward a belt of timber stretching across the front. The Confederates had a strong skirmish line part way up this rise; their main battle line, protected by the usual piles of logs and rails, ran along the northern edge of the belt of woods.

Custer, on the right, deployed his regiments so that his left connected with the right of the XIX Corps, his line generally facing Cedar Creek. Shortly after noon he was attacked by Rosser, who had been quiescent since his predawn attack across Cupp's Ford; the attack was beaten off by three regiments of Pennington's brigade.

As the late morning wore away, the artillery and small-arms fire of both sides became sporadic, and in the early hours of the afternoon "an ominous silence succeeded. Even the batteries were still"; but, Colonel Kidd noted, "it was the calm that precedes the storm. To those on the left, it seemed that the dispositions were a long time in making. When one has his courage screwed to the sticking point, the more quickly he can plunge in and have it over the better. The suspense was terrible."[79] The minutes and hours passed, and not until nearly four o'clock did Sheridan have all his troops deployed where he wanted them and judged that all was ready for the attack. Now the order to advance was given and passed down the line. Sheridan intended to have the infantry on the right swing toward the east and across the Valley Turnpike, so as to cut the Confederates off from the turnpike bridge across Cedar Creek and the fords adjacent to it, but Merritt's and Custer's horsemen were too aggressive and too fast for him.[80] Early's fear of being attacked in flank by the powerful Federal cavalry—a fear that in the opinion of a competent judge "caused him to extend his lines to such an extent that they were nowhere of sufficient strength"—was about to receive its justification.[81]

79. *Ibid.*, 421.
80. Sheridan, *Personal Memoirs*, II, 88.
81. Davies, *General Sheridan*, 157–58; see also Gordon, *Reminiscences of the Civil War*, 347–48, and *Official Records*, Vol. XLIII, Pt. 1, p. 581.

As the cavalry bugles sounded "Forward," Colonel Kidd, from his position on the left flank, could see the entire Federal line surge ahead. The whole of Merritt's division swept forward against the concentrated fire of Confederate infantry and artillery, across the depression, the creek, and the two ravines. The division was nearly up to the main enemy position on the edge of the timber when Devin's brigade, on the right, was caught in a cross-fire on its flank from enemy infantry on the turnpike; the brigade fell back, drawing the entire division with it. The regiments reformed in the shelter of the depression, and after a brief pause the charge was again sounded. On went the division a second time across the ravines and up the slope toward the woods, only to be brought to a halt again, this time by a check to the VI Corps infantry to its right. Once against the cavalry reformed, the infantry rallied and moved forward, and for the third time Merritt's troopers charged up the rising ground toward the timber. This time the charge was pressed home, and the Confederate line, its left compromised by the advance of the VI Corps infantry, gave way "in disorder."[82] The cavalry followed them into the woods, "and then it was every regiment for itself." Devin, nearest the turnpike, was the first to reach the Cedar Creek bridge, and his lead regiment, the 6th New York, charged across it; his other regiments drove across the stream over a ford just below the bridge and then veered right and across the turnpike. The Michigan regiments, crowded off to the left, galloped straight for the Shenandoah below the mouth of Cedar Creek, capturing "seemingly, more prisoners than . . . [they] had men."

Meanwhile, on the right, Custer had a decision to make. His First (Pennington's) Brigade was still engaged in a desultory fire fight with Rosser's cavalry. Should he join Pennington with his Second Brigade, drive Rosser across Cedar Creek, and thus make his fight on the right, out of contact with the advancing infantry? Sitting his horse on the ridge from which Pennington's artillery was shelling Rosser, Custer could see, away to the left, the advance of the VI and XIX Corps, and it became "apparent" to him "that the wavering in the ranks of the enemy betokened a retreat,

82. This and the two quotations that follow are from Kidd, *Personal Recollections*, 423–24.

and that this retreat might be converted into a rout."[83] He hesitated, but only for a moment; then, without waiting for orders, he made the decision that any cavalry commander worth his salt should have made. Leaving Pennington with three regiments to maintain pressure on Rosser, he wheeled the rest of the division into column and "moved to the left at a gallop." What Custer intended was to "gain possession of the pike in rear of the enemy, and by holding the bridge and adjacent fords, cut off his retreat." But he was too late. Devin had already crossed the bridge when Custer came within sight of it. Nonetheless, the onset of Custer's regiments had the classic textbook effect: "Seeing so large a force of cavalry bearing rapidly down upon an unprotected flank and their line of retreat in danger of being intercepted, the lines of the enemy, already broken, now gave way in the utmost confusion."

Custer's regiments had become somewhat strung out in the gallop toward the bridge; Custer himself was where he should have been, at the head of his two lead regiments, the 5th New York and the 1st Vermont. Seeing the bridge already secured by Devin, Custer veered right and led the two regiments at a gallop to a ford a half mile upstream, splashed across, charged ("when within short pistol range") and routed a line of Confederate infantry that attempted to make a stand. From that point well into the night his men and Merritt's enjoyed a cavalryman's dream, a grand and glorious chase of the enemy, who were fleeing south along the Valley Turnpike.[84] This time, unlike at the Opequon and at Fisher's Hill, the cavalry was in its proper place; Confederate Captain Hotchkiss noted that they "dashed along, killing horses and turning over ambulances, caissons, &c., stampeding the drivers . . . as there was nothing to defend them and we had no

83. All the quotations in this paragraph are from Custer's report, *Official Records*, Vol. XLIII, Pt. 1, p. 524. Here is Custer's charge, as viewed from the other side: "As the tumult of the battle died away, there came from the north side of the plain a dull, heavy swelling sound like the roaring of a distant cyclone, the omen of additional disaster. It was unmistakeable. Sheridan's horsemen were riding furiously across the open fields of grass to intercept the Confederates before they crossed Cedar Creek. . . . As the sullen roar from horses' hoofs beating the soft turf of the plain told of the near approach of the cavalry, all effort at orderly retreat was abandoned." Gordon, *Reminiscences of the Civil War*, 348–49.
84. *Official Records*, Vol. XLIII, Pt. 1, p. 525.

organized force to go after them."[85] Before the pursuit ceased, halted by exhaustion and the darkness, sixteen hundred prisoners had been taken, the eighteen guns captured by the Confederates in the morning had been recaptured together with twenty-five to thirty of Early's guns, and nearly all his transport was smashed, burned, or in Sheridan's possession.[86]

The tally of Confederate prisoners would have been far greater had it not been for the headlong pace and confusion of the pursuit and the total darkness. John DeForest was told the next morning by a lieutenant of the 2nd South Carolina Infantry that he had surrendered five times during the night. "Two hundred of our men," he said, "would throw down their arms to twenty or thirty of your cavalry. Then the chief of the troop would order, 'now you stay there!' and spur off after more prisoners. Then we officers would tell our men, 'Now scatter, boys; take to the bushes and hollows; get back to Fisher's Hill.' Well, what with the nightfall and the rough country, the biggest part of us sneaked out of our scrape."[87] Confederate losses were increased by the enterprise of a group of blue cavalrymen, who circled around Spangler's Mill, west of Strasburg, broke down a bridge over a tributary of the Shenandoah, and thereby blocked the escape of everything north of that point. Nevertheless, most of Early's men escaped. They marched through the night, across Fisher's Hill to New Market, thirty miles south of Cedar Creek. It says much for their morale that even after this smashing defeat, the third within a month, "most of the men . . . [had] sorted themselves and order [had] been somewhat restored" by the time they reached New Market at daylight.[88]

85. Ibid., 581.

86. Freeman, Lee's Lieutenants, III, 608. Early estimated his loss in killed and wounded at "less [than] 1,000," and in a second dispatch as "not more than 700 or 800" (Official Records, Vol. XLIII, Pt. 1, pp. 560, 564), which Freeman believed was "probably too low"; Freeman, Lee's Lieutenants, III, 610. In a dispatch to Grant on October 21, Sheridan wrote, "For ten miles on the line of retreat the road and country was covered with small arms, thrown away by the flying rebels. . . . Forty-eight pieces of captured artillery are now at my headquarters. I think not less than 300 wagons and ambulances were either captured or destroyed." Official Records, Vol. XLIII, Pt. 2, pp. 436–37.

87. DeForest, A Volunteer's Adventures, 229.

88. Freeman, Lee's Lieutenants, III, 608; Official Records, Vol. XLIII, Pt. 1, p. 582.

The captures, particularly the captures of guns, which, together with regimental battle flags, were prize trophies, led to bad blood between Custer and Merritt. The total number of guns recaptured and captured was reported variously as forty-three, forty-five, and forty-eight. Custer claimed for his command the capture of forty-five, both in his official report and in a congratulatory order issued to his division after the battle. Merritt, who had obtained an acknowledgment of the receipt by the army provost marshal of twenty-two pieces of artillery captured by Devin's brigade, had his attention called to Custer's congratulatory order after it was published in a New York newspaper. At once he let fly with an indignant missive to Major William Russell, Jr., Torbert's assistant adjutant general, protesting against "this official recognition of overweening greed of some of the Third Division for the rightful captures" of his own division and stating that it was his duty to declare Custer's claim to be "wholesale robbery" and "without foundation in truth." One of the many reporters with the army sent a copy of this dispatch to the New York *Times*, which duly published it as a "card." Ten days later, Custer sent Major Russell a clipping of the "card," repeated the claim that his division had indeed captured forty-five pieces of artillery, and requested "respectfully but most earnestly" that either Torbert personally adjudicate the conflicting claims of the two divisions, or that he appoint a board of disinterested officers to summon witnesses, hear testimony, and reach an official decision on the question. The records are silent on the subsequent fate of this grave issue.[89]

October 19 was a great day for Sheridan, a day of an unparalleled personal triumph. Grant wired Secretary Stanton the next day, "I had a salute of 100 guns from each of the armies here fired in honor of Sheridan's . . . victory. Turning what bid fair to be a disaster into glorious victory stamps Sheridan, what I have always thought him, one of the ablest generals."[90] It is safe to assume that the secretary, who had questioned the wisdom of appointing Sheridan to the Valley command, did not fail to note the "I told you so" tone of the message. The president, fully aware as always of political realities, was overjoyed. A dramatic victory for the Union

89. *Official Records*, Vol. XLIII, Pt. 1, pp. 526, 528, 453–54, 528–29.
90. *Ibid.*, Pt. 2, p. 423. For Grant's reaction to the news of Sheridan's victory, see Porter, *Campaigning with Grant*, 306–308.

was doubly welcome, coming as it did three weeks before the presidential election, and Lincoln sent Sheridan the thanks of the nation and his "own personal admiration and gratitude . . . for the splendid work of October 19."[91] In due course, Sheridan, his officers and men were voted the thanks of Congress for the "brilliant series of victories achieved by them . . . and especially for their services at Cedar Run [sic]."[92] Sheridan received more substantial recognition when, by presidential order, he was promoted to the rank of major general in the Regular Army. But perhaps the most gratifying of his rewards came from the men he commanded, exemplified by the diary entry of Trooper Luman Harris Tenney of the 2nd Ohio: "The victory complete. All worship Sheridan who turned a complete rout into the most complete victory of the war."[93]

Be it said to Sheridan's credit that he was prompt to share the glory of his victory; two days after the battle, he wired Grant, "I want [the self-assurance of that "I want," addressed to the general-in-chief, is to be noted] Getty, of the Sixth Corps, and the brave boys, Merritt and Custer, promoted by brevet," and promoted they were, to major general.[94] Custer received the further honor of being detailed to take to Washington and deliver to the War Department the ten battle flags captured in the battle, each carried by the man who had captured it. Indeed, there was sufficient glory for everyone, but it had been purchased at the cost of 644 killed, 3,430 wounded, and 1,591 captured or missing; included in these losses were those of the cavalry: 28 killed, 116 wounded, and 42 captured or missing.[95] The highest ranking cavalryman killed was the commander of the Reserve Brigade, the greatly admired Charles Russell Lowell, Jr.[96] Painfully wounded early in the day,

91. Facsimile in Sheridan, *Personal Memoirs*, II, 91; *Official Records*, Vol. XLIII, Pt. 1, p. 62.
92. *Official Records*, Vol. XLIII, Pt. 1, p. 63.
93. Tenney, *War Diary*, 133.
94. *Official Records*, Vol. XLIII, Pt. 2, p. 437.
95. *Ibid.*, Pt. 1, pp. 136–37.
96. See Merritt's splendid encomium in *ibid.*, 450–451. John DeForest, riding the day after the battle over the ground covered by the charge of Merritt's division, wrote, "A remarkable number of slaughtered horses showed how freely the cavalry had been used and how severely the artillery had suffered. There were so many of them in front of a stone wall east of

Lowell insisted on continuing to lead his men and was killed in the forefront of the late afternoon charge of Merritt's division against the enemy in the "belt of timber."

On the Confederate side, Major General Stephen Dodson Ramseur—a West Point classmate of Wesley Merritt—was gravely wounded and later captured by the 1st Vermont. Union army surgeons joined a Confederate surgeon in trying to save Ramseur's life, but without success. "A Union officer—a friend—watched by his side in his last moments and conveyed to his southern home his last words of affection." The Union officer and friend was General Merritt, and some of General Ramseur's "last words of affection" that he conveyed were for a child born to his wife three days before the battle, whom its father was fated never to see.[97]

---

the pike which had been charged and carried by our troopers, that I did not stop to count them, but guessed the lot as about a hundred." DeForest, *A Volunteer's Adventures*, 228.

97. *Battles and Leaders*, IV, 520; Freeman, *Lee's Lieutenants*, III, 610.

XII

Soldiers of the Sword

WEAKENED BY ITS LOSSES IN THREE SUCCESSIVE BAT-
tles, the Army of the Shenandoah was incapable of mounting a
major effort for some time after Cedar Creek. Fortunately, it did
not need to. Sheridan claimed that his cavalry had been particularly hard hit; in addition to its losses in the three battles, it had suffered casualties in daily brushes with the enemy; moreover, men
who had enlisted in the late summer and fall of 1861 and had not
"veteranized" were leaving in appreciable numbers for muster-out.
Perhaps even more damaging was the loss of horses. Writing to
Grant on October 25, Sheridan said that his mounted force was not
"half so strong as it was six weeks ago."[1] His statement seems to
be disproved by his monthly strength reports, which show an increase, not a decrease, in the numbers of Torbert's two divisions
"present for duty," from 6,343 (exclusive of the horse artillery) in
September to 7,078 in October and 7,978 in November.[2] The term
"present for duty" was used in notoriously imprecise and inconsis-
tent ways: thus the only basis on which these reports can be rec-
onciled with Sheridan's statement to Grant is by assuming that
the former included all men on detached duty, all partially
equipped men, and all dismounted men present with their units,

1. *Official Records*, Vol. XLIII, Pt. 1, p. 34.
2. *Ibid.*, Pt. 2, pp. 248, 501, 716.

whereas Sheridan counted as available for service only fully equipped mounted men actually in the ranks.

Whatever Sheridan's exact strength may have been, it was inevitable that some units should have been harder hit than others. On October 22 the 1st Vermont lost 283 of its three-year veterans, who left that day for Vermont and muster-out.[3] Four days later, Colonel Powell reported that his Second Division had shrunk from 2,287 on September 23 to 1,129 on October 26, a loss of just over 50 percent in a month.[4] Company C, 2nd Ohio, after losing since May 1 five killed, thirty wounded, and seventeen missing, was down to eleven, rank and file.[5] On the other hand, the more enterprising or more fortunate regiments were receiving recruits; the 1st Vermont got 140 shortly before the departure of its 283 time-expired veterans; the 17th Pennsylvania got 200, raising its strength to "about 600," a large regiment for the time.[6] The 2nd New York received no fewer than 400 fully equipped recruits in one lot. "For a time," wrote Roger Hannaford, "their arrival, [their] appearance, equipments, &c., created an excitement, & many were the surmises that many of them would be minus some of their fancy equipments before another week; they all had nice red . . . horse blankets . . . I recollect Lieut[enant George M.] Adams [Co. M, 2nd Ohio] expressing an ardent desire to possess one & know moreover that not long after he had the coveted article, but how or where he got it I dont know."[7] Later in the fall and during the winter the wastage of nearly six months, particularly the wastage of horses, was made good. "Many fresh horses were obtained, and the numerical force was increased by the return of convalescents [and] the re-equipment of dismounted men."[8]

The least of Sheridan's concerns after Cedar Creek was General Early's army. The Federal pursuit after the battle halted at Edenburg, and Early was able to pause for a time at New Market to get his remaining forces into some sort of order.[9] In a disconso-

3. Benedict, Vermont in the Civil War, II, 671.
4. Official Records, Vol. XLIII, Pt. 1, pp. 506, 510.
5. Tenney, War Diary, 137.
6. Moyer, History of the 17th Regiment, 142.
7. Hannaford, "Reminiscences," 213(d).
8. Davies, General Sheridan, 204.
9. Early had to admit that "the rout was as thorough and disgraceful

late dispatch to General Lee he offered to surrender the Valley command, but the offer was declined. Sheridan meanwhile retreated a short distance down the Valley and established a defensive line at Kernstown, to facilitate the transfer of some of his troops to Grant. Early led a reconnaissance in force to "feel" Sheridan's new position, but he had neither the forces nor the supplies to remain that far north for any length of time; having established Sheridan's whereabouts, he returned to New Market.[10]

In General Davies' opinion, Early's cavalry had been so "disorganized and broken up as no longer to be considered a factor in hostile operations" after Cedar Creek.[11] "Demonstrations" and reconnaissances by portions of the Federal cavalry were now meeting negligible opposition or none.[12] On November 12, moving along the "Back Road," abreast of Early's advance to Kernstown, two brigades of Rosser's cavalry were charged and routed by Pennington's brigade and were driven "at a run four or five miles across Cedar Creek."[13] Nevertheless, it is clear from the reports of the Federal commanders who were in this fight that however "disorganized and broken up" Rosser's command may have been, the men he had left had not lost all their old bite. Rosser had reached the Federal picket lines, manned by the 1st Vermont, attacked, drove them back, and engaged in a "heavy skirmish" until dark with Pennington's brigade, which had come to the aid of the Vermonters. The following morning it was Rosser once again who took the initiative; he attacked and forced back the 2nd Ohio and the 1st Connecticut, and not until Merritt appeared at nightfall to help out Pennington was Rosser checked and eventually routed.[14]

---

as ever happened to our army." On this occasion, he had no fault to find with Sheridan's generalship. *Official Records*, Vol. XLIII, Pt. 1, p. 563.

10. Sheridan, *Personal Memoirs*, II, 98.

11. Davies, *General Sheridan*, 193.

12. *Official Records*, Vol. XLIII, Pt. 1, p. 35. On November 10, Sheridan reported to Grant that he had sent "a small division of cavalry" (presumably the Second Division) east of the Blue Ridge, to the Upperville-Paris-Bloomfield area. The expedition found no enemy other than guerrillas, but brought back a "lot of stock, horses, sheep and cattle" and destroyed a "lot of grain, barns, subsistence, &c." *Ibid.*, 36.

13. *Ibid.*, 36 (Sheridan's report).

14. *Ibid.*, 548, 533–34. Major William G. Cummings, commanding the Vermont regiment, wrote that "it never fought better, though some 250 of

At the same time that Pennington and Merritt were having their fight with Rosser, Colonel Powell had a fight with Lomax. Advancing along the Winchester-Front Royal Pike, Powell was attacked by Lomax at Nineveh; moving his whole line forward "with drawn sabers," he met the attack with a charge of his own and routed the enemy, killing and wounding 55, taking 161 prisoners (including 19 commissioned officers), and capturing Lomax's two pieces of artillery, at a cost of 2 men killed and 15 wounded.[15]

Ten days later Torbert led the Second and Third Cavalry Divisions on a reconnaissance forty miles up the Valley as far as Rude's Hill. He had a fight with Confederate cavalry, not identified in his report, and brought back precise and accurate information about the enemy infantry, even reporting that Kershaw's division had left Early and begun entraining at Waynesboro for a journey to Richmond "at 2 o'clock Friday morning, 18th instant." He reported further that Early still had left an army of four divisions of infantry and one of cavalry.[16] General Torbert's succinct report makes no mention of the conditions in which this expedition took place—information that is supplied by a trooper of the 2nd Ohio:

Nov. 21. We left camp . . . in the midst of a heavy rain . . . it rained all day steadily. . . . Just before dark we came to Woodstock . . . and camped on a hill south of town. . . . The wind was now beginning to blow from the north, & the rain . . . was driving & getting much colder. . . . the ground was covered with water . . . it was near 1 A.M. of . . . [the] 22nd . . . the bugle blew. . . . A terrible time we had getting our stiff muddy blankets, tents & ponchoes rolled up & packed. . . . The boys walked half the time to keep from freezing.

In a fight with Confederate cavalry later that day, the Federal troopers had an unpleasant surprise: "the weather was very cold, freezing hard all the time, and our 'Spencers' did not act well, the

---

its members were recruits just from the State, and had never seen a day's drill." *Ibid.*, 549. On the other hand, Colonel Pennington reported that the 18th Pennsylvania had "set a very bad example to the brigade." *Ibid.*, 534.

15. *Ibid.*, 512. Torbert stated that Powell captured 180 prisoners, including 18 officers. *Ibid.*, 437.

16. *Ibid.*, 437, 534; Pt. 2, pp. 661, 663. Colonel Pennington again criticized the 18th Pennsylvania, this time for "having gone to the rear without orders and avoided the fight." *Ibid.*, Pt. 1, p. 534.

tallow on the cartridges was as hard as clay, besides they were all slightly damp from the rain . . . so that fully one half of the cartridges did not explode. . . . a man who finds his gun out of order, is sure to take a back track, at least for awhile."[17]

While these reconnaissances and small-scale fights were taking place, the Union cavalry had a generally grim time of it. One of Sheridan's reasons for establishing his army at Kernstown was that by reconstructing the Winchester & Potomac Railroad from Harper's Ferry to Stephenson's Depot, he would be well placed to keep his men and animals in rations and supplies, but to get the railroad service restored took time, and in the interim there was much suffering. As usual, the horses were the chief victims; Sheridan reported them on November 14 as "suffering very much from the cold weather and insufficiency of food."[18] The men's rations too ran short, and after the repeated marches of Sheridan's and Early's armies up and down the Valley and the devastation of October, foragers needed above-average enterprise and luck to find anything worth taking back to camp. When Thanksgiving Day came, Roger Hannaford recorded that "according to the pictures in Harper's Weekly . . . every Soldier became the happy possessor of a mammoth turkey together with various etceteras. . . . for our part there were 5 old skinny, tough, bony, half-starved, dried-up chickens distributed to our Co[mpany] & one or two small cans of tomatoes or dried corn or something of that kind, & we fared as well as any of the [Third] Div[ision]."[19]

17. Hannaford, "Reminiscences," 217(b)–218(a), 220(a).
18. *Official Records*, Vol. XLIII, Pt. 2, p. 624.
19. Hannaford, "Reminiscences," 222(c). The Confederate cavalry, stationed in the devastated portion of the Valley, was far worse off than the Federal. As winter came on, wrote the historian of the Laurel Brigade, "Hope and fortitude would not feed and clothe the men, nor keep alive the horses. . . . Day by day the brigade was diminishing in numbers. Many went home by permission for fresh horses; many took 'French leave' not as deserters, but for temporary absence without furlough. . . . Many whole companies were permitted to go home and recruit." McDonald, *A History of the Laurel Brigade*, 331–34. At Christmas, the 2nd Virginia of Wickham's brigade received twenty-five days' ration of salt—"No bread, no meat, or anything." And, added a member of the regiment, "Of course we had to steal everything we ate, for we had no money to buy anything with." R. H. Peck, *Reminiscences of a Confederate Soldier of Co. C, 2nd Va. Cavalry* (Fincastle, Va., 1913), 59.

Despite the discouraging prospects, foragers continued to go out in the hope of finding something edible for themselves and their horses. Returning after nightfall with another trooper from one such expedition, Hannaford recalled, "a really beautiful vision lay before us, there lay our camp half a mile distant but as it was so much lower, it seemed almost at our feet, it was laid out very regular . . . & now before each tent a fire was burning, the glimmer of the lines of fire around which we could see forms flitting was really like fairy land."[20] Having found their way back to camp, the foragers had next to locate their units:

[You have] no idea where your Co[mpany] or Reg[imen]t or even Brig[ade] is encamped; before you is perhaps an hundred acres sparkling with bright camp fires, which dazzle your eyes just come from darkness, by asking those you meet you learn the place your Brig[ade] is camped, slowly walking your horse when near it you begin calling at the top of your voice the name of your Reg[imen]t . . . soon the welcome sound comes back "here" and you steer in the direction, calling the letter of your Co[mpany] . . . soon a dozen voices echo back crying "here, here" & you soon find where your bunkee is established.[21]

But the hardships of late October and November were eased by some pleasant and interesting incidents. On October 22, the paymasters made a long overdue appearance, and the cavalry received eight months' pay. Many of the troopers of the 2nd Ohio wanted to send home a portion of their pay, and the paymasters announced that anyone who wanted to do so could place his money in an envelope, seal it, and mark the amount and the destination on the outside. The paymasters would then have the envelopes delivered by express. The Ohioans, who had "weak faith in the honesty of P[ay] M[asters] as a class" were dubious, but after the regimental town meeting had discussed the proposal at great length, they decided to accept it. Roger Hannaford, trusted by everyone, had the job of collecting the envelopes and delivering them to the paymasters. When he added up the sums marked on the envelopes, he was surprised to find that he had nearly three thousand dollars in his hands.[22]

20. Hannaford, "Reminiscences," 207(b).
21. Ibid., 172(b).
22. Ibid., 208(a)–(b).

Then came November 8, the day of the presidential election. Ohio was one of the states that allowed its soldiers to cast their ballots in the field, and on election day, after the pickets had been posted in the morning, the 2nd Ohio "went busily to work voting. . . . by six o'clock the ballot of every man entitled to vote was cast. . . . It was quite interesting to see the clerks and judges sitting under a large tree, questioning & at times swearing the men as they came up; the ballot box was a hat covered by another."[23] Luman Tenney of the Ohio regiment saw November 8 as "the decisive day of the nation. If the cause of the Union prevails today, liberty and union will be ours forever." His regiment did not disappoint him; it voted 201 for Lincoln, 4 for McClellan. "Glorious for the 2nd Ohio," wrote Tenney in his diary when the results were announced.[24] The vote in many another regiment, East and West, was equally "glorious," and as self-consciously motivated as was Tenney's vote by a determination to see the war fought to a victorious finish. And these were not the votes of stay-at-home civilians, but of the men, many of whom had already borne all the hazards and hardships of war for two or three years, who would have to continue to do the fighting and the dying if the war was to go on to a final victory for the Union.

On November 25 every cavalryman was issued—much to the "dissatisfaction" of many of them—a forage cap, with instructions to have added to it the crossed sabers insignia of the cavalry, and regimental number and company letter. Stringent orders came down from the army commander himself that the caps were to be worn thereafter in place of the heterogeneous assortment of hats of all shapes, types, and colors that the men had been wearing.[25]

23. Ibid., 212(a).
24. Tenney, War Diary, 134. A reason for the small vote was the number of men under twenty-one in the regiment. Illinois did not allow its soldiers to vote in the field, but before November 8 the 8th Illinois received orders to grant furloughs to "all who were unfit for active duty . . . that they might go home and vote; and large numbers thus obtained leaves . . . the government furnishing transportation." Hard, History of the Eighth Cavalry, 314. The regiment formed by the consolidation of the 1st Maine and the 1st District of Columbia voted 329 for Lincoln, 46 for McClellan. Most of the regiment being on picket on election day, "Col. [Jonathan P.] Cilley and other officers rode along the picket line . . . taking the vote." Tobie, First Maine Cavalry, 367.
25. Tenney, War Diary, 136.

In the weeks following Cedar Creek, Grant, who had developed an absolute fixation about the Virginia Central Railroad, sent Sheridan a series of messages urging him to send his cavalry to destroy the road.[26] The orders were discretionary, but they made quite clear Grant's great desire to have the road broken up; it would, he said, "go far toward starving out the garrison of Richmond." Sheridan was equally persistent in voicing his objections to such a raid. He wrote on October 25 that the movement "would be exceedingly difficult, on account of supplies and forage, and would demoralize the troops, now in magnificent trim."[27] In early December he shifted his ground and took a position that he would hardly have tolerated in one of his own subordinates; he disputed the validity of the general-in-chief's basic premise, arguing that the breaking of the road would not be "very important" and that he was "satisfied that no supplies go over the road toward Richmond from any point north of the road or from the Shenandoah Valley."[28] When Grant repeated his contention that the breaking of the road would starve out Lee, Sheridan replied on December 13 that the inclement weather—snow several inches deep and an intense cold—made any movement on the roads impossible. He repeated his belief that no supplies for Richmond were being carried on that route and implied that the raid would be a waste of effort; he did end, however, with the promise that he "would break the railroad, if possible, as soon as the weather will permit."[29] Grant had to be satisfied with that considerably less than firm assurance.

It is an interesting coincidence that at the very time in mid-December that Grant quietly swallowed the latest of Sheridan's essentially negative, argumentative messages, he was on the verge of superseding General George H. Thomas at Nashville, because Thomas claimed, with complete justification, that it was a physical impossibility for him to attack the Army of Tennessee over the sheet of ice that covered the hills south of the city. Clearly, the scales of justice in Grant's hands were not held level between

26. *Official Records*, Vol. XLIII, Pt. 2, pp. 645 (November 19), 740 (December 5), 778 (December 12); see also Grant to Halleck, October 11, *ibid.*, 339.
27. *Ibid.*, Pt. 1, p. 35.
28. *Ibid.*, Pt. 2, p. 743.
29. *Ibid.*, 780.

Sheridan and Thomas, any more than Sheridan had held them level between Averell and Torbert.

Sheridan evidently sensed just how far he could go in opposing the general-in-chief's wishes, because he notified Grant on December 20 that he had sent all his cavalry, about eight thousand mounted men, without artillery or supply wagons, on the raid.[30] His plan was for Torbert, with the First and Second Divisions, to ride south via Front Royal, cross the Blue Ridge over Chester Gap, and then, marching along the eastern foot of the Blue Ridge, strike the railroad at Gordonsville and follow it, destroying track, culverts, and bridges as he went, as far as Charlottesville and Lynchburg. Custer and the Third Division were at the same time to march up the Valley to Staunton and then on to the James River Canal, destroying it as much as possible, and meet Torbert at Lynchburg.[31] Sheridan was careful to tell Grant that the weather was "so very bad" that he was "not sanguine of success," a most sensible disclaimer.[32]

Both "wings" of the raid departed on the morning of December 19. Torbert, with about five thousand men in his command, reached Chester Gap the same evening. Rain had been falling nearly all day and was followed by an all-night storm of sleet and hail. Nevertheless, Torbert was able to cross the Blue Ridge on the twentieth. After a second night of sleet and hail, the march was resumed on the twenty-first. A few enemy vedettes, belonging to John McCausland's and William L. Jackson's brigades of Lomax's division, were met that day and brushed aside. Progress was

30. *Ibid.*, 810. Since Torbert reported his "present for duty" strength in December as 10,117 (*ibid.*, 847), the 2,117 not going on the raid were presumably the sick, men on detached duty, dismounted men, and men whose horses were deemed unfit to make the march.

31. *Ibid.*, 810, 804. There is a major discrepancy between the two dispatches concerning Custer's role. In the earlier, Sheridan wrote that he ordered Custer to march "as far as Staunton" and stay out as long as his forage lasted; in the later dispatch Custer's assignment is as given in the text. Contrary to what he told Grant, Sheridan wrote in his memoirs that he intended Custer's march to be "a demonstration in Torbert's favor, hoping to hold the enemy's troops in the Valley." Sheridan, *Personal Memoirs*, II, 102.

32. *Official Records*, Vol. XLIII, Pt. 2, p. 804. Sheridan repeated the next day: "The weather is so very bad—rain, snow and sleet—that I feel a great deal of anxiety about the horses." *Ibid.*, 816.

General Sheridan and his cavalry commanders. From left to right:
Wesley Merritt, David Gregg, Sheridan, Henry Davies, James Wilson, A. T. A. Torbert.
Courtesy of the Library of Congress

Major General David McM. Gregg and staff. General Gregg third from right, seated.
Courtesy of the Library of Congress

Officers of the 1st Massachusetts Cavalry. Charles Francis Adams, Jr., second from right.
Courtesy of the Library of Congress

Wesley Merritt
Courtesy of the Library of Congress

George Crook
Courtesy of the Library of Congress

August V. Kautz
Courtesy of the Library of Congress

slowed not by enemy opposition but by a heavy fall of sleet and snow and by the state of the road, described by Torbert as "one of the worst" he had ever encountered. On the twenty-second the march continued toward the bridge across the Rapidan at Liberty Mills, where in October of the year before Stuart, caught between Buford and Kilpatrick, had narrowly escaped a severe defeat. Retreating before Torbert's overwhelming strength, the Confederates destroyed the bridge in his face. The ford adjacent to the bridge was "barricaded and defended" by McCausland's and Jackson's dismounted cavalry "in rifle pits and artillery in position behind earth-works." Judging a frontal attack impractical, Torbert decided to try to flank the Confederates out of their defenses. Rounding up some local people to serve as guides, he sent two of his brigades to cross the stream at a ford two miles above Liberty Mills, and a third brigade to cross at a ford three miles downstream. Neither ford was as good as the guides claimed, and the crossings, made single file, took much longer than Torbert had anticipated. Then the roads on the other side, leading to the rear of the Confederate position, turned out to be more roundabout and longer than he had been led to believe. Consequently, it was dark by the time the two flanking columns reached Liberty Mills and drove the Confederates out of their defenses and in the direction of Gordonsville. The day had been intensely cold, and after nightfall it grew even colder. Nevertheless, the advance was resumed at daybreak on the twenty-third. The Confederate cavalry was driven with the loss of their two pieces of artillery to a gap through Southwest Mountain, two and a half miles from Gordonsville. This narrow gap through a steep-sided mountain was ideal for a defensive stand, and the Confederates made good use of it; Torbert was unable to break through. He sent a column to cross the mountain by way of another gap several miles to the north and swing around into the Confederates' rear, but before this flanking column could fulfill its assignment, the dismounted cavalry in the gap was replaced by two brigades of infantry belonging to Longstreet's corps, rushed to the scene by rail from the Richmond defenses. This caused Torbert to conclude that "it was useless to make a further attempt to break the Central railroad," and he gave orders to return to his base. He reached Winchester on De-

cember 28 after a five-day march, bringing back with him the two
captured guns and about a thousand head of "stock," but at a cost
of 102 of his men killed, wounded, "accidentally hurt," and missing, 258 horses lost, and many of his troopers badly frostbitten.[33]
The march back to Winchester was undisturbed by the enemy, but
was hampered by the continued foul weather, which caused suffering "almost beyond description."[34] Not mentioned in Torbert's report was another difficulty, which, however, mitigated the effects
of the snow and the cold for at least some of the men. A participant in the raid recalled that on the return march, there was "an
abundance to eat and drink; too much of the latter. Applejack,
apple brandy, and blackberry wine flowed like water . . . in some
regiments scores of men had to be strapped to their horses. . . . It
was indeed a sorry scene."[35]

Custer's share of the expedition was no more productive than
Torbert's. Leaving camp with three days' rations and one day's
forage, Custer was shadowed by Confederate scouts from the start.
He did not expect to meet serious opposition until he was beyond
Staunton, south of the devastated area, where he also expected to
find food for his men and animals. On the second day out, near
Mount Jackson, Custer assembled the entire division in a tight
circle, mounted a gun carriage in the center, and treated his men
to "a few words of encouragement," that is, an oration. He told
them that General Thomas "was drubbing the rebels in grand
style," which was certainly true, Thomas and Wilson having
destroyed Hood at Nashville a few days earlier. Then he reported
"a rumor that 'Jeff Davis' had tried to commit suicide," and he
ended "by adjuring the men to take great care of their ammunition, not to expend it hastily or foolishly." The morale-building

    33. This account of Torbert's Gordonsville Raid is based on his report
in *ibid.*, Pt. 1, pp. 677–79; all quotations are from that source unless otherwise identified. See also *ibid.*, 38, 39, and Pt. 2, p. 829. For lack of transportation Torbert had to leave behind some of his thirty-eight wounded.
Ibid., Pt. 1, p. 678; Sheridan, *Personal Memoirs*, II, 104. Sheridan was "disappointed" by the failure of the raid; added to Torbert's failure in the Luray
Valley in September, it caused him to "mistrust" the latter's "ability to conduct any operations requiring much self-reliance." Sheridan, *Personal Memoirs*, II, 112.
    34. *Official Records*, Vol. XLIII, Pt. 2, p. 829.
    35. Bowen, *Regimental History of the First New York*, 273.

exercises concluded "by a rousing 3 cheers for our Gen[era]l who was very popular with his men."[36]

Evidently Custer was in one of his more expansive moods this day, for he sent a message back to Sheridan from Woodstock, where the division had bivouacked for the night, that he hoped to spend Christmas in Lynchburg.[37] This, the twentieth, had been a fine day; "the weather . . . was most beautiful . . . it was as warm as Oct[ober]; the sky was perfectly cloudless & of a deep blue, the men too were in good temper, enjoying the march, remarking what a splendid trip it was."[38] The division marched through New Market that day and stopped for the night at Lacey Springs, nine miles north of Harrisonburg.

The First Brigade bivouacked to the east of the Valley Turnpike, a half mile south of the "mansion at the Springs" where Custer made his headquarters for the night; the Second Brigade, with the ambulances and supply wagons, bivouacked about the same distance north of the "mansion," and to the west of the turnpike. Many of the men were already out of rations and went foraging to the farmhouses near their camps, and "most of them came back well loaded."[39] When after a good supper the men bedded down for the night, the sky was still blue and clear, so much so that not a tent was put up. Soon after midnight, however, clouds driven by a strong northwest wind covered the sky, and a heavy fall of sleet mixed with snow and rain came pelting down. At the four o'clock reveille, as the men crawled out from under their blankets and ponchos, there were already five inches of sleet and snow on the ground, and there was no letup in the storm.

A short time later, the troopers of the First Brigade were finishing their breakfast, "Boots and Saddles" and then "Lead into Line" were blown, and the men, in no great hurry, were straggling in the storm and the darkness to form up, when suddenly they heard shots, followed quickly by the rebel yell and the sound of pounding

36. Hannaford, "Reminiscences," 235(b)–(c).
37. *Official Records*, Vol. XLIII, Pt. 2, p. 816.
38. Hannaford, "Reminiscences," 236(a).
39. The recital of the events of the night of December 20 at Lacey Springs is based on the eyewitness account of Hannaford, "Reminiscences," 236(a)–239(a), and all quotations in this and the next paragraph are from that source.

hoofbeats muffled by the snow underfoot, coming toward them from the north. The camp of the Second Brigade had been surprised and attacked from the north and west by Payne's, Rosser's, and Wickham's cavalry. The surprise was complete; the single vedette posted only three hundred yards from the camp in the direction from which the attackers came was shot down, and before Colonel Wells's men, still in the process of packing their gear and saddling up, could assemble, the enemy was upon them, "fairly into the camp, riding over beds, fires, horses & men, firing at everything they . . . [saw]." Fortunately for the Federals, it was still pitch dark, and most of them were able to scatter out of harm's way; hence casualties were few. Contrary to what happened at Cedar Creek two months before, the Confederates did not leave the ranks to plunder the camp; they remained in their places and, riding as fast as the state of the road would permit, moved down the turnpike to attack the First Brigade camp. But the few minutes' warning Colonel Pennington's men had had was enough to save them. The line they formed in great haste was neither as full nor as orderly as it should have been, but it was sufficient. The onrushing Confederates were brought to a halt by a volley and were then countercharged and driven down the turnpike toward Harrisonburg.

After his return to Kernstown, Custer received a "communication" from Sheridan, asking him to explain "how it happened that his camp was charged by the enemy."[40] Custer's response, in his report on the expedition, was an elaborate description of the posting of his pickets, followed by a series of statements of questionable accuracy—that the enemy "found the command in the saddle," that they, and not Custer's command, were the "surprised party," and that their losses greatly exceeded his.[41] Sheridan's memoirs make it sufficiently clear that he accepted Custer's "explanation" with a large grain of salt; he wrote that Custer "had to

40. The "communication" is not in the *Official Records*; Sheridan's query is, however, quoted in Custer's report, *Official Records*, Vol. XLIII, Pt. 1, pp. 676–77.

41. *Ibid.*, 676. In fairness to Custer it should be said that, as reported by Hannaford, some of the *First* Brigade were "in the saddle" when the Confederates attacked. It may be conceded to him also that the attackers were "surprised" to meet with any organized opposition.

abandon his bivouac and retreat down the valley, with the loss of a number of prisoners, a few horses, and a good many horse equipments, for, because of the suddenness of . . . [the] attack, many of the men had no time to saddle up."[42] It might have been better if Custer had admitted frankly that he had been caught by surprise and had pointed out the mitigating circumstances—that he had been assured there were no Confederate troops north of Staunton, and that the weather and the darkness enabled the attackers to make an undetected approach to the Second Brigade camp.[43]

To cap a report replete with what General Beatty called "exaggerations—romances, founded upon the smallest conceivable amount of fact," Custer then proceeded to detail his reasons for deciding to call off the expedition and start on his journey back to Kernstown as soon as the Confederate attack had been beaten off. The hopes—or mere bombast—of spending Christmas in Lynchburg went up in smoke in the chill, murky dawn at Lacey Springs. Custer reasoned, he said, that his men's rations would be exhausted that night, that for the next two days no more could be obtained by foraging, and that he lacked the means of caring for the men wounded in the predawn attack; finally, he said, "if it was decided to return, the sooner . . . [the] return was accomplished, the better it would be"—a splendid example of circular reasoning, eminently worthy of the "goat" of the West Point Class of 1861.[44]

The low intellectual quotient of Custer's decision is obvious enough; all the same, the retreat was ordered and the journey of the next two days was the most trying experience the veterans of the division had ever undergone. "The pike was too slippery for our horses not one of them rough shod to stand on, so we had to take to the fields. . . . the wind steadily increased in violence & the mercury fell with unparalleled velocity. By the time we reached Edinburgh the cold was intense." The second day of the retreat was even worse than the first:

42. Sheridan, *Personal Memoirs*, II, 102.
43. *Official Records*, Vol. XLIII, Pt. 1, p. 674.
44. *Ibid.*, 676. James H. Kidd, who served under Custer as colonel of the 6th Michigan and may be presumed to know whereof he spoke, wrote of Custer, "there are in his official reports many inaccuracies, not to employ a stronger term." James H. Kidd, "The Michigan Cavalry Brigade in the

It was most intensely cold[,] the men having to dismount & walk fully half the way to keep from freezing to death. . . . I say freezing to death not as a figure of speech but as a fact. . . . While passing over Fisher's Hill & the high knoll between Cedar Creek and Middleto[w]n I found it perfectly impossible to walk in the middle of the turnpike without support, for the road was high and rounding & very slippery & the wind was blowing so hard that I could not keep my footing.[45]

Thus, both Torbert's and Custer's expeditions ended in failure. The Virginia Central remained unbroken, and mercifully, the state of the weather and of the roads ruled out major military operations for the rest of the winter.

Early and his army were no longer a cause for concern to Sheridan, but despite the snow, the cold, and the barely passable roads, the guerrillas became an even more serious problem than they had been. "Refugees" from Early's army remained in the lower Valley and joined existing guerrilla bands or organized new ones. After Cedar Creek and Sheridan's move back to Kernstown, whole companies of cavalry were furloughed from Early's army "to operate in the lower Valley"; typically, the men of one such unit, Company B of the 12th Virginia, scattered to their homes after getting within the Federal lines, but assembled on call to swoop down on Federal wagon trains and on parties of soldiers small enough to be attacked safely—and profitably. The men of this unit operated in the neighborhood of Winchester, and before the end of the winter, "in various sorties and assaults killed, wounded and captured . . . more than three times . . . [their] own numbers, besides inflicting other losses on the enemy." There were numerous other groups of the same sort, there were the more "formal" Partisan Ranger units, Mosby's in particular, and there was the ubiquitous lone bushwhacker.[46]

Wilderness," MOLLUS, Commandery of Michigan, *War Papers, No. 11* (Detroit, 1888), 8.

45. Hannaford, "Reminiscences," 240(c)–(d), 243(d)–244(a). Luman Tenney of the same regiment noted in his diary, "The most uncomfortable day I ever passed. 45 2nd Ohio men with frozen feet." Tenney, *War Diary,* 140.

46. Baylor, *Bull Run to Bull Run,* 262, 264; most of the Laurel Brigade, many of whose men were residents of the Valley, were furloughed in this manner. Sheridan, *Personal Memoirs,* II, 110.

Sheridan wrote, and may actually have believed, that the guerrilla bands were a "benefit" to him, "as they prevented straggling and kept . . . [his] trains well closed up, and discharged such other duties as would have required a provost guard of at least two regiments of cavalry."[47] One must note, however, that this comment is to be found in Sheridan's report of the Shenandoah Valley Campaign, written nearly a year after the end of the war. His tune in the fall and winter of 1864 was quite different and with good reason. It was certainly not a benefit to the morale of his cavalry or of his command as a whole to have the troopers of the 17th Pennsylvania declare, as they did "frequently" in October and November, 1864, that "they would rather go on duty on the picket line, or go into battle, than do patrol duty on the highway between Harper's Ferry, Martinsburg, Winchester and the front."[48] Even less of a boost to cavalry morale was the Michigan Brigade's knowledge that of the 104 of their men killed or mortally wounded from the beginning to the end of the campaign 18 were victims of what they called "Mosby's men," that is, of guerrillas in general.[49] Nor is it likely that even Sheridan considered it a benefit that, as Colonel Oliver Edwards told him on October 2, it would require an escort of "at least 2,000 men" to move a train of 250 wagons from Winchester to Harrisonburg, or to be told that to ensure the delivery of dispatches between those two points, an escort of not less than five hundred "good cavalry" was needed.[50] Officers like Colonel Edwards had good reason to be concerned about the safety of the trains and dispatches they were called upon to forward, for only a short time before Mosby had attacked a train of 250 wagons escorted by General John P. Kenly's brigade of infantry and "a large force" of cavalry, and, after destroying 75 of the wagons, carried off between five and six hundred horses, two hundred head of beef cattle, and two hundred prisoners.[51]

47. *Official Records*, Vol. XLIII, Pt. 1, p. 55.
48. Moyer, *History of the 17th Regiment*, 135.
49. Kidd, *Personal Recollections*, 431.
50. *Official Records*, Vol. XLIII, Pt. 2, p. 263. Colonel Edwards wrote later, "Escorts with dispatches from the front have to cut their way through and generally lose half their men. . . . I think a train of 200 wagons should have an escort of 1,000 infantry and 500 cavalry." *Ibid.*, 277.
51. Mosby, *Mosby's War Reminiscences*, 290–92.

In point of fact, Sheridan was not nearly so casual about the guerrillas in late 1864 as his postwar report would lead one to believe. He wrote Grant on October 7, "Since I came into the Valley, from Harper's Ferry up to Harrisonburg, every train, every small party, and every straggler has been bushwhacked by people, many of whom have protection papers."[52] General Halleck urged him to use his cavalry to "completely clean out Mosby's gang of robbers"; Sheridan in turn blamed his lack of success in doing so on the poor quality of the regiments of cavalry posted in the lower Valley. He told Halleck on October 27 that one good regiment could at any time "clean out" "Mosby and the numerous robbers that now infest the country" if "the regimental commanders had spunk enough to try." He had, he said, cavalry regiments at Harper's Ferry, Martinsburg, and Winchester, a sufficient force to keep the lower Valley clear of guerrillas, but that "they do not do it." A month later he wrote General John D. Stevenson, in command at Harper's Ferry, that "if the Twelfth Pennsylvania Cavalry cannot keep that country clear of guerrillas," he would "take the shoulder straps off of every officer belonging to . . . [it] and dismount the regiment in disgrace."[53] This was tough talk, even if not entirely grammatical, but the threat remained just a threat; no action followed.

The divisional and brigade commanders of cavalry in the field did not need to be spurred to action by Sheridan. Colonel Powell, in the Luray Valley with his division of West Virginians, had two bushwhackers, taken prisoner on October 4, shot the next day "in retaliation for the murder of a soldier belonging to . . . [his] command by a bushwhacker"; ten days later, "having learned of the willful and cold-blooded murder of a U. S. soldier by two men (Chancellor and Myers, members of Mosby's gang of cut-throats and robbers)" he ordered the execution of a member of "Mosby's gang" captured the day before and left the body with a "placard on

52. *Official Records*, Vol. XLIII, Pt. 1, p. 30.
53. *Ibid.*, Pt. 2, p. 273; Pt. 1, p. 35. Halleck also wrote in this dispatch, "The two small regiments [the 13th and 16th New York] under General Augur have been so often cut up by Mosby's band that they are cowed and useless." The 8th Illinois, however, also in Augur's command, Mosby and his men considered to be their "most formidable enemies." Virgil C. Jones, *Ranger Mosby* (Chapel Hill, 1944), 221. See also *Official Records*, Vol. XLIII, Pt. 2, p. 665.

his breast with the following inscription: 'A. C. Willis, member of Company C, Mosby's command, hanged by the neck in retaliation for the murder of a U. S. soldier by Messrs. Chancellor and Myers' "; then, to complete the job, he sent a detachment to burn down Chancellor's house and farm buildings and drive off all his livestock. He concluded the report in which he described these events with the following statement:

> On the 5th and 15th instant it became my duty, though painful and repugnant to my own feelings, to order the execution of three . . . bushwhackers, in retaliation for two Union soldiers murdered by guerrillas, believing it to be the only means of protection of our soldiers against the operations of all such illegal and outlawed bands of horsethieves and murderers. . . . I wish it distinctly understood by the rebel authorities that if two to one is not sufficient I will increase it to twenty-two to one, and leave the consequences in the hands of my Government.[54]

In early October, near Dayton, Custer had a bushwhacker tried by court martial; the man was found guilty and shot.[55] A scouting party of the 1st New York (Lincoln) captured two of Harry Gilmor's men, and they were shot as spies the next day. It may perhaps be assumed that they were wearing Federal uniforms when caught. "One of Mosby's men" captured by the same regiment on October 12 was "hanged to the limb of a tree by the roadside, labeled 'In retaliation.' "[56] Toward the end of the month a trooper of the 6th Michigan named Briggs ("a favorite with all his company") was killed by a shot fired from one of two adjacent houses. The owners of the two houses were taken prisoner. Lieutenant H. H. Chipman of the Michigan regiment, sent out with a nine-man detail to bring in Brigg's body, concluded that one of the two prisoners had shot Briggs, "but which . . . [he] could not determine." "Only by the greatest effort" was he able to prevent his men from killing both prisoners out of hand, but ultimately he himself gave up the effort to determine which was guilty and, after having both houses set on fire, had both men shot.[57]

54. *Official Records*, Vol. XLIII, Pt. 1, pp. 508–10.
55. Hannaford, "Reminiscences," 178(c).
56. Beach, *First New York (Lincoln) Cavalry*, 439, 441. Gilmor himself was captured at Moorefield in January, 1865, by Major H. K. Young, Sheridan's chief of scouts, and imprisoned in Fort Warren. Sheridan, *Personal Memoirs*, II, 105–107; see also *Official Records*, Vol. XLVI, Pt. 1, pp. 455–57.
57. *Official Records*, Vol. XLIII, Pt. 2, p. 470. Chipman reported that

The most notorious instance of retaliation occurred following an attack by 120 of Mosby's men (Mosby had been wounded on September 15 and was not himself present) on a Union ambulance train near Front Royal on September 23. Unnoticed by the guerrillas, Merritt's Reserve Brigade was marching a short distance behind the ambulances. When the attack came, the Reserve Brigade galloped to the rescue, routed the guerrillas, and killed eighteen of them. According to the Federals, an officer of the brigade, Lieutenant Charles McMaster, 2nd United States, "was mortally wounded in this affair, being shot after he was taken prisoner and robbed." The claim of "some" of the guerrillas that McMaster was shot down while "fighting at the head of his detail in an attempt to cut off the enemy's retreat" is unconvincing.[58] Custer, at any rate, then still in command of Merritt's First Brigade, preferred to believe the Federal version and in retaliation had six of the captured prisoners executed. Four of the unfortunates were shot and two were hanged; one of the latter was left with a placard on his chest, reading "This will be the fate of Mosby and all his men."[59]

In a lengthy dispatch to General Lee five weeks later, Mosby spoke of the execution of the six men and of Colonel Powell's execution of another and declared that he intended "to hang an equal number of Custer's men." General Lee thought it proper to authorize Mosby to do as he proposed, and his decision was "cordially approved" by James A. Seddon, the Confederate secretary of war.[60] On November 6 at Rectortown, Mosby had twenty-seven Federal prisoners lined up and made to draw slips of paper out of a hat; twenty of the slips were blank, seven were numbered. Of the seven who drew numbered slips—as innocent of Custer's deed as

---

he "tried to procure ropes to hang the men," but without success. Thereupon he asked for volunteers to shoot them, and all nine men of his detachment—all of whom belonged to the same company as Briggs—stepped forward.

58. Jones, *Ranger Mosby*, 202–204, 207–208; *Official Records*, Vol. XLIII, Pt. 1, p. 441.

59. Jones, *Ranger Mosby*, 211. The fight of the Reserve Brigade is mentioned in a report of Merritt's, *Official Records*, Vol. XLIII, Pt. 1, p. 441, but not the execution of the six prisoners. There is no report from Custer on the incident in the *Official Records* but there seems to be no question that it occurred.

60. *Official Records*, Vol. XLIII, Pt. 2, pp. 909–10.

were the six Custer executed to avenge the murder of Lieutenant McMaster, if murder it was—two escaped, three were hanged, and two were shot.[61]

The grisly process of bushwhacking and murder followed by retaliation went on in a seemingly endless round, contributing nothing to the progress of the war except dead bodies, bitterness, and hatred. Sheridan himself furthered the process by ordering General Stevenson, if the railroad from Harper's Ferry to Winchester was "interfered with by guerrillas," to "arrest all male secessionists in Charlestown, Shepherdstown, Smithfield and Berryville, and in the adjacent country" to be jailed in Fort McHenry, and to "burn all grain, destroy all subsistence, and drive off all stock" belonging to the individuals arrested.[62] On October 3, Sheridan's topographical engineer, Lieutenant John R. Meigs, son of Quartermaster General Montgomery C. Meigs, was murdered near Dayton, well within the Union lines, by a group of three Confederates wearing Federal uniforms, "without resistance of any kind whatever, and without even the chance to give himself up."[63] This was the version of the incident reported to Sheridan by one of Meigs's two companions who escaped. The killers, Sheridan believed, had been visiting their homes in the vicinity and had been "secretly harbored by some of the neighboring residents," and he decided to teach the "abettors of the foul deed" a lesson they would never forget. He ordered burned every house within a five-mile radius of where the murder had been committed. The burning was actually begun the following morning, but after "a few houses in the immediate neighborhood of the scene of the murder had been burned," the order was countermanded.[64]

61. In a letter he sent to Sheridan under flag of truce, Mosby said that seven men had been executed. Jones, *Ranger Mosby*, 226–27.
62. *Official Records*, Vol. XLIII, Pt. 2, p. 565.
63. Sheridan, *Personal Memoirs*, II, 51. Sheridan's version is directly contradicted by General Early, who wrote that "Meigs was ordered to surrender by one of our scouts, to which he replied by shooting and wounding the scout, who in turn fired and killed the lieutenant." *Battles and Leaders*, IV, 525n. Early's version loses much of its credibility by his statement that the scouts wore "their uniform." If they did, they were a rare exception to the almost universal habit among Confederate scouts and guerrillas of wearing either civilian clothes or, more commonly, Federal uniforms or overcoats.
64. Sheridan, *Personal Memoirs*, II, 51–52; Hannaford, "Reminis-

In mid-August, as has been mentioned, Grant had suggested to Sheridan that if he could spare a division of cavalry, he should send it "through Loudoun County, to destroy and carry off the crops, animals, negroes, and all men under fifty years of age capable of bearing arms. In this way," Grant wrote, "you will get many of Mosby's men."[65] From mid-August to mid-November Sheridan's cavalry had other work to do, but on November 26 he wrote General Halleck, "I will soon commence work on Mosby. Heretofore I have made no attempt to break him up, as I would have employed ten men to his one, and for the reason that I have made a scapegoat of him for the destruction of private rights. . . . I will soon commence on Loudoun County, and let them know there is a God in Israel."[66] This was brave talk, and the next day, in a dispatch that was as much a dissertation as an order, he directed General Merritt to cross the Blue Ridge with his division and "operate against the guerrillas in the district . . . bounded on the south by the line of the Manassas Gap Railroad . . . on the east by the Bull Run range, on the west by the Shenandoah River, and on the north by the Potomac.[67] This area, covering a large part of Loudoun County, was "Mosby's Confederacy," the scene of many of his exploits and the chief source of his strength in men, information, and shelter. Merritt was ordered to "consume and destroy all forage and subsistence, burn all barns and mills and their contents, and drive off all stock"; he was told that the order "must be literally executed," but that "no dwellings are to be burned and . . . no personal violence offered to citizens." Merritt was out for the five days the orders specified and on his return reported that Sheridan's directions "were most fully carried out; the country on every side of the line of march was in every instance swept over by flankers . . . and in this way the entire valley was gone over."[68]

Neither Merritt nor the commanders of his First and Second

---

cenes," 179(d). Sheridan does not explain why he countermanded the order.

65. *Official Records*, Vol. XLIII, Pt. 1, p. 811.
66. *Ibid.*, Pt. 2, p. 671.
67. *Ibid.*, 679. The order is signed and was presumably written by James W. Forsyth, Sheridan's chief of staff.
68. *Ibid.*, Pt. 1, pp. 671–72, 55–56; Sheridan, *Personal Memoirs*, II, 99–100.

Brigades reported in detail on the property destroyed or seized, but Lieutenant Colonel Casper Crowninshield, 2nd Massachusetts, who had succeeded Colonel Lowell in command of the Reserve Brigade, reported that his small unit, which did not join the expedition until the second day out, had captured 87 horses, 474 beef cattle, and 100 sheep and burned 230 barns, 8 mills, 1 distillery, and an estimated 10,000 tons of hay and 25,000 bushels of grain.[69] As to the guerrillas themselves, however, it was a different story. General Merritt was forced to confess a total lack of success in that respect; he reported, "Efforts were made to run them down or capture them by stratagem, but these in most instances failed. The sides of the mountain[s] bordering Loudoun Valley are practicable throughout their entire extent for horsemen, and the guerrillas, being few in numbers, mounted on fleet horses and thoroughly conversant with the country, had every advantage."[70] The raid fulfilled expectations as far as the destruction or seizure of property was concerned, but none of the groups of guerrillas, Mosby's or any of the others, was broken up, and guerrilla activity in the area remained endemic. Within a month, however, Mosby himself, who had recovered from his September 15 wound and had been promoted to full colonel, was shot and gravely wounded while having dinner with friends near Rectortown, in the area lately devastated by General Merritt. Had it not been for the stupidity of the officer commanding the detachments of the 15th and 16th New York, one of whose troopers had shot Mosby, his career as a raider would have been at an end. As it was, he escaped, eventually recovered from his wound, and resumed his guerrilla operations.[71]

Merritt's sweep through Loudoun County, Torbert's unsuccessful

69. *Official Records*, Vol. XLIII, Pt. 1, p. 673. Sheridan wired General Stevenson at Harper's Ferry on the morning of Merritt's departure, "Should complaints come in from the citizens of Loudoun County tell them that they have furnished too many meals to guerrillas to expect much sympathy." *Ibid.*, Pt. 1, p. 687.

70. *Ibid.*, Pt. 1, p. 672.

71. *Ibid.*, 843–44. The officer, who was said to have been under the influence of liquor, did not recognize Mosby and thought that he was mortally wounded and not worth taking along as a prisoner. Jones, *Ranger Mosby*, 245–48.

raid toward Gordonsville, and Custer's discomfiture at Lacey Springs ended major operations in the Shenandoah Valley for 1864. Early sent off to General Lee Kershaw's division, followed a short time later by the division of Robert Rodes. With the weather making further operations impossible, Sheridan too reduced his forces and sent the VI Corps to reinforce Grant. The remaining infantry of the Army of the Shenandoah went into winter quarters around Kernstown; the cavalry did the same a short distance to the north, near Winchester.

Setting up a winter camp, building the log huts roofed over with shelter halves, had become well-rehearsed arts by the winter of 1864. Frame buildings—except churches, protected from desecration by stringent orders from headquarters—and fences were stripped of their boards to make rafters and doors; even stone walls were dismantled for material to build the indispensable fireplaces. Axes for felling trees for building logs and firewood were in short supply, and so were grindstones to sharpen them. Nails too were "exceedingly scarce," and Roger Hannaford had to smile when, after the war, he recalled "what pains we took to straighten out a lot of crooked, abominable rusty things that I worked nearly one whole afternoon to extract from the remains of an old ruined hut."[72]

Christmas came before any of the huts were built, and it was a cheerless affair. Custer's division had returned from Lacey Springs two days before the holiday. The weather turned mild, and the division's camps became "one perfect sea of mud; the horses stood nearly to their knees in mortar & it was nearly impossible to go from tent to tent."[73] There was no Christmas turkey for the cavalry; there was instead an issue of whiskey on Christmas Eve, which in the 2nd Ohio divided up into "a small horn for each man." Other regiments appear to have done better, notably the 3rd New Jersey, which, imbued with a combination of holiday and alcoholic spirits, marched in a body to Colonel Pennington's quar-

72. Stephen Z. Starr (ed.), "Winter Quarters Near Winchester, 1864–1865; Reminiscences of Roger Hannaford, Second Ohio Volunteer Cavalry," *The Virginia Magazine of History and Biography*, LXXXVI (1978), 329, 331, 336.
73. *Ibid.*, 321–22.

ters and gave him three cheers; later in the night, however, one of their men nearly killed his sergeant "for some real or fancied insult."[74]

On December 28, the day Torbert got back to Winchester, came good news from headquarters: permission for corps commanders to grant fifteen- or twenty-day leaves of absence to officers and furloughs of the same length to enlisted men. The latter were eligible for a furlough only if they had "faithfully performed their duties"; the absence of any such qualification for officers suggests that it was assumed they had all done so.[75] Only one field-grade officer and three line officers, and not more than five of every hundred enlisted men were permitted to be on leave from any regiment at one time. Then came New Year's Eve, and doubtless it was observed throughout the cavalry camps in much the same fashion as in the camp of the 2nd Ohio, described by Roger Hannaford:

When evening came on, the boys gathered around our fire, chatting of home and absent friends, relating incidents of other New Years, & debating whether it would be worth while to sit up & watch in the New Year; the crowd gradually fell away, until at ten o'clock I sat solitary & alone. . . . thinking of home & the loved ones there, hoping if spared life to spend my next New Year's eve with them; at last near eleven o'clock I grew tired & sleepy & crawled into our tent, with the comfortable feeling of a good night's sleep before me.[76]

Duty in winter quarters this year was generally light. The horses needed daily attention, of course—Custer's regiments cut large quantities of cedar and pine boughs and built high screens to protect their horses from the "terrific" winds ("Oh! the winds, they swoop down over Great North Mountain as if they intended to take everything bodily over the Blue Ridge")—but there was

74. *Ibid.*, 321. The 15th New York's "cold, cheerless" Christmas was made more bearable by the issue of a gill of whiskey to each man. Chauncey S. Norton, *"The Red Neck Ties," or, History of the Fifteenth New York Volunteer Cavalry* (Ithaca, 1891), 61. Instead of a turkey dinner, the 8th New York had an inspection on Christmas Day. Norton, *Deeds of Daring*, 105.
75. *Official Records*, Vol. XLIII, Pt. 2, p. 834. The twenty-day furloughs were to be given to men from Maine, New Hampshire, Vermont, Ohio, and Michigan, and states west of the last two.
76. Starr, "Winter Quarters," 323.

little drill, and dress parades were held only when there were orders to be read out. The picket duty was on a far less demanding scale than it had been in the first three winters of the war. Men were detailed for a variety of duties at headquarters, and other details were sent to Stephenson's Depot to load supply wagons. There were inspections, and officers' schools met in the evenings, but generally life was anything but strenuous, and the men had most of their afternoons free to spend as they liked.[77]

A story told by one of Custer's officers concerning shelter for the horses is worth repeating:

In our thickly wooded country there is positively no excuse . . . for a cavalry colonel letting his horses stand out in winter. . . . In the winter of 1864–65 . . . the [19th] New York . . . was commanded by a first class cavalry officer [Colonel Alfred Gibbs]. . . . The 6th New York Cavalry possessed for its commander a recently promoted . . . lieutenant-colonel [Charles L. Fitzhugh] . . . ignorant of horseflesh. . . . [Gibbs] in one week from his arrival had stables, with good straw roofs overhead, for all his horses. The other built good quarters for his men, and left his horses almost unstabled, entirely uncovered.[78]

One of the orders read out at dress parade came from Sheridan himself. Every company commander in the "Cavalry Corps" was directed to report to his regimental headquarters the "name of every man whom they considered unfit for the cavalry service either thro. abuse or neglect of their horses, or thro. cowardice or any other cause," for transfer to the infantry. Troopers of the 2nd Ohio (their numbers are not known) so reported were transferred to Colonel Rutherford B. Hayes's regiment, the 23rd Ohio Infantry, as "being unfit for the honor of the Cav[alry] service."[79]

The cavalry camps lay within five or six miles of the southern terminus of the Winchester & Potomac Railroad; hence there should have been ample rations for men and animals alike, but there were shortages just the same. Roger Hannaford, who, as quartermaster sergeant of his company was ideally placed to know, asserted,

77. Gause, *Four Years with Five Armies*, 350.
78. [Whittaker], *Volunteer Cavalry*, 55. As a former commander of a battery of horse artillery attached to the Cavalry Corps, Fitzhugh should have known better.
79. Hannaford, "Reminiscences," 186(b)–(c).

while we lay in winter quarters we did not draw enough to eat. . . . our own mess would never make their 5 days' rations go over 4, often indeed 3 to 3½ days, this notwithstanding that bitter experience had taught us strict economy. . . . We used to be short on bread more than any one article, yet I used to think we got our full rations, for we drew 2 days' fresh bread & 3 days of crackers & most of the men would have their bread finished at the end of the first day, that is, a loaf that weighed 2¼ lbs., at least that is what it should have weighed & it may have done so. . . . With crackers it did rather better, but with even these we fell short. . . . These are the plain facts, & the men used to live on parched corn, &c. for a day or so before we would draw rations, & would be so utterly ravenous when they came that at least one day's rations would go at a meal.[80]

Still, the situation of Custer's and Merritt's regiments near Winchester was relatively comfortable compared to that of regiments in outlying posts. The 22nd Pennsylvania was stationed at New Creek, West Virginia, on the line of the Baltimore & Ohio, near Cumberland. The regiment camped "in the large bottom above the railroad station, between the station and the river." The regimental historian has recorded that "As a train of coal cars would approach, a number of the men would board the moving train and toss off large lumps of coal while the train was passing camp. This practice soon brought a complaint from the shippers and from the railroad company, which resulted in a sufficient supply of coal being furnished to the camp."[81] The men were thus enabled to keep warm without the necessity of cutting their own firewood. In the absence of any complaint in the regimental chronicle, it may be assumed that the men also received adequate issues of rations. It was far otherwise for the horses.

[They] were obliged to stand out in zero weather and driving storm with no protection but a blanket. Oftentimes without feed or hay for a day or longer. . . . the suffering of the poor animals from cold and starvation must have been terrible. They gnawed and literally ate up the rails to which they were hitched, and their cries at night were heart-rending. A large number, 200 at least, died right there, starved and frozen to death through incompetency and inefficiency . . . some-

80. Starr, "Winter Quarters," 325.
81. This and the following quotation are from Farrar, *The Twenty-Second Pennsylvania*, 444, 446; see also *Official Records*, Vol. XLIII, Pt. 2, p. 469.

where higher up. . . . Why baled hay was not supplied in abundance by railroad, was a wonder then and is today.

The reader of Comrade Farrar's regimental history might wonder also why, with miles of forest surrounding its camp, the 22nd Pennsylvania did not build some sort of shelter, however crude, for its miserable animals. Obviously, not all the "incompetency and inefficiency" were "somewhere higher up."

On January 6, 1865, the entire Third Division was turned out to witness the execution of two deserters, "Germans" belonging to the 3rd New Jersey. The two men had a grievance against some of their officers and decided to desert and "join 'the rebels' " Riding up the Valley, they fell in with a detachment of what they took to be " 'grayback' Cavalry," but was actually Major H. K. Young, Sheridan's chief of scouts and a group of his men, wearing as always Confederate uniforms. The would-be deserters answered freely Young's questions about the "picket posts, how & where posted, where each Brigade and Regiment were, how situated, the strength of each Regiment" and said they were willing to "guide a force between the pickets at night, for the purpose of capturing General Custer & the 1st Brigade." At a signal from Young, the deserters were surrounded and disarmed. They were escorted back to camp, and when a few days later "they were brot out as an example to the whole Division & shot, not a single dissenting voice was there to the verdict, 'served them right.' "[82]

Toward the end of February, rumors of peace filled the camps. In a letter to his wife, Hannaford tried to express what he took to be the "universal opinion" of his regiment: "the soldiers talk over these rumors with a quiet smile & turn away with some expression of disdain or disbelief on their lips; they believe that Grant, Sherman, Sheridan, Thomas & Co. are the best peace commissioners. Yet we desire peace, no men more than we do, but we *want an honorable peace or none at all.*"[83] These were the feelings of men

82. Starr, "Winter Quarters," 334; Norton, *Deeds of Daring*, 106, supplies the information that the two would-be deserters belonged to the 3rd New Jersey. Sheridan reported to Halleck that he had ordered the execution of the two men because he "thought it best to make an example of them at once. We have lost a great many men by desertion, particularly in coming from Washington to join their regiments." *Official Records*, Vol. XLVI, Pt. 2, p. 56.

83. Starr, "Winter Quarters," 334. Hanaford wrote his letter two days

who, at the same time, shared a revulsion from war that Hannaford expressed in another letter home: "Folks at home know nothing of war. God grant they never may. May you all be saved from
seeing such scenes of desolation & ruin as I have witnessed the
last 10 Mos. . . . I *cannot* help pitying the suffering of the Southern
women, and still more the little children. Yet I don't want peace
at the sacrifice of honor."[84] Hannaford's feeling of pity for the
women and children of the South had its source partly in his in-
nate decency, and partly in the friendship that grew between him
and the family of John L. Grant, on whose farm the 2nd Ohio had
its winter camp. As quartermaster sergeant and company clerk,
Hannaford had a great deal of writing to do—records to keep, reports to be compiled and prepared—which he could not do well in
the dark cramped hut he shared with two other men, and he got
into the habit of taking his work to the Grant farmhouse. He grew
fond of the Grants, their two little girls and their infant son
(named Lee Grant) and they of him, and he was able to repay
their hospitality with an occasional bushel or two of oats for
Grant's horses.[85]

The changeable winter weather of the Valley invited sickness.
On January 1, the 1st Vermont, an exceptionally large regiment,
had 292 men on the sick list out of the 593 it had present for
duty.[86] The winter was also the time for recruits to join their regi-

---

after the "Hampton Roads Conference" between President Lincoln and
commissioners appointed by Jefferson Davis. In a letter Hannaford wrote
his wife on February 17 he said, "peace rumors have died entirely away. We
do not feel disappointed or very bad about it, for we never believed it would
amount to anything." In yet another letter, on February 25, he wrote, "we
want . . . [the South] whipped worse yet & I think it necessary, before we
can make a peace honorable or lasting; we may be mistaken, we indeed
hope so, for we do not want one single life, or drop of blood, to be spent unnecessarily." *Ibid.*, 333–34.
    84. *Ibid.*, 329–30.
    85. In mid-January, the officers of the 2nd Ohio decided to begin work
on a regimental history. The committee in charge of the project requested
all company commanders to "furnish a complete history of their Companies,
the name of every man that ever belonged to it, & a full history of him since
he joined, also a list of the killed, wounded, &c., &c." The work of assembling this mass of data fell on the company clerks, of whom Hannaford
was one. Winter camp was broken up before the work had progressed very
far, and the history of the 2nd Ohio was never written. *Ibid.*, 334; Tenney,
War Diary, 146.
    86. Benedict, *Vermont in the Civil War*, II, 664.

ments, but not without the organizational problems that persisted throughout the war. Thus, of the 629 recruits credited to the 17th Pennsylvania at this time, 54 never showed up.[87] The 2nd Ohio had an even more disturbing manpower problem. The regiment had been without a colonel since the muster-out of George A. Purington upon the expiration of his term of enlistment. Lieutenant Colonel A. Bayard Nettleton was exceedingly anxious to possess a colonel's eagles, but the regiment did not have enough men to entitle it to muster a full colonel, so Nettleton, Hannaford reports, "hunted up a long list of recruits. . . . to our Company was added (I think) seventeen recruits, not one of whom ever joined, or indeed were ever heard of excepting 2 or 3; beside[s] this, men that we knew to be dead or deserters . . . were put on the Muster Rolls. . . . Indeed it was on this fictitious strength that more than one 2nd Lieutenant was mustered into service." And, Hannaford adds, "This will account to a civilian for the great disparity between the Official returns & the actual strength in the field."[88] One may indeed wonder how prevalent such falsifications were, to confuse army commanders no less than historians.

The weather began to turn mild toward the end of February, and signs of an early move began to appear. Orders came down from headquarters requiring that the points and edges of sabers be sharpened. On Sunday morning, February 26, Custer staged a review of his division. "The sun shone down very warm and bright" that day, but the roads were "flooded with water from the melting snow." The men of the Third Division were up early and, as Hannaford recorded, "had our arms & equipments in nice order, our clothes slicked up so that both man & horse were in the best possible condition for the review." The review went off well and shortly after noon, when the regiments returned to their quarters, came word that the cavalry was to leave winter quarters at daylight the next morning. Then came a frenzy of activity. Damaged and worn-out equipment had to be collected and officially con-

87. Moyer, *History of the 17th Regiment*, 288.
88. Starr, "Winter Quarters," 330–31. Hannaford's statement is unquestionably correct, since, as company clerk, it was his duty to maintain the company muster roll. Nettleton was not mustered as colonel until April 22, 1865; in the meantime, however, he commanded the regiment as lieutenant colonel.

demned, with a proper record made of each and every piece; clothing had to be drawn, issued, and charged to the men who needed
it; five or six days' rations had to be distributed; in short, "a thousand & one things to do & a short time to do it in."[89]

Before Roger Hannaford tumbled into his bunk late that night,
he dashed off a letter home, as did many of his comrades. He
wrote his wife, "everything belonging to Uncle Sam is moving,
and if we wish to win new laurels in what I hope will be the death
blow to the rebellion, why it is *time* we were up & doing."[90]

Long before dawn on the twenty-seventh the division was in
the saddle and began moving out, halting on the road in front of
the Grants's farmhouse to wait for daylight. Then, wrote Hannaford,

We had gone at least a quarter of a mile toward Winchester when I
determined to ride back & bid farewell to Mr. Grant's family . . . I galloped back & found Mr. G[rant]. . . . He gave me a hearty shake of the
hand & then I turned to Mrs. Grant . . . she said she was glad I thought
enough of them to come & bid them good bye, then she bid me good
bye, hoping that I would live to rejoin my wife & child & that soon, &
then with a tear in her eye & a hearty shake of the hand she bid me
"good bye, God bless you" then I bid good bye to the two little girls who
stood behind their mother gazing at me . . . & with a tear standing in
my eye I put spurs to my horse & soon overtook my Company.[91]

89. *Ibid.*, 335–36.
90. *Ibid.*, 337.
91. *Ibid.*, 338.

XIII

Marching as to War

WHILE HIS MEN WERE MAKING THE BEST OF THEIR STAY in winter quarters, Sheridan was occupied with the manifold administrative duties of the commander of a large and complex military division and had to deal besides with the excursions and alarums caused by the ever-active guerrillas. In an occasional dispatch to Grant he spoke of the bad weather in the Valley, extremely cold, as much as twelve inches of snow on the ground, the coldest and worst winter he had ever experienced, which made it "utterly impossible to do anything"; it was not so bad, however, as to stop the activities of the guerrillas, or of the small groups of regularly organized Confederate horse that remained with the colors throughout the winter.[1]

On November 28, in broad daylight, the Federal post at New Creek, West Virginia, "was completely surprised by the enemy and captured almost without resistance." The garrison, commanded by Colonel George R. Latham, consisted of 200 artillerymen and 500 dismounted cavalry, only 160 of the latter being armed, "and they principally with arms which had been condemned." The attackers were Rosser's and Payne's brigades of cavalry, commanded by Rosser himself, and numbering according to the Federals about

1. *Official Records*, Vol. XLVI, Pt. 2, pp. 545, 27, 496, 780.

2,000.[2] Warned the previous day to expect an attack, Latham arranged to have picketed the approaches to the post as much as eight miles out. Rosser's force, with the men in the front ranks wearing Union army overcoats, was taken by the pickets for a returning scouting party Latham had sent out the day before. The pickets were captured before they realized their error or could give the alarm; with the men clad in the Union army overcoats still in front, the attackers rode boldly into the town. They were not recognized as Confederate cavalry until they began shooting. The garrison was not under arms, as it should have been after the warning Latham had received, and all 700 men were taken prisoner. After plundering and setting on fire the government warehouses in the town, the raiders departed with their prisoners.[3]

On December 6, Sheridan ordered Latham dishonorably dismissed from the service "for the shameful and disgraceful conduct in allowing the enemy's cavalry to capture his strong post . . . without firing a gun."[4] Sheridan held Latham's immediate superior, General Benjamin F. Kelley ("In command of Forces West of Hancock") partially to blame, but in his case confined himself to sarcasm in dispatches to Kelley himself and, about Kelley, to General Halleck, but he also wrote the latter, "I very much fear that, until all the troops of Western Virginia are sent to points remote from their homes, there will be a recurrence of dishonorable conduct."[5] Ten days later Sheridan ordered dismissed from the service

2. *Ibid.*, Vol. XLIII, Pt. 1, pp. 660, 656. In his brief report, Rosser does not mention the size of his force (*ibid.*, 669–70), It is hardly likely that he would have had more than half the force with which the Federals credited him.

3. The numerous dispatches covering this affair are in *ibid.*, 653–68, 669–70.

4. Stanton ordered Sheridan to revoke his dismissal order and to have Latham tried by court-marital; "If he be guilty of cowardice or disloyalty, as you allege," Stanton wrote, "he should be shot. It is necessary that an example be made of officers surrendering their posts." Sheridan revoked the dismissal order and convened a court-martial, which found Latham guilty and sentenced him to dismissal from the service. On March 19, 1865, however, the court-martial sentence was revoked and he was given an honorable discharge at his own request. *Ibid.*, Pt. 2, pp. 747, 746, 780; Pt. 1, p. 662n. In some dispatches, Latham is incorrectly identified as colonel of the 6th West Virginia; he was colonel of the 5th West Virginia.

5. *Ibid.*, Pt. 2, p. 717.

Lieutenant Nelson B. Holcomb of the 21st New York for allowing a scouting party of fifty men of his regiment to be surprised by the enemy, with the loss of three men killed and twenty-seven taken prisoner.[6]

A few days before Christmas, Governor Andrew I. Boreman of West Virginia wired Secretary Stanton that Rosser, with three thousand cavalry, had left Petersburg on a raid aimed at the Baltimore & Ohio as far west as Grafton. In accordance with standing orders, the message was repeated to Sheridan by the War Department telegraph office. Sheridan responded by wiring Stanton, "If I were to make disposition of the troops under my command in accordance with the information received from the commanders in . . . Western Virginia, whom I have found . . . always alarming in their reports and stupid in their duties and actions, I certainly would have my hands full. . . . It was only yesterday that Rosser was at Crab Bottom—according to their reports . . . it was only two or three days previous that Rosser was at Romney, &c."[7] As Sheridan was about to learn, this was not the sort of dispatch to send to the "Ogre of the War Department." Stanton was not to be trifled with by the victor of the Opequon, Fisher's Hill, and Cedar Creek, any more than by the most recently commissioned second lieutenant. Sheridan received a reply from Stanton that had all the delicacy of a solid shot from a 12-pounder Napoleon:

No one, that I am aware of, has asked you to make disposition of your troops in accordance with the information received from the commanders in . . . [Western] Virginia. Governor Boreman's dispatch was . . . sent . . . in accordance with general instructions to give military commanders every report that comes here in respect to movements of the enemy in their commands. They are expected to form their own judgments of its value. It has been supposed that such information might be useful and desired by you, as it is by other commanders who are your seniors in the service, without provoking . . . [a] disrespectful reply. With your subordinate commanders you will take such action as you please, but such reports as come to this Department in relation to the movements of the enemy will be forwarded as heretofore, and will be expected to be received with the respect due the Department of which you are the subordinate.[8]

6. *Ibid.*, 765, 752, 753. Holcomb himself was badly wounded in this affair.

7. *Ibid.*, 822, 823.

8. *Ibid.*, 824.

As it turned out, Governor Boreman's information was in error only with respect to Rosser's destination, and Sheridan not only had to swallow Stanton's rebuke, but to eat his own words as well. On the night of January 11, with a force estimated by the Federals as seven hundred and reported by General Early as three hundred, Rosser attacked the Union garrison at Beverly, West Virginia, made up of the 34th Ohio Infantry and the 8th Ohio.[9] In command at Beverly was Lieutenant Colonel Robert Youart of the cavalry regiment. Made careless by "the severity of the weather, the high water of the rivers, and the statements of the citizens 'that it was impossible for the enemy to attack at that time of the year,'" Youart had single sentries posted at night, only four hundred yards from his camp and three hundred yards from each other. Rosser's men, wearing U.S. Army overcoats as usual, captured the lone sentinel posted on the byroad on which they made their approach before he could give the alarm. The first knowledge the men in the camp had that the enemy was upon them was when they heard them pounding on the doors of their huts, demanding that they surrender. "The surprise was complete; our forces did not have time to rally even one company together." Nevertheless, some resistance was attempted, resulting in the killing of 6 and the wounding of 23 Ohioans, 580 of whom were taken prisoner. The only credit the cavalry could claim from this affair was that the majority of the casualties—5 of the killed, 17 of the wounded, and 338 of the prisoners—were theirs.

Colonel Nathan Wilkinson, 6th West Virginia Infantry, sent to investigate "the late disaster," reported that the regimental officers had "repeatedly" called Colonel Youart's attention "to the insufficiency of the guard for picket duty," that "the whole command was latterly in a loose state of discipline," and that on the evening before the attack there was a ball in the town, "largely attended by officers, who remained there until a late hour." On the strength of Wilkinson's report, General Crook recommended that both Youart and the officer commanding the 34th Ohio Infantry be "dismissed

9. For the Federal estimate of Rosser's numbers see *ibid.*, Vol. XLVI, Pt. 1, p. 448; the number three hundred, based on information from General Early, is given in General Lee's dispatch to Secretary of War Seddon, *ibid.*, 451. The account in the text of Rosser's capture of Beverly is based on Colonel Wilkinson's report, *ibid.*, 447–50, and all quotations in this and the succeeding paragraph are from that source.

the service for disgraceful neglect of their commands."[10] In his notification to General Halleck of the incident, Sheridan commented, "there seems to be a total want of discipline or soldierly qualities about troops in this section of country."[11] He may well have been right on both counts, but the main problem seems to have been a lack of self-disciplined and soldierly regimental commanders, and not in Beverly alone, a state of affairs not surprising in a military backwater. Wisely, Sheridan notified Halleck two days later, "I am now on my way to make an inspection of the Department of West Virginia."[12]

All in all, there was little comfort for anyone like Sheridan, as demanding of his subordinates as he was of himself, in the winter's events in his sprawled-out military division. The pursuit of a casual group of thirty-eight furloughed Confederate cavalrymen, who on February 4 derailed a Baltimore & Ohio freight train three and a half miles from Harper's Ferry and robbed the engineer and fireman of their money and watches, was mismanaged by Lieutenant Harlow M. Guild of the 12th Pennsylvania, whom his commanding officer forthwith recommended for dismissal from the service.[13] With the horse well out of the stable, Sheridan ordered General Devin to send a strong regiment to the area to protect the railroad, commenting:

The neighborhood has of late been infested with guerrillas and men from the rebel army who are visiting their friends, getting clothes, plundering, &c. . . . The commanding officer will . . . dispose of the lawless ruffians who are committing the outrages spoken of. No quarter will be given these persons who have destroyed by their actions the right to be treated as prisoners of war. When a guerrilla is found on a plantation or at a habitation, the fences, &c., of the farm will be destroyed, and the citizens generally will be given to understand that if they continue to harbor these villains they will be turned from their homes and sent through our lines.[14]

10. *Ibid.*, 449.
11. *Ibid.*, Pt. 2, p. 108.
12. *Ibid.*, 142.
13. *Ibid.*, 384, 411. The comment on Guild by his commanding officer, Colonel Marcus A. Reno, was, "I do not design that he be court-martialled, as that would occupy more time than he is worth. He is entirely unfit for a commission . . . although never what you could charge as drunkenness, he is always full, and when not stupefied with whiskey he is with opium." *Ibid.*, Pt. 1, p. 455.
14. *Ibid.*, Pt. 2, pp. 411–12.

Two weeks later came another failure; a 224-man force made up of men from the 14th Pennsylvania and the 21st New York, commanded by Major Thomas Gibson of the Pennsylvania regiment, was sent across the Blue Ridge with two deserters from Mosby's command as guides, to search houses as far east as Upperville for guerrillas and furloughed Confederate soldiers. The expedition was mismanaged from the start; the men were armed only with their carbines, and then the two halves into which Gibson divided his command so as to search a wider area failed to meet as planned for the return to base. The group led by Gibson himself was ambushed and routed, with the loss of the forty prisoners and hundred horses it had captured, plus an unknown but large number of its own men taken prisoner.[15] Sheridan forwarded the reports of the expedition to General Halleck with the comment that there was "no doubt that this scout was badly managed by all concerned," and that the affair was being investigated.[16] To cast an even more unfavorable light on this badly bungled operation, Captain Henry E. Snow, 21st New York, in command of the second group, reported that he had taken ten men to search a house a mile from Upperville, leaving the rest of his detachment in the village; when he returned he found about a third of his men "very much under the influence of liquor" and had to leave six of them behind, they being "so intoxicated it was impossible to get them along."[17]

Sheridan made a brief mention of this fiasco in one of his reports to Grant, who replied that "the number of surprises in West Virginia indicate negligence on the part of officers and troops. . . . Hereafter, when these disasters occur, cause an investigation to be made . . . and when there has been neglect, punish it."[18] Considerably less helpful, and certainly no salve for Sheridan's pride, was a dispatch from Assistant Adjutant General E. D. Townsend; "The Secretary of War directs me to inform you," Townsend wrote, "that . . . [t]he frequent disasters in your command have occa-

15. *Ibid.*, Pt. 1, pp. 462, 463–67; Pt. 2, p. 605.
16. *Ibid.*, Pt. 1, p. 463.
17. *Ibid.*, 467.
18. *Ibid.*, Pt. 2, p. 619. Sheridan replied to Grant, "There is and has been an inexcusable carelessness on the part of the officers and troops in the Department of West Virginia. I have dismissed, subject to the approval of the President, in all cases."

sioned much regret in this Department, as indicating a want of vigilance and discipline which, if not speedily cured, may occasion greater misfortune."[19] But even before this dispatch was sent, Sheridan had still another humiliating episode to report, one that at least symbolically was harder to swallow than any that had preceded it. At three A.M. on February 21, a party of about thirty men of Jesse McNeill's Partisan Rangers entered Cumberland after capturing the picket, rode directly to General Crook's head-quarters, and took prisoner Crook himself, General Kelley, and the latter's assistant adjutant general. Ten minutes after entering the town they rode off into the night with their three prisoners and fifteen or twenty horses. The raiders were pursued by a fifty-man cavalry detachment from Cumberland; other detachments, from New Creek and from Custer's division at Winchester, joined in the pursuit, but the raiders, mounted on good horses, escaped. The three prisoners were taken to Richmond, but within a month Crook was exchanged and was able to resume active duty.[20]

Despite their numerous successes, the guerrillas did not have things all their own way. On February 18 a scouting party of the 1st Michigan brought in the dead bodies, clad in Federal uniforms, of "two of the most notorious guerrillas, Augustine and Cox."[21] The following day a detachment of the 8th Illinois, stationed at Fairfax Station, brought in fifteen prisoners, members of "Kinche-loe's band," and two days later they came in with another haul of

19. *Ibid.*, 683. Sheridan replied on February 25, "Most of the captured have come in. This party was stampeded, and the whole affair badly man-aged." At the same time that Stanton had Townsend write Sheridan, he him-self wrote to Grant, "The frequent surprises in Sheridan's command has [*sic*] excited a good deal of observation recently. . . . There has been negli-gence, I am afraid, along that whole line for months, and I have been in daily apprehension of disaster." *Ibid.*, 702, 608.

20. The capture of the three officers and the subsequent pursuit of the raiders (who are reported in Federal dispatches as numbering 50, 60, 50 to 60, 50 to 150, and 100) are the subject of numerous reports and orders; see in particular *ibid.*, 621, 620, 622, 625, 684; and Pt. 1, pp. 468, 471. Major E. S. Troxel, 22nd Pennsylvania, with 150 men, actually caught up with the raiders beyond Moorefield, attacked their rear guard, and captured three of their men and five horses. He then "learned," presumably from his prison-ers, that the raiders had been reinforced (he actually outnumbered them five to one), and, his horses being "much worn down," he gave up the pur-suit. *Ibid.*, Pt. 2, p. 667.

21. *Ibid.*, Pt. 2, p. 592.

eight prisoners, including the colonel of the 1st Virginia and three members of Mosby's battalion; Colonel Gamble proudly reported that the regiment had taken thirty-four prisoners in five days without sustaining any loss.[22]

In the course of these events, Sheridan's time in the Shenandoah Valley was drawing to a close. On February 8, Grant, dwelling as he unceasingly did on the problem of the railroads keeping Richmond and Petersburg supplied, wrote Sheridan that Rodes's division and Wickham's cavalry had joined Lee; hence, Grant thought, the enemy troops left in the Valley could not stop Sheridan from reaching the Virginia Central and the James River Canal when the weather made it possible for him to resume active operations.[23] Sheridan assured Grant that he was "very certain" of being able to break both the railroad and the canal as soon as the end of wintry weather allowed a campaign to get under way, but that, with twelve inches of snow still on the ground, he was as yet unable to move.[24] A week later Sheridan was in Baltimore, and his chief of staff sent him word that the snow around Winchester was beginning to melt. Back at his headquarters on the twenty-first, Sheridan wired Grant that the snow was "going fast," and that he hoped to start his move south on the twenty-fifth.[25] When the day came, however, he had to tell Grant that he had not been able to leave as scheduled; he was awaiting the arrival of Devin's brigade from Loudoun County and of some pontoons from Washington which he needed because "all the streams in the country are at present unfordable," but he added that he would get off on Monday, February 27.[26] This time he was as good as his word; at daylight on the twenty-seventh the First and Third Divisions and a brigade of the Second Division were on the road south.

Sheridan himself directed the expedition, and under him, in

22. *Ibid.*, 595, 627.
23. *Ibid.*, 495.
24. *Ibid.*, 496. Grant wired in reply that Sheridan need not move "until the weather and roads are such as to give assurance of overcoming all obstacles." *Ibid.*, 553.
25. *Ibid.*, 619–20.
26. *Ibid.*, 701. Devin and his brigade, then "cleaning out" Loudoun County (which had been "cleaned out" by Merritt only three months before) were ordered on February 21 to return to Winchester as quickly as possible. *Ibid.*, 622, 667.

immediate command of the cavalry, was Wesley Merritt as acting chief of cavalry. Torbert was away on leave in the latter part of February and Sheridan decided not to recall him, making it abundantly clear that he no longer wanted Torbert to command his cavalry, and that he was much relieved to be able to relegate him to the command of the greatly reduced cavalry force he was leaving behind in the Valley.[27] Torbert had had his chance and by Sheridan's lights had failed to measure up. Under Merritt were Thomas C. Devin, now a brigadier general, in command of the First Division, and Custer in command of the Third. The First Division had Colonel Peter Stagg's First or Michigan Brigade (5th, 6th, and 7th Michigan and a detachment of the 1st Michigan), Colonel Charles L. Fitzhugh's Second Brigade (6th, 9th, and 19th New York, 17th and 20th Pennsylvania, and four companies of the 4th New York), and Brigadier General Alfred Gibbs's Reserve Brigade (2nd, 5th, and 6th United States, 2nd Massachusetts, 6th Pennsylvania, and four companies of the 1st Rhode Island). Colonel Alexander C. M. Pennington, Jr., commanded the First Brigade (1st Connecticut, 3rd New Jersey, 2nd New York, and 2nd Ohio) of Custer's division, and Colonel John J. Coppinger commanded the Second Brigade (8th, 15th, and 22nd New York, 1st Vermont, two companies of the 3rd Indiana, and a detachment of the 1st New Hampshire); added to the division as its Third Brigade was that of Colonel Henry Capehart (1st New York (Lincoln), 3rd West Virginia, seven companies of the 2nd, and a detachment of the 1st, West Virginia), formerly a part of the Second Division. Outside the divisional organization was the two-regiment (14th and 22nd Pennsylvania) brigade of Brigadier General William B. Tibbits.[28] The horse artillery taken

27. Sheridan, *Personal Memoirs*, II, 112.
28. Two of the brigade commanders, Colonels Fitzhugh and Pennington, and the commander of the 2nd New York of Pennington's brigade, Colonel Alanson M. Randol, were Regulars. They had all, with the rank of lieutenant, commanded batteries of horse artillery when they were given high rank in the volunteer service and the opportunity for distinction. When Merritt became acting chief of cavalry and Devin succeeded him in command of the First Division, Fitzhugh succeeded Devin in command of the Second Brigade. Then, as always, West Point looked after its own. If the appointment of "outsiders" to regimental command was resented by the units affected, it is not reflected in the regimental histories. It is worthy of notice

on the expedition consisted of a mere two sections of four guns.

Sheridan began the march with 9,239 mounted men and 554 gunners, a total force of 9,793, rank and file.[29] He told Grant that "the cavalry officers say the cavalry was never in such good condition." The officers may well have been right. With the exception of a relatively small number of recruits, the force was made up of tough veterans, inured to every kind of hardship, able to take care of themselves in any situation, all of whom had had a restful two months in camp, or even a furlough at home. The historian of the 2nd West Virginia described them as enjoying "the best of health and spirits."[30] Most of the horses were in good condition also; they too had had two months' rest and plenty of feed. Judging from a report General Meigs sent Secretary Stanton on February 23, all broken-down animals at Winchester had been replaced; indeed, the replacement program had been on a lavish scale, and Meigs complained, "The great consumption of horses in the Shenandoah Valley is a most serious expense. . . . the last reports show a cavalry force in that region . . . present for duty 11,214 men, and . . . there have been forwarded . . . [there] between the 1st of December, 1864, and 20th of February, 1865, 8,255 . . . remounts. The Government has apparently replaced the horses of three-fourths of the men present for duty in less than three months, during which time there has been no great battle."[31]

---

also, as an indication of the reduced strength of many regiments and the attrition of the officers' corps, that of the twenty-six whole regiments listed, only two were commanded by full colonels; twelve were commanded by lieutenant colonels, seven by majors, two by captains, and one by a lieutenant; the three last, however, were regiments of Regulars.

29. *Official Records*, Vol. XLVI, Pt. 2, p. 754. The slightly higher total of 9,987 given by Sheridan in his report on the march is labeled as his "effective force." *Ibid.*, Pt. 1, p. 475. At Kernstown, where the entire command assembled shortly after the start, there was a hurried inspection of men and horses, and all those "judged unable to stand a hard march were sent back to Winchester." Hannaford, "Reminiscences," 265(b). The number thus weeded out does not appear in the records.

30. Sutton, *History of the Second Regiment*, 185.

31. Notwithstanding the 8,255 horses delivered to Sheridan in three months, plus the unknown number of horses captured from the enemy or seized from farmers when he marched from Winchester, he left behind 3,553 men who were dismounted and also lacked "horse equipments" and carbines. *Official Records*, Vol. XLVI, Pt. 2, pp. 656, 724.

Sheridan's orders for the march required every trooper to carry on "his person" seventy-five rounds of ammunition and five days' rations, plus thirty pounds of grain ("short forage" in army language) for his horse. Wheeled transport was to be limited to a total of thirty wagons loaded with small-arms ammunition, coffee, sugar, salt, and the pontoons, and, for each division, one headquarters wagon, five ambulances, and two wagons for medical supplies.[32] Three days after the march began, Merritt ordered that "Strong foraging parties . . . be detailed by brigade commanders. . . . Great care must be taken in selecting competent officers for this service. . . . No soldier will be allowed on any pretense whatever to enter private dwellings. All pillaging and marauding will be punished summarily. Division commanders will issue strict orders . . . to prevent their men from obtaining liquor."[33] General Devin's report on the campaign strongly suggests that to some extent at least, the prohibition of pillaging and marauding was no more effective on this occasion than it had ever been; "such excesses as may have been committed," he wrote, "are chargeable to the lawless men, whom of late there has been scant opportunity to ferret out and punish."[34] The phrase "may have been committed" in such reports is a transparent euphemism for "*were* committed." There is no mention of the fate of the warning about liquor in any of the reports of the expedition, but an order of Merritt's to Custer, issued after Charlottesville was occupied, suggests that alcohol too remained a problem. Custer was told that "in order to preserve the command intact it is necessary that every exertion be made to prevent the men of your command from entering this town. . . . timely warning should be given to the men that . . . the most severe punishment will be inflicted on such as are found in the town without express permission."[35]

The objectives of the campaign on which Sheridan was now setting out were spelled out for him by Grant in a dispatch of February 20. They were to be modified out of all recognition partly by

32. *Ibid.*, 702–703. Sheridan took along fifteen days' supplies of coffee, sugar, and salt.
33. *Ibid.*, 778–79.
34. *Ibid.*, Pt. 1, p. 493.
35. *Ibid.*, Pt. 2, p. 834.

events and partly—and deliberately—by Sheridan. Grant desired
Lynchburg to be Sheridan's first objective. With the town occupied
and serving as his base, he was to destroy the railroad and canal
"in every direction, so as to be of no further use to the rebellion";
then, if the information he was able to collect there justified it, he
was to strike south, pass to the west of Danville, and join Sherman, then on his way north through the Carolinas. On the day
after he sent these instructions to Sheridan, Grant wrote General
Meade that "Sherman has but little over 4,000 cavalry. . . . The
main object is to re-enforce . . . [him] in that arm of the service."[36]

At the beginning of the march, Sheridan's only problem was
the weather; he, his men, and his animals were made to pay the
penalty for setting out on a long march just as the winter snows
were melting and the spring rains beginning. The first two days'
march, as far as Lacey Springs, was made in a steady downpour,
but the Valley Turnpike, on which the command was moving
south, was still in fair condition notwithstanding four years of
hard usage and neglect. The crossing of the North Fork of the
Shenandoah at Mount Jackson on the second day was, however,
a difficult operation. Part of the command crossed on the pontoons
they had brought along, but some of the units had to swim their
horses across the swollen stream.[37] Pennington's brigade, one of
the units that had to swim the stream—"which . . . was in a fearful state, between the melting snow of the mountain and the rain
of the valley"—lost one man drowned, "and many others would
have been drowned had it not been for the superhuman efforts of
a number of officers and men . . . who rushed into the stream, and
at great personal risk brought them to the shore." Gibbs's Reserve
Brigade fared much worse; seven of its men drowned.[38]

Before the crossing of the Shenandoah on February 28 began,
"Officers' Call" was blown. Roger Hannaford noticed, as the officers returned to their units after an open-air conference with
Sheridan, that "each wore a very solemn countenance; the men
were now drawn up, & certain points and parcels of information

36. *Ibid.*, 605–606, 609.
37. Sheridan, *Personal Memoirs*, II, 113.
38. *Official Records*, Vol. XLVI, Pt. 1, pp. 504–505; Gracey, *Annals of
the 6th*, 319.

[were] doled out to them; 1st we were told that we were on a big march of not less . . . than 350 or 400 miles, that it behooved us to take the best care of our horses, to ease them whenever possible, to save our forage, not waste a grain, & most of all to see that our ammunition be kept with the most scrupulous care."[39]

The first enemy reaction to the march materialized on the third day, March 1. General Early learned of Sheridan's advance on the previous day. He had Rosser collect as many of his men as he could on short notice and sent him to Mount Crawford to try to block the crossing of the Middle Fork of the Shenandoah.[40] Rosser got to Mount Crawford just ahead of the Federals and set fire to the long covered bridge across the river, but Colonel Capehart sent two of his regiments to swim the river above the bridge and attack Rosser in flank, while he himself charged across the burning bridge with the rest of his brigade. Rosser, with a handful of men, had no chance against a full brigade. He was driven away from the bridge, and while some of Capehart's men put out the fire, the rest chased Rosser to within four miles of Staunton, capturing a number of his ambulances and wagons and taking prisoner thirty-seven of his men.[41]

The crossing of the Shenandoah secured, Sheridan reached Staunton the next day. There he learned that Early had collected most of his remaining troops at Waynesboro, on the direct road to Charlottesville via Rockfish Gap, and had let it be known that he intended to fight Sheridan at that point. Sheridan now had a decision to make. From Staunton he could go directly south to Lynchburg and then on to Danville and North Carolina, as Grant wished him to do, or he could turn east, fight Early at Waynesboro, and after defeating him (with the manpower odds five to one in his favor there was little question but that he could do so), cross the Blue Ridge and go on to Charlottesville. He chose the latter course, apparently (his explanation is far from clear) because he did not

39. Hannaford, "Reminiscences," 266(a).
40. Sheridan, in *Personal Memoirs*, II, 113, gives Rosser's strength at Mount Crawford as five or six hundred, but in his report on the march he credits him with "200 or 300" men; *Official Records*, Vol. XLVI, Pt. 1, p. 475. It seems likely that the latter estimate is correct.
41. *Official Records*, Vol. XLVI, Pt. 1, p. 501. The figure in Sheridan, *Personal Memoirs*, II, 113, is slightly higher.

want to leave Early behind him in the Valley; one might properly ask what harm Sheridan thought Early could do in the Valley with the mere two thousand men he had left in his command.[42] It seems much more likely that Sheridan turned east at Staunton because he had had no intention to begin with of going south to Lynchburg and North Carolina.

Having chosen the Charlottesville route, Sheridan sent Colonel Fitzhugh's brigade to destroy the commissary and quartermaster's stores—blankets, boots, clothing, beef, and pork—that the Confederates had stockpiled at Swoope's Station, ten miles west of Staunton.[43] Meanwhile Custer, followed by Devin, went forward to Waynesboro with rather puzzling verbal orders (if Custer has reported them correctly) directing him, as Custer wrote, to "ascertain something definite in regard to the position, movements, and strength of the enemy, and, if possible, destroy the railroad bridge over the South River at that point"—the same bridge Torbert had failed to destroy three months before.[44] More important than these orders, which in any event Custer chose to ignore, was the fact that the Valley Turnpike ended at Staunton. From there east to Waynesboro, Charlottesville, and beyond, the cavalry had to use unimproved dirt roads, "bad beyond description," deep with the mud of melting snow and four days of an almost uninterrupted torrential downpour. Custer's men reached Waynesboro so bespattered with the soft mud thrown up by their horses' hooves that they were unrecognizable.[45]

Early's defenses at Waynesboro were on a ridge immediately to the northwest of the town. The ridge was in effect the chord of a shallow arc described by a loop of the South Branch of the Shenandoah (the "South River"). The position violated the most basic of military rules; Captain Jed. Hotchkiss commented justly that "the general committed an unpardonable error in posting so small a force with a swollen river in its rear and with its flanks wholly

<hr/>

42. Sheridan, *Personal Memoirs*, II, 114; *Official Records*, Vol. XLVI, Pt. 1, p. 476.
43. *Official Records*, Vol. XLVI, Pt. 1, p. 497; Pt. 2, p. 849. The modest amount of material destroyed, itemized in Colonel Fitzhugh's report, becomes "immense quantities" in Merritt's. *Ibid.*, 485.
44. *Ibid.*, 502.
45. *Ibid.*, 476.

exposed, the left having an interval of one-eighth of a mile between it and the river and with a body of woods that concealed every movement [upon it] that might be made."[46] To man his defenses, Early had two weak brigades of Gabriel C. Wharton's infantry division, a dozen pieces of artillery, and "some" (probably not more than a few dozen) cavalry under Rosser, a total of about two thousand men altogether.[47]

At about two o'clock in the afternoon, shortly before Custer reached Waynesboro, Early had sent orders to his infantry to move back from their lines into the woods and build fires "to protect themselves from the cold sleet which was constantly falling."[48] Before these orders could be executed, however, Custer arrived and ordered Colonel Wells's brigade to deliver a probing attack against Early's line. The result convinced him that if he attacked the defenses frontally, "success would be doubtful, [and] it would involve a large loss of life."[49] In a fast reconnaissance of the enemy line, he discovered the gap mentioned by Captain Hotchkiss between the left end of the defenses and the river. He ordered Lieutenant Colonel Edward W. Whitaker of his staff to take charge of the 2nd Ohio, 3rd New Jersey, and 1st Connecticut (the three regiments of Pennington's brigade armed with Spencers), assemble them under cover of the woods facing the gap, and attack through the gap, dismounted.[50] While this flank attack was preparing, Colonel Wells's brigade was to "keep the enemy's attention engaged in front by displaying a heavy force of mounted skirmishers," and Colonel Capehart's brigade and Pennington's 2nd New York were to make ready to charge the enemy in front the moment the attack through the gap was launched. Lieutenant Carle A. Woodruff's section of horse artillery was brought to the front and ordered to begin firing on the enemy breastworks to compel the infantry behind them to lie down. When everything was ready, Custer gave the signal; every part of his neatly inte-

46. *Ibid.*, 516.
47. *Ibid.*, 476.
48. *Ibid.*, 516.
49. *Ibid.*, 502.
50. *Ibid.*, 502. But Colonel Pennington does not mention Colonel Whitaker at all in his report; he does not say so directly, but he implies that he himself led the charge of the three regiments.

grated plan fell into place, and within moments the three flanking regiments, attacking at a run, were in the left rear of Early's infantry, whereupon the entire defense collapsed in "one of the most terrible panics and stampedes" Captain Hotchkiss had ever seen.[51]

Roger Hannaford, who was in the flank attack with his regiment, was told by prisoners "that it was useless to try to stand against our seven shooters. . . . to see us coming at a run, never stopping to load, but running & firing. . . . 'Beside[s], you came with such a rush, so different from an infantry charge . . .' said an Officer, 'the men are really afraid of the seven shooters, they dread them, a panic seems to possess them as soon as they see them coming.'"[52] The description by the Confederate officer of the Union cavalry charging with a "rush" may be contrasted with the comment of a German observer who feared that an excessive reliance by the Federal cavalry on firearms and dismounted attacks would endanger "the so-called cavalry spirit."[53] The opposition at Waynesboro may have been negligible, but there seemed to be no lack of the "cavalry spirit" in the troopers who made the flank attack.

In the battle itself, if indeed it can be called a battle, and in the subsequent pursuit to the western end of Rockfish Gap twelve miles away, sixteen hundred of Early's two thousand men were taken prisoner. The captures also included eleven pieces of artillery, seventeen battle flags, all the men's weapons and ammunition, and nearly two hundred ambulances and wagons complete with their teams, including Early's headquarters wagon containing all his records.[54] The Federal loss was extraordinarily small; a

51. *Ibid.*, 516; Pt. 2, p. 794.
52. Hannaford, "Reminiscences," 271(b)–(c). The "seven shooters" were the Spencer carbines.
53. Jay Luvaas, *The Military Legacy of the Civil War; The European Inheritance* (Chicago, 1959), 65, quoting Major Justus Scheibert of the Prussian army, who was present as an observer in several campaigns of the Army of Northern Virginia.
54. *Official Records*, Vol. XLVI, Pt. 1, p. 476. These are the figures in Sheridan's report. Custer claimed eighteen hundred prisoners and fourteen guns captured, but Colonel John L. Thompson, who marched the prisoners back to Winchester, reported that he had thirteen hundred, including fifty-six officers, in his charge. *Ibid.*, 528. The 8th New York, charging mounted over the Confederate breastworks, took eight hundred prisoners (nearly twice their own numbers), five pieces of artillery, and large numbers of

total of nine killed and wounded, the combined loss of the three regiments making the flank attack being one man wounded.[55]

The rout of Early's little army on March 2 removed the last body of any size of organized Confederate troops from the Shenandoah Valley, the scene of one campaign after another from the summer of 1861 on. Except for guerrilla operations, which were to continue to the formal end of the war and even beyond—Mosby did not disband his battalion until April 21, 1865, and not until June 21 did he himself deign to surrender and accept a parole—the Valley was now at long last to be at peace.

On the morning after Custer's victory, Sheridan organized a force of twelve hundred officers and men to escort the prisoners and captured artillery back to Winchester. The force was made up in part of the smallest regiment taken from each of the seven brigades; indicative of the greatly reduced strength of many cavalry regiments by the early spring of 1865 is that these seven regiments totaled only six hundred officers and men, half the strength of a single twelve-company regiment in the palmy days of 1861. The remainder of the escort consisted of the dismounted men and those with the poorest horses, taken from throughout the command. Colonel John L. Thompson, 1st New Hampshire, was given command of the escort.[56] He left Waynesboro with no forage for his animals and no food for his prisoners or his own men, other than a three days' supply of coffee, sugar, and salt, on a march that could not have been made in less than five or six days. Thompson solved the problem of feeding his prisoners when he

---

wagons, ambulances, forges, small arms, horses, and mules. Norton, *Deeds of Daring*, 109.

55. *Official Records*, Vol. XLVI, Pt. 1, pp. 504, 505. Fifteen Congressional Medals of Honor were awarded for this fight, one of which went to Major (later Colonel) Hartwell B. Compson, 8th New York, who, as mentioned in Vol. I of this work, ran away from home in 1861 at the age of seventeen to enlist in the regiment and, after promotions through every rank, was commissioned colonel of it at age twenty-one; as a well-deserved compliment, his colonel's commission was postdated to March 2, 1865, the date of the fight at Waynesboro. Norton, *Deeds of Daring*, 182.

56. *Official Records*, Vol. XLVI, Pt. 1, p. 528. The account in the text of Colonel Thompson's march is based on his report, *ibid.*, 528–29, and the quotations in this and the succeeding paragraph are from that source. See also *ibid.*, 477, 486, 489, and Pt. 2, p. 793.

reached Staunton on the morning of the second day. He announced to the townspeople that "they could have a half hour to provide food or I should take it from the insane asylum. They brought none, and I took flour and bacon from the asylum, upon which . . . [the prisoners] subsisted until they arrived at Winchester." His own men lived on what they could forage in an area that had been fairly thoroughly devastated five months before.

Thompson learned in Staunton that Rosser, who had escaped from Waynesboro, was collecting his furloughed men and would try to free the prisoners. In fact, from Staunton northward Thompson's rear guard, commanded by Lieutenant Colonel Theodore A. Boice, 5th New York, had to fight off a succession of attacks, including a final attack in some strength at Rude's Hill, the only result of which was to increase the convoy of prisoners by thirty-four of Rosser's officers and men. The stand made by the rear guard at Rude's Hill was for the purpose of giving the rest of the escort and the unfortunate prisoners time to cross the North Fork of the Shenandoah at Mount Jackson; "the dismounted men and prisoners forded the stream in groups of fifty or sixty, holding each other by the arm. It was impossible for a single footman to ford, the water being breast high, with a rapid current." Not mentioned by Colonel Thompson was the fact that at the beginning of March the water, fed by mountain streams, was icy cold. Nevertheless, crossing the Shenandoah was the last hazard Thompson had to surmount, and on the eighth he marched his command and his prisoners into Winchester. General Torbert forwarded Thompson's report of the march with a thoroughly well-deserved tribute: "The harassing difficulties overcome, and the skill, genius, and judgment displayed by Colonel Thompson in bringing safely to Winchester more prisoners than he started with, is deserving of the highest commendation and worthy of more than an ordinary notice."[57]

Sheridan considered the defeat of Early and the destruction of his tiny army important from a military standpoint, for it opened the way to Rockfish Gap at a time when "crossing . . . the Blue Ridge, covered with snow as it was, at any [other] point would

57. Ibid., Pt. 1, p. 529.

have been difficult."[58] On the morning after the battle, while Colonel Thompson organized his command for the march back to Winchester, and the Reserve Brigade blew up the iron bridge of the Virginia Central and destroyed the wagons, caissons, muskets, ammunition, and supplies captured the previous day, the rest of the cavalry, with the Third Division in the lead, started on the march across the Blue Ridge to Charlottesville.[59]

The difficulties of this march were not caused by the enemy, but were solely the result of the state of the roads. There is complete unanimity on this point; all the contemporary reports, from Sheridan's on down, all the regimental historians and the writers of memoirs, are alike at a loss for words to convey an adequate idea of it. Merritt writes of the "fearful condition of the roads" which "defies description," explaining that the "heavy rains, which fell during the march, rendered the stiff, yellow clay, soft and almost impassable."[60] The historian of the 9th New York tells of the sets of fours throwing up the soft mud in ridges as much as two feet high; the historian of the 6th New York writes of mud from eighteen inches to two feet deep, in which "frequently a horse was abandoned through inability to extricate him," and he adds that "men and horses, teamsters and mules, wagons and negroes, were literally plastered [with mud] from one end to the other, but the men were good natured, laughing and singing and joking, for the enemy was in the last ditch, the war was nearing its end, and home, sweet home, was almost in sight."[61]

58. *Ibid.*, 476.
59. *Ibid.*, 489; Pt. 2, p. 794.
60. *Ibid.*, Pt. 1, p. 486.
61. Cheney, *History of the Ninth Regiment*, 248; Committee on Regimental History, *History of the Sixth New York*, 254, 256–57. The identification of cavalry regiments in the last few months of the war becomes more and more difficult. Some regiments disappear altogether. Others shrink to a few dozen men, but retain their identity. Others in the same situation become a three- or four-company battalion, but retain the name and number of the original regiment. Still others, reduced to 100–150 men, are consolidated into two or three companies, added to another regiment, and lose their identity altogether. For example, the reenlisted veterans and recruits of the 3rd Pennsylvania become the "Veteran Battalion, 3rd Pennsylvania Cavalry," and those of the 1st Pennsylvania, the four-company "First Pennsylvania Veteran Cavalry Battalion." The 6th Pennsylvania, down to a hundred, rank and file, remains officially a regiment, but the remnant of the

Roger Hannaford, whose reminiscences are particularly valuable because of his habit of noting specific facts instead of dealing in broad generalities, reports that shortly after the march began, his regiment "came to a place where the wagons had been detained, it was a piece of road about 400 yards long, a deep cut only wide enough for a single wagon, in this place which it was impossible for the wagons to pass around the mud appeared bottomless & it was an absolute fact that the wheels would so sink that the bed would rest on the mud, now a dark reddish brown mass the consistency of soft mortar."[62]

Destroying the large railroad bridge over Mechum's River on the way, Custer's division and Devin's First and Second Brigades reached Charlottesville late in the afternoon of March 3.[63] They were met on the outskirts of town by the mayor and a delegation of prominent citizens. Familiar from their reading of history and of Sir Walter Scott with the correct procedure for surrendering a city to the enemy, but, due to the absence of a city wall and gates, lacking the keys that the time-honored surrender ceremony required, they substituted the keys to all the public buildings in the town, and "General Sheridan found himself in full possession and control of the courthouse, the jail, the University of Virginia, and several taverns and churches."[64]

Difficult as the march to Charlottesville had been for Custer's and Devin's horsemen, it was far worse for the Reserve Brigade, shepherding the trains and artillery on roads already cut and churned up by the passage of the cavalry. Indeed, the train did not arrive at Charlottesville until the evening of March 4, having taken two full days to cover a distance of just over twenty miles.[65]

1st District of Columbia is added to the 1st Maine and disappears as a regiment, as does the 4th New York, whose reenlisted veterans and recruits become Companies B, E, and L of the 9th New York. Regimental History Committee, History of the 3d Pennsylvania, 454; Lloyd, History of the First Reg't., 114; Tobie, First Maine Cavalry, 355; Cheney, History of the Ninth Regiment, 246.

62. Hannaford, "Reminiscences," 275(d).
63. Official Records, Vol. XLVI, Pt. 1, p. 477.
64. Davies, General Sheridan, 210.
65. Merritt states that the trains arrived at Charlottesville on March 4; Sheridan writes that "Gibbs's brigade, which was bringing up the much-impeded train, did not arrive until the 5th." Official Records, Vol. XLVI, Pt.

By common consent, they would not have reached Charlottesville at all had it not been for the mules captured from Early, which were used to double and triple the teams pulling the wagons and guns, and, more importantly, for the Negroes, who, as was always the case, flocked from all sides to join the column—there were to be three thousand of them by the time the march ended on the Pamunkey—and who oftentimes literally lifted mired wagons out of the muck.[66]

The delay in the arrival of the trains at Charlottesville made it necessary for Sheridan to give the cavalry a day's rest before resuming the march. For some of the troopers it was indeed a rest, one that, as the historian of the 7th Michigan noted, would

always be remembered. . . . For several days we had been marching over the rain-soaked roads of red Virginia clay. . . . Mud-covered and water-soaked, hungry and sleepy, we reached the dry and solid pike leading into the town. The sun, which had been hidden behind rain-clouds, now shone out warm and bright. . . . The General assigned us quarters in and about the residences formerly occupied by the officers and professors of the University of Virginia. . . . many of the men betook themselves to the numerous, but now unoccupied rooms once used by the university students, each soldier having a room to himself.[67]

The 1st New York (Lincoln) had its own distinctive arrangement for making enjoyable its stay in Charlottesville; "some of the men, who were practical printers, took possession of a printing office and issued a special edition, advertising, with the old-time cuts of runaway slaves, offering large rewards for the finding and return of 'My boy Jube,' and 'My man Rosser.' "[68]

1, p. 486; Sheridan, Personal Memoirs, II, 118. The activities of the cavalry in and about Charlottesville on March 4, 5, and 6 suggest that Merritt's date is probably correct.

66. Cheney, History of the Ninth Regiment, 252. Merritt credits "Capt. W[illiam] H. Brown, chief quartermaster . . . and his able assistants . . . [with] getting the train over the road. . . . they worked night and day, using every exertion and means which a settled determination to succeed could provoke or human ingenuity invent." Official Records, Vol. XLVI, Pt. 1, p. 486. Merritt did not think it necessary to mention the Negroes, who provided much of the "exertion."

67. Isham, An Historical Sketch, 77–78.

68. Beach, First New York (Lincoln) Cavalry, 477.

For most of the command, however, the stay at Charlottesville was anything but restful. Colonel Stagg's brigade, reinforced by three regiments of Fitzhugh's, was sent to destroy the Virginia Central trackage in the direction of Lynchburg; three miles of the road and two bridges, each fifty feet long, were "thoroughly destroyed."[69] Custer was sent in the opposite direction to destroy the railroad for a distance of eight or ten miles toward Gordonsville, as well as the massive iron railroad bridge over the Rivanna River. For good reasons or bad, he did not act fast enough in destroying the bridge to satisfy Merritt and was therefore reminded that it was "of the utmost importance" to get the job done; he was directed to "send an officer or man into town to find powder . . . to blow up the piers. . . . It is more important to destroy bridges than miles of railroad track. Have it done completely. Your provost guard in town must collect all the negroes and send them to work on the bridge."[70]

At the same time the work of destruction was going on, preparations were also being made for the next stage of the march. Seven days' rations of coffee, sugar, and salt were issued to the men to lighten the loads in the wagons, deficiencies of ammunition were made good, tents were burned; a thorough inspection of the supply train and headquarters wagons was made and "All material not absolutely necessary" was discarded. Merritt was ordered to see to it that every man in the command had a horse to ride. "The commanding general is satisfied," he was told, "that every enlisted man in the command can be mounted, and it must be done. You will please issue orders that the dismounted men seize the [captured] horses ridden by enlisted men or negroes, unless they have a pass showing the horses are private property, and every officer giving a pass to a soldier or negro for captured horses will be dismissed the service."[71]

Sheridan could have gone on from Charlottesville to Lynchburg, Danville, and North Carolina, but he decided not to do it. He explains in his memoirs that he made his decision on the strength of information brought in by Major Young's scouts that the garri-

69. *Official Records,* Vol. XLVI, Pt. 1, p. 490.
70. *Ibid.,* Pt. 2, p. 833.
71. *Ibid.,* 881; see also 833, 849, and Pt. 1, p. 490.

son at Lynchburg was being reinforced and the fortifications strengthened. In his report on the march, however, he ascribes his decision not to try to capture Lynchburg to the "necessary delay" at Charlottesville.[72] What he did instead was to send the First Division in the direction of Howardsville, with orders to destroy the bridges and mills on the James River at Scottsville and New Canton and on the Rivanna at Palmyra, and all the locks on the James River Canal that the division could reach. Meanwhile the Third Division, with the trains in tow, was to march along the Virginia Central track, destroying it as it went, as far as Amherst Court House, sixteen miles from Lynchburg. The two columns were then to meet at New Market. From New Market the united command was to march to Duguidsville, cross on the bridge there to the south side of the James, strike for the Southside Railroad at Appomattox Station, and destroy it as far as Farmville.[73]

With an important exception that could not have displeased Sheridan, these operations proceeded as planned. At two A.M. on March 7, the 19th New York started out to seize the bridge at Duguidsville, but "for some time previous . . . [the bridge] had been filled with straw, and saturated with tar and turpentine," and when the Confederate scouts reported the approach of the Yankees, the guard at the bridge set it on fire.[74] The structure was destroyed, and another bridge over the James at Hardwicksville was set ablaze and destroyed in a similar manner. The eight pontoons Sheridan had hauled along with great effort were found to reach only half way across the swollen, unfordable river.[75] Thus it was here, because of his inability to get across the James, that Sheridan's decision "to join the armies in front of Petersburg" became final and irrevocable. Given the sequel, one may suspect that he never intended to do anything else. Indeed, he makes it evident that he was greatly relieved not to be able to march south to join Sherman. He writes that he "now decided to destroy still more thoroughly the James River canal and the Virginia Central rail-

72. Ibid., Pt. 1, p. 477.
73. Ibid., 478; Pt. 2, p. 848. On this occasion, the division commanders were given maps with their orders.
74. Ibid., 491; Pt. 2, p. 881.
75. Ibid., Pt. 1, pp. 478, 49.

road and then join General Grant in front of Petersburg. I was master of the whole country north of the James as far down as Goochland; hence the destruction of these arteries of supply could be easily compassed, and feeling that the war was nearing its end, I desired my cavalry to be in at the death."[76]

The destruction of the two bridges across the James that made it impossible for Sheridan to cross to the south side of the river made it equally impossible for any sizable force of Confederates to cross to the north side to interfere with his progress. Hence the work of destruction, itemized in great detail in the reports of the brigade and division commanders and in an appendix to Sheridan's own report, could go on without hindrance.[77] The final stages of the march, which ended at White House on the Pamunkey, were relatively uneventful. Forage for the animals and food for the men was found in great abundance around Charlottesville and on the way east from there.[78] It is a sorry commentary on the efficiency of the Confederate supply system that while General Lee's troops at Richmond and Petersburg were living on inadequate rations, Sheridan's command of about eighty-five hundred soldiers, plus the nearly three thousand Negroes who were marching with the column, found ample food for themselves and their animals seventy miles away at the farthest. Colonel Fitzhugh, for example, reported that his brigade had "never suffered from scarcity of forage or rations; good foraging parties under competent officers having been able to meet every want."[79] The two division commanders were told before they left Charlottesville that they would be held responsible for providing meat and bread for their commands; "there are numerous mills that can be run at night, with a little enterprise on the part of division and brigade commanders, which will furnish the bread ration, and more." No excuses would be accepted for any "delinquency" in that respect, they

76. Sheridan, *Personal Memoirs*, II, 119; see also *Official Records*, Vol. XLVI, Pt. 1, p. 478.

77. *Official Records*, Vol. XLVI, Pt. 1, 481–82.

78. *Ibid.*, 477. When the command reached Columbia on March 10, Hannaford noted that they "found this whole country overflowing . . . with food of every description for both man & beast, yet it was within 50 or 60 miles of Richmond." Hannaford, "Reminiscences," 280(b).

79. *Official Records*, Vol. XLVI, Pt. 1, pp. 499, 507; Pt. 2, p. 918.

were told, but they were also warned that foraging was to be "done properly and without outrages being committed."[80]

The principal impediment encountered by the cavalry continued to be the weather and the state of the roads. It rained almost uninterruptedly during the last two weeks of the march, but with the aid of the Negroes marching along with the train, and by replacing worn-out mules with animals captured at Waynesboro and subsequently, along the way, the command, although "much worn and fatigued . . . managed to get along in very good shape."[81]

At Columbia, which the troopers reached on the evening of March 10, Sheridan decided to give his men and animals a day's rest.[82] From there, too, he sent Grant a lengthy account of the experiences and accomplishments of his force since leaving Waynesboro. He wrote that he planned to continue his march east along the Virginia Central, destroying it as he went, then to strike and destroy the Richmond, Fredericksburg & Potomac, and, after "finishing" that railroad, to join Grant, unless directed otherwise. He asked that forage, rations, and pontoons be sent for him to White House. "I have no opposition," he concluded; "everybody is bewildered by our movements. . . . I cannot speak in two [sic] high terms of Generals Merritt, Custer and Devin, and the officers and men of their commands. They have waded through mud and water during this continuous rain, and are all in fine spirits and health."[83] Two of Major Young's scouts, J. A. Campbell (aged nineteen) and A. H. Rowland, Jr., delivered the dispatch to Grant at City Point on the evening of March 12; they had ridden 145 miles without sleep and without food, pursued part of the way by enemy cavalry. The dispatch had been written on tissue paper and rolled up in a ball of tinfoil, which Campbell carried in his mouth.[84]

80. *Ibid.*, Pt. 2, p. 847.
81. *Ibid.*, Pt. 1, p. 478.
82. *Ibid.*, 477.
83. *Ibid.*, Pt. 2, pp. 918–19.
84. Colonel Horace Porter describes the arrival of the two scouts at Grant's headquarters, as well as their adventurous journey. The distance he says they covered, 145 miles, seems a great exaggeration. Even by making a wide circuit around Richmond, as they would have had to do, it is doubtful that they traveled more than about 80 miles, but even that was a considerable distance to cover in two days. Porter, *Campaigning with Grant*, 396–99.

Having received Sheridan's message, Grant sent him one in return to be handed him when he arrived at White House, to congratulate him and his command "on the skill and endurance displayed" on their long journey and to assure him that "the importance of . . . [his] success can scarcely be estimated." More to the point, Grant also wrote that he had ordered a hundred thousand rations for the men and ten days' forage for the animals sent to White House. Furthermore, mindful of Wilson's disastrous homecoming from his raid nine months before, Grant ordered General Edward O. C. Ord (who had succeeded Butler in command of the Army of the James, which, possibly in an effort to wipe out its dismal past, was renamed the Army of Virginia) to send his cavalry to the Chickahominy, to keep the Confederate cavalry as far away as possible from White House. An indication of the progress the Federal cavalry had made over the years is that Colonel Robert M. West, temporarily in command of Ord's cavalry, wired back as soon as he received his orders that he would be ready to start "in a few minutes."[85]

A brief moment of excitement in the final stages of Sheridan's march from Columbia to the Pamunkey was provided by General Early. At Frederick's Hall Station on the Virginia Central Custer captured the telegraph office, where he found a message from Early about to be sent to General Lee, in which Early announced that with the two hundred cavalrymen he had somehow collected, he was about to attack the Federals. Custer did not wait to be attacked; he sent the 1st Connecticut and a battalion of the 2nd Ohio to find and attack Early. This, in the language of contemporary reports, was "handsomely done." Within two hours the men from Connecticut and Ohio found Early's party, charged it, and "captured or scattered [it] in every direction." Early himself, with a half-dozen orderlies and two staff officers, managed to escape down a side road. Pursued by a few of the best mounted men of the 2nd Ohio, Early and one staff officer, the last remnants of the army he had led to the outskirts of Washington the summer before, outdistanced their pursuers and reached safety in Richmond; the others were captured.[86]

85. *Official Records*, Vol. XLVI, Pt. 3, pp. 24, 11, 12.
86. *Ibid.*, Pt. 1, pp. 506, 479.

Of greater practical, as distinguished from symbolic, importance was an exploit of the 5th United States of the Reserve Brigade. On March 14, General Devin ordered the 2nd Massachusetts to proceed to the Virginia Central bridge over the South Anna and destroy it; the 5th United States was to follow and provide support if needed. The two regiments took different roads to reach the bridge. The road the Regulars took turned out to be shorter, and they were first at the bridge, which was guarded by an artillery unit of three 3-inch rifled Parrott guns. Lieutenant James Hastings, leading the advance, dismounted thirty of his men, charged across the bridge, drove off the gunners, and captured the guns intact. When the artillerymen rallied eight hundred yards away and showed signs of being about to make a charge of their own to retake their guns and the bridge, Hastings turned the guns around and, with his men serving them, dispersed the Confederates with the fire of their own artillery.[87]

When Sheridan reached Frederick's Hall Station his scouts brought him word that Longstreet, with George E. Pickett's division of infantry and Fitzhugh Lee's cavalry, had been sent north from Richmond to intercept him. To throw the enemy off the scent, Sheridan sent both his divisions across the South Anna at Ashland Station to create the impression that he was about to move in the direction of Richmond. Then, leaving only Pennington's brigade at Ashland for a few hours to "amuse" the enemy, he had the rest of his command recross the river and march east to the Pamunkey, opposite White House, continuing the work of destruction as they went. He reported to Grant that his men "totally destroyed" fifteen miles of the Virginia Central, from Tolersville to Beaver Dam Station, including five of its bridges over the North and South Anna, and he added proudly, "there is not a bridge on the railroad from the South Anna to Lynchburg."[88]

On March 19, Sheridan's entire command crossed the Pamunkey and reached the end of their long journey. "There perhaps never was a march," Sheridan wrote, "where nature offered such impediments and shrouded herself in such gloom as upon this; incessant rain, deep and almost impassable streams, swamps, and

87. *Ibid.*, 479, 487, 492, 494, 500; Pt. 2, pp. 981, 994.
88. *Ibid.*, Pt. 2, pp. 993–94, 981; Pt. 3, p. 14.

mud, were overcome with a constant cheerfulness which was truly admirable. Both officers and men appeared buoyed up by the thought that we had completed our work in the Valley of the Shenandoah, and that we were on our way to help our brothers-in-arms in front of Petersburg in the final struggle."[89]

Roger Hannaford stood at the southern end of the decked-over railroad bridge across the Pamunkey on which the command crossed the river and watched the Negroes who had followed the column, walking across.

They were beginning to come, first by ones & two[s] then by squads, at last a constant stream. I stood and watched them as they flocked by . . . it was curious to observe how each seemed affected, old men & women that could after their exhaustive [sic] journey scarcely totter, would go by, the tears rolling down their withered cheeks, looking upward crying "tank God Ise free"; most of them seemed however almost wild with joy, singing & dancing as they hurried down to the landing.[90]

89. *Ibid.*, Pt. 1, p. 480.
90. Hannaford, "Reminiscences," 286(b).

XIV

The Essence of War

THE SECOND DIVISION OF THE CAVALRY CORPS REMAINED
with the Army of the Potomac when the First and Third Divisions
left for the Shenandoah Valley in August, 1864. In command of
the division was steady, reliable, patriarchally bearded David
McM. Gregg, to whom James Wilson, not normally given to eulo-
gizing fellow cavalry commanders, paid a splendid and thoroughly
well deserved tribute:

In Gregg the cavalry had one of its very best officers . . . noted for ster-
ling ability and great experience. Steady as a clock and as gallant as
Murat . . . he was the best all-'round cavalry officer that ever commanded a division in either army. Somewhat lacking in enthusiasm
and possibly in aggressive temper, he was a man of unusual modesty,
but of far more than usual capacity. He had done splendid service
wherever called upon . . . but for some reason not easy to define he
had not impressed himself sufficiently upon his immediate commanders to secure the position which was given to Sheridan. . . . he resigned
. . . in early February, 1865. Whether this was due to pique or disappointment, he was always too proud to explain. But whatever may have
been the real cause, it is due to him to add that it cost the army . . . the
services of a most gallant and useful officer.[1]

1. Wilson, *Under the Old Flag*, I, 364–65. Appointed to West Point
from Pennsylvania, Gregg graduated in the Class of 1855 and was commissioned a second lieutenant in the cavalry. He served on the frontier until his
appointment in January, 1862, as colonel of the 8th Pennsylvania.

The First Brigade of Gregg's division, made up of the 1st New Jersey, the 1st Massachusetts, 10th New York, 6th Ohio, and 1st Pennsylvania, was commanded by Henry E. Davies, Jr.; J. Irvin Gregg (David Gregg's cousin) commanded the Second Brigade, consisting of the 1st Maine, and the 2nd, 4th, 8th, 13th, and 16th Pennsylvania.[2] Thus, with the exception of the 6th Ohio, the division was made up entirely of eastern regiments. Frequently associated with the division was August Kautz's small cavalry division, organizationally a part of B. F. Butler's forces. Kautz too had two brigades, the 3rd New York and 5th Pennsylvania making up the First, under Colonel Robert M. West, and the 1st District of Columbia and 11th Pennsylvania the Second, under Colonel Samuel P. Spear.

The First and Third Cavalry Divisions departed for the Valley within a few days after the lamentable fiasco of the Petersburg Mine, a failure that made it necessary for Grant to look for another way to break through the Petersburg defenses.[3] On the basis of an erroneous report that General Lee had depleted his lines north of the James by sending three divisions of infantry to the Valley—actually, only one division of infantry and Hampton's division of cavalry had been withdrawn—Grant decided to repeat the operation he had tried on July 26, when the II Corps had the job of breaching the Confederate line to enable Sheridan to march his cavalry through the gap and destroy as much as he could reach of the Virginia Central Railroad. On this second try, the II Corps, aided this time by two divisions of the IX Corps, was again to be the spearhead; under cover of the infantry attack, Gregg's division was to slip past Lee's left flank to the railroad. The operation, covering the seven days from the fourteenth to the twentieth of August, was essentially a failure. Lee had to move six brigades of infantry from Petersburg and to recall Hampton, who had

2. *Official Records*, Vol. XLII, Pt. 2, pp. 618, 622. In Davies' and J. Irvin Gregg's absence later in the month (Gregg was wounded in a fight with Confederate cavalry in August), Colonel William Stedman commanded the First Brigade and Colonel Charles H. Smith the Second.

3. Not until the end of September were detachments of the 1st Vermont and the 3rd New Jersey, serving as escorts and orderlies in the II and IX Corps, relieved of those duties and sent to join their regiments in the Valley. *Ibid.*, 1125.

reached Culpeper on his way to the Valley, to help General Charles W. Field's division of infantry and W. H. F. Lee's division of cavalry blunt the II Corps attack, which they succeeded in doing. Gregg's cavalrymen were unable to break through to the railroad, but they acquitted themselves well; they drove W. H. F. Lee's pickets out of the southern edges of White Oak Swamp and their subsequent attack up the Charles City Road in the direction of Richmond threatened to outflank Field and created a momentary crisis for General Lee.[4]

In the attack up the Charles City Road, Colonel J. Irvin Gregg was wounded and had to go to the rear. Thereupon General Gregg, with only his bugler and one of his aides by his side, took command of the Second Brigade and led it in a charge against the Confederate cavalry.[5] Later in the day it was the Confederates' turn; they attacked Gregg north of Deep Run with a "large" combined force of infantry and cavalry and "after a sharp fight compelled . . . [him] to retreat across Deep Run with considerable loss."[6]

Unsuccessful in this attack from his right—except that he believed that it prevented the transfer of troops from Lee's army to reinforce Early—Grant decided to try next an attack from his left, south of Petersburg. The target was to be the Petersburg & Weldon Railroad (commonly called the Weldon Railroad). Since this line was continued by connecting roads north to Richmond and south to Goldsboro and Wilmington, North Carolina, Grant rightly considered it "very important to the enemy. The limits from which his supplies had been drawn were already very much contracted, and I knew he must fight desperately to protect it."[7] And so, on August 18, G. K. Warren's V Corps of four divisions, accompanied by the 1st District of Columbia and 3rd New York of Kautz's division, moved out beyond the southern end of the Federal lines and, opposed by only a single brigade of cavalry (later reinforced by

4. Grant, *Personal Memoirs*, II, 321–22; Freeman, *R. E. Lee*, III, 480–84; *Official Records*, Vol. XLII, Pt. 1, p. 81; Pt. 2, p. 1172 .For General Lee's congratulations to Hampton, expressing his "gratification" at the conduct of the cavalry in these operations, see *Official Records*, Vol. XLII, Pt. 2, p. 1189; for the "crisis," see Freeman, *Lee's Lieutenants*, III, 588.
5. Pyne, *First New Jersey Cavalry*, 284.
6. *Ibid.*, 285; see also *Official Records*, Vol. XLII, Pt. 2, p. 230.
7. Grant, *Personal Memoirs*, II, 304.

"some" infantry P. G. T. Beauregard sent down from Petersburg), got across the railroad between Globe Tavern and Reams' Station, three and a half miles and about eight miles south of Petersburg, respectively. After he had gained a foothold across the railroad, Warren was attacked in force by General A. P. Hill; he lost heavily in prisoners but was nevertheless able to maintain his position astride the railroad.[8]

Grant's assumption that General Lee would "fight desperately" for the railroad proved to be correct. Lee met the immediate problem of the break in the road by organizing convoys of wagons to haul supplies from Stony Creek Depot, which Warren's success had made the northern railhead, twenty miles to Petersburg over roads well to the west of the breach; at the same time he launched powerful attacks to dislodge Warren. Despite his own presence to coordinate the attacks and encourage his men, the attacks failed, and on August 21 Lee had to reconcile himself to the fact that the road had been broken beyond recovery.[9]

After the Confederate attacks came to a halt, the V and II Corps, the latter having been brought back from north of the James and posted on Warren's left, began to tear up the Weldon track, working south from Globe Tavern. On August 22, Gregg was ordered to move his division to the railroad and "cooperate with General Warren"; a subsequent order directed him to drive the Confederates away from Reams' Station.[10]

The summer of 1864 on the Tidewater was exceptionally hot and dry. On August 15, in the operation north of the James, the 1st Maryland, then fighting as infantry in the First Division, X Corps, had "as many as thirty cases of sunstroke."[11] Finding water

8. Freeman, *R. E. Lee*, III, 485–87; *Official Records*, Vol. XLII, Pt. 1, pp. 428–30, 851; Pt. 2, p. 260.
9. Freeman, *R. E. Lee*, III, 485–87; Grant, *Personal Memoirs*, II, 323–24; *Official Records*, Vol. XLII, Pt. 1, p. 851.
10. *Official Records*, Vol. XLII, Pt. 2, pp. 375, 408. Later still, Gregg was ordered to send a brigade (Colonel Spear's was suggested) to accompany the infantry tearing up the track and, with the rest of the cavalry, to cover the left flank of the infantry and be "ready to operate as circumstances may require." *Ibid.*, 435, 436.
11. *Ibid.*, Pt. 1, p. 751. Two days later, but still in the course of the battle of Deep Bottom, the Maryland regiment had an even more trying experience. Its pickets were driven in by the enemy, "and about the same time . . . [its own] artillery opened from the left almost directly upon . . . [its] lines. Several men were killed and wounded. . . . An unfortunate panic originated

for their horses became a major problem for the cavalry; Gregg wrote General Hancock on the evening of the fourteenth, "search was everywhere made, but no water could be found. . . . My horses have not been watered since last night."[12] The weather broke at last when Hancock and Gregg were about to march south to help Warren with the Weldon Railroad operation, and as is not uncommon, one extreme was succeeded by another. They found the roads east of the railroad "impassable with fresh mud. . . . all the approaches [to the railroad] were flooded with standing water; and the passage of a wagon over the light, porous ground made deep ruts of gradually thickening mud. There seemed no really solid bottom to the soil. Wagon after wagon cut in deeper; until . . . unloaded wagons sank above the axles, and had to be abandoned until the rains were over."[13]

Despite these difficulties, Gregg made his way to Reams' Station and found it unoccupied. He learned after he got there that Spear's brigade of Kautz's division had had a fight with the enemy a mile and a half west of the station, so he rode out with two of his regiments to see what force the Confederates had in that direction.[14] He found what he estimated to be a division of cavalry, dismounted and deployed for action, moving toward him. He dismounted his two regiments, sent orders back to the station for the rest of the division to join him, and, in a fire fight lasting from five in the afternoon until eight-thirty in the evening, held off the enemy. Eight of the Federal regiments present fought dismounted; the ninth remained mounted, to protect the flanks and to be ready for a countercharge if the enemy made a mounted charge on the dismounted regiments.[15]

. . . caused in great measure by this fire." *Ibid.*, 751. One may choose between the foregoing report of the regimental commander, and that of the officer commanding the 4th New Jersey Battery of Light Artillery, who, ordered to bombard the woods in his front, tried to do so, but was "much interrupted by officers and men of the . . . [1st] Maryland dismounted Cavalry, who persisted in getting in front of my guns as they hurried to the rear." *Ibid.*, 786.

12. *Ibid.*, Pt. 2, p. 179.
13. Pyne, *First New Jersey Cavalry*, 287–88.
14. *Official Records*, Vol. XLII, Pt. 2, p. 408; Pt. 1, p. 606.
15. *Ibid.*, Pt. 1, p. 606; Pyne, *First New Jersey Cavalry*, 290.

The fight Colonel Spear had had before Gregg's arrival placed a greater strain on the colonel's nervous system than it could readily bear, for he reported in evident perturbation that he had

encountered Hampton's cavalry; hard fight; the enemy were ten times my number. I fought them one hour. Sent for re-enforcements; could get none. . . . My loss is 8 killed, 32 wounded . . . I left dead on the field 184 rebels. I hold my own; have sent to General Gregg for help. He returned me word he had nothing to do with me. I then sent word to General Miles; he sent me word he could give me but 100 men. The enemy are in strong force on my left. I can do great execution and rout them if I have one or two regiments of infantry. . . . My men are exhausted; but will protect General Warren's left at all hazards.[16]

What Gregg had replied to Spear's plea for help is not on record, but it is doubtful that it was quite so bluntly worded, or so unhelpful, as the distraught colonel claimed. It is nevertheless a fact that no one had any clear idea of the command relationship between Gregg and Kautz. The latter was unsure of the status of Spear's brigade; Gregg had told him that he (Gregg) had ordered Spear to report to him (Kautz), whereas Spear claimed that he had been directed by General Meade to report to Gregg.[17] Gregg himself was at sea in the matter, for he asked General Humphreys, chief of staff of the army, if Kautz was to receive his orders from, and send his reports to, General Meade.[18] Humphreys' response can hardly be said to have clarified the situation; Kautz, he wrote, was to receive his "instructions" from, and make his reports to, Gregg, but he was also to communicate with Meade's headquarters directly on "anything requiring immediate attention for it."[19] Orders Gregg received from Humphreys a few days later directed him to "concentrate *your* cavalry (your division and that of Kautz)."[20] The doubts the two cavalrymen must still have had about their precise relationship remained unresolved, and it speaks well for their good sense that in a war in which such prob-

16. *Official Records,* Vol. XLII, Pt. 2, p. 427. General Meade asked for an explanation (which, if furnished, is not in the records) of Gregg's and Miles's alleged failure to assist Spear. *Ibid.,* 426, 427.
17. *Ibid.,* 549.
18. *Ibid.,* 464.
19. *Ibid.,* 549.
20. *Ibid.,* 644; italics added.

lems frequently led to disputes, bitterness, and downright insubordination, their relations remained correct and harmonious.

General Lee's experiment, unavoidable at the time, of having each of his divisions of cavalry report directly to him and receive its orders directly from him ended on August 11, with the appointment of Wade Hampton as chief of cavalry of the Army of Northern Virginia.[21] Two days later Hampton proposed the establishment of a "bureau of cavalry" in the War Department at Richmond, to be charged "specifically with the care, direction, and organization of the cavalry arm of the service" and suggested that General Richard S. Ewell, a dragoon in the "Old Army," was "the officer best qualified by experience, information, and service," to head the bureau. It is indicative perhaps, of the state of military administration in Richmond in the last few months of the war that Hampton's suggestion was not referred to General Ewell for his comments until December 8, four months after Hampton had submitted it. In the event, nothing came of the proposal.[22]

Of more immediate importance to the Confederate cavalry was Hampton's way of using that arm. His sober, conservative leadership—an expression of his personality—had about it none of the flamboyance of the glory days of Jeb Stuart. Unlike his great predecessor, who "would attempt his work with whatever force he had, and often seemed to try to accomplish a given result with the smallest possible number of men," Hampton believed in concentration, the use of every available man in every operation, and in careful planning in place of Stuart's "cavalry instinct."[23] Equally important, and perhaps inevitable in the face of the

21. *Ibid.*, 1171, 1173. In a dispatch of July 2, 1864, Lee wrote President Davis, "I am convinced that the cavalry service will be benefitted by having one officer to control its operations and to be held responsible for its condition. . . . You know the high opinion I entertain of Gen. Hampton, and my appreciation of his character and services . . . and although I have feared that he might not have the activity and endurance so necessary in a cavalry commander, and so eminently possessed by Gen[.] Stuart, yet . . . I request authority to place him in command." D. S. Freeman and Grady McWhiney (eds.), *Lee's Dispatches: Unpublished Letters of General Robert E. Lee to Jefferson Davis . . . 1862–1865* (New York, 1957), 268–69. Hampton was promoted to lieutenant general in February, 1865.

22. *Official Records*, Vol. XLII, Pt. 2, pp. 1173–74, 1174–75. General Ewell's comment on the proposal that he head the bureau was that he had had "no experience whatever as a bureau officer." *Ibid.*, 1174.

23. Wellman, *Giant in Gray*, 143.

quality and numbers of his cavalry mounts, was Hampton's increasing reliance on dismounted action, little to the taste of those of his men whose ideas of cavalry tactics were formed under Stuart. In the dismounted fighting that became more and more the lot of Hampton's troopers, the rifles with which many of them were armed, a handicap in mounted action, became an asset. They were no match for the Federal carbines in volume of fire, but they had the advantages of greater accuracy and range.

Hampton's first major opportunity after his formal appointment as chief of cavalry came after the failure of the Confederate infantry to drive Warren back across the Weldon Railroad. Warren had made haste to build well-sited breastworks west of the track, which would have made another frontal attack too costly for the depleted ranks of the Confederate army. But south of Warren's lines the II Corps at Reams' Station had not been equally foresighted; the works they occupied, constructed originally by the VI Corps in June, were described as "feeble"; moreover, there was a sizable gap between their right and the southern end of Warren's lines. In a reconnaissance in force toward Reams' Station, Hampton discovered the weakness of Hancock's lines as well as the gap between his corps and Warren's. On his return, he suggested to General Lee that an attack in that area by Confederate infantry supported by his own cavalry would produce good results. Accepting the suggestion, Lee ordered ten brigades of infantry down to Reams' Station to make the attack under the command of A. P. Hill. Hampton was to contribute to the operation his own former division, now commanded by Matthew C. Butler, and the division of W. H. F. Lee, commanded by General Rufus Barringer.[24]

The Confederate forces told off for the operation were in position on the morning of August 25 and launched their attack early in the afternoon. The main thrust of the infantry onslaught was directed at the right of Hancock's line—that is, at a point just south of the gap between him and Warren—while Hampton crossed the railroad south of the station, pivoted his two divisions on their left, and, with all his men dismounted, attacked Hancock's left flank. Tactically, the operation was a brilliant success; Hancock lost nine guns and ten caissons, and 2,150 of his men

24. Freeman, *R. E. Lee*, III, 488–90.

were taken prisoner, but the strategic results were nil; Warren's grasp on the railroad remained unbroken, and all that the operation accomplished was to prevent for the moment the tearing up of the track farther south.[25]

Gregg had reported to General Hancock with his division on the twenty-fourth; on the morning of the twenty-fifth he had his regiments, some mounted and some dismounted, disposed in a rough semicircle to the west and south of the station, with pickets out on all the access roads. Gregg's sparse report merely states that when the Confederate infantry drove in Major General Nelson A. Miles's division on the northern end of Hancock's line, his own dismounted cavalrymen, plus a miscellaneous lot of about a hundred infantry, "maintained a telling fire upon the enemy"—presumably the "enemy" was the right flank of the Confederate infantry attacking Miles—until they themselves were flanked and had to retreat.[26] One must turn to General Hancock's narrative—otherwise a sorry tale of regiments of infantry "giving way in confusion," of brigades that "could neither be made to go forward nor fire," of orders to retake a lost position being "responded to very feebly," of a regiment "running away without firing more than one or two shots"—for a more informative account of Gregg's contribution. When Hampton's cavalrymen attacked John Gibbon's division, which held the left of Hancock's line, they met little opposition. Hancock reported:

This division offered very little resistance, though the attack was feeble compared with that of the enemy's infantry, and the enemy, elated at their easy success . . . were pressing on with loud cheers when they were met by a heavy flank fire from the dismounted cavalry, occupying the extreme left, and their advance summarily checked. General Gregg, with his own command and one regiment and a squadron from Colonel Spear's command, rendered invaluable service at this point, and the steadiness of his men contrasted more than favorably with the conduct of some of the infantry commands.[27]

25. According to Grant only five guns were lost; *Personal Memoirs*, II, 325. General Lee gave the correct figure of nine in his report to Secretary Seddon and said that "one line of breast-works was carried by the cavalry under General Hampton with great gallantry, who contributed largely to the success of the day." *Official Records*, Vol. XLII, Pt. 1, p. 851; see also Hampton's report and Hill's dispatch, *ibid.*, pp. 942–44, 940.
26. *Official Records*, Vol. XLII, Pt. 1, p. 607.
27. *Ibid.*, 227.

The cavalry had little rest following this battle at Reams' Station. There were operations of greater or lesser magnitude on September 2, September 15–17, September 29–October 2, October 7, October 11–12, October 13, October 22, October 24, October 27–29, October 31, another in November, and two more in December, some by the cavalry alone and others in which all or a major part of the cavalry assisted the infantry. In the days between these operations and often concurrently with them, the cavalry was kept busy picketing the large area, easy of access at many points and particularly so south of the James, in rear of the Federal trench system facing the Richmond-Petersburg defenses.[28] Kautz deemed it necessary to call General Gregg's attention on September 19 to the impossibility of adequately picketing a line "in all its windings of nearly fifteen miles" with a division reduced to not more than fourteen hundred men.[29] Gregg provided some relief by taking over a portion of the line with one of his own regiments, but Kautz's situation, and hence that of the army he was responsible for guarding, remained precarious; he was careful to point out that he lacked the manpower to hold his line anywhere if it was attacked in any strength; "the best he could do was to furnish the earliest intelligence of an advancing force."[30] Within three days of taking over a portion of Kautz's picket line, Gregg too thought it well to point out, for Meade's benefit, and in nearly the same words Kautz had used, that "the line occupied by this [i.e., Gregg's own] division is so long that at many points a forcible attack of the enemy could not be seriously resisted, but the dispositions are such that with vigilance timely notice will be had of the advance of the enemy on any of the roads."[31]

28. On September 1 Gregg was ordered to assemble his and Kautz's commands in the night and "at daylight make a sudden and rapid dash upon the enemy's line of communication between Petersburg and Stony Creek Depot for the purpose of capturing wagon trains and straggling escorts." Gregg moved out as ordered but found access to the wagon road blocked by a brigade of enemy cavalry backed by infantry in earthworks, and he returned without having accomplished his goal. Ibid., Pt. 2, pp. 644, 670, 671.
29. Ibid., 932–33.
30. Ibid., 1006.
31. Ibid., 1057. Gregg's and Kautz's statements about their numerical weakness were echoed by Meade in a dispatch to Grant on September 17; ibid., 880.

At the root of Gregg's and Kautz's common problem was the steadily shrinking manpower of their divisions. At the end of August Gregg's was down to 3,332 officers and men "present for duty equipped," and Kautz's to a mere 1,453.[32] In the mid-August operation north of the James, Gregg had lost 258 men killed, wounded, and captured or missing, and in the fighting at Globe Tavern and Reams' Station later in the month another 75; Kautz's losses in the latter engagement were 82.[33] As Kautz had noted in repeated warnings to Gregg, Meade, and Butler, the departure of time-expired men was also a major factor in the shrinkage. In two cases certainly, and perhaps in others as well, notably the 1st Pennsylvania and the 1st New Jersey of Gregg's division, the men leaving for muster-out represented the majority of their regiments.[34] It was unnecessary for Gregg and Kautz to make the further point that the loss of so many veterans was far more serious than the mere drop in numbers.

There was, however, a favorable side to the story. Kautz and Gregg learned that a number of regiments, originally enlisted as cavalry, were serving as infantry in various corps in Meade's and Butler's armies. Following their strenuous representations, these regiments were mounted and rearmed, as horses and cavalry equipment became available, and assigned to Kautz's or Gregg's divisions. This process, however, took time; not until nearly the end of the year was the last such unit rescued from the ignominy of having to serve as infantry. Kautz acquired by this means the 1st Maryland from the X Corps. In asking for the regiment, Kautz took pains to point out that it was a veteran unit "much discouraged by not being allowed to receive their horses," and that its commander, Colonel Andrew W. Evans, was not only a West Pointer, but was also a captain in the 6th United States of the

32. *Ibid.*, Pt. 1, p. 39. At this very time Grant thought he had a cavalry force of 9,000. He ordered Meade to make "such disposition . . . of the cavalry at once as will give from 3,000 to 4,000 ready for a service" the nature of which he would make known to Meade later. What operation Grant had in mind appears neither in the *Official Records* nor in his *Personal Memoirs*, possibly because Meade at once corrected his figure, informing him that the cavalry numbered "5,500 at the outside." *Ibid.*, Pt. 2, pp. 935, 936.
33. *Ibid.*, Pt. 1, pp. 121, 131.
34. *Ibid.*, Pt. 2, p. 646; Pyne, *First New Jersey Cavalry*, 292.

Regular Army.[35] Butler approved Kautz's request and ordered the regiment mounted "as soon as horses can be procured." On September 27 the regiment was relieved of duty with the X Corps and ordered to proceed to Bermuda Hundred "for the purpose of being mounted and equipped as cavalry." But the next day Butler ordered the regiment back to the X Corps because it could not be mounted and reequipped in time to take part in the attack on Forts Harrison and Gilmer of the Richmond defenses, planned for the twenty-ninth. Four days passed and then, on October 4, the Marylanders were again ordered relieved of duty as infantry and turned over to the cavalry division, and at last they and Kautz had their hearts' desire.[36]

The transfer to the Second Cavalry Division of four of these regiments was handled in more orderly fashion. The regiments involved were the 24th New York, 13th Ohio, 2nd New York Mounted Rifles, serving in the IX Corps and numbering 962 officers and men, and the 21st Pennsylvania, a comparatively large regiment with a roster of 608, serving in the V Corps.[37] Orders were issued on September 27 transferring these regiments to Gregg, but strangely, execution of the transfers was "suspended for the present" in a subsequent paragraph of the *same* order.[38] A week later the suspension was lifted and Gregg was directed to have his ordnance officer requisition the weapons and equipment the four regiments would need to serve as cavalry. The regiments would be transferred to him as rapidly as he had the horses and cavalry gear for them. Based on this practical arrangement, the 21st Pennsylvania and the 24th New York were converted to cavalry in October, the 2nd New York Mounted Rifles in mid-November, and the 13th Ohio on December 19.[39]

The 13th Ohio had been organized in the winter of 1863–1864 by the consolidation of two formerly independent battalions of

35. *Official Records*, Vol. XLII, Pt. 2, pp. 908–909.
36. *Ibid.*, 960, 1061, 1081, 1090.
37. *Ibid.*, 999, 1042. The 24th New York was armed with the Star carbine, hardly a suitable weapon for a regiment serving as infantry, and a technically poor weapon besides.
38. *Ibid.*, Pt. 2, p. 1053.
39. *Ibid.*, Pt. 3, pp. 77, 86, 250, 627, 987. The first unit added to Kautz's division was the 1st New York Mounted Rifles.

cavalry and the enlistment of enough recruits to fill it up to regimental strength.[40] Mustered in on May 6, 1864, the regiment "received its first heartache by being required to take Springfield rifles and infantry equipments, when the expectancy was horses and cavalry arms"; there was much "growling and swearing," but on the assurance that they would have to serve as infantry for only sixty days, the men accepted the situation.[41] As part of General Orlando B. Willcox's division of the IX Corps, the regiment fought in the battle of the Crater, in which it lost 19 killed, 103 wounded, and 59 taken prisoner.[42] Serious trouble broke out a short time later. The sixty days of the supposedly temporary infantry service came to an end without a sign of the promised conversion to cavalry. The resulting dissatisfaction came to a head with "some of the boys" declaring that "they won't take muskets any more, but if given cavalry equipments they were ready to do their duty as such, according to their enlistment," which in their view was a contract imposing obligations on the government no less than on themselves. Twenty-one men of Company F went beyond talk; they refused to shoulder their muskets when ordered to do so. Placed in arrest, the twenty-one spent the following day "carrying logs in front of brigade headquarters, within range of rebel shells."[43] Perhaps these difficulties and frustrations account for the misbehavior of the regiment on September 30, when, to take advantage of the transfer of Confederate troops to deal with the Union attack on Forts Harrison and Gilmer, the V and IX Corps advanced westward from Globe Tavern. The enemy counterattacked Colonel Samuel Harriman's brigade of the First Division, IX Corps, and forced it back; three regiments of the brigade retired in good order, reformed, and checked the enemy, but the 13th Ohio, also a part of the brigade, was "thrown into a panic and part of them fled ingloriously from the field."[44]

40. Whitelaw Reid, *Ohio in the War: Her Statesmen, Her Generals and Soldiers* (2 vols.; Cincinnati, 1868), II, 826.
41. Howard Aston, *History and Roster of the Fourth and Fifth Independent Battalions and Thirteenth Regiment Ohio Cavalry Volunteers* (Columbus, 1902), 8.
42. Reid, *Ohio in the War*, II, 826.
43. Aston, *History and Roster of the Fourth*, 21.
44. *Official Records*, Vol. XLII, Pt. 1, p. 553 (General Willcox's report).

Hardly had Kautz and Gregg learned that the five regiments of unwilling infantry were to be transferred to them, when they requested their respective army commanders to authorize the reorganization of their divisions from two brigades to three. Permission to do so being granted, the tables of organization of October 31 show both divisions divided into three brigades.[45]

The cavalry pickets protecting the rear of the infantry in the siege lines facing Petersburg had no Mosby or other Partisan Ranger groups to contend with, but they had their hands full just the same with the responsibility of guarding a curved line more than twenty miles long, running from Grant's headquarters and the army's huge supply base at City Point on the James River to Reams' Station to the southwest. There were no mountains to provide hideouts for guerrillas, but the area was seamed and checkered with small watercourses, swamps, ravines, thickets and wooded areas, and obscure plantation and woods roads provided

---

The brigade commander's report was even less flattering. "The Thirteenth Ohio," Colonel Harriman wrote, "were thrown into a panic by a few shots and fled, the greater part of them, from the field. A part of them . . . were afterward collected and placed on the line." *Ibid.*, 558.

45. *Ibid.*, Pt. 3, pp. 233, 241, 259, 463, 466. Kautz made up his third brigade from the two newly acquired regiments, the 1st Maryland and the 1st New York Mounted Rifles. Gregg reshuffled his regiments completely. From October 31 on, his First Brigade (Davies) was made up of the 1st Massachusetts, 1st New Jersey, 10th and 24th New York, and 1st Pennsylvania (four companies); the Second Brigade (Colonel Kerwin) included the 2nd, 4th, 8th, 13th, and 16th Pennsylvania; the Third (Colonel Charles H. Smith) was the 1st Maine, 6th Ohio, and 21st Pennsylvania. One of Kautz's organizational problems involved the 1st District of Columbia. Originally a battalion raised in the District to perform mounted patrol duty in Washington (where it became known as the "Terror of Evildoers"), it became a regiment when in February and March, 1864, eight companies raised in Maine were added to it. It had the distinction of being the only cavalry regiment armed with the 16-shot Henry rifle. In the late summer of 1864, it was decided to fill up the ranks of the 1st Maine by transferring to it the eight Maine companies of the 1st District of Columbia. Kautz wrote on September 4 to Gregg, "There is great dissatisfaction in the regiment about the order. . . . It virtually breaks up . . . one of the most efficient regiments in the service. They are much discontented by the order, as they have heretofore felt great pride in their regiment on account of being armed with a peculiar and effective weapon." Nevertheless, the transfer was made, but not until after the regiment had lost about 220 men in Hampton's Cattle Raid. Merrill, *Campaigns of the First Maine*, 227–28; Tobie, *First Maine Cavalry*, 320–23; *Official Records*, Vol. XLII, Pt. 2, p. 694.

ready access to and through the cavalry picket lines for those who knew the country, and many did. And, as in the Shenandoah Valley, guerrillas could rely on a friendly population for food, shelter, and information. Kautz and Gregg reported time after time that their pickets and picket reserves had been pounced upon by guerrillas, or, as both generals thought was frequently the case, by Confederate cavalrymen on the prowl for horses to remount themselves.[46] There were other, relatively minor, incidents, of telegraph lines cut and of Federal scouting parties fired on from ambush, but it was the constant harassment of pickets that caused the greatest concern.[47] With the attackers nearly always dressed in Federal uniforms and operating mainly at night, complete safety was unattainable, but General Kautz proposed a scheme that came surprisingly close to accomplishing it. The wonder is that it was not thought of and put into practice two years earlier—another case, perhaps, of Columbus and the egg. In a mid-September report, Kautz explained that "quite a number" of his pickets had been killed, wounded, or taken prisoner in the previous month, and that the losses would have been far greater had he not started the practice of dismounting his pickets and having them stand guard on foot. "The restlessness of the horses," Kautz wrote, "revealed the sentinel's position in the night to the lurking foe, who generally were on foot and made their attacks from the inside of the line." But, Kautz went on,

When it becomes necessary to dismount the men and separate them from their horses to perform their duty, it seems to be a legitimate duty of infantry, and it would be economy to perform all the duty that can be done by infantry by that arm. . . . The maintenance of such long picket lines for weeks at a time by cavalry exclusively is destructive of discipline and ruinous to the horses, and destroys its efficiency for sudden and quick movements, which I consider to be the legitimate duty of . . . cavalry. It is too expensive an arm of the service to be wasted away and broken down for defensive purposes that can be as well or better performed by infantry, with the assistance of a relatively small force of mounted men to carry intelligence.[48]

46. For example, Official Records, Vol. XLII, Pt. 1, pp. 611, 630; Pt. 2, pp. 241, 583, 708, 715, 878–79.
47. Ibid., Pt. 3, pp. 242, 526.
48. Ibid., Pt. 2, p. 933. At almost this same time, General Lee queried Hampton on the possibility of having picket duty performed by his "dismounts." Ibid., 1231.

The first part of Kautz's proposal was generally adopted, and dismounting the pickets, posting them so that "each will have in view those immediately upon his right and left, and . . . within easy communicating distance," posting additional dismounted sentinels "to the rear as well as in front" of the picket line and of the picket reserve posts, and protecting the pickets as well as the reserve posts "by constructing barriers to obstruct the approach of the enemy" and by sending out frequent scouting parties, became standard practice.[49] On the other hand, Kautz's unanswerable argument for the use of infantry to do picket duty was ignored, and only rarely were footsoldiers given that duty to perform. The dead weight of doctrine and habit was too great; besides, Meade and Butler were as shorthanded for infantry to maintain the siege of Petersburg and Richmond as they were for cavalry to protect the siege lines.[50]

It was at this time also that Kautz issued orders to his brigade commanders and they in turn to their regimental commanders that "dismounted [enemy] cavalrymen, seeking to obtain horses to remount themselves . . . if captured, are not to be sent in as prisoners."[51] The records do not indicate, nor could they be expected to do so, to what extent the obvious implications of this harsh order were actually acted upon.

A particularly distasteful task the cavalry had to perform at this time as part of their picket duty was to try to stop desertions from the Union army to the enemy, and the escape of bounty-jumpers, drafted men, and substitutes, to the rear.[52] On December 20, General Butler directed Kautz to "instruct . . . [his] officers and men on outpost and picket duty to . . . arrest all whom they may see trying to desert, if necessary pursue and shoot them down. . . . for every deserter apprehended a reward of $30 and a month's furlough will be granted to the soldier making the arrest."[53]

49. *Ibid.*, Pt. 3, p. 1010.
50. *Ibid.*, Pt. 2, pp. 959, 1006. At the end of August, Meade and Butler between them had only forty-six thousand infantry, many of whom were untrained or partially trained recruits of questionable reliability. Catton, *Grant Takes Command*, 352.
51. *Official Records*, Vol. XLII, Pt. 2, p. 716.
52. *Ibid.*, 951.
53. *Ibid.*, Pt. 3, p. 1049. So far as the records show, no would-be de-

General Hampton demonstrated on September 16 that the Union cavalry had something more serious than the intrusion of an occasional scout, guerrilla, or would-be horse thief to worry about. The possibility of a sweep around the southern end of the Federal lines for a damaging blow against their base at City Point had not escaped General Lee's attention. On September 3, he wrote Hampton that he judged from the reports of the latter's scouts "that the enemy . . . [was] very open to attack at City Point, and other points where his wagons are parked in his rear. . . . A sudden blow in that quarter might be detrimental to him"; he asked Hampton to give this possibility his best attention and to study the available roads and the distances for such a foray.[54] Two days later Hampton received a report from Sergeant George D. Shadburne (signed "Your obedient scout, Shadburne") of the Jeff. Davis Legion, which settled the question of what he should do to comply with General Lee's suggestion. Shadburne's communication deserves to be used as a textbook model of what such reports should be. It listed, location by location, the Federal installations around City Point—the "immense hospital and ambulance and wagon train," "large pontoon train," and the "immense amount of supplies," and the type and number of troops at each of these locations. Then came the location of each of the Federal army corps, and lastly, full information on the points on the Federal picket line from which these facilities and encampments could be reached. Shadburne also reported the presence at Coggins' Point (about five miles east of City Point and almost directly across the James from Westover Landing) of "3,000 beeves, attended by 120 men and 20 citizens, without arms. At Sycamore Church [three miles south of Coggins' Point] is one regiment of cavalry (First District of Columbia) about 250. This is the nearest point on the picket line to Coggins' Point." Then, following a list of the distances from Coggins' Point to the Jerusalem Plank Road (the main north-south highway), came Shadburne's conclusion: "The greatest danger, I think, would be on the Jerusalem plank road in return-

---

serter was ever shot pursuant to this order. Only one case is in the records of a Union cavalryman deserting to the enemy at this time; this was a private in the 3rd New York. *Ibid.*, 158.

54. *Ibid.*, Pt. 2, p. 1233.

ing." His choice of words implies either that the scout had decided on his own that the capture of the herd should be the objective of the operation, or that Hampton had done so and sent Shadburne to make an on-the-spot investigation of its feasibility.[55]

The vulnerability to attack of the cattle herd, from which beeves on the hoof were issued to supply the army with fresh meat rations, had for some time been a cause for concern to the commissary officers in charge of the herd and to the officers of the cavalry guard. Major J. Stannard Baker, commanding officer of the 1st District of Columbia, reported as early as August 13 that the herd, then at Cocke's Mill, six miles south of Coggins' Point, was "exposed to guerrillas that are very numerous."[56] Two weeks later, on August 29, the herd was moved to Coggins' Point, but not until the officers in charge had asked for and received reassurance from army headquarters "that beef-cattle can be safely herded and grazed there."[57] Guarding the herd, in addition to the 1st District of Columbia at Sycamore Church, were 50 civilian herdsmen and about 150 men of the 13th Pennsylvania.

On September 9, General Lee approved Hampton's proposal of a raid to capture the herd, but warned, as Shadburne had, that the "only difficulty of importance" would be the return march, encumbered as Hampton would then be with a large, slow-moving herd. Lee also warned Hampton to be on his guard against an attack on his flank by Gregg, who was thought to be near the Weldon Railroad, and he offered to send two brigades of infantry down the Boydton Plank Road to assist Hampton on his return.[58]

Hampton left on the raid on the morning of September 14, with W. H. F. Lee's division, Rosser's and James Dearing's brigades, and a detachment of 100 men from John Dunovant's and P. M. B. Young's brigades, a total of perhaps 4,000 to 4,500 men, estimated by the Federals as a force of about 6,000.[59] He had decided to attack the cavalry at Sycamore Church, "as being nearest

55. *Ibid.*, 1235–36. The Jerusalem Plank Road ran southeast from Petersburg, between the Weldon Railroad on the west and the Norfolk & Petersburg Railroad on the east, to Jerusalem, on the Nottoway River.
56. *Ibid.*, 166; see also 695, 697.
57. *Ibid.*, Pt. 1, pp. 27, 26.
58. *Ibid.*, Pt. 2, p. 1242.
59. *Ibid.*, Pt. 1, p. 28.

the cattle, and . . . [as] the largest force of the enemy"; "by dispersing them there," Hampton reasoned, he would make it "impossible for them to concentrate any force in time to interfere with the main object of the expedition." Shadburne's report indicated that against the small regiment at Sycamore Church and the 150 cavalrymen guarding the herd Hampton would have a superiority of nearly ten to one. Nevertheless, he took no chances; he sent Lee to guard the left and Dearing to guard the right. Rosser was given the job of attacking the cavalry at the church and those guarding the herd, and then to round up and bring out the cattle. At five A.M. on the sixteenth, Rosser charged the 1st District of Columbia camp. The Union pickets and picket reserves put up a stout fight —Hampton wrote that "for some time . . . [they] fought as stubbornly as I have ever seen . . . [the enemy] do"—but they were up against hopeless odds; they were surrounded and overrun, and nearly all of them were taken prisoner. The herd had been corraled for the night less than two miles behind the picket line. Rosser had already driven away the 13th Pennsylvania detachment and had the corral surrounded before Captain N. A. Richardson, who appears to have kept his head better than any other Union officer present, could carry out his intention to have the corral fence torn down and the cattle stampeded in all directions. By sunrise the Confederates, who, according to Richardson, had brought along "a large number of hounds and herding dogs," had their prisoners, a number of wagons, all the horses and mules they could catch, and the entire herd of 2,486 beef cattle rounded up and were on their way south at the best speed of the herd.[60]

It was nearly noon before reliable information about the raid reached army headquarters. Orders were sent at once to Kautz, and to Davies, who in Gregg's absence was temporarily in command of the Second Division, to start after the raiders with all the men they could collect in a hurry. The two officers did their best,

60. The main sources on the raid and the Federal pursuit are Hampton's and Captain Richardson's reports, *ibid.*, 944–47 and 27–30, but there are numerous additional orders, dispatches, and reports dealing with this affair, *e.g.*, *ibid.*, 25–26, 26–27, 34–35, 614–15, 821–22; Pt. 2, pp. 859, 861, 868, 869, 874, 877, 879, 891, 897, 947. Hampton's losses were 10 killed, 47 wounded, and 4 missing. He claimed the capture of 304 prisoners. *Ibid.*, Pt. 1, pp. 823, 946.

but their task was hopeless. Kautz had to pursue with fewer than 500 men, only half of whom were armed with carbines, and Davies with about 2,100. The raiders had a long start, and the distances Kautz and Davies had to cover to catch up with them were too great, about fifteen miles from Davies' camps, and nearly twice as far from Kautz's. Nevertheless, both of them managed to make contact with the powerful rear and flank guards Hampton had told off to check any pursuit, but were unable to break through them to the main body and the fast-moving herd. Late that night they gave up the chase, with nothing accomplished other than the recapture of about twenty of the cattle.

Having their herd of cattle driven off practically from under their noses—anyone, including the people back home, could see on a map or learn from the reports in their newspapers how near Coggins' Point was to the general-in-chief's headquarters—was a humiliation for the Union army, not too different from Stuart's rides around McClellan. One evening, shortly after the raid, Grant was asked by a visitor, "When do you expect to starve out Lee and capture Richmond?" and he answered ruefully, "Never, if our armies continue to supply him with beef-cattle."[61] Fortunately for the Union cavalry, no one seemed to hold them responsible for the loss. On the other side of the line, the windfall of nearly 2,500 well fattened steers provided the Confederate troops with a welcome improvement of their diet, and gave their spirits an equally welcome lift. In a fight at McDowell's farm two weeks later Hampton's cavalry, fighting dismounted as usual, had perfect ammunition with which to taunt their blue-coated opposite numbers by "bellowing like bulls, and shouting over to the Yankees, 'Good fat beef over here, come over here and get some,' and then a fellow would jump up and bellow and by the time he dropped, bullets would be whistling over our heads and rattling against the rail piles."[62] Clearly, the Civil War owes much of its special flavor and at least some of its fascination to the fact that the men on both sides spoke the same language. Of greater importance than such japes was the boost that this well planned, crisply executed, and

61. Porter, *Campaigning with Grant*, 299. On the day of the raid Grant was meeting Sheridan at Charlestown and so was absent from City Point.
62. Brooks, *Butler and His Cavalry*, 330.

eminently successful operation gave Hampton's standing with his own men and throughout the Confederate army.[63]

Grant's objective in a succession of operations in the late autumn of 1864 was to force Lee to stretch and strain his limited and declining manpower by having to meet a steady succession of alternate or simultaneous attacks on the two ends of his ever-lengthening defense lines. Secondarily, Grant wanted to extend southward his grip on the Weldon Railroad, to interrupt the wagon routes on the Vaughan and Boydton Plank roads to the west of it that General Lee was forced to use after Warren's initial success at Globe Tavern, and lastly to reach and break still another of Lee's major supply arteries, the Southside Railroad.

The first of these operations was the attack on September 29–30 on Forts Harrison and Gilmer, north of the James, mounted by General Butler. Kautz's division took part in this operation by attacking along the Creighton Road, north of the Chickahominy, at midnight on the night of the twenty-ninth. The attack brought them within sight of Richmond, but it came up against a continuous defense line, with light and heavy artillery commanding all the approaches. "In the darkness the command became confused in the fallen timber, which was very extensive and difficult to get through"; consequently, Kautz was forced to halt the attack and to recall his men.[64]

To coincide with this operation north of the James, Meade sent the IX Corps, with Gregg's cavalry attached, to get across the Vaughan Road to the Boydton Plank Road and if possible to the Southside Railroad beyond. The initial attack by the IX Corps infantry drove M. C. Butler's cavalry back to Hatcher's Run, about two miles short of the Vaughan Road, but could not break through the well sited and well protected rifle pits at that point. Gregg in the meantime had sent some of his division south "to dash upon Reams' Station . . . [and] drive off or capture" whatever enemy troops were there. This force succeeded in driving Confederate

63. See General Lee's congratulatory message to Hampton; *Official Records*, Vol. XLII, Pt. 1, p. 952.

64. *Ibid.*, Pt. 2, p. 1149; Pt. 1, p. 20. Kautz does not say so, but it may be assumed that the "fallen timber" was an abattis protecting the Confederate line.

cavalry, whose numbers are not given, a mile west of the station, but then it ran into barricades held in strength and could get no farther.

In command of the defenses in this sector was Hampton. When the Federals launched their attack, he decided to retain W. H. F. Lee's division, which had been ordered north to help deal with Butler's attack and had actually begun its march. Just before dark Hampton launched an attack on Gregg that was sufficiently successful to enable him to reestablish his picket line east of the Vaughan Road, but Gregg, with his men fighting dismounted, managed to maintain a perimeter west of the station and, with the bulk of his forces, around Wyatt's farm. The following afternoon the V Corps, attacking in support of the IX, drove Dearing's brigade, now commanded by Colonel Joel R. Griffin, out of its position northwest of the station. Thereupon Hampton arranged with Henry Heth, commanding the infantry rushed down from Petersburg to help him, for a repetition of the manoeuver that had worked so well against Hancock a month earlier; Heth was to deliver a frontal attack against the Federal infantry while Hampton with the cavalry attacked their exposed left flank and rear. This time Gregg was not present to protect the open flank. The Confederate attack, which Hampton called "one of the handsomest" he had ever seen, was a success, producing nine hundred prisoners and "ten standards."[65] It was in the face of this attack, which struck Orlando Willcox's division, that the 13th Ohio gave way in panic, and it was in the fighting at McDowell's farm the next day that the Confederate cavalry taunted the Federal cavalry opposite by "bellowing like bulls."

The next serious incident involved Kautz's division, now numbering about 1,700. Kautz held an advanced position in front of the X Corps, on the Darbytown Road, which ran southwest from Richmond toward Malvern Hill. The position was poorly chosen, with a swamp on its right and another to its rear, and the men did not have sufficient tools (or enterprise?) to entrench properly. On the evening of October 6, Kautz was warned by "refugees" to expect a reconnaissance in force of his position the following morn-

65. *Ibid.*, Pt. 1, pp. 947–48, 553; Pt. 2, pp. 1106, 1107, 1108–1109, 1140, 1141.

ing. Hence the command was standing to arms at 6:30 A.M. on the seventh when the enemy did in fact attack. As it turned out later, this attack, which was easily repulsed, was a mere probe, but with the danger apparently past, everyone relaxed. An hour went by, and then, without warning, came the real attack. Two brigades of infantry charged Kautz's left and a third brigade attacked his right, while the 7th South Carolina, making a wide circuit, got into his rear. Kautz's entire division was driven back; the first of the guns, leading the retreat of his artillery over the single, badly cut-up road through the swamp, became mired, blocking the road, with the result that all eight of the guns he had with him, together with their caissons, were lost to the enemy. Lost also were 18 men killed, 54 wounded, and 202 (of whom 14 were known to have been wounded) taken prisoner.[66]

On October 27 came another expedition toward the Boydton Plank Road with the Southside Railroad as its ultimate objective. The movement was to be made by three columns of infantry: the IX Corps on the right (north), the V Corps in the center, and two divisions of the II Corps—John Gibbon's, commanded by General Thomas W. Egan in Gibbon's absence, and General Gershom Mott's—on the left. Supporting the II Corps and marching on its left flank was to be Gregg's cavalry.[67] In overall command was General Hancock. On the morning of the twenty-fifth, Egan's and Mott's divisions were quietly withdrawn from the trenches before Petersburg; they moved the next day to Fort Dushane, three quarters of a mile south of Globe Tavern. The plan called for the entire force to move out at 3:30 A.M. on the twenty-seventh. Egan and Mott were to march on the Vaughan Road, cross Hatcher's Run to reach the Boydton Plank Road, march on it to a second crossing of Hatcher's Run at Burgess' Mill, and then proceed northwestward to the Southside Railroad. Gregg was to move along their left flank

66. *Ibid.*, Pt. 1, pp. 823–25, 826–28, 830–31, 832–33. Quite properly, Kautz blamed himself for allowing his division to be caught in a tactically untenable position and for mistaking the 6:30 probing attack for the real attack.

67. This account of the action at Burgess' Mill is based on the reports of Generals Hancock, Gregg, and Hampton; *ibid.*, 230–38, 608–10, 949–50. Burgess' Mill was located on Hatcher's Run, immediately to the west of the Boydton Plank Road crossing.

by way of Rowanty Post Office and the Quaker Road. On the route specified by his orders, Hancock would have had to march about eight miles to reach the nearest point on the railroad; the cavalry, being on the outer flank, would have had to cover another two or three miles.

The troops moved out on time. The head of Egan's column made good the first crossing of Hatcher's Run; as his and Mott's divisions resumed their march northwest to Dabney's Mill, they could hear Gregg's guns off to their left, as the cavalry fought its way across Rowanty Creek, driving back the dismounted cavalry of M. C. Butler's division, posted behind breastworks to block the crossing. The attack at this point was spearheaded by the 6th Ohio and the 1st Maine. Having crossed the creek, Gregg turned north on the Quaker Road and hastened forward to make contact with Egan and Mott. He now learned from captured Confederate couriers that W. H. F. Lee's division was in camp on Stony Creek, three miles to the southeast, and that Butler's divison, having regrouped, was holding a position athwart the Quaker Road, up ahead. Ignoring the potential threat by Lee to his rear, Gregg continued his advance, which brought him to the crossing of Gravelly Run, defended by a major portion of Butler's cavalry and backed by a section of artillery on a "commanding eminence" above the west bank of the stream. Gregg ordered the 6th Ohio and the 1st Maine to force a crossing; they dismounted, waded the stream, and, aided by a mounted charge of the 21st Pennsylvania, drove back the opposition and cleared the crossing.

While Gregg was fighting on the left, Hancock's infantry reached Dabney's Mill. With Egan still in the lead, they covered the three miles from the mill to the Boydton Plank Road and followed it northward to the bridge over Hatcher's Run at Burgess' Mill. Then followed one of the more confused actions of the war. As Egan's division, supported by a brigade of Mott's and preceded by a regiment of cavalry, deployed under the fire of fourteen pieces of Confederate artillery to force a crossing of the stream, Byron R. Pierce's brigade of Mott's division, some distance to the rear, was attacked in flank by portions of Henry Heth's and William Mahone's divisions of infantry, emerging from the "very dense" woods to the east of the Boydton Plank Road. After driving

Pierce beyond the road, where, with the help of Regis deTrobriand's brigade, the Union line was stabilized, Heth and Mahone
formed line of battle facing south. They were then attacked in
rear by Egan, who, at the sound of the fighting behind him, called
off the attempt to cross Hatcher's Run, turned his men around,
charged Heth and Mahone from the rear, and drove them back into
the woods from which they had emerged, with the loss of "two
colors and several hundred prisoners."

All this time Gregg was fighting a battle of his own below the
intersection of the Quaker Road and the Boydton Plank Road,
somewhat—perhaps a half mile—to the south of the area in
which the fight between the Confederate and the Federal infantry
was swirling first in one direction and then in the other. Gregg
had sent the 6th Ohio and the 1st Maine to help deTrobriand and
Pierce stem the Confederate attack coming in from their right,
when he himself was attacked from the south and west by two brigades of W. H. F. Lee's division. At first, Gregg had only one of his
regiments, the 21st Pennsylvania, at hand to contain Lee's attack,
but he was joined shortly by the 6th Ohio and then by the 1st
Maine. The arrival of these reinforcements could do no more than
to slow down Lee's advance; the three regiments were being
pressed back, step by step, by the "very determined" Confederate
attack, and at length Gregg had to ask General Hancock to send
back to him as many more of his cavalry regiments as he could
spare. Hancock, hard pressed on three sides as he was, had no
choice but to comply, for if Gregg had been driven in, the entire
command, infantry and cavalry, would have been hemmed in on
every side and in imminent danger of being bottled up. He therefore ordered back to Gregg the 2nd, 4th, and 13th Pennsylvania,
which, so Gregg reported, came on "successively as fast as their
legs could carry them, entered the fight, and at dark the enemy
retired repulsed without having accomplished [anything] other
than his own punishment."[68]

The operation clearly a failure, Hancock was now faced with

68. This fight, in D. S. Freeman's opinion "a brilliant addition to
Hampton's record," also resulted in a personal tragedy for him. One of his
sons, Lieutenant Thomas Preston Hampton, was killed in one of Butler's
charges, and another, Lieutenant Wade Hampton, Jr., was severely wounded
when he went to his brother's aid. Freeman, *Lee's Lieutenants*, III, 615–16;
Official Records, Vol. XLII, Pt. 1, p. 949.

the unpalatable necessity of ordering a retreat. His forward progress was effectively blocked, his line of retreat back to Dabney's Mill was in jeopardy, a heavy rain had begun to fall, and his entire force, particularly the cavalry, had run low on ammunition.[69] The retreat of the infantry, minus many of the wounded who had to be left behind for lack of ambulances to carry them, began at ten P.M. The retreat of the cavalry began a half hour later and was effected without interference by the enemy.

This action at Burgess' Mill was a costly fiasco, with a loss to the Union army of 123 killed, 754 wounded, and 625 captured by the enemy or missing. It also closed active operations for the year, which, from the beginning of May on, saw six months of almost continuous, bloody fighting.[70] In his report of the operation, Hancock paid tribute to Gregg's "stubborn and successful resistance to Hampton's attack," and he, as well as Gregg, called special attention to the "conspicuous gallantry" of Major Sidney W. Thaxter, 1st Maine, who had received his orders to return to Maine with a portion of his regiment for muster-out, but volunteered to stay on for this operation and commanded the skirmish line of Gregg's Third Brigade throughout the day.[71]

The end of "active operations" for the year did not by any means inaugurate a period of peace and rest for the Federal cavalry. It had, as always, its picketing and scouting duties to perform, activities that became increasingly demanding and hazardous as Hampton's cavalry grew in strength throughout these autumn months. On October 24, Hampton reported to General Lee that his command was "growing stronger every day" and was "in good condition for a fight." He said that with the continued success of his efforts to augment the effective strength of his command, he expected to be able to take "upward of 5,000 men into action."[72] Indeed, only a week later, on October 31, he reported an "effective total present" (presumably the total of his mounted and fully equipped men) of 5,654.[73] He had in addition "a large num-

69. *Official Records*, Vol. XLII, Pt. 1, p. 235.
70. *Ibid.*, 238; Grant, *Personal Memoirs*, II, 341.
71. *Official Records*, Vol. XLII, Pt. 1, pp. 237, 609.
72. *Ibid.*, Pt. 3, pp. 1162, 1176–77.
73. *Ibid.*, 1187. Two separate reports show Hampton as having on November 30, 6,208 "effective total present," and 4,999 "effective present." The difference between the two figures is not explained. *Ibid.*, 1236–37. By

ber" of dismounted men, whom he used to man trenches in the Petersburg defenses.[74]

The Federal cavalry too was growing in numbers; despite a steady toll of casualties, which in the four and a half months from August 13 to the end of the year mounted up to 181 killed, 731 wounded, and 509 taken prisoner or missing, and despite the discharge of men for disability and the departure of time-expired veterans, Gregg's numbers rose from 3,435 "present for duty equipped" at the end of August to 4,869 on September 30, and, after a drop to 3,864 on October 31, rose again to 6,160 at the end of November and 6,136 at the year-end. Similarly, Kautz's division grew from 1,585 on August 31 to 1,624 on September 30, to 2,244 on October 31, and after a slight decline to 2,117 on November 30, to 3,226 on December 31.[75] But if these gains in numbers suggest that lack of manpower was no longer the critical problem it had been, there were other difficulties to cause concern. On November 14, Gregg deemed it necessary to issue the following circular to his division: "A recent inspection of the division shows a great deficiency in the arms and equipments of the men present for duty. Regimental commanders will ascertain accurately the deficiencies in carbines, pistols, and sabers . . . and . . . will make requisitions at once to supply the deficiencies. If, after a reasonable time, the stores required are not furnished, it is desired that official information to that effect be sent to these headquarters."[76] Why such directions should have had to be issued in the fourth year of the war to commanders of regiments in daily contact with the enemy, "passeth all understanding."

Equally difficult to understand is an incident that occurred

December 31, however, the "aggregate present" had dropped to 3,463. *Ibid.*, 1286. Contrary to this officially reported figure, the historian of Hampton's command states that "by the return of December 31, 1864 . . . [the cavalry] had increased to 7,063. . . ." Besides this there were about a thousand men absent on horse furloughs." Edward L. Wells, *Hampton and His Cavalry in '64* (Richmond, 1899), 388.

74. *Official Records*, Vol. XLII, Pt. 3, p. 1159.

75. *Ibid.*, Pt. 1, pp. 116–62, 39–41. The strength figures given include all ranks, and, in the case of the Second Division, the horse artillery attached to the division.

76. *Ibid.*, Pt. 3, p. 618.

THE ESSENCE OF WAR

while Gregg was absent on Warren's December 7–11 railroad-wrecking expedition. He had left behind Colonel Michael Kerwin with the 13th Pennsylvania and the 6th Ohio to guard the installations around City Point and, generally, the rear of the army. On the evening of the tenth, Kerwin was ordered to move out as quickly as possible and join an infantry column "sent to communicate with Warren." The departure of the expedition was delayed for several hours by a lack of ammunition for the Burnside carbines with which the two cavalry regiments were thought to be armed. After Warren's and Gregg's return to the army, General Meade ordered an investigation of the incident. Gregg reported that three quarters of the men in the two regiments were armed with Sharps carbines, "for which there was an abundance of ammunition," and that the shortage affected only 176 men in the two regiments who were armed with Burnside carbines.[77] Entirely apart from Colonel Kerwin's lack of judgment in failing to make a movement he knew to be urgent with the men—the majority of his command—who had plenty of ammunition, it may also be asked how it was possible so late in the war to have men in the same regiments armed with carbines that required two different types of ammunition, and whose commanders therefore had to cope with all the problems, particularly in combat, that such a situation entailed. It should be added also that this inefficient distribution of firearms was not by any means confined to the two regiments mentioned.

The replacement of horses lost by the cavalry seemed not to be a major problem in the late summer and early autumn of 1864. Even the horses needed to mount the regiments transferred from the infantry to Gregg and Kautz appear to have been supplied reasonably promptly. On January 6, 1865, Grant wrote to Halleck to suggest that the purchase of horses in the East (which had apparently been halted some time before) be resumed, "and that all the horses that can be got elsewhere between this and spring ought to be purchased. If we can start out in the spring with a reserve of 20,000 or 30,000 . . . cavalry horses they will be worth as much to us as that number of veteran troops." But the sugges-

77. *Ibid.*, 981, 1004.

tion brought to light a fresh problem; Halleck replied that "without the greatest care and energy we shall not be able to feed the animals we have . . . due precaution should be taken not to purchase cavalry horses till they are actually required, otherwise large numbers will actually starve."[78] Indeed, within two days of his dispatch to Halleck, Grant had to tell him that the army's supplies of forage had run short, and that for the past week the cavalry and artillery horses had been on half rations. Whatever the reason for the shortage may have been, it was corrected quickly; on January 13, Grant was able to direct Meade to have full rations restored.[79]

Some of the scouting expeditions the cavalry had to make at this time were on a major scale. Thus, on November 6 Gregg was directed to take his entire division, except for the men on picket duty, on a reconnaissance "well down in the direction of the Weldon railroad" to see if the enemy might be trying to take advantage of any election-day slackness in the Union lines by a movement toward the Federal rear.[80] Again, on November 30, he was ordered to "make a reconnaissance in the direction of Dinwiddie Court-House" to see if "any portion of Hampton's cavalry has gone south, as reported," and to "ascertain if the enemy are building a railroad from Stony Creek through Dinwiddie, and if so . . . [to] destroy it."[81] Moving out on December 1 in response to this order, Gregg, with J. Irvin Gregg's brigade leading the way, captured and destroyed Stony Creek Depot, "defended by infantry and cavalry, with artillery in strong works"; after destroying large quantities of supplies stored at the station and spiking two pieces of artillery he was unable to move, he came away with 190 prisoners, eight wagons, and thirty mules. He was, however, unable to obtain information about any portion of the enemy cavalry moving south.[82]

78. Ibid., Vol. XLVI, Pt. 2, pp. 53, 68.
79. Ibid., 74, 113.
80. Ibid., Vol. XLII, Pt. 3, p. 536; Pt. 1, p. 610.
81. Ibid., Pt. 3, p. 758.
82. Ibid., Pt. 1, p. 24. The "infantry" Gregg refers to was actually a group of Hampton's dismounted cavalry. There is the usual conflict of evidence on the amount of supplies (corn, hay, bacon, clothing, ammunition, etc.) destroyed by Gregg at the station, as well as on the circumstances of his retreat. Compare ibid., 610–11 and 854.

On December 7 in bitterly cold weather—five of Hampton's pickets are said to have frozen to death that night—Gregg and 4,200 of his men accompanied Warren's V Corps and Mott's division of the II Corps on an expedition to wreck the Weldon Railroad from Stony Creek Depot south eighteen miles to the Meherrin River.[83] The cavalry not only cleared the way for the infantry by driving off parties of Hampton's horsemen, some in regimental strength, that tried to block its progress, but also helped with the work of destruction, tearing up track by the usual method of burning the ties and heating and twisting the rails, and destroying a series of bridges, one 160 feet long over the Nottoway, and two others 60 and 100 feet long respectively over two branches of Three Creeks. After reaching the Meherrin at Hicksford, Warren decided to return, and thereafter, until the arrival of the command at its camps late on the night of December 11, the cavalry protected the flanks and rear of the marching infantry from the harassment of Confederate cavalry and lost in the process 17 killed, 64 wounded, and 56 taken prisoner or missing.[84]

According to General Warren, "the railroad destruction was carried over a distance of about seventeen or eighteen miles, and was so complete that I think the enemy will not deem its use of

83. Wellman, *Giant in Gray*, 165; for reports of the operation, see *Official Records*, Vol. XLII, Pt. 1, pp. 443–49, 611–13, 950–52; also Pt. 3, pp. 833, 834, 855, 885, 886.

84. *Ibid.*, Pt. 1, p. 613. This expedition appears to have had more than a normal by-product of atrocities. The historian of Butler's division relates, "Our scouts were instructed that when they caught Yankees in the act of robbing and burning, to take the vandals by the arms and legs and swing them in the flames, drunk or sober." The historians of the 3rd Pennsylvania record that "the bodies of several Union soldiers were found hanging to trees along the road, having been murdered by guerrillas. In retaliation, every man who could be found within some distance of the road was treated in the same manner and the houses burned to the ground. It was a sad though a grand sight to see the whole country illuminated by the flames." General Warren reported officially, "Scarcely a man was to be found. . . . We had evidences, however, of the men lurking about in the woods, for on our retreat it is reported some of our men were found dead along the route, in one instance with the throat cut. Whether this was true or not, it soon became the belief of all the men in the command, and in retaliation almost every house was set on fire. Every effort was made by the officers to stop this incendiarism . . . with partial success." Brooks, *Butler and His Cavalry*, 387; Regimental History Committee, *History of the 3d Pennsylvania*, 469; *Official Records*, Vol. XLII, Pt. 1, pp. 445–46.

sufficient importance to rebuild it." General Lee, on the other hand, reported to the Confederate War Department, on the basis of information supplied by the superintendent of the railroad, that "about six miles of the track" had been broken up.[85] Whatever the correct figure may have been, Hampton gave General Butler the job of getting the road back into service. Butler impressed three hundred Negroes from the nearby farms and plantations and set between eight hundred and a thousand of his own men to cutting down and sawing up trees for crossties, and to straightening the rails by the same heating process the Yankees had used to bend them. Within two weeks the first train, with Butler riding in the engine, steamed over the rebuilt track.[86]

There was to be another raid, ordered by Grant in early February ("to take advantage of the present good weather") to destroy or capture one of the wagon trains hauling supplies to Petersburg around Warren's position astride the Weldon Railroad. Gregg went west as far as Dinwiddie Court House, met little opposition, and captured eighteen wagons and fifty prisoners.[87] Apart from this expedition, drill when the weather and the footing allowed, an occasional scout, and the routine of picket duty, the cavalry had little to do in these late-winter weeks but to take care of themselves and their horses and to enjoy life in their log huts. Mindful perhaps of Hooker's accomplishments in the winter of 1862–1863, General Meade saw to it that the army was well supplied with necessities and even some comforts. Every company had its log cookhouse, and every regiment a bakery that supplied the men with freshly baked bread every day. The cattle driven off by Hampton were replaced promptly, and the troops were issued fresh beef three or four times a week; there were also plentiful

85. *Official Records*, Vol. XLII, Pt. 1, p. 444; Pt. 3, p. 1271.
86. Brooks, *Butler and His Cavalry*, 387; Wellman, *Giant in Gray*, 165.
87. *Official Records*, Vol. XLVI, Pt. 2, pp. 365, 367, 368, 380, 388. The cavalry raid, Gregg's last, was incidental to a larger, three-day operation, known as "Second Hatcher's Run." As might have been anticipated, the good weather mentioned by Grant did not last. The historian of the 13th Ohio wrote of the night of February 6, "We are too close to the enemy to build fires so will have to shiver through the night in our cavalry jackets as our overcoats are with the horses, strapped to the saddles. Where the horses are we do not know. . . . Spent a miserable night covered with sleet our clothing seemed like a coat of mail." Aston, *History and Roster of the Fourth*, 29.

issues of beans, peas, desiccated vegetables, coffee, and tea. Even the paymasters appeared more frequently than they had in the summer and autumn. The general opinion was that Meade "certainly fed, clothed, and paid his troops better and more promptly than any other commander the Army of the Potomac had ever had."[88] The Christian Commission too was much in evidence. It not only ministered to the spiritual wants of the men, assisted in looking after the sick and the wounded, and supplied reading matter, but it also had at City Point a "mammoth coffee-boiler on wheels, with heating apparatus attached . . . drawn by two horses," which regularly toured the lines and camps and dispensed coffee to the boys. All in all, as the historian of the 1st Maine, writing after the war, noted, "it may be questioned if the boys did not enjoy themselves as well and quite as thoroughly as many of them have done since in civil life."[89]

When David McMurtrie Gregg returned on February 8 from the raid to Dinwiddie Court House, he completed his final mission as commander of a division of Union cavalry. He had submitted his resignation some time before, as the regulations permitted him to do, and on February 8 he received notice from the adjutant general's office that it had been accepted.[90] As his colleague, General Wilson, indicated, Gregg, with a Scottish reticence, did not

88. Augustus C. Buell, *"The Cannoneer": Recollections of Service in the Army of the Potomac* (Washington, D.C., 1890), 249. Tobie, *First Maine Cavalry,* 377. Contrary to this favorable, but postwar, testimony, General Davies, then in command of the Second Division, complained to General Meade on March 14 that "the supply of fresh vegetables and antiscorbutics furnished to this command is entirely insufficient. . . . From reports of the medical officers . . . I learn that several well-developed cases of scurvy have recently occurred, and they report that among the men there is generally a low state of health and predisposition to disease, resulting from continued living upon salt provisions and the absence of vegetables." *Official Records,* Vol. XLVI, Pt. 2, p. 975. Also, although the troopers' pay was not so badly in arrears as it had been, delayed pay was still the norm, and in February, 1865, when Grant asked for an improvement, Halleck replied, "If we pay the troops to the exclusion of other creditors of the Government, supplies must stop. . . . What we want is some more great victories to give confidence in our currency." Ella Lonn, *Desertion During the Civil War* (New York, 1928), 133.
89. Tobie, *First Maine Cavalry,* 378, 377. The 1st Maine also built log stables for its horses, and it may be assumed that several other, if not most, regiments in the division built some sort of shelter for their animals.
90. *Official Records,* Vol. XLVI, Pt. 2, p. 494.

choose to offer a public explanation of his reasons for leaving the service when, as he must have realized, the war was in its last stages, and his reasons remain unknown to this day. It would be gratifying to know that someone, perhaps Meade, or even Grant, had tried to persuade a fine and valuable officer to remain, but there is nothing in the records to indicate that anyone did so. Indeed, his departure from the army, which he left without the nearly obligatory farewell order to his division, is not even mentioned in Grant's *Personal Memoirs*. On February 10, Gregg turned over command of the division to J. Irvin Gregg, the senior officer present, and left for Washington.

Henry E. Davies, Jr., absent on leave when David Gregg left, ranked J. Irvin Gregg and took over command of the division when he returned to the army. He may or may not have had a claim to be given command of the division on a permanent basis in succession to David Gregg, but there is nothing in the records to suggest that he was considered for the post. Instead, the command was offered successively to Generals Romeyn B. Ayres and Samuel W. Crawford, both of whom commanded divisions of infantry in the V Corps, but neither of them "[felt] like taking the cavalry under existing circumstances."[91] In the absence of any firm evidence, it may be suspected that the "existing circumstances" were the prospect of having to serve under Sheridan in the likely event of his return to the Army of the Potomac. Having been turned down by Ayres and Crawford, Meade suggested that Kautz be transferred to the command of the Second Division, as "the best and only arrangement" that could be made "for immediate action," but Grant did not care for the idea.[92] Presumably there were further discussions about the cavalry command between Grant and Meade, but nothing was done until March 21, when Grant "recommended" to Stanton that General George Crook, who had been released from captivity, exchanged, and reinstated in command of the Department of West Virginia, be given the post.[93] Why Crook should have been chosen is another decision on which the records shed no light; they do show, however, that the secretary of war did not

91. *Ibid.*, 614, 630. Meade spoke to both generals on February 21.
92. *Ibid.*, 630.
93. *Ibid.*, Pt. 3, p. 61.

think Crook a suitable choice.[94] In a dispatch to Grant, curiously deferential in tone—Stanton was not normally deferential to anyone, not excepting the president of the United States—he suggested "a careful consideration of the propriety of giving . . . [Crook] a command so important as . . . [that] of your cavalry," but, he added, "with this suggestion the matter is left entirely to your own judgment. Anything you may do in regard to it will be approved."[95] Grant thereupon made the appointment.

In the meantime, the cavalry division of what had been B. F. Butler's Army of the James also had a change of commanders. After his abject failure at Fort Fisher, Butler had at long last been relieved of his command and sent home. Command of his department and army was given to General E. O. C. Ord. In what may well have been a case of "new men, new measures," it was decided to replace Kautz in command of the cavalry division. As is usual in such cases, the records provide no clue as to the reasons for the change, nor do they indicate at whose request or by whom the decision to relieve Kautz was made. Brigadier General Ranald Mackenzie, who had been considered for the command of the Second Division when David Gregg left (he could not be given the post because he was junior to Davies, who would have been one of his subordinates; it was apparently considered inadvisable to solve the problem by removing Davies from the division) was chosen by Grant himself to take Kautz's place. It was so ordered on March 20.[96] At the time of his appointment, Mackenzie, a native of New York City, was twenty-four years old; he had graduated at the top of the West Point Class of 1862 and, after serving

94. The explanation may be the high opinion Sheridan was known to have of Crook, who had been his roommate at West Point. Following the fight at Fisher's Hill he requested that Crook, then a major general by brevet, be commissioned in that rank. "His good conduct," Sheridan wrote, "turned the tide of battle in our favor, both at Winchester [i.e., the Opequon] and Fisher's Hill." Ibid., Vol. XLIII, Pt. 2, p. 153. The fact that Grant had been Crook's company commander in the 4th United States Infantry in the early 1850s may also have had a bearing on the appointment.
95. Ibid., Vol. XLVI, Pt. 3, p. 78. Stanton's reasons for questioning the wisdom of giving Crook the post were "Your [Grant's] account of the way Crook talked on his return from Richmond, and other circumstances." Ibid., 78. There is nothing in the records to explain this statement.
96. Ibid., Pt. 2, pp. 947, 967, 977; Pt. 3, p. 55.

for two years as an engineer officer in the Fredericksburg, Chancellorsville, Wilderness, and Spotsylvania campaigns and in the
siege of Petersburg—operations in which he was twice wounded
and received four brevets for gallantry in action—was given command of the 2nd Connecticut Heavy Artillery in July, 1864. In the
fighting in the latter half of 1864 he was awarded three more
brevets and had the distinction therefore of being a major general
at the age of twenty-four. Grant regarded him "as the most promising young officer in the army," who had made his way "upon his
own merit and without influence."[97] In an act of justice, General
Ord was directed to provide a suitable infantry command for
Kautz. He did so on March 27, assigning him to the command of
the First Division of General Godfrey Weitzel's XXV Corps.[98]

Thus, in the last week of March, 1865, as the Second Division
of the Cavalry Corps, Army of the Potomac, and what had been
known as Kautz's cavalry division, Army of the James, faced the
campaigning season which, as everyone knew, was to start within
a matter of days, they did so under new commanders, both strangers to their respective commands.[99]

97. Grant, *Personal Memoirs*, II, 541.
98. *Official Records*, Vol. XLVI, Pt. 3, p. 212.
99. This chapter has focused on the operations of the two organized
divisions of cavalry involved in the Richmond-Petersburg siege. It would
burden the narrative unduly to recount in addition the activities of the
numerous detached companies, battalions, and even regiments of cavalry
that were performing auxiliary services—provost, guard, escort, courier,
etc.—in the Army of the Potomac throughout this period.

XV

To Summon His Array

SHERIDAN'S LONG JOURNEY FROM WINCHESTER TO White House had taken its toll in many ways, from cast horseshoes to lost weapons. His two divisions were in urgent need of a period of rest and refurbishment. Even before the command crossed the Pamunkey, Merritt ordered a "thorough inspection" by the two division commanders, to determine and report "the number of horses needed to mount their commands, as also the number of unserviceable horses which will have to be sent to the rear," what weapons were needed to rearm the men who had lost theirs on the march—the value of which, Merritt pointed out, was to be charged to the men responsible for losing them—and the ammunition required to replenish stores up to standard.[1]

Replacing ammunition was a simple matter and so was the replacement of lost weapons, only 427 unarmed men having been found in the entire command.[2] Replacement of horses was, as always, a more difficult problem. Before anything else, however, horseshoes cast on the march had to be replaced. Colonel Orville Babcock wired for twenty-five forges and sets of shoeing tools to be sent to White House; he was told that they would leave City Point within the hour. Three days later a second set of twenty-five

1. *Official Records*, Vol. XLVI, Pt. 3, 35–36.
2. *Ibid.*, 58.

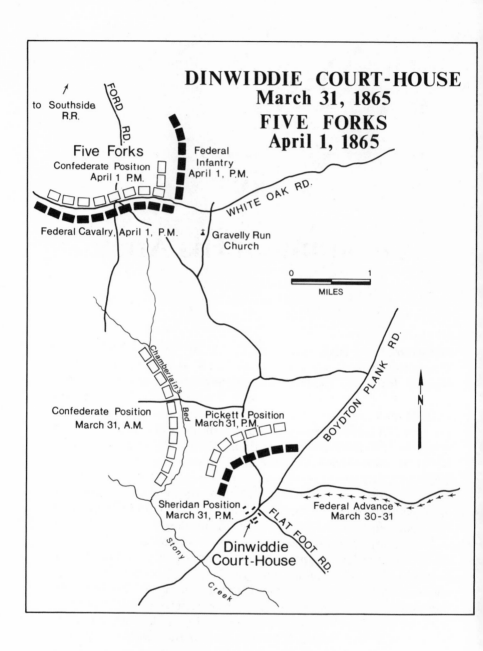

DINWIDDIE COURT-HOUSE
March 31, 1865
FIVE FORKS
April 1, 1865

to Southside R.R.

FORD RD.

Five Forks
Confederate Position
April 1 P.M.

Federal Infantry
April 1, P.M.

WHITE OAK RD.

Federal Cavalry, April 1, P.M.

Gravelly Run Church

0   1
MILES

Chamberlain's Bed

Confederate Position
March 31, A.M.

Pickett Position
March 31, P.M.

BOYDTON PLANK RD.

N

Sheridan Position
March 31, P.M.

Federal Advance
March 30-31

FLAT FOOT RD.

Stony

Dinwiddie
Court-House

Creek

forges was sent to speed the reshoeing process.[3] But there was a greater need for replacement horses than for shoeing the serviceable animals. Contrary to the statements of some of his subordinates that more than enough horses were captured on the march to replace losses, Sheridan reported that "over 1,000 men" had reached White House dismounted or riding captured mules; in addition, 2,161 horses were found to be unserviceable because of "hoof rot" caused by three weeks of marching in liquid mud by day and standing in it by night.[4] The records do not indicate how many of the men who needed horses got them before the start of the Appomattox Campaign ten days later, but the total appears to have been considerably below 3,200. General Halleck, after he had been asked by Sheridan for 3,000 horses to be delivered to him immediately, wired Grant that there were only 600 on hand in Washington.[5] The depot at City Point had available about 1,200 animals; it is possible that General Ingalls' appeals to Washington for additional horses produced an increase over 600 in the number sent from there, but in the end, as Sheridan reported, "nothing like enough horses were at hand to replace those that had died or been disabled . . . so a good many of the men were . . . without mounts."[6]

Another of Sheridan's problems was to dispose of the three thousand Negroes who had joined his column on its way south. In a harshly worded order, Merritt directed a "most rigid" inspection of every regiment to collect all the Negroes who had attached themselves to the command, including the many "employed by both officers and men."[7] Considering the great service the Negroes had performed in getting Merritt's trains through the mud, their dismissal might have been managed in a less abrupt, more compassionate fashion. It was nothing more than justice, perhaps intentionally so and perhaps not, that Grant subsequently ordered the Negroes delivered to the provost marshal at Fort Monroe, who was to find work for the able-bodied men and send the rest to

3. *Ibid.*, 35, 68.
4. *Ibid.*, Pt. 1, p. 498; Pt. 3, pp. 36, 58, 67.
5. *Ibid.*, Pt. 3, p. 87.
6. Sheridan, *Personal Memoirs*, II, 124–25; see also *Official Records*, Vol. XLVI, Pt. 3, pp. 52, 68, 74, 80, 81, 87.
7. *Official Records*, Vol. XLVI, Pt. 3, p. 35.

whatever settlement General Ord thought could best employ them.[8]

These activities proceeded, and the men rested, while messages came from Grant to Sheridan urging him to move his force to City Point as promptly as possible. The first such message was sent on the very day of Sheridan's arrival at White House, but it gave him ample latitude, for it asked him to start as soon as he could do so conveniently. The same message indicated the operation Grant had in mind for the cavalry. "When you start out from here [*i.e.*, from City Point]," Grant wrote, "you will be re-enforced by about 6,000 cavalry. I will also move out by the left at least 50,000 infantry and demonstrate on the enemy's right, and probably remain out. Your problem will be to destroy the South Side and Danville roads, and then either return to this army or go on to Sherman, as you may deem most practicable."[9] Grant's thinking about the shape the forthcoming campaign should assume underwent a change within a few days, but for the moment he seemed preoccupied with the need to prevent what he thought was the "possibility, if not the probability, of Lee and Johnston attempting to unite." Hence, although he professed not to want to hurry Sheridan, and indeed said that he appreciated fully his need to have his "horses well shod and well rested before starting again on another long march," Grant nevertheless told him that he had better start "by Saturday next," that is, by March 25, so as to be in a position to act promptly if the two Confederate generals attempted to form a junction.[10] Sheridan replied the next day that he would leave White House on the morning of the twenty-fifth and that as soon as his command reached Harrison's Landing he himself would cross over to City Point for a discussion of the plans Grant had proposed.[11]

When Sheridan arrived at City Point on the morning of the twenty-sixth he found the general-in-chief entertaining visitors; Mrs. Grant and President and Mrs. Lincoln were at headquarters, and Sheridan was thus caught up in some unavoidable but unwel-

8. *Ibid.*, 41.
9. *Ibid.*, 46.
10. *Ibid.*, 67; see also *Battles and Leaders*, IV, 708.
11. *Official Records*, Vol. XLVI, Pt. 3, p. 79.

come socializing. Time was found, however, for the military purpose of his visit.[12] The two issues to be resolved were the role the cavalry was to play in the forthcoming campaign, and Sheridan's place in the military hierarchy that would direct operations. The second problem, raised apparently by Grant, not by Sheridan, was settled quickly. By giving up the command of the Middle Military Division for that of the cavalry, Sheridan sacrificed a great measure of independence and even more prestige. To make the change more palatable Grant gave him the status of an army commander; he would report to and receive his instructions directly from Grant, and not through General Meade with whom, after their angry confrontation of the previous May, Sheridan's relations would not have been of the best. Whether Meade agreed to this arrangement, or had even been consulted about it, does not appear in the records.

The more important problem, namely the role the cavalry was to play, was not settled so easily. With the fervent encouragement of General John Rawlins, Grant's chief of staff, Sheridan objected strenuously (in what he termed "a somewhat emphatic manner") to being separated from the Army of the Potomac.[13] He had remarked to his own chief of staff, General James W. Forsyth:

This campaign will end the war. I have been anxious for fear Lee would commence to move west before we could get to Grant's army. The Army of the Potomac will never move from its present position unless we join them and pull them out. If I obeyed these instructions and . . . joined Sherman, the Army of the Potomac would rest where they are and Sherman, with our assistance, would close the war. . . . This cavalry corps and the Army of the Potomac, of which it is a part, have got to wipe out Lee before Sherman and his army reach Virginia.[14]

If as is probable—for Sheridan had no more fear of the general-in-chief than he had of the enemy—this was the reasoning and language he used in his discussion with Grant, they had the effect

12. Porter, *Campaigning with Grant*, 411–16.
13. Sheridan, *Personal Memoirs*, II, 128.
14. James H. Wilson, *The Life of John A. Rawlins* (New York, 1916), 307–308. Forsyth quoted these remarks of Sheridan's in a letter to Wilson written in 1904, forty years after the event, and explained that he was repeating "in substance" what Sheridan had said.

he hoped for. Grant ended the conversation by assuring him in confidence that the direction that he join Sherman after destroying the railroads was just a "blind," that it was his (Grant's) intention to "close the war" before Petersburg and Richmond, and that he wanted Sheridan to remain with the Army of the Potomac to bring about that result.[15] This labored "explanation" lacks credibility (what purpose could the "blind" have had, and who was to be taken in by it?) notwithstanding that it appears in Grant's *Personal Memoirs* and is faithfully repeated in Sheridan's. General Sherman, another visitor to City Point on March 27 and the commander who, next to Sheridan, was most closely concerned in the matter, was either not made privy to what Grant claimed were his real intentions with respect to Sheridan, or, being a realist, put no stock in the "blind" explanation, for early on the morning of the twenty-eighth he tried hard but without success to persuade Sheridan to change his mind about joining him.[16] The likelihood is that Grant did in fact want Sheridan to join Sherman, but that the cavalryman with his blunt and aggressive self-assurance simply bowled over his essentially diffident commander; nor was this the last time he was to do so. He would do it again only three days later on an even more critical issue.

These questions settled, Sheridan returned to his headquarters at Hancock Station to get his troops ready to move the next day.[17] The Army of the Potomac and the Army of the James had already received their orders for the movement. Two corps of the former and three divisions and the cavalry of the latter were to cross Hatcher's Run and advance in the direction of Dinwiddie Court House in a move essentially similar to that attempted by Hancock in the previous October but on a far more ambitious scale, "for the double purpose of turning the enemy out of his present position

15. Grant, *Personal Memoirs*, II, 437–38; Sheridan, *Personal Memoirs*, II, 128–29. It is repeated also in Porter, *Campaigning with Grant*, 411–12, in *Battles and Leaders*, IV, 708–709, and in Catton, *Grant Takes Command*, 437.

16. Sheridan, *Personal Memoirs*, II, 133. There is no mention in General Sherman's memoirs of this early morning discussion with Sheridan.

17. "Hancock's Station" is what Sheridan called it. Orders issued by his chief of staff the next day are datelined "Gregg's Station." These stations were on the military railroad running the length of the Union lines from City Point down to Petersburg.

around Petersburg and to insure the success of the cavalry under General Sheridan, which will start at the same time, in its efforts to reach and destroy the South Side and Danville railroads."[18] On March 28 Grant drew up new orders for Sheridan, based on their discussion two days earlier. He was to move out as early as possible on the morning of the twenty-ninth "without being confined to any particular road or roads" past the left wing of the V Corps, and "passing near or through Dinwiddie, reach the right and rear of the enemy." If the Confederates left their trenches to attack the Federal advance, Sheridan was to "move in with . . . [his] entire force in . . . [his] own way." If the enemy remained in its trenches, Sheridan was to "cut loose and push for the Danville road" and the Southside Railroad and destroy both as completely as possible. Then came the controversial point. "After having completed the destruction of the two railroads, which are now the only avenues of supply for Lee's army," the order concluded, "you may return to this army, selecting your road further south, or you may go on into North Carolina and join General Sherman."[19]

It will be noted that except for the March 29 starting date, nothing in these orders was mandatory; Sheridan was given complete latitude with respect to the roads he was to use, whether or not and in what manner he was to attack the enemy, and whether he was to return to the Army of the Potomac or join Sherman.[20] Repeating in these orders the option that he join Sherman, which, as Grant well knew, Sheridan had no intention of doing, sheds a curious light on Grant's mental processes or perhaps on the mental processes of command in general.

On March 28, on the eve of the campaign, Sheridan had under his command three divisions of cavalry. The First under Thomas C. Devin and the Third under Custer were in the shadowy area of belonging both to the Army of the Shenandoah and the Army of the Potomac. The two divisions constituted an unofficial corps commanded by Wesley Merritt. The Second Division, formerly

18. *Official Records*, Vol. XLVI, Pt. 1, p. 50.
19. *Ibid.*, 52.
20. Even the permissive "you may go on . . . and join Sherman" language of these orders "disturbed" Sheridan, which certainly suggests that he had not been taken in by Grant's claim of a "blind." Sheridan, *Personal Memoirs*, II, 134.

Gregg's, now commanded by George Crook, belonged without question to the Army of the Potomac. In Devin's division were three brigades, Colonel Peter Stagg's First (1st, 5th, 6th, and 7th Michigan), Colonel Charles L. Fitzhugh's Second (6th, 9th, and 19th New York, 17th and 20th Pennsylvania), and Alfred Gibbs's Third or Reserve Brigade (2nd Massachusetts, six companies of the 6th Pennsylvania, and the 1st, 5th, and 6th United States). Custer's division also had three brigades: Colonel Alexander C. M. Pennington, Jr's First (1st Connecticut, 3rd New Jersey, 2nd New York, and 2nd Ohio), Colonel William Wells's Second (8th and 15th New York, 1st Vermont), and Colonel Henry Capehart's Third (1st New York (Lincoln), 1st and 3rd West Virginia, and seven companies of the 2nd West Virginia). The First Brigade (1st New Jersey, 10th and 24th New York, and five companies of the 1st Pennsylvania) of Crook's Second Division was commanded by Henry E. Davies, Jr.; the Second Brigade (4th, 8th, 16th, and 21st Pennsylvania) by J. Irvin Gregg and later by Colonel Samuel B. M. Young; and the Third Brigade (1st Maine, 2nd New York Mounted Rifles, 6th and 13th Ohio) by Charles H. Smith. Attached to the three divisions were four batteries of horse artillery, Batteries C and E of the Fourth, Battery A of the Second, and Battery H of the First United States Artillery.[21]

Assigned to Sheridan's command from April 1 on was General Ranald Mackenzie's Cavalry Division of the Army of Virginia. The division had reverted to a two-brigade organization, the First (20th New York and 5th Pennsylvania) under Colonel Robert M. West, and the Second (1st Maryland, 11th Pennsylvania, and a battalion of the 1st District of Columbia) under Colonel Samuel P. Spear. Attached to the division was the 4th Battery, Wisconsin Light Artillery.[22]

Sheridan's numbers at the start of the campaign cannot be given with any degree of confidence. He claimed in his report on the campaign that he started with an "effective force" of 9,000, presumably comprising only the mounted and fully equipped men, but the trimonthly returns for March 31 show 13,143 officers and men plus 290 gunners "present for duty" in the three divisions.[23]

21. *Official Records*, Vol. XLVI, Pt. 1, pp. 575–76.
22. *Ibid.*, 580.
23. *Ibid.*, 1101. For the March 31 returns see *ibid.*, Pt. 3, p. 391. Sheri-

Grant's orders for the movement directed that "all dismounted cavalry . . . not required for guarding property belonging to their arm of the service, will report to Brigadier-General [Henry W.] Benham, to be added to the defenses of City Point." It is possible that these dismounted men accounted for the surprisingly large difference of 4,133 between Sheridan's figure and the official returns.[24] Yet it is difficult to believe that almost exactly one third of the Cavalry Corps lacked horses or equipment or both. Whatever the correct number may have been, there should be added to it the numbers of General Mackenzie's division on which, however, there is a similar conflict of testimony, Sheridan reporting that the division consisted of "about 1,000 effective men," whereas as of March 31 Mackenzie himself reported 1,798 of all ranks "present for duty."[25]

The Confederate cavalry with which Sheridan's horsemen would have to contend had diminished from the robust force of nearly 5,700 "effective men" Hampton had reported to General Lee on October 31. The shortage of forage had played havoc with the horses to such an extent that in December, General Longstreet suggested in all seriousness that the large numbers of dismounted cavalrymen be mounted on mules.[26] In mid-January on orders from President Davis, M. C. Butler's division was detached from General Lee's army and sent to South Carolina to obtain horses for its dismounted men and then to reinforce William J. Hardee in an

---

dan gives the 9,000 figure in his memoirs, explaining that the men were actually counted while crossing Rowanty Creek on March 29. General Davies gives the same 9,000 figure, but does not indicate whether it is his own independent estimate or is based on Sheridan's report. Sheridan, *Personal Memoirs*, II, 148; Davies, *General Sheridan*, 226. The only two subordinate commanders who gave in their reports the exact strength of their commands at the start of the campaign were General Gibbs of the Reserve Brigade, whose four regiments and six companies of a fifth had a total strength of 457 of all ranks, and Colonel West, whose brigade of Mackenzie's division numbered 566. *Official Records*, Vol. XLVI, Pt. 1, pp. 1127, 1248.

24. *Official Records*, Vol. XLVI, Pt. 1, p. 50.

25. *Ibid.*, 1104; Pt. 3, p. 390. In his report on the campaign Mackenzie wrote that he began it with 1,638 officers and men. *Ibid.*, Pt. 1, p. 1244. If, as is evidently the case, Sheridan understated Mackenzie's strength by 40 percent, he may have committed the same error with respect to his own three divisions.

26. Ramsdell, "General Lee's Horse Supply," 772.

effort to block Sherman's northward march. What horses the division still had, plus enough others to make up a total of 2,700 were shipped to recuperate part to North Carolina and part to South Carolina, where there was still forage available.[27] The effect of the winter's adversities was that Lee faced the opening of the campaigning season with two weak divisions of cavalry, 2,020 officers and men "present for duty" in Fitzhugh Lee's division and 2,691 in W. H. F. Lee's.[28] In a postwar letter about the Appomattox Campaign, General Lee wrote Hampton, "The absence of the troops which I had sent to North and South Carolina was, I believe, the cause of our immediate disaster. Our small force of cavalry (a large portion of the men who had been sent to the interior to winter their horses had not rejoined their regiments) was unable to resist the united Federal cavalry under Sheridan."[29] General Hampton, whose leadership and skill might have added substantially to the effectiveness of the cavalry General Lee did have was absent also. He had been sent to South Carolina, in the expectation, General Lee wrote, that he would be "of service in mounting his men and arousing the spirit and strength of the State."[30] Commanding the Cavalry Corps in his absence was Fitzhugh Lee.

General Grant's orders to the cavalry were received on the evening of March 28; later the same evening General Forsyth issued orders to the subordinate commands for the following day's march. Crook was to lead out at five A.M., destination Dinwiddie Court House via the Jerusalem Plank Road, Reams' Station, and a crossing of Rowanty Creek. All the wagons, formed into a single train, were to bring up the rear, escorted by a brigade of the Third Division. Since a large body of Confederate troops was known to be to the south, in the neighborhood of Stony Creek Depot, strong scouting parties were to be sent out on all the roads coming in on

27. *Official Records*, Vol. XLVI, Pt. 2, p. 1101.
28. *Ibid.*, Pt. 1, p. 390; Ramsdell, "General Lee's Horse Supply," 775. Rosser had reached Richmond at the end of March; he was given command of a small division of cavalry made up of the brigades of James Dearing and John McCausland. On February 23, the Confederate Congress passed a law authorizing the quartermaster general of the army to purchase horses and supply them to the cavalry, but it is doubtful if any action was taken under the law before the collapse of the Confederacy.
29. Ramsdell, "General Lee's Horse Supply," 777.
30. Freeman, *Lee's Lieutenants*, III, 639.

the left flank of the column to prevent a surprise attack.[31] The men were to carry five days' rations, thirty pounds of forage, and forty rounds of ammunition.

The historian of the 1st Maine of the Second Division describes the frame of mind in which he and his fellow troopers of that division set out on the campaign. He writes that they "felt somewhat blue" as they formed in line on the morning of the twenty-ninth in preparation for the march;

They were going to enter upon a campaign which they had every reason to expect would be a fighting campaign, under a new and untried commander, Gen. George Crook, who had taken command of the . . . division on the twenty-seventh, and whom the men knew but little about (Gen. David McM. Gregg, their tried commander for two years, whom they loved and believed was the peer of any division cavalry general in the field, having resigned). . . . Therefore they were not at that time in a really enthusiastic mood. But while waiting in the line they saw a force approaching, and soon recognized "Little Phil Sheridan's" headquarter flag. The cheers that rent the air told no uncertain tale, and with those cheers went out all the distrust and forebodings with which the men had been tormented. They had begun to believe that under . . . [him] they could whip anything that could be brought against them, as they had already done on many fields.[32]

The first day's march was uneventful. Rowanty Creek was crossed on a bridge made passable "by a covering of rails, then some hay, another layer of rails and more hay."[33] By five in the afternoon, Crook's and Devin's divisions had reached Dinwiddie Court House. The trains, however, were still near the Rowanty Creek crossing, "greatly retarded by the almost impassable roads of that miry section."[34] The Federal infantry, having much shorter distances to cover, had made good progress, and by nightfall Grant had a continuous line, infantry to the right and cavalry on the

31. *Official Records*, Vol. XLVI, Pt. 3, p. 324; Pt. 1, p. 1116. Merritt reported at the last minute that he was short two hundred thousand pounds of forage. The needed forage was supplied at once. *Ibid.*, Pt. 3, p. 325.

32. Tobie, *First Maine Cavalry*, 385–86. Passages such as this in regimental histories are normally suspect, being probably colored by the later successes of Sheridan and the cavalry. There is, however, enough unquestionably contemporary evidence of the impact of Sheridan's personality to justify acceptance of this passage at face value.

33. Aston, *History and Roster of the Fourth*, Appendix, 3.

34. *Official Records*, Vol. XLVI, Pt. 1, p. 1101.

left, reaching from the Appomattox River to Dinwiddie Court House, well beyond the southern end of General Lee's intrenchments.

Encouraged by this auspicious start, Grant sent Sheridan a dispatch that evening—this was the dispatch containing the much-quoted sentence, "I now feel like ending the matter, if it is possible to do so, before going back"—in which Sheridan's bugbear, the march to join Sherman, was finally exorcised. "I do not want you . . . to cut loose and go after the enemy's roads at present," Grant wrote; "In the morning push around the enemy if you can, and get on his right rear."[35] These were precisely the instructions Sheridan wanted to receive, and what made them even more to his taste was that the means he was to use and the route or routes he was to follow to get on the enemy's right rear were left entirely up to him.

But now the unpredictable late spring weather took a hand in the proceedings. It began to rain in the late evening of the twenty-ninth, and for the next thirty-six hours, until midmorning on the thirty-first, it rained "in torrents." With uniforms, blankets, and rations waterlogged, the men shivered in the chill downpour, and so did the horses. The mostly low-lying country south of the Appomattox became a vast quagmire in which it was nearly impossible for men and animals to move, and totally so for anything on wheels; "in every by-way and every field wagons were hopelessly imbedded in the glutinous mud. Drivers and mules had given it up."[36] Early in the afternoon of the thirtieth the 2nd Ohio came upon a brigade corduroying a road that had become a sheet of water; "first a force was cutting down the pine trees that grew near by, these flung into the road were laid as near together as the[y] would lie, then other[s] were covering these with fence rails, & still another force were dragging the tops of the pine trees & covering the rails with pine limbs, even all this was disappear[ing]

35. *Ibid.*, Pt. 3, p. 266.
36. Frederick C. Newhall, *With General Sheridan in Lee's Last Campaign* (Philadelphia, 1866), 58. When the cavalry went into camp at Dinwiddie Court House on the evening of March 29—and this was before the rains began—Merritt reported that his trains were seven miles behind, and that the artillery of the First Division was "stuck not far back." *Official Records*, Vol. XLVI, Pt. 3, p. 267.

a foot or two under the water & mud when the wagons were on it, the bottom seemed literally to have tumbled out."[37]

General Ingalls told Colonel Theodore Lyman of General Meade's staff that the thirtieth "was the worst day for moving trains he ever had had in all his experience. A train of 600 wagons, even with the aid of 1000 engineer troops, was fifty-six hours in going five miles."[38] Corduroying a road did not invariably help; "the logs that had been put in, were in many instances floating, and they were an obstacle instead of a benefit."[39] The cavalry had the worst of it, because they had to leave the better roads to the infantry, and "the country cross roads . . . [they were] obliged to use were the worst to be found in that hopeless region."[40] However difficult the corduroyed roads were to negotiate, these by-roads were even worse; horses sank to their bellies in the liquid mud. The mishap of Trooper Conrad Bauer, 2nd Ohio, was not at all unique; his horse fell in a water-filled hole in the middle of the road "& he came off in the middle of it & came blame near drowning, disappearing entirely in the mud & water," loaded down as he was with weapons, forty rounds of ammunition, and a full haversack.[41]

Dinwiddie Court House, located thirteen miles southwest of Petersburg, "was far from attractive in feature, being made up of a half-dozen unsightly houses, a ramshackle tavern propped up on two sides by pine poles, and the weather-beaten building that gave official name to the cross-roads."[42] Its importance on March 30, 1865, lay in its location at the intersection of five roads, one leading north to the Southside Railroad by way of Five Forks, another giving access to the southern end of General Lee's Petersburg defenses, and a third, the Boydton Plank Road, providing good communication with the left rear of General Warren's V Corps, Sheridan's nearest neighbor to the right. The terrain to the north and northwest of Dinwiddie was heavily wooded and mostly low-lying; the timber and underbrush were particularly heavy

37. Hannaford, "Reminiscences," 293(d).
38. Agassiz, Meade's Headquarters, 330.
39. Gause, Four Years with Five Armies, 366.
40. Davies, General Sheridan, 223.
41. Hannaford, "Reminiscences," 293(d).
42. Sheridan, Personal Memoirs, II, 139.

about one and a half miles to the west and northwest of the settlement, where Chamberlain's Creek, or "Bed," the local word for a
swamp, flowed sluggishly southward to empty into Stony Creek.

At dawn on the thirtieth, with the continuing heavy rain driven
by a strong southwest wind, Sheridan rearranged his dispositions
to enable him "to push around the enemy and get on his right
rear," as Grant's orders of the previous evening directed him to do.
He sent Devin's division and a brigade of Crook's forward on a
reconnaissance in the direction of Five Forks, which led to a lively
scrap between the 6th Pennsylvania, 2nd Massachusetts, 7th
Michigan, and the 1st United States, and a brigade of Confederate
cavalry.[43] Another brigade of Crook's division was sent to hold the
Boydton Plank Road crossing of Stony Creek, thereby forcing
W. H. F. Lee, who was known to be coming up from the south, to
make a wide swing to the west to reach the Dinwiddie area. The
third brigade of Crook's division Sheridan held back at Dinwiddie
as a reserve.[44] Custer's division was several miles to the south of
Dinwiddie, still struggling to bring on the trains through the mud.
"Shortly after the troops began to move," however, Sheridan received a dispatch from Grant which in effect called off the entire
operation.[45] "The heavy rain of to-day," Grant wrote, "will make it
impossible for us to do much until it dries up a little or we get
roads around our rear repaired. You may therefore leave what
cavalry you deem necessary to protect the left . . . and send the
remainder back to Humphreys' Station, where they can get hay
and grain."[46]

Having "pondered" this message, Sheridan decided to ride to
Grant's headquarters to "get a clear idea of what it was proposed
to do," for, he wrote, it seemed to him "that a suspension of operations would be a serious mistake."[47] Phrased in less politic terms,
he obviously decided that it was up to him to put some backbone

43. Gracey, Annals of the 6th, 329–30.
44. Sheridan, Personal Memoirs, II, 142; Official Records, Vol. XLVI,
Pt. 3, pp. 325, 325–26.
45. Sheridan, Personal Memoirs, II, 142; Official Records, Vol. XLVI,
Pt. 1, p. 1102; Pt. 3, pp. 323, 324.
46. Official Records, Vol. XLVI, Pt. 3, p. 325. The dispatch does not
show when it was sent, but evidently it was quite early in the morning.
47. Sheridan, Personal Memoirs, II, 143.

into the general-in-chief and his staff. Getting from Dinwiddie to Grant's headquarters south of Gravelly Run was anything but easy, Sheridan's powerful pacer "Breckinridge" "plunging at every step almost to his knees in the mud," but measured by its ultimate results, this was the most important ride of Sheridan's life, more deserving of being immortalized in poetry than his well-publicized ride from Winchester to Cedar Creek. Arriving at headquarters, he found a state of despondency and apprehension. Standing around in the rain near a campfire "on boards and rails placed here and there to keep them from sinking in the mire" were disconsolate groups of staff officers. Rawlins and Grant were in the latter's tent, debating—heatedly, on Rawlins' part—the suspension of operations to which Rawlins was "strongly opposed."[48] Colonel Horace Porter has given a colorful and justly famous account of the effect of Sheridan's arrival on this scene of gloom and the impact of his sturdy personality:

[Sheridan] said: "I can drive in the whole cavalry force of the enemy with ease, and if an infantry force is added to my command, I can strike out for Lee's right, and either crush it or force him so to weaken his . . . lines that our troops . . . can break through and march into Petersburg." He warmed up with the subject as he proceeded, threw the whole energy of his nature into the discussion, and his cheery voice, beaming countenance, and impassioned language showed the earnestness of his convictions. . . . "I tell you, I'm ready to strike out to-morrow and go to smashing things"; and pacing up and down, he chafed like a hound in the leash.[49]

The staff officers around the fire caught the infection of Sheridan's determination and enthusiasm, but there was also the general-in-chief to be won over. Sheridan did it in a brief private conversation. He reminded Grant of the ridicule Burnside had incurred when he called off his "Mud March" two years before, and he bore down hard on the thesis that halting the operation would be considered by the country as a disaster. Whatever arguments Sheridan used, these or others, they were probably of less moment than the intensity and the vehement self-assurance with which he urged them. Once again his advocacy had the result he wanted;

48. *Ibid.*, 144.
49. Porter, *Campaigning with Grant*, 428–29.

Grant was won over and ended the discussion with the remark, "We will go on."[50]

Late that evening, after his return to Dinwiddie, Sheridan received Grant's orders for the next day's operations. If the situation next morning justified the expectation that with the aid of a corps of infantry he could turn the Confederate right—the operation Sheridan had proposed to Grant at the close of their meeting—he was to notify Grant accordingly; the V Corps, which was nearest him in line, would then be sent to him and would be under his command for the operation.[51] The situation had, however, changed in a vital respect before Sheridan got back to his headquarters. The reconnaissance toward Five Forks and Major Young's scouts located five brigades of Confederate infantry, three of George Pickett's division and two of Richard Anderson's corps, with Pickett in command of the whole, marching out from the southern end of the Petersburg defenses toward Five Forks, by way of the White Oak Road, the main east-west road in the area.[52] Sheridan had this information "about dark" and promptly sent it on to Grant, who had it before he issued the above-mentioned orders for the operations he wanted executed on the thirty-first.[53] General Lee had reacted to the threat to the Southside and Danville railroads just as Grant had anticipated he would have to do; he had to protect the railroads, either to continue the defense of Petersburg and Richmond, or, as had become inevitable by March 30, to evacuate

50. Not surprisingly, Grant's version is directly contrary to Sheridan's. Grant states that it was Rawlins who urged that the operation be called off, and he implies that his decision to continue did not require Sheridan's persuasion; *Personal Memoirs*, II, 438–39. Porter's obviously secondhand account (*Campaigning with Grant*, 427–28) agrees with Grant's.

51. *Official Records*, Vol. XLVI, Pt. 3, p. 325. In the meeting with Grant in which he proposed this operation, Sheridan asked for General Horatio Wright's VI Corps, but that corps was a considerable distance east of Dinwiddie, with Ord's three divisions and Warren's corps between it and Sheridan. Given the state of the roads, it would have been impossible for Wright to reach Sheridan in time to be of use.

52. Freeman states that in addition to his own three brigades, Pickett had two brigades of Richard Anderson's corps. Sheridan, presumably on the basis of information obtained from prisoners, identified the latter two brigades as belonging to Bushrod Johnson's division. Freeman, *Lee's Lieutenants*, III, 658; Sheridan, *Personal Memoirs*, II, 148; see also *Official Records*, Vol. XLVI, Pt. 1, pp. 1116, 1122.

53. *Official Records*, Vol. XLVI, Pt. 3, p. 324.

the Petersburg-Richmond defenses and try to form a junction with Joseph Johnston's army in North Carolina. Pickett's orders were to use his five brigades of infantry and the cavalry commands of Rosser and the two Lees to attack Sheridan at Dinwiddie and drive him away from the railroads at all costs.[54]

The rain, which had continued to fall heavily all day on the thirtieth, stopped for a short time in the evening and then began again as hard as ever, "aggravating the swampy nature of the ground and rendering the movement of troops almost impossible."[55] Even if it had not been for the elements, the presence of Pickett's infantry and the massing of the Confederate cavalry at Five Forks ruled out the attempt to turn the Confederate right that Grant's orders on the evening of the thirtieth specified as the program for the next day. Instead, Sheridan found himself having to fight for his life against a combined force of Confederate infantry and cavalry.

Reveille for the Federal cavalry on the thirty-first was at two A.M., and at first light on a murky, overcast morning, the First and Second Brigades of Devin's division, with Davies' brigade of the Second Division guarding their left rear, moved forward in the direction of Five Forks. Smith's brigade of Crook's division was posted to guard the crossings of the Chamberlain's Creek swamps, a short distance northwest of the Dinwiddie settlement. Gregg's and Gibbs's brigades remained at Dinwiddie as a reserve. The first of Sheridan's forces to be seriously engaged that day was Smith's brigade. Pickett had sent some of his infantry, preceded by W. H. F. Lee's cavalry, by way of a "concealed wooded road" west of Chamberlain's Creek to turn and attack Sheridan's left flank.[56] On picket along the east (left) bank of the creek were the 2nd New York Mounted Rifles of Smith's brigade. In midmorning the New Yorkers were attacked by Pickett's flanking force, and General Smith moved his entire brigade forward to support them.[57] A

54. Freeman, *Lee's Lieutenants*, III, 656, 658.
55. *Official Records*, Vol. XLVI, Pt. 1, p. 1102.
56. *Ibid.*, 1299.
57. General Smith calls Chamberlain's Creek "Little Stony Creek" in his report; Crook calls it "Stony Creek" and adds that "the country in the vicinity of the creek was covered with a dense thicket, so that cavalry could only fight with advantage on foot." *Ibid.*, 1141.

battalion of the 1st Maine that he had sent across the creek on a reconnaissance earlier in the morning was attacked by a strong force of the enemy's cavalry "and driven back in confusion, the men seeking refuge among the led horses and fording the stream up to their necks. The enemy pursued in hot haste, plunged into the stream in heavy force . . . drove back the . . . [6th Ohio and the 2nd New York Mounted Rifles] and effected a lodgment on the . . . [left bank]."[58] But they did not remain there long. General Smith dismounted and deployed the rest of the 1st Maine and the 13th Ohio, rallied the 6th Ohio and the 2nd New York Mounted Rifles, and, with the four regiments charging in unison, drove the Confederates back across the swamp "in confusion and with considerable loss."[59] Davies, then about a mile north of Smith, had been ordered to move to Smith's support. To do it, he had to dismount his men, "the road being impassable for mounted troops"; he also left behind a line of pickets at the crossing of Chamberlain's Creek that he had been guarding with his entire brigade. Riding forward ahead of his men, he arrived after Smith had already driven the Confederates back across the creek and no longer needed help. Hearing heavy firing on his own picket line to the north, Davies countermarched his men at the double, but he was too late. The enemy, whom Davies took to be nearly the whole of Pickett's division, had driven off his pickets and had crossed the stream in full force. It was now Davies who was in serious trouble. He tried to restore the situation by attacking the enemy, but his attack was beaten off, and he was then driven in a northeasterly direction, that is, away from Dinwiddie, as far as the Dinwiddie-Five Forks road. He managed to save his led horses, but the direction of his retreat took him out of contact with Smith, and between him and the latter there was now a solid wedge of Pickett's infantry.[60]

In midmorning the rain at last stopped, the sun came out, and

58. *Ibid.*, 1156–57; see also 1148–49.
59. *Ibid.*, 1157; see also Tobie, *First Maine Cavalry*, 387–92. In the 1st Maine, one enlisted man in every four and one of every three officers were killed or wounded at Dinwiddie. Tobie, *First Maine Cavalry*, 392, 400.
60. *Official Records*, Vol. XLVI, Pt. 1, p. 1144. The whereabouts of Gregg's brigade, while Smith and Davies were engaged with the enemy, is a mystery. According to Sheridan Gregg was guarding the left bank of Chamberlain's Creek to the right (north) of Smith; according to Crook, Gregg

it turned into a "bright, beautiful day."[61] But it was anything but that for Sheridan. Pickett, W. H. F. Lee, and Rosser had made good the crossing of Chamberlain's Creek, and the direction of their advance east of the stream split the two divisions Sheridan had immediately available. Stagg's, Fitzhugh's, and Davies' brigades were to the north of the Confederates, and Gibbs's, Smith's, and Gregg's to the south. Each of these two segments of Sheridan's cavalry was outnumbered nearly three to one by the Confederates between them, and in danger of being destroyed in detail. Custer's division was still several miles to the rear, struggling to bring up the trains through the bottomless mud.

By midafternoon on this last day of March, Sheridan was on the ragged edge of a major defeat. Not only was his own command in imminent danger of being engulfed, but in addition Pickett was now in a position from which he could attack the left flank of the infantry of Warren's corps. There was only one chance of escaping defeat, and Sheridan took advantage of it. The northeasterly direction of Pickett's advance took him past the front of Gibbs's and Gregg's brigades and exposed his right flank and rear to attack. Sheridan ordered the two brigades forward. Their carbine fire was sufficiently effective and their advance sufficiently threatening to cause Pickett to halt his advance and wheel to his right to meet this attack. Sheridan had already sent orders back to Custer to leave one of his brigades with the trains and, with the other two, to make for Dinwiddie with all speed. Smith, who in the meantime had been forced back from the Chamberlain's Creek crossing and was hard pressed by enemy cavalry in front and infantry on his right flank, was ordered to retreat toward Dinwiddie as slowly as the enemy pressure would allow. Merritt was directed to get word to the three brigades that had been cut off by Pickett's advance to make a wide circuit to the east and get back to Dinwiddie by way of the Boydton Plank Road.[62] Sheridan himself rode forward and selected a line, about

was in reserve. In either case, why and by whom was Davies, and not Gregg, sent to help Smith? Ibid., 1102, 1141.

61. Hannaford, "Reminiscences," 295(a). But, Hannaford adds, "the roads Oh! they were horrible, indescribable."

62. On the fighting retreat of Smith's brigade see Tobie, *First Maine Cavalry*, 393–96.

three quarters of a mile north of the village, for his troops to occupy as they arrived. The success of Grant's plan depended on the ability of the cavalry to retain possession of Dinwiddie Court House, and Sheridan meant to hold on there "at all hazards."[63]

It was "past 3 p.m." when Custer reached Dinwiddie. An officer of the 6th New York saw him come thundering up "at the head of a long escort carrying the seventeen battle flags he had captured at Waynesborough, and followed by two brass bands."[64] He had ridden ahead of his troops to get his instructions from Sheridan. As the two brigades behind him neared the settlement, the men could see that "matters were really serious, here were the cooks, ostlers & underlings of every kind, all ready for a hurried retreat, only waiting to find out the right road, many a wounded man too was seen."[65] Pennington's brigade was still some distance from the village when

some Officer (Staff) came dashing down toward us & in a moment we were in fours & . . . dashing up the road . . . & when near a mile from the C[ourt] H[ouse] we [see] Custer & his Staff, who are waiting for us, dash to the head of the column & we turn into a field & form line at a gallop. "Dismount! prepare to fight on foot" is the word . . . "Forward march" & away we go on a dead run, making for a little knoll distant 450 or 500 yards . . . scattered all over the fields before us are our men, now rapidly falling [back], occasionally turning to fire at the swift[ly] advancing rebel skirmishers; they give a hearty cheer as we draw toward them & our Officers call to them for help to hold the enemy [but] not a man of them stops.

The cavalrymen retreating through Custer's advancing line were the troopers of Gregg's and Gibbs's brigades, who had slowed

63. Sheridan, *Personal Memoirs*, II, 150–51; *Official Records*, Vol. XLVI, Pt. 1, pp. 1102–1103.

64. E. P. McKinney, *Life in Tent and Field* (Boston, 1922), 151. Custer's costume had become somewhat less flamboyant; "the old blue shirt, with its star in the corner, remained, but the velvet jacket was replaced by a blue sack with major-general's shoulder straps, and his trousers were now of the regulation sky blue. The cavalier hat, long curls, and flaunting red necktie, were as conspicuous as ever. There were more shocks of long, shaggy, unkempt hair in the Third Division than anywhere in the army. As for neckties, Custer's division could be recognized a mile off by fluttering scarlet handkerchiefs." Whittaker, *George A. Custer*, 284.

65. This and the following quotation are from Hannaford, "Reminiscences," 295(a)–(b).

down Pickett's southward advance long enough to allow Custer to get to Dinwiddie, and for Smith, though "severely pressed," to make good his retreat to the curved line, about a mile long, on which Sheridan had decided to make his stand. Smith's brigade occupied the left of the line, nearest the Chamberlain's Creek position from which it had been driven. On its right were the brigades of Capehart, Pennington, Gibbs, and Gregg, in that order, sheltering behind hastily thrown-up breastworks, "the familiar barricades," as Sheridan called them. The horse artillery, which had at last been extricated from the mud, had come up, and all its guns were in the line.[66]

Smith's brigade was the first to be attacked, but in charging it, the Confederates exposed themselves to an enfilade fire on their left flank from Capehart's brigade. This brought the attack to a halt. Then came a pause; Sheridan took advantage of it to ride along the full length of his line to encourage his men. Then just at sundown Pickett's infantry in full force advanced to the attack. "It was really magnificent to see them, as they came, a double line, the men standing shoulder to shoulder; on they come over the open field as tho' on parade."[67] Two of Pennington's regiments, the 2nd Ohio and the 3rd New York, were flanked and driven back some distance, but the Union line as a whole held and the Confederate advance was checked, first by the fire of the artillery, and then, at short range, by the carbines of the cavalrymen.[68] This

66. Sheridan, *Personal Memoirs*, II, 152. The whereabouts of Gregg's brigade is again a puzzle. Sheridan says in one place that "the brigades of Gregg and Gibbs took position in the line to the right of the space that was to be occupied by Pennington's brigade," but in describing the repulse of the Confederate attack, he speaks of the same space as occupied by "Capehart and Gibbs." The map of the battle in the *Official Atlas* (Plate LXXIV, No. 2) shows Smith, Capehart, Pennington, and Gibbs, in that order from left to right, occupying the line, and Gregg posted a considerable distance east of Dinwiddie. Gregg himself wrote no report on the battle, and his successor in command of the brigade, Colonel Samuel B. M. Young, states that after retreating before the advance of Pickett's infantry "a new line was formed," but he does not say where this "new line" was located. The historian of the 6th Pennsylvania, a part of Gibbs's brigade, speaks of Gregg's brigade being in the main defense line to the left of his regiment. Sheridan, *Personal Memoirs*, II, 152, 153; *Official Records*, Vol. XLVI, Pt. 1, pp. 1154–55; Gracey, *Annals of the 6th*, 334.
67. Hannaford, "Reminiscences," 295(c).
68. *Ibid.*, 296(a); *Official Records*, Vol. XLVI, Pt. 1, pp. 1134–35.

proved to be the final encounter in the day's fighting. When it was over, the two armies settled down for the night on lines that in some places were only a hundred yards apart.

As soon as the firing ceased, Sheridan sent his brother Michael, who was one of his aides, to inform Grant of the day's events and of the prospects for the next day. He had escaped defeat by the narrowest of margins, three of his brigades were cut off from the main body, and he had every reason to expect that he would have to meet a full-scale attack by Pickett's infantry in the morning. For once, therefore, the message his brother carried lacked the buoyancy and optimism usual in his messages to the general-in-chief. He told Grant that he would hold on at Dinwiddie if possible, but if driven out, would retreat by the Vaughan Road to Hatcher's Run.[69] A short time after Michael Sheridan's departure with the dispatch to Grant, Stagg's, Fitzhugh's, and Davies' brigades reached Dinwiddie after making a wide circuit to the east around Pickett's infantry, and Sheridan began to view his situation in a more optimistic light. He sent Colonel John Kellogg, another member of his staff, to Grant with a second dispatch, in which he wrote that the enemy in his front was too powerful for him, but, he said, "I will hold on to Dinwiddie Court-House until I am compelled to leave."[70]

Both Michael Sheridan and Colonel Kellogg stopped at Meade's headquarters on their way to Grant's. It may have been the tone of Sheridan's two dispatches, or more probably the remarks of the two staff officers about the state of affairs at Dinwiddie, that caused both Meade and Grant to conclude that Sheridan's situation was desperate and that a rescue operation to save him had to be mounted in hot haste.[71] Altogether, the thirty-first of March had not been a good day for the Army of the Potomac. Two of Warren's divisions had been severely mauled and driven back by an attack of Confederate infantry, with losses in wounded alone of six hundred. Pickett, having driven Sheridan back to Dinwiddie, was now in a position from which he could attack Warren's left, and if in the course of the morning he should succeed in forcing Sheridan

69. Sheridan, *Personal Memoirs*, II, 153–54.
70. *Official Records*, Vol. XLVI, Pt. 3, p. 381.
71. *Ibid.*, 339, 340.

out of Dinwiddie, Grant's entire operation would be ruined. This had to be prevented, and Grant ordered that Mackenzie's cavalry and General Charles Griffin's division of the V Corps be rushed to Dinwiddie to reinforce Sheridan.[72]

In the light of what occurred between Sheridan and G. K. Warren at Five Forks on the evening of the next day, April 1, it is ironic to find that the first to see that Sheridan's plight had in it the seeds of a major Union victory was General Warren. Having learned from Meade that Sheridan had been forced back to Dinwiddie, Warren offered to hold his position with one of his divisions and to take the other two to attack Pickett on one side while Sheridan attacked on the other; "Unless Sheridan has been too badly handled," he wrote, "I think we have a chance for an open field fight that should be made use of."[73] An hour later Meade queried Grant, "Would it not be well for Warren to go down with his whole corps and smash the whole force in front of Sheridan? . . . Warren could move at once . . . and take the force threatening Sheridan in rear, or he could send one division to support Sheridan at Dinwiddie and move on the enemy's rear with the other two."[74] Grant immediately fell in with the second of Meade's alternatives; "Let Warren move in the way you propose and urge him not to stop for anything. Let Griffin go as he was first directed."[75]

At some point late in the afternoon or in the evening, Sheridan too realized, as Warren, Meade, and Grant had already done or were to do, that "by following . . . [him] to Dinwiddie, the enemy infantry had completely isolated itself, and hence there was now offered the Union troops a rare opportunity."[76] Pickett's command, a substantial portion of General Lee's greatly diminished army, had moved out from behind the protection of the Petersburg de-

72. *Ibid.*, 341, 340. It was agreed later to substitute Ayres' division for Griffin's, as Ayres' position was such that he could get to Dinwiddie faster than Griffin.

73. *Ibid.*, 365.

74. *Ibid.*, 341.

75. *Ibid.*, 342. Orders to this effect were sent to Warren at 10:15 P.M., as marked on the order. If Grant's orders to Meade are marked correctly as having been sent at 10:15, the orders to Warren could not have been sent before 10:30–10:45. Meade's acknowledgment of Grant's orders is marked 10:45 P.M.

76. Sheridan, *Personal Memoirs*, II, 154.

fenses and was exposed to attack. Moreover, by going as far south as Dinwiddie, Pickett had made himself particularly vulnerable to just such an attack as Warren suggested, by Federal infantry on his left flank and rear and a simultaneous frontal attack by the cavalry at Dinwiddie. Sheridan saw this and asked that the VI Corps, which had been with him in the Valley, be given the infantry's share of such an attack. In his reply, sent late in the evening, Grant explained why that corps could not be sent, and he also told Sheridan that the V Corps, which had been ordered to march to his support, should reach him by midnight; he was to assume command of the whole force and use it to the best of his ability to "destroy" the enemy.[77]

The difficulties between Sheridan and Warren, which culminated in Sheridan abruptly relieving Warren of his command, unquestionably originated in this unfortunate message of Grant's. The dispatch in which he approved Meade's suggestion that the entire V Corps be ordered to assist Sheridan was sent at 10:15 P.M. It would have taken Meade until 11:00 P.M. at the earliest to get corresponding orders to Warren. How Grant could have imagined that a corps whose men were tired after their fight that day, whose bivouacs were scattered over a wide area in the woods, could be assembled and organized for the march, and then, in the dark and on roads still barely passable after the two-day downpour, cover the six miles that separated them from Dinwiddie, all within an hour, is beyond human comprehension.[78] Sheridan, who had no knowledge of Warren's actual situation, and did not know when Warren had been ordered to march, cannot be faulted for being disturbed by the latter's failure to arrive at the time indicated in Grant's dispatch.

After their attack at sundown on Sheridan's line had been re-

77. *Official Records*, Vol. XLVI, Pt. 3, pp. 380, 381.
78. To enable Crawford and Griffin to reach the point indicated in Meade's orders, Warren had to build a forty-foot bridge over Gravelly Run, which after the heavy rains of the two previous days was unfordable. Warren informed Meade of that fact and said that the march might well be delayed as a result, but there is nothing in the records to indicate that the information was passed on to Sheridan. *Ibid.*, 366. Colonel Porter's account appears to have been written without an examination of the sequence of Grant's and Meade's orders, and is therefore wholly misleading; *Battles and Leaders*, IV, 711.

pulsed, the Confederate infantry went into bivouac. Anticipating a resumption of their attack at first light, Sheridan forbade the lighting of fires on his line. The weather had turned chilly after the rains, and without fires the Federal cavalrymen spent a cold, sleepless night. Not so the Confederate infantry, much to the envy of their blue-coated opponents, shivering through the night a short distance away: "the rebels . . . had built up rousing great fires, around which they were moving, singing, yelling & shouting until near midnight, we could hear the sound of their voices plain . . . could see them busily getting supper. . . . By midnight the fires of the enemy were mostly but a twinkle, a few still burned brightly, flaring up every once in a while, showing it had been replenished & a figure could be seen moving about."[79]

The Federal generals were not alone in realizing that by following the Federal cavalry to Dinwiddie Court House, Pickett had placed himself in an exceedingly vulnerable position. Pickett too realized it. Shortly before three A.M. he ordered his troops to break camp and march back to the breastworks at Five Forks that they had constructed on the thirtieth. The departure of the enemy was of course observed from the Federal lines a short distance away:

About 3 oclock A.M. some movement was seen [in] the rebel camp, the fires sprung up & figures were seen moving around, but there was no noise, all was still. . . . Long before daylight we could see the camp was empty, the fires nearly out & no figures moving. . . . Before it was fully light, & a slight mist added to the indistinctness, Genls Sheridan & Custer & staffs came riding out from the C[ourt] H[ouse]. I fancy I can see "Little Phil" now as he passed out beyond our line peering toward the rebel camp, with his hand up to his eyes.[80]

At some time during the night but before there was any indication of Pickett's retreat, Sheridan sent word to Warren that the division (Ayres') of the V Corps advancing along the road at "J. Boisseau's" (an east-west side road, known as the Crump Road, which intersected the Dinwiddie-Five Forks Road a little over two miles north of Dinwiddie) was "in rear of the enemy's line and almost on his flank." If, Sheridan went on, Pickett attacked him

79. Hannaford, "Reminiscences," 297(a).
80. *Ibid.*, 297(b). Freeman's statement that the retreat was ordered at 4 A.M. and the march north began at daybreak, at 5 A.M., does not agree with Hannaford's eyewitness account. Freeman, *Lee's Lieutenants*, III, 661.

(Sheridan) at daylight, Ayres should attack from the Crump Road, and in that way Pickett's entire force could be captured. "Do not fear my leaving here," Sheridan added; "If the enemy remain I shall fight at daylight."[81]

But the enemy did not remain; furthermore, neither at daylight nor for a good many hours thereafter was there any sign of the forces that Warren was leading to what Sheridan hoped would be Pickett's rear. Both these factors made it necessary for Sheridan to recast his plans.

The controversy over the justice or injustice of Sheridan's impetuous decision to relieve Warren that day, and thereby wreck an army career whose distinction is attested by Warren's statue on Little Round Top at Gettysburg, is outside the scope of the present study. A good case can be made for each of the two generals, and both have had their defenders. Without taking sides in the controversy, one may nevertheless ask if this tragedy would have occurred if there had been better communication between the two men and if Grant's absurdly unrealistic dispatch, promising the arrival of Warren's infantry at Dinwiddie by midnight, had not aroused expectations completely beyond Warren's ability to fulfill.[82]

Mackenzie's cavalry and Ayres' division of the V Corps had

81. *Official Records*, Vol. XLVI, Pt. 3, pp. 419–20. Warren, an engineer officer. was exceptional in having the time of receipt marked on the dispatches and orders sent to him. He received Sheridan's dispatch at 4:15 A.M. The time sent is not marked on the dispatch, but Sheridan states that it was 3 A.M. Sheridan, *Personal Memoirs*, II, 156.

82. Sheridan sets forth his own case in *Personal Memoirs*, II, 155–70, especially 165–70, and in *Official Records*, Vol. XLVI, Pt. 1, pp. 1103, 1105. The pro-Warren case is made by Warren himself, in *Official Records*, Vol. XLVI, Pt. 1, pp. 818–27 and 828–37, and by Joshua L. Chamberlain, *The Passing of the Armies* (Dayton, 1974), 82–106. (General Chamberlain commanded the First Brigade of Griffin's division; his account of Five Forks is that of a highly intelligent participant.) A pro-Sheridan but balanced view is presented by Bruce Catton, "Sheridan at Five Forks," *Journal of Southern History*, XXI (1955), 305–15. Augustus Buell, who had no axe to grind, was of the opinion that Sheridan "expected too much of the infantry," and that "the faults he attributed to Warren were mainly due to the frightful condition of the roads." "Then, I think," Buell wrote, "Sheridan had a prejudice against engineer officers as commanders of large bodies of marching and fighting troops. . . . It was not possible for me to help noticing the wide and irreconcilable 'incompatibility of temperament' between . . . Warren and Sheridan." Buell, *"The Cannoneer,"* 358–59. See also *Battles and Leaders*, IV, 723–24.

arrived at Dinwiddie at daylight, but by that time Pickett, with Devin and Custer at his heels, was already past the point where Sheridan had hoped that Warren's other two divisions could trap him. As Pickett marched toward Five Forks, the cavalry kept him moving with repeated dashes at his rear guard, but the statements in Federal reports, including Grant's, that Sheridan "drove" Pickett to Five Forks, stretch the facts by a considerable margin.[83] Indeed, whenever the Federal cavalry came too close, it was the Confederates who did the "driving."

By two o'clock in the afternoon, Pickett's infantry was safe behind its defenses on the White Oak Road, but there was still no sign of the other two divisions—Griffin's and Crawford's—of Warren's corps. Bitterly disappointed over the loss of a great opportunity—"we accomplished nothing but to oblige our foe to retreat"—Sheridan deployed Devin's division and part of Custer's in the woods facing the Confederate breastworks.[84] Thrown together as usual of logs, brush, fence rails, and scooped-up earth and strengthened with a wide abattis of felled trees in front, the defenses ran in a nearly straight east-west line from about a mile west of the intersection of the White Oak Road and the Ford Road (the latter running north to the Southside Railroad) to a point about three quarters of a mile east of the intersection; at that point there was a sharp angle, from which the breastworks continued for about one hundred yards in a northeasterly direction. Having lost the opportunity to fight Pickett in the open, Sheridan now decided to attack him behind his entrenchments.

Pickett had his five brigades of infantry and ten pieces of artillery lined up behind his breastworks; beyond its two ends, Fitzhugh Lee's (now commanded by T. T. Munford) division of cavalry, dismounted, protected his left and W. H. F. Lee's cavalry his right. Dearing's and McCausland's brigades of cavalry, under Rosser, were posted as a reserve about two miles to the north, near Hatcher's Run.[85] Sheridan's plan was to keep Pickett pinned down behind his breastworks with the carbine fire of Devin's and a part

83. *Official Records*, Vol. XLVI, Pt. 1, pp. 54, 1117.
84. Sheridan, *Personal Memoirs*, II, 158. Crook's division was left behind at Dinwiddie to hold the crossings of Stony Creek and Chamberlain's Creek and to guard the trains.
85. Freeman, *Lee's Lieutenants*, III, 663–64; see also Sheridan, *Personal Memoirs*, II, 159.

of Custer's dismounted cavalry. The rest of Custer's division, mounted, was to stage a diversionary attack against the western end of Pickett's line. The real attack was to be made by Warren's three divisions of infantry and was to be aimed primarily at the angle between Pickett's main line and its northeasterly extension, or "return." As soon as the dismounted cavalry facing the main east-west line of breastworks heard the musketry of Warren's infantry attacking the angle, they too were to go over to the attack and force their way through the entrenchments.

After a long delay which drove Sheridan nearly frantic, the operation finally got under way late in the afternoon; when it did, it worked flawlessly.[86] The delay was caused by the late arrival of Crawford's and Griffin's divisions; when at long last, at some time past three o'clock, they reached Five Forks, they were either misdirected or lost their way in the woods and came in some distance northeast of where Sheridan wanted them to be. In the meantime, mistaking some firing on their right for the all-out infantry attack, the dismounted cavalry charged the breastworks three separate times. They were repulsed each time, but more importantly, they used up most of their ammunition in these unsuccessful charges.

Eventually the two strayed divisions of Warren's infantry were deployed where Sheridan wanted them to be. Then Ayres, supported by Griffin, launched his attack on the angle. To reach it, the footsoldiers had to struggle over a patch of boggy ground, through dense woods and underbrush. At an early stage of their advance and still some distance short of the breastworks, the Confederate musketry caused Ayres' skirmish line to waver. Thereupon, wrote Colonel Horace Porter, who was at Sheridan's side as an observer, "Sheridan began to exhibit those traits which always made him a tower of strength in the presence of an enemy. He put spurs to his horse, and dashed along in front of the line of battle from left to right, shouting words of encouragement, and having something cheery to say to every regiment." Thus encouraged, the skirmish-

86. For Sheridan's impatience, see Porter, *Campaigning with Grant*, 436. Sheridan himself wrote in his report, "I was exceedingly anxious to attack . . . for the sun was getting low, and we had to fight or go back. It was no place to intrench, and it would have been shameful to have gone back with no results to compensate for the loss of the brave men who had fallen during the day." *Official Records*, Vol. XLVI, Pt. 1, p. 1105.

ers resumed their advance, but a short time later Ayres' main body was "staggered by a heavy fire from the angle, and fell back in some confusion." Then "Sheridan . . . rushed into the midst of the broken lines, and cried out, 'Where is my battle-flag?' As the sergeant who carried it rode up, Sheridan seized the crimson-and-white standard, waved it above his head, cheered on the men, and made heroic efforts to close up the ranks . . . [he dashed] from one point of the line to another, waving his flag, shaking his fist, encouraging, entreating, threatening, praying, swearing."[87] Inevitably, such leadership had its reward. Ayres' men responded to it. They rallied, resumed their advance, and broke through the angle with a rush, followed closely by the men of Griffin's division.[88] Sheridan, riding forward abreast of the charging infantrymen, spurred his horse up to and over the breastworks to urge them on.

The 6th Pennsylvania of the Reserve Brigade, weakened in the fighting at Dinwiddie the previous day, was in the advance to Five Forks. When the regiment reached the Confederate breastworks and "for the last time dismounted to fight on foot, there stood in the ranks but 48 men bearing carbines. These all went into the fight. There were no Nos. 4 left behind to hold horses that day . . . the horses were given in charge to officers' servants."[89]

Hearing the roar of battle on their right, the dismounted cavalry in the center and on the left the mounted regiments of the Third Division, led by Custer himself, all dashed forward. There were minor hitches; the mounted attack made no headway against the resistance put up by W. H. F. Lee's troopers, and in the dismounted attack in the center there was some confusion and delay

87. Porter, *Campaigning with Grant*, 438–39; Sheridan, *Personal Memoirs*, II, 163; *Official Records*, Vol. XLVI, Pt. 1, pp. 869, 838–39; Townsend, *Rustics in Rebellion*, 255.

88. Porter, *Campaigning with Grant*, 439. It was the "giving way" of a portion of Ayres' division, "simply from a want of confidence on the part of the troops, which General Warren did not exert himself to inspire" that proved to be the last straw. Sheridan sent Warren orders relieving him of his command. General Griffin, the senior divisional commander, took over command of the V Corps. *Official Records*, Vol. XLVI, Pt. 1, p. 1105; Pt. 3, p. 420; Sheridan, *Personal Memoirs*, II, 165.

89. Gracey, *Annals of the 6th*, 336–38. Five Forks was the 6th Pennsylvania's last fight. On the following morning, Merritt, rightly thinking that forty-eight men were too few to do duty as a regiment, ordered the 6th Pennsylvania to his headquarters to serve as his escort. *Ibid.*, 340.

at the boundary between the right-hand regiment of Pennington's brigade (which, according to General Devin's report, "gave way" twice) and the left-hand regiment of Devin's division (which, according to Colonel Pennington, "failed to keep up proper connection"), but the success of the attack on the angle proved decisive. It broke the resistance of the Confederate infantry, most of whom abandoned the breastworks and made for the rear, which then made it possible for Devin's and Pennington's troopers to get through the abattis and breastworks with little loss.[90]

With the back of Confederate resistance broken, the pursuit and the rounding up of prisoners began. There were small islands of resistance here and there, where some officer managed to hold a few men together. Most of the Confederate cavalry got away, but by far the greatest part of the infantry—nearly six thousand of them—that Pickett had taken into the fight were taken prisoner. Other trophies were six of Pickett's ten guns, eight thousand muskets, and eighteen battle flags.[91] The cost to the Union was sufficiently high, perhaps as many as a thousand killed, wounded, and missing, but as the price of the ultimate results of the victory, the loss was infinitesimal.[92]

Gravelly Run Meeting House, a mile to the east of Five Forks, was visited late that evening by a newspaper correspondent, George Alfred Townsend; he saw "a little frame church, planted

90. Sheridan, Personal Memoirs, II, 164; Official Records, Vol. XLVI, Pt. 1, pp. 1129, 1124, 1135–36. Merritt, however, reported that "the right of Pennington's brigade was thrown into some confusion on account of a deficiency of ammunition." Official Records, Vol. XLVI, Pt. 1, p. 1118.

91. Sheridan, Personal Memoirs, II, 165; Townsend, Rustics in Rebellion, 259. The latter states that twenty-eight battle flags were captured.

92. The cavalry's losses at Five Forks are not reported separately from those at Dinwiddie Court House. Griffin reported the losses of the V Corps as 633 killed, wounded, and missing; the losses of the cavalry may, perhaps, have been about half of those of the infantry. On that assumption, Sheridan's total loss would have been about a thousand, which is also D. S. Freeman's estimate. Official Records, Vol. XLVI, Pt. 1, p. 840; Freeman, R. E. Lee, IV, 40n. Sheridan told reporter Townsend immediately after the battle that the cavalry's loss was "no more than eight hundred men," and the total "no more than fifteen hundred"; both figures seem excessively high. Townsend, Rustics in Rebellion, 259. Luman Tenney noted in his diary that the 2nd Ohio's losses on March 31-April 1 were 35, including 5 officers, killed and wounded; he commented on Five Forks, "Brilliant affair —but oh the cost." Tenney, War Diary, 149, 151.

among the pines, and painted white, with cool, green window-shutters . . . I found its pews moved to the green plain over the threshold, and on its bare floors the screaming wounded. Blood ran in little rills across the planks, and, human feet treading in them, had made indelible prints in every direction . . . Federal and Confederate lay together, the bitterness of noon assuaged in the common tribulation of the night."[93]

A short distance to the west of the little church, on what had been the battlefield,

The White Oak Road presented a scene of chaotic confusion and disorder only to be witnessed after a battle. Here and there huge camp-fires were already blazing . . . and the horses of hurrying staff officers kicked over coffee pots and had anathemas hurled after them as they galloped up and down; hundreds of soldiers called out for their regiments, and hundreds of officers advertised theirs for the benefit of those astray; for it was after dark now and fighting so long in the woods had scattered the troops in all directions. Drums were tapped and bugles blown and cries resounded for these enfants-perdus. The muddy road was blocked with horse and foot and strewed with abandoned arms; and mingling with the crowd came wounded men, limping slowly back to the hospital, or carried in blankets if badly hurt.[94]

Colonel Porter rode back to Grant's bivouac with the tidings of Sheridan's great victory. He found the general-in-chief, surrounded by many members of his staff, sitting before a blazing campfire. Porter began shouting his news while he was still some distance away, and "in a moment all but the imperturbable general-in-chief were on their feet giving vent to boisterous demonstrations of joy. For some minutes there was a bewildering state of excitement, and officers fell to grasping hands, shouting, and hugging each other like schoolboys. The news meant the beginning of the end, the reaching of the 'last ditch.' "[95]

General Wilson was to write of the effect of Sheridan's victory that it "literally pulled the Army of the Potomac out of its hesitation and delay, and started it in earnest upon its last and most victorious campaign. Nothing could stop it; nothing except a failure to press forward with the utmost speed could mar the complete-

93. Townsend, *Rustics in Rebellion*, 259–60.
94. Newhall, *With General Sheridan*, 121–22.
95. Porter, *Campaigning with Grant*, 442.

ness of its success."[96] This was precisely what Sheridan intended to achieve by staying with the Army of the Potomac. His cavalrymen did not have the benefit of Wilson's after-knowledge, but they could sense as soon as the battle was over that they had won an all-important victory. They realized also that Sheridan's presence and personal leadership had been the key factors in their triumph. And so, on the morning after the battle, "marching up the railroad, they greeted . . . [Sheridan] all along the column with such hearty cheers as had been seldom heard in that army since the old enthusiastic days, when everybody believed that the generals were born to command and that every campaign was to end the rebellion."[97] Nor were these feelings, and these demonstrations, confined to Sheridan's own cavalrymen. General Joshua L. Chamberlain, the very able commander of a brigade in the V Corps, wrote after the battle:

We had had a taste of . . . [Sheridan's] style of fighting, and we liked it. . . . We had formed some habits of fighting, too. . . . We went at things with a dogged resolution; not much show. . . . But we could give credit to more brilliant things. We could see how this voice and vision, this swing and color, this vivid impression on the senses, carried the pulse and will of men. . . . We had a habit, perhaps drawn from dire experience . . . when we had carried a vital point or had to hold one, to entrench. But Sheridan does not entrench. He pushes on, carrying his flank and rear with him—rushing, flashing, smashing. He transfuses into his subordinates the vitality and energy of his purpose; transforms them into part of his own mind and will. He shows the power of a commander—inspiring both confidence and fear.[98]

Indeed, the verdict was unanimous that in the most literal sense Five Forks was Sheridan's personal victory;

96. Wilson, *John A. Rawlins*, 315.
97. Newhall, *With General Sheridan*, 131.
98. Chamberlain, *Passing of the Armies*, 153–54. This passage is from the pen of an officer whose corps commander Sheridan had relieved of his command—unjustly, in Chamberlain's opinion. Colonel C. S. Wainwright of the V Corps wrote in his diary on April 2 that when he heard the infantry of his corps cheering, he "supposed that Sheridan was riding by; for he excites the greatest enthusiasm among the men, and is greeted whenever seen with such cheers as I have not heard given to any officer since McClellan's day." Nevins (ed.), *A Diary of Battle*, 516, (It turned out that the cheering Colonel Wainwright heard was occasioned not by Sheridan, but by news of the fall of Petersburg.)

His presence on every part of that contested field . . . had as much to do as generalship with the final result of that battle, where everything depended on the persistence of the attack on the weak point which Sheridan had discovered. It is doubtful if success would have followed the efforts of a general who had been content to direct the battle. Sheridan led. He was in the front line, under the heaviest fire, at all times, waving his sword, encouraging his men, exhorting them . . . and as usual with him, swearing alternately at the enemy and at his own skulkers.[99]

As John Rawlins wrote his wife on the evening of the victory, "The hero of the Shenandoah stands afront of all on the Appomattox. His personal gallantry and great genius have secured us a great success to-day."[100]

General Grant saw that the essential preliminary to Sheridan's victory at Five Forks had been his stand at Dinwiddie Court House on the previous day. At Dinwiddie, Grant wrote, "Sheridan had displayed great generalship. Instead of retreating with his whole command on the main army, to tell the story of superior forces encountered, he deployed his cavalry on foot, leaving only mounted men enough to take charge of the horses. This compelled the enemy to deploy over a vast extent of wooded and broken country" and created the conditions that made possible the next day's victory.[101]

The problem facing Grant on the late evening of April 1 was how best to exploit the victory Sheridan had won for him. And the problem facing General Lee was to try to cope with the crisis created by the seemingly irretrievable disaster—"a dark and humiliating tragedy"—of Pickett's defeat.[102]

99. William F. G. Shanks, *Personal Recollections of Distinguished Generals* (New York, 1866), 158.
100. Wilson, *John A. Rawlins*, 316.
101. *Official Records*, Vol. XLVI, Pt. 1, p. 54.
102. Freeman, *R. E. Lee*, IV, 39.

XVI

"Hasty as Fire"

ESSENTIALLY, FIVE FORKS SETTLED THE FATE OF CON-
federate resistance in Virginia. Joseph Johnston in North Carolina,
heavily outnumbered, could do no more than annoy Sherman's
northward advance; he had no chance whatever of arresting it.
The Army of Northern Virginia, its numbers shrinking day by day
through attrition and desertions, had reached the last ditch even
before Five Forks. By mid-March its numbers were already wholly
inadequate to break through the Federal siege of Richmond and
Petersburg or even to maintain its defense lines against an all-out
Federal attack. Then on March 25 came General John B. Gordon's
superbly planned but ultimately unsuccessful assault on Fort Stedman, in which his casualties "certainly reached 4,400 and perhaps 5,000."[1] A week later at Five Forks, Pickett lost upwards of
six thousand men, mostly as prisoners. These were losses on a
scale General Lee could not sustain. With his already exiguous
forces reduced by eleven thousand in the space of a week, he had
no choice but to evacuate the fortifications he had held against
heavy odds for the better part of a year and then to try to outdis-

---

1. Freeman, *Lee's Lieutenants*, III, 651. The attack of the Federal infantry on the southwest end of the Petersburg defenses on the morning of
April 2 was equally calamitous for Lee, the VI Corps alone taking three
thousand prisoners. *Official Records*, Vol. XLVI, Pt. 3, p. 447.

tance the Federal pursuit and join Johnston at or below Danville, Virginia. Even this was no better than a forlorn hope, based not on military realities, but on spirit, a sense of honor, and dedication to a patently sinking cause.

To make certain that the lesson of Five Forks was not lost on Lee, Grant ordered three corps of the Army of the Potomac and one of the Army of the James to assault the Petersburg defenses before them on the morning of April 2. The assaults of the II, IX, and XXIV Corps met with varying success, but that of General Wright's VI Corps drove a wedge through the defenses and broke out into open country beyond. Wright's success merely underlined the obvious and in a sense simplified Lee's problem. It was no longer a question of whether he should or should not continue the defense of Richmond and Petersburg. That issue was settled for him by the Federal successes that morning and on the previous day. He was forced now to try to hold out until nightfall so that the unavoidable retreat could be organized and the army withdrawn from the fortifications without alerting the enemy to the evacuation in progress.

Lee planned to march his army southwest, following generally the line of the Richmond & Danville Railroad to Burkeville, about fifty-five miles below Richmond, and thence to Danville.[2] To begin with, however, he had to arrange for the commands of Generals Longstreet and Ewell, which were manning the Richmond defenses north of the James, to join the troops that were leaving the defenses of Petersburg. He designated Amelia Court House, south of the Appomattox River and about equidistant from Richmond and Petersburg, as the point where the two forces were to meet. From Amelia Court House the twenty-eight thousand to thirty thousand infantry to which the Army of Northern Virginia had now been reduced was to endeavor to reach Danville, 120 miles away, encumbered with a train 30 miles long of well over a thousand wagons and two hundred guns, drawn by weakened and emaciated horses and mules.[3] A handicap even more serious than

2. Burkeville, or Burke's Station, was where the Southside Railroad crossed the Richmond and Danville and continued west to Lynchburg and on into Tennessee.

3. Freeman, *R. E. Lee*, IV, 58–59.

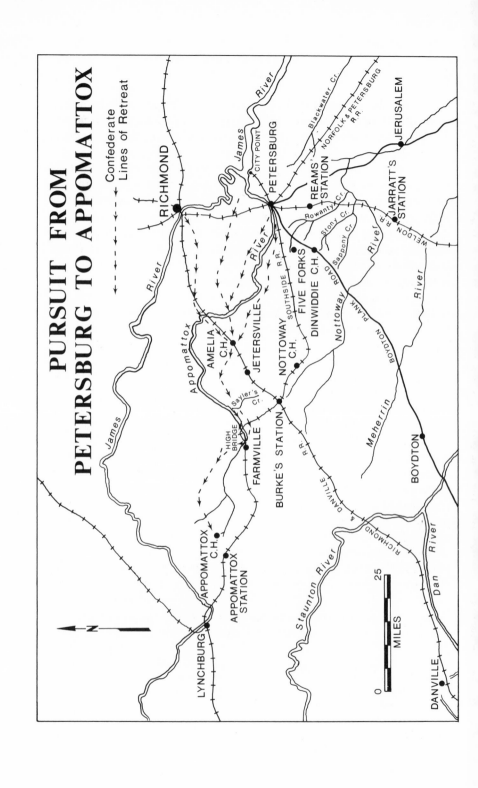

PURSUIT FROM
PETERSBURG TO APPOMATTOX

- - - → Confederate
Lines of Retreat

RICHMOND

James River
City Point
PETERSBURG
Blackwater Cr.
Norfolk & Petersburg R.R.
JERUSALEM

Appomattox River
REAMS' STATION
Rowanty Cr.
JARRATT'S STATION
Weldon R.R.

AMELIA C.H.
JETERSVILLE
NOTTOWAY C.H.
Southside R.R.
FIVE FORKS
DINWIDDIE C.H.
Stony Cr.
Sappony Cr.
Nottoway River

Sayler's Cr.
HIGH BRIDGE
FARMVILLE
BURKE'S STATION
Plank Road
Boydton Plank Road
Meherrin
BOYDTON
Danville R.R.

APPOMATTOX C.H.
APPOMATTOX STATION
Staunton River
Richmond & Danville R.R.
Dan River
LYNCHBURG
DANVILLE

N

25
MILES
0

the huge, slow-moving train and the mass of artillery was a lack of rations. Lee's orders to move the 350,000 rations that had been accumulated in Richmond to Amelia Court House became a casualty of the confusion of the last day and were not carried out.[4] Moreover, the line of retreat ran through the relatively poor lowlands south of the Appomattox River, an area in which farmers had little food to sell or give the soldiers. Even the cavalry, expert at living off the country, went hungry; a trooper of the 2nd Virginia recorded that if the men of his regiment, in common with the rest of the army, "got anything to eat at all, they begged it from citizens in passing by or stole it, and the great trouble was there was so little left to steal. The country was stripped."[5] The wagons General Lee sent out from Amelia Court House on the fourth to collect food from the countryside, after he learned that the rations from Richmond he expected to find there had not been shipped, came back the next day nearly empty, notwithstanding the personal appeal he had sent out with them to the "generosity and charity" of the farmers in the area for "provender in any quantity that can be spared."[6] This unsuccessful attempt to find food for his hungry men and animals cost Lee the day's lead he had on the pursuing Federals and further compromised his ill-omened attempt to escape. Indeed, the retreat, from the first day to the last, can be viewed as only incidentally a military operation; its most urgent objective, to which all else had to be subordinated, was to find food somewhere, somehow, for a starving army.

President Lincoln was at City Point on April 2. Grant kept him informed by means of a series of dispatches meant for his eyes, addressed to Colonel Theodore S. Bowers of his own staff. In one of these messages, sent on the morning of the second, Grant wrote, "I have not yet heard from Sheridan, but I have an abiding faith that he is in the right place and at the right time."[7] The right

4. *Ibid.*, 66. The train of W. H. F. Lee's division, containing "20,000 good rations," had come to within four miles of Amelia Court House on the morning of April 5 when it was attacked and destroyed by a detachment of Federal cavalry. Neither General Lee, nor any of the Federal reports, identify the unit that made this attack. *Official Records*, Vol. XLVI, Pt. 1, p. 1296.

5. Peck, *Reminiscences*, 71.

6. Freeman, *R. E. Lee*, IV, 67, 71.

7. *Official Records*, Vol. XLVI, Pt. 3, p. 449.

place that morning, in Sheridan's opinion, was the southwestern end of the Petersburg fortifications. He therefore directed General Miles's division of the II Corps, backed by two divisions of the V Corps, in an attack on this "vital point." After an initial success, however, Sheridan thought it advisable, in order to "avoid wrangles," to surrender command of Miles's division to its corps commander, General Humphreys, and he withdrew from the operation.[8] Meanwhile he had sent Merritt to drive off the Confederate cavalry, much of which had collected between Hatcher's Run and the Southside Railroad, north of the Five Forks battlefield. Merritt met little opposition. The enemy—mainly W. H. F. Lee's division —put up only a token resistance. This made it possible for Merritt to cross the railroad and break up a short stretch of its track before going into bivouac for the night.[9]

By midafternoon of April 2, Sheridan's intuition told him not only that Lee was about to evacuate the Richmond-Petersburg defenses but also that his retreat would be along the Richmond & Danville Railroad in the direction of Burkeville. After receiving a dispatch from Grant directing him to cross to the north side of the Appomattox with his cavalry and the V Corps, presumably to attack Petersburg from the rear, he countered with a dispatch of his own to Grant, saying, "From what has transpired . . . I think, beyond a doubt, that the enemy's troops, wagons, and, in fact, everything that is left of them, have moved off and are moving toward Burkeville. . . . I think everything has left Petersburg or is leaving it."[10] Based on this assessment of the situation, which of course proved to be correct, he questioned the wisdom of crossing to the north of the river, the effect of which would have been to leave open for the enemy the most direct route to Burkeville, the so-called River Road, which ran south of the river.

8. Sheridan, *Personal Memoirs*, II, 172.
9. *Official Records*, Vol. XLVI, Pt. 1, pp. 1118–19, 1106; Pt. 3, pp. 489–90, 490, 490–91. The absence of serious opposition is suggested by one of Merritt's dispatches: "We are all right and will give them fits." *Ibid.*, Pt. 3, p. 490.
10. *Ibid.*, Pt. 3, pp. 488, 489. As had now become his habit, Grant gave Sheridan maximum latitude. He instructed him to cross the river "where you please. The position and movements of the enemy will dictate your movements after you cross."

Unlike Sheridan, Grant had not anticipated the evacuation of Petersburg on the second; in fact, he ordered a bombardment of the defenses to begin at five A.M. on the third, to be followed by a full-scale assault an hour later.[11] In the event, the bombardment and the assault were called off, for Grant learned that the Confederate fortifications were unoccupied. Acting on this information, he sent Major Peter T. Hudson of his staff to Sheridan with orders that do not appear in the *Official Records*, but whose tenor can be deduced from a second dispatch, sent at 10:20 A.M., in which he told Sheridan that his primary objective was to intercept Lee's army on its march south, and secondarily—and that was clearly based on the unspoken assumption that Lee might not be intercepted—to occupy Burkeville, rebuild the railroad from Petersburg to that point, and hold it as a base "until . . . [Lee's] policy is indicated."[12]

Sheridan was not the man for alternate strategies, one of which implied the failure of the other, nor did he think it necessary to wait for Lee's "policy" to be revealed; he already knew what that policy was, as indeed it had to be. He acknowledged receipt of Grant's orders without referring to the establishment of a base at Burkeville, but could not resist the temptation to write, "Before receiving your dispatch I had anticipated the evacuation of Petersburg and had commenced moving west"; he said, further, that he was marching for the Danville Railroad with all speed.[13] Having decided to his own satisfaction where Lee was going, Sheridan's one thought was to destroy or capture Lee's army before he could get there. Moreover, he already knew how he would go about doing it. As his chief of staff has written:

his decision as to the method to be pursued by the cavalry corps was immediate and simple. It was to pursue and attack the left flank of the retreating army at any possible point with the cavalry division that first reached it, and, if possible, compel it to turn and defend its wagon trains and artillery, then to send another division beyond and attack

11. Grant, *Personal Memoirs*, II, 453.
12. *Official Records*, Vol. XLVI, Pt. 3, p. 528. To make the Danville Railroad usable by the U.S. Military Railroad, not only did the roadbed have to be repaired, but also the gauge had to be changed from 5′ to 4′8½″. Grant, *Personal Memoirs*, II, 458.
13. *Official Records*, Vol. XLVI, Pt. 3, p. 529.

the Confederate army again at any possible point, and to follow up this method of attack until at some point the whole army would be obliged to turn and deliver battle.[14]

General Forsyth's summary spells out clearly the concept that was to guide Sheridan's operations from April 4 to the end. Before he could begin to put this strategy to use, however, he had to catch up with the enemy. Shortly after sunrise on the third, the cavalry moved out and marched at a fast walk nearly all day;

The roads in places were horrible, the terrible rain of Thursday & Friday before having covered the level land & the road was badly cut up by the enemy's train; in many of the low bad places the enemy had been obliged to abandon wagon[s], caisson[s], forges, &c., while the roadside was thickly strewn by ammunition of every kind and sort. . . . We moved rapidly forward, having now the Appomattox River on our right, distant half a mile to a mile, at one place we could distinguish a large wagon train going west.[15]

The wagons Sheridan's troopers saw moving along beyond the Appomattox were a portion of Lee's trains marching on one of the several roads they used to get to Amelia Court House. This was only the first day of the retreat, but already signs of disintegration were manifest. Sheridan reported to Grant in the afternoon that by eleven A.M., Custer, leading the advance of Merritt's two divisions, had captured one gun and ten caissons abandoned by the enemy, and that

the resistance made by the enemy's rear guard was very feeble. The enemy threw their artillery ammunition on the sides of the road and into the woods and then set fire to the fences and woods through which the shells were strewn. . . . We captured the enemy's rear guard, numbering between 200 and 300 men. . . . The roads are strewn with burning and broken-down caissons, ambulances, wagons, and debris of all descriptions. Up to . . . this hour we have taken about 1,200 prisoners . . . and all accounts report the woods filled with deserters and stragglers. . . . One of our men, recaptured, reports that not one in five of the rebels have arms in their hands.[16]

14. Forsyth, Thrilling Days, 175–76. To the old saw that "no man is a hero to his valet" may be added the corollary that commanding generals are seldom heroes to their chiefs of staff. The Sheridan-Forsyth relationship is a pleasing exception.
15. Hannaford, "Reminiscences," 305(a).
16. Official Records, Vol. XLVI, Pt. 3, p. 529. By noon Merritt was re-

Except at the crossing of Namozine Creek, which Custer was able to force by flanking the dismounted cavalry defending it out of the breastworks commanding the ford, there was no opposition until near nightfall, when Custer's advance was checked by what he believed to be six brigades of infantry.[17] To make up for the absence of enemy opposition, however, there was the eternal mud to hamper the advance. In addition, there was also hunger; the Federal cavalry too marched on empty stomachs.[18] The men had only what remained of the rations issued to them four or five days previously, which meant that most of them had nothing. Their trains had not been able to keep up with the rapid advance. Merritt reported bravely that he had to have "rations if possible, but will, of course, in the emergency hurry through if possible." He actually did so. Thus the pursuers, no less than the pursued, were "half starved."[19]

The spirits of the Federal cavalry had been raised early in the afternoon, when the regiments at the head of the column heard great cheering

afar distant in the rear, which seemed rapidly coming up the column; looking back we could see . . . Capt[ain Charles H.] Miller, our A[ssistant] A[djutant] G[eneral] & his Ord[erly], galloping along the column . . . as he came near we could catch what he was repeating, "Hurrah! Richmond is taken, Grant has taken Richmond! hurrah" in a moment we were as wild as he was, yelling & cheering long after he was past, hunger, hardship & danger all were overlooked, it was a proud moment.[20]

While Merritt, with the First and Third Divisions, pursued the enemy on the direct road to Amelia Court House, Crook and the

porting that "twenty-three miles of wagon trains are ahead. If a division of infantry is pushed up their capture is insured," and a short time later, "I think there is no doubt . . . that a force of infantry pushed into Amelia Court-House would get the entire rebel army. . . . The whole thing is gone up." *Ibid.*, 530, 531.

17. *Ibid.*, Pt. 1, pp. 1131–32.
18. Newhall, *With General Sheridan*, 138.
19. *Official Records*, Vol. XLVI, Pt. 3, p. 531; Hannaford, "Reminiscences," 305(b). Merritt reported later in the day, however, that he was finding plenty of forage. For once the horses seem to have fared better than the men. *Official Records*, Vol. XLVI, Pt. 3, p. 560.
20. Hannaford, "Reminiscences," 305(b)–(c).

Second Division, followed by the V Corps infantry, swung to the south, with orders from Sheridan to set up a blocking position across the Danville Railroad at or near Jetersville, eight miles southwest of Amelia Court House and ten miles northeast of Burkeville Junction.[21] This was a move that to all intents and purposes sealed the fate of Lee's army, for it not only barred its direct route toward Danville but also cut the only practicable means by which the food they desperately needed could reach them either from Danville or from Lynchburg. Sheridan in fact hoped that if he could hold Jetersville, Lee might be forced to surrender at Amelia Court House.

After telling Grant, "If we press on we will no doubt get the whole army," Sheridan rode on ahead of his troops to Jetersville with his two hundred-man escort of the 1st United States. He deployed this handful of men across the railroad to try to hold the position until Crook could get there; he also sent orders back to Merritt to join him as quickly as possible.[22] Then he dashed off a dispatch to General Meade to ask that the II and VI Corps be hurried forward to Jetersville. His message elicited a response greatly to Meade's credit and of a kind that was not as common in the Civil War as it might have been: "The Second and Sixth Corps shall be with you as soon as possible," Meade wrote; "In the meantime, your wishes and suggestions as to any movement other than the simple one of overtaking you will be promptly acceded to by me, regardless of any other consideration than the vital one of destroying the Army of Northern Virginia."[23]

Merritt had already gone into camp at Beaver Dam at six P.M. after a twenty-mile march when Sheridan's orders to join him at Jetersville reached him. At ten P.M., within a half hour after receiving the orders, he had his men back on the road; after "a long and exhausting" all-night march, his leading regiments reached Sheridan at daylight. During the last few hours of the march,

21. Sheridan, *Personal Memoirs*, II, 174. Sheridan regularly spells Jetersville with two t's.

22. *Official Records*, Vol. XLVI, Pt. 3, pp. 556, 560. Sheridan, *Personal Memoirs*, II, 175. Crook, who had struck the railroad south of Jetersville, was ordered to march up there and join Sheridan. *Official Records*, Vol. XLVI, Pt. 3, p. 561.

23. *Official Records*, Vol. XLVI, Pt. 3, pp. 557, 558.

wrote the historian of the 19th New York, "scores of men could be seen swaying in their saddles, sound asleep."[24]

Shortly after noon on April 5, General Lee, riding forward with General Longstreet, came upon Sheridan's lines—"a well-chosen position"—at Jetersville and saw that the direct road to Burkeville and Danville was barred. If nothing more than Sheridan's cavalry had been in the way, Lee might well have decided to mount a direct attack by his infantry to drive it out of his path, but his son Rooney, whose cavalry had the advance, reported that the Federal infantry was nearby.[25] For an army weakened by two days of hunger, its numbers reduced by the thousands who had dropped out on the march, to make a direct attack on Federal infantry posted behind defenses they would have had ample time to build and strengthen, was not to be thought of. The only alternative—other than a capitulation, which was as yet not even considered—was a march past Sheridan's left flank to reach the Southside Railroad at Farmville, twenty-three miles away by the poor roads the army would have to use. At Farmville, if all went well, there would be rations, sent down by rail from Lynchburg for the hungry army, and from there the march could be resumed southwest to Danville. There was an important prerequisite, however: Lee had to outdistance the pursuit by forces he knew were several times the size of his own. The march to Farmville would therefore have to start at once, which meant that much of the twenty-three miles would have to be covered at night.[26]

On the previous afternoon, a short time after Sheridan deployed his escort across the railroad at Jetersville, his pickets captured "a man on a mule," apparently a civilian; a search of the

24. *Ibid.*, Pt. 1, pp. 1119, 1125. Bowen, *Regimental History of the First New York*, 291. Devin's division did not get to Jetersville until noon. As the two divisions began their march, they rode past their pioneers, "each with a box of Spencer ammunition which they were anxious to get rid of. As most of the men had from sixty to eighty rounds already they did not want to take any more, but the orders were for each man to have 125 rounds, a very unusual order, 75 rounds being the utmost we usually carried." Hannaford, "Reminiscences," 307(b).

25. Freeman, *Lee's Lieutenants*, III, 692–93; Freeman, *R. E. Lee*, IV, 74. By one P.M. on April 5, the V Corps was in position at Jetersville, the II Corps was arriving, and the VI Corps was only a short distance away.

26. Freeman, *R. E. Lee*, IV, 74–76.

man turned up messages from Lee's commissary general to the quartermaster officers at the depots at Danville and Lynchburg, directing each of them to send in all haste three hundred thousand rations to Burkeville. The messenger said that he had been ordered to send on these instructions by telegraph from the nearest point along the railroad beyond which the lines were still in operation. Here Sheridan perpetrated what southern writers would be justified in describing as a low Yankee trick. He sent out two pairs of scouts, each pair with one of the originals of the order, with instructions to locate the ends of the telegraph lines to Danville and Lynchburg, respectively, and get the orders transmitted. He intended to intercept for the use of his own troops the rations he hoped would be sent forward in response to these orders.[27] General Lee of course did not know that the messenger had been captured, and it was the rations sent forward from Lynchburg in response to the orders the messenger carried that he expected to find waiting for him when he reached Farmville.

While the entire Cavalry Corps and three corps of infantry waited at Jetersville for an attack that failed to materialize, Sheridan ordered Crook to send Davies' brigade on a reconaissance north to Paineville, about seven miles from Jetersville.[28] When Davies reached Paineville, he learned that Lee's wagon train, which had started for Farmville over a series of by-roads north and west of the route the cavalry and infantry were to use, was four miles ahead. Davies at once went after the wagons, the 1st Pennsylvania at a gallop, the rest of the brigade following at a trot. Charging through a "deep swamp," Davies struck the train near its head. He rode along the long line of vehicles, captured 320 of the guard, and drove off the rest. Deciding that the weakened draft animals were in no condition to haul the captured wagons to Jetersville, he burned two hundred ammunition and headquarters wagons, caissons, and ambulances and started back to Jetersville with five guns, eleven flags, 320 white prisoners, the same number of Negro teamsters, and four hundred horses and mules.[29] His retreat, however, turned into a more difficult opera-

27. Sheridan, *Personal Memoirs*, II, 175–76.
28. *Ibid.*, 176–77; *Official Records*, Vol. XLVI, Pt. 1, pp. 1107, 1145. Paineville is called Paine's Cross Roads in some reports.
29. *Official Records*, Vol. XLVI, Pt. 1, p. 1145.

tion than the attack on the train had been. Led by Martin W. Gary's brigade, Munford's and Rosser's cavalry repeatedly attacked and drove in Davies' rear guard; at one point, they circled around his column and attacked his lead regiments at the same time that his rear guard was attacked from the rear and on both flanks. Thanks to the help of Smith's and Gregg's brigades, which Crook sent on to his support, Davies succeeded in cutting his way through to Jetersville with all his prisoners and other captures.[30] Fitzhugh Lee claimed in his report (written after the surrender and without benefit of reports from his subordinate commanders) that in the attacks on Davies, "30 of the enemy were killed, principally with the sabre, and 150 wounded and captured." Since, however, Davies' losses for the entire period from March 31 to April 9 were 31 killed, 130 wounded, and 83 missing, General Lee's tally appears to be exaggerated.[31]

Davies' reconnaissance had a much more important result than the destruction of wagons or the capture of the prisoners, guns, and animals he brought back with him. His report of finding the Confederate trains so far north of Jetersville and headed northwest was a clear indication that Lee was leaving, or had already left, the direct road to Danville and would attempt to escape encirclement by making a flank march to the northwest in the direction of Farmville and Lynchburg, Sheridan may have been disappointed by the failure of his concentration at Jetersville to produce the encirclement and capture of the Army of Northern Virginia, but he also saw the opportunity of so delaying Lee's march toward Farmville with repeated flank attacks by his cavalry—the tactics he had described to his chief of staff—that the Federal infantry, much of it still a day's march behind, would be given time to catch up and block somewhere the roads toward Lynchburg and Lee's last remaining chance of escape. First, however, there was a difference of opinion between himself and Meade that had to be re-

30. Ibid., 1145, 1142, 1149–50, 1301; Preston, History of the 10th Regiment, 248–49; Tobie, First Maine Cavalry, 411–12.
31. Official Records, Vol. XLVI, Pt. 1, pp. 1301, 1147. Davies fails to give casualty figures in his report of this operation, nor does he mention the help he received from Smith and Gregg, other than to say that one regiment (which he does not identify) of Smith's brigade joined two of his own regiments in driving off the Confederate cavalry that had gotten ahead of his brigade and blocked its way back to Jetersville.

solved. In midafternoon on the fifth, Sheridan sent a dispatch to Grant, who was with General Ord's infantry on his way to Burke-ville; it told Grant of Davies' exploit at Paineville and closed with "I wish you were here yourself. I feel confident of capturing the Army of Northern Virginia if we exert ourselves. I see no escape for Lee. I will put all my cavalry out on our left flank, except Mac-kenzie, who is now on our right."[32] From the sentence "I wish you were here yourself," Grant evidently sensed that difficulties had arisen between Sheridan and Meade that required his intervention to clear up. Leaving Ord's column, he set off with a few members of his staff and a small escort of cavalry to ride sixteen miles to Sheridan's bivouac.

Earlier that day, Meade had notified Grant that if his infantry was not needed at Jetersville, he intended to assemble his troops and set off after Lee's army in the morning.[33] Grant approved this plan, but after he reached Jetersville late in the evening, Sheridan explained what he thought Lee was trying to do and convinced him that "Meade's orders, if carried out, moving to the right flank, would give . . . [Lee] the coveted opportunity of escaping and put-ting us in rear of him."[34] This meant a stern chase and was direct-ly contrary to Sheridan's conception of the correct strategy to be employed. It was now near midnight; nevertheless, Sheridan and Grant decided to ride to Meade's bivouac. What occurred there, as described in Grant's and Sheridan's reminiscences, is one of the many mysteries of the Civil War. Grant's language to Meade was just what Sheridan wanted; "we did not want to follow the enemy," Grant claims to have said; "we wanted to get ahead of him, and . . . his [Meade's] orders would allow the enemy to es-cape, and besides that . . . [he, *i.e.*, Grant] had no doubt that Lee was moving right then."[35] Thereupon, still according to Grant,

32. *Ibid.*, Pt. 3, p. 582. Sheridan sent Grant with this dispatch a cap-tured letter written earlier in the day by Confederate Colonel John Taylor to his mother, which began, "Our army is ruined, I fear." Earlier in the day, Sheridan had written Grant, "From present indications the retreat of the enemy is rapidly becoming a rout. . . . Everything should be hurried for-ward with the utmost speed." *Ibid.*, 582.

33. *Ibid.*, 576. Grant replied, "Your movements are right. Lee's army is the objective point, and to capture that is all we want."

34. Grant, *Personal Memoirs*, II, 469.

35. *Ibid.*, 469; Sheridan, *Personal Memoirs*, II, 178–79.

"Meade changed his orders at once . . . [and directed] an advance on Amelia Court-House at an early hour in the morning." As Sheridan tells the story, it was Grant who in effect dictated Meade's "advance on Amelia Court House."[36] Since Meade wanted all his infantry available for the attack in the morning, he withdrew the V Corps from Sheridan's control.

Orders to the Cavalry Corps on the evening of the fifth directed the command to be "in readiness to move at 6 a.m." the next morning "with a full supply of ammunition."[37] The seemingly superfluous reminder that the men carry a full supply of ammunition was coupled with a circular announcing that "firing along the line of march or in camp is strictly prohibited, and any men violating this order will be severely punished."[38] This order, issued four days before the end of the war, was identical with hundreds of others to the same effect issued by a long line of regimental, brigade, division, corps, and army commanders, in the West as well as in the East, from the very beginning of the war on. It probably had as little effect as its innumerable predecessors had had.

For the cavalry, "readiness to move at 6 a.m." meant reveille long before daylight. Nonetheless, wrote a regimental historian,

the men awoke in fine spirits. Never before during their three years or more of service had there been any prospect of the end. All the hard marching and fighting of three summer campaigns, and the long hours on picket and in dull winter quarters, had been with no such encouragement as they now had. . . . Richmond was captured . . . the goal for which they had marched and fought, and for which so many brave boys had died, was reached—the backbone of the rebellion . . . had now been broken . . . and was beyond healing. . . . It was exciting to even think of the situation, that spring morning.[39]

36. There seems to be a serious flaw in Grant's and Sheridan's accounts of their midnight meeting with Meade. On the evening of April 5, Meade's infantry was at or near Jetersville. To attack Amelia Court House in the morning, they had to march northeast—to the right—whereas to get ahead of Lee they would have marched west, or to the left, as Sheridan actually did. Why, in any case, did Grant order an attack on Amelia Court House if, as he says, he believed that Lee was "moving right then" and would therefore be gone from there by morning, as in fact he was? Grant, *Personal Memoirs*, II, 469; Sheridan, *Personal Memoirs*, II, 178–79.
37. *Official Records*, Vol. XLVI, Pt. 3, p. 583.
38. *Ibid.*, 583.
39. Tobie, *First Maine Cavalry*, 413.

General Charles H. Smith remarked as his brigade of the Second Division took the road that morning, "To-day will see something big in the crushing of the rebellion."[40] General Smith was a good prophet. April 6 did indeed prove to be what he predicted, the "Black Day," in D. S. Freeman's words, of the Army of Northern Virginia.

Sheridan remarks in his reminiscences that he was satisfied that Lee would make a night march on April 5 and would be gone from Amelia Court House long before Meade was in a position to make his attack on the morning of the sixth. Hence he "did not permit the cavalry to participate in Meade's useless advance, but shifted it out toward the left to the road running from Deatonville to Rice's Station."[41] Crook was in the lead, with Custer and Devin right behind him. Near Deatonville, at a small tributary of the Appomattox called Sayler's Creek, they beheld a short distance to the north a sight to gladden a cavalryman's heart; there, on a road parallel to theirs, was a line stretching as far as they could see, of Lee's wagons, protected by "heavy masses of infantry and cavalry."[42] Crook at once deployed his division into line and charged, but could make no impression on the defense. Sheridan ordered him to withdraw, turn west, and look for a less well defended section of the line of wagons to attack. To give time for Custer and also the VI Corps, which was now only a short distance behind the cavalry, to come up, he ordered a section of Captain Marcus P. Miller's horse artillery to open on the line of wagons, and Colonel Peter Stagg's Michigan Brigade of the First Division to "demonstrate" against it.[43] After Miller's gunners had found the range,

40. *Ibid.*, 413.
41. Sheridan, *Personal Memoirs*, II, 179. But see preceding note 36. If Meade, having changed his orders to conform to Grant's and Sheridan's wishes, was doing what they wanted, why was his attack "useless"?
42. *Official Records*, Vol. XLVI, Pt. 1, p. 1107.
43. *Ibid.*, 1107, 1126. Meade did move forward to attack Amelia Court House, but when his infantry was still three or four miles short of the village his scouts reported that the enemy was gone, just as Sheridan claims he predicted they would be. Thereupon the infantry was turned around and marched west, over the route Sheridan had taken earlier in the morning. The VI Corps happened to be in the van and was the first to catch up with the cavalry, arriving at Sayler's Creek at just the right time and in the right place. *Ibid.*, 305, 604.

Sheridan ordered Stagg to charge the trains in earnest, an order that the men from Michigan carried out "most gallantly" in Sheridan's opinion and "brilliantly" in General Devin's; they brought back three hundred prisoners from their attack.[44]

While Stagg was making his attack, Pennington's brigade of Custer's division arrived on the scene;

after some turning and twisting we crossed the Danville R. R. . . . moving thro' fields & bye roads in a nearly west direction. . . . we could look away over to our right nearly 2 miles, and see a large wagon train moving. . . . A mile or so farther, we came on the 2nd Cav[alry] Div[ision], & from them learnt that it was indeed Lee's wagon train. A portion of their Div[ision] had attacked it, & had been repulsed . . . we soon came to a lot of their wounded . . . the effect of such a sight on a lot of men just going to attack the enemy is exceedingly bad.[45]

Nevertheless, attack they did, after moving, as Sheridan's orders required, to the left of the point where Crook's attack had been beaten off. When the order to charge was given, the brigade "took off through the fields . . . on the gallop, gradually making for the train, yelling like Indians . . . we soon flanked the train guard, who had been hastily drawn up in line to oppose us. This done we came on the wagon train where there was not a single guard, or, indeed, often a man, for most of the drivers jumped off & ran away on our approach or ran toward us swinging their hats in token of surrender."[46]

Custer's attack on the train was a smashing success, resulting in the capture of what was variously reported as either three or four hundred wagons plus three batteries of artillery.[47] But then Custer in turn was attacked by what remained of the divisions of Joseph B. Kershaw and G. W. Custis Lee; he was so roughly handled that he had to ask Devin, who in the meantime had ridden

44. *Ibid.*, 1108, 1126.
45. Hannaford, "Reminiscences," 308(b)–(c).
46. *Ibid.*, 309(a).
47. Custer claimed "over 300" wagons in his report. Colonel Pennington claimed "about 300 wagons, about 800 horses and mules," and ten guns. The figure of four hundred for the wagons captured is in Sheridan's report, but when he wrote his reminiscences he changed it to "several hundred." *Official Records*, Vol. XLVI, Pt. 1, pp. 1132, 1136, 1107; Sheridan, *Personal Memoirs*, II, 180. Given the circumstances, it is doubtful if anyone had the opportunity to make an accurate count.

behind and past him to the left with two of his brigades, looking
for another soft spot in the Confederate column to attack, to come
to his aid. General Devin's report describes with obvious unction
Custer's plea for help, and his own subsequent success in checking the enemy and relieving the pressure on the Third Division.[48]

Satisfying as it doubtless was to the morale and spirits of the
cavalry to have captured several hundred decrepit wagons which
had to be burned when Kershaw and Custis Lee attacked Custer,
the irruption of the Federal cavalry into the Confederate line had
another and far more devastating sequel. Other factors—mis-
understandings, mistakes, and failures, due perhaps to exhaustion
—were also at work, but they combined to allow a large gap to
open up between Longstreet's corps in the van, and the commands of Anderson, Ewell, and Custis Lee in the rear of the column.[49] It was through this gap that Custer was able to break into
the wagon train. Moreover, to make a perilous situation more ominous still, as the result of another misunderstanding General
John B. Gordon, whose corps had done yeoman work in protecting
the rear of the column, had gone off on an eccentric march to the
north. The effect of all these accidents and errors of omission and
commission was that the troops to the rear of the gap, amounting
to nearly half of Lee's army, were brought to bay. To the north of
them, between the two branches of Sayler's Creek, lay nearly impassable terrain. The Federal cavalry in full strength barred the
way to the west and south. The VI Corps, which Gordon's march
to the north had allowed to come in on the Confederates' rear, lay
to the east. For the Federals, it was now a case of "every man to
the attack." The entire Cavalry Corps, some regiments mounted
and some on foot, attacked in a great semicircle facing east and
north; Frank Wheaton's and Truman Seymour's divisions of infantry of the VI Corps attacked facing west and southwest. The
Confederates fought with desperation, and some of Custis Lee's
men even mounted a counterattack, but their situation was hope-

48. *Official Records*, Vol. XLVI, Pt. 1, pp. 1125, 1132. Roger Hannaford of Custer's division wrote, "Now talking about the size of our Div[ision]
it always used to be called 5000 in the newspapers, reports, &c.; now I have
it on excellent authority, being from a staff Officer at Div[ision] H[ead]
Q[uarte]rs, that on the morning of Ap[ril] 6#, 1865, the total number of
men reported for duty was exactly 2121." Starr, "Last Days of Rebellion," 8.
49. Freeman, *Lee's Lieutenants*, III, 699–703.

less. Nearly encircled, exposed to the concentric fire of what must have been nearly sixteen thousand Federal cavalry and infantry, almost the entire Confederate body, including Generals Ewell, Custis Lee, Seth M. Barton, M. C. Corse, Dudley M. Dubose, and Joseph B. Kershaw and their staffs and between nine and ten thousand men and lesser officers, were taken prisoner. Only a small minority, perhaps as many as two thousand, escaped through the woods and swamps.[50]

The most spectacular of the charges that broke the back of Confederate resistance at Sayler's Creek was that of Colonel Henry Capehart's brigade, called the "Virginia Brigade" by the rest of the Third Division, because in it were one partial and two full regiments of *West* Virginia cavalry.[51] This is how their charge appeared to a member of another brigade of the Third Division:

as they came on in double line we could see them plainly . . . the fire as they neared the rebel line was terrific, opening gaps in their lines, but if a horse was shot & the rider unhurt he would jump up [and] take his place, firing as he went. "Never was such a charge seen," was the universal comment; as they emerged from the woods they began firing, keeping it up steadily, their gait was a slow walk . . . there was not another Brig[ade] in the Cav[alry] Corp[s] that had such trained horses, they kept in line almost as well as on parade, forward they move, never once checking, not even wavering, pouring in their deadly fire as they go, at last when almost into the enemy's line, the word is given to charge & like a bullet . . . they are away into & over the enemy's breastwork with a rousing cheer in which we now join . . . for we had been spell bound with admiration at their coolness & bravery & splendid discipline.[52]

Be it noted that these troopers of the 1st, 2nd, and 3rd West Vir-

50. *Ibid.*, 703–707. Sheridan claimed "from nine to ten thousand prisoners" in his reminiscences, but in his official report he had written, "I have never ascertained exactly how many prisoners were taken in this battle." F. C. Newhall of his staff wrote, "how many [prisoners there were] we never knew exactly. . . . From the best information we could get, though, there is no doubt that the day gave us from eight to ten thousand." D. S. Freeman states, without citing his source, that the seventeen hundred men Gordon lost by capture "and those who straggled and fell into the hands of the enemy during the day, brought the Federals' haul of prisoners to at least 6,000." Sheridan, *Personal Memoirs*, II, 184; *Official Records*, Vol. XLVI, Pt. 1, p. 1108; Newhall, *With General Sheridan*, 177–78; Freeman, *R. E. Lee*, IV, 93.
51. The brigade also included the 1st New York (Lincoln).
52. Hannaford, "Reminiscences," 312(d)–313(a).

ginia—and the 1st New York (Lincoln) of their brigade must not go unmentioned—had not forgotten, in the process of fighting dismounted for the most part, that they were *cavalry*. When the occasion called for it, as it did at Sayler Creek, they were able to deliver a mounted charge with all the dash and all the effectiveness of any gaudily uniformed European cavalry brigade.

The victory at Sayler's Creek was the product, once again, of Sheridan's strategic intuition, his drive, his skillful use of cavalry, infantry, and artillery in effective combination, and his God-given ability to raise the potential of his subordinates, from major general to rear-rank private, to higher levels. Like James H. Wilson's capture of Selma on April 2, Sheridan's victory of April 6 was overshadowed by the crowning glory of Appomattox only three days later. Nonetheless, it was Sayler's Creek that made the surrender at Appomattox a virtual certainty.

At the regimental and brigade level, claims were staked out for the largest possible share of the credit for the victory at Sayler's Creek. Colonel Isham, former commander of the Michigan Brigade, claimed that the brigade, under his able successor Colonel Stagg, by interposing between the rear of Ewell's infantry and General Gordon's command, completely isolated Ewell and made possible the capture of his entire corps.[53] The historian of the 1st New York (Lincoln) points out that his regiment had "the choicest position in . . . [Custer's division] as they rode among, and over, and through, the disorganized masses. . . . The regiment, Capehart's brigade, and Custer's whole division never did more heroic work." Moreover, the New Yorkers had the trophies to lend their claims credibility; Captain Edwin F. Savacool, Company K, captured three battle flags before he was wounded and disabled; Captain Samuel Stevens, Company C, captured General Ewell himself, with all his staff, "and the general presented him with his field glasses as a *souvenier* of the occasion."[54] The 1st Maine, on

---

53. Isham, "The Cavalry of the Army of the Potomac," 326.

54. Captain Savacool had enlisted in the regiment as a private on its formation in 1861 and was one of several of its officers who had been promoted from the ranks. He died on June 2, 1865, of his Sayler's Creek wound, but not before he had received the Congressional Medal of Honor for his gallantry in that battle. Beach, *First New York (Lincoln) Cavalry*, 503, 572; Stevenson, "*Boots and Saddles*," 345.

the other hand, had a grievance; it had charged dismounted with the other three regiments of General Smith's brigade and all of J. Irvin Gregg's. The result of their attack was that "the rebel line was broken through. The sowing and the reaping, however, were not done by the same hand. A large mounted force immediately rushed in and secured the game their dismounted brethren had brought down." The "large mounted force" thus maligned was Davies' brigade of their own division, whose charge was described by General Crook as "one of the finest . . . of the war, riding over and capturing . . . [the enemy's] works and its defenders."[55]

Before the fight at Sayler's Creek began, Sheridan had written Grant, "The [enemy] trains and army were moving all last night and are very short of provisions and very tired indeed. I think that now is the time to attack them with all your infantry. . . . I am working around farther to the left." He closed a later dispatch in which he reported the outcome of the battle, with the confident declaration, "I am still pressing on with both cavalry and infantry. . . . If the thing is pressed I think Lee will surrender."[56] When Sheridan wrote this second dispatch, he did not yet know that at the same time that he was fighting the enemy near the headwaters of Sayler's Creek, Gordon was being driven across the creek near its mouth by an attack of two divisions of General Humphreys' II Corps, with the loss of seventeen hundred prisoners, over three hundred wagons and ambulances, four guns, and thirteen battle flags.[57] The situation of the Confederate army, desperate even before Sayler's Creek, had now become critical.

General Lee had himself witnessed some of the fighting at Sayler's Creek; then, in the course of the afternoon, news of Gordon's defeat reached him. His catastrophic losses of men, guns, and ammunition and the near certainty that the Federal cavalry would be across his path in the morning, ruled out any possibility

55. Merrill, *Campaigns of the First Maine*, 349; *Official Records*, Vol. XLVI, Pt. 1, p. 1142.
56. *Official Records*, Vol. XLVI, Pt. 3, pp. 609, 610. Sheridan's second dispatch, wired by Grant to the president at City Point, elicited the classic reply, "Gen. Sheridan says, 'If the thing is pressed, I think Lee will surrender.' Let the thing be pressed." Catton, *Grant Takes Command*, 455.
57. *Official Records*, Vol. XLVI, Pt. 1, p. 682; Freeman, *Lee's Lieutenants*, III, 709–10.

of his march to Danville on the shortest route, south of the Appomattox River. Only one avenue of escape was left: to cross the Appomattox on the bridges at and near Farmville, burn the bridges behind him to delay for however short a time the Federal pursuit, and then make for Lynchburg over roads north of the river. Information that reached him during the day that rations sent down from Lynchburg were waiting for him at Farmville left him no choice; Farmville was where he had to go in any case. But to reach the town and cross the river before he was again intercepted made it necessary that he call upon his dead-tired and starving troops to make another all-night march. He did so, and at nightfall the march began, Longstreet going northwest from Rice's Station on the Southside Railroad on the direct road to Farmville, and Gordon, Mahone, and the cavalry going west along the right bank of the Appomattox toward High Bridge, about three and a half miles east of the town.[58]

The Federal cavalry, widely scattered in the fight at Sayler's Creek and the subsequent hunt for fugitives, got itself sorted out during the night. On the morning of April 7, as soon as it was light enough to see, the troopers stood to horse. Their first task that morning was to start the thousands of prisoners to the rear:

they marched past [Third] Division headquarters in immense ranks. . . . They had some spirit in them, notwithstanding all the hardships they had gone thro'. The Division Bands were playing as . . . they marched; when they played "Yankee Doodle," "Hail Columbia" & kindred tunes, they would groan, but as . . . they struck up "Dixie," this called out rousing cheers from them. . . . it was a noble sight [as] they moved off, with the manner & tread of trained soldiers, & it was impossible not to accord them respect as brave men. Often enough had we met them to prove this.[59]

As soon as the prisoners left, under escort of the 1st Connecticut of Pennington's brigade, the First and Third Divisions began their march west to Prince Edward Court House to block any attempt by Lee to veer off in the same direction and attempt to break through toward Danville. The Second Division was sent to

---

58. Actually three bridges were involved: a wagon and a railroad bridge in the town, and High Bridge, a double-deck structure, with the wagon bridge below and the railroad tracks above, east of the town.
59. Starr, "Last Days of Rebellion," 8.

follow directly behind Lee toward Farmville. As Crook's horsemen took the road, they found the Federal infantry

already on the move, singing, laughing, joking and apparently happy as they marched along, though a little inclined to growl at being obliged to let the cavalry have the road, while they took the rougher, harder-to-march-over ground at the side. Along the side were evidences of the rapid retreat of the enemy—all sorts of munitions of war laying around in loose profusion,—a dead rebel soldier lying on the road where he halted his last time, with every appearance of having died from hunger and exhaustion,—dead horses, the infallible army guideboards, lying where they dropped, and others abandoned because unable longer to carry their riders,—all informed the men that the men ahead of them were in a great hurry, and had an exhilarating effect upon their spirits.[60]

Now occurred another of the series of disasters that made Lee's retreat a long nightmare. Through a misunderstanding or a failure to carry out orders, the wagon deck of the High Bridge—the bridge three and a half miles east of Farmville—was not set on fire behind Mahone's division, the last Confederate troops to cross, until too late. General Francis Barlow's division of the II Corps arrived in time to put out the flames and save the bridge.[61] The time to issue rations and allow his men a chance to rest that General Lee had hoped to gain by his night march was snatched from him, for as soon as the High Bridge was saved the II Corps began to cross, and in a short time the entire corps was on Lee's side of the river and on his flank.

In the meantime, however, the Confederate cavalry had scored the last of their victories. Crook's division reached Farmville after

60. Tobie, *First Maine Cavalry*, 418. The infantry Tobie mentions belonged to the VI Corps.

61. Freeman, *Lee's Lieutenants*, III, 714–16; *Official Records*, Vol. XVI, Pt. 1, p. 683. On April 6 General Ord had sent an expedition from Burkeville to destroy the bridge. The troops sent were two small regiments of infantry, the 54th Pennsylvania and the 123rd Ohio, and his own cavalry escort, an eighty-man detachment of the 4th Massachusetts. In command was Ord's chief of staff, General Theodore Read. Within about a mile of its objective the expedition ran into Confederate cavalry leading Lee's advance to Farmville and, after a desperate resistance by the cavalry detachment, was overrun. Read, Colonel Francis Washburn, and two other officers of the 4th Massachusetts were killed, three officers of that regiment were wounded, and most of the rest of the cavalry and infantry were taken prisoner. *Official Records*, Vol. XLVI, Pt. 1, pp. 1161–62, 1168–69, 1302–1303.

the two bridges there had been destroyed, and also after General Lee, having learned that the II Corps had crossed the river and was marching to cut the road to Lynchburg well to his rear, broke off the issuance of rations and hurried his men north to prevent the II Corps from getting across the Farmville-Lynchburg road. Crook had his men ford the river, with J. Irvin Gregg's brigade leading. Made careless by the events of the past few days, Gregg rode into a neat trap the Confederates prepared for him; they used what remained of their trains as bait, and when Gregg charged to capture the wagons, he was met by a countercharge of Munford's cavalry in front and a simultaneous charge by Rosser on his flank. He was routed with "severe" loss; he himself and two officers of his staff were among the many taken prisoner. Those of his men who escaped rallied behind Davies' brigade.[62] At dark the division was recalled across the river and ordered to bivouac at Prospect Station, eight miles west of Farmville. They had left Sayler's Creek at daybreak on April 7 and reached Prospect Station at two A.M. on the eighth, nearly twenty-one hours later; during that entire time, they were either in action or on the march.

Gregg's unfortunate encounter with Munford and Rosser was the only fighting of any consequence on April 7. Threatened by Crook's cavalry and the VI Corps in rear and the II Corps on his right flank, Lee had to put into motion once again what was left of his army. The issuance of rations was stopped well before it could be completed, the railroad train containing the unissued rations was started up the track to be out of harm's way, and the troops began a weary march toward Appomattox Court House and Lynchburg.[63]

At five in the afternoon of this day, Grant, having reached Farmville, sent off the first of his messages to General Lee, inviting "the surrender of that portion of the Confederate States army

62. *Official Records*, Vol. XLVI, Pt. 1, pp. 1155, 1303. Colonel Samuel B. M. Young, who succeeded to the command of the brigade, stated that it was attacked by "Rosser's division of cavalry and Gordon's infantry." Given the circumstances, Fitzhugh Lee's report, on which the statement in the text is based, is more likely to be correct. Rosser's attack was, nevertheless, supported by infantry—a brigade, reduced to two hundred muskets, of what had been Jubal Early's division. Freeman, *Lee's Lieutenants*, III, 718.

63. Freeman, *R. E. Lee*, IV, 99–100.

known as the Army of Northern Virginia." The dispatch, carried across the lines under flag of truce, was delivered to Lee late in the evening. He read it "without a word or sign and then silently passed it to Longstreet, who was sitting near him. Longstreet read it also, and handed it back. 'Not yet,' he said."[64]

Crook's report of Gregg's encounter with the Confederate cavalry made it obvious to Sheridan that "Lee had abandoned all effort to escape to the southwest by way of Danville. Lynchburg was undoubtedly his objective point now"; the correct countermove, he decided, would be to intercept him with his cavalry and "hold him till the infantry could overtake him."[65] To prepare for this operation, he reunited his cavalry. Merritt, who had bivouacked for the night at Buffalo Creek, was ordered to join Crook at Prospect Station. At Farmville, the previous day, Crook's men had found and appropriated "tobacco in great plenty and of the best quality—the best to which the boys ever helped themselves in Virginia soil"; on the morning of the eighth, at Prospect Station, when the 2nd Ohio "came along the 13# Ohio Volunteer Cavalry, the men of that Regiment stood alongside the road with their arms full of tobacco, calling out as the column passed bye, 'are you Buckeyes? where are the Buckeyes?' and when we came to them crowded up, offering us, yes, pressing us, to take tobacco; if one kind did not suit, take some other."[66]

What caused Sheridan to decide on Appomattox Station as the point where he wanted to position his cavalry to block Lee's march to Lynchburg was the report, brought to him by Sergeant James White of Major Young's scouts, that there were four trains of cars loaded with rations waiting for Lee's army at that point. These were the rations sent from Lynchburg to meet Lee, in response to the orders of his commissary general which Sheridan had inter-

64. *Official Records*, Vol. XLVI, Pt. 3, p. 619; Freeman, *R. E. Lee*, IV, 104.

65. Sheridan, *Personal Memoirs*, II, 188.

66. Tobie, *First Maine Cavalry*, 421; Starr, "Last Days of Rebellion," 11. Tobacco was not all that Crook's men "appropriated" at Farmville; "many of the boys confiscated articles of underclothing, and enjoyed a change then and there. . . . The boys helped themselves to anything they wanted . . . till almost every one had as much as he could carry." Tobie, *First Maine Cavalry*, 421.

cepted at Jetersville and then forwarded to their destination. White, dressed in the Confederate uniform that Young's men habitually wore, had decided, apparently on his own, to patrol the railroad line on the lookout for the trains that he expected would be sent forward in response to these orders. The trains were sent, and White located them "several miles west of Appomattox Depot, feeling their way along, in ignorance of Lee's exact position." The enterprising sergeant did more than merely observe; with the Confederate uniform and the original of the commissary general's orders as his credentials and by taking "pains to dwell upon the pitiable condition of Lee's army, he had little difficulty in persuading the men in charge of the trains to bring them east to Appomattox Station."[67] He then hurried off to Sheridan with his information.

Sergeant White's feat, a remarkable combination of intelligence and daring, was only one of the many exploits of Young and his scouts that caused Sheridan to hold them in high regard. When he reported on the march of his corps from Winchester to White House, he wrote, "To Maj. H. H. Young . . . chief of scouts, and the thirty or forty men of his command, who took their lives in their hands, cheerfully going wherever ordered, to obtain that great essential of success, information, I tender my gratitude. Ten of these men were lost."[68] Then, in a special report to the secretary of war after Appomattox, recommending the promotion of a number of his subordinates in recognition of their contributions to the success of the campaign, he wrote:

I desire to make special mention of the valuable services of Maj. H. H. Young . . . chief of my scouts. . . . His personal gallantry and numerous conflicts with the enemy won the admiration of the whole command. In the late campaign from Petersburg to Appomattox Court-House he kept me constantly informed of the movements of the enemy and brought in prisoners from brigadier-generals down. The information gained through him was invaluable. I earnestly request that he be made a lieutenant-colonel by brevet.[69]

67. Sheridan, *Personal Memoirs*, II, 189.
68. *Official Records*, Vol. XLVI, Pt. 1, p. 481.
69. *Ibid.*, 1113. The brigadier general Sheridan referred to was Rufus Barringer, commander of a brigade of North Carolina cavalry, whom Young captured on April 3.

Colonel Newhall described Young as "an excellent officer, fond of adventure, brave, and a good disciplinarian"; later, after commenting on the worthlessness of the general run of scouts, he wrote, "Young's men were differently managed, and were of great service. They were much more afraid of the general [Sheridan] and of the major [Young] than they were of the enemy, for the general has a way of cross-examining that is fatal to a lie, and as Young was constantly off in the enemy's country himself, his men never knew but that he had been following their trail, so there was no use trying to shut up his eye, as a scout would say."[70] Volunteering for duty as scouts had the same appeal for men in the Union cavalry as joining a Partisan Ranger unit had for Confederate cavalrymen, and in some cases, at least, the results were much the same. Major Robert B. Douglass, who had been sent on March 2 to destroy the Confederate stores at Swoope's Station near Staunton, reported that shortly before his arrival at the station, "a party of fifteen men, clad in rebel uniform, whom . . . [he had] every reason to believe belong to our scouts, had preceded him, and had been bribed by a farmer in the vicinity to spare his barn, containing a large amount of stores."[71] It was doubtless such incidents that caused Sheridan to order that "No division, brigade, or regimental commander will be allowed to have men of their commands clad in gray or rebel uniform and acting as scouts."[72] It must also be said that the admiration of Young and his scouts by the Cavalry Corps was not so universal as Sheridan professed to believe. Frederick Whittaker, for one, wrote after the war, "Nine out of ten of the headquarters scouts in our service . . . [were] simply reckless scoundrels, who brought in but little valuable information, and stole horses from the farmers to sell for a consideration. There were exceptions, but this was the rule. A more useless body of men, take them all in all, was seldom met with." And, he added, "Our own headquarters scouts, when Sheridan commanded the cavalry corps, were very much disliked by the men on account

70. Newhall, *With General Sheridan*, 52–54. Newhall added, "The men were well paid for this hazardous work, and often received a bonus for special acts of daring and good service."
71. *Official Records*, Vol. XLVI, Pt. 2, p. 848.
72. *Ibid.*, 847–48.

of their assuming the rebel uniform. I have known them even to be fired at deliberately by our own men, under pretence of mistaking them for enemies."[73]

While Sergeant White was engaged in hoaxing the Confederate trainmen, the Cavalry Corps, marching at a fast walk and with the advantage—unusual in that campaign—of good roads and a beautiful spring day, "exceedingly pleasant, the sky cloudless, [the] air still and serene," covered the twenty miles from Prospect Station to Appomattox Station in excellent time; Pennington's brigade of the Third Division, in the lead that day, reached the Southside Railroad well before sundown. The roads the cavalry used ran south of the tracks; Lee's army marched north of the rail line on roads that led to Appomattox Court House, two and a half miles northeast of the station.[74] Custer, with his staff and escort, had ridden ahead of his division and at Appomattox Station found the trains that Sergeant White said would be there, the locomotives with steam up. Without waiting for his command to arrive, Custer made a dash for the trains, captured all four, and started three of them down the track toward Farmville to remove them from the danger of being recaptured by the enemy. The fourth train was burned, but the records do not indicate if it was set on fire accidentally, or by Custer's men, or by the Confederate train guards. The locomotive engineers driving the trains toward Farmville were Custer's own men; given the great variety of civilian skills to be found in the cavalry, it is not at all surprising that there should have been locomotive engineers among them.[75]

Custer had little time for gloating over the capture of the four trains before he was attacked by Confederate infantry and artillery in considerable strength. The artillery attacking him was part of the large number of surplus guns that Lee had sent on ahead of

73. [Whittaker], *Volunteer Cavalry*, 84, 86; see also Nevins, *A Diary of Battle*, 517.

74. The II Corps followed directly on the tracks of Lee's army, but was about four miles behind it.

75. Sheridan recalled that these men "were delighted evidently to get back to their old calling. They amused themselves by running the trains to and fro, creating much confusion, and keeping up such an unearthly screeching with their whistles that I was on the point of ordering the cars burned. They finally wearied of their fun, however, and ran the trains off to the east." Sheridan, *Personal Memoirs*, II, 190.

the army from Amelia Court House. The identity and strength of the attacking infantry are a mystery; whoever they were, and however many of them there might have been, they gave Custer as much as he could handle. Once again he had to call for help and two brigades of the First Division were ordered to reinforce him. Most of Custer's division fought dismounted in the woods ("very much of the wilderness order") and clearings. The 15th New York, on Custer's right, was driven back nearly to the railroad in his rear, but he succeeded in restoring the situation by sending a force to attack the enemy's right flank and rear, while he personally led what mounted men he could collect in "nearly a dozen" charges against them, in which he "had a horse or two killed under him." For the last two hours of the action the men fought in total darkness, aiming at the flashes of the enemy's guns.[76] When at about nine o'clock the firing at last ceased, Custer had possession of the field. In addition to the four trains, he had captured all of W. H. F. Lee's wagons, twenty-four guns, and a sizable number of prisoners. For good measure, a small detachment he sent forward to Appomattox Court House "charged fairly into the rebel camp . . . riding over & between the tired & sleeping rebels & out again before they were sufficiently awake to stop them."[77]

In the course of this day, Generals Lee and Grant had exchanged additional messages. Grant's dispatch, which Lee received at about dark, offered honorable terms, what was called a "cartel": the release of the entire force under Lee on the same parole that had been used by both sides throughout the war.[78]

76. Starr, "Last Days of Rebellion," 16. Custer claimed in his report that he was attacked by two divisions of infantry, which he did not identify. This would have been impossible; the nearest bodies of Confederate infantry of that size were four or five miles away, on the far side of Appomattox Court House. On the other hand, D. S. Freeman's statement that Custer was opposed by two companies of artillerymen serving as infantry is also impossible to accept. Even with the aid of darkness and the wooded terrain, a mere two companies of untrained men could not have held off the attack of Custer's division, to say nothing of forcing him to call for help. Sheridan's statement that Custer was opposed by the "advance-guard of Lee's army . . . bent on securing the trains" seems to fit the facts most accurately. *Ibid.*, 12–16; *Official Records*, Vol. XLVI, Pt. 1, pp. 1132, 1136–37, 1120, 1126; Freeman, *Lee's Lieutenants*, III, 723; Sheridan, *Personal Memoirs*, II, 190.
77. Starr, "Last Days of Rebellion," 18.
78. *Official Records*, Vol. XLVI, Pt. 3, p. 641.

When Lee received this message, his cavalry was in bivouac in and around Appomattox Court House, Gordon's corps a mile to the east of the village, and Longstreet just to the east of Gordon. Lee had between twenty-one hundred and twenty-four hundred cavalry, about eight thousand infantry (he thought he had about fifteen thousand), and just under twenty-one hundred artillerymen still in the ranks, with sixty-one guns and thirteen caissons.[79] The rations he needed for his men and animals had been captured by Custer. And as the sounds of Custer's fight northeast of the station died away in the night, General Lee could see from his bivouac near the courthouse, reflected against the dark sky, the glow of Federal campfires to the east, to the south, and to the west; only to the north was there a narrow belt of darkness. The Army of Northern Virginia was practically surrounded.

It was with full knowledge of these circumstances that late in the evening Generals Lee, Gordon, Longstreet, and Fitzhugh Lee held their last council of war. General Lee summarized the situation in which the army found itself, read the messages he had exchanged with Grant, and asked for the others' advice. Agreement on the course to be taken was reached quickly. There was to be no surrender without one last desperate effort to break free. On the assumption that the campfires to the west were those of Sheridan's cavalry alone, it was decided that the army should try to cut its way through in that direction. Fitzhugh Lee's cavalry, followed by Gordon's infantry, were to make the attack; Longstreet was to follow, ready at the same time to repel any attack on the army's rear by the II Corps.[80] The Army of Northern Virginia had satisfied and more than satisfied the utmost demands of honor and pride since leaving the Richmond-Petersburg defenses, but a few more dozen men had to die, and a few hundred more had to be wounded or maimed, before the inevitable could be accepted.

Sheridan made his headquarters on the night of the eighth in a little frame house just south of Appomattox Station. At some time during the day he had received word from Grant about his exchange of messages with Lee; "I think," Grant wrote, "Lee will surrender to-day. . . . We will push him until terms are agreed

79. Freeman, R. E. Lee, IV, 118–19.
80. Ibid., 114–15.

upon."[81] Sheridan had no doubts about the form the "push" should take. In a dispatch sent off at 9:20 P.M., after Custer's fight had ended, he wrote Grant, "If General Gibbon and the Fifth Corps can get up to-night we will perhaps finish the job in the morning. I do not think Lee means to surrender until compelled to do so."[82] He had already sent a staff officer to General Gibbon, then five miles away, to urge him to hurry forward with the XXIV Corps. "If it is possible to push on your troops," he told Gibbon, "we may have handsome results in the morning."[83] Gibbon's response was less than Sheridan had hoped for; the XXIV Corps had been marching since five A.M., and the most Gibbon could promise was to reach Sheridan early next morning.[84] General Ord, to whom Sheridan had sent "staff officer after staff officer" also, to urge a maximum effort, kept the V and XXV Corps moving through the night; he himself reached Sheridan's headquarters ahead of his troops, just before sunup, and agreed readily to Sheridan's suggestion that he march them to the rear of the cavalry, west of the village.[85]

Orders to the cavalry directed that the men be in the ranks and on the alert at four A.M. Sheridan posted Mackenzie on the left, Crook in the center, and Devin on the right, all facing east; Custer was held in reserve. If the Confederates attacked, as Sheridan expected, Mackenzie, Crook, and Devin were to fight a delaying action, retreating step by step, as slowly as possible, to allow time for Ord's, Griffin's, and Gibbon's infantry to come into line behind them, and were to veer off to their own right so as to give their infantry a clear field of fire at the oncoming enemy.[86]

Neither Sheridan, nor Merritt, Custer, Crook, Devin, Mackenzie or their staffs, had any sleep on the night of the eighth. They were borne along on the exciting prospect that the next day—Palm Sunday—would at last bring them to the goal of their efforts

81. *Official Records*, Vol. XLVI, Pt. 3, p. 652.
82. *Ibid.*, 653.
83. *Ibid.*, 654.
84. *Ibid.*, 654.
85. Sheridan, *Personal Memoirs*, II, 191. Since Ord was his senior in rank, Sheridan could not order him to do anything, but Ord had the good sense to act on Sheridan's "suggestion."
86. *Ibid.*, 192.

and end their long travail. The men in the ranks, who had learned long ago never to let pass an opportunity for sleep, however short, had slept until the three A.M. reveille. From March 29, when they left their camps before Petersburg, through April 8, a period of ten days, they had fought three major battles and innumerable lesser scraps and skirmishes; action was so nearly continuous that, as the historian of the 19th New York remarked, "it would sometimes be hard to indicate when one battle ended and another began."[87] And when they were not in a fight, they were on the march, mostly on miserable roads and sometimes with insufficient rations. Hence when they had a chance to rest, they took it.

The Third Division being in reserve, its men had time to cook and eat a leisurely breakfast, to curry, feed, and water their horses, and to allow them to graze while they themselves washed and talked over the previous evening's events. But the idyll did not last long. Up ahead of them Crook and Devin were already in action;

it was plain as could be to us that the fighting was drawing nearer . . . the bullets began every once in a while to crash among the tree-tops overhead. This made us very anxious, & much speculation was indulged [in] as to how many & what Infantry were already up, for over-estimating as we did Lee's strength . . . & feeling certain that we had all of it to cope with, we felt sure we would be thrashed. . . . Our horses were already saddled, & we were waiting for the order to mount, which we felt must soon come; come it did. . . . Moving down toward the R. R. . . . we saw a sight that revived our dropping spirits wonderfully. The main road was full of colored troops of the 25# Corps, who, though it was plain to see were almost ready to drop from fatigue . . . were now hurrying by . . . as we saw the poor tired fellows, many of them reeling with fatigue . . . & almost all limping . . . we gave them a hearty cheer, which . . . seemed to infuse new life for a moment in the poor, footsore, weary fellows.[88]

As Custer's cavalrymen reached the ridge north of the railroad and overlooking Appomattox Court House, they saw before them infantry of their own army in a double line of battle, "the men lying flat on their faces, & glad enough no doubt to rest after their terrible march; they were the 24# Corps . . . and so worn out were

87. Bowen, *Regimental History of the First New York*, 282. Bowen adds (p. 291) that "from constant marching, fighting and picket duty, the men had scarcely enjoyed an hour of undisturbed rest for a week."
88. Starr, "Last Days of Rebellion," 18–19.

most of the men that but very few lifted their heads to observe the passing Cavalry." A few moments more passed, and then,

All of a sudden the column came to a . . . halt. Why, no one knew, but soon rumors flew like wildfire that Lee had sent in a flag of truce. Not many minutes elapsed before General Custer, in an almost frenzied excitement, hat in hand, rode along the column, informing us that General Lee had sent in a flag of truce to arrange terms of surrender. . . . never in all my experience did I see men so utterly beside themselves. Every one seemed to catch the excitement of our beloved commander . . . & so wild a body was never before seen or heard. We yelled & cheered, threw our caps in the air, shook hands, danced, & cut such capers as at any other time we would have been ashamed of. . . . Not until we were almost exhausted, which was in about 10 minutes, did we begin to talk about it in a rational manner.[89]

The terms of surrender were yet to be settled and written out, but for all except diehard General Martin W. Gary, the war in Virginia was ended, three days short of the fourth anniversary of its start in Charleston Harbor.[90] Fitzhugh Lee's and Gordon's attack had gone in at five A.M. as planned, a half mile west of the settlement. Crook's and Devin's cavalry facing them were driven back and two of Crook's guns were captured, but from that point on the fight developed exactly as Sheridan, and not General Lee, had planned. The retreat of the Union cavalry to their own right unmasked the masses of Union infantry in line of battle behind them, and Gordon and Fitzhugh Lee at once recognized that the game was up. Then the Federals prepared to go over to the attack themselves, Crook and the infantry on the left, Devin and Custer, mounted, on the right. Sheridan was about to order the two mounted divisions to charge the enemy, when Custer sent him word that he had received a request under flag of truce—actually

89. *Ibid.*, 19.
90. General Gary and his brigade (7th Georgia, 24th Virginia, 7th South Carolina, and the Hampton [South Carolina] Legion) arrived on the scene not knowing that hostilities had been suspended and opened fire on the Federal cavalry. Sheridan asked General Gordon to send a staff officer to Gary with orders to stop the firing. Gordon had no one to send, so Sheridan lent him Lieutenant Vanderbilt Allen of his own staff. Told by Allen to stop firing as "there had been a surrender," Gary replied that he would not accept orders from an officer of the Union army, that he knew of no surrender, and that "We are South Carolinians and don't surrender." The tragicomic episode ended with the arrival of Colonel W. W. Blackford, C.S.A., whose authority Gary was willing to recognize, and he ordered the firing stopped.

a none-too-clean towel—for a suspension of hostilities pending a reply from Grant to Lee's dispatch asking for an interview to arrange for a surrender of his army.[91] General Lee had sent his message to Grant as soon as he learned that Fitzhugh Lee's and Gordon's attack had come up against Federal infantry. The truce having been agreed to, Merritt, and then Sheridan, rode to the village, each to a great ovation as he rode past the lines of the Third Division.

Lee and Grant met at the Wilmer McLean house at 1:30 in the afternoon, and the final instruments of surrender were signed and exchanged two hours later, but for the men the war was over well before its official end. For their officers too the war was at an end, and visiting began back and forth across the lines to hunt up West Point classmates and Old Army friends.

No doubt dissenters could have been found in General Meade's headquarters, but there was at the time, and there can be now, little question that the four divisions of cavalry were entitled to the lion's share of the credit for forcing the surrender of the Army of Northern Virginia at Appomattox Court House.[92] The role played by the infantry and of course the artillery cannot be minimized; it was the V Corps infantry to whom the overwhelming victory at Five Forks was mainly due, and the VI Corps infantry was a major factor in producing the victory at Sayler's Creek. The timely arrival at Appomattox Court House after grueling marches of two divisions of the XXIV Corps and of the division of Negro troops of the XXV Corps drove the last nail into the coffin of the proud Confederate army and caused its leaders to face the inevitable. But it was the unrelenting pressure, the ceaseless attacks of the Federal cavalry on the left flank of the Army of Northern Virginia, and, equally important, its interception of the food that army needed

91. *Official Records*, Vol. XLVI, Pt. 3, p. 664.
92. A passage in a letter of Colonel Theodore Lyman of Meade's staff to his wife, written on April 5, explains much about the relations of Meade and Sheridan, their respective staffs and subordinates. "That's the way with those cavalry bucks," Lyman wrote, "they bother and howl about infantry not being up to support them, and they are precisely the people who are always blocking up the way. . . . They are arrant boasters and to hear Sheridan's Staff talk, you would suppose his ten thousand mounted carbineers had crushed the entire Rebellion . . . they are useful and energetic fellows, but commit the error of thinking they *can* do everything and no one else *does* anything." Agassiz, *Meade's Headquarters*, 346.

for survival, first by blocking the railroad at Jetersville, and then by capturing the trains at Appomattox Station, that made surrender unavoidable. And the motive power of the cavalry's great success was without question Sheridan—his driving energy, strategic insight, and tactical skill. Colonel G. F. R. Henderson, a great student of the Civil War and of the art of war in general, wrote that "there is no finer instance of a pursuit than that of Lee's army by Sheridan in 1865."[93] This statement by a high authority can stand as the final verdict on Sheridan's achievement.

But there was yet another major contributor to the success of the Federal cavalry in these closing days of the war. Next to Sheridan in credit for the accomplishments of the cavalry in the Appomattox Campaign stood George Custer. Not yet twenty-six years old, not quite four years out of West Point, a major general by brevet since the winter of 1864, victor at Waynesboro in March, 1865, everything he did in the Appomattox Campaign was a resounding success—his intervention in the battle of Dinwiddie Court House, the fight his division put up at Five Forks and then at Sayler's Creek, and at the last, his capture of the trains at Appomattox Station. And all these achievements of his division came about under, and largely because of, his leadership—personal in the most literal sense. He was in tight quarters at Sayler's Creek and again at Appomattox Station and needed help to extricate himself, but he led and fought with skill, gallantry, and the headlong vigor Sheridan expected of his subordinates. And he inspired the admiration and love of his troopers, if not, perhaps, of his senior officers. It was fitting that the flag of truce asking for a suspension of hostilities should have come into his lines, and equally so that after the surrender Sheridan should have made him a present of it with the message, "I know of no one whose efforts have contributed more to this happy result."[94] Later, after Sheridan bought from Wilmer McLean for twenty dollars in gold the little table on which Grant had written out the terms of sur-

93. Henderson, *The Science of War*, 56. Colonel Henderson wrote in another context, "with one single exception . . . [American] generals seem to have been unequal to the task of handling the three arms together on the field of battle. The single exception was Sheridan, and his operations, both in the Shenandoah Valley and during the 'last agony' of the Confederacy, are well worth the very closest study." *Ibid.*, 279.

94. Whittaker, *George A. Custer*, 308. But, said his biographer, Custer's

render, he gave it to Custer as a gift for his wife, and in a graceful note that accompanied the present, wrote, "there is scarcely an individual in our service who has contributed more to bring . . . [the surrender] about than your very gallant husband."[95]

But what of the cost of the final victory? From March 29 to April 9, the Army of the Potomac and the Army of Virginia sustained total casualties of 10,780 officers and men; included in this figure are the losses of the four divisions of cavalry, which came to 1,630: 197 killed, 1,037 wounded, and 396 missing, or 15.1 percent of the total.[96] The significance of this figure is pointed up by the fact that (accepting Sheridan's figures of the strength of his own and Mackenzie's commands at the start of the campaign) the mounted troops, a mere 8.3 percent of the forces employed in the campaign, sustained 15.1 percent of the casualties, nearly twice as many, proportionately, as did the infantry and artillery. This disproportion in the casualty figures may be taken as the measure of the cavalry's contribution to the final victory.

But now the victory so dearly bought was a reality. The physical and moral strain were ended. Then let Trooper Roger Hannaford, 2nd Ohio, speak for the men in the ranks, the men in blue and the men in gray alike, cavalry, infantry, and artillery, as they pulled their blankets around them on the night of April 9:

never shall I forget the feeling that passed over my soul just before retiring, the knowledge that *now we* could go to bed & *feel sure* of enjoying a full night's rest . . . be *certain* that we would not be aroused by war's wild alarm; the feeling of perfect quiet & safety, the feeling of being able now to enjoy perfect peace, was delightful, & occupied my mind until I went to sleep. The thought that I was certain, yes, certain of having a quiet night, the idea of security, was ineffable.[97]

---

success "attracted much envy. . . . Hardly a cavalry officer outside of his own commands but was intensely jealous of him and detraction was ready to belittle all his exploits." *Ibid.*, 282.

95. O'Connor, *Sheridan the Inevitable*, 272. But see Govan and Livingood, *The Haskell Memoirs*, 94–95.

96. *Official Records*, Vol. XLVI, Pt. 1, pp. 591–92, 597. The casualties of the First, Second, and Third Divisions totaled 1,490 (190 killed, 961 wounded, 339 missing); the Second Division's share was 827, more than half of the total. *Ibid.*, 1111.

97. Starr, "Last Days of Rebellion," 27.

XVII

Taps

THE CAVALRY CORPS OF THE ARMY OF THE POTOMAC WAS
not to play a part in or even to witness the ceremonies, sanctified
by eighteenth-century military usage, marking the formal end of
the Army of Northern Virginia: the defeated army assembled in
proper formation, unit by unit, the men fixing bayonets, stacking
arms, hanging cartridge boxes on the stacks of rifles, folding regimental flags, all to be surrendered to the victors. Wesley Merritt,
John Gibbon, and Charles Griffin had been appointed to meet with
James Longstreet, John Gordon, and William Pendleton on the
Confederate side to arrange for the mechanics and details of the
surrender, and Ranald Mackenzie's division was ordered to remain at Appomattox Court House to accept the surrender of the
1,559 Confederate cavalrymen who had either been unable or had
chosen not to escape on the morning of the ninth when it became
clear that the surrender of the army was inevitable.[1] Late on the
afternoon of the ninth, Devin's, Crook's, and Custer's divisions
received orders to leave for Burkeville the following morning.[2] An-

1. *Official Records*, Vol. XLVI, Pt. 3, pp. 685–86; Freeman, *Lee's Lieutenants*, III, 768. General Gibbon gives the number of cavalrymen paroled at
Appomattox as 1,714. John Gibbon, *Personal Recollections of the Civil War*
(New York, 1928), 394.
2. *Official Records*, Vol. XLVI, Pt. 3, p. 676. One of Crook's brigades

other order issued at the same time, and greatly resented by the men, directed that the cavalry pickets prevent enlisted men and line officers from "visiting the camps of the enemy or approaching them from any direction." Not knowing that the order was issued at General Lee's request "so that personal encounters would be avoided," the men thought it was just another example of unfeeling West Point officiousness, thought up by their own officers.[3] Sheridan, however, saw to it that some of the sting was taken out of the order by directing that the journey to Burkeville the next morning begin with the entire Cavalry Corps marching through Appomattox Court House "by fours and well closed up."[4] The cavalry was to have its chance after all to see and to be seen by its former antagonists. And as an indication, if one were needed, that the fighting days of the cavalry were over, the march was to get under way at the unheard-of late hour of eight A.M.

The cavalry bivouacked at Prospect Station on the evening of the tenth. The orders for the second day's march included another and less welcome reminder that the war in Virginia had indeed ended. Officers were told that they would be held responsible for the "good conduct" of their men and that forage was to be collected by "authorized forage parties" only.[5] Whether this order had any more effect in preventing "depredations" than the hundreds, perhaps thousands, of similar orders that had been issued previously, may be doubted. A few days later Mackenzie, who was ordered to accompany with his cavalry two divisions of the XXIV Corps to take possession of Lynchburg, announced in orders that "any soldier . . . who shall be caught pillaging private houses, or committing any outrageous acts upon the persons of citizens . . . upon proof of such offenses committed the soldier committing the same shall without trial be hanged."[6]

---

was, however, detached to escort Grant to Burkeville, starting at six A.M. on the tenth. *Ibid.*, 693–94.

3. *Ibid.*, 677; Starr, "Last Days of Rebellion," 24; Freeman, *R. E. Lee*, IV, 142.

4. *Official Records*, Vol. XLVI, Pt. 3, p. 676.

5. *Ibid.*, 694.

6. *Ibid.*, 694–95, 748. In fairness to Mackenzie's troopers it should be added that the order was issued at General Gibbon's request; doubtless similar orders were issued to the XXIV Corps infantry.

Burkeville had been chosen as the destination for the Cavalry Corps partly because it was on the direct road to Sherman's army in North Carolina, and partly because it was believed that the rations, forage, and supplies the corps needed could be delivered to it there over the Southside and the Richmond & Danville roads, which General Ingalls reported would be "in working order" by the eleventh.[7] The Appomattox Campaign had been brief but uncommonly hard on clothing, weapons, and "horse equipments"; supplies of all sorts were badly needed. Sheridan reported on the fourteenth that the men of Devin's and Custer's divisions were in particularly sore straits, having only the clothing they wore when they started out from Winchester six weeks before.[8] After reaching Burkeville, however, he decided for reasons that do not appear in the records to move the cavalry to Nottoway Court House on the Southside Railroad and ten miles nearer Petersburg, where he thought he would be in "an excellent place to refit the command."[9] On closer acquaintance, however, Nottoway Court House proved to be no more satisfactory than Burkeville; on the sixteenth Sheridan notified Grant that he could not get his command in good condition there either. "The railroad is in such bad condition," he reported, "that it cannot furnish the necessary allowance of forage and other supplies. Thus far I have not been able to get anything," and he proposed moving the cavalry all the way back to City Point.[10]

On the previous day, in a dispatch that was evidently delayed in reaching Sheridan, Grant told him that Sherman was then moving north and that "instead of surrendering, Johnston may follow his usual tactics of falling back whenever too hard pressed. If so, Sherman has not got cavalry enough to head off and capture his army. I want you to get your cavalry in readiness to push south and make up this deficiency if it becomes necessary."[11] The next day, suspecting that Sheridan had not received this dispatch, Grant wired him again to ask if he could not move "with from

7. *Ibid.*, 686.
8. *Ibid.*, 733.
9. *Ibid.*
10. *Ibid.*, 794.
11. *Ibid.*, 760.

6,000 to 8,000 to join Sherman," but then, after receiving Sheridan's message that he could not "refit" his command at Nottoway Court House, approved his proposed return to the "vicinity of Petersburg."[12] Accordingly, on the seventeenth, the cavalry resumed its march and on the evening of the next day was comfortably encamped about a mile from Petersburg. There Sheridan was met by another dispatch from Grant, directing him to return Crook's division to the Army of the Potomac as soon as he thought it could be done; no doubt to make the loss of a third of his command more palatable, Grant promised in the same dispatch to restore Sheridan to his Middle Military Division command or give him "some new one." Sheridan told him in reply that he could not send Crook back to Meade immediately, because the horses of the entire corps were weak, having been "on short allowance of grain for some time without any long forage" and needed a "short time to recuperate."[13]

But now an entirely new situation was created for Sheridan and for Grant as well by events in North Carolina. On the seventeenth Generals Sherman and Johnston met near Raleigh to negotiate the surrender of the latter's army. Unfortunately, unlike Grant's arrangements with Lee at Appomattox, the agreement Sherman entered into and signed on the eighteenth went well beyond the strictly military terms of an instrument of capitulation; it was virtually a treaty of peace with the South and provided for political arrangements that Sherman had not the authority to negotiate.[14] Sherman had explicitly made the validity of the agreement conditional upon approval of it by the authorities in Washington; despite this, when the document reached the capital, it produced a violent explosion. To the accompaniment of an excessive amount of publicity, unjustly hostile to Sherman, the agreement was disapproved, Sherman was disavowed, and Grant was directed to proceed at once to North Carolina to negotiate a new agreement, which was to provide for nothing more than the surrender of Johnston's army. Orders were sent at the same time by

12. *Ibid.,* 794, 495, 796, 811, 825.
13. *Ibid.,* 825.
14. Lloyd Lewis, *Sherman: Fighting Prophet* (New York, 1932), 534–42.

Halleck to Sheridan to move "immediately" to Greensboro, North
Carolina, to be available in case the repudiation of the Sherman-
Johnston agreement resulted in a resumption of hostilities.[15]
Meade was ordered to march the VI Corps to the same destination
to reinforce Sheridan.

In his dealings with Grant, Sheridan had demonstrated more
than once that he would not begin an operation before he thought
his command was ready, and he now showed that he was not prepared to do for the chief of staff what he had not done for the
general-in-chief. He countered Halleck's orders with the query if
moving three days hence, on April 25, would meet the latter's
wishes, but added as a sop that he could be ready to march on the
twenty-fourth "by forcing."[16] Whether he did so voluntarily or
under pressure does not appear in the records, but the cavalry did
in fact move out on the twenty-fourth. One of those who made the
march wrote, "A more delightful morning never gladdened the
earth. In early spring, the roads for the most part dry, and yet free
from dust, the weather mild without heat, the forests clothed in
beauty, and the earth covered with a luxuriant vegetation . . . the
men jubilant from recent victories and the prospect of soon ending the war and returning to their homes, the march was as delightful as could be wished." The first evening's bivouac was at
Dinwiddie Court House, which inspired the same chronicler to reflect, "It seemed strange to bivouac so quietly on ground which but
a few days ago resounded with the din of arms and when the utmost vigilance was demanded to guard against surprise. 'Is this a
dream or a reality?' was a question often asked."[17]

General Wright and the VI Corps had moved out from Burkeville on the twenty-third and reached Danville on the twenty-
eighth. There had been "many" complaints to General Meade's
headquarters of "depredations committed by stragglers from the
Sixth Corps"; when General Wright's attention was called to these
complaints, he explained that for the most part the depredations
had not been committed by his own men, but by "paroled prison-

---

15. Grant, *Personal Memoirs*, II, 516; *Official Records*, Vol. XLVI, Pt. 3,
p. 895.
16. Official Records, Vol. XLVI, Pt. 3, p. 895.
17. Merrill, *Campaigns of the First Maine*, 357.

ers from the rebel army," some of whom he had arrested for marauding, and by Sheridan's cavalrymen. He cited as an example of the latter two cavalrymen who, arrested for marauding, admitted "that they . . . [had] not seen their commands since the battle of Sailor's [sic] Creek" three weeks before.[18]

Sheridan and the cavalry had started for Greensboro a day later than the VI Corps and had a considerably greater distance to cover. They got as far as South Boston Station, nearly thirty miles short of Danville, when Grant's dispatch of the twenty-sixth to Halleck, forwarded via Meade and Wright, reached Sheridan, announcing the surrender of Johnston on the same terms that had been granted General Lee. In the same dispatch, Grant directed Halleck to "order Sheridan back to Petersburg at once."[19] Sheridan acknowledged receipt of these orders on the evening of the twenty-eighth, writing that he would "commence the retrograde movement" the following morning.[20] As still another and evidently necessary reminder to the cavalry that the Civil War was a thing of the past, the orders for the next day's march were accompanied by a circular announcing that the "seizure of animals or private property of any description . . . [was] positively forbidden" except pursuant to special authority from Sheridan's headquarters; all commanding officers were "charged to keep their commands from straggling and pillaging."[21]

The journey back to Petersburg was made in easy stages. Those who made the march remembered it as

glorious . . . a sort of pleasure trip. The weather was fine; all nature was bright and cheery in its fresh spring green, and fairly laughed; the march was through a country for the most part not devastated by war; foraging was easy and forage was plentiful, though the men were allowed to forage only what was necessary; there was no picket duty to do, no advance duty to perform . . . at night the men, with the exception of the few detailed for guard, turned in and went to sleep with no fear of war's alarms . . . and yet . . . it may be doubted if the lack of excitement on that march did not rob it of some of its enjoyment.[22]

18. *Official Records*, Vol. XLVI, Pt. 3, pp. 997, 998.
19. *Ibid.*, 954, 991, 999.
20. *Ibid.*, 999.
21. *Ibid.*, 1001.
22. Tobie, *First Maine Cavalry*, 443.

On May 3 the cavalry was back in its old camps near Petersburg and shortly thereafter came portents of its approaching end as an organized force. There were already as many, if not more, cavalrymen in dismounted camp as there were fully equipped mounted men with the colors; General Hancock reported that in the Middle Military Division, he had sixty-three hundred of them in a camp at Harper's Ferry, and another three thousand were performing a seemingly needless guard duty on the railroads near Burkeville.[23] In a dispatch to Secretary Stanton on May 2, Grant recommended that all cavalrymen whose terms of enlistment were to expire before September 1 be mustered out of the service at once and that all who remained be "consolidated." He suggested also that the quartermaster general sell all horses and mules on hand that were unfit for immediate issue to the troops.[24] Nevertheless, there was still some work for the cavalry to do. Colonel Charles Francis Adams, Jr.'s 5th Massachusetts, a Negro regiment commanded by white officers, had been the first unit of the Army of the Potomac to enter Richmond on April 3, greatly to the delight of its colonel, and was now patrolling the Southside Railroad near Petersburg.[25] Following the assassination of President Lincoln, the 16th New York and the 8th Illinois were sent out to scour the countryside for the assassin, John Wilkes Booth, and his accomplices; it was Company L of the New York regiment that tracked down Booth and David Herold in a tobacco barn near Port Conway, Virginia, and Sergeant Boston Corbett of that unit who shot and killed Booth.[26]

23. *Official Records*, Vol. XLVI, Pt. 3, pp. 869, 748.
24. *Ibid.*, 1066. The orders issued by the adjutant general on May 8 pursuant to this dispatch directed the muster-out of cavalrymen whose terms of enlistment expired before October (not September) 1, the consolidation of the remaining men into full-strength regiments (but with the proviso that only organizations from the same state were to be consolidated with each other), the selection by army and department commanders of the officers and noncommissioned officers for the consolidated units, and the muster-out of all those not so selected. *Ibid.*, 1112–13.
25. Adams wrote his father on April 10, "To have led my regiment into Richmond at the moment of its capture is the one event which I would most have desired as the culmination of my life in the army." Ford (ed.), *A Cycle of Adams Letters*, II, 261–62.
26. Hard, *History of the Eighth Cavalry*, 320; *Official Records*, Vol. XLVI, Pt. 3, pp. 818–19, 901. The 16th New York and the 8th Illinois also

The fall of Richmond and Petersburg had produced a major change for the better in the morale of the 3rd Pennsylvania.

The spirits of everyone rose, the stolid, solemn, resigned aspect of countenance so evident among the officers and men ever since Grant started out on May 4 . . . for the long bloody "campaign of attrition" vanished. Enthusiasm became intense. Nothing like it had been seen since the victory of Gettysburg. It had not been our habit on the march to carry unfurled the regimental . . . standards and company guidons, but now that the beginning of the end was in sight . . . the colors were kept flying until everything was over.[27]

Within a month of General Lee's surrender, however, disillusionment came to the men from Pennsylvania. Ordered to do provost duty in Richmond, they were assigned quarters in a group of buildings known as the "Winder Hospital" ("Every part of the place was filthy beyond words and alive with vermin") a mile outside the city. Moreover, they found "playing mounted policeman, especially in the excessive heat which characterized that spring and summer . . . monotonous after the excitement of active campaigning and marching. Occasionally, however, the men were treated to excursions into the country on other business, especially in the hunting down of prominent Secessionists."[28] The 11th Pennsylvania was given a more pleasant assignment; on May 4 it was ordered to cross the Blue Ridge to Staunton to accept the surrender of General Rosser and those of his officers and men who had escaped with him from Appomattox Court House before General Lee's capitulation.[29]

It was on May 4 also that Halleck informed Sheridan and Crook that there was "an armed body of rebels in Lynchburg which resisted a detachment sent there by General Meade. Also,

---

furnished the escort for President Lincoln's funeral procession to the Capitol and thence to the funeral train. *Official Records*, Vol. XLVI, Pt. 3, pp. 801–802, 829.

27. Regimental History Committee, *History of the 3d Pennsylvania*, 488..

28. *Ibid.*, 497.

29. *Official Records*, Vol. XLVI, Pt. 3, pp. 1088–89. Lieutenant Colonel Franklin A. Stratton, commanding the regiment, was warned to hold it "to the strictest rules of discipline and order, giving protection to persons and property." *Ibid.*, 1089.

that guerrillas . . . [were] collecting arms and horses under orders
of Governor ["Extra Billy"] Smith and the sheriff of Appomattox
County"; wherefore he ordered them to send immediately a brigade of cavalry "to capture these rebels and bring them to Richmond." As was now his habit, Sheridan asked for a delay, on the
ground that the cavalry was "much reduced in flesh and wants a
short rest."[30] However valid or invalid these pleas for delay may
have been in the past, it would seem that on this occasion his only
possible motive could have been a reluctance to accept orders
from Halleck; his men and horses had had nearly a month's recuperation since Appomattox. Eventually, but not until after Sheridan himself had left the Cavalry Corps and gone to Washington,
Colonel Samuel B. M. Young's Second Brigade of the Second Division was sent to Lynchburg, where on May 15 Colonel Young
found "all quiet."[31] In the surrounding countryside, however,
there was "trouble brewing," and the four regiments of the brigade
—the 4th, 8th, 16th, and 21st Pennsylvania—were kept busy in
what was essentially a peacekeeping operation. Sheriff William D.
Hix of Appomattox County, backed by an armed posse of "citizens
and paroled prisoners" was taking horses "from what he terms
common people" and turning them over "to those that hitherto
have been termed wealthy planters." Thereupon the "common people" organized an armed force for their own protection. To add to
Colonel Young's difficulties, there was widespread robbery in the
area, perpetrated "by paroled prisoners and men who . . . [had]
never been paroled . . . together with some bounty jumpers from
the U. S. Army."[32] These were the inescapable troubles of an in-
terregnum of lawlessness between the collapse of one government
and the reestablishment of the authority of another. Coping with
such problems was unglamorous police duty, but it is safe to assume that the men of the four Pennsylvania regiments preferred
it to the increasingly irksome round of "busy work" that was the
lot of the regiments remaining in camp. Typically, for the 1st
Maine,

30. *Ibid.*, 1087. "Extra Billy" Smith was the last Confederate governor
of Virginia.
31. *Ibid.*, 1137, 1157.
32. *Ibid.*, 1157–58.

there was little to do except the usual routine of camp and guard duty, with a goodly quantity of fatigue duty, and it was not long before the men got heartily sick of soldiering in time of peace. They missed the excitement and rapid changes of actual war—camp duty was always distasteful to them—they preferred to be on the move. Although few if any of them really loved to fight, they would accept that with all its risks, in preference to this inactivity, and, besides, they felt that the need for their services no longer existed. When are we going home? What good are we doing now? The war is over, why can't we go home? were thoughts that arose daily and hourly in the minds of the boys.[33]

The more restless spirits ("quite a number of men") of the 18th Pennsylvania, and of many other regiments as well, made their escape from the burdens of peacetime soldiering by simply deserting.[34]

There was one more duty for the cavalry as an organized whole to perform, but this was a duty that was undoubtedly relished by the great majority of cavalrymen still with the colors. On May 7 Crook, who seemed to be in command of the Cavalry Corps in the absence of Sheridan, was ordered to move the command to Alexandria, in preparation for the grand review of the Army of the Potomac to be staged in Washington on May 23.[35]

On the nineteenth, orders came to the cavalry to cross the Potomac and set up its camps at Bladensburg. Merritt, now in command of the corps, was directed at the same time to report to General Meade's headquarters to receive his instructions for the review. There he learned that the brigade of horse artillery, under Colonel James M. Robertson, was to march with the cavalry in the review, just as it had done in all the cavalry's campaigns. This was as it should have been; on a less pleasing note, Merritt also learned that his command was to be subject to Meade's orders for the re-

33. Tobie, *First Maine Cavalry*, 444–45. Much to the disgust of its men, the 13th Ohio was given a daily dose of drill. Aston, *History and Roster of the Fourth*, 33.

34. Publication Committee of the Regimental Association, *History of the Eighteenth Regiment of Cavalry, Pennsylvania Volunteers, 1862–1865* (New York, 1909), 179.

35. *Official Records*, Vol. XLVI, Pt. 3, p. 1108. The march to Alexandria was made in easy stages and took from May 10 to May 16. The "atmosphere" of the march is indicated by the fact that the wives of Custer and Pennington "rode the whole distance at the head of the column." Benedict, *Vermont in the Civil War*, II, 687.

view, which meant in effect that the cavalry was to march as part
of the Army of the Potomac and not as the independent organization it had been under Sheridan.[36] This may have been an appropriate act of justice to Meade, but it is hardly likely to have pleased
the cavalry chauvinists, particularly those in the upper ranks.
Nonetheless, two days later, on the twenty-first, the cavalry moved
to Bladensburg; like so many of their marches in the past, this too
was made in a rainstorm. The same day clothing was issued to all
who needed it. On the next day there was great currying and
grooming of horses, cleaning and polishing of tack, boots, and
weapons, slicking up of uniforms, and shining of buttons. Everyone, officers and men alike, spruced himself up as much as he
could for the grand occasion.

The review of the armies of the Republic was to be a two-day
affair; the Army of the Potomac was to have its day in the lime-
light on the twenty-third and Sherman's armies the next day. In
front of the White House, facing Lafayette Park, a large covered
pavilion was erected and "decorated with flags and flowers and
evergreens and surmounted by the names of the great battles of
the war."[37] The pavilion was to seat the new commander in chief,
Andrew Johnson, the general-in-chief, Ulysses S. Grant, members
of the Cabinet, the diplomatic corps, and guests especially favored. Facing the pavilion across the avenue was a similar structure for the governors of the loyal states, justices of the Supreme

36. *Official Records*, Vol. XLVI, p. 1177. There is a state of utter confusion in the records on the status of Merritt and Crook in relation to the
Cavalry Corps and each other. On the same day the orders here quoted were
sent to Merritt as "Commanding Cavalry" by Colonel Bowers of Grant's
staff, Lieutenant Colonel Babcock, also of Grant's staff, sent orders to Crook
as "Commanding Cavalry" to "report to Maj. Gen. George G. Meade . . .
with your command, for the review to take place on the 23d." It was Merritt
who determined the order in which the divisions and brigades of the cavalry
were to march; his directive (issued from "Headquarters, Cavalry Corps"
and signed "W. Merritt, Major-General Commanding") does not mention
Crook at all; it shows Davies as commanding the Second Division, but it
also shows him as commanding the First Brigade in that division. To add to
the confusion, on the day Merritt issued his directive on the order of march
in the parade, Colonel Bowers sent orders to "Maj. Gen. George Crook, Commanding Cavalry Corps" to send a brigade of the First (not his own Second) Division to St. Louis. *Ibid.*, 1177, 1190.

37. Margaret Leech, *Reveille in Washington, 1860–1865* (New York,
1941), 414.

Court, and members of Congress. Other stands, farther down Pennsylvania Avenue, were set aside for high-ranking officers of the army and navy, the press, official delegations from the northern states, disabled veterans, and a miscellany of invited guests. The black streamers that had marked the death and funeral services of Abraham Lincoln were taken down, and every building and lamppost along the line of march was gay with the national colors. To add to the festive air of the occasion, tens of thousands of visitors came streaming into the capital and packed every hotel and lodging house to capacity.

At sunrise on the twenty-third—a clear, mild, late-spring day —the crowds of spectators began to gather, lining both sides of Pennsylvania Avenue, a solid mass of humanity from the Capitol to the Treasury, around to the reviewing stands, and as far beyond them as the eye could see. The soldiers too had an early reveille: the troopers and gunners of the Cavalry Corps, and the infantrymen, pioneers, gunners, and pontoniers of the II, V, and IX Army Corps of the Army of the Potomac.

The cavalry and their fellows of the horse artillery, in recognition of their decisive role in the Valley and the Appomattox campaigns, and perhaps too to make up in some degree for being deprived of their independent status, had been assigned the place of honor in the parade; they were to be at the head of the marching column, immediately behind the army commander, General Meade. Wesley Merritt was to ride at the head of the Cavalry Corps in the review, and not the man to whom the place rightfully belonged and to whom the corps owed its glory insofar as it was indebted for it to any one man. Sheridan had led the Cavalry Corps from victory to victory for twelve action-packed months, but he was not to lead them, as he badly wanted to do, on this their day of glory. He had been ordered on May 3 to report to Grant in Washington and, as a clear indication that he had earned membership in the Grant-Sherman-Sheridan triumvirate at the head of the armies, was told of his appointment to the command of the huge area west of the Mississippi, with the mission of forcing the surrender of E. Kirby Smith, restoring western Louisiana and Texas to the Union, and preparing to deal with Maximilian in Mexico, should the United States decide on military intervention in that situation. Sheridan asked Grant's permission to remain in Washington long enough to lead his troopers in the "Grand Review" but was told that it was "absolutely necessary" that he leave at once for his new command.[38] The reader may decide whether Sheridan's arrival there was as urgent as it was represented to be (E. Kirby Smith surrendered while Sheridan was still on his way to New Orleans) or whether he had to be hustled out of Washington to forestall the painful decision of just where, in relation to Meade, he was to take his place in the review.[39]

Sheridan was not the only high-ranking officer previously identified with what had been the cavalry of the Army of the Potomac who was not present on the twenty-third of May. There were many others. George Stoneman, exiled to the West after his failure in command in 1863, was in North Carolina, after leading a highly successful raid from east Tennessee through southwest Virginia that was brought to a halt in North Carolina when Generals Lee and Johnston surrendered. James Harrison Wilson too was absent, his triumphant march east after the capture of Selma halted also by Johnston's surrender. Others too, who had led the cavalry or portions of it in its early days of incompetence and humiliation, were absent: John Buford, dead of disease; George Bayard, Elon Farnsworth, Benjamin Davis, killed in action; John McIntosh, crippled; Alfred Pleasonton, Alfred Torbert, William Averell, Alfred Duffié, exiled or in the outer darkness; David Gregg, resigned. Missing too were many thousands more, men of every rank, killed in action, dead of wounds or disease or in prison camps in the South, discharged for disability, mustered out after serving faithfully for their terms of enlistment, transferred out of the cavalry to become officers of Negro regiments—the 8th Illinois alone had furnished twenty-two such men—officers who had resigned, and thousands of dismounted men.[40] But enough were left to give the spectators an eye-filling show. The many thousands watching the trim cavalrymen riding past were not aware of it, but

38. Sheridan, *Personal Memoirs*, II, 209.
39. On May 22, Merritt and Custer were ordered by the adjutant general to report to Sheridan in New Orleans, no doubt at the latter's request. *Official Records*, Vol. XLVI, Pt. 3, p. 1195.
40. Hard, *History of the Eighth Cavalry*, 329.

of the ten mounted regiments that sustained the highest number of casualties in the war—all ten had served in the East—six were in the parade: the 1st Vermont, 2nd and 19th New York, 1st New Jersey, and the 5th and 6th Michigan, and it was only an accident of the service that two others, the 1st Maine and the 8th New York, were not also present. Also in the line of march was the first volunteer cavalry regiment raised in the far-away summer of 1861, the 1st New York (Lincoln).

Merritt had had the invidious task of deciding the order in which the divisions, brigades, and regiments of the corps were to march in the review. Whether he handled it to everyone's satisfaction may be doubted; at any rate, he, his staff and escort (the 5th United States) were to lead; next, in the place rightfully theirs, would march George Custer and the Third Division, followed by the Second Division, and then the First; bringing up the rear would be the horse artillery.[41]

At nine A.M. on May 23, with the streets and fields north of the Capitol filled with sixty-five thousand soldiers of all arms, the signal gun was fired and General Meade, a garland of flowers around his horse's neck, his battle flag, staff, and mounted escort behind him, rode out past the Capitol. Then came Merritt, and after the proper interval, George Custer, dressed for the occasion in the regulation uniform of a major general of cavalry, except for his trademarks, the large scarlet kerchief around his neck and the broad-brimmed, low-crowned hat aslant on his head. His devoted troopers behind him added a loud splash of nonregulation color to the cavalry uniform by sporting in imitation of their commander scarlet kerchiefs with flowing ends outside their jackets, the unofficial badge of their division. Henry E. Davies, Jr., and the Second Division came next, and then Thomas C. Devin at the head of the First Division, with Colonel Peter Stagg's Michigan Brigade at the head of the division, a distinction they had amply earned.[42] Each regiment of cavalry, many, like the 1st New York, mere skeletons of what they had once been, came riding out of the side streets behind the Capitol, its regimental standard and

41. *Official Records*, Vol. XLVI, Pt. 3, pp. 1190–91.
42. The Michigan Brigade was under orders to entrain for St. Louis as soon as the review was over. *Ibid.*, 1190.

guidons unfurled, to take its place in the marching column. These were not the frightened novice horsemen of 1861. As they marched on a carpet of flowers strewn in their path by the cheering, handkerchief-waving spectators, they kept their horses in perfect alignment. There was only one contretemps. As Custer approached the White House, his horse bolted and went thundering past the reviewing stand, the president, and all the dignitaries, Custer's sabre at the salute, before he succeeded in reining in the animal. Then he trotted back to his proper place at the head of his division, and this time at a sedate walk, marched past the reviewing stand a second time. Had the horse been frightened by a "thrown wreath," as some thought, or was the incident a manifestation of Custer's irrepressible showmanship?[43] No one will ever know, but it should be said for the instruction of believers in the "thrown wreath" theory that Custer's horsemanship was legendary.

It took over an hour for the cavalry, its regimental lines filling Pennsylvania Avenue from curb to curb, to march past the presidential reviewing stand, and it was well into the afternoon before the last battery of artillery, at the tail of the long column, rumbled past the end of the parade route. Back once more in Bladensburg, the troopers resumed the familiar routine of a cavalry camp, watering, feeding, and grooming their horses, attending to their own suppers, and then spending a leisurely evening talking over the sights, sounds, and experiences of a memorable day.

And now indeed the shadows were closing in on the Cavalry Corps. The men to be mustered out under the terms of the adjutant general's order of May 8, issued pursuant to Grant's recommendations of May 2, had already begun to leave. They were followed by the muster-out of returned prisoners of war, convalescents in military hospitals, and all the dismounted men. Then, one by one, in June, July, and August, complete regiments—or more accurately, the remnants of complete regiments—turned in their horses, equipment, and weapons, received their final pay, were mustered out, and ceased to be, except in the memories, refreshed and kept green by the regimental reunions

43. Leech, *Reveille in Washington*, 415.

that were a prominent part of American life in the postwar decades, of the men who had belonged to them. In some cases, too, the memories were preserved for posterity in the laboriously compiled pages of a regimental history, true labors of love, published for the benefit of surviving comrades and the families of those who were gone.

The army being a bureaucratic machine, the massive muster-out process was not always free from errors of judgment, mistakes, and delays. Even if it had been, it would not have satisfied men eager to be done with the army and get home. Some cavalry regiments were kept in the service, or threatened with being kept in the service, to perform in strange surroundings duties the authorities deemed necessary but the men most definitely did not. Thus, the Michigan Brigade and a short time later the 2nd Ohio were ordered to St. Louis to try to restore peace and order in Missouri, where the immediate postwar months were nearly as grim and deadly as the war years had been. Two brigades of cavalry were ordered to Louisville, possibly as an intermediate stop leading to eventual deployment on the Mexican border. The 8th Illinois, ordered initially to St. Louis, was intended ultimately to go on to Fort Riley, Kansas, destined in later years to be the premier cavalry post and school of the United States Army. Such orders invariably resulted in ill feeling between officers and enlisted men, protests, a wave of desertions, the threat of mutiny, and the enlistment of whatever influence, military or political, the regiment could muster, to obtain its discharge from the service.[44] By the late autumn of 1865, however, the volunteer cavalry of the Union army had ceased to be.

From the beginning of the war to its end, the national government had in its armies the huge total of 203 regiments and 67 un-

44. The orders to proceed to Fort Riley "gave great dissatisfaction" to the Illinois regiment; "the men claimed that they had reenlisted for three years or during the war; that now the war was over and having fulfilled their part of the contract they should be mustered out. A petition embodying these views was signed by all the officers . . . and sent to General Pleasonton." On the strength of Pleasonton's "hearty endorsement" of the petition, the orders to proceed to Fort Riley were canceled and the regiment was mustred out on July 17. Hard, *History of the Eighth Cavalry*, 325.

attached companies of mounted troops raised in the loyal states (including the officially loyal states of Missouri and Tennessee, and the District of Columbia) for the standard terms of enlistment of three years or longer. If cavalry raised in the far western states and territories, and in states officially part of the Confederacy are included, and if mounted troops raised for terms of less than three years are added, the total becomes 245 regiments, 1 unattached battalion, and 158 unattached companies.[45] What this meant in terms of manpower is impossible to determine accurately. In light of the fact that with recruits added from time to time, many of the three-year regiments had anywhere from 1,500 to more than 2,000 men on their rolls over the period of their existence, it is not unlikely that nearly 300,000 men served in the cavalry and the mounted infantry in the course of the war.[46] The numbers at any given moment were of course substantially less, and the number of fully equipped and mounted men available for duty at any one time was never more than half, and frequently less than half, of the number on the rolls. Nevertheless, there were those in the high command who questioned the need for mounted troops on so large a scale. General Halleck reported to

45. Frederick Phisterer, *Statistical Record of the Armies of the United States* (New York, 1883), 12–20, supplementary volume of *Campaigns of the Civil War.* It should be emphasized, however, that not all these units were in existence at the same time. The western states and territories (California, Oregon, Nebraska, Nevada, New Mexico, Colorado, and Dakota) raised 7 regiments and 14 unattached companies for the three-year service. In the states of the Confederacy (North Carolina, Florida, Alabama, Mississippi, Louisiana, Texas, and Arkansas) there were raised for the Union 12 three-year regiments and 7 unattached companies of mounted troops. In addition, the loyal states and territories and the seceded states contributed a total of 23 regiments, 1 unattached battalion, and 70 unattached companies of cavalry for terms of less than three years: thirty, sixty, ninety, or a hundred days, three, six, nine, and twenty months, and one year. *Ibid.*

46. For example, 2,297 in the 1st Vermont, 3,226 in the 1st Maine, 3,224 in the 1st Michigan, 1,998 in the 5th Michigan, 1,779 in the 7th Michigan, 1,963 in the 5th New York, 1,963 in the 9th New York, 1,733 in the 11th New York, and 1,618 in the 1st New Jersey. Benedict, *Vermont in the Civil War,* II, 694; Tobie, *First Maine Cavalry,* 659; John Robertson, *Michigan in the War* (Lansing, 1882), 566, 568, 572; Boudrye, *Historic Records of the Fifth,* 310–33; Cheney, *History of the Ninth Regiment,* 282; Thomas W. Smith, *The Story of a Cavalry Regiment: "Scott's 900," Eleventh New York Cavalry* (Chicago, 1897), 6; Pyne, *First New Jersey Cavalry,* 321–50.

Grant on February 13, 1865, on the basis of data collected by the Cavalry Bureau, that as of January 1 of that year, of the 160,237 cavalrymen then on the rolls, 105,434 were "present for duty," but only 77,847 of them had serviceable horses. To keep cavalrymen in such numbers in the field—the great majority of them in the West—the War Department had purchased, in 1864, 154,400 horses and replaced 93,000 destroyed, damaged, or lost carbines, 71,000 pistols, 90,000 sabers, and 150,000 sets of horse equipments. The total cost of the cavalry in the year 1864, in horses, pay, forage, rations, clothing, ordnance, equipments, and transportation, was estimated by the bureau at $125,000,000.[47]

What did the army and the nation receive in return for expenditures on this scale? For the cavalry in the eastern theatre, the subject of this and the preceding volume of this study, the answer is self-evident. Before mid-1863—more precisely, before June 9, 1863, the date of the battle of Brandy Station—the Union cavalry in the East was simply not worth its keep. There were occasional indications, under commanders like John Buford and George Bayard, of better days to come, but by and large the performance of the Federal cavalry east of the Appalachians was woefully poor. Operating under every conceivable handicap—lack of a clearly defined or understood mission, faulty organization, poor leadership, unreliable weapons, inexperience at every level— its efforts to find a place in the military constellation, to perform a useful function, were a humiliating failure.

But the two years of fumbling and incompetence at the start of the war were not wasted. Like the jewel in the head of the basilisk, the miseries of 1861, 1862, and the first months of 1863 had in them the seeds of future success. Many of the ingredients

47. *Official Records*, Series III, Vol. IV, 1167. Halleck pointed out that the cavalry had actually received 180,000 horses in 1864, as, in addition to the 154,400 newly purchased animals, "a considerable number of team and captured horses have been issued to the cavalry and also recuperated animals." Halleck's prognostication in the same dispatch of the likely outcome of Wilson's Selma Campaign is not without interest in the light of what actually happened. "It will not be possible," Halleck wrote, "for such a cavalry force to be subsisted in any operations against Selma or Montgomery. Like all extravagant operations, its very magnitude will defeat it. The horses will starve, the equipments be lost, and the men left on foot along the road." *Ibid.*, 1169.

of an eventual high level of competence were already there and
had existed from the beginning: dedication, loyalty, adaptability,
self-reliance, ingenuity, and an incredible toughness, both physical and moral. It did not take long for the weaker vessels and the
misfits of all ranks to be weeded out, and, as one by one the handicaps were eliminated or corrected, mostly by a process of trial and
error, the underlying strengths had a chance to emerge and de-
velop. The men and their officers became veterans. Then, organized at last as a corps, and under commanders like Sheridan,
Custer, Merritt, David Gregg, Wilson, McIntosh, Davies, Gibbs,
Lowell, Wells, Kidd, Stagg, Charles Smith, Pennington, Capehart,
and many more, and hundreds of regimental officers who had
learned the tricks of the trade, the eastern cavalry began to assert
a domination of the battlefield that was to culminate in its spectacular successes in the Appomattox Campaign. Beginning with
an uncertain grasp of a European cavalry tradition wholly inap-
propriate to American conditions, the cavalry evolved its own
highly effective tactics, becoming equally adept in attack or defense, in mounted action as at Tom's Brook, Cedar Creek, and
Sayler's Creek, or in dismounted fighting as at Dinwiddie Court
House and Five Forks; and at the last, under Sheridan, it achieved
what was nothing less than a strategic independence.

Despite the heavy losses the cavalry sustained in the final year
of the war, its troopers developed and maintained a splendid
morale, based on an ever-growing conviction of invincibility, of
being members of an elite corps. In the perspective of more than
120 years, the cavalry as an organization, its difficulties and accomplishments as an arm of the service, its success in adapting
its tactics to the greatly increased effectiveness and importance of
firepower, are a fascinating and challenging study for the military
historian. But far more satisfying is the human dimension of the
Union cavalry, the opportunity to make the acquaintance of the
men who made it up, from major general to trooper. It was they
who starved, froze, sweltered, died, were wounded, crippled,
killed, or had to suffer the abominations of Andersonville and
Salisbury. It was they who lived with fear but stuck it out. And it
is not at all surprising to learn, in the process of getting to know
these men through their letters, reminiscences, and regimental

histories, that with all its hazards and hardships, taking the rough with the smooth, service in the cavalry had a tremendous appeal for those who knew it best, the cavalrymen themselves; this was an appeal that can best be expressed in the words of one of them: "There is a marvelous fascination in the life of a cavalryman. The wondrous activity, the ceaseless daring, the constant danger, the perpetual adventure, the well-known companionship of man and horse, the exhilarating experience of open-air life—all combined to give the cavalryman's life a keener zest."[48]

48. Sutton, *History of the Second Regiment*, 180.

Addenda to Bibliography

Catton, Bruce. *A Stillness at Appomattox*. Garden City, N.Y.: Doubleday, 1953.

———. *Never Call Retreat*. Garden City, N.Y.: Doubleday, 1965.

Davis, William C. *The Battle of New Market*. New York: Doubleday, 1975.

Dornbusch, C. E. *Military Bibliography of the Civil War*. 3 vols. New York: New York Public Library, Arno Press, 1971.

Freeman, D. S. and Grady McWhiney, eds. *Lee's Dispatches: Unpublished Letters of General Robert E. Lee to Jefferson Davis . . . 1862–1865*. New York: G. P. Putnam's Sons, 1957.

Gordon, John B. *Reminiscences of the Civil War*. New York: Charles Scribner's Sons, 1905.

Leech, Margaret. *Reveille in Washington, 1860–1865*. New York: Harper & Brothers, 1941.

Macartney, Clarence E. *Grant and His Generals*. New York: McBride Company, 1953.

Phisterer, Frederick. *Statistical Record of the Armies of the United States*. New York: Charles Scribner's Sons, 1883. Supplementary volume of *Campaigns of the Civil War*.

Randall, J. G. *Lincoln the President*. 2 vols. New York: Dodd, Mead, 1945.

Starr, Stephen Z. "Hawkeyes on Horseback: The Second Iowa Cavalry." *Civil War History*, XXIII (1977), 212–27.

———, ed. "The Last Days of Rebellion." *The Cincinnati Historical Society Bulletin*, XXXV (1977), 7–30.

————, ed. "The Wilson Raid, June, 1864: A Trooper's Reminiscences." *Civil War History*, XXI (1975), 218–41.

————, ed. "Winter Quarters Near Winchester, 1864–1865; Reminiscences of Roger Hannaford, Second Ohio Volunteer Cavalry." *The Virginia Magazine of History and Biography*, LXXXVI (1978), 320–38.

U.S. War Department. *Atlas to Accompany the Official Records of the Union and Confederate Armies*. 3 vols. Washington, D.C., 1891–1895.

Williams, T. Harry. *Hayes of the Twenty-third: The Civil War Volunteer Officer*. New York: Knopf, 1965.

Index

Upton, Emory: wounded at the Opequon, 271

Wade, James: reports supplies destroyed, 168
Wainwright, Charles S.: on John Buford, 77
Warren, G. K.: Mine Run Campaign, 31; Weldon RR wrecking raid, 415–16; suggests attack on Pickett, 443; mentioned, 28, 389, 390, 406, 413, 444, 445, 446
Wells, Charles A.: reports 1st New York (Lincoln) carbines unreliable
Wells, William, 428, 507
West, Robert M.: tries to reach